Irresistible Empire

Irresistible Empire

America's Advance through Twentieth-Century Europe

VICTORIA DE GRAZIA

The Belknap Press of Harvard University Press
Cambridge, Massachusetts · London, England
2005

Library of Congress Cataloging-in-Publication Data

De Grazia, Victoria.
Irresistible empire : America's advance through twentieth-century Europe /
Victoria de Grazia.
p. cm.
Includes bibliographical references and index.
ISBN 0-674-01672-6 (alk. paper)
1. Consumer behavior—Europe—History—20th century.
2. Consumers—Europe—Attitudes—History—20th century.
3. Consumption (Economics)—Europe—History—20th century.
4. Social values—Europe—History—20th century.
5. Social values—United States—History—20th century.
6. United States—Civilization—20th century. I. Title.
HF5415.33.E85D4 2005
306.3'094'0904—dc22   2004059943

To Al and Jill
on the shores of Lake Michigan

Contents

Irresistible Empire

Introduction

The Fast Way to Peace

ON MONDAY MORNING, July 10, 1916, President Woodrow Wilson was in Detroit to address a convention hall full of salesmen. The occasion was the first World's Salesmanship Congress, the time a dire one for world civilization. All Europe was at war. Over the next several months Wilson would be weighing the nation's options: whether to stay clear of the conflict and benefit from the ruin of the Old World or to commit to the Entente, crush the German nemesis, and occupy the high ground at the peace table. Meanwhile, in view of the fall elections, the Salesmanship Congress offered a convenient venue to spell out a more expedient way to regain global concord than the calamitous path of armed conflict.

America's "democracy of business" had to take the lead in "the struggle for the peaceful conquest of the world," Wilson said.[1] And to start, it had to set new standards for consumer-friendly trade. Seeing how "the great manufacturing countries" conducted their affairs with "the rest of the world," it had to choose between two antithetical ways. One was "to force the tastes of the manufacturing country on the country in which the markets were being sought." That way was typical of the rapacious commerce of Europe's powermongers, especially German monopolists. The other was "to study the tastes and needs of the countries where the markets were being sought and suit your goods to those tastes and needs." That was the American way. Accordingly, a truly statesmanlike salesmanship would "press for manufacture of goods that they desire, not [that] you desire." It would "keep pace with your knowledge, not of yourself and of your manufacturing processes, but of them and of their commercial needs."

By insisting that salesmanship and statesmanship were "interrelated in

outlook and scope," Wilson infused contemporary statecraft with a strik-
ingly modern consumer sensibility. "The great barrier in this world is not
the barrier of principles, but the barrier of taste," he went on to say.
Given that "certain classes of society" find "certain other classes of society distasteful to them" because of their poor dress, uncleanliness, and
other unpleasant habits, "they do not like to consort with them . . . and
therefore, they stand at a distance from them and it is impossible for
them to serve them." Conflict, then, arose not from ideology or politics,
but out of the incomprehension generated by differences in manners of
living. For that reason salesmanship could assist statesmanship, "by in-
structing in that common school of experience which is the only thing
that brings us together and educates us in the same fashion." Wilson had
every reason to believe that his fellow Americans understood this pre-
cept. For no nation on earth showed so immense a capacity to produce
and sell standardized goods. None so widely cherished the belief that material comforts were an inalienable corollary of the rights to life, liberty,
and the pursuit of happiness. And none was so effectively blending away
its own diversity through the great mixmaster of mass consumption.
Hence his jollied-up audience of three thousand could well grasp his
"simple message":

> let your thoughts and your imagination run abroad throughout the
> whole world, and with the inspiration of the thought that you are
> Americans and are meant to carry liberty and justice and the princi-
> ples of humanity wherever you go, go out and sell goods that will
> make the world more comfortable and more happy, and convert
> them to the principles of America.

Against the prevailing disposition to believe that political convictions
and social injustice rather than differences in lifestyle provoke conflict,
here was this standoffish, austere man, poised at his lectern, the world's
first leader to recognize that statecraft could find leverage in the physical
needs, psychic discomforts, and situations of social unease being unleashed by the new material civilization of mass consumption. Equally remarkably, Wilson stressed not the warm, disinterested person-to-person
contacts for which his open diplomacy would be acclaimed, but rather
the hustle-bustle, seductive wiles, and calculated empathy we identify
with mass marketing. Here too he endorsed a peculiarly American notion
of democracy, that which comes from having habits in common rather
than arising from equal economic standing, freedom to select far-fetched

alternatives, or recognizing diversity and learning to live with it. The flip side of the exhortation to Americans to let their "imagination run abroad throughout the whole world," "go out and sell goods," and "convert them to the principles of America," was equally remarkable. Here America's most renowned foreign policy idealist was authorizing a global traffic in values as well as commodities. This traffic wouldn't hesitate to disregard other nations' sovereignty. Its goal was to bring down the "barriers of taste" that were deemed to cause revulsion, distrust, and conflict, as well as to pursue profits. Its ulterior aim was to promote America's "peaceful conquest of the world."

Wilson's words struck me as altogether apt to introduce the subject of this book, the rise of a great imperium with the outlook of a great emporium. This was the United States during the reign of what I call the Market Empire. An empire without frontiers, it arose during the first decade of the twentieth century, reached its apogee during its second half, and showed symptoms of disintegration toward its close. Its most distant perimeters would be marked by the insatiable ambitions of its leading corporations for global markets, the ever vaster sales territories charted by state agencies and private enterprise, the far-flung influence of its business networks, the coin of recognition of its ubiquitous brands, and the intimate familiarity with the American way of life that all of these engendered in peoples around the world. Its impetus and instruments derived from the same revolution in mass consumption that was ever more visibly reshaping the lives of its own citizens. It ruled by the pressure of its markets, the persuasiveness of its models, and, if relatively little by sheer force of arms in view of its wide power, very forcefully by exploiting the peaceableness of its global project in a century marked by others' as well as its own awful violence.

Today it is not news that global mass marketing has been central to fostering common consumption practices across the most diverse cultures. It is equally evident that if the commonalities encouraged by its models of material life have stimulated new living standards, communication, and mutual recognition, they have also aroused rancor, incomprehension, and clash. Belying the great hopes of the twentieth-century Pax Americana, globalizing consumer habits have established only the most tenuous foundation for a peaceful, egalitarian global society. Is that the fault of Wilson's vision? Critics and apologists alike recognize that the United States has almost invariably had an edge in innovations in the realm of consumer culture, and this edge has played some significant role in its global hegemony, alongside its great economic power, political alliances, and military force. Yet it is not at all clear how as elusive a force as consumer culture, being the sum of myriads of marketing strategies, second-order decisions of government, and mundane choices about getting and spending, was converted into great power. Nor is it clear how the United States exercised this great power to promote democracies of consumption elsewhere, much less to advance global concord. These are the fundamental questions this book addresses.

At the time President Wilson spoke, the revolutionary precepts of the Market Empire were nowhere more self-consciously being put into practice than in Detroit, the world headquarters of the Ford Motor Company, whose booming Highland Park plant the president was driven over to visit that afternoon, with Henry Ford himself at the wheel. It was here that over the previous decade Ford had exercised his genius as organizer of the moving assembly line, engineer of the all-purpose Model T, philosopher of the five-dollar-a-day minimum wage, and promoter to the world of the necessity of "Fordism," the eponymous manufacturing system designed to spew out standardized, low-cost goods and afford its workers decent enough wages to buy them. Here too his publicists invented the idiomatic expressions of the language of "efficiency," "progress," and "service" that supplied the key words of the empire's vernacular.

But American hegemony was not forged here, as is commonly held, nor in Hollywood, the world capital of cinema, nor in New York City, the world's emerging financial center, nor in Washington, D.C., the nation's political capital. Nor, for that matter, was it forged in Chicago, then the headquarters of Rotary International, the world's largest service club movement, nor Dayton, Ohio, the seat of National Cash Register, the world's leading manufacturer of accounting machines, nor in Boston, the hometown of the Gillette Company, which, as the Europeans went to war in 1914, built a global monopoly over the production of safety razors. Not that these sites of great entrepreneurial prowess were unimportant to inventing and propelling American market culture abroad.

America's hegemony was built on European territory. The Old World was where the United States turned its power as the premier consumer society into the dominion that came from being universally recognized as the fountainhead of modern consumer practices. For America to establish its legitimacy in this domain, it had to confront the authority that the European region had accumulated since the age of merchant capitalism as the center of vast imperial wealth, astute commercial know-how, and great good taste. Under the old regime of consumption, the global wheels of commerce spun out of the Mediterranean, then out of the Dutch and British Empires, splendid royal courts cradled the aristocratic luxury born of merchant empires, and European industries led the world in producing ingenious machinery, luxury items, and useful crafts. Down through the early twentieth century, the European bourgeoisie set the pattern for Western hierarchies of cultural and social distinction. And down to the 1970s, the European left set the model for critiques and movements to resist the inequalities, conspicuous frivolity, and wastefulness of capitalist consumption. In the process of challenging Europe's bourgeois commercial civilization and overturning its old regime, the United States established its legitimacy as the world's first regime of mass consumption. Thereby it did far more than step into the gaps created by the failed diplomacy, military overreach, and travailed liberalism of the European great powers, failures that are well known. It also established an alternative to the foundering effort of European societies, both to satisfy their own citizens' mounting demands for a decent level of living and, building on the legacy of earlier revolutionary traditions, to champion such a standard for the larger world.

Though the main lines of advance were clearly visible as early as World War I and pursued an erratic, often obstructed course until World War II, the Market Empire pressed its advantage from the outset of the Cold War. Once the pillars of the old regime of consumption had been knocked from under it and western European societies resolved to build anew on the basis of the right to a decent standard of living, all forces grasped the stakes. And all sides played the card of consumer desire. Starting in 1948 with the Marshall Plan, the Market Empire acknowledged as much, both by trying to bind western Europe to its own concept of consumer democracy and by warring to overturn the Soviet bloc's state socialism. For the planned economy was also a legacy of Europe's old regime of consumption, as well as being the last holdout against America's claim to establish global norms for a market-driven consumer modernity. Thus continuing its advance through Europe, America's Market Empire reinforced its overweening confidence in its own parvenu identity as a "new material civilization," cast disrepute on the Old World's claim to rule by virtue of its imperial civilizing mission, heritage of art, and bourgeois revolutionary values, and unceasingly retooled the machinery of its own consumer-oriented capitalism to engineer similar consumer revolutions elsewhere.

By speaking of a great multitude of trends and actors coalescing in the unique historical formation of the Market Empire, and by emphasizing the nonmilitary dimension of U.S. rule, I intend here to clarify the legitimacy that the United States acquired as the premier consumer society differed from the hegemony exercised by other imperial systems. Empire is usually taken to mean a formal system of hierarchical political relationships in which the most powerful state exercises decisive influence. In its classic Western form, an empire has more or less well-defined territorial boundaries. The capital of the metropolis is likely also to be the center of the empire. It exercises its power largely through political authority delegated to subordinate states or to colonial authorities. It establishes political monopolies over trade and resources. For most of its history, the American empire did not act along these lines. If anything, it offered a model of informal empire, with its outright colonial adventures aberrant, circumscribed, and generally short-lived. In post–World II western Europe, to the degree that U.S. power has been characterized as imperial, it has been to distinguish its light touch as befitting an "empire by invitation," an "empire by consensus," or an "empire of fun."[2]

But all empires rely for their power on the means that are historically available to them. If we hold to orthodox definitions, we miss the specific powers accumulating to the leading capitalist state in the twentieth century. These powers derived not just from being front-runner in the consumer revolution, but from recognizing the advantages that derived from that position and developing these into a system of global leadership.

Five features mark the uniqueness of the Market Empire's rule, the first and most fundamental being that from the outset it regarded other nations as having limited sovereignty over their public space. Once the classical liberal principle of free trade had been accepted, it was to naught that nations abroad protested that American foreign trade violated local cultural traditions. What is more, the Market Empire recognized that its trade could be a cultural infringement, yet found numerous ways to justify it. So peoples elsewhere would be benefiting not just from the traffic of goods, but also from the principles embedded in them. Say the commodity was Hollywood cinema: its promotion would stimulate not only more trade, but also a lively local market in new identities and pleasures. Consequently, the foreign power that tried to close off trade with tariffs, quotas, and the other barriers showed itself to be not just protectionist in the conventional economic sense, but culturally intolerant and backward. The paradoxes of this position are only magnified by the fact that throughout most of the twentieth century, the United States' home market was the hardest to crack in the capitalist West.

The *second* feature is that the Market Empire exported its civil society—meaning its voluntary associations, social scientific knowledge, and civic spirit—in tandem with, if not ahead of, the country's economic exports. And both had a subtle, sinuous, and inventive backer in a government that was thoroughly responsive to the ethos of a modern consumer-oriented economy. Initially acting solo, even at cross-purposes, at the apogee of American power at the turn of the 1960s, state and civil society operated with the impeccable synchronicity of a movie dance routine, resonating with that enthusiastic unity of purpose called the "national interest" that was the hallmark of the Cold War consensus. There was a surprising affinity of action whether on the part of the cinema producer operating out of Hollywood, the car dealer, the link in the long commodity chain coming out of Detroit, the American-trained German manager of a leading advertising agency, or the commercial consular officer responding to directives from the State or Commerce Department. In turn, though the local movie exhibitor in rural France, the household efficiency expert in Milan, or the German adolescent rock-and-roll fan had direct contacts neither with each other nor with their American counterparts, they acted within a common framework, whose terms of dialogue, however differently inflected, directed their attention toward the Market Empire.

The *third* feature was the power of norms-making. This was the Market Empire's winning arm. No royal patents, formal codes, or binding legislation governed it so much as the rules of "best practice" as spelled out by enterprising businessmen, civic leaders, and conscientious bureaucrats, each according to their specific expertise. Best practice could come out of the Hollywood studio system, chain-store operation, scientific advertising, or club life. Whatever the source, it involved devising procedures flexible enough to accommodate local knowledge, reworking them to foster trust, and making hyperbolic claims for their universal applicability. Arising out of Americans' own efforts to communicate with each other across their own vast continent, rejuggled under the pressure of brutal competition, enlivened by the jargons of new professions, best practice was invariably inflected with metaphors from market relations, with nods to the constitutional niceties of *Robert's Rules of Order*. In principle, then, the Market Empire's rules of procedure were pragmatic; their guide was the reasonable self-interestedness of Adam Smith's market exchanges rather than the inexorable rationalization of Max Weber's bureaucratic iron cage. Exuding transparency, they claimed to be norms, not laws. And by virtue of appearing to be the natural, modern, and good way to do things, they resisted being characterized as the "micro-powers" of modern governmentality, to use the French philosopher Michel Foucault's term, though that is exactly what they were. Typically, the Market Empire's power was so mobile and transitory that it was never all-determining. Therefore, it has been easy to conclude that its subjects could take what they liked and ignore the rest. Just as characteristically, it never created a stable center. For that reason too, it never generated any "single locus of Great Refusal."[3]

The *fourth* feature was the Market Empire's vaunted democratic ethos, democracy in the realm of consumption coming down to espousing equality in the face of commonly known standards. Sociability was the key word here: it showed up in the personalizing of commodities with brand names, the cult of customer loyalty, the restless quest to engage more and more consumers, and the persuasive claim to offer new comforts and services, but also in new occasions of togetherness; until eventually the lifestyles thereby created pivoted around the commodity rather than the commodity merely offering a convenience for living. Sociability had a revolutionary resonance to the degree that it was counterposed against the solidarities of Old World commerce. Solidarity implied community, its ties drawing on traditions and rights; it empowered, but it also excluded; it was said to be based on ideology rather than on convictions, and those who spoke in its defense were said to ply propaganda rather than information. By contrast, sociability defined liberty as freedom of choice, privileged the marketplace and individual acquisitiveness as the means to access it, and tranquilly asserted that a vote in politics was not significantly different from making a choice in the market. The power that derived from this democracy of consumption had the effect of detaching authority from local communities even when it did not necessarily accrue to the Market Empire. And the response to this subversion of old habits often took the path of reinforcing national, class, and racial hierarchies. In turn the sociability of mass consumer society presented itself as the jauntily progressive alternative to dourly exclusive, provincial, or, worse, reactionary solidarities.

The Market Empire's *fifth* and most confounding feature was its apparent peaceableness. Born as an alternative to European militarism, it progressed as a model of governing the good life in a century beset by

successive decades of total war, fratricidal civil conflict, nuclear holocaust, and genocidal murder. It made soft power seem a distant alternative to hard power, and thereby it largely absolved itself from accusations
of committing another kind of violence, that whose objective was to
show mastery over market exchanges, whose winning weapons came
from the arsenal of a super-rich consumer culture, and whose victims
were people wrenched out of their customary habits, their livelihoods
disrupted, their lives disoriented by fast-paced commercial change. Its
claim to rule by the consensus of consumer well-being also obscured the
facts that the Market Empire advanced rapidly in times of war and that
its many military victories—and occasional defeats—were always accompanied by significant breakthroughs to the benefit of its consumer industries and values. Its great boast with respect to all other empires of the
modern period was that it never failed to supply its own people with both
guns and butter. And when it did impose itself militarily elsewhere, it
promised to follow up with substantial aid to rebuild the ruins in its own
image.

To explain so multifaceted a power, my approach to the Market Empire
takes account of three perspectives. The first focuses on the forces pushing out from the United States, which caused the consumer revolution in
the first place and propelled its institutions and practices into Europe.
Some developments, such as the tendency toward larger and larger units
of production, an increasingly inventive application of technologies to
consumer goods, and an ever more intense effort to secure shares of the
market by gaining customer loyalty, were general to capitalist societies.
But conditions peculiar to American history gave these trends a particularly dynamic character. One was the absence of a heritage of aristocratic
customs that in Europe continued to make sumptuary habits a source of
social division, another the pressures from contending with European
competition and wave after wave of emigration which early inclined
Americans to regard their consumer practices as having a distinctive national character. So too, American business culture, in the absence of Europe's rich legacy of commercial institutions, was freer to imagine the
market as unbounded except by the seller's fantasy and the buyer's purchasing power. This outlook helped turn what initially looked like great
commercial disadvantages such as vast distances, varied climates, and a
mobile, needy, racially segregated, ethnically diverse customer base into
significant advantages. All told, products of every ilk, having been tried

out on a vast, diverse, fiercely contended home market, had a strong competitive edge by the time they were exported. Backed by solicitous government and rich in capital and knowledge, entrepreneurs saw foreign sales territories as extensions of the domestic market and planned to engage customers abroad with the same techniques they used at home, from the stimulation of wants and the study of national psychology to the spread of mass purchasing power.

The second perspective brings into focus Europe, to reconstruct the commercial civilization that confronted American consumer culture with a rival vision of market institutions and values. Recalling the intense animation of its city centers, its High Streets anchored by fabulous department stores, its arcades and kiosks festooned with luminously colored posters, its trade fairs and expositions that secured prospering regional markets, reexamining the legacy of beliefs about luxury, austerity, and trust achieves three purposes. First, it shows the challenge that was posed to the United States as the harbinger of the "new material civilization," from a market culture that in the early twentieth century was still economically competitive, aesthetically formidable, and deeply troubling in its sensuality, social inequalities, and disdain for American "civilization." Second, it highlights how distant this "old" bourgeois regime of consumption was from what we conventionally call modern mass consumer culture and how different a trajectory might have developed had the European ones not been under constant pressure from New World forces. Finally, it shows the larger European framework within which these forces would operate. Never a straightforward march, the American advance accentuated the sustained conflict both within and among European nations over the distribution of the region's still significant economic resources. The campaigns and battles that ensued pitted the United States' upstart mass consumer society, with its middle-class profile and huge industrial output, wide and deep markets, and the social cement that came from broad access to similar sets of goods and services, against a venerable market culture as it fissured under the pressure of narrow markets, stumbling technological advance, and unevenly distributed material wealth that turned consumer goods and services into sources of social divisiveness rather than social cohesion.

The outcome was a transatlantic clash of civilizations. The first major conflict reached its climax around 1940 with a monstrous paradox: that Hitler's Third Reich, as heir to Germany's huge economic potential and brilliant cultural legacy, could present itself to a demoralized continent as the one European power capable of offering a winning alternative to American dominion. The second and final conflict would end with a more pathetic dénouement: that the Soviet Union, isolated from the West, impoverished, war-wrecked, a dictatorship obsessed with deploying its centralized plans to catch up with the Western standard of living, came to be regarded as offering the leading global alternative to the hegemony of American consumer culture for practically the entire period from 1945 to its disintegration in the late 1980s.

My third perspective brings into focus the new transatlantic dialectic fostered by America's consumer revolution. More than a pace-setter or the first to get there, American consumer culture catalyzed discontents, produced ruptures, and pushed aside obstacles. In that sense, it acted much like the French and Bolshevik Revolutions in overthrowing old regimes that proved incapable of reform and were obstructive and reactionary. For the Europe entrenched in the bourgeois regime of consumption down to the 1940s and for the Europe of the Soviet bloc that until 1989 was dominated by the failures of planned consumption, the consumer revolution arrived in the shape of a "passive revolution." In Antonio Gramsci's definition, that was the overturning of institutions that occurs when a society is no longer capable of staying the same and, having tried in turn revolutionary and reactionary alternatives, is finally compelled by the pressure of outside forces to break out of the old mold and recast itself according to a different model of development. By the 1970s the outcome was indeed a New Europe, but a close ally of the Market Empire rather than the exact image of the United States. Forming a "White Atlantic" with its American partner, it had as its most conspicuous feature the striving for the satisfaction of consumers' every desire, the most basic being the comfort and convenience offered by the kitchen, the porcelain whiteness of its new material civilization all the brighter as it was viewed against the darkness of Third World poverty and the dinginess of state socialism. Thereafter one could put to rest the old tropes that counterposed Europe's lofty high culture to America's vulgar material civilization, the Old World's dissipating militarism to the New World's constructive peaceableness, quality to quantity, solidarity to sociability, and refined taste to cheap convenience. With Europe too developing according to this new dialectic of growth into a first world of mass consumption, the problem henceforth was to confront the meaning of consumer democracy for the 80 percent of people in the rest of the world. Their right to the same standard of living had been recognized, but with no probability of its being realized.

This book is a sequence of interlinked histories, each pivoting around a single social invention, moving forward in succession across the twentieth century. Each of these social inventions was a key carrier of American consumer culture, and each provides a different measure of the Market Empire's advance through European societies. Some, like the Hollywood star system, the leading brands, modern advertising, and the supermarket, are so familiar that they hardly need special introduction. Other social inventions, like the service ethic, the standard of living, the consumer-citizen, and Mrs. Household Consumer, are less familiar. Yet how would consumer society as we know it exist without, say, the elaboration of a new ethic of service to make elites accept, as Wilson said, that barriers of taste had to be overcome, and that in principle the creature needs of those at the top of the social hierarchy were no different from those at the bottom? That was the message that the high bourgeoisie of Europe was supposed to learn from the American men who founded Rotary International. How could consumer society as we know it exist without widespread acceptance that access to goods is based on income, not on status, special privileges, or hard and fast class lines? That was the lesson America's high standard of living taught in Europe, threatening to disrupt class-based distinctions in living styles that were key to maintaining social hierarchies. In the name of what rights were consumers to be allowed to consume? The Market Empire engaged in a sustained struggle with Europeans over whether their right to consume should be based on the liberal freedom of choice in the marketplace or, as Europeans asserted, on the basis of equality, which the state would guarantee should markets fail to provide the appropriate level of goods and services. "Sell the family" was an American advertising slogan from the 1920s. But who was in command of family choices? It took until the 1960s for the European Mrs. Consumer to be anointed as the sovereign shopper. Thereupon the Market Empire finally stepped over the threshold separating public spaces from the private sphere into the intimacy of the home.

As much as this book is about the hegemony that arises from the transfer of procedures and institutions, it is also about the people involved in the process, joined in puzzling over the words, concepts, and practices appropriate to translating them from one milieu to another. "Approach politics from behind and cut across societies on the diagonal": Foucault's advice struck me as sound to map the hidden and unexpected connections of a new cross-Atlantic civilization in the making.[4] So I have zigzagged across the North Atlantic and around Europe to capture the leaps of imagination that brought seasoned European reformers to argue over the meaning of the good life with optimistic American social scientists, proletarian spectators in makeshift cinemas to converse with Garbo about being a woman or with Humphrey Bogart over what it takes to be a man, and supermarket managers from the American Midwest to chat up fussy Italian shoppers.

Cutting across societies on the diagonal has also revealed unanticipated protagonists. The most obvious is the multitude of anonymous workers who were summoned forth from their subaltern status by America's consumer revolution to demand the right to a high standard of living, only to discover that they had to submit to the rules of the market, moderate their political convictions, and restrain their appetites to gain access to it. Jewish entrepreneurs turned out to be unexpectedly visible protagonists in this history. Their prominence in cross-national commerce gave them a leg up in sectors identified with American innovations—the cinema industry, chain-store operations, and marketing. Their experience of intra-European and transatlantic emigration also put them at ease with international networks. Both factors fed their vulnerability to anti-Semitic claims that they embodied the rootlessness and out-of-control desire of high capitalism, exposing their livelihoods and lives to destruction in the name of rerooting European values.

The most subdued presence at the outset of this history, only to become its most outspoken by the end, was female. America's empathetic imperialism had a distinctly feminine sensibility, and women emerged as the Market Empire's main interlocutors. So a book that starts with men meeting with men to debate the meaning of the new ethic of service-oriented capitalism as a means of reaffirming bourgeois male individualism ends with the leaders of the warring superpowers debating the standards of living appropriate to championing the desires of their female citizens.

Cutting across society on the diagonal reveals that the Market Empire much preferred to have as its main interlocutor not the national state, but a generic entity called Europe. For American foreign policy idealists, states were all-important entities, not only to interpret the commonality of views people had acquired from their shared contacts, but also to calm the turmoil generated by opening up markets. However, for American manufacturers and marketers, foreign states were also nuisances to the degree that they passed tariffs, quotas, and other protectionist barriers to trade. There is some truth to a joke that circulated at the turn of the 1950s: this had an American marketing man flying over Europe poring over his sales charts. When his assistant excitedly shouts: "We're flying over France!" his boss cuts him off with "Don't bother me with the details." In similar vein, Henry Ford was as much a father of the European idea as anyone from Europe, given his company's pioneering effort to treat the European region as a single sales territory. A good decade before the consumer appeared as an item on the European Community's agenda, *Reader's Digest* ran the first European-wide surveys of a "Europe of 220 million consumers." National states figure prominently in the following pages, but largely as settings to illuminate more general patterns of complicity or resistance. So Great Britain, though still a global power in its own right, as well as being known for its special relationship with the United States, occupies a less prominent place than France. And France, though notorious for its intellectuals' traditions of anti-American sentiment, occupies less space than Germany, which under the rule of the Third Reich coalesced into the most complete and awful alternative thrown up against the American advance. But readers can expect to move off the beaten path of the big powers to turn up in Italy, Belgium, Spain, Switzerland, and Czechoslovakia, following the tracks of American social inventions as they restlessly traced their course around the "far-flung edge of the empire."

Again and again, the American encroachments showed that if Europe was to resist, it needed to be united. And as Europe moved toward unification—as its militarism dissolved into material well-being and its cultural pride was sacrificed on the altar of consumer progress—it came to demonstrate as no other place in the world the confidence Wilson placed in the pacifying powers of allying salesmanship to statecraft. But it is also true that Europe became a place of great well-being, it became less relevant to the United States as a testing place for its hegemonic models; in the larger scheme of global transformation, the conflicts between the United States and Europe turned around contrasting lifestyles, material interests, and political ambitions rather than deeper-lying clashes of civilization.

CHAPTER 1

The Service Ethic

How Bourgeois Men Made Peace with Babbittry

*Trouble with a lot of folks is: they're so blame material;
they don't see the spiritual and mental side of American
supremacy.*

GEORGE F. BABBITT, fictional
American businessman, 1922

*The Babbitt idealism of the American method terrifies us by
its monotony . . . Europe without her individuality would
be only one continent among many; she would cease to be
the yeast which leavens the rest of the world.*

ANDRÉ SIEGFRIED,
European intellectual, 1935

IF THE WESTERN world at the outset of the twentieth century had been
mapped to show how men of wealth and power viewed their everyday surroundings, High Street, Germany, would have marked one anti-
pode, and Main Street, U.S.A., a far-distant other. To visualize the distance between them, we might pinpoint centuries-old Dresden in Saxony
as the easternmost limit and locate upstart Duluth, the half-century-
old Minnesota town overlooking Lake Superior, as the westernmost extreme. High Street in central Dresden was the refined Prager Strasse.
Moving from Vienna Square by the grand railway terminal down to the
Johannes Ring, with the bulging domes, spires, and steeples of the Old
City's baroque palaces and churches soaring into view at its end, Prager
Strasse coursed through unbroken blocks of ornately façaded, harmoni-
ously proportioned buildings, with stylish cafés, hotel atria, art galleries,

banks, and busy shops crowding the street level. In Duluth, Main Street was the ten-block stretch downtown where West and East Superior met just behind the expanse of train tracks and docks lining the lake shore. Overshadowed by the steel and cement office towers of the Folz Building, Superior Street's implacably straight course gave order to a hodgepodge of self-important civic and commercial buildings. Each was unto itself an imaginatively overwrought architectural style, set amidst nondescript clapboard rooming houses, frame storefronts, and cement garages.

Downtown Dresden circa 1930 showed the accumulated largesse of six centuries of princely patronage. Prospering at the juncture where the Elbe River traffic intersected with the Silver Road eastward, the Electors of Saxony had turned their munificent power, accrued from lording over the trade in saltpeter and arms and consolidated by warmaking, to endowing palaces, churches, theaters, and museums. As much as Weimar, the birthplace of Goethe and Schiller, the Dresden shaped by the Wettin dynasty came to embody the German ideal of *Kultur*, a refinement of taste and spirit so lofty and untainted by market forces that only an elite with *Bildung*, meaning a firm sense of personal vocation and rigorous cultural formation, could aspire to attain it. "Florence on the Elbe," the Romantic poet Herder had dubbed it. In the late nineteenth century, as the city industrialized together with the rest of the Saxon region to become Germany's most urbanized area as well as having its densest concentration of machine-tool and craft manufacture, its leading families cultivated both material prosperity and cultural propriety, which is to say both *Besitz* and *Bildung*. Weimar, the saying went, was where Germany's cultural heroes had been born, but Dresden where they found nurturing patrons. Pride in this legacy grew in proportion to the nation's disarray after Germany's calamitous defeat in World War I. Given its proximity to the hodgepodge of new states formed out of the breakup of the Austro-Hungarian realms, Germans could dream of Dresden as the spiritual capital of a rebuilt Reich, whose boundaries would stretch from the North Sea to the Adriatic and from Flanders all the way east to Russia's Pripet Marshes and southward to the Black Sea.[1]

By contrast, downtown Duluth showed the material wealth of a mere six decades of growth. From 1855, when the canal at Sault Ste. Marie opened up the Great Lakes to the Atlantic shipping lanes, and speculators bet that the scrubby hillock verging on Lake Superior would become the area's major railroad terminus, the frontier settlement named after the intrepid fur trapper Daniel Greysolon Sieur Du Lhut quickly sloughed off its uncouth origins as a French and Indian trading post turned gambling

center and barge pier. Incorporated in 1876, the year that Dresden celebrated its 660th anniversary, the jerry-built village rapidly turned into a
robust manufacturing center and port. By the 1920s Duluth was a bustling entrepôt; its warehouses brimmed with grain, its wharves were piled
with iron ore from the Mesabi, lumber, foodstuffs, and equipment ready
to load. Sailing out across Lake Superior, the boats passed through the
elaborate system of canal locks to the open sea, to move southward to the
freighters crowding the narrow docks of the eastern seaboard or across
the North Atlantic, where their cargoes were unloaded at Southampton,
Antwerp, Rotterdam, Bremen, or one or another of the lesser European
ports.

For the city fathers, Duluth was "the Zenith City of the Unsalted
Seas." Boundlessly ambitious as they were for their hometown, their
pride was only slightly tempered as the town's growth was outpaced by
that of Detroit, Minneapolis, and, of course, Chicago. Even when they
had to settle for more modest sobriquets like "the Pittsburgh of the
West" or "the Chicago of the Northern Great Lakes," they still regarded
their Duluth as embodying in clapboard and concrete the industriousness, optimism, and patriotic spirit that in their eyes made the United
States the greatest nation on earth. With equal gusto they boosted the
vim and vigor of Rotary luncheon speeches, the fanciful architecture
of Superior Street, the eclectic repertoire of the Opera, Orpheum, and
Strand Theaters, and the efficiency of the city jail. One and all were worthy enterprises, conceived to satisfy universal human wants for comfort,
decencies, diversion, and order.[2]

Manners too could not have seemed further distant between the two
cities. At noontime on Prager Strasse, the formalities of a bourgeois culture graced with aristocratic gestures was still palpable. The prewar hierarchies were fading, if one was to judge from the swagger of boyish
young women, the war-decorated mutilees crouched begging on city streets,
and the insolent posture of youthful men in uniform clustered at the main
crossings. Yet form was still a point of honor, visible in the drape of suit,
the doff of hat, the click of heels and sharp bow over the lady's hand, the
courteous deference of shopkeepers, and the fixity of leisure habits. After
dining, the Kaiser Café or the Hülfert under the hotel Europa-Hof at the
corner of Waisenhausstrasse was the place to be seen. Teatime was at
Brülsche Terrace, where one could chat until dusk, the river traffic maneuvering in the distance, undistracted except by the fast-moving cloud-
light glinting off the Catholic High Church's spire and the murmur of
groups of tourists agape at such magnificence. From this perspective, it

was hard to imagine Dresden as a city also inhabited by hard-scrabble working poor, crowded into the dreary brick slums abutting the machine industries that drove the local economy. It was equally incongruous to imagine the calm, cobbled avenues swept by street battles—in 1919, when cavalry troops from the Police Presidium faced down rioting veterans with the rat-tat-tat of machine guns, and again in 1920, when the right-wing Kapp Putsch was crushed and the city wracked by civil war. In its sublime beauty, cosseted by its ring of gray-ocher walls, the Old Town seemed unshakable.

By contrast, Duluth was all a-flurry. Around noon, East Superior Street saw crowds of Fords and Phaetons disgorge gray- and brown-suited men at the Kitchi Gammi Club, the Masonic Lodge, or, if it was Thursday, at the Rotary luncheon in the nearby Hotel Spalding while smartly coiffed women maneuvered family cars into parking spaces before hopping out to do their shopping. The workers crowding out of Fitger's Brewery sat side by side at the diner counters with salesgirls from Wirth's Drug Store and sales managers from the Folz Building, and secretaries in bright printed dresses rushed over to the five-and-dime to pick up odds and ends. Everybody was talking, with hellos to one and all, hearty handshakes, and big pats on the back; everybody looked so perky, well-dressed, and well-nourished that their class provenance was hard to discern. Calm descended only at evening when the center emptied out, the middle classes heading home to gardened suburbs, the workers to the grimy frame houses of West Duluth. This calm had been broken only once in recent times by an event whose memory was quickly suppressed. That was on June 15, 1920, when several thousand of the town's residents, many out-of-work and panicky from the postwar recession, had rushed the city jail, overpowered the police, and yanked from the cells three black youths, workers from a traveling circus being held on trumped-up rape charges. They were lynched from the lightpost just off East Superior, the one by the crosswalk between First Street and Second Avenue East.[3]

One might be tempted to say that Dresden with all its magnificent culture was inimitable, whereas Duluth was just another average American town. Dresden had aura. It was authentic. Duluth, by contrast, spunky, optimistic, philistine, was practically indistinguishable from scores of similar middle-American places. Even so, Duluth was as central to defining American civilization as the unique beauty of world-weary Dresden was to defining European culture. Under the guise of Zenith, Duluth had

✗ become world-famous through the novels of <u>Sinclair Lewis</u>. It was in Zenith-Duluth, the closest big town to his birthplace, tiny Sauk Centre, that Lewis sited his tragic-pathetic story of George Babbitt, the real estate agent who was the hero of his eponymous 1922 novel. It was in this place, a fictional composite of a score of similar towns, that Lewis situated the capital of <u>middle-class mores</u> and <u>consumption habits</u>. It was here that he exposed the new business rackets in real estate and car insurance, the nuclear family's bickering over bathroom time, the pious displays of churchgoing, the demagogic politics, and the clubby conventions of fraternizing made to order for the inveterate joiner—the Babbitt—whose anxious status fears, indulgent materialism, and complaisance made him the nemesis of the well-marked individuality, inner spirit, and skepticism of the true bourgeois man of culture.[4]

When the Nobel Foundation awarded Sinclair Lewis the prize for literature in 1930, the citation underscored that he was the first American ever to win the prize. The intention of the award was to recognize the capacity of a new literary realism to vivify the average man's way of life. It was also to acknowledge a style that Europeans regarded as typically American, one that Lewis exemplified: the use of deft humor to put critical distance on the dejecting human condition epitomized by the everyday existence of the middle classes. Wanting to choose an American, they preferred the "cheerfulness and alacrity" that gave "a festive air to his crusading social criticism" to the "weightily serious" realism of their other favorite, <u>Theodore Dreiser</u>, who like Emile Zola was too Old World in his emphasis on exposing a "consistently dark view of life."[5] The award to Sinclair Lewis thus showed the Old World self-consciously bowing to America's still uncertain cultural prestige. It also acknowledged that in Lewis's work, world literature had given life to a new human type, one in which at present a whole nation with "greater or lesser pleasure recognized itself." This was the get-up-and-go businessman, whose tragi-pathetic existence was chronicled in the figure of George F. Babbitt.

With this questionable choice, the Swedish Academy placed Lewis in the company of the greatest and most controversial of all contemporary novelists. This was <u>Thomas Mann</u>, whom they had finally honored only twelve months earlier after years of misgivings. The Mann they celebrated was first and foremost the author of *Buddenbrooks,* his prewar epic narrative of the inexorable decline of a merchant dynasty. In the accolades and ceremonies accompanying the prize, Mann's most challenging (and recent) work, *The Magic Mountain,* was mentioned only *en passant,* as if his reflections on the sickly denizens of the Alpine sanitarium at Davos were a too-depressing commentary on the moral decline of *Homo europeensis.* For the Academy, Mann's contribution to world literature stood in his capacity to trace the degeneration of bourgeois figures from "self-contained, powerful, and unselfconscious characters to reflective types of a refined and weak sensibility."[6] Accepting the prize as a token of sympathy for his "much injured and misunderstood" nation, Mann spoke of German culture's uniquely "productive and problematic genius." Like a Mannerist *Saint Sebastian,* painted bound to the stake, his alabaster-white body pierced from all sides, his agonized face illuminated with a smile, German culture was uniquely able to turn "anguish into pleasure." Through its terrible travails, the German nation safeguarded, indeed reinforced, "the Western and European principle of the dignity of form in the face of an almost Eastern and Russian chaos of passions" at the same time as "combining the essence of sensual intellectual adventure, of the cold passion of art of the South, and the heart, the bourgeois home, the deeply rooted emotion, and innate humanity of the North."[7]

When his turn came to address the Academy, Sinclair Lewis could not but allude to the traditions embodied in his intimidatingly erudite predecessor, in whose *Magic Mountain* he saw "the whole of intellectual Europe." Europe had the critical spirit and cultivated manners lacking in those small-town American elites that elsewhere he chided as "a sterile oligarchy," "men of the cash-register." Far be it from them to conceive of the "community ideal" in "the grand manner." Their self-esteem swelled not from contemplating their heritage of art or music, but from surveying the number of cheap appliances in the kitchen and calculating the upward spiral of land values.[8] On the European side of the Atlantic, drawing-room conversation touched on love, courage, and politics, whereas on the American, homey evening chats on front porches turned to the workmanship of safety razors, the artfulness of colored ads for Crisco and Maxwell House coffee, and the joys of cruising around in flivvers.[9] Making this contrast, Lewis wanted to show neither servility nor snobbery so much as his own paladinship of a new synthesis. This was a straightforward, superbly crafted middle-brow culture, one that despaired at the frivolity, escapism, and hypocrisy of the new material civilization yet was deeply indulgent about rendering its human comforts, democratic mores, and sociable ways. Many Americans of average culture shared his views.

As each man was decorated at the Nobel ceremony, first Mann, then Lewis, each was indirectly the interlocutor of the other; not that they had ever met each other, nor would they for another half-dozen years. However, both framed their thoughts for the occasion in terms of the conflict of cultures that was coming more and more sharply into view between the New and the Old Worlds, especially as this had been framed by the vexed opposition between *Kultur* and Civilization.[10] However, until the war, Germany had been the embodiment of *Kultur,* whereas Germany's rivals, England and France, were the standardbearers of Civilization. When European culture had been split and Germany crushed by World War I, the torch of civilization had been passed to the United States. For many Europeans, this outcome posed the risk that Western civilization would be thoroughly tainted by the materialism peculiar to American society. But few Americans saw it that way, including prominent intellectuals. True, the everyday culture they saw around them was not high culture, certainly not in the sense that Germans intended when they used the word *Kultur.* But it was culture nonetheless, at least in the sense anthropologists use the term, to speak of commonly held ways of living and patterns of belief that impart a sense of unity to a people and give significance to their daily lives. American culture rested on shared assumptions, civilizing manners, and mutual recognition, and most Americans didn't worry that there was nothing transcendent about this sense of belonging. In that respect, their culture was akin to what French anthropologists at the time called a "habitus," and it wouldn't have particularly bothered them to know that the French term had first been conceived to characterize the fetishes, rituals, and superstitions of primitive peoples.

How much distance, then, ran between Mann, who during the war spilled out his torment in countless pages to defend the value of German *Kultur* against the Western powers, and Lewis, the articulate American spokesman for improving the cultural quality of civilization.[11] Mann, the novelist-philosopher, had as his frame of reference the pessimism of Schopenhauer, Goethe's idealism, and Nietzsche's mordant critique of civilization. Lewis, the novelist-journalist, had as his the optimism of populist reformers, the market researcher's familiarity with the American vernacular, and the engaged intellectual's malaise about cultural conformism. Like Babbitt and the Buddenbrooks, the cultural worlds these men represented were immeasurably far apart. Dresden was the homeland of a cultivated bourgeoisie still struggling to live in the grand manner; Duluth was the habitat of the striving businessman of America's myriad Middletowns. True culture in both places demanded that vulgar commercialism be despised. But what each saw as the ultimate token of crassness differed radically. For Mann, it was epitomized by the merchant countinghouse of his native Lübeck fallen on hard times; for Lewis, by the Rotary club gathering where Babbitt consorted with his cronies. Lewis, like other intellectuals critical of the lowbrow in American life, would have smirked in agreement at the caustic views of his friend, the journalist H. L. Mencken, when the latter excoriated his fellow Americans, especially the Babbitts, whom Mencken regarded as prime exemplars of a new species of humanity, the *Boobus americanus,* strutting about clucking the clichés of its class and calling, and wholly possessed by its possessions. Rotary clubs, in his view, were the "pillar of a commonwealth of morons."[12]

But here reality is stranger than fiction. If we actually go to Dresden around 1928, to the exact corner where Prager Strasse once intersected with Waisenhausstrasse, if we peer behind the brocade curtains of the Europa-Hof, once one of Dresden's two or three most fashionable hotels, we catch one of those minute details that confound the observer who wants to draw cultural differences with broad strokes and a thick layering of tropes. There, in the hotel's best sitting room, every Monday, punctually at 1:30 P.M., at least thirty but more often forty of the city's most prominent men assembled for an hour-and-a-half luncheon and talk. The minutes of these encounters began to be recorded on September 28, 1928. Over the next nine years, until late August 1937, when they disbanded under pressure from the Nazi dictatorship, the group met 440 times. The occasion was the weekly gathering of the Rotary Club of Dresden.

The incongruity of these assemblies in the peerless capital of German culture is only magnified when we discover the eminence concentrated in the membership list. This was straightaway visible at the inaugural ceremony conducted on Tuesday evening, November 6, 1928, as the forty-one hosts, the club's founding members, welcomed their guests in the chandeliered ballroom of the Bellevue, Dresden's premier hotel. Circulating in the very rooms Prince Bismarck had honored with an overnight stay while en route to Vienna in 1892, the crowd represented a veritable who's who of the cultural, political, and economic leadership of the city. There was the founding president, Dr. Grote, chief surgeon at Dr. Lahmann's Sanatorium. The tall, angular fellow with the supercilious air moving from group to group was the club's major animator and secretary, Karl von Frenckell, the Finnish consul, sometime diplomat and

banker, and a well-known patron of the arts, married to a local woman,
the renowned chamber-opera singer Minni Nast. Lord High Mayor Dr.
Blüher was there too, introducing the out-of-town visitors to other leading officials of the city and regional government. As usual, Dr. Hugo
Grille, lately chief of the Police Presidium and now counsel to the State
Court, stood out in the crowd with his impressive aquiline profile and the
impeccable bearing that recalled his long career as a military man. The
stately Heinrich Arnhold, director of Germany's second-largest private
bank, Bankhaus Gebr. Arnhold, and well known locally for his generous philanthropy, leaned over in intense conversation with the painter
cum state theater artistic director Leonhard Fanto and the scion of another assimilated Jewish family, Viktor von Klemperer. The latter's family
was twice represented that evening: in the pudgy, jovial figure of Viktor
in his vest as head of the Dresdner Bank, and by his younger, more reticent brother Ralph, a can manufacturer. Everybody knew the mercurial
Julius Ferdinand Wolff, editor-in-chief of the liberal *Dresdner Neueste
Nachrichten,* and they could tick off the heads of the city's major cultural
institutions: Professor Haenel of the State Historical Museum and the
Green Vault; the famed musician Maestro Fritz Busch, musical director
of the Dresden State Opera; and the Magnificent Rector Nägel of the
world-famous Polytechnic. The credentials of the thirty other founding
members were no less eminent.[13]

Yet if the mix of gravitas and good-hearted fellowship marking the occasion was unmistakably German, and the black-tie dress stipulated by
the invitation recalled old-regime gentility, the paraphernalia of membership would have been recognizable to the business elite of Duluth.
Draped beside the entrance was the royal-blue banner embossed with the
gold-colored cogged wheel inscribed with "Rotary International." The
founding charter, its typed-in number marking Dresden as the 3010th
club to join Rotary International, would soon be on its way from Chicago, while the pamphlets of rules and notices and the stack of correspondence signed off alternately with "Rotarily yours" or "With heart-
felt Rotary Wishes" *(Mit herzlichen Rotarygrüssen)* were squirreled
away by the recording secretary, von Frenckell, in his office around the
corner at the Arnhold Bank at 24 Waisenhausstrasse. Speeches, toasts,
and small talk expressed in sonorous phrases sentiments akin to those
more boisterously voiced by thousands of American men in praise of the
cordial fellowship, comity of nations, and spirit of community service
embodied in Rotary ideals.

To leap from the middle-class Babbitts of Duluth to the high bourgeoisie of Dresden is a real stretch of the imagination. What then to make of discovering that the charter members of the Rotary Club of Munich, founded at about the same time, included a certain "Dr. Professor Thomas Mann, profession writer"? So it was: just about the time Mann accepted the Nobel Prize for literature, he had become a fervent Rotarian. Busy though he was finishing the first of the *Joseph* novels, on Tuesday, October 9, 1928, he had met with a dozen friends at Walterspiel's Restaurant at the Four Seasons Hotel to draw up their application.[14] Three months after forwarding it to Chicago, the application approved, the Munichers celebrated the arrival of the founding charter, theirs numbered 3009. To commemorate the occasion, Mann signed the gilt-edged guest album, adding a thought to relate Rotary to his profession. Below Adolf Stöhr's wordplay "I am a builder, let nothing befall me," and law professor Heinrich Rheinstrom's wry legal gloss on the sign "Give the Grass a Chance," which he had seen on a lawn in Washington, D.C., and which he admired as "grass-friendly rather than people-hostile," Mann had the philosopher Lessing address Martin Luther: "Great man, you broke the yoke of tradition, but who will save us from the unbearable yoke of the written word?"[15] This little conceit, elaborated over another ten lines, would later be developed at a Rotary luncheon talk, one of a half-dozen occasions on which he entertained his fellow members. Though he professed himself a non-orator "instinctively repelled as a writer by the improvised and noncommittal friendly character of all talk," he took to the podium to speak about "Idealism in a World of Reality" at Rotary International's first Regional Conference for Europe, held at The Hague on September 12–14, 1930. When he won the Nobel Prize, his club was the first to toast him, the master of ceremonies, Oscar Walterspiel, joking that the wine, a 1921 Erbacher Honigberg Cabinet, was so "noble" that he was afraid to uncork it for fear it was dynamite. When Mann was forced to depart from Germany in February 1933 under threat of physical harm and jail by the Nazis, the minutes recorded him as absent for a month before he was unceremoniously dropped from membership in April 1933.[16] Later, in exile in the United States, Mann would occasionally be drawn to speak on the Rotary luncheon circuit against the growing menace of Nazi Germany, urging conservative American businessmen to back the war effort on the grounds that "the preservation and stewardship of the West's cultural inheritance has passed to America."[17]

Our conundrum is not just how Rotary got to Dresden (or to Munich or Leipzig or Hamburg or Frankfurt) or why it appealed to men like Mann. It is how it operated under conditions so different from its place of origin in the American Midwest; what it meant that a club life ordained for one kind of elite was arrogated by another so distant in place, political circumstances, and cultural sensibility. This puzzle could not be answered in terms of Dresden alone, much less in terms of Germany, where by 1937 there were forty-four clubs with 1,082 members. Rotary was a widespread European phenomenon by the mid-1930s, with 300 branches in Great Britain and on the continent. And in the latter area it so clearly appealed to a different social constituency than in the United States—an Old World high bourgeoisie rather than the New World middle class—that it would be equally intriguing to know how its members in Barcelona and Budapest, Paris, Louvain, Glasgow, and Milan used their clubs to engage with the world around them.

To explain a transatlantic circuitry of social contacts that Americans said was their invention—though available for the whole world to use—and that Europeans wanted to make their own, we must first go to the place in the United States where Rotary first sprang to life. And there we can begin to treat the words "Babbitt" and "Babbittry" not as pejoratives but as terms invented by a fast-changing social lexicon to characterize new ideal types of middle-class identity and social behavior. To do otherwise would be to fall prey to the invidious comparisons that inevitably arise—from both sides of the Atlantic—whenever the U.S. middle class and European bourgeoisie are juxtaposed for purposes of scrutiny and analysis. The second move is to explore how this new sociability was appropriated across Europe. In doing so, we show how European elites "made peace with Babbittry"; which is another way to say that we are going to use the spread of Rotary clubs to show how those elites began to accommodate to a new life that emphasized the material commonality of daily needs.

Harking to Woodrow Wilson's admonition that barriers of taste were harder to overcome than barriers of principle, men of the elites had to disembarrass themselves of castelike notions of cultural distinction. They had to learn to accommodate a new standard of living that was income driven and potentially open to all. They had to accept entrepreneurs who engaged in the new service-oriented professions like salesmanship as legitimate members of the elite. They had not to be afraid that changing notions of culture, though frighteningly rocking the old ways of respecting hierarchies of class, would overturn their social rank. They had to embrace the new spirit of consumer-oriented corporate capitalism, embodied in the ethos of service, in order to establish a more empathic relationship with the community around them. "Making peace" also meant accommodating differences across national cultures. Across their continent, Americans used the fraternities of men's service clubs to network. The place to start to alert men of goodwill everywhere that all people were similar in their wants and fears was the weekly gathering at midday with food and talk. That was the Rotary Club's universal trademark.

America's Ardor for Association

If Rotary had been an artifact of the U.S. eastern seaboard, concocted for the genteel old money of Edith Wharton's drawing rooms, Henry James's refined Bostonians, or the golden alumni of F. Scott Fitzgerald's Ivy League, it would be less difficult to imagine its appeal to Europe's bourgeois elites. But it was far from that. A newly minted outfit for upstart businessmen and striving professionals, it was as much of a mass-produced invention as Henry Ford's Model T. And like the earliest automobile assembly lines, it was a midwestern invention. The first Rotary club was crafted on the shores of the Great Lakes, a couple of hundred miles distant from Detroit, on Lake Michigan's windswept south shore, where American capitalist growth was most dynamic and ruthless.

Rotary's birthplace was Chicago, the world's fastest-growing city in the early twentieth century. Its population nudging 3.5 million by 1930 and sprawled over 520 square miles, the city could be a place of dreadful solitude for newcomers, inducing a desperate inventiveness in the search for social relations. This effort was perhaps most self-conscious and pressing among those for whom making sustained contacts was most arduous—namely small-town, native-born, unattached, white Protestant males. The socially prestigious circles of old elites shunned their modest backgrounds and urgent need to talk shop. Unless they married downward into the new communities of Irish, Italian, or Polish immigrants, they were excluded from the protective neighborhood and kin ties of the striving working classes, parish churches, and the ever better-greased patronage systems of big-city machine politics. For their own part, they snubbed the mixed worker/small business fraternities and were aggressively antilabor. It was said of Rotary's founder, Paul P. Harris, the lanky, gentle-faced lawyer who specialized in fraud suits, that he had numerous acquaintances but few friends. Solitude was personally painful for this amiable, peripatetic native of Racine, Wisconsin, balding, bespectacled, and still a bachelor at age thirty-seven. Solitude was also bad for business. No mockery was implied when Rotarians later celebrated Harris's machine for socializing as the product of his "facile brain" and "lonely heart."[18]

Rotary lore has placed the first gathering on February 23, 1905, in the coal dealer Sylvester Schiele's cluttered office in the Unity Building on Dearborn Street. The purpose of subsequent meetings, hosted weekly over lunch and rotating among members' places of work, became clearer over time: Rotary meetings enabled each member in turn to expound on his line of activity and thereby develop social contacts and business connections. Through these encounters, Rotarians would recapture the good feelings that people who had been habituated to transacting business in small communities allegedly felt toward one another. The club thus afforded protected niches from which they could operate in the face of the cruelly competitive environment of large-scale corporate enterprises. The occupations of the founders—an attorney, a coal dealer dabbling in insurance, a merchant-tailor, and a mining engineer, soon to be joined by a printer and a real estate agent—underscore the club movement's small-business social origin and defensive purpose.

Male bonding was by no means new to a country famous for the fraternal orders that had grown by leaps and bounds over the previous quarter-century, their solidarity underpinned by an ethos of mutuality and brotherly support and enlivened by fabulous and corny rituals. Association, in German sociologist Georg Simmel's poignant words, was everywhere being stimulated by "a growing distance in genuine inner relationships and a declining distance in more external ones." White men bonded across class and craft, the circles of fraternity widening to include European immigrants of all ilk; women, blacks, and orientals were rigorously excluded.[19] America's "aptitude for association," Tocqueville's phrase, clearly drew on European associational traditions. Any time two Germans got together, the old saying went, they formed a *Verein*. And they brought this proclivity to the United States, especially to regions like the Midwest, where they made up a large percentage of the newcomers. It couldn't be dismissed as accidental, chauvinist German Rotarians insisted, that two of the first Rotary club's founding members, Sylvester Schiele, a coal dealer before dabbling in insurance, and the mining engineer Gustavus H. Loehr, were of German origin. However, after the turn of the century, this "aptitude" turned into a mania for joining that paralleled "the extension of manufacturing and selling which gave uniformity to life from one end of the continent to the other," commented Charles and Mary Beard in 1927. As communication networks and routines of economic activity grew national in scope, the country was crisscrossed by federations and superfederations for profit, pleasure, diversion, and self- and social improvement.[20]

However, the Rotary movement represented a significant leap in the scale and scope of fraternizing. For the drive to associate was excited not just by the intense competition arising from the integration of the national market and the possibilities of communication opened up by this trend, but also by the determination of local elites to secure position, power, and profits as the prevailing status lines and styles of command were shaken up by big business, the rise of organized labor, the professionalization of town management, and the realignment of national political parties. Rotarians saw their first and foremost goal as renewing the personal contacts lost to anomie and the personal animosities engendered by roughshod business manners. But by facilitating face-to-face encounters, they acquired a cultural resource of particular value to so mobile a society, namely a never-ending accumulation of local knowledge. With leverage from this small-town know-how, Rotary staked first a national, then an international claim to establishing the rules and manners of a new capitalist business civilization. By the time the sociologists Robert and Helen Merrell Lynd conducted their investigation of "Middletown, U.S.A." in the late 1920s, only to discover a brand-new civic culture "in which everything hinges on money," Rotary stood out front and center as "the oldest and most coveted of all clubs." The members, "carefully selected for prowess in business, highly competitive, and constituting a hierarchy in the prestige their membership bestows," exemplified "the prepotent values of the dominant group of businessmen in the city." The combination the group offered—of "utilitarianism and idealism, linked with social prestige and informal friendliness"—made it "almost irresistible."[21]

Though still best known for its influence in small towns, by the turn of the 1930s the network was solidly ensconced in big cities as well. The second-born Rotary was the San Francisco club; the fifth, Los Angeles. In 1909 a Rotary club was established in cosmopolitan New York City, a johnny-come-lately never to have much clout. In Chicago, however, "Old Number One" had become the city's premier men's civic club by the

1920s. Its members, leading business executives, high management, and professional men culled from all over the city, were almost all native born, moderately wealthy, church-going, and Republican in their party preference. Though they belonged to other social clubs, fraternal organizations, and professional associations, Rotary was special to them for its citywide interests and national vision.[22] By the late 1930s practically every medium-size town also had its Rotary club. Flourishing down to the 1960s, when American club life hit the doldrums, its membership was revived in the 1990s by globalization, the reinvigoration of voluntary work, and the inclusion of women.[23] Today Rotary International is the world's largest service club organization; its 30,000 circles, each signaled by the blue-and-gold Rotary wheel, though not as conspicuous, are currently about as numerous as McDonald's Golden Arches.

At the outset, Rotary's surging growth seemed to confirm nothing so much as Americans' peculiar "aptitude for association." That was Alexis de Tocqueville's phrase, written in the context of his penetrating if often misinterpreted remarks that "Americans of all ages, all stations in life, and all types of disposition are forever forming associations."[24] His point was not, as often asserted, that American life was rich in associations and that this phenomenon made it notably democratic, nor its corollary, that continental Europe was association-poor and therefore prone to authoritarianism, neither of which was true. Tocqueville's point was rather that American associations lent themselves to promoting a democracy of recognition, based on the effusive ritual that both fascinated and appalled upper-class Europeans, combined of hearty handshakes, jocular talk, first-name intimacy, and loud chorus singing. Individualistic, yet tamed by small courtesies, this sociability encouraged a mutable new social self, conformist yet enterprising, withholding judgments or expressing them in circumlocutory conventions, yet confident enough to recognize and be recognized by others in distant worlds. "Normatively ordained" organization makes Americans feel equal to their neighbors, as well as denoting "efficiency," observed the Dutch historian Johan Huizinga in 1927, remarking on the degree to which "uniform and well-defined technical nomenclature" had become the "ideal of civilization."[25]

In turn, local associations empowered local elites to speak out knowledgeably about local affairs and with at least the pretense of having digested national and even international events. In George Babbitt's boastful words, the 100 percent red-blooded American business man differed from the effeminate European in that he "knows how to talk right up for himself, knows how to make it good and plenty clear that he intends to run the works. He doesn't have to call in some highbrow hired-man when it's necessary for him to answer the crooked critics of the sane and efficient life. He's not dumb, like the old-fashioned merchant. He's got a vocabulary and a punch." Babbitt wasn't sure how "they," meaning the Europeans, "did it over there." But he was certain that unlike American men, they were "willing to take a lot off the snobs and journalists and politicians."[26] Here we could perhaps conclude that fiction was born of fact.

Rotary clubs, if they helped business America to speak out locally, also showed that it could be a good listener. Tocqueville's observation that associations can enhance the plurality of voices, making politics less strident and polarized, makes sense.[27] Insofar as civic associations grew up alongside and independently of political parties in the United States, they tuned into community issues that in their reasonableness could claim to transcend partisan interests—such as public health, the standard of living, or good government. It was only sound politics for elites to recognize the needs of others, at least some of them. This profession of interest in the needs of the community was certainly nurtured by Judeo-Christian charitable impulses, but it was also greatly bolstered by the self-publicity of emerging service industries.

These sensitivities were also bolstered by Rotary's responsiveness to the women's movements of the early twentieth century and to women generally in the form of the female relatives of its members. No national rules specifically barred women, though in practice they were completely excluded from club membership until 1987, when the U.S. Supreme Court ruled that a California law requiring service clubs to admit women did not violate First Amendment rights to freedom of assembly. However, the club movement regarded itself as women-friendly. Which is to say that its commitment to do-gooding causes, sense of decorum, and use of social courtesies, which its forebears, the fraternal societies, would have regarded as effeminate, resonated with and were perhaps even learned from the practices of the early twentieth-century women's club movements. Rotarians met over lunch on the grounds that supper was family time. In turn, family togetherness was used to reaffirm the practice of "men only"; to include the growing numbers of businesswomen in the community, some of whom were heirs to family firms, others principals in new undertakings like real estate, would only result in what British Rotarians delicately called "family complications." It would have been disrespectful of the "real Women of Rotary" to "open our doors to those women who in recent years have felt that the call of business . . . was of more service to humanity than the responsible occupation of home building."[28] Wives and daughters of members were encouraged instead to form auxiliary groups, though these were firmly deterred from efforts to obtain official recognition. If the women were sufficiently motivated they could choose a more prestigious option, namely the women's own service club circuit, notably Altrusa, the Soroptimists, and Zonta, with which the Rotary movement enjoyed good relations and some of whose members provided highly educated stalwarts to manage the European office. In sum, women were treated as valuable assets, most conspicuously on occasions of state, when the wives of incoming presidents were introduced from the podium to testify to their spouses' value. The teetotaling Scots Presbyterian Bonnie Jean Thomson, married to Paul Harris in 1910, became as much an icon of the international movement as the unprepossessing guru himself. Her hovering presence offered further evidence of a mystery that European men sometimes pondered, namely that abroad and in public American men appeared to dominate the world while at home and in their personal lives they supinely deferred to their domineering mates.

In the last analysis, Rotary's vision of social connectedness addressed the ever-equivocal relationship under capitalist exchange between the commercial impulse that could make society whole and the cut-throat competition that could tear it apart. For that reason Rotarianism was regarded by contemporaries as a helpmate of Fordism, the one putting a check on out-of-control robber-baron capitalism by standardizing factory output, the other by systematizing social relations. So the "Age of Fordism" was also the "Rotarian Age." Like Ford, Paul Harris was an idolized celebrity, whose unmemorable face made him equally hard to pick out of the crowd. Both men's down-home musings were accorded the status of philosophy and translated into a myriad of languages. Ford provided the machinery for the new era, it was said, Harris the morality. Ford put America on wheels; Harris gave America the Golden Wheel. Like Ford's assembly lines in Detroit, Rotary International's headquarters in Chicago turned out a standardized means of communication with long runs. By minutely specifying rules, procedures, and rituals, the clubs produced the world's first mass-manufactured sociability. Factory test-driven first through the obstacle-riddled Chicago environment, road-tested across the U.S. continent, they were then tried out abroad—first in the English-speaking markets of Canada and Great Britain, then in 1916 in the culturally more distant bustle of Americanized Havana. As Rotarianism moved farther from its original market niche, the fast-growing cities of the Midwest, the Rotary management speedily worked out all the possible dysfunctions that might beset such an invention. These included competition and dissension among members' interests, inertia from lack of compelling external goals, and loss of prestige as its novelty diminished, its size grew, it faced obsolescent practices, or its market share was threatened by other entrepreneurs in the sector.[29] Learning from successful business entrepreneurs about how to operate in wide markets and in competition with a proliferation of clubs similarly devoted to the service ideal, including the Lions, Kiwanis, Exchange, Civitan, and Gyro, Rotarians brought to bear to their product, male fellowship, all the rules of successful sales promotion, from building up brand-name recognition and product uniformity to introducing quality control and tie-ins.

Their instincts for salesmanship showed in the felicitous name: Rotary could refer to both a wheel and a dynamo, unlike "Rotation," the founders' ponderous first idea. Rotary spoke to the constant turnover of leadership and the fast pace of the local meetings, but also to the dynamism of the organization and the egalitarian ties, like spokes on a wheel, that connected members around the world. Rotary also worked wonderfully well in translation, as its club bulletins showed. Chicago One had its *Gyrator,* and the staid newsletter *The Rotarian* was the organ of the international movement. British English inspired linguistic playfulness: In addition to several *Cogs,* there were *In Gear* (Gloucester), *Live Steam* (Sheffield), *Spokes* (Walsall), *Rotula* (Ipswich), *Flywheel* (Belfast), and *The Gear Box* (Bristol). Translated into continental languages, it acquired the same charm and allure as any number of other American big brand names, from Ford, Gillette, Coca-Cola, and Kodak to Xerox, Nike, McDonald's, and Microsoft. Depending on the tongue, the *r*'s could be intoned as guttural, rolled, or throaty, and the tonic stress shifted from the first syllable (in Italian and Spanish), to the second (in German), to rest on all three (French). Breaking *Rotarier* into syllables, fanciful German philologists discerned two opposite forces, namely "Red" *(rot)* and "Aryan" *(arier).* Rotarianism was the synthesis that would save their nation from being torn asunder.[30]

Then there was the inimitable emblem, the golden wheel. The product of the inventiveness of local printers, reproduced in scores of versions in the first decade, it was eventually reduced to twenty-four cogs, with a keyway added to dynamize the gearshaft. This escutcheon was officially fixed at the Duluth Convention in 1912, with meticulous injunctions about the proportions and colors, before being redesigned one final time in 1924 to reduce the number of spokes to six. A brilliant advertising image, it has proved as lasting and recognizable as any corporate symbol in history and is vigilantly protected by patent to bar commercial misuse. Rotary's slogans too were ingenious marketing devices. The original motto, the overly selfless "Service, then Self," became the excessively self-regarding "Service after Self" before being rephrased around 1910 as the disinterested-sounding "Service above Self." The phrase persists today, translated into as many languages as the people speak who belong to Rotary International. Lest the motto be interpreted too liberally, the clause "He profits most who serves best" was tacked on at the first annual convention at Chicago in August 1910, its author the self-touted founder of American salesmanship, the Michigan-born Arthur Frederick Sheldon. His handiwork would persist long after many Rotarians had come to regard the slogan as morally inappropriate and obstinately refractory to translation.[31]

Rotary's trickiest balancing act was to link the intimacy of fellowship with the outward "extension" of the world movement. The more Rotary went abroad—it dropped the adjective "foreign" in 1921—the more indispensable it was that its goals be stated coherently and without any trace of the salvationist rhetoric of small-town America. A big step toward this goal was to delegate the clarification of principles to English as opposed to "American" speakers. Over many years, amateur British constitutionalists pared away the verbiage to highlight the goal of international peace and clarify the two basic organizing principles, namely the classification system and service principle.

The classification system was the means devised to select membership. Since each club had to be relatively small to be effective, each profession could be represented by only one member. The original rationale for this requirement was that competition might ruin the atmosphere of good fellowship. Over time the classification principle was given a more sophisticated rationale. Unlike occult cliques, which used black balls and secret ballots to recruit members, or the snobbily exclusive old boys' circles, which discriminated on the basis of social pedigree, Rotary selected the top representative of each profession or classification. Since no club intent on thriving would choose members uncongenial to those already in it, the founders still had a large say in deciding which among these to choose. Even so, much was made of the club's having nothing to hide. To mark this transparency, the men forsook the privacy of mahogany-paneled club rooms, the Masonic temple, Elks lodge, or reclusive dining chambers to meet in conspicuously public venues, usually the grandest hotel or best-known restaurant in the area. Places and times of meeting were emblazoned on Rotary signs on public roadways, the name and topic of the lecturer announced in the local paper, and the annual rotation of officers well publicized.

Rotary's second founding principle, "service," was thick with at least three centuries of meaning. In the notion of "Service above Self" there was the Calvinist idea of individual redemption through on-earth social action. The slogan "He profits most who serves best" alluded to the trust between seller and buyer and the promise of after-sales maintenance congenial to an emerging consumer-oriented business civilization. The service ethic held that the community's needs were rich and the level of shared comforts should be high, but also that the profit system recommended a parsimonious pragmatism in satisfying them. Accordingly, Rotarians were uninterested in any notion of public solidarity in the populist or welfare sense. Nor did they intend their notion of service to be paternalistic. Rotary community projects were selected with an eye to feasibility and strict nonpartisanship, so as to avoid controversy or treading on special interests, especially those of one or another powerful member. One should serve conscientiously, but without eccentric convictions.

Hence projects might involve improved lighting for Main Street or establishing a downtown parking lot. But avoid disputes over zoning laws! Rotarians might supply hospital wards with iron lungs or x-ray equipment, campaign to inoculate children, provide free eye examinations, and, if there was an oculist in the group, perhaps even supply gratis eyeglasses for myopic schoolchildren. But never debate health care as an issue! Rotary stood for world peace. But never be a pacifist, or discuss divisive issues like going to war, much less war debts! Rotary should be in the forefront in promoting the Golden Rule that you "do unto others as you would have them do unto you" and encouraging "constructive citizenship" by voter registration, doing jury service, and celebrating the Fourth of July. But these projects, however conscientiously they were pursued, were never to be confused with partisan politics. The whole point was to act in place of politics, the claims of which to improve civic life were at best dubious and certainly inferior to concerted community action. Thereby Rotarians aggressively stepped in to steward the public domain in order to have a significant say in reshaping it.

Sing, You Rotarians!

By Sigmund Spaeth
Musician and Author

"A singing Rotary club is a good Rotary club": Harry L. Ruggles, composer of "Rotary," leads the "boys" of the Chicago club. The Rotarian, *June 1938.* By permission of the Rotary Club of Chicago.

This was the service ideal, the new ethic of consumer-oriented capitalism. It is best grasped in operation, and perhaps nowhere so viscerally, in the first civic undertaking of the founding Chicago club. The project, grandly announced over dinner at the Great Northern Hotel on October 24, 1907, called for public lavatories at the corner of La Salle and Washington Streets, near City Hall. The problem it addressed was the crowds of immigrants and others who ended up urinating or worse in public places while waiting to attend to civic obligations such as visas, taxes, and licenses. The solution was to salvage their dignity as individuals but to safeguard public hygiene while doing so. Not every local interest showed such sympathy for the plight of Everyman or such sensitivity to the community's well-being. Marshall Fields, the department store, saw potential customers in the people who straggled in to use their facilities. So did the bar owners around the Loop. Accordingly, both opposed any public provision. Thus, a certain unembarrassed civic courage was required to go forward with the project in addition to two years of wheeling and dealing to surmount zoning and other obstacles. Then speeches were given, the ribbons cut, and the lavatories opened for business.[32]

Crossing the White Atlantic

The very strengths that made the Rotary movement triumph across America catapulted it abroad. At the Duluth convention of August 1912, following the establishment of its first foreign club in Winnipeg, Manitoba, in 1910, and just a year after clubs were founded in Dublin, Belfast, and London, delegates representing all of forty-one clubs voted with raucous unanimity to designate themselves "The International Association of Rotary Clubs."[33] Expansion abroad continued to be the handiwork of single businessmen in search of the same occasions to socialize abroad as they had at home until the war in Europe gave a new impetus to thinking globally. Meeting in Kansas City in 1916, the convention voted "to have Rotary clubs in all commercial centers throughout the world." In Los Angeles on June 6, 1922, following the surge of growth that accompanied the first international conference held abroad in Edinburgh, Scotland, in 1921, conventioneers unanimously voted to rename their movement Rotary International. They could not have been unaware of the Communist International, founded in 1919. But then branding never had inhibitions about exploiting phrases that resonated with the Zeitgeist, without, of course, conceding any power to the original. By the mid-1920s, with business in Europe picking up, and with anxiety mounting that the independent-minded Rotary of the British Isles might preempt American organizers on the continent, and in response to a goodly number of inquiries arriving from over there, Rotary International decided to leap across the Channel.

This decision made Ostend, a Belgian beach resort reportedly like Atlantic City, the ideal site for the 1927 congress, the eighteenth in Rotary history. From a moral perspective, neutral Belgium, the chief victim of the Great War, was the perfect location. It showed Rotary International's dedication to world peace, especially in bellicose Europe. From a logistical point of view too, it was perfect, being easily accessible via Antwerp, the continent's main port of arrival for transatlantic shipping. Preparations for the crossing, the largest, its organizers boasted, since the launch of the American Expeditionary Force in 1917, boarded 4,000 U.S. and

Canadian Rotarians onto six Cunard ocean liners sailing from New York Harbor on May 25. Regrouping after a rough passage, they paraded past the southern coast of Britain, the *Carinthia* in the lead, the other vessels following a half-mile apart, before proceeding up the Scheldt River, where they berthed simultaneously on June 2, 1927. From Antwerp, the conventioneers were joined by 3,000 others, mainly from the British Isles, to go by special train to Ostend. The movement, coming just two weeks after Charles Lindbergh landed the *Spirit of St. Louis* at Paris's Bourget Airport on May 21, impressed all who witnessed it with the potential of face-to-face diplomacy: "World neighborhood brought together by modern transportation is truly a world brotherhood."[34]

Within the grand glass-and-iron Kursaal built with wealth pillaged from the Congo, the timbre of continental European voices resonated at a Rotary assembly for the first time. King Albert, who had graciously accepted an honorary membership, welcomed the assembled 15,000 in the name of peace. When this admirably ordinary monarch had finished, the public-address system amplified the voices of the other European speakers. "Mother Europe, the cradle of white civilization is in crisis, and its offspring, of the same race, youth infused with the old country's vitality, offers the means of teaching Europeans to become practical idealists." The "Rotary bridge" would span the "White Atlantic." It would recognize the challenge the Old World faced as it turned toward the United States, "teeming with wealth, with new cities," whereas "in Europe, our material life is outwardly changing slowly; we are more inclined to philosophize over life; we emphasize the value to the individual of art, literature, and music; but we suffer possibly from superculture, and it might be well, if we exchange some of it for the energy and elementary force of a young country like the U.S.A." Against the "diplomacy of isolation and intrigues," Rotary stood for complete "moral disarmament" carried out not by "soft headed pacifists or feebleminded idealists, but [by] practical, hard headed business men with warm hearts."[35] "Rotary would teach us to speak European," a Frenchman intoned. A Dutch businessman brought his neighbor's rhetoric down to earth. Peaceful relations would start with "the smile of gratitude on the face of the member coming from another country when you sit by him and tell him what is going on and translate the jokes the members are laughing at." Now Europe had to take its own destiny in hand. The movement's "extension . . . does not depend on Rotary International, it depends on ourselves, on the way we handle and live Rotary."[36]

These impassioned words would have been lost on the Dresdeners, none of whom went to Ostend. The fact is that all Germans were excluded from the movement until the autumn of 1927. True, the Americans and British had been keen to organize in Germany as soon as the issue of its war reparations was settled by the Dawes Plan in 1924, laying the way for the country to be admitted to the League of Nations in September 1926. Their interest was as much practical as idealistic. Mostly, they just wanted to facilitate business connections, but they also worried that as giant Germany's industry recovered, Europe would be overwhelmed by "commercial travelers' clubs" with Teutonic businessmen trying to fob themselves off as Rotarians.[37] Ordinary people were still deeply wary about the resurgence of German power.

Still, the Anglo-Americans couldn't dismiss outright the opposition from the continental clubs. No Germans, the French said: at the Leipzig trade fair, the entire crowd at the Central Market "with its cold German discipline" had doffed their hats and scraped and bowed when Reich President General von Hindenburg passed in his car. To think how quickly German groups might proliferate if encouraged: not 50 or 100, when the French were barely pushing a dozen clubs, but as many as 200. If the Americans had glimpsed the hillocks and fields dotted with ghastly war cemeteries, they could grasp the depth of the objections from "trustworthy types" who described the Germans as utterly unrepentant, "fanatic nationalists and dreaming of revenge, [though] otherwise perfectly correct in business." If Old World notions of honor insisted that the sight of Germany's black-red-gold banners unfurled amidst the flags of thirty-eight nations would be an affront to King Albert and the Queen, then it was worth postponing the organizing drive until after Ostend.[38]

Meanwhile, to preempt any German misbehavior, plans shaped up under American supervision to establish a European Area Committee with representatives from all of the eight countries surrounding Germany. Experience had shown that the founding members set the tone for subsequent recruits. So the goal was to recruit from the highest social classes, as if high bourgeois or aristocratic men could better vouch for their countrymen's conduct than the plain middle classes. Anglophile Hamburg was to be the jumping-off place. Famous for its codes of business ethics, the city had been the area's leading port since the medieval Hansa League, as well as the capital of Germany's merchant marine. It was thus appropriate that its sponsor be the Rotary of the venerable port town of Oakland, California, and its founding president the general director of the Ham-

burg-American Steamship lines, Count Wilhelm Cuno. Chancellor of the
Weimar Republic in 1922–23, he, like several of the other founding
members, was recruited from the Overseas Club, the most prestigious in
the city.[39] Under Hamburg's patronage, Catholic Cologne was brought in
next, its founding president the lord high mayor Konrad Adenauer. Then
came Frankfurt under Baron Moritz von Bethmann-Hollweg; he was the
scion of the banking line of the family, suspicious Belgians were reassured, not the offspring of the German chancellor infamous for issuing
Austria-Hungary the "blank check" to bully Serbia in July 1914, thereby
concatenating the events that led to the Great War.[40] After Munich and
southern Germany, organizers pointed northeastward toward less familiar regions, first Dresden and, via Dresden, Leipzig, Germany's fourth-
largest city. Finally, there would be Berlin, which because of its size and
complexity was regarded as the hardest place of all to organize a club.

To explain how Rotarian ideals arrived on the Elbe, the Dreseners
would have recalled a mid-September day when the Finnish consul, the
fatuous but endearing Karl von Frenckell, rounded up sixteen of his colleagues and friends to meet Rotary's special emissary, T. C. Thomsen. A
Dane by nationality, he made a vivid impression since he was just forty
years old at the time, tall, handsome, with thick blond hair, and a good
fifteen years younger than the men he was being introduced to. He had
been the chief engineer of the Vacuum Oil Company of Britain for a decade, then the managing director of the giant Company of Denmark,
which had made him a fortune trading in copra, soybeans, and other colonial staples, and at the time he headed his own firm, Aarhus Oil Factory.[41] Engineers were the darlings of the European elite at the time,
and the fact that his business thrived while he dedicated nine months
out of twelve to attend to Rotary business marked him as a managerial
genius. He was also not only fluent in German, but a Germanophile
with a passion for opera. And he had come impeccably introduced. Max
Hans Kühne, the Saxon architect who had built the Leipzig train station,
Europe's largest, was his contact via a mutual acquaintance, Rotarian
Gerbel, Austria's leading road and bridge engineer, who that year was
president of the Rotary of Vienna.

Since Kühne had to be away, the expansive von Frenckell squired
Thomsen around, though he made it clear that he himself was not interested. He didn't have the time. Through von Frenckell, Thomsen met
the Finnish consul's friend and longtime business associate Heinrich
Arnhold, whose prospering bank was just opening a branch in New York

City. In turn, Arnhold introduced him to yet another banker, Victor von Klemperer, who in turn brought Thomsen to meet other members of his luncheon club. Thomsen recalled the men as a "happy mix of *Ernst und Scherz*" (probity and playfulness). Later, the others would tease von Frenckell, an indefatigable enthusiast, voluble in six languages (in addition to Esperanto) and soon to be famous in German Rotary annals as "Magister Rotariensis," by recalling that he had "No Time" for all of this.[42]

Rotary arrived in the middle of Europe packing little if any of the obvious American baggage it had landed with at Ostend, where it was already visibly less encumbered than when it had shipped out of New York Harbor. From the weekly minutes the Dresdeners compiled, starting from the moment they banded together on this new venture, nothing suggested that they were guided by the long arm of the American Market Empire, much less that their choice had anything to do with the mania for everything American sweeping 1920s Germany with "import articles." Nothing evidenced the erotic displacement of shopgirls seduced by America's idols, Mary Pickford and Douglas Fairbanks, or the repressed libido of scruffy clerks gawking at the robotic kick lines in the style of the Tiller girls, or the wanderlust of the hard-nosed radical aesthetes—like Bertolt Brecht or John Herzfield—who delighted in the Wild West, bloody knockdown boxing matches, advertising slang, and the down-to-earth crassness of the New World, or the rationalist disenchantment with the world of industrialists who were fascinated by Henry Ford's assembly lines and F. W. Taylor's systems of clocking and timing men's work, or cinema-goers' awe at the spooky fantasies of Fritz Lang's *Metropolis*. Nothing would have brought them into contact with, much less given credence to, views that called Rotary in Europe a "form of commercial back-scratching."[43]

What, then, disposed these busy, established, cultivated men to embrace so passionately an invention that they nonetheless recognized as having originated in the United States? Clearly, it was not for lack of other occasions to socialize. For they were already heavily scheduled with their luncheon groups, fraternities, veteran officers' associations, the local Esperanto section, international friendship societies, sports clubs, and churches and synagogues, as well as occupying demanding positions of leadership in their professions. They were also patrons of the fine arts, the opera and chamber music societies, and various important charities, in addition to being patriarchs of large families with obligations to entertain relatives, friends, and acquaintances regularly and generously. Recognizing that this new commitment was very demanding—that they would have to pay high dues—a 50-Reich Mark entrance fee, 50 RM annually, and an additional 4 or so RM for the luncheons, in addition to being obliged to attend regularly and to serve the group in some capacity— they justified their enthusiasm by joking that Germans were inveterate joiners. "The Garden of Eden, Inc." had gone bust, abandoning mankind to create its own little community. That was the sense of the inaugural evening's entertainment, expressed in amiable doggerel by the brewery financier Herr Dr. Johannes Krüger:

> Nobody was made to go it alone.
> Either they marry or a club they join . . .
> Club life is as old as mankind itself
> Club life, the dance around the golden calf.[44]

But the real reasons were more pressing, and ever more intimate and involved as time passed. The most urgent was to rejoin the international community from which Germany had been ostracized by the war. Rotary Article Six's goal of international peace appealed to the liberal pacifists among them, a *rara avis* in Germany, one being Heinrich Arnhold, who had long been active in the German Friendship Society. It was also congenial to onetime nationalists like Mann, who by the mid-1920s had succumbed to the Hungarian Count Coudenhove-Kalergi's seductive projects for a pan-European confederation. Belonging to Rotary also promised to reestablish the business trust to support Germany's export economy. It gave patriotic men the opportunity to show what a renascent Germany could contribute culturally to an international movement. Above all, the invitation marked the cessation of the embarrassing personal hostility Germans sometimes encountered doing business abroad or on holiday, even on family vacations skiing or hiking at St. Moritz, Montreux-Vevey, Chamonix, or Davos, where they saw their calm, rosy-cheeked children taunted: "little Boches, bullies, warmongers." It flattered them by reaffirming their own transcendent purpose as an elite of culture and property in this deeply disquiet nation. It brought them into a global community of 2,930 other clubs in forty-four other lands, together with 137,000 other men.

Rotary's moral code offered yet another attraction. In Rotary's business ethics, German Rotarians saw the general values of bourgeois humanism, or *Bürgerlichkeit*. It confirmed that their culture was not the privilege of class, as critics vehemently argued, nor was it self-serving, but rather the bearer of timely universal values. Thereby it also validated the worth of their profession or calling, their *Beruf*. Rotary taught that, perforce, modern life called for the habit of a more democratic way of living, but also one that was orderly and civilized. True, Rotary didn't contemplate the familiar *du*, except among those who were already close friends. But it encouraged a comradeship that enabled members to call each other by their family names rather than verbally bowing and scraping as one addressed "Herr Doctor" this and that. What mattered for Rotary was "not who you are, but what you are."[45] Because it was based on leadership in the professions, it was an open elite, relatively speaking, and in principle inclusive: Catholic and Protestant, gentile and Jew, Saxon and Bavarian, the sophisticated citizen of merchant Hamburg or Leipzig but also the upstanding provincial from Plauen, Görlitz, Zwickau, and Baden-Baden.

Yet another attraction was the club's procedure. The authority of precedent and the imprimatur of a charismatic founding leader, Harris, were happily combined with a clear constitution, a president who rotated from year to year, a committee structure, and endless rules. This was not the cloddy togetherness *(Vereinsmeierei)* of the masses, but a new model of orderly coming together. This newness was best expressed through the use of English rather than German nomenclature. The group was not a *Kreis* but a "club"; they joined together in a "district" rather than a *Bezirk;* and were responsible to a "governor," not a *Gouvernor.* They signed off on their correspondence with a more democratic "With Rotarian good wishes" rather than one or another of the obsequious conventions: "With deepest respect your very devoted . . ." The expectations placed on the members were rigorous: that they attend regularly, that they excuse themselves if they could not, that on occasion they deliver an after-luncheon talk. Each, in turn, would speak about his professional interests, intended broadly of course: not mere shop talk, but serious, informed conversation about one's vocation, not without humor, and never to exceed fifteen to twenty minutes. The point was to enable real discussion. This was the kind of presentation that Mann savored.

Predictably, the Germans took the rules to heart. The British proved to be far better constitutionalists, the French better at ferreting out the politics embedded in procedure, and the Italians expert at flouting the rules or simply ignoring them altogether in the name of their own pleasurable but self-involved notions of conviviality. Alone among the European clubs, the Germans punctiliously wrote up weekly minutes and mimeographed, circulated, and stored them. Alone, they drew on their interest in genealogy to draw up meticulous family trees of clubs. Alone, they applied their philological skills to translating the arcana of the Chicago rules. The Americans, as if uncertain about their identity, often commissioned studies of themselves and in turn were the human subjects of curious, often irreverent, academic sociologists. The Germans displayed no such insecurities. Practically from the outset, their undertaking was judged worthy of being inscribed in the historical record. Rotary, for those who were disposed to think according to Hegel's dialectic, was "the synthesis of the world-historical club spirit perfected across the ages."[46]

On the basis of this appeal, the grouplet at Dresden cohered; the original sixteen selected another twenty-five founding members, then co-opted three more each month until they numbered an expansive sixty or so in 1931. What a diverse group it was, at least by American standards. There were the high civil servants as well as a handful of manufacturers, doctors, and the notary public, the museum director, artists, and even a leading opera singer. Five among the founders were of Jewish belief—a significant number, given that only about 3,500 of the city's population of 650,000 were Jewish. At least one other, like Mann, had a Jewish wife.[47] Their presence testified to the success of two prominent families, the Arnholds, intermarried with the Bondi and Maron families, and the von Klemperers, relative newcomers from Austria. Sometimes joining gentile organizations was part of an effort to assimilate, hence self-conscious and a little uncomfortable. Not in this case: it was a pleasure to come in on the ground floor of an organization, especially one that was world-famous, and in Germany almost all Rotary clubs had at least one Jewish member, and a few, like Dresden, several. In Dresden, if not elsewhere, the Jewish members felt especially at home, at least for the time being. The same could not be said for their contemporaries in small-town America. Since there was such a premium on belonging to Rotary, there were relatively few Jews, and prejudice against including more than one, if even that.

Rotary in Dresden also yielded the profile of a generation, modern Germany's most favored. Born during the *Gründerzeit,* or founding era, the boom years immediately following the establishment of Kaiser Wilhelm's empire in 1871, they came of age when Germany's power was at its peak. Most were too old to serve in World War I, though some, out of patriotism, had volunteered anyway. Rotarians everywhere were engaged in a "battle with senility," as a Baltimore member put it irreverently. "The struggle to get to the top was so harsh, their tops were grey or balding." In Germany too people complained that the clubs were "Only for Honorable Officials *(Herr Kommerzienrate)*"; that "we need youth, as in the United States."[48] All were conservative after a manner, their class, experience, and age making them loyal to the Weimar Republic out of duty, though they disdained its lowly social democratic birth and rabble-rousing politics.[49] They believed in serving the Fatherland. And they feared for its fate as the small rightist parties they voted for shrank in proportion to the advance of the Nazis and the Communists.

No arm-twisting, then, was ever required to bring the Dresdeners into Rotary. Still, one wonders whether they knew that the movement in Germany was the result of Allied strategy, leveraged by Americans with indispensable support from the men of the nations surrounding Germany to wedge it back into Europe. Perhaps not. Clearly, they had their own reasons for belonging, and what they ignored only added to the originality of their interpretation of its workings. Nonetheless, they were mistaken, these superbly cosmopolitan, sophisticated gentlemen: they had been subjects of a project of "extension" and not, as they believed, its protagonists. Quite correctly, they had glimpsed that Germany's debacle—which in their mind was also Europe's defeat—demanded that they live differently. And Rotary was the institution they had seized upon to reestablish themselves in the world. But they had done so as provincials being edged toward the periphery, and showed themselves historically naive in their lack of reflection that its appearance in their midst signaled that old Europe now followed, not led.

Special emissary Thomsen's report of his mid-September visit as an unmitigated success was resoundingly endorsed the following December 5, 1928, when the Dresdeners' application came up for approval at Rotary International's headquarters on East Wacker Drive in Chicago. By then a staff of about fifty men and women was handling as many as a dozen applications a week from all over the world, and it mainly limited itself to checking whether the aspirants' membership roster conformed to the stipulation that there be only one representative from each classification or profession. Good American democrats that they were, they noticed the bristle of titles in front of the applicants' names: four *vons,* twenty-four *Drs.* of various ilk, ten *Herr Direktors.* . . . Hegemony is never so sweet as when it involves lording it over one's social betters. When the application went to the Board of Directors for approval, it carried Thomsen's note: "this is the finest baby that has so far been born into Rotary."[50] Adept though they were at fitting this attractively shaped puzzle piece into their own picture of the world, the "men of Chicago," as they were called in Europe, were inept at figuring out how it fitted into another social panorama. Consequently, it was not for them to ask how this "finest baby" would survive in an environment so different from the American heartland.

With its export-dependent economy, overextended banks, and impoverished agriculture, the Saxon heartland of central Europe had become known in those decades as the "weathervane of the business cycle." Saxony was also the bellwether of bum politics. A hotbed of anti-Semitism, its class-riven political system incapable of lending itself to compromise, the region had been in a state of endemic civil war since 1918. The Great Coalition patched together by the liberal-conservative statesman Gustav Stresemann, which brought some stability to German politics from 1926 to 1929, never gained support there, so acute were the animosities between left and right. Saxony was where Hitler made his first electoral breakthrough in the May 1928 elections and where, in the crucial January 1932 parliamentary vote, his party won more than 50 percent of the ballots. The liberal center wasn't holding. With no middle ground, conservatives of the region wandered toward the far right, at least so long as the far right was willing to accommodate them.[51]

In that context, it is not surprising that Rotary took on such a charmed life and its German members were so devoted. At the Dresden club's prime, three-quarters of the members were always in attendance. Luncheons at the Europa-Hof had at least a handful of guests each week, and often the half-dozen or so men who were excused because they were away on business or holiday dropped in at clubs elsewhere and signaled their affection by sending postcards of salutations. Rotary presented them with a new traditionalism, combining the familiarity of the old with the freshness and pleasures of the new.[52] Far from indulging in the hysterical *Kulturpessimismus* that affected other groups of the German educated middle class, Rotarians confidently espoused a tamed version of Friedrich Nietzsche's damning criticism of German bourgeois conformism. So their talks and writings attacked a blinkered, mechanistic conception of culture, short-sighted utilitarianism, and blind faith in technological panaceas.

The paradox, then, was that Rotary in Germany emerged as a vehicle of a powerful, if ambiguous cultural critique. And the antagonist, if not directly named as such, was the new culture that elsewhere numerous authoritative critics identified quite simply as *Amerikanismus*. Although the dazzling conqueror from overseas was never named, the antagonist was nonetheless the myth of limitless opportunity, the power that based its claim to legitimacy on its prodigious financial and economic strength, notions of unimpeded efficiency and untrammeled innovation, the disturbing immediacy induced by the mass media, and the shapeless informality of everyday life. Rotary in Germany thus stood firmly against the suppression of the ethics of the Old World by the New, as well as against the displacement of the strong self of traditional culture by the immature personhood of the fragile males of mass society. In sum, far from the world of the Babbitts, Rotary in Germany stood against all those trends of modern life that, in a Kantian view, contaminated the world of aesthetic consumption with the world of ordinary consumption, in such a way as to collapse the distinction between facile pleasure as the play of the senses and feelings, and pure pleasure that sublimates the senses to express the truly moral man.[53]

All of this resonated with a sense of their difference not only from Americans, but from other Europeans as well. Their distinctiveness was given voice right away in the decision to found their own journal *Der Rotarier,* at first to be published in Dresden, but then delegated to the Munich club, which with Mann and other distinguished writers and artists promised more intellectual heft. "Our impression [is] that the clubs of our district are on the whole not insignificantly different from American or even from a part of the European clubs," said Count Cuno in announcing this undertaking. "We want to express this difference in our newsletter . . . We hope that our peculiarity can enrich not only the life of our clubs, but gradually even the life of Rotary International."[54]

With real sympathy the Dresdeners must have read "On A Beautiful Room," the little essay Thomas Mann published in *Der Rotarier's* very first issue. True creativity no longer called for "princely pomp" or "sumptuous rooms." The "era of princes is over"; likewise "the bourgeois luxury-style has outlived its epoch and died out on aesthetic grounds." But the functionality, or *Sachlichkeit,* of the new aesthetic of modernism shouldn't require living like sterile cogs in a gearbox. Nor should the desire to join productivity with comfort be dismissed as bourgeois. Rotary members would have recognized their own orderly effort to create a "beautiful room" in Mann's plea to "put together inherited and acquired pieces to create interiors of [one's] own with intimations of elegance," to cultivate "pleasant but by no means pompous quarters" seated at one's desk or relaxed while reading in one's Empire chaise.[55] They would also have recognized their world-historical mission in *Bambi* author the Viennese Felix Salten's "Remarks on the Rotary Idea" in the same issue: Europe's problem was not profitmongering or cruel individualism, unlike the land of Rotary's origins (whose civilization he capsulized in *Five-Minute America*, his 1930 travel memoir). The problem was the class struggle. And the only way to placate that was for the bourgeoisie to redouble the compactness and civility of its way of life.[56]

In sum, the goal of Rotary in Germany was to be an exemplary organization rather than one open to emulation; its qualities were its compactness and deep passion, its inner life, as it were, rather than the exteriorized vernacular of procedure the Americans favored as a means of connecting to other cultures. It was graced by inimitable manners rather than, like the Americans, showing off its codes and rituals in order to be imitated. All told, it was transcendent rather than universal, cosmopolitan rather than global. So the very sociable Rotary brought these men into a world movement only to see them mark it with their righteous conviction that they represented an alternative way of thinking about the material world.

This self-involvement in no way precluded displays of exquisite hospitality toward outsiders, nowhere more visible than when a party of forty-eight Americans stopped over in Dresden in mid-June 1931 on their way to the sixteenth Rotary World Congress in Vienna. It fell to Victor von Klemperer, who that year was the club's president, to welcome the Americans. Times were terrible: the collapse of Austria's Kreditanstalt the previous May had shaken the soundest of German financial institutions, his own Dresdner Bank included. With the knowledge that the financial crisis had been aggravated when U.S. banks cut credit lines and pulled out capital, von Klemperer welcomed the Americans into their midst. "Never has Paul Harris's thought been more pertinent than today," he intoned, addressing his audience first in German, then English, "when the whole world is in crisis and Europe bleeds from a thousand wounds. Just as the child has to remember with gratitude its parents' good deeds, so America has to be mindful of the good earlier generations brought it. American good will would so greatly help us now."[57] President Herbert Hoover

*Germanic centaurs at play with Lady Liberty in a bookplate
engraved for the Rotary of Steyr, Austria, circa 1930.*
By permission of the Collection of Monroe and Aimée Brown Price.

would indeed declare a moratorium on German war debts on June 20.
But that move didn't prevent the run on German banks a week later.

If their American friends grasped the drama of the appeal, their club
repertoire afforded nothing to voice an adequate response. Rotary was
not a forum for controversial topics at home, not a place to discuss tariffs, much less debt moratoriums. None of them would have influence in
politics as Rotarians in Europe might have had. Anyway, Rotary was rich
with a repertoire to stimulate fellowship, not to display solidarity in the
face of disaster. To show their thanks for the hospitality—which was now
culminating in this breakfast for 149 people, gifts of Meissen china dishes
for the ladies, and a rousing performance of "Home on the Range" and
other American folk tunes arranged by the house pianist and performed

with his delicate conservatory touch—the foreign guests regaled their hosts with several choruses of Ruggle's anthem, "R-O-T-A-R-Y":

R-O-T-A-R-Y That spells Ro-ta-ry
R-O-T-A-R-Y is known on land
And sea; From North to South, from East to West,
He prof-its most who serves the best; R-O
T-A-R-Y, That spells Ro-ta-ry.

"So for the first time we experienced this custom from overseas," the minutes show von Frenckell, the father of Saxon Rotary, observing with a touch of condescension.[58] The unanticipated novelty only made them redouble their impeccable hospitality. That afternoon they brought their guests to the exquisite Painting Gallery, toured the Green Vault, with its treasury of exotica, and took them at teatime to Brülsche Terrace. The next day von Frenckell, with a score of others, accompanied the Americans to the Central Station, where, with fervent farewells and pride in the graciousness displayed by their beautiful city, even in the face of such hard times, they waved their guests good-bye with sincere hopes for their safe journey and a return visit. Their generosity could not be reciprocated, as their aristo-bourgeois gift economy demanded. The Dresdeners knew this. And this knowledge could only have reinforced the sense of their superior place in the order of things.

All Power to Procedure

One can't but admire a network that had small-town America hobnobbing with the aristo-bourgeoisie of central Europe: Rotary was their invention, an extension of their new power. Whether these close encounters helped Americans grasp the otherness of the Europeans they came in contact with is more problematic. Did they consider that their own rituals of jollification seemed folkloric, even puerile for men for whom *Gemütlichkeit* came naturally, for whom conviviality over good food and drink was as natural as the day was long, who belonged to communities that used military decorations, state ribbons, and professional emblems rather than commercial brand names or club badges to show, if not who they were, where they were positioned in the world at large? Not likely: Rotary had thrust Americans into a world of great variety at the same time as it blunted their grasp of the reasons for its diversity. Abroad, as at home, the Rotary badge encouraged the half-narcissistic, half-altruistic belief in the omnipresence of like-minded people. This was all a very comforting and positive feeling for rising hegemons.

The initial problem for "the Europeans," as the Americans called them, was to accept that the uniformity indispensable to the cohesiveness of the movement was not a straitjacket, that some distant administration was not going to standardize out of existence the strong individuality that was fundamental to their Europeanness. Over meetings, they heard the reassuring sales pitch well practiced on American soil. Every community has its "peculiarities." It is "almost always" necessary to "demonstrate to a new community Rotary's fundamental soundness, that it is suitable and adaptable to local needs." Gathered around the conference table at Frankfurt, representatives at the European Advisory Meeting heard Rotarian Adams, sent by headquarters in 1929 to take the pulse of European sentiment, reiterate this point with one of those puerile mechanical metaphors popular at the time: "We are traveling the same road, same piece of machinery. The raw products are different in the different clubs, perhaps the method of manufacturing may differ, but we are all trying to turn out the same product."[59] Europeans seized on the metaphor, turning it to their own interests. If Rotary was like a Model T, it had to be customized for a more discriminating clientele. Not for the Europeans, Ford's slogan "All colors, so long as it's black." The question was whether these exigent and diverse clients merely wanted to upgrade the machine—say, with wood paneling, leather accouterments, or bright tail lights. Or did they want to trade it in for a custom-crafted, mahogany-paneled European model—say, a Hispano-Suiza or a Bugatti or a Daimler-Benz?

On the road to customizing their clubs, "the Europeans" had to be convinced of yet another premise, namely that the rules of procedure that all clubs had to follow did not emanate from some old-fashioned administrative power like the long arm of imperial bureaucracy they extended into their own colonial lands. The Americans intended procedures as a new form of rules-sharing among an international elite, acting in compliance with common standards of reasonableness and functionality. On the constitutional level, Rotary strived to appear egalitarian and transparent. It was governed by a board of directors whose fourteen members were elected by the delegates at the annual convention. Meeting in Chicago twice a year, the board debated suggestions passed on to it from all over, formulated recommendations, and sent any measures requiring constitutional amendment to a vote at the annual convention. Although the composition naturally favored American delegates in particular, and the Anglophone world more generally, since they were the founders and accounted for the largest percentage of overall membership, continental Europeans were more and more visibly represented by the 1930s.

Nonetheless, the real power of decisionmaking rested with the imperturbable "Men of Chicago." Headquarters was ruled by a general secretary who from 1910 to 1941 was embodied in the athletic figure of Chesley R. Perry—"Dear Ches" as he was known to acquaintances in the movement; "Dear Secretary Perry" to his scores of hundreds of other correspondents. A veteran of the summer war in Cuba and a librarian by training, Perry was perfectly scripted for the position. Thirty-six years old when he started, he had the appeal of a familiar film star to faraway viewers: his air of authority, lean silver-haired handsomeness, and yawningly bland conservatism suited him equally to playing the upright civil servant, midwestern military officer (which he was, as a lieutenant in the reserve), and righteous small-town minister. A skillful businessman whose first successful investments were in Mexican bonds, he was above all a joiner, who, once he had attached himself to Paul Harris, funneled his virtuoso organizational talents into the Rotarian cause. This he interpreted in the America-first style of midwestern isolationists, his zealous one-worldism tempered by the unshakable belief that America always knew best.[60]

For most of Perry's three-decade-plus tenure, the operation's goals were to boost the number of clubs and establish them in ever more countries while avoiding controversy, especially controversy that would impugn Chicago's authority. Will R. Manier, the charming Nashville, Tennessee, lawyer who was president of Rotary International in the *annus horribilis* 1936–37, asked: "What use is it to be hurtful if we let pass what we don't expect will eventuate and we hope won't eventuate?"[61] This tactful inaction justified not vetoing out of hand the Danes' earnest proposal to compile European membership lists profession by profession so that businessmen in the same line of work could make contact with one another. Words could be spent to condemn this outlandish corporatism; the whole point of the movement was to socialize *across* the professions. But why bother when the matter would disappear for lack of time and energy? Tactful inaction also justified not blasting a cockamamie proposal from the European Extension Committee to open clubs in Stalin's Russia. Why quibble about principles? Nothing could come of it, since no business elites existed in the land of the Bolsheviks. Tactful in-action also justified neutrality in the face of the European dictatorships down to 1941.

It was already a large concession to the complexity of Europe that an overseas "office" (not a "headquarters," it was often stressed) was estab-lished on the continent in 1925 to supervise regional affairs. The purpose first and foremost was to improve communication with and among conti-nental Europeans, not to foster national, much less regional, autonomy. Like many other international agencies, the office was located in Switzer-land to take advantage of that country's central position, neutrality, and multilingual labor force. However, Zurich was chosen over Geneva, to put it closer to German-speaking central Europe and farther away from the League of Nations and other agencies of European internationalism for which the American officialdom, unlike European Rotarians, showed scant sympathy. Working out of modest quarters on the fourth floor of the Basler Bank on 21 Börsenstrasse in the gabled center of Old Zurich, the European office hummed along like a powerfully charged little trans-former, routinely switching among five languages to respond to the 2,000 or so queries a month, and if necessary arranging translations into an-other five. It took instructions from and referred questions back to Chi-cago, all the while making the arrangements for and presiding over the European Advisory Committee's meetings, which in the best of circum-stances took place in Baden-Baden, where one could also take the baths, and in the worst in Belgrade, which from west of the Rhine was a two-day trip on the Orient Express.

If one imagines Rotary International as European elites' first experi-ence of extra-European rule, the importance of showing that the rules were not specifically American, much less arbitrary, coercive, or undemo-cratic, can be better appreciated. "All power to procedure" could have been the slogan. "Put things through channels," "follow traditional us-age"—those phrases "worked like magic," according to the European secretary, Alex Potter. Whenever this doggedly patient Canadian was faced with complaints "that rules, regulations, constitutional provisions, etc. . . . have been put in force by Americans and therefore are not suited to European conditions," he found it "psychologically . . . better to tell them: 'Well, let's study the matter and see if we can find anything better'" rather than to say, "Now boys, you must do this because Rotary Interna-tional says so." When seemingly irreconcilable differences arose with the European leaders, he turned over the problem for review by the "Aims and Objects Committee," "Classification Committee," "Extension Committee," or some other. This strategy worked like a charm: "invariably they arrive at the same result that has been arrived at previously. But having arrived at that result themselves, they are much more satisfied in carrying out the regulation than if they feel that it is imposed on them by Rotary International."[62]

The urgency to maintain oversight on operations yet not appear to control them was brought home by the tendency of all the European clubs to develop national "characters," some even more obstinate and disagreeable in their own way than the Germans'.

The British established an especially negative example, as far as Chicago was concerned, by insisting on autonomy of action. Founded in London in 1911, Rotary International of the British Isles, or RIBI, had experienced the same impetuous growth as in United States before World War I, and its membership came from men with similar small and middle-size business and professional backgrounds. But once the club movement got going, the civic-political outlook tended to differ, reflecting the declining fortunes of the British Empire. Though conservative, it was reform-minded in the Lloyd George tradition, reflecting the perception of the middle classes that they were being squeezed between the "aristo-snobs and the plebs"—meaning corporate capital and organized labor. Later Winston Churchill would try to exploit this sentiment by having Ernest Bevin, the Labour leader in his wartime coalition, present the first glimpse of the government's plan for postwar reform to London Rotarians at their weekly luncheon at the Connaught Room in 1940. This deference to the opinion of Rotarian businessmen, who very warmly received the proposals that in 1942 would lead to the Beveridge Report, would do the Conservative Churchill little good over the long run. Many of the "Brothers," along with other middle-class voters, swung to Labour in 1945, putting him out of office.[63]

It was at British Rotary's initiative that Chicago had held the first conference abroad, in Edinburgh in 1921, only to discover that its securest European ally had become its organizational nemesis. A practically autonomous power, Rotary in Britain was now found to have its own London headquarters, around which about 60 of the 375 clubs of Great Britain and Ireland clustered. That arrangement went contrary to the notion that there should be only one club to a city. It also had its own governing board, which appointed its own independent district chairs, its own publications, and its own plethoric contingents of articulate committee men, some of whom were also gifted amateur constitutionalists cheerfully intent on criticizing and correcting the injudiciously mercenary, salvationist, sometimes abstruse, and occasionally plain wrong language in the proliferation of documents by their American brothers. It had its own system of assessing dues that it had no intention of forwarding to Chicago. Last, it had its own thick relationship with the clubs popping up all over its imperial dominions, first in Canada and soon afterward in South Africa, New Zealand, Australia, Singapore, and other outposts of the empire.

Worse, the British presented a model that Rotary International's constitution vetoed elsewhere. The district, which was never formally to be congruent with the nation-state, was the basic unit of administration. Once the number of clubs reached fifteen, they were grouped in a district. In practice, clubs were established along national territorial lines. Nevertheless, irrespective of numbers or inclination, there was never to be an entity called "French Rotary," much less "German Rotary." Hence Rotary in mid-1930s France officially consisted of three districts of Rotary International, and the German clubs were officially called District 73 and also included the Austrian circles.

Italian Rotary was the outstanding exception. And its peculiarity could indirectly be blamed on the British, for Rotary had been brought to Milan in 1923 via Glasgow by the gregarious Scots expatriate James Henderson, general director since 1911 of the Italian-British textile firm Cucirini Cantoni Coats, and by the Irish-Italian Leo Giulio Culleton, the chief engineer and managing director at the Italian subsidiary of Worthington Pumps. Its first recruits were drawn from the exclusive Anglo-American Circle. The combination of hard-edged British textile manufacture, Italian *bella figura,* and American corporate capitalism produced an anglophilia, snobbery, and suave good fellowship unmatched anywhere in the world outside the club life of the British Raj. The Italian model, the founders reiterated, was the self-governing RIBI. Its membership was elitist, "aristocratic" as opposed to "vulgarly democratic." Expanding slowly, picky about who joined, Italy's Rotary was firmly controlled by the high bourgeoisie of the North. Finding that lowbrow Chicago deeply misunderstood who they were when at the outset they were lumped with the motley club life of Cuba, Spain, and Portugal in the first "Latin" district, the founders lobbied fiercely to become a separate entity, District 46. The moment they acquired that status in 1925, having reached the ten-club minimum, the Italians installed a permanent national council and secretariat in Milan, recruited a who's-who of the professional and business elite, and obtained honorary membership, a category that didn't officially exist, for the king, nine princes of the royal blood, and, for good measure, the journalist Arnaldo Mussolini, younger brother of Benito. Through the voice of Achille Bossi, the club's permanent secretary, a lawyer by training and signally clever, Italian Rotary expressed the conviction that true world citizenship began at home with acts of homage to the government. It therefore cultivated close relations with the Fascist regime, taking great pride in being able to say that Mussolini, as the head of the government, was its protector. This claim was useful in protecting the clubs from accusations that they were an extension of the "demo-plutocratic" nations that disdained "proletarian" Italy. The claim remained plausible until 1938, when the tyrant withdrew his favor.[64]

What would "the Europeans" have wanted if granted autonomy? Americans posed that question rhetorically and often with a certain tendentiousness to prompt their brethren to recognize how important this putatively neutral movement was to their cohesiveness as Europeans. Indeed, all the Europeans looked after their nations' interests in some measure. What kind of elites would they have been if they hadn't? Thus Rotarian M. B. Gerbel, the master Austrian road and bridge engineer, was a major patron of Balkan clubs as a means of reinforcing German-Austrian business in the area, as well as enlarging the German-language bloc. In turn, the French, out of fear of German expansion, played an especially dynamic role in the international leadership. District 46 hosted the international conference on May 5–8, 1937, at Nice, a huge success in spite of the bad times; moreover, its onetime governor, Maurice Duperrey, an abrasives manufacturer, was the first continental European to hold the presidency of Rotary International, an event he commemorated during his tenure in 1937–38 with a twenty-day trip round the world, the thrust of which was to show that French universalism was as dynamic as the American version. The small neutrals were bigger players than their size denoted, with all due difference between, at one extreme, the Swedes, whose idea of impartiality contemplated strong ties to Germany and overlooked its expansionist impulses toward eastern Europe, and, at the other, Belgium, whose vulnerability made it a small but shrill guard dog against big-power nationalism.

The dilemma was indeed to find some middle ground between European self-rule and American-led globalism. "Whispering voices" wanted to put an end to "the so-called American supremacy," as Kurt Belfrage, the distinguished Swedish banker, acknowledged. But if these efforts were successful, he doubted that a "united and unanimous European Rotary" would survive. To protect the internationalism of the movement given the tempestuousness of intra-European relations, members had to be as pragmatic as the Americans, but even more idealistic. "Let us stand with our feet on solid earth but with our eyes turned upwards," he exhorted his fellows. That was high-flown language for a banker. Louis Steinmann, a Belgian, put the problem in more down-to-earth terms: "Europe is not ready for Area Administration. We are too national for this."[65]

Using American to Speak European

In turn, as if to clarify that American leadership stemmed from best practice rather than bureaucratic manipulation, the Americans underscored: "We care nothing about administration"; "we want to be assured that the program of Rotary is finding a way into the hearts of the people."[66] Practically speaking, this meant first and foremost the literal translation of its principles, disseminated in pamphlets of astounding prolixity, number, and abstruseness of language. The bigger problem was to embrace these principles: for Europeans, "It was not simply a question of form but of thought," as Edouard Willems, Rotary of Belgium's founder, remarked. "In the process of translation, European thinking has somehow to replace the Anglo-Saxon."[67]

Translation in the literal sense was indispensable nonetheless. Although English was the leading global language by the 1920s, it was certainly not the language of European bourgeois civilization. Within all of Europe it was the first language of only 47 million people, most all of them living in the British Isles. Far more people, at least 80 million, spoke German, which was also the second language for many minorities of central Europe. French, in addition to being spoken by 41 million French citizens and tens of thousands in France's empire, was also the second language of intellectual elites thanks to the prestige of its literature and the legacy of the Enlightenment. Spanish, though spoken by only 16 million people in Europe, was the lingua franca of Latin America, where there was an active Rotary movement. Italian may have been spoken almost exclusively in Italy, in onetime Venetian outposts in the eastern Mediterranean, and by hundreds of thousands of immigrants. But that language, too, accounted for at least 40 million speakers.[68]

The translation of Rotarian terminology into European was further complicated by what Antoine Meillet, professor of Indo-European languages at the Collège de France, called the "crisis of European languages." By that he meant, first, the fracturing of the European language map with the proliferation of national languages—Czech, Polish, Hungarian, Serbo-Croatian—as new states were founded in east-central Europe after World War I. He also meant the end of the so-called universal tongues, meaning those written and spoken by elites: his own French, the language of international conferences; and German, the language that had dominated central and eastern Europe. The "crisis" of tongues was further reflected in the jargons of new professions like the cinema and advertising, as well as the vocabularies of movements and institutions like Rotary itself.[69] Rotary International's language, then, was not yet English—at least not in principle. It simply couldn't be. Too few continental Rotarians spoke it. In Dresden one-fifth of the club members indicated that they knew English, more than knew French.[70] Wisely, then, the European secretariat recognized four official languages—French, German, Italian, and Spanish—in addition to English, and they supervised the task of translating documents into five more. Occasional motions to use English as a universal language to simplify communication, at least at the world congresses, were resoundingly defeated. European businessmen were canny in their recognition that to accept English as the official language was to sanction a wholesale transfer of cultural capital to the Anglo-American world.

Even so, the language of procedure was loaded with words whose translation implied the transfer of the civic culture in which they originated. True, some words didn't catch on, like "brothers." National notions of male companionship dictated the preservation of "Brat," "Brüder," "amico," "campañero," or "comrade," each suggesting a different notion of fraternity, friendship, and intimacy.[71] However, the translation of the founding organizational principles, and especially the translation of the classification principle and the principle of service, involved real linguistic struggles. Here the stakes were high.

The classification principle was "unerringly" to guide the selection of members. To help aspirant clubs to identify prospective members, Rotary International generated a universal list of professions. By the 1930s this general catalogue included around 2,300 lines of work, from Aeronautics to Wool. Most of the choices reflected the list's American origins: Beverages and Broadcasting were juxtaposed with Building and Burials; and

Real Estate and Recreation were followed by Religion. These major classifications were in turn subdivided; Real Estate, for example, could encompass business properties as well as private homes. Religion demonstrated the liberality of the U.S. conception of belief; organized with the impartiality of the alphabet, the subdivision started with Buddhism, followed by Christianity (subdivided once more into Established Churches, Free Churches, Roman Catholicism), and moved along through Confucianism, Hinduism, Judaism, Muhammadanism, and Taoism to Zoroastrianism. In effect, a profession was defined by the capacity to offer the community a ware or service. By that token, priests, ministers, imams, rabbis, gurus, and the like all provided religious offices; and, similarly, realtors supplied home purchases, veterinarians animal care, and concertmasters artistic enjoyment.

Though the universal list was formulated for the express purpose of avoiding controversy, no aspect of the "rules of Chicago" generated more perplexity, ridicule, and protests. Not that Rotary International was inflexible about deviations from the norm, provided the local clubs could provide some plausible sociological explanation. Indeed, local clubs-in-formation took a certain self-absorbed pleasure in measuring the eccentricities of their social profile with respect to the larger scheme of things, especially in view of the end result, which was for a faraway authority to certify that they were indeed a "representative cross-section" of the local community. To establish the club at Vichy, Rotary International recognized a whole roster of medical subspecialties—liver doctors; plastic surgeons; eye, nose, and throat specialists; dieticians—as befitted treatment of maladies under cure at the world-famous French spa town. At Plauen, a somber Saxon manufacturing center eighty miles southwest of Dresden, the sponsors, after having had to make a special plea for membership because their town's population was under 100,000, were hugely gratified to discover that their backwater's main claim to fame, namely felt cloth processing, had made it onto the universal list of classifications. This recognition salved the sense of mortification of the founding secretary, whose poor English caused the initial application to generate a flurry of correspondence. His German-English dictionary had supplied him with a "false friend," *Filz,* which could be translated as "felt" but also as "skinflint." How embarrassing to have chosen such a word to describe the occupation of Mr. Rüdiger, Rodewisch Felt Manufacturing's chief sales manager.[72]

Nothing could prevent the Italians from giving the principle "their own interpretation," as the British chair of the subcommittee on classification ruefully put it. Aside from listing honorary members, mainly royalty related to the House of Savoy and high government officials, a practice that went wholly against the notion that Rotary should not be considered an honorific title, they included the *federali* of the Fascist party, sometimes real thugs, by listing them under the category "charities and public works, directors of." The prince of Niscemi, a Sicilian *bon vivant* living off his vast landed estates, was classified as a "horse trainer."[73] It would be simple to write off these classifications as spurious or to argue, as Europeans themselves sometimes did in self-criticism, that the system only encouraged lying. Behind these original interpretations, there was a different notion of elites, one not bound up with hard-and-fast definitions of professions, and with a different notion of the community as well, one disinclined to open old hierarchies to new professions or to elaborate a new ethic of service.

Take Elbe-Florence. For the Dresdeners, it was first and foremost a city of finance and industry, the arts, and men devoted to service to the state. Their pride in the city's cultural mission was especially notable. Not only did they include the heads of all of the leading cultural institutions, from the State Opera and the State Symphony Orchestra to the State Historical Museum and the famous Hygiene Museum, but they also wanted to include leading artists. That was perfectly fine, Chicago replied, provided the prospective members' renown as artists provided them with an independent income. Can we detect the hand of the corresponding secretary, von Frenckell, the husband of singer Minni Nast, in the request that the fine arts classification be further subdivided to include both the baritone and the tenor of the State Opera? That query clearly bollixed the Men of Chicago. Only after consulting the board's Committee on Classifications and corresponding with the Zurich office did they finally deliver their Solomonic decision. A singer was a singer. The service he provided came from the quality of voice that made his reputation. The public didn't care whether he was a tenor or a baritone provided it was satisfied with his performance. Hence, by proposing two singers, Dresden was mistakenly "proposing a duplication of services."[74] Dresden wisely, perhaps with hilarity, let the matter drop. What could be expected from cultural philistines, unable to distinguish a tenor from a baritone, understand their amour-propre, or appreciate their rivalry for public admiration?

If Dresdeners were perplexed by Chicago's commodification of artists, the Chicagoans must have puzzled over the Dresdeners' devaluing of commerce. In the United States, professions related to commerce were omnipresent; in Britain as well. But as a rule, the farther east and south one went on the European continent, the more conspicuous was their absence. Dresden never had any representative from commerce. Most retailers could be described as petit bourgeois; their manners, education, culture, and schedules were so different from those of the high bourgeoisie that no luncheon club could bridge the chasm. The other complication was that when retailing did become big business, mainly in large cities, most proprietors were Jewish. True, Georg Tietz, the Jewish principal of the Hermann Tietz Department Store, was a sometime member of the Berlin Rotary. And his cousin Alfred Leonhard, the head of Tietz's Rhineland branch, was a leading member in Cologne. So was the latter's friend at the Saarbrücken Club, Martin Cohen, the chief of the Passage-Department Store. But given a choice, the preference was for Jews from other professions. In Paris and elsewhere, to speak of the overrepresentation of commerce among members was to employ a code word for too many Jews.[75]

To translate "service," the other fundamental principle of organization, was equally challenging. Ethics of noblesse oblige, altruism, and solidarity ran deep in the European upper classes, in different measure among all faiths, Catholic, Protestant, and Jewish. In Catholicism it was attached to charity; in Protestantism, to the Calvinist calling. However, the notion of "good works" was divorced from the particular meaning that "service" had acquired in the United States, where it resonated with connotations of uplift, neighborliness, helpfulness, but also the attentiveness of provider to customers and clients.

As we will often find here, struggles over transferring a concept were reflected in struggles over translation. The French played with *solidarisme*—though that evoked late nineteenth-century reform movements. *Servir* caught on quickly enough, though as the French pun on the word suggested, too few local Rotarians grasped the distinction between "to help out" *(servir)* and "to help oneself to" *(se servir)*. Italians played with *altruismo* and *noblesse oblige,* an atavism, before embracing an equivalent of the English word, *servizio,* at first putting it in quotation marks "as if it were a dirty word." Local Rotarians liked the neologism; it reflected the times, which shunned vapidly passé humanism for the Fascist New Man's efficient action. They also liked to recall that service was by no means a new concept for ancient merchant cultures. On a sixteenth-century Spoleto doorway, somebody noted the inscription: "To serve, you gain—Serve as much as you can."[76] And at the Mann family's merchant offices in Lübeck, somebody remembered seeing the motto "Enjoy your business during the day, but do it so you can sleep well at night." The closest German word, *Dienst,* sounded like domestic service, some complained, and the common rendering, *Dienstleistung,* or "service-performance," was ridiculed as incorrect German. Rotarian purists like von Frenckell thought the best term was a neologism, *Der Service-Gedanke.* Few Germans were convinced. Von Frenckell also thought that the perfect translation for "Service above Self" was the phrase *Gemeinnutz vor Eigennutz,* or "public need before private greed." That had become a favorite Nazi slogan, drawn from the lexicon of medieval solidarity. Nobody outdid the Italians in semantic sleights of hand: embarrassed by the firestorm that broke out abroad upon Italy's invasion of Ethiopia in 1935, the Italian Rotary urged their European brethren to regard the Fascist regime's mission in East Africa as a "service to civilization" (*servizio alla civiltà*).[77]

If we look at how the Rotary clubs of Duluth and Dresden approached the problem of building bridges, quite literally, the differences become clear. The Duluth Rotary's first and proudest achievement, completed in only two months in 1917, was to raise $2,000 to build a wooden span across the nearby Pigeon River to link the United States with Canada. Before then, the only way to cross the roiling torrent was by steamship three times weekly or by a chartered boat. The "Outlaw Bridge," as it was proudly named, offered the only local crossing until 1930, when the U.S. and Canadian governments cooperated to put up a steel structure.[78] In a similar affirmation of cross-border communication, the Dresdeners contemplated as their club's first activity to petition the German State Railroad System about the frustrating delays at the border between Saxony and Czechoslovakia, and they were greatly pleased that the Prague club, founded by Jan Masaryk, did likewise by forwarding a complaint to the Czech Ministry of Transportation. On the Dresdeners' side, however, doubts arose as to whether the club as a whole should be involved or only the members whose interests would benefit. This one initiative, it was decided, was justifiable on the grounds that several other groups were backing it as well. But beyond this modest lobbying, there was no further action.[79] Admittedly, the worlds of possibility were incomparably different: in the case of Duluth, the virtual absence of government, an unguarded wilderness frontier, a habit of action unfettered by rules and regulation, in contrast to Dresden, where the organization of the railroad system was an affair of high politics, organized interests, and state bureaucracy and the frontier lined with heavily policed customs points. But it is also true that the bourgeoisie of Dresden regarded their club as *Kultur*, and would have been appalled to sully it with base economic considerations.

Dresden's dilemma was common on the continent, not because European clubs were egotistical, indifferent, or benighted, but because the "service ideal" was hard to imagine, much less to implement, in communities wracked by partisan, religious, and regional splits. When the socially conscious bourgeoisie of France, Belgium, and the Netherlands took up service in the cause of social reform in the politically polarized world of the 1930s, they risked splitting clubs down the middle, between partisans of Popular Front movements and loyalists of far-right groupings. When, in the aftermath of the bloody repression of the Asturian miners' strikes in October 1934, the Rotarians of Spain wanted "to bring [their] grain of sand to relieve so much pain," they were determined to abide by "absolute nonpartisanship" because "suffering knows no ideology." Hence the Madrid club voted to pay the expenses for raising five boys, orphans of the civil guard killed in the course of confronting the miners. To be even-handed, they also proposed to pay an equivalent sum in money, clothing, food, and medicine to the defeated workers' families. In the end, though, their goal of "peace and cooperation" was a chimera in the face of near–civil war conditions, and their action "served, sadly, to very little effect."[80]

Of course, there were cases in which the service ideal was narrowly self-serving, designed solely to benefit the elite. In Milan, an egregious case, service took the form of building the first golf club at Monza, subsidizing the publication of automobile guidebooks for the Touring Club of Italy, raising Rotarian monies for fellowships and prizes for university students, and, in the face of intense soliciting by the local Fascist "directors of charity," making generous contributions to the Fascist Winter Help funds.

The Businessman's Church

For Europe, Rotary raised the specter of religion. In America, it had not. Or had it? Tocqueville had asserted that Christianity in the United States was an "established and irresistible fact which no one seeks to attack or to defend."[81] Rotary asserted that it was ecumenical, true to the religious pluralism of American society. Nonetheless, though no records were kept on members' religion, the vast majority of Rotarians were Protestant churchgoers. Moreover, the salvationist rhetoric of Rotary resonated with a religious vocabulary. So Paul Harris, "like the Apostle Paul, was converted on the Road to Tarsus," and the brothers, like all good Christians, subscribed to the Golden Rule, which was incorporated into a Rotary Code of Ethics to guide business practice. Lacking the religious intensity of Christian cults, the Rotarian "faith" was like a dab of cologne that exuded a pleasant odor of sanctity. It was thus perfectly suited to societies in which religious creeds were sworn to like advertising pitches: "I believe in this product, not that one." Since Rotarianism was not a creed, from the American perspective, there was no reason for it not to flourish even where church and state had not been blessed as in America by being separated by the Constitution.

Initially clubs did pop up in Catholic countries, including France, Italy, Austria, and Spain; in predominantly Protestant Sweden and England; and in religiously mixed countries, notably Germany and Holland. Perhaps because Rotary's literature was written mainly in American English, perhaps because the Vatican was preoccupied elsewhere, mainly with the Marxist atheism of Bolshevik Russia, for two decades Rotary eluded the vigilance of the Jesuits, the Catholic Church's guard dog against religiously suspect movements.

However, all roads eventually lead to Rome. In 1927 the sharp-eyed bishop of San Miguel in El Salvador alerted the Vatican's secretary of state to a newly founded businessmen's club in San Salvador that, after consulting his synod, he denounced as "a suspicious, seditious, and secret association" akin to freemasonry, Communism, and the egregiously heretical sect Theosophism, known for combining oriental mysticism, Protestant fundamentalism, and an eccentric feminism. The matter was immediately delegated for study to the competent congregations of the Apostolic See, namely the Consistory, which oversaw the clergy, and the Holy Office, which rendered judgments on questions of faith. Meanwhile the Jesuits set to work. In Spain, where they worriedly saw clubs forming in sixteen cities toward establishing a local district, the investigation was entrusted to the thirty-four-year-old professor of theology Felipe Alonso Barcena, S.J., expert in the study of apologetics. The brilliant young zealot's conclusions, presented in a two-part article in *Razon y Fe* (Reason and Faith), were devastating. Aside from condemning the frivolous social climbing, ostentatiously expensive weekly luncheons, and moral hypocrisy of parvenu elites—all vices, but none major transgressions—he exposed the kinship with freemasonry and the doctrinal heterodoxy of this "businessman's Church." These acts could be cardinal sins.[82]

Barely a year later, on June 16 and July 21, 1928, the voice of the Vatican reverberated through the quasi-official *Civiltà Cattolica,* the mouthpiece of the Jesuits. By ordaining itself as a moral authority, Rotary had been found to encourage "the common heresy, condemned by Leo XIII in his 1884 Encyclical, *Humanus Genus,* that man was sufficient unto himself when it came to interpreting moral law, no specific religion was obligatory, and any creed could be his guide." Moreover, even if Rotary wasn't actually in league with freemasonry, the Church's two-century-old nemesis, it certainly acted as if it were, displaying the same "utilitarian individualism," the same "religious indifferentism." The Consistory soon prescribed penalties: any priest who joined Rotary did so under "pain of mortal sin and excommunication" from the sacraments. Pending further study, the Vatican left action on the moral danger wrought by membership among lay Catholics to the discretion of individual archdioceses.[83]

The Church's reaction was so ferocious because it had been engaged in a full-fledged counter-reformation since at least 1917. Faced on the one hand with atheistic Russia and on the other by materialistic, immoral America, while in Europe itself secular religions tugged on the faithful—on the left in the form of messianic communism, and on the right, fascist paganism—Pius XI boldly moved to reconstitute an integrally Catholic society. Once he had obtained recognition of the Vatican's statehood by means of the Lateran Accords signed with Fascist Italy in 1929, he laid the basis of a civil society in his postage-stamp kingdom, first in the form of public services, such as a radio transmitter, railroad station, and government post office. Then, using all the weapons in his power—anathema, conciliation, but also the Church's grip over Catholic elites, who operated in the arenas of business, military, and civil service—Pius appealed to a restoration of Christianity. Based on the idea of class reconciliation, Christian solidarity, austerity, and benevolence, the Catholic counter-reformation of the early twentieth century was advancing a subculture as distant from market culture as could be tolerated under a capitalist system.

Inevitably this endeavor portrayed the United States in an ambiguous role. On the one hand, America was the crucible of religious experimentation. On the other hand, it was the homeland of millions of Catholic faithful. When Leo XIII composed his apostolic letter, *Testem Benevolentiae* of January 22, 1899, to denounce religious modernism, meaning the belief that doctrine should be updated with popular ideas and methods, he called it by the name that the Curia used, namely Americanism. At the same time Leo made it clear that his usage wasn't intended to condemn "the characteristic qualities that reflect honor on the people of America." The problem for later popes who fulsomely praised the American Legion of Decency, the Hays Code, and other institutions typical of American moral policing was that for every example of this positive civic action, there was a score of lay movements of dubious religious inspiration claiming to offer ethical guidance. Rotary International was even more problematic because of its global pretensions. Hitherto the ecclesiastical potentates close to the Curia had stayed clear of pronouncing on the morality of great powers, the Soviet Union with its dangerous atheism being a special exception. However, in the spread of Rotary, the Jesuits condemned the "gigantic efforts of the United States to expand and consolidate its political and economic expansion throughout the world," using "moral interferences to consolidate economic hegemony."[84]

These were fulminating words, opening the prospect of excommunication. Turning to the Americans, Europeans appealed for help to explain that Rotary was neither religious nor freemasonic. In response, the Americans launched a massive, sustained public relations campaign to appeal to common sense and educated opinion. Everybody was a target, from the holy pontiff to the lowliest prelate, from the agnostic layman to the religiously devout. The campaign underscored that Rotary membership did not interfere with churchgoing or with the plurality of religious beliefs. If Rotary's district governor for Mexico sent a message of congratulations to the new President Calles (who like all presidents of Mexico in the wake of the Revolution was zealously anticlerical), he was merely being respectful of public authority; if Rotary in Mexico made a donation to the Young Men's Christian Association, this was not religious propaganda, but good deeds. The goal was simply to provide playgrounds and other help to the wretchedly poor youth of the metropolis. As for the allegations of freemasonic ties: yes, Paul Harris had once been a Mason, but not at the time he founded Rotary and certainly not at present. As for the good faith of Catholics who belonged: who could doubt the devotion of Germany's Count Cuno or Count Henry Carton de Wiart, the onetime premier of Belgium and the head of the Catholic party, not to mention the 273 Roman Catholic clergymen, members in good standing in the United States and Canadian clubs?[85] Like other American Catholic Rotarians of high standing called on to speak about "Why you enjoy being a member of Rotary," John Cavanaugh, the longtime president of the University of Notre Dame, publicly endorsed this "beautiful and beneficent movement." "I am a member of Rotary myself and I strongly recommend it to European Catholics."[86]

The accusations by the Catholic hierarchy, inflamed by right-wing movements, were hard to lay to rest. Through the connection to freemasonry, Rotarianism was associated with all the bugaboos of the counterrevolutionary right, including the world Zionist conspiracy, Bolshevism, and the racially and religiously hybrid Theosophism. At bottom, the Catholic Church was saying that under the pretext of moralizing, honest people acting in good faith were forgetting the true fonts of morality. In rejoinder, European Rotarians said that honest people joined not to partake of a new religious ethic, but to express a new public ethos.[87] The difference was measured by a thin line—one the devout had crossed innumerable times since Calvin. By the 1920s the Americans had practically erased the distinction, so bent were they on promoting the new spirit of service capitalism. Following in the Protestant tradition, Rotary was urging European Catholics too to believe that religion worked not by means of doctrinal persuasion, much less ecclesiastical power, but by individually interpreting scripture as a guide to social conduct. At Rotary's urging, Catholics were to become not *less* religious, but differently religious.

Toward that end, European Rotarians subscribed to what had previously been regarded as American models of religious pluralism. When, in the wake of the riots attending the Stavisky corruption scandals of 1934, Rotary in France came under attack from the far right as a freemasonic, antireligious secret society, Governor Fabvre strongly recommended that each incoming president start by making a round of courtesy calls: the first stop was the prefect, the representative *in loco* of the national government, followed by the heads of all the religious communities, including Israelites, Protestants, and Catholics.[88]

That Rotary was able to defend itself from the most censorious assaults of the Catholic Church (at least outside Spain) depended not so much on tactfulness as on the degree to which religious practice was becoming more privatized, more informal, and more religious in the most formal sense—by partaking in the rituals of churchgoing. In Italy, Rotary played on this growing separation. But it also found a backup in nepotistic relations. Pius XI's nephew, the engineer Count Franco Ratti, was one of the Milan Rotary's most distinguished members. His Holiness had given him permission to join, it was said, and Pius also gave his blessings to his nephew's society marriage to the daughter of Senator Silvio Crespi, the textile magnate, another prominent Rotarian. *Vox populi* had it that the blessing forgave at least one other peccadillo as well.[89]

In Spain, by contrast, religiosity was practically synonymous with everyday material existence among Catholics. It was a nation whose King, Alfonso XIII, had consecrated it to the Sacred Heart of Jesus in 1919. "You will reign in Spain," said the dedication inscribed on the giant statue on a hilltop outside Madrid in consolation for the ingratitude of the modern world. The country was beset by cultural civil war well before General Franco's insurrection against the Republic in June 1936, agitated by the new Constitution in 1931, which declared church and state separated.[90] When one reads of the vicissitudes of everyday life for Rotarians—all men of considerable substance and standing—the effect is at once risible and harrowing. In Valencia the president of Rotary, Leno de Respinosa, was prevented from buying a piece of property and then forced to withdraw his sons from their Jesuit school. The Infante Don Jaime, heir to the Carlist pretender to the throne, was constrained to postpone his entrance into the Madrid Club, lest his son be barred from making his First Communion. At Majorca, President Forteza withdrew on the grounds that his mother had already suffered too much on behalf of his convictions. After making her habitual donation to the parish charity, she reminded the priest to make his usual visit to the house to bless her son. When in all innocence she let drop that Forteza had become a Rotarian, the good padre imprecated so furiously that he was a sinner unworthy of a visit from a minister of God that she collapsed from grief. Out of sympathy, the club agreed to suspend meetings to await better times.[91] It reopened briefly, only to close down when the civil war broke out. Like other Rotary clubs, it was permanently banned by the Franco dictatorship in 1940, not to reopen until 1978, two years after Generalissimo Franco's death.

Drawing the Line

Left to their own devices, there is no reason to believe that Rotary clubs would not have spread in Europe, the economic crisis being only a momentary deterrent. The only place where clubs had ever actually closed of their own volition, Rotary boasted, was in the United States, and, more than anything else, this phenomenon testified to the volatility of U.S. society. Occasionally members simply became bored. More often sudden economic busts caused enterprises to go out of business, making their heads ineligible for Rotary membership or dooming whole townships to collapse together with their club life.

Europeans faced another kind of problem, namely that more and more insistently their governments demanded proof that their citizens were first and foremost nationalists rather than internationalists. As soon as they began to join Rotary, Europeans started to debate over how to divide their loyalties. The Italians, having had to live with a dictatorship from the start, were especially open to professing their dual faith. At the 1929 Dallas Congress it was they who brought to a vote a measure affirming that allegiance to one's own nation was not just compatible with, but the very premise for, being a good internationalist. At the time the concept was unproblematic, especially for American empire-builders, who took it for granted that it was their patriotic duty to be globally minded.

This dilemma—where to place one's loyalties—would be brought home to the Dresdeners with shocking immediacy after Adolf Hitler became chancellor in January 1933. Though numerous members had been sympathetic to an authoritarian solution to the crisis of the Republic, as a group they felt no joy in this turn of events. Almost immediately they were faced with a party diktat, which was then tempered, calling for civil servants and Nazi party members to give up membership. Worse, they were mortified to read that their clubs, born of such good intentions, were being excoriated by the National Socialist press as "freemasonic, pacifistic, internationalist and big capitalist organizations in disguise, directed from abroad and alien to our lifestyle"; that they were aristocratic dueling societies or even vile gambling circles. In the next couple of months the clubs experienced a spate of resignations. Some came from civil servants abiding by the injunction to quit; others from sitting lord mayors and other public officials who, after being replaced by Nazi loyalists, lost the classification that had made them eligible for membership; still others were well-known liberals and Freemasons. Then the anti-Jewish laws caused Jewish members to resign. Their departure was voluntary, it was said, like all the others. And sometimes it was, out of solidarity with the effort to keep the club alive.[92]

The whole movement in Saxony would have collapsed had not von Frenckell devised a cunning step to take the situation in hand. Acting according to what its members were convinced was an honorable end— to serve the state, and especially to repair Germany's tarnished image abroad—the Dresden Rotary committed an act that according to International Rotary procedure was illegal: it dissolved itself and reformed with a new membership, one of its own choosing, vetted to conform to the diktats of the Nazi regime that barred non-Aryans, Freemasons, and various and sundry other personae non gratae. By law, three of its Jewish members could legally belong, and the new organization invited them back, all of them front-line veterans of the Great War, whose sacrifices for the Fatherland were still being honored by not depriving them of citizenship. The two von Klemperers together with a more recent member, Friedrich Salzburg, a prominent notary public specializing in family law, agreed to rejoin, though only after talking the matter over with the Jewish members who had not been invited back. Together they decided that their continued presence would help to uphold the aims and objects of the Rotary movement.[93]

Who knows what discomfort this threesome felt over the next two years? The von Klemperer brothers continued to come, but more and more infrequently as, surreptitiously, they prepared to leave Germany. By contrast, Fritz Salzburg always attended. Being a newcomer, the company was important to him, especially since his best friend, Ernst Winckler, also nicknamed Fritz, a gentile with whom he had passed two years on the Western Front, was a fellow member. As the club became more fully immersed in the Nazi new times, the beautiful room lost its protective charm. True, members "grumbled" about Hitler and thought that Nazism was "against culture" and "unhealthy."[94] But the political tone of the times was closely reflected in the obsequious message that President Grunert sent in the name of the club to local political and military authorities on March 18, 1935, to celebrate Hitler's orders to rearm Germany; it said: "Best wishes on the occasion of this historic decision."[95] Invitations to attend the weekly get-togethers went out to local Nazi officials, even to the Saxon Gauleiter Mutschmann, who, to their discomfort, continued to snub them.

In October 1935 directives from the Nazi party lifted the exemption for Jewish front-line soldiers. The von Klemperers were prepared for this move; both had ceased to attend meetings. Fritz Salzburg was not. He recalled being puzzled when Dr. Grunert, the club president, showed up at his home in person early in the morning of October 16. Grunert apologized for having to "convey something that is infinitely horrible": at a hastily called meeting the evening before, club members had voted to end his membership. Even the membership secretary, his best friend,

Winckler? Salzburg asked in disbelief. Yes, all of them. "That's Unro-tarian," Salzburg burst out. "No," the president corrected him; "It's in-human." Salzburg immediately sent off a long letter of protest to under-score that he had not resigned and that the action violated Rotarian statutes. The members ignored it. To show him that nothing personal was intended, Winckler continued to invite Salzburg and his wife to dine at his home, reminding him of the "time they faced death together" con-fronting the French enemy; and the elegant Kühne, who made a special point of having him attend a soirée at his home, tried to salve his hurt feelings by seating him next to the Rotary president. A few weeks later, after he was notified that non-Aryan notaries had been banned from work, Salzburg patched together what he could of his property. In 1937 he and his family fled to Switzerland and after long travels took up resi-dence in Berkeley, California.[96]

For Rotary in Germany to survive under the Third Reich in the pride-ful, meaningful way its members wanted, it needed recognition from the new regime. That was the conclusion of its leaders as membership dropped and they worried over the still-pending threat that civil servants and Nazi party members would be barred. If Rotary was to serve the na-tion, especially if it was to help to counter mean criticisms from the for-eign press, it could not be a second-class club network. Nor could they, as the cultivated elite, be treated as second-class citizens. The dispute was over how low they should stoop for these ends.

Fate had it that Rotary's future was placed in the graceful hands of one of Dresden's charter members. Hugo Grille, a former head of the judicial police and founder of the Saxon Artist's League, had served as presi-dent of the Rotary of Chemnitz before retiring to Berlin in 1935. The men of Chicago, in the belief that he was a "high Nazi," were convinced that Grille could handle the tricky local situation. Good civil servant that he was, Grille had indeed obtained a party card in 1933. But as a man of the old school, a former member of General Lüdendorff's circle, he was prickly about which Nazis he intended to deal with: the poten-tate Goering ideally; possibly the S.S. chief, Himmler; and Koch, the ad-ministrative head of the Nazi party. But never that vulgar Goebbels: "I wouldn't proffer him my hand!" Gossips had overheard his original words. When somebody quoted them to him, he dismissively said he had been misquoted; his actual words had been: "[Goebbels] didn't want to shake hands." Like many conservative nationalists, he hoped that Hit-ler's rule was a passing phenomenon. But after the foreign minister, the traditionalist Konstantin von Neurath, lost influence and was finally re-moved in November 1937, nobody was left in high places to champion Rotary's alleged usefulness to quell anti-German "hate propaganda."[97]

Nevertheless, Grille, like other conservatives, continued to place hope in the German legal system. In an effort to clarify Rotary's status, he put the case in the hands of a lawyer, Dr. Krueger, an expert on gambling re-sort licenses, also known for having excellent connections with high-placed party men. Meticulously, he set about clarifying three issues. The first was that Rotary was not a refuge for Freemasons. The three "first-degree" Masons who had been identified had long since left the move-ment. The second issue, whether Rotary was friendly toward Jews, was trickier. The evidence showed that all Jewish members had been ejected. If it was true that in their travels abroad Rotarians occasionally come into contact with Jews, that was the nature of international business. And that was surely not a problem Rotary could be expected to solve. The final clarification involved Rotary's status as an international organiza-tion. With tacit approval from Rotary International, District 73 dropped mention of Objective 6, namely international peace. More and more, members spoke of it as "German Rotary." They completely Germanized the American-English terminology. When they gathered for the district meeting in Hanover in May 1937, it took tactful prompting from T. C. Thomsen's self-possessed wife, the opera singer Thomsen-Bjorg, to elicit a toast, even a halfhearted one, to the health of Rotary International.[98]

Above all, Rotarians in Germany sought just a word from high up that Nazi party members and civil servants could remain members. How, oth-erwise, could Rotary dedicate itself to serving the Fatherland? That per-mission was not to come: in late summer, a decree from the Nazi party's Supreme Arbitration Court spelled out that by December 1937 all mem-bers of the party who were also members of the club had either to resign their party membership or resign from Rotary. It would have been sense-less, even dangerous, to dally; on September 7, 1937, the Rotary of Dis-trict 73 declared itself dissolved.

In Italy by late 1937 Mussolini was more and more isolated from the Western powers and more and more in league with Hitler. Now, to show off the pure vigor of Fascist Italy, the regime embarked on its so-called re-form of custom. To call somebody a cosmopolitan, much less a covert in-ternationalist, became nasty invective. The civilized bourgeois manners cultivated by Rotarians in the form of handshakes, luncheon meetings, and the little courtesies of friendship aroused the fury of fisticuff Fascists.

When the news arrived that Rotary had disbanded in Germany, high-placed members rushed over to the Duce's official residence at Palazzo Venezia to urge him to censor the news. He obliged. In June, as a further token of his favor, he took time from his famously overburdened schedule to welcome 150 Japanese and American Rotarians who, on their stopover in Rome on return from the Nice conference, came by to pay their respects to the Duce.[99] Barely six months later, however, the Duce had become indifferent to their fate. The anti-Jewish laws of November 1938 required that all organizations purge their non-Aryan members. And many of the northern clubs had at least one, if not a handful, of Jewish members, mostly engineers and professors. Some of these men had been in the clubs for over a decade.

Later it would be said that resistance to the anti-Jewish laws decided the Italian clubs to disband. If so, it would have been the first time Italian Rotarians had acted on firm principles. Having long made a virtue of being flexible about the rules of Chicago, if they could have they would certainly have flouted this one too. At Como, which had some Jewish members, Angelo Luzzani, a lawyer, volunteered that his group was willing to "sacrifice and accept the racial laws if it [is] so decreed by the government."[100] When the matter was discussed at Messina, where there were no Jewish members, Professor Martino, holder of the chair in physiology at the university, surely got nods of agreement when he made the point that "no Rotary rule actually prescribes that there have to be Jewish elements in the single districts."[101] Above all, it was what Milan thought that mattered. And the Milanese, from their long dealings with the British and American movements, knew enough about international procedure to realize that Rotary International would not tolerate outright expulsions, even though it had shown itself remarkably tolerant regarding the so-called resignations of the Jewish members in Germany. Indeed, the ever-pliable President Bill Manier had made a point of coming to Europe to work behind the scenes with Lester Struthers, the new European commissioner, to smother the protests of members who, instead of departing quietly like the Jewish members at Dresden, noisily agitated to revoke the club charters for violating the rules.[102]

The highly placed Milanese had by now concluded that even if their cherished Jewish members had resigned as a token of solidarity, nothing was going to save the clubs. Rome had become more and more outlandish in its philo-German behavior. Practical enough to know that nothing would pacify the regime, the leadership followed the German example, disbanding the groups in December 1938 with a panache that von Frenckell would have appreciated. The reason officially given—which Chicago gratefully publicized—was that Italian Rotary's goals were now being fulfilled by government policies. In other words, Fascist totalitarianism had reached such an acme of perfection in its services that the men's clubs were simply no longer needed. In Milan on December 20, witnesses recorded the sobs of the female secretary who had been employed there twelve years. President Portaluppi, choking back tears as he addressed the ninety people present, offered consoling words to the effect that their "mission had been fulfilled" and their "patrimony of ideas would remain alive." After rolling up the banner and packing away the registers, they spent several minutes toasting and embracing one another. In unison, before leaving the room at 2:30, they shouted, "Long live the king, long live Savoy!" Then somebody called out, "Let's meet next Tuesday at Tantalo's restaurant."[103] The aristo-bourgeois lifestyle still had other cultural resources.

Dresden was not graced with so glorious a finale. The process of saving Rotary from the Nazis had been going for three years and was completely mired in arcane legalisms, rumor about which would filter back to the Dresden club, whose members, with the old guard departed, were now out of the loop. The quality of membership had declined. The art of the luncheon talk had degenerated, so that often lunch was accompanied by a fifty-minute political rant. The bitter joke circulated that the goal of the old club members (notably Heinrich Arnhold) had been 100 percent attendance whereas 100 percent absence was the aim of the new.[104] Still, the occasional attendance of eleven of the founders, including the fun-loving Blücher and the amiable architect Kühne, recalled the good old days. But the charm was gone. In the spring of 1937 the founding father, von Frenckell, retired with his wife to his estates in Finland. His withdrawal showed his impeccable manners.[105] By then his former employer, the Arnhold Bank, had been put in the hands of an Aryan receiver. With the vile Gauleiter Martin Mutschmann setting the social tone, von Frenckell's gracious ways, if not suspect, were not a significant social asset. Anyway, he never made good on his gracious promise to return to visit with his old friends.

On August 30, 1937, in the expectation that the Nazi party's Supreme Arbitration Court would reaffirm its veto on Rotary membership for civil servants and party members, Dresden's Rotarians gathered for the last time. Arriving at the Europa-Hof in business dress (as the invitation to the emergency meeting prescribed), they agreed to the motion to dissolve their group.[106] The meeting over, they straggled out onto Prager Strasse, though not before some stickler for the rules charged the secretary to wrap up the charter and mail it back to Chicago. That was the procedure to follow in the event of dissolution if one went by the book, which clubs rarely did. So Charter 3010 of Rotary International made its way back to be archived in the offices on East Wacker Drive.

Conceivably, the Dresden group, like the Italians or members from the clubs in Hamburg, Munich, Stuttgart, and elsewhere, continued to meet as "circles of friends." The Parisians recalled that after Rotary was banned by the occupying German forces, they would gather in the large hotels and brasseries, moving from place to place to avoid notice, combining resistance with a small *r* with companionable dining. Once when eating at La Rotonde they were caught off guard by the sudden approach of an imposing German military officer. As they shrank down behind their table, they recognized Karl Schippert, the onetime governor of District 73, a charter member of the Stuttgart club, and the former chief executive of Daimler-Benz. At present he was a general in the Wehrmacht in command of the Renault automobile works, and it was hard for Duperrey, a former president of Rotary International, and his fellow dining companions to think of him as other than what he was, the enemy. Their exchange of pleasantries was civil but brief.[107]

If the Dresden Rotarians did continue to meet informally as a circle of friends, the real end came on the night of February 13–14, 1945, when Allied planes, the spires of the Old City centered in their bomb sights, blitzed the city for fourteen hours. Undeflected from their targets by paltry bursts of antiaircraft fire, the bombardments ignited an inferno of fire that engulfed eleven square miles of the city, killing scores of thousands. Prager Strasse lay at the epicenter, and all the buildings lining its graceful course were pulverized into burning mounds rising two stories high, including the Europa-Hof, where the club had met 400 times.[108] Around the same time, Duluth, its industries booming from the last wartime commissions, reached the acme of its prosperity. At the Hotel Spalding on bustling Superior Street the Rotarians met imperturbably every Thursday at noon.

CHAPTER 2

A Decent Standard of Living

How Europeans Were Measured by the American Way of Life

> *Nowhere in the history of the world is there evidence that*
> *any country has ever deliberately set about raising the stan-*
> *dard of living of its neighbors, let alone that of the entire*
> *world.*
>
> STANLEY HILLER,
> San Francisco businessman, 1945

> *International relations between nations have become so*
> *easy and close through modern technology and the commu-*
> *nication it makes possible, that the European, often without*
> *being conscious of it, applies American conditions as a stan-*
> *dard for his own.*
>
> ADOLF HITLER,
> Nazi party head, 1928

IN 1945 STANLEY HILLER was just an ordinary American citizen. A San Francisco businessman active in the U.S. war effort, he was so fervid about an idea that he paid a vanity press to bring his version of it to the public. His thought was that "so long as there are millions of people who are confined to living on the barest subsistence level, we have in them the potential soldiers who will rise under another Hitler or Mussolini to wage future wars." His prescription was ambitiously high-minded: "we must reorder the economy of the world [so] that all people will have the opportunity to work for a fair remuneration."[1]

In 1928, when Adolf Hitler dictated the quotation above, he was a demagogue with a flagging cause. The subject of his musing—the famously rich "American Standard of Living"—had intrigued him since 1924, when, to celebrate his release from Landsberg Prison, his friend Ernst Haftstängl made him a present of Henry Ford's just-translated autobiography.[2] An ardent motoring fan, Hitler had long marveled at Ford's capacity to pay high wages yet turn out a wonderful machine at a reasonable price. But now he was worried that *Fordismus* might prove successful in Germany. If mass production boosted supply and high wages raised demand, then his dire predictions about Germany's future would be disproved, and he risked becoming just another right-wing irritant. He consoled himself that "the standard of living is not autarchic"; that the masses "want to lead a life like others and cannot."[3] He would exploit that need, as he said elsewhere, to convince them that the "bread of survival" was the "fruit of war."

In radically different ways, each of these men was speaking to the issue of the *standard of living*. No issue in the modern world has generated greater dispute or more disparate remedies than the minimum that humans require to live in dignity. Indeed, by the early twentieth century a whole science had developed around the problem of measuring and improving living standards, inspired at times by the quest for social justice and at others by fear of social disorder, the search for economic stability, or embarrassment over national backwardness.[4] To start with two of the least competent authorities on the matter, one a dilettante, the other a demagogue, might thus be regarded as a scholarly disservice. Yet in their own different ways both men saw a new twist to this vexed problem, namely that with the growing internationalization of cultural models, living standards became an everyday element of the struggle among great powers for global leadership. Accordingly, Stanley Hiller limpidly expressed the imperial project that had matured in the United States over the previous half-century. This had the *high* standard of living as a uniquely American invention whose universal spread was at once economically advantageous to American trade, a force for world order and political democracy, and generative of no significant negative effects, at least none regarded as pernicious enough to excite probing discussion. In turn, Adolf Hitler presciently captured a dilemma that eluded contemporary statesmen, namely that in a global world, as changing standards of living spilled over from one nation to another, old demands for social justice became intertwined with new strivings for consumer satisfaction. Deprived, discontented people were lured by the prosperity and possessions common in other, better-off countries; and for their rulers, "the fight against the child begins."[5]

On how to placate these invidious comparisons, optimistic American mass consumer culture and pessimistic European bourgeois commercial civilization clearly parted ways. Like many other Americans of his time, Hiller believed that with increased productivity from technology and open trade, material well-being would become global. In that belief he was the child of Woodrow Wilson and a direct descendant of Adam Smith. Like many other Europeans of his time, the Nazi leader believed that growth was zero-sum: if some people gained, others would lose. Barring checks on birthrates—which Hitler abhorred as damaging to the race—or the accumulation of new resources—which he declared impossible without expanding empire—the German nation was destined to expire. In his apocalyptic pessimism, he was the spawn of the turn-of-the-nineteenth-century English parson Thomas Malthus, who calculated that as population grew in geometric ratio and the means of subsistence grew arithmetically, the human species would periodically be culled by famine, disease, and strife. In the coming global struggle over resources, whole nations would be excluded from nature's feast, and the weak would fall prey to the strong. This bleak vision resonated widely in the wake of the ruinous conflict of World War I as the terms of trade definitively shifted, and the Old World could no longer count on the New for the magnificent ghost acreage of bygone centuries, precious remittances from millions of emigrants, cheap staples, or high returns on invested capital. The United States had escaped the Malthusian vise, whereas Europe was being choked in its grip. Worse, the United States offered models of new ways of living that completely bypassed political control, multiplying wants and desires, exacerbating feelings of social exclusion, and increasing pressures for radical change.

In the previous chapter we saw how European elites were nudged by the new spirit of capitalism to change their conception of everyday culture by embracing the service ethic. Closed off by their class and cultural outlooks from grasping the sense of the American project or faced with its unfeasibility because of their surroundings, they saw the fate of their clubs bear witness to a Europe radically diverging from America. Defining the "high" or "decent" standard of living as a function of income, the goods that income could buy, and the individual choices these purchases entailed, Americans also confronted European society with a different conception of norms of living. In the face of bourgeois legacies of invidious social distinctions, political cleavages, and, in increasing measure, legalized ethnic and racial bias, American consumer practices advanced the promise of leveling away differences with a neutral standard, namely money income, higher wages, and the access these provided to a plethora of mass-produced goods.

Even as the American standard of living spoke to the need to raise purchasing power to promote recovery from the Great Depression, it sparked fears of out-of-control consumption. European business leaders, eager though they were to experiment with Fordism to increase output, were also under intense pressure from reformers and workers to introduce the whole package—not just technologies to increase productivity, but also higher purchasing power, with who knew what effect on everyday habits. The American standard also distressed cultural elites, who feared a debasement of taste, craftsmanship, and civility. But social reformers too were wary that the American standard, by shaking up the familiarly austere hierarchies of wants, would cause organized labor to lose its political edge and workers their ethical compass.

Making Detroit the Measure of All Europe

The frustrating predicament faced by reformers turns up unexpectedly in the records of the very statesman to whom contemporaries turned for calm and clear-cut answers on the subject of the standard of living. *Zut* (damn), *tant pis* (tough), *impossible* (no way), *Je n'accepte pas* (unacceptable), *tant pis encore* (tough again), "They expect us to do all that for 25,000 dollars"—these intemperate words were out of character for Albert Thomas, the revered French socialist who in 1920 had become chief of the International Labor Organization in Geneva, the very first agency set up to monitor and improve standards of living on a global scale. But they are clearly his, tidy marginalia on the typewritten letter dated July 16, 1929, from Major Lyndall Urwick, head of the International Management Institute. The matter that the shrewd Britisher was trying to negotiate regarded what would come to be known as the Ford-ILO Inquiry.[6] This inquiry would be the first effort to compare systematically the living conditions of workers in the United States and Europe in the twentieth century. It was also the first to impose on Europeans the urgency of grappling with what the Americans meant by a "decent" standard of living.

Why Thomas—a man who was famed for his steely-nerved constancy at surely the most thankless job in the world—should have been repeatedly caught off guard as the Inquiry proceeded over the next two years requires a glance backward to April 23, 1929, when a request for help from Ford Motor Company Limited was received at the International Labor Organization. At the time, the world's best-known company had just begun another big push into global markets, and it was seeking information on living costs in the European region in order to determine the pay scales in the seventeen cities in twelve different countries where it either had already established or intended to set up its plants.

The avowed purpose sounded innocent enough: this was to know "how much a Parisian, German, etc. worker would need to expend if his general standard of living was to be approximately equivalent to that of his Detroit counterpart." This "general standard of living" should be treated as a monetary sum, advised Sir Percival Perry, chairman of Ford's London-based European operations. More precisely, it should be calculated as the total monies the worker family disbursed each year on food, shelter, clothing, taxes, and so on. Accordingly, the first step was to find out how the lowest-paid, regularly employed wage earners at Ford's Detroit assembly plants spent their paychecks in a given year. The next was to determine what it would cost workers in each of the selected European cities to consume an equivalent basket of goods and services. If in Paris, for example, the commodity basket cost 85 percent of what it cost in Detroit (adjusted for currency differences), the Ford Company would pay the Parisian automobile assembler 85 percent of the Detroit wage. The aim, Sir Percival reiterated, was to help the Ford Company "determine the maximum efficiency" of the worker regardless of where he lived.[7]

Now in principle, a request of this kind was not inappropriate. Inquiries about the nuts and bolts of working-class existence fitted right in with the lofty mandate of the International Labor Organization. Conceived in the side chambers of Versailles in the course of drawing up the treaties to end World War I, the ILO was intended to support the League of Nations' peacekeeping machinery. Its specific task was to reform the "conditions of labour," guided by the humanistic principle that "Labour is not a commodity."[8] At the time there was so little public and official knowledge about the unequal treatment of workers from one region of the world to the next that simply to collect and disseminate information on wages and prices performed an invaluable public service.

That the Ford Company had turned to the ILO out of self-interest nobody doubted. Even so, this could be regarded as a gratifying development. For up to then, official America had kept its distance not just from the League of Nations but also from its other agencies, the most important being the ILO. This isolationism vexed Thomas, who, like other internationalists, was sympathetic to America's democracy but appalled by its self-isolating foreign policy. By boycotting the ILO, the United States had absented itself from scores of international agreements drawn up to regulate conditions of work. This absence was especially irksome given that American enterprises were the major beneficiary of accords that, by reducing industrial unrest, fostering cooperation between workers and employers, and curbing the influence of the Soviet-backed Red International of Labor Unions, favored American investment abroad. The Ford request, it was hoped, would be a step toward recognizing that "economic internationalization" had important social dimensions.

Thomas hesitated nonetheless, out of concern that Ford's request for a European-wide study was too complicated an undertaking for the ILO. Who except the Americans could think that such data were easy to come by, as if there were some ready-made reference collection on standards of living for places as far-flung as Cork on the Irish Sea and Istanbul on the Bosphorus and for people as far apart in their daily needs as the hard-drinking, potato-fed workers of Catholic Ireland and the abstemious, flatbread-eating laborers of Muslim Turkey? European statisticians had made little headway in performing calculations about standards of living on the basis not just of how much workers received in wages, but of what Americans called their "purchasing power," meaning the goods and services they could buy with their wages. And there had been little investigation on "expenditure on consumption habits," meaning how workers actually spent their income. What's more, nobody even spoke of a common European standard of living. Nor for that matter was it common usage to speak of a French, German, or Belgian standard of shared national preferences for this or that set of consumer goods. Up to then, figures on the spending habits of workers, much less any other social group, though plentiful, were piecemeal.[9]

Such an inquiry would thus require travel to the United States, trips back and forth across the Channel, and grueling forays around the continent. It could never be completed within the six-month time frame that the Ford Company demanded. And for the sake of scientific accuracy, it could not be pursued in the narrow terms that the Ford Company specified it wanted, namely by taking the standard of living of its workers at Detroit as the model for all of Europe. In sum, the whole undertaking was considered of dubious worth even if the ILO had had the funds to conduct it. But these it lacked, since its only income came from the modest government grants and employer and union dues of its member states.

The matter would assuredly have been shelved after perfunctory consultations in the ILO offices had not the *New York Times*'s Geneva correspondent, Clarence Streit, turned it into an appealing news story. A convinced internationalist himself, practiced at making the League of Nations appear newsworthy to the *Times*'s locally absorbed readership, the American journalist made the Ford request out to be an ambitiously modern all-American operation that deserved philanthropic support if it were not to fail in the face of Old World ineptitude.[10] Early 1929 was a perfect time for his pitch. Henry Ford was fully back in the public eye after reopening the factories he had shut down in 1927 to retool the assembly lines to produce his new Model A. The cars were now available in salesrooms all over the country, and for the first time, Ford was advertising. Moreover, June 1929 was the most affluent moment yet recorded in the history of the American economy, if one believed the index of output of producer goods. American philanthropists, hugely enriched on the stock market, were keen to adopt European causes. They had every interest in supporting the spirit of peace augured by the 1929 Pact of Paris, brokered by American secretary of state Kellogg and the French foreign minister Briand to swear all of the Great War belligerents to end wars of aggression. Aside from doing good, American philanthropy was heavily invested in the stability of the European area as American banks poured in hundreds of millions of dollars in short-term loans.

The Inquiry immediately found a benevolent angel in the figure of Edward Filene, the Boston department-store magnate, a devoted internationalist, and a great fan of Henry Ford. He pledged his own foundation, the Twentieth Century Fund, to contribute $25,000 to the project, promising to pay it out of his own pocket if the fund's board of governors had any objections. In the page-and-a-half-long telegram addressed to the ILO announcing the gift, Filene lauded Henry Ford's "announced intention to establish the same scale of real wages for all employees, regardless of the country in which they work." Mr. Ford paid a "high cultural wage" to his own employees in Detroit while turning out an automobile "at a price the masses could buy" and making "a record breaking profit in the process." Filene continued: "If [Ford] can help to bring about the same changes in Europe, it will mean higher wages, lower prices, greater total profits, and higher standards of living in Europe and as a result greater world prosperity and an enormous impetus to world peace."[11]

Now we find out why Thomas was so angry: not because of the self-serving nature of the Ford Company's initial request, nor because of its ingenuousness, which some regarded as characteristically American, nor because of Edward Filene's fanciful posturing about Ford's contribution to peace in Europe. What Thomas could not abide was the Twentieth Century Fund's presumption to impose conditions on the conduct of the Inquiry. Acting as if the American foundation world were ideologically Simon-pure whereas a foreign-based international agency dedicated to labor reform was impeded by ideological baggage, the U.S. donors demanded that outside consultants be hired to ensure the "authoritativeness" of the results. They also insisted on monthly progress reports to release the monies as if the Geneva staff were layabouts. The most irksome matter was that they insisted on a six-month deadline to finish and circulate the results, as if science could be rushed.[12] And "all this for 25,000 dollars," as Thomas had commented in his infuriated scribbles. It was one matter to accept donations to conduct scientific research. That was Thomas's conception of the relationship. It was another to be paid to do market research on behalf of a giant U.S. corporation under the pretext that the whole world would profit.

But Thomas's ambition was not only to do good social science. He had a political agenda as well. And that was what finally decided him to abandon his usual prudence, accept the money, and push ahead with the Inquiry subject to the conditions demanded by the donor. Like other European socialists, Thomas was committed to the politics of high wages, which the Ford Company claimed to have pioneered in the United States. This commitment made him willing to risk irritating labor delegates, who were always suspicious of capitalist motives, disturb fellow reformers worried about Ford's intrusiveness, and infuriate European employers fearful of Ford's competition. When word of the agreement reached Paris, the business press declared itself aghast at this latest "insidious maneuver" by U.S. capitalism: it bore all the hallmarks of the "American triptych," namely "all-out super-protectionism, financial hegemony . . . and economic imperialism manifested in multiple and varied guises." Anybody with a business mind at all would have treated Ford's request as pure demagoguery. Everybody, except perhaps those naive socialists at the ILO, knew that management calculated wages not on the basis of the local cost of living, but on the basis of labor productivity, investment in machinery, the supply of workers, production plans, and the costs of raw materials and other expenses, not to mention estimates about their market position vis-à-vis competitors.[13]

Moderates too, notably the Belgian government's delegate, the esteemed statistician Max Gottschalk, head of the Solvay Sociology Institute, the country's leading social research center, cautioned Thomas against getting the ILO involved. Thomas had to know that the Ford Company was engaged in dumping; that is, it was selling parts and equipment under cost on the European market. If it made cars entirely in Europe for European consumption, it wouldn't be paying high wages. Then, the social fallout from the Inquiry had to be gauged. Not much imagination was needed to foresee the "general malaise"—indeed "real danger"—that would result when documents showed in black and white that Ford workers in Detroit were paid weekly, say, the equivalent of 216 Belgian francs. In real terms, that was equivalent to a far smaller sum, 108 Belgian francs. But the average Belgian worker was paid only half that, a miserable 54 francs. To see the risks, it sufficed to look at what had happened in Antwerp, where the Ford Company already operated an assembly plant, using parts that had been "knocked-down" and crated in Kerny, New Jersey, and shipped over on the S.S. *Oneida*. The prodigious output had already contributed to wiping out ten of the fifteen craft-based automobile firms that had been Belgians' pride in the early 1920s. If Ford upped his wage rate to 108 Belgian francs, the rest of the firms were doomed. Even worse was to come: as the best skilled workers were stolen away by the Americans and the rest began to agitate for higher pay, the whole metallurgical sector would be thrown into turmoil.[14] The sagacious Gottschalk, no radical, was only urging caution.

In sum, this "Ford business"—as it was coming to be called—was clearly a can of worms. In retrospect it is also possible to see a certain self-promotional chicanery at work as the company, by publicizing its desire to promote a high wage, sought allies in the labor movement to override resistance from protectionist national manufacturers. Notwithstanding, Thomas was now resolved to go ahead. Such a study appealed to him as a politician, restive at intransigent opposition to experiments that might lead to higher wages. It appealed to him as an intellectual, head of his class at the elite Ecole Normale Supérieure, by enabling him to deepen his familiarity with America's fast-growing fields of applied social science. He already had a good friend in Herbert Feis, the Harvard-trained economic historian, who in 1927 precociously published the first empirical evidence linking global trade expansion to improved wage conditions. And at various meetings cosponsored by the Rockefeller-funded Social Science Research Council, he deepened his acquaintance with Charles Merriam, the University of Chicago sociologist in charge of the SSRC's project on international wage comparisons.[15] These men were not socialists, of course. They were progress-minded Americans who at times seemed naive, even vulgar in their quest, as they put it, to know "what kind of life incomes can purchase" and what the "competition between different commodities" revealed about "ideals and values in the daily life of people." That said, their eagerness to connect to the world made them fresh spirits compared to the shriveled academicism of much contemporary European social science. And they were much to be admired for their confidence that massive data collecting would yield a rich fund of common knowledge, free of manipulation by government and powerful interests, that could be used "to fix things up."[16]

Confident that he could master New World money and know-how, Thomas reiterated how "deeply gratified" the ILO was for Filene's generous offer of financial help, and without consulting again with his restive board, on October 8, 1929, five and a half months after Sir Percival's initial request, he officially launched the Inquiry.[17] The deadline set for completing the report was six to eight months later, by May 1930 at the latest. That week, trading on the New York Stock Exchange was running ragged after its astronomical highs in September. The panic occurred two weeks later, followed by the great plunge in stock values the following Tuesday, October 29.

As the investigation began, it was immediately clear that nobody had an exact idea of the living standards of the so-called average Ford worker in Detroit. Though the company had a well-deserved reputation for snooping in the private lives of its employees, it had disbanded its infamous Sociological Department in 1921. Thereafter it destroyed the thousands of confidential files accumulated by the scores of investigators it had employed since 1914, the year the five-dollar day was introduced, to inspect whether Ford workers were spending their pay envelopes according to the idiosyncratic standards of efficiency and puritanism that the boss had designed as the condition for getting the whole payment. Edsel, Henry's brow-beaten son, who was delegated to handle such minor issues, explained that the company could not help out because it lacked the facilities.[18]

In truth, knowledge of how workers spent their wages and free time no longer engaged the busybody paternalism of intrusive employers. It had become society's responsibility generally, as evidenced by the sheer number of government offices, corporate marketing departments, and assorted private agencies devoted to collecting data about consumer behavior. Having enlisted help from the two most reliable institutions, the U.S.

Bureau of Labor Statistics and the Michigan-based National Bureau of Economic Research, the Inquiry promised to proceed expeditiously.

The investigators' first task was to establish a "commodity budget" for all their subjects. As soon as they figured out the yearly amount the average automobile worker earned, they would pore over checkbooks, credit records, wives' estimates, and various miscellaneous measures to calculate how the take-home pay was apportioned. But nothing was straightforward here. To start, workers were said to earn $1,750 annually, or seven dollars a day, five days a week. But this pay rate, though an increase from the celebrated five dollars of 1914 and the six-dollar day to catch up with inflation in the 1920s, had been established under political pressure the previous November 22, 1929. That was when Herbert Hoover had summoned Henry Ford and other U.S. business leaders for an emergency meeting at the White House. There the president pleaded with them to support recovery from the October stock market panic by reaffirming as publicly as possible their commitment to the New Era's "doctrine of high wages." Henry Ford himself took the lead. But within a year, as the financial panic spread, he reneged on his commitment, and the wage fell back to six dollars, sometimes even lower.[19]

Another obstacle was that calculations were based on the budget of the lowest-paid "average worker." This figure was defined as a fully employed family man, meaning he had worked at least forty-five weeks the previous year, was the sole support of a wife and two or three children, and had no other source of income or additional dependents. This must have been a rare creature. Out of a workforce in excess of 100,000, the company supplied a list of 1,740 men, from which the investigators culled its sample of 100.[20]

Just to determine what workers spent their wages on in Detroit took eight months. Reaching the Geneva offices in July 1930 (two months after the putative deadline), the results required another several weeks to be converted into the metric system, for prices to be recomputed in seventeen currencies, and for the myriad terms of comparison to be translated into a half-dozen languages.

Meanwhile the European investigators, fanning out from the cities closest to Geneva—Marseilles, Genoa, Trieste, and Frankfurt—and then moving in ever-wider circles to visit Barcelona, Antwerp, Stockholm, and Helsinki, toward the most distant, Cork and Istanbul, found their tasks rough going. Sometimes governments stinted on offering help, either out of indifference or, as in France, to show disagreement with the Inquiry's goals and methods. Sometimes they were overly solicitous, as in Great Britain. There officials followed the project closely for fear that if the Trade Union Council learned how much pay varied from place to place, they would agitate for wage adjustments. To deter leaks, they insisted that pounds and shillings not be used in the final report, only index numbers.[21]

It was harder to overcome skepticism that it was possible, much less desirable, to make rigorous comparisons about different ways of living. Even if the money cost turned out to be equal, was a loaf of American white bread really the equivalent of a loaf of Scandinavian rye? Swedish nutritionists were studiously neutral when they posed the question. French investigators were vocally skeptical. As the old French proverb went, "One stick of wood is not the same as another." The same held for a brioche as well as a pat of butter. Any housewife at a Parisian market could tell you that the price of butter could vary by 15 to 20 percent, depending on whether it came from hay-fed Normandes or from a herd of Salers grazed in the Auvergne. It was common sense, then, that if the comparison between Detroit and Europe truly took account not just of the cost and quantity of products, but also of the quality and the myriad of individual tastes and preferences, the margin for error was infinite.[22] Not only different classes within the nation, but also different communities, experienced their ways of life in incommensurably different fashions. The U.S. Bureau of Labor Statistics was only being disingenuous or naive when it affirmed that the Detroit study was "entirely objective and colorless, as can only be expected from a Government report."[23] "Speaking frankly," said Pierre Laval, who was France's minister of social security and labor at the time, the methods being used were "not susceptible to" or even close to "approximating" a "scientific solution."[24] Hence the French government could not lend the Inquiry its official support.

Observers did indeed seem susceptible to invidious comparisons. Who would refrain, for example, from making a value judgment about the fact that the abstemious but fun-seeking Detroit worker spent his fifty cents of disposable income at the moviehouse whereas his bibulous Berlin counterpart spent his five pfennigs at a beerhall? How to dissuade investigators from reflecting on the "psychological, sociological, and hedonistic considerations" that went into the workers' choices? The response designed to check these "instinctive" judgments showed positivistic social science at its most fetishistic. The goods were to speak for themselves. Accordingly, investigators would collect physical specimens of the De-

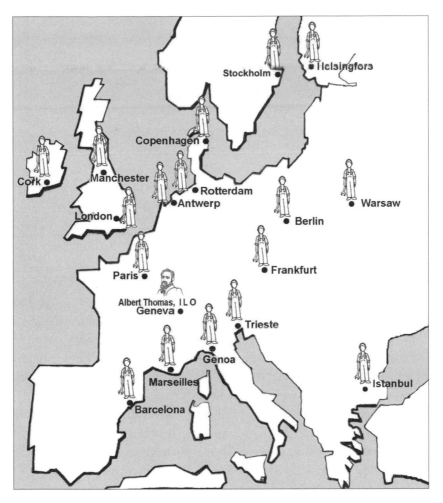

Henry Ford's Europe: sites of the Ford-ILO Inquiry, 1929–1931.
By permission of the author.

troit commodity basket and ship them to Europe to make them available on site. So, in addition to compiling lists with the nutritional and caloric content of perishable items and drawing up estimates of the 100 households' expenditures on commodities and services, the women experts of the Department of Agriculture's Bureau of Home Economics packed two wooden trunks with samples of clothing and household dry goods and sent them off.

The years 1930 and 1931 were a tumultuous time for unaccompanied baggage to be crisscrossing frontiers. Though furnished with special diplomatic waivers to expedite customs formalities, the trunks' progress around the continent was travailed. One was inexplicably sidetracked for a month while en route from Berlin to Warsaw. The trunk destined for Barcelona arrived amidst the turmoil following the collapse of the dictatorship of General Miguel Primo de Rivera at the end of January 1930, and with the staff of the state labor and statistical offices out on strike, nobody was on hand to receive it. It was an unpropitious moment anyway to do anything in the name of the Ford Company, since, without warning, it had just shut down its Barcelona assembly plants to retaliate against the higher customs duties the Spanish government had imposed on auto parts. This measure had been taken to retaliate against the Hawley-Smoot Act that Hoover had signed into law in June 1930, jacking up U.S. tariffs against European imports.[25] Fortunately, the trunk was eventually consigned to officials kindly disposed toward the ILO, who proceeded to complete the assignment.

So felicitous an outcome was not fated for the trunk destined for Italy, whose arrival found the northern regions gripped by labor unrest and Fascist leaders on full alert as a result of the fall of their brother dictatorship in Spain. In the best of circumstances, the Duce's regime, which had outlawed free labor unions to replace them with puppet Fascist syndicates, was out of sympathy with the International Labor Organization. However, the real obstacle to cooperation was Giovanni Agnelli, the head of Fiat, who intended to preserve his company's monopoly over Italian car production. Lobbying hard against the Ford Company, he had his wish gratified in October 1929, when Mussolini ordered Ford's Trieste plant to close down and denied the company authorization to build any new ones.[26] Consequently, the cargo was returned unopened to the sender, and Genoa and Trieste, the two Italian cities selected for the study, were dropped from the comparison.

When the trunks did reach their proper destinations, they revealed a material culture that was visibly bountiful compared with the European. From the sets of attire provided for a family of four—a mother and father and two children, a boy and a girl—as well as from the notation that they spent 12 percent of their annual budget on clothing, it was clear that American workers were investing in smart dressing. They renewed their wardrobes constantly. In 1929, when wages were at their postwar peak, an average husband bought annually five shirts, two ties, two cotton union suits, fourteen pairs of cotton socks and one pair of what looked like dress socks made of silk or rayon, one pair of suspenders, two pairs of shoes, two pairs of leather and nine pairs of cotton work gloves. From the look of it, the quality of the wool suit, purchased on average every two and a half years, was first-rate; likewise the quality of the slouching silk-banded felt hats, famous from Hollywood movies, purchased on average one every two years; so also the wool overcoat, made to last about seven. The typical worker's wife renewed practically her entire wardrobe every two years. In 1929 alone she had purchased two colorful cotton, rayon, or silk dresses, eight pairs of stockings, including four of silk or rayon, three housedresses, a variety of underwear and night-gowns, and two pairs of shoes. Even more was spent on the children's garb than on the adults, the equivalent on average of one-twentieth of the family budget. The labels and handiwork showed that all of it was store-bought, right down to the ruffled rayon petticoats to go under the plaid, back-sashed school dresses. By contrast, European working-class children wore clothing that was almost always home-made and often patched together from adult castoffs and hand-me-downs. The house-hold linens folded up beneath the clothing showed the prodigious use of cotton in U.S. manufacturing; whether the sateen-bound wool blankets were comparable to German and Scandinavian eiderdown was more debatable. The food lists showed that Detroit workers ate a remark-ably varied, plentiful, and nutritious diet. By contrast, though their own workers were well-fed, Swedish investigators observed, they consumed hefty quantities of a far smaller range of products, and they dosed these with prodigious quantities of tobacco and alcohol, a habit, it was prud-ishly commented, that added spark to the diet but little in the way of nutrition. The quality of American housing looked so good as to raise troubling questions of comparison. Single-family houses averaging 4.1 rooms, equipped with gas, electricity, central heating, bathroom, and windows with views, were rare in European cities, where the average worker shelter, averaging 2 to 3 rooms, was in a decrepit state. In Berlin and Frankfurt, to find something equivalent in size and comforts, one would have to look at the housing of upper civil servants. As for personal services, American workers spent goodly sums out of pocket on doc-tors and, not infrequently, dentists too, and some had taken out life in-surance policies as well. Compared with the Europeans', their budgets showed skimpy outlays for social insurance and mutual aid societies and, unsurprisingly, none at all for union dues, as Ford ran a closed shop.[27]

The most remarkable difference was that Ford workers were con-stantly renewing an ample stock of mass-produced home conveniences, from radios, phonographs, and electric irons to electric washing ma-

chines and vacuum cleaners. Nearly half of the families owned an automobile, some of which may well have been purchased new, as the price of
the Model T had dropped to $440 by the 1920s. Most cars had been pur-
chased for recreation, not strictly to commute, and installment payments
and maintenance costs weighed heavily on the family budget. By contrast, no European workers had a car or dreamed of getting one. Minute
percentages of young males owned motorcycles, some with sidecars. Bicycles were precious possessions. But then, relatively few European bourgeois households owned automobiles either. France and Britain, the two
most motorized countries in Europe, had only one car for every twenty
people at the end of the 1930s; Germany, one for every forty; and Italy,
about one for every hundred; while in the United States there was one automobile for every four.[28] Clearly, it was pointless to price the cost of living for a European worker by putting a car in his commodity basket.

Yet another significant difference was that Detroit workers commonly
used consumer credit. Indeed, credit enabled them to outspend their annual incomes, if only by a little. By contrast, consumer credit was little
practiced by European workers. Experiments with installment buying on
furniture and larger articles failed as soon as there was an economic
downturn. In Great Britain, workers still ruefully knew credit as the
"never-never." To get from one payday to the next, European workers relied on informal arrangements with shopkeepers, who sized up their
creditworthiness for the basics, food and fuel, and recorded their debits
and payments in the store ledger.[29]

In sum, the more the ways of living were brought into contact, the
more the complicated process of comparing them stretched on. Finally, in
November 1931, two and a half years after Sir Percival's initial request,
twenty-five months after the Inquiry was authorized to begin, and seventeen months after it was due to be finished, stung by the U.S. donor's accusations that it was engaging in "sharp practices" by not producing
results, the ILO released the final report.[30] Realizing that his own governing board was in turmoil over the findings and fearful that the brouhaha would lead to its suppression, Thomas avoided sending it up for
final approval.[31] Meanwhile, in New York City, at the behest of the
Twentieth Century Fund, Edward L. Bernays, the founding genius of
American public relations, prepared a barrage of publicity to celebrate
the English-language edition's release. By then, however, it was unclear
whether the point was to celebrate the success of international collaboration, the generosity of U.S. business philanthropy, or the American politics of high wages.

One thing was certain: released at Christmastime 1931, this "most bullish" account of the American Standard of Living belonged to another time.[32] Most of the 100 workers interviewed in 1929–30 were now jobless as skyrocketing unemployment rates withered the American auto industry. Ford himself, still denying that there was an economic crisis, had put 75,000 workers on "indefinite holiday" under the pretext that the company had to retool the assembly lines for a brand-new model. Whoever survived the layoffs could still earn seven dollars a day, provided he could fulfill his new daily productivity quota, which was as much as half again higher, so that by the end of his shift he would have staggered out of the factory gates limp and ashen-faced. Of the thousands laid off, none were eligible for relief, since the Ford workers were bereft of unemployment insurance. They weren't even eligible for the modest sums doled out by the municipality, which tided over other jobless people until 1935, when the New Deal finally cobbled together the country's first national unemployment compensation scheme. Local government initiatives depended on business taxes, and Ford's fifty-seven-acre Highland Park plant and its River Rouge branch had been deliberately placed outside the Detroit city limits to avoid paying municipal levies.[33]

In the calm of lakeside Geneva, the rush to publication provoked the proverbial tempest in the bureaucratic teapot. As the ILO's governing board protested that it had not approved the final version (nor even authorized it properly in the first place), some delegates picked apart its more idiosyncratic findings while others wondered at the conspiracy that had caused the volume to be published in English but not in the ILO's other official tongues, French and German.[34] To mollify critics, the editors quickly put out a second, significantly revised edition, this time in all three languages. The new edition also offered the opportunity to make certain changes, such as the title, from the ambitious *An International Enquiry into the Costs of Living* to the more self-effacing *A Contribution to the Study of International Comparisons of Costs of Living*. The study's real scope was presented more modestly too: a statistical "exercise," it aimed to compare "costs of living," it was underscored, not "standards of living."[35]

By 1932 the value of even that goal had been thrown into question. As the economic crisis spread across the globe, prices declined sharply and unemployment shot up. As one country after another pulled off the gold standard, currencies capered this way and that, tariff barriers mounted, and governments increasingly manipulated statistics for political ends.[36] In London in April 1931, when Sir Percival was solicited for his views on the report, his cherub-pink clergyman's face pursed with perplexity as he disarmingly confessed to having let the whole matter slip his mind. By then, softening sales and rising tariffs had cut catastrophically into Ford's European market, and the company was closing down plants and pulling back from the continent. Back in 1929, well before the company could get feedback from the ILO, it had gone ahead and set its workers' wage scales "empirically." Following its usual practices abroad, management had checked the going pay rates, set the wage just high enough to cream off the best laborers from the region, and required that unions be banned in exchange for better wages. The "high" or "efficiency wage," as Henry Ford himself once confessed, was "a flexible concept." With an affable nod to the effort put into the report, Sir Percival sportingly offered to check its findings against the wage scales the Ford Company had actually adopted, off the record, the only point being to test whether management was on its toes.[37] This was as much thanks as the ILO got for this thankless project. For Albert Thomas, his bearlike constitution notwithstanding, it was one more checkmate for European social reformism. On May 8, 1932, at age fifty-seven on a visit back to Paris, he died in a boulevard café after collapsing from a pulmonary embolism.

What a Pandora's box, to compare conditions of living in the United States and Europe: the first such effort since the United States had become hegemonic; and the first occasion for Europeans and Americans to debate what it meant to define a "decent" standard of living. Out of the confrontation, Europeans saw two market cultures sharply divided over the meaning of standards. They would have found much to agree with in James Bryce's remark that Americans had a "habit of destroying all qualities by relating them to their measurable monetary value" and dismissing "situations where . . . it is no longer possible to apply the monetary standard." This outlook fostered a high regard for quantity and the measurement thereof and, by extension, "a tendency to mistake bigness for greatness."[38] When the ILO's governing board met to discuss the report's findings, the normally reticent Armand Julin, a Belgian statistician, burst out: "To compare a real man with a phantom" was indecent; it was ethically wrong to treat workers as if they lived under "conditions of free choice"; their existence depended "not just upon conditions of employment and wages" but also upon "circumstances of life" over which they had little control. Hard figures gave "an impression of precision" that was "false." Far from being "reassuring in their fixity," they provoked "a sense of insecurity"; they aroused envy, yet failed to impart any sense of what workers really wanted when they spoke of wanting a "decent" existence.[39]

As France's preeminent labor economist François Simiand put the final touches on his three-volume study *Le salaire,* he voiced similar concerns. Wages could take many forms, not just pure cash, but also goods in kind, gifts, and services. Likewise, to consider the significance of how wages were spent in terms of only one factor, the standard of living, was inadequate to understand the norms shaping people's choices. He advised two terms: "manner of living," or *train de vie,* which was akin to "standard of living" and investigated choices based on income; and "style of life," or *genre de vie,* which called attention to other complex noneconomic considerations that shaped spending, especially social standing, but also community values and religion, not to mention climate and other physical factors.[40] From the moment he had heard about the Ford-ILO Inquiry, Simiand had been dismissive. What could possibly be learned from an experiment with human subjects that treated people like draft animals, itemizing the calories they ingested? The whole exercise, he joked with colleagues and students, was like calculating an elephant's upkeep in Lapland as if it still lived in India or a reindeer's in India as if it still lived in Lapland.[41]

To Americans, this continental hauteur about the quality of life was nothing more than Old World elitism. Arguments that cited the complications created by the diversity of tastes from one group to another sounded like scientific ineptitude or social hypocrisy camouflaged behind cultural highmindedness. It was fine to be skeptical about comparisons. Nobody would accuse Europeans of social bias if they said that car-owning was a luxury for workers in Europe, and not a good indicator of the standard of living, whereas it was a necessity for American workers, who lived in sprawling municipalities with no public transportation. But when the same investigators remarked that European workers lacked the indoor plumbing "to permit of washing oneself properly," and then let it slip that, even when water was available, the workers displayed an "aversion" to frequent bathing, that was social bias.[42] For who could really say to what standards of cleanliness would they have held themselves if the climate had not been so damp and cold, if there were public baths, or if they and their parents before them had homes equipped with running water, even a cold-water kitchen tap, much less a whole separate warm, even sunny bathroom, set up with a flush toilet, sink, tub, shower, and hot and cold running water? What would their standard have been had they been surrounded, like American immigrants, with cheap, brightly packaged milled soap, subjected to the wrinkled-up noses and pained looks of teachers, supervisors, and fellow citizens if they smelled, and bombarded with newspaper and magazine advertisements for Camay, Palmolive, or Ponds soap that made it gross behavior to exude a new discovery called "body odor"?

In sum, one conclusion might be that the wants of the Detroit workers were expansive because of several decades of high wages. If so, it could equally be said that the wants of European workers had been depressed by several decades of low wages.[43] European statistical science could well scoff at the American notion of measuring the standard of living in terms of the preferences revealed by the goods and services that a given sum of money could buy. Still, like it or not, money notoriously offers a universal form of measurement in capitalist societies, and consumer goods are nothing if not tangible choices that people are making about their own well-being. Surely, the total sum of the comforts in goods and services that a certain level of income afforded a nation's citizenry provided a plausible index of its rank in the world scale of civilized well-being. That was what many Americans believed, and were convinced others believed as well.

Anyway, the "facts" were now circulating as part of the public record, and the dense little book larded with charts and statistics took on a life of its own, often mis-cited and the butt of ridicule as misguided, superficial, or, worse, biased social science. So Detroit came to set the terms of comparison: the measure of bread was a loaf of processed white flour, not a round of rye or a crusty baguette; the measure of bedding, mass-produced cotton and wool rather than the eiderdown; the measure of children's clothing, store-bought outfits rather than home-sewn goods; the measure of social security, private spending on insurance rather than state pensions or other collective social provisions. Even critics of the minute sample, the crude comparisons, and the ambiguous results ended up speaking knowledgeably of a cluster of habits they called "the American Standard of Living."

Yet the American standard had not won in some objective comparison, for the question of which continent offered a better life and to whom could never be answered conclusively. Rather, American consumer culture had seized the high ground by asserting that the good life consists of a decent income for lots of people spent individually by purchasing goods that they believe enable them to live comfortably. And they defined it by claiming to be able to measure it scientifically by the amount of wages, the expansion of purchasing power, the bountiful output of mass production, and the range of individual choices provided by private enterprise.

But what, then, did Europeans intend when they spoke of the norms implicit in their "way of life"? The experts spoke of nonmarket considerations. But how to calculate these? They spoke of incommensurable needs. How then could people be compared without making invidious distinctions or, worse, legitimating some people's needs as lesser or more worthy than others'? These questions prompt us to ask how these two very different conceptions of identifying the appropriate and necessary arose and how, in turn, responding to America's advance, Europeans defended their "way of life" in a more and more reactionary way.

Advancing the American Standard

The Ford-ILO Inquiry resonated with Henry Ford's own fabulous story of how his company had achieved "the greatest revolution in the matter of rewards for its workers ever known to the industrial world."[44] This self-edifying tale was rehearsed in three brief, widely translated books; *My Life and Work*, published in 1922, Hitler's bible; *My Philosophy of Industry*, coming out in 1929; and *Moving Forward*, dating from 1930. Personable and didactic, these little how-to books offered nostrums about living efficiently in the modern world. They also lent an altogether false coherence to the narrative about the coming of mass consumption, making it a matter of huge efficiency, big supply, heightened wages, and sharpened demand.

The five-dollar day gave the story a touch of magic. Announced to the world on January 5, 1914, the new compensation scheme was pure genius from the point of view of labor management and publicity. Doubling the prevailing daily wage rate of $2.43 for an eight-hour five-day week, it crowned the decade-long transformation that had turned the Ford Company, founded in 1903, from being one of several scores of craft shops, with a payroll of 150 employees and turning out a fraction of the total U.S. output of 1,700 cars a year, into a megafactory employing 14,000 people and producing nearly half of all American cars. After settling on the design of the all-purpose vehicle known as the Model T, the farmer's son turned mechanic-entrepreneur speeded up the tempo of innovation. First perfecting the breakdown of tasks, then lining up single-purpose machinery, thereafter incorporating the time-and-motion studies of the renowned industrial engineer Frederick W. Taylor to compel the men to keep up with the machines, finally management had the whole process hoisted off the ground with a power-driven conveyor system—the assembly line—to move pieces from one factory hand to the next. There was only one hitch: by the time the finished cars rolled off the line, one every ninety-three minutes, an average of half of Ford's employees were quitting every month. Worse, as exhausted laborers finished their shifts, International Workers of the World organizers were waiting in front of the factory gates to persuade them to join the union drive. Without some measure to reduce turnover and foreclose unionization, the firm could not profit from its huge investments, much less expand as intended. The offer of the pay hike plus bonus proved to be right on the mark. The day after it was announced, 12,000 applicants crowded into the company lot to line up for 4,000 openings. From then on, the Ford Company got the pick of the labor force, speeded up the assembly line, eliminated the disgruntled, incapable, and absentee, and forestalled unionization for fully two decades. Ford himself, notoriously a man of few words, summed up the experiment as "one of the finest cost-cutting moves we ever made."[45] Overnight, he became a folk hero and the Model T a household name.

The policy of so influential a company had a lasting effect by making the high wage seem central to the success of the twentieth-century American economy and the supply from production the *primum mobile* of the demand central to mass consumer society. Accordingly, the United States had become a high-wage economy compared with Europe, because land and capital were abundant whereas labor remained scarce, inelastic, and hence costly. Consequently, the cost of labor relative to capital was higher than in Europe, entrepreneurs had an incentive to introduce more and perhaps superior labor-saving machines, and high productivity yielded increased wages. In turn, high wages, freely disposed of by the worker, unencumbered by heavy taxation, union dues, and other withholdings, yielded mass consumption, which then fed profits, which in turn promoted investment. Any business management that failed to rejoice in this virtuous circle, so its boosters argued, was technologically backward, shortsighted, or plain mean-spirited.

European elites were judged guilty on all scores as the Americans seized the moral high ground during the 1920s boom. Much as in the nineteenth century, when American republicans had argued that the Union was superior to European aristocratic society in terms of property distribution, in the twentieth-century, American progressives argued that

U.S. civilization was superior to European bourgeois society in terms of income distribution. Europe squandered its men and hoarded its resources, went a familiar refrain, whereas America hoarded its men and squandered its resources—a strategy that was no vice in a pre-ecological age. On one side of the Atlantic, economic retribution yielded a "mere living wage" resulting in economic stagnation; on the other, it yielded "a high standard of living" that generated prosperity. The difference was as simple as it was fundamental, explained Paul Mazur, the genius merger manager and economist, in his bestselling book *American Prosperity:* Europe tightened its belt to the last notch, whereas the United States let its out to the first. The goal should be to feed the man to fill out the belt, not to yank it tight to fit a shrinking waistline.[46]

Yet it isn't at all obvious how the industrial productivity that yielded relatively high wages in the United States—an economic strategy that plainly could be afforded by only a few score of the giant consumer-oriented industries—could convert a whole society to the tenets of a full-blown mass-consumer culture. Other factors also play a role in explaining the coming of age of the American Standard of Living and why the United States took the high road to consumer abundance, whereas European society, already embarked on a low road, moved first toward the American model, then veered sharply away from it, before being pitched onto the tracks of the German-dominated New Order.

The first element, plainly, was the United States' unusual set of resources. When narratives about American economic greatness speak of plentiful natural reserves, the imagination goes to coal, iron, tin, copper, abundant water, petroleum, or any of the other staples that go to industrial production and in which the nation abounded. Not enough is said about the remarkably precocious industrialization of agriculture or the bounty from a vast informal empire that early established what the historian William Appleman Williams called "the imperial confusion of an economically defined *standard* of living with a culturally defined *quality* of life."[47] Vast resources of food were indispensable to the modern consumer in order not just to avoid perennial shortages, but to push down food costs so that even slight increments of wage could go to other goods like clothes and shelter. Whereas many Europeans were haunted by recurring food shortages down to the 1950s, from the 1870s urban Americans were becoming accustomed to a varied and nutritious diet, one that by offering a wide menu of choices also familiarized people with assortment in other domains. Prospering agriculture turned rural lands into wealthy markets, peopled by mail-order customers. And fast transportation, in addition to making Americans the world's largest consumers of sugar and tobacco, made coffee, chicle gum, coca extracts for cola drinks, pineapples, and banana bunches everyday decencies. The banana, speeded from quasi-colonies in Central America by refrigerated express cargo and quick freight carriage, turned up by the ton in the Philadelphia Ghetto, Chicago's North Side, and New York's Lower East Side, where it sold at six cents a dozen. By "its simplicity, economy of preparation, and low price," the Wharton School economist Simon E. Patten wrote, it "added . . . permanently to the laborers' fund of goods."[48]

The second element to account for the rise of mass consumer culture was the breadth and depth of the U.S. domestic market and the large size of American industry. Nobody can ignore the huge scale and scope of consumer-oriented enterprises, and how these capitalized on a single market whose fast-growing population reached 123 million by 1930, a third of Europe's 370 million, spread over a land mass of 3 million square miles compared with Europe's 2 million.[49] Wedded to the three S's of high productivity, namely simplification, standardization, and specialization, giant American manufactures tended to narrow the range of products, aiming for profits on quantity with low unit costs.[50] In turn, these giants' grip on markets was periodically loosened by smaller flexible, regional firms, which, finding outlets in chain-store outlets like Woolworth's, contributed to the precocious growth of mass retailing. Even when these smaller enterprises went bankrupt or were bought out, they teased government into antimonopoly legislation, set the pace of consumer innovation, and encouraged an ethos of service.[51] The net outcome was a home market, constantly expanding outward and downward, the widest, deepest, and fastest-growing of any nation in the world.

The third element was the precocious development of a proletarian consumer consciousness. Ensuring decent wages to pay for a decent standard of living was as much a labor as a business strategy. To resist employer efforts to drive down wages in the late nineteenth century, native-born white male laborers defied being reduced to "wage slaves"; their labor was their flesh and blood, not to be negotiated away in paltry wages. Having imposed by strikes and sabotage the principle that their manhood was not for sale, they accepted payment on other grounds: not to alienate their labor, but to acquire the necessaries for a dignified existence.[52] This populist consumerism worked for the socially best-armed and most skilled laborers because they conceived of their struggle as aimed at two enemies: one was the extortionist boss, and the other, their contemptible competitors in the labor market, in the figure of scrounging Paddy the Irishman, spineless John the Chinaman, and indolent Negroes, dagos, and wops "who live like vermin, whose families cost nothing, and whose food and clothing are but nominal in cost."[53] To bargain with the former while forestalling the latter, workers authorized their unions to negotiate special relations with business and government to damp down competition from alien labor (which could be foreign-born, black, or female) and to engage in pugnacious "buy American" campaigns.

Populist consumerism was thus not at all incompatible with bloody labor struggles. Collective action, combined with a fundamentally individualist use of social goods, would build a Big Rock Candy Mountain of well-being for all who earned a fair day's wage for a fair day's work. When the good fight was finally won, labor militants saw a wonderfully materialist fantasy of the world to come: gymnasiums, great swimming pools, and bathrooms of marble; industrial plants decorated with collections superior to the displays at the Metropolitan Museum of Art; and for laborers, the comfort of Morris chairs in which to rest their weary limbs.[54] Nor did populist consumerism preclude a peculiarly American form of working-class internationalism. Claiming for itself the right to a decent livelihood, American labor set itself on a different course from both the continental socialist movements, which under Marxist influence battled for socially just retribution and political representation as universal rights, and British trade unionism, which in the name of the age-old right of John Bull to the basic decencies built a strong common front among workers by battling for across-the-board wage hikes.[55] But the American labor movement also stood for keeping on the lookout for unfair competition from low-wage foreign lands and exhorting the oppressed workers of those benighted places to rally to the "high-wage doctrine."

Naturally, populist consumerism was reinforced by rising wages. However, high wages are to be understood not simply as a quantity, but rather as a sum paid in cash, regularly, and to a larger and larger proportion of working people. It replaced payments in kind like company housing, food rations, and other dribs and drabs of employer paternalism. There were few withholdings on the pay envelope, but equally slight government or company entitlements to compensate if it stopped. With cash wages, workers could dispose of their income flexibly, stimulated by floods of innovative goods, advertising, fast-changing consumer mores, and the availability of credit. Unable to rely on state help in times of need, workers had to learn to manage their wages to take account of the booms and busts of the business cycle. In flush times, the whole family was free-spending; in hard times, it was provident. In sum, training that taught workers to treat their income as a form of capital, to be invested in household equipment, if possible in home ownership, testified to their entrepreneurship as consumers as well as to their apparent freedom of action.[56]

Populist consumerism would have been inconceivable unless filtered through "the democratic style of public life." Werner Sombart, Europe's most acute observer of turn-of-the-century capitalist growth, is often cited as having argued that socialism in America foundered on "shoals of roast beef and apple pie," which is to say that workers were bought off by mass consumption. He said nothing of the kind. His point was that in the United States "the style of living," meaning new goods and habits, was experienced through "a situation of social ease," whereas in Europe it was filtered through enduring legacies of class discrimination. Hence it was not the "finely fitting dress suit, patent leather boots and elegant clothes of the latest fashion that made trade union leaders move about with the same grace as any aristocrat in Germany—it was the self assurance, the absence of stigma of being a class apart that almost all European workers have about them." Income inequality was not the issue, for it was greater in the United States than elsewhere. But the absence of the status distinctions inherited from feudal relations "made the distance . . . even smaller in the consciousness of the various classes than it really is."[57] So as new goods flooded onto the market and businesses in search of customers knocked off cheaper models, the sumptuary lines between classes became more and more porous. In a country of immigrants, the newcomers wanted to make themselves as much like those who had already arrived as possible. Since mass goods like the Model T or brand-name soaps lacked a specific class connotation—though marketers would always be working to invest them with status connotations—the most obvious means of indicating this likeness was a sumptuary one, by possessing objects like everybody else's. Which is not to say that this equality of access to innovative goods was in any way incompatible with racial prejudice, inequality of material circumstances, and vicious acts of social snobbery.

Nothing marked American consumer culture's precocious development more than the wide consensus that had emerged by the 1920s that all its citizens partook more or less of the American Standard of Living.[58]

The very notion of a "decent," "high," or "cultural" wage marked a clear departure from the nineteenth century, when "standard of living" denoted the absolute minimum necessary for workers to survive, and the main issue was whether, in accordance with early nineteenth-century British economist David Ricardo's "dismal law" on wages, the minimum would be pushed below the subsistence rate as workers competed for scarce jobs. Adding the omnibus word "American" to the term imparted to it an altogether new sense: that shared material habits were the single most palpable evidence of the unity of the American people, that a set of norms guided the American people, and that in turn the American people revealed these in their individual choices.

Behind this belief stood a revolution in outlooks toward mass consumption that endorsed America's passage from what Simon Patten called a "deficit" or "pain" to a "surplus" or "pleasure" economy. Out of the "new bases of civilization" in moviegoing, banana-eating, and the other humble pastimes of contemporary life, the philosopher saw a new morality coming into being. Its basis was the proper management of national economic resources, such as raising the minimum standard without dropping the consumption levels of other classes. Hence Malthus's catastrophic prognosis about mankind's animal-like predicament, to fornicate and procreate until the food supply was outstripped, then to perish fighting over the scraps, was declared dead; and likewise, Marx's fearsome dialectic of class struggle to divide the surplus generated out of advances in the means of production. Forsaking Judeo-Christian asceticism, Patten declared that with a "higher standard of living" would come "a higher threshold of desire." Novelty in experience and taste not only quickened the wits but refined the senses. The true gluttons were primitive men; the well-fed became epicures. More consumption thus resulted in a more ethical society; no higher good, no natural law, no transcendent principle of human justice needed to be invoked to justify the right to a decent standard of living.[59]

Now only two more elements were needed to establish the American standard. The first was to reveal what Americans wanted. Regardless of the high value accorded personal privacy, Americans exposed their every nook and cranny to probes and tests in the name of consumer science. As public and private national surveys of consumer expenditure multiplied into the hundreds by the early 1930s, no self-respecting study of the direction of American civilization could ignore consumer trends. The result was a cacophonous public voice around what constituted an "adequate, healthy and decent standard of living."[60] From "expenditures, the status of housing, and hundreds of other things," the new sciences of consumption produced the outlines of the "American standard." For Margaret Reid, the well-known home economist, it was "characterized by absence of class distinction, and by a measurement of values in terms of money; much importance is attached to the new, to speed, to time-saving. One family dwellings are common and home ownership rates high. Health and formal education, although not necessarily learning, are conspicuous among the things people strive for."[61]

The final element was to classify Americans according to their capacity to achieve this standard. With his "standard of living groups," Columbia economist and business consultant Paul H. Nystrom produced the first complete profile. At the bottom, regrettably, there were still the lower orders, by which he meant the 18.5 percent (counting "the work shy and tramps") who lived at the level of bare subsistence and thus "lacked the necessities and much of the comforts and conveniences of life." Those numbers, presumably, would have included most of the African-American population at the time, along with impoverished rural whites and Native Americans. However, the great bulk of the American people, 71.4 percent, partook of the consumer market for all classes of goods, their consumption or use of necessities, comforts, conveniences, and luxuries increasing in quantity, quality, and price with advances in their level of income. Above them, a relatively small 10 percent of the population showed "well-to-do and liberal" standards of living, representing "higher levels of purchasing power and expenditure for all *classes* of consumer goods."[62] Henceforth there were classes of goods, but no longer classes of people. About that time, advertising, pollsters, and economists appropriated Nystrom's categories, to divide all of the nation's people into income bands ranked from A to D.

The standard of living, then, connoted not just the sum total and types of goods the American people owned, but also the means by which they were acquired, through higher and higher levels of income. The American Standard of Living affirmed that the habit of breaking habits demonstrated social vitality; that as desires matured, they became more varied and complex; that social emulation in using goods was natural and positive; that no class monopolized standards of taste; and, finally, that as new goods came on the market, being in theory available to one and all (depending on income), the whole society became more cohesive and communicative. Of course, there was vast room for improvement, with a fifth of the population practically completely cut out and levels of access very unequal. Yet even at the lower-middling levels, consumers were recognized as having acquired a real if small power in their capacity to make choices. Thereby consumer habits came to be hailed as a daily plebiscite about the quality of life, a minimalist exercise of citizenship reinforcing a feeling of national belonging. Eliminating inequality required not overhauling the system, but maintaining wages and improving consumers' skills in order to increase their purchasing power. The agenda of social justice could thus forgo any ambitious overhauling of the system for the opportunity to pick and choose among alternative offers. From the early 1920s, Americans spoke of the "freedom of demand [as] the first essential of freedom in general."[63]

The power granted to consumers to exercise this freedom seemed to be hugely enhanced as the term "consumer sovereignty" entered the American vocabulary scarcely a decade later. A London-born political economist, H. A. Hutt, a professor at the University of Capetown before moving to the United States, was the first to insist that in the face of authoritarian regimes and command economies, free societies had to champion the power citizens might exercise by means of their choices as consumers.[64] His point was not that the consumer had the last word or that unfettered consumer rule would efface class inequalities. Market economies existed not to equalize or liberate, but to allocate and preserve existing freedoms in the face of the encroaching state. However, to speak of sovereign consumers with their own specific needs and rights represented progress of a kind. If this generalization represented a leap in hypocrisy concerning the reality of social relations, it also contemplated a leap in the civility of public discourse. It thus made it possible to speak about other people's collective habits without obvious bias, cruel hyperbole, or denigrating epithets. Regardless of wealth or power, all people were consumers.

Defending the European Way of Life

When the self-anointed Tocqueville of the twentieth century, André Siegfried, asked what American democracy portended for European liberalism, his answer was full of trepidation. The "technical talk" coming out of the United States sounded neutral, France's leading political sociologist wrote in 1926, only when, in reality, it was suffused with "a whole conception of man, of society, and of life" at odds with the European way of existence. Europe had to live as "befitting a great old civilization, in knowledge of her handicaps, the lack of raw materials on the spot, the scarcity of available capital, the poor buying power of her European clientele." Her "treasures" lay in "the individual resourcefulness of her sons, their creative ability, their tradition for work, and their simplicity of life." This way of existence risked being devastated by "the somewhat unreasonable and excessive standard of living of the New World."[65] So spoke a cosmopolitan liberal who repeatedly professed admiration for the land where "for the first time the white race is achieving something independent of European leadership." Most of Europe's elites thought as he did.

The problem is not whether the American Standard of Living was detestable or desirable, a point that recurred time and again as Fordism with its offer of a quick economic fix worked its demagogic charm across the political spectrum. On the far left, there were the Communists, notably Antonio Gramsci, who wrote passionately and idiosyncratically about "Americanism and Fordism" in his *Prison Notebooks*, endorsing in it the power to sweep away the detritus of Europe's feudal-bourgeois past.[66] On the extreme right, the academic baron Friedrich Gottl-Ottlilienfeld, professor of political economy at the University of Berlin, where he was Sombart's colleague, was an exemplary figure. In the 1924 pamphlet book he tentatively titled *Fordismus?*, he popularized a reactionary "white socialism" that would collectivize the abundance spilling out of the assembly line to deflect the masses from the revolutionary "red" variety.[67] It was the enduring popularity of this misbegotten screed among right-wingers that in 1928 had alerted Hitler to the need to clarify his own view on the matter.

The problem is rather whether it was realistic at all to expect a standard akin to the American to develop in early twentieth-century Europe. After all, no overhaul in the regime of consumption had occurred in the European states such as had taken place in the United States over the previous fifty years in consequence of its vast resources, its democratic heritage, and the accumulation of numerous deep, subtle, and sustained changes in the country's economic institutions, demographics, social relations, and cultural outlooks.

The most ingenious responses rested not so much on reforms on the national level as on projects to unify European nations in order to create a consumer market equal in size to the American. French economist

François Delaisi presented one especially searching plan at the cusp of the 1930s, his goal nothing less than to harness "horse-power Europe" to "horse-drawn Europe," by which he meant the northwestern area, with its modern industry and relatively high consumption, to the southern and eastern regions, with their low levels of urbanization, scattered rural population, and subsistence agriculture. The first step this imaginative pan-Europeanist proposed was to rechannel toward eastern Europe the big flows of American capital that were going into Germany, where they produced an excess of manufacturing capacity and recession. In 1932, faced with the Depression and emboldened by Soviet-type planning, Delaisi advanced a second, more ambitious proposal. The so-called Delaisi Plan would bring producers together with consumers by retooling Europe's commercial infrastructure, including transportation, postal systems, and other means of communication. It also called for Europe's colonial great powers to take a lesson from the United States, end formal empire, which was only a waste of resources and a source of conflict, and "return to Europe." Then, to widen and deepen their domestic markets, European governments had to take a lesson from Ford and treat the European region as a single market. With purchasing power on the rise and cheap goods pressing the market, Europe would pull out of stagnation and develop along American lines.[68] Though prescient, Delaisi's utopia foundered on the shoals of the Great Depression.

Anyway, it would be mistaken to see early twentieth-century Europe's problem as a dearth of consumer-oriented production. Admittedly, everything about the European area was scaled and shaped differently from the American: from the size, output, and intrafirm arrangements of its enterprises, modes of distribution, and notions of profit, to the very concept of the consumer. The best face that can be put on Europe's consumer-oriented economy is that it was based on flourishing but segmented regional markets. Innovations with a view to widening these local areas of exchange could not depend on investment in vast new assembly plants operating with single-purpose tools and unskilled labor, as in the United States, but rather on installing general-purpose machinery to turn out a more varied array of customized products.[69] Relying on a versatile, stable labor force, enterprises could have kept their workers more or less continuously employed by changing their batches of goods. But they could never have raised their wages. European manufacturers had barely recovered from the dislocations of supply from World War I and inflation during the 1920s before being knocked flat by the Depression. Desperate to reduce costs, they whittled back money income, upped nonmonetary compensations, jettisoned safety measures, and skimped on product quality. Whenever possible, firms making similar lines of products struck deals to keep prices at remunerative levels and divided up markets in the hope of reducing competition. Most sought tariff protection. The net effect was low productivity, high prices, slow turnover, and insignificant innovation in consumer goods.

Had there been real prospects of increasing demand, business strategies could conceivably have changed. However, Europe's population growth had been slowing to an average of 6.5 percent per decade from 1890 on, whereas in the United States population growth from immigration and strong birthrates leaped ahead by 19 percent. In "horse-drawn Europe," large swathes of people lived in semiautarchy, making sparse use of money and purchasing little from local markets. Generally, overall purchasing power grew slowly. Whereas the United States saw a remarkable 23 percent increase from 1913 to 1929, western Europe averaged only 5.5 percent. In the United States, per capita income, adjusted to the cost of living, after doubling between 1869 and 1899, nearly doubled again from 1909 to 1942 following some wild fluctuations in the early 1930s. Sweden alone kept pace. France showed no visible gains at all in per capita income from 1913 to 1947. Nor did Germany or Italy.[70]

Although income was not evenly distributed, consumer habits showed change nonetheless. So Europeans experienced boomlets in the 1920s and even in the 1930s as bourgeois clients purchased automobiles, unionized workers bought dining sets and other household appliances, urban shopgirls who lived at home indulged in small personal luxuries such as scarves, hair clips, or lipstick, and people of all classes made a habit of moviegoing and purchasing home radio sets. However, these trends did not add up to a rise in the standard of living in the American sense. Nor did they result in that virtuous circle that had mass production push prices lower, made the consumption of new goods more general, enriched the businessman, fostered new investment, and shook up the old hierarchies of needs.

Instead, the very demand for new goods and pastimes ran up against a fortress of obstacles. Class-bound norms of consumption formed one bulwark, the culture of poverty of the socialist and working-class movements another. Pressing up against these barriers, new consumer behav-

iors acted as a source of social fragmentation rather than social integration; they produced new sources of differentiation and exclusion rather
than making standards more homogeneous and accessible. At best, consumers were worrisomely ill-understood, unpredictable social figures. At
worst, their needs were identified with the demands of the lower orders,
volatile, ravenous, capricious, hence contributing to the unpredictability
of economic trends, political polarization, and the degradation of national culture.

Above all, new consumer habits pressed up against European societies'
barriers of "distinction." The term, though largely identified with French
sociologist Pierre Bourdieu's massive empirical study published in 1976,
first appeared in a slim interpretative essay called *La barrière et le niveau*,
published in 1925. The author, Edmond Goblot, was a professor of logic
with an unconventional mind, who assiduously took note of the lines of
exclusion and inclusion within French society as he slowly advanced in
his career through the French provinces.[71] By "distinction" Goblot meant
several features peculiar to the bourgeois classes' social relations: from
their habits of purchase and air of refinement to their incessant if subtle
struggle to set themselves off materially from other social classes. Admittedly, no sociologist could have documented this way of life scientifically,
since bourgeois families regarded the privacy of their domiciles as a prerogative no snooping surveyor dared to breach. However, Goblot was familiar enough with the milieu to sketch out several general rules that distinguished the bourgeoisie's behaviors as consumers from others. First,
there was the abode, which whether house or apartment and no matter
how poor, was furnished with a reception room, separate quarters for the
children, and a kitchen nook adjacent to the servants' area. The last were
indispensable to the operation of a household in which modern comforts
such as running water, elevators, gas stoves, and adequate illumination
were often lacking, and the women of the class were not held to perform
menial labor. Though expenditure for food was frugal, dining was elaborate, supplies attentively purchased and prepared, the timing of presentation impeccable, the place settings just so, the napery immaculate. Others remarked on the distinctive manners, from handwriting and style of
dress—noting the prescriptions about when to wear a bowler and when a
top hat, and those regulating the etiquette of receiving at home—to the
regularity of spa treatments, automobile touring, and family vacations at
the seaside and mountains. To be bourgeois also meant the capacity to
monopolize the major means of social reproduction, including higher

education and control over art patronage, and to set taste and influence public opinion. Reflecting this remarkably formalized way of life, irrespective of profession, income, family size, and place of residence, the bourgeoisie was ineffably set apart by dress, body movement, and physical affect. Goblot made the point as a matter of fact: "One can tell a bourgeois from a man of the people simply by a glance as they pass in the street; a gentleman simply isn't to be confused with a man, much less a lady with a woman."[72]

The origins of this singularly cohesive style of life lay in the society of orders of the old regime, and the efforts made by the bourgeoisie, in the slow process of displacing aristocratic elites, to seize their aesthetic sensibility and power to pattern taste and fashion to establish their own influence. At its acme on the eve of World War I, the bourgeoisie's lifestyle appeared to be so well defined, clear-cut, and exclusive that Goblot was tempted to characterize it as castelike. However, distinction arose not from birth, as under the prerevolutionary old regime, but through inherited economic power, and especially through the capacity of bourgeois families to use their social standing to establish monopolies over goods and services. From Karl Marx, the analyst of capital, we learn that cultural power depends on class position, which in turn depends on relations to production, and that the former will be eroded and eventually overthrown as the latter are revolutionized. From Max Weber, the analyst of the sticky power of social stratification, we learn that social status, when enhanced by the control of access to goods and services, can be quite impervious to declining economic fortunes.[73]

Far from declining, new forces weighed in to reinforce the social barriers within the old regime of consumption. Governments protected craft industries dedicated to luxury production. They also made certain that regardless of their productivity, their functionaries were accorded the salaries and prerequisites appropriate to upholding a way of life redounding to the decorum of the nation. Governments also upheld the elites' monopoly over the educational system. The fact that cultural goods were so treasured, yet so stingily and unevenly distributed, raised the prestige of the traditional cultural establishment. More important, it raised its prestige in the eyes of all the professions that in some way benefitted from its organization, from the newspaper editorial writer and leading trade union leader down to the local head of the public library and the elementary school teacher. This attachment alerted a wide if socially disparate elite to dig in their heels in the face of potential changes in national taste and styles.

In its formality and conservatism, how distant this European bourgeois regime of consumption appears from the relations Thorstein Veblen detailed in *The Theory of the Leisure Class* (1899). In contrast to the perpetuation of social distance, monopolies over goods, and conspicuous displays of separation, Veblen's admittedly fanciful picture told of threatening proximity, competition over goods, and the volatility of the Gilded Age's new wealthy acting out their craving for social recognition in atavistic warrior displays. The dynamics of "invidious comparison" ran up and down the class pyramid in a general frenzy of emulation. "Conspicuous consumption," also Veblen's term, had the superrich in their burnished carriages ostentatiously setting off to charity balls; and it had workers at the taverns on payday outdoing each other in offering rounds of drinks to all comers.[74] Fifteen years later, Veblen would have observed the impact of innovative goods like canned foods, the safety razor, or automobiles, whose rapid diffusion was associated with rising income and new needs rather than the demonstration of social rank. Purchasers paid for them by economizing on some other object. Thereby, such goods gave a further jolt to an already contentious social hierarchy, yet a jolt that could be absorbed, as new purchases could be paid for out of rising income and had been legitimated as appropriate to the whole society's move to a higher American standard of living.

In Europe, by contrast, slow and uneven growth inhibited the flow of innovative goods onto the market even while making their social impact more disruptive. Lacking economic means, the lower levels of the bourgeoisie had trouble emulating the higher. Yet they couldn't turn their backs on them either, for they accepted bourgeois standards as their own, and neither the market nor another social authority sanctioned an alternative. To make their circumstances harder, they were trapped in a struggle over the "positional goods" of bourgeois society: goods like entry to the higher educational system, with its deluxe ornaments, the study of Greek and Latin, which, as they were democratized, lost their status value.[75] Newcomers similarly wanted access to libraries, hotels, spas, and the seaside, not to mention the first-class compartments of trains, the box seats at the opera, and the motor roads transited by the wealthy in their touring cars. But once newcomers had access to them, these goods and services could not yield the same satisfactions. Thus an excess of demand for bourgeois lifestyles outstripped bourgeois opportunities, inflating prices and conflict over claims. To democratize scarce status goods was an affront to their original proprietors; to maintain their exclusivity, an affront to new aspirants.

The classes in between were the worst hit, those whom the Germans classified as the *Mittelstand* and other cultures called the petit bourgeoisie. Suddenly, it was they rather than the unemployed worker, the ragged peasant or the inveterate poor, who elicited an outpouring of public pity for the sag in their means of living from inflation and unemployment. From the early 1920s, stories abounded about the upstanding lampshademaker around the corner, the dutiful accountant at such-and-such a state ministry, and the loyal bank clerk who were to be observed quietly cadging from passersby, while their prematurely aged wives, stressed by economic worries, threw themselves on the mercy of storekeepers for credit and bundled up the family lace, drapery, and silver plate for furtive trips to the pawnshop.[76] Drawn from the artisan economy, state bureaucracies, and the modern service sector, their incomes often differed little from the wages of the unionized, skilled working classes, though in terms of lifestyle and mental habits they couldn't live like workers, any more than they or their wives could engage in manual labor. It was their intimate distress about the crumbling hierarchies of the old regime of consumption that made for an emotional war zone, and their fear of losing this struggle with a Medusa-like enemy—the workers, America, the rich, the Jew—that pitched them onto the side of reactionaries in the 1930s. Meanwhile, the more volatile the political situation, the more weight was given to constancy in everyday culture. The American, it was said, never having had to face down revolutionary upheavals, could live with unending restlessness of taste and style; the European, having experienced the press of revolutionary mobs, panicked if his slippers and dressing gown were misplaced.[77] Faced with cutting back, the middle classes tried to defend their common interests by means of organizations more apt to represent their outward marks as a status group than their economic interests. In this endeavor they were usually ineffective.[78] Nothing seemed to stop this bleeding of the social body, short of another way of thinking about standards, one that would attach them to a new mass middle way of life. How such an existence could be conceived, much less instated, was the question of questions.

Why Was There No Consumerism in Europe?

The creation of any new standard was greatly complicated by the fact that the other face of the society of distinctions was the working-class subculture, whose features shaped and were shaped by the socialist

movement. Around 1900, Werner Sombart's sympathy for Europe's socialist working-class movement had provoked him to ask whether consumer abundance had obstructed its spread in the United States. Suppose
the "Red Prince" of European sociology had turned the question back to
his own world to ask: "Why is there no consumerism in Europe?" Would
he have successfully highlighted the peculiarities of his own society that
obstructed the advance of populist consumerism?

To start, European socialists had rich if deeply divided traditions of
thinking about the standard of living. On the one hand, socialism as a political movement supported the demand for higher wages both to improve working-class material life and to demonstrate the limits of capitalism as an economic system by advancing demands that it could not
deliver on. On the other hand, socialism was ethically and culturally invested in Western traditions of asceticism. The socialist good life drew on
the egalitarianism of Christian poverty as well as the austerity of humanism. It spoke of Christ breaking bread with his followers and Saint Francis' vows of poverty. It resonated with Erasmus of Rotterdam's charming
words: "When I have a little money I buy books; when I have a little
more, food and clothes." It rejoiced in visions of natural abundance:
"There is no wealth but life," the gentle guild socialist John Ruskin used
to say. True poverty was not a lack of things, nor could the whole arc of
life's possibilities be conceived as finding satisfaction through market exchanges. In recognition of the great variety of human sensual, physical,
and intellectual needs, Karl Marx imagined that when the chains of private property had finally been broken off, mankind would be free at last
to hunt in the morning, fish in the afternoon, and read in the evening.

Nineteenth-century socialism had nurtured this rich view of life's
pleasures. In the oft-reprinted *The Right to Laziness* (1887), Marx's own
son-in-law Paul Lafargue, the creole husband of his beloved chestnut-
haired daughter Laura, gave a particularly seductive French twist to the
utopian dreams of satisfactions that were also a leitmotif of the fantasizing of Charles Fourier's Phalansterian movement, the American Edward
Bellamy's *Looking Backward,* and the whole range of folksy orators at
May Day festivities who conjured up with fanciful rhetoric the promise
of the fabled land of Cockaigne. For Lafargue, the workers' "rights to laziness" were "a thousand times more noble and sacred" than the "con-
sumptive Rights of Man concocted by the head-in-the-clouds lawyers of
the bourgeois revolution." As scornful of Judeo-Christian asceticism as
his contemporary Nietzsche, Lafargue called on the bourgeoisie to re-

nounce the work ethic, to force itself "to work but three hours a day, to do nothing and play around the rest of the day and night." Thus "liberated from its task as universal consumer, it will hurry about dismissing the mob of soldiers, judges, hangers-on, pimps, etc., which it retired from useful work to help it consume and waste." In turn, the working class "will have to stretch its consumer capacities infinitely. Instead of eating one or two ounces of spoiled meat a day, if it eats meat at all, it will eat joyous beefsteaks of a pound or two; instead of drinking bad wine in moderation, more Catholic than the Pope, it will gulp down huge, deep tankers of Bordeaux, of Burgundy, undiluted, and leave the water to the animals."[79]

Why these European visions of the Big Rock Candy Mountain should have turned into doctrinal blasphemy by the early twentieth century, superseded by the austere notion of needs we associate with twentieth-century Communism, is hard to pinpoint. Partly, it resulted from the destruction in dreary urban ghettos of workers' ties to the Rabelaisian play of rural festivities. Partly, it grew out of the insufferable regimentation of the mass-production factory. Partly, it was the effect of the killjoy austerity of socialist leaders who truly believed in the redemptive value of misery and that their constituents' poverty made them worthy of any sacrifice in the struggle for socialism. Anyhow, by the 1920s European socialism was notably unimaginative about the copious, useful, and attractive output of manufacture, especially standardized, mass manufacture. And to the degree that it reflected upon this production, it was to argue that it satisfied inauthentic, as opposed to real, needs. The two types of socialists who were the most insufferably unimaginative about what workers could do with material possessions were also those most enamored of Fordism. One was the Communist revolutionary who had broken away from the tedium of social reformism in the name of vanguard politics. The other was the efficiency-minded trade unionist who, though intent on winning higher wages for his constituents, was remarkably inhibited about spelling out what they might actually do with them.

The machine could be the "workers' friend," exhorted Hyacinthe Dubrueil, the well-known French trade unionist; just imagine the bounty of aluminum pots and pans that could be turned out from spanking-new assembly lines![80] Between the minimum of bread and shelter and the maximum, a small-cylinder automobile, it was as if nothing existed worth fantasizing about. The multitudinous household conveniences a working-class woman might imagine, including the aluminum pots, but also warm water, down-filled pillows, or a crank-driven washing machine, much less silk stockings, a flower vase, or lace doilies, lay outside the ken of the hard-nosed male socialist's imagination.

Ideally, socialism would accomplish the great leap from the realm of necessity to the realm of freedom by allying the intellectual who had renounced everything with the plebs, who had nothing. On the one hand, the self-mortifying asceticism of the left argued for extinguishing the self in the collective, especially insofar as the self gave expression to worrisomely contradictory desires. To concentrate on the nonnecessary was a diversion and source of self-dissipation, and to renounce the bourgeois lifestyle was the way to overcome the material separation between the classes. Communism had "an appeal to the ascetic in us," the pleasure-loving John Maynard Keynes remarked, speaking of the left-sympathizing university students of the 1930s. "Cambridge undergraduates were never disillusioned when they took their inevitable trip to 'Bolshiedom' and found it 'dreadfully uncomfortable.' That is what they are looking for."[81]

On the other hand, left asceticism saw the worker as innately possessed of animal vitality that was easily diverted into crude material wants unless refined by political consciousness and the discipline of party organization. Once he had stepped onto the hedonic treadmill, he could very well end up like his counterpart in Detroit who on payday, as he stepped out of the factory gates, was mobbed by wives, bookies, salesmen, bill collectors, representatives of installment credit firms, and sheriffs' bailiffs with bankruptcy writs to attach wages.[82] In the United States, however, there were puritanism and Prohibition to keep workers in check. Lacking these checks, the New Man of European socialism needed to have his desires sublimated by measures to steer him clear of the degraded social behaviors of petit-bourgeois strivers and anchor him solidly in the working-class community. The more urgent problem was that the working-class family lived in a cramped, dark apartment, ate large amounts of carbohydrates, wore remade and mended clothing, stayed mostly within walking distance of home except for going to work, and hung around the neighborhood as its main social activity. But these issues had to be addressed collectively. Here properly was the space for the most capacious and lovely thinking about the good life: functionally laid out subsidized apartments, stately parks, public transportation, decent schools, fine theater with discounts and special matinees for the masses, organized vacations.

Until the 1950s most European workers would not have traded harder work for more money in any case, even if their bosses had been disposed to negotiate higher wages in return for higher output. Lacking new needs, it was futile to argue for sacrifice of time and labor today for the gratification of goods tomorrow. If anything, the preference was for more leisure: there was plenty to live for provided one wasn't working.[83] Anyway, nothing indicated that high productivity in itself was a worthwhile goal, or that improved compensation was in any way related to more intense labor. Unlike American businessmen, who were legendary for working round the clock, Europe's *rentier* classes were legendary for being parasites, living off the fat of the land and producing nothing except for their own selfish pleasure. And enough of them lived that way to justify the legend. Likewise, the pay of the myriad of government functionaries was tied to their station as servants of the state rather than to the level of services they provided the public. Emergencies like war caused pay to increase, especially in military-related employment. Otherwise, it was well known that the workers best organized politically had the best chance of obtaining higher wages, not the ones who were most productive.

All said, obtaining social justice was a far more tangible goal than getting goods. Around 1950, when sociologist Paul-Henry Chombart de Lauwe queried Parisian workers around contract negotiation time what they wanted from life, they answered: to secure what little they already had. "The issue," to use the French sociologist's elegant synthesis, was "subsistence, not future substance, immediate survival, not future flourishing."[84] In turn, employers believed that if they raised wages, the workers would "waste their surplus buying power in vulgar and transient satisfactions." Whoever expected workers to live austerely because of their poverty found their behavior as consumers unpredictable, if not capricious. The workers on the dole at Wigan Pier took sugar and sweets with their cup of tea, George Orwell noted, to twit tongue-clucking do-gooders.[85] Wanting for everything, Chombart de Lauwe's Parisian workmen were in turn anxious and playful, depressed and expansive, pinched and generous. On the eve of payday, their wives fretted whether they could put food on the table, they were so burdened with debt. Yet the day afterward, with the storekeeper placated, they loaded up on meat and sweets as if there were no tomorrow.

Given that workers were conceived as a group apart, their habits shaped less by income than by life choices imposed by their condition as manual laborers, how could their standards of living ever be expected to change? This was the conundrum that the French sociologist Maurice

Halbwachs, a socialist, returned to again and again in the course of his wide-ranging intellectual life. Born in 1877, just a year older than Albert Thomas, whose classmate he had been at the Ecole Normale Supérieure and under whom he worked during World War I, Halbwachs was such a cosmopolitan and a polymath that he seemed unlikely to nurse any preconceptions about the needs of different classes in contemporary society.

Yet Halbwachs's first book, an investigation into "the hierarchy of needs in contemporary industrial societies," only reaffirmed what seemed intuitive at the time, namely that social classes lived in ways utterly segregated from each other even if they had similar incomes. Accordingly, the family of a salaried man partitioned his income like a bourgeois family, spending as little as possible on food, stretching its budget to pay for respectable housing, the children's education, help for Madame, and the summer holiday. By contrast, the working-class family spent relatively large sums on food while putting aside little for housing. The differences were a surprise, for the only real "law" regarding consumption, Engel's Law, formulated by Ernst Engel, the head of mid-nineteenth-century Prussia's Office of Statistics, said that the less a family's income, the more proportionally would be spent on food. At equal revenue, then, both salary and wage earners should be spending the same. To explain this difference, Halbwachs drew from Emile Durkheim, his teacher, the argument that the styles of life of groups were conditioned by their collective self-image; the workers, by being "forced into contact with inanimate things," hence "becoming cut off from the rest of the human community," to compensate for the absence of companionability at work, overspent (in view of their income) on sociable afterwork pastimes, on food in particular. By comparison with the petit bourgeoisie, they invested proportionally little in housing, since it would only reinforce their isolation. The conclusion was a familiar one: different classes thought of themselves differently. More income for the worker simply meant that he and his family ate more. Bourgeois blinkers prevented Halbwachs, though a socialist and expert on the housing "problem," to consider whether the impossibility for workers of finding decent housing may not have been the most trenchant factor.[86]

The only socialists fully committed to considering workers in their fullness as consumers were the leaders of the consumer cooperative movement. But socialist consumerism, unlike American populist consumerism, was too politicized to fit easily into the bourgeois regime of consumption, as it reinforced the workers' subcultures even while increasing the working-class standard of living.

The annals of the European labor movement celebrated as one of its most noble moments the day in 1844 when twenty-eight impoverished flannel weavers from the bleak little valley town of Rochdale in the English Midlands, each subscribing two or three pounds for the cause, collected a tidy capital to open an outlet to sell flour, butter, sugar, and oatmeal. Before this effort, workers in the valleys of Lancashire and Yorkshire had banded together against exploitation by local shops, manufacturers' outlets, and distributors' monopolies to provide unadulterated foods and decently made clothing at low prices only to splinter over the vexed problem of how to distribute the profits. It was the genius of the Rochdale "pioneers" to have solved the problem of profiteering by paying out 5 percent interest on the share capital in proportion to their subscribers' investment and purchases. Any excess was paid out in the form of a dividend to the members. Accordingly, cooperativists, as they became known, saw it as being to their advantage to make purchases at their store and to welcome new subscribers from among their neighbors. Spreading with industrialization, the movement had millions of members globally by the turn of the twentieth century, from Seattle and Minsk to Calcutta.[87]

Every region and country had its prophet. France's was Charles Gide. A political economist, the founder of the so-called Nîmes School, he was hugely influential not only in French-speaking areas but in Europe generally. For Gide, the consumer was "king." Consumer sovereignty, as he used the concept, was a great force arising out of the sentiment that consumers were the "forgotten third estate." Like the common people who had banded together to overturn the tyranny of the old regime of aristocrats, they would join forces to overturn the oppression of the old regime of the producers.[88] In contrast to the American concept of consumers, which was the clustering of individual desires revealed through market choices, the will of Gide's consumers operated collectively by means of a myriad of cooperative outlets. At their apogee in the 1920s, their entryways marked by a "lode star" rather than by "a lowly store sign," they oriented the norms of consumption of thousands of working-class communities.[89]

However, socialist cooperativism did not lead an easy existence, as is demonstrated by the grandest of cooperative undertakings, centered in Belgium, the heartland of European labor reformism, and housed in the grandest of buildings, the Maison du Peuple of downtown Brussels. When Victor Horty's six-story art nouveau structure was inaugurated in 1899, fully half of it was dedicated to the cooperative's business. The scores of delegates from abroad, the chants of "Long live the International," the fireworks, the tens of thousands of celebrants were also celebrating a working-class undertaking that in its layout, merchandising techniques, and quality of product rivaled any bourgeois department store. Yet this was a poor man's consumer sovereignty. First, it could not sustain material standards, much less set them: styles were still set by bourgeois fashion leaders, and the workers' purchasing power wobbled up and down according to the business cycle. When the economy turned sour, niceties suffered; dress passed from being fashionable to merely decent, and bread became the biggest-selling item. Second, sourcing presented a problem: to find the cheapest prices, buyers sought stingier-paying manufacturers, and it was entirely conceivable that these were not just not unionized workers, but not even Belgian.[90] Third, "buying for socialism" enhanced social distance rather than closing it. Emulation works when the upper classes take pride in being imitated, as business elites in the United States did, in effect, by promoting the mass production of knock-offs, not when they feel intimidated by emulation and bitterly stigmatize it as class envy.

The cooperatives' most trenchant critics came not from the bourgeois elites, however, but from the cultural milieu closest to them, the one shaped by the neosocialist faction of the Belgian Workers Party. The most qualified and prominent of the critics, Hendrik De Man, scion of a leading Flemish family from Antwerp and the boldest and best-known reviser of socialism during the interwar years, had been a great admirer of the United States, which he had visited in the last year of the war and where, completely disillusioned with Europe, he had intended to go to live, moving his whole family to Seattle to find "new spiritual anchorage" and restart his life as a university professor. In his paean to the United States, *Au pays du Taylorisme,* he made light of Sombart's worry that the American working class had been seduced away from radical politics by material comforts, and he spoke of his special affection for the West Coast's efficient cooperatives. Belgian workers should learn from their successes. That, at least, was his line until the moment he recalled as "the worst day of his life."[91] This occurred sometime in the mid-1920s when he suddenly realized that the European working class was being suborned from socialism by similar material influences. With a stroke of brilliance, he turned Sombart's question on its head: the problem to be investigated was not "Why is there *no* socialism in America?" but "Why *is* there socialism in Europe?"

De Man's answer was that socialism in Europe responded not to the misery caused by industrialization, but to deep needs for democracy, equity, and ethical meaning absent in European bourgeois civilization. To build an effective agenda of reform, the socialist movement had to set its sights high. Workers suffered not just from economic deprivation, but from a sense of social inferiority. If given the opportunity, they would try to placate their envy by "buying into" a "culture of imitation." His conclusion, apostate for the time, was that the battle for socialism had to position itself around ethical issues as opposed to material acquisitions. But if the goal was a revolution in values, then America's materialist culture stood as a real threat. Turning against American mass culture in the late 1920s, by the mid-1930s the socialist widely regarded as the European movement's leading intellectual embarked on a search for a "national" socialism. In 1940 De Man would embrace Hitler's New Order.[92]

Around the same time, Werner Sombart, the onetime "red prince" of German sociology, arrived at similarly damning conclusions about proletarian consumerism. During the 1920s he had become more and more convinced that in the era of what he called "high capitalism," the bourgeoisie's goal in accumulating capital had once more changed character. In early capitalist times, it had sought profits at the same time as aiming to satisfy its own well-defined needs. In the contemporary world it was motivated by pure desire—infinite, unleashed, and destructive of all values. The Americans had set the pace, but the true prototype of the modern capitalist was the Jew, a figure who, though admirable for his clairvoyance, was much to be deplored for his cultural rootlessness. Converted to Nazism after 1933, Sombart was increasingly outspoken in his belief that German socialism, by which he meant the ideology of the Nazi regime, needed to spell out new "good" standards of consumer taste and well-being. Neither the old bourgeois classes with their futile luxury nor the "uniformity of gray proletarian poverty" was capable of generating a principled vision of living. A "simple state" like old Prussia offered a convincing model, and so did the outlook of its sovereign, Frederick the Great, who, though he "wore a shabby uniform . . . knew how to distinguish between noble and ignoble needs."[93]

Commanding Consumers

As Sombart's reactionary call makes clear, the 1930s brought a sea change in perspectives on the standard of living. In the 1920s it was rare to hear consumption spoken of outside the cooperative movement.[94] Liberal economists recognized that it existed as a problem. After all, World War I could not have been fought without rationing and other regulations on consumption on the home front. However, until the debates over improved wages were recast as debates over increasing purchasing power to salvage the whole capitalist system from the Great Crisis, scarcity was treated as an underlying condition of human existence, free markets as the device to allocate them, and consumption as just another liberty, like commerce, subject to the vicissitudes of politics and the market. For conventional liberal political economy, there was more consumption in good times, less in bad. Consequently, liberal commentators had ignored major new trends. First, governments had long been regulating consumption in one way or another by rationing, wage restraints, "buy national" campaigns, taxation, tariffs, and so on. Second, as Keynes said, the Great War, by "disclosing the possibility of consumption to all," had spelled "the end of the true religion around non-consumption of the cake of production"; not only could pressures to redistribute wealth not be put off forever, but the bourgeois ethic of saving rather than spending promised to become an obstacle to capitalist development.[95] Finally, the Depression, whether it was diagnosed as resulting from overproduction or from underconsumption, failed to respond to traditional liberal deflationary remedies that would cut government spending to the bone to drive down costs, wages, and prices until the moment was again ripe for the capitalist to invest.

Indeed, government response to the Great Depression spelled the death knell of the political economy underpinnings of the old regime of consumption. Across the board, from left to right—from the British Labourite Ramsay McDonald to Germany's conservative Catholic Chancellor Brüning—governments deflated economies and wrought political havoc. To aid the jobless, none of the provisions currently available worked: neither the meager dole, nor improvised public works projects, nor spotty unemployment insurance. It was only a question of time before they were all turned out of office by protest movements, massive shifts of votes to the parliamentary opposition, and the reinforcing of antiparliamentary movements.

One remarkable outcome was that pumping up purchasing power began to be viewed as indispensable to the recovery of capitalism. Keynes is invariably credited with explaining the hitherto little-understood determinants of effective demand by emphasizing the need to understand the overall level of consumer expenditures. Leaving aside conventional distinctions between the producer and the consumer, a distinction favored by liberal economists who held that it was impediments between the two—such as cartels, bureaucracy, and bad regulations—that had caused the crisis and prevented rapid remedy, Keynes developed the notion of a consumption function to complement other economic aggregates such as the investment function or the demand for money. Exploring this function, he discovered that richer people saved proportionately more and thus consumed proportionately less, thereby reducing rates of investment. This unexpected conclusion spelled out that the unpredictable force was the investor, the capitalist producer, and the bourgeois customer, who failed to use their potential savings, rather than the mass consumer, whose demand was capable of being properly managed through monetary and fiscal policy. A social snob, Keynes assumed an agnostic position on what consumers actually did with their purchasing power, provided they used it.[96]

In the event, Keynes's theories had hardly begun to circulate before the measures required to elevate purchasing power moved to the center of debate. Inevitably eyes turned toward the United States, where Franklin Roosevelt, by means of the New Deal, looked as if he were successfully raising purchasing power, empowering the people, and checking organized business. In reality he was engaged in a different undertaking: by recognizing collective rights to bargaining at the same time as setting up social security, he greatly strengthened both U.S. capitalism and American democracy. However, his government regarded the consumer not as a political force, but as an aggregate in economic growth. Policies energized the economically diffuse interests of the consumer to offset the power of the strong and concentrated, but not to the point of impeding free enterprise, overseeing any redistribution of wealth, or investing substantial new regulatory authority in the federal government.[97]

In Europe, however, projects to augment purchasing power immediately opened the vexed question of how masses of people would use it. Suddenly European nations faced problems that Americans had either resolved over time, such as the assimilation of immigrants to national norms of living, or had ceased having to face at all after 1914, like pressure from imported goods and foreign models of consumption. In other words, the idea that the economy's recovery depended on giving free rein to consumer choice came into vogue just as these very theories were going out of favor. What forces, then, were to moderate changes of consumer habit, protect against the exaggerations of foreign customs on both cultural and economic grounds, and set positive standards, aligning market trends and cultural messages to the appropriate national resource mix? All of a sudden it was clear how very useful the concept of a *national* standard of living could be.[98]

By the second half of the 1930s, then, Europe became the stage for various experiments to establish new national standards of living, with the right and the left in competition with each other and both having the American experience in mind. Two more different politics with respect to the standard of living could hardly be imagined than those taken by the French Popular Front of Léon Blum and by Hitler's Third Reich. Blum's left-wing coalition aimed at raising purchasing power across the board, redistributing wealth, and empowering workers through collective bargaining. By contrast, the Nazi regime aimed at "as much butter as necessary and as many guns as possible."[99] Within the constraints of a closed economy, more and more oriented to war preparation, it endeavored to supply cheaply the consumer goods whose lack had made Germany seem backward, modify the class-divisive nature of cultural goods, and distribute scarce resources by rewarding and depriving consumers according to their place in the hierarchy of utility and race of the so-called People's Community, or *Volksgemeinschaft*.

For conservatives, the French Popular Front presented the worst-case scenario: not only were they hostile to higher wages, but they were terrified about the changes in the way of life that the left in power boded. Winning the elections in May 1936, the radical socialist alliance thought it was following the New Deal when it undertook to raise purchasing power by across-the-board salary and wage increases. For that purpose, the government of the socialist Léon Blum took three measures: it reduced the work week to forty hours without cutting wages, thereby spreading employment; it undertook public works to increase jobs; and it raised agricultural prices to augment peasant incomes.[100] Audacious though it was on these issues, it didn't want to risk devaluing the franc for fear of hurting the middle-class way of life based on savings and income or to give the big bourgeoisie an even bigger fright by establishing controls over capital. Consequently, the overvalued franc made it hard to export goods, and the lack of controls permitted capital flight, provoking the financial crisis that brought down the government.

Yet what a time it was, the nearly two years the Blum government lasted in power. Unfettered by the forty-hour work week, the institution of the weekend, the first paid holidays, the festive atmosphere and strikes at the workplace that caused labor productivity to plunge, the working class came as close to achieving Lafargue's "right to laziness" as could be imagined in a modern industrial society. With the appointment by the Cabinet of the first undersecretary for sports and leisure, Leo Lagrange, who spurred tourism with discounts on rail fares, the Popular Front celebrated the consumption of leisure as well as the consumption of goods.[101]

The Popular Front's confidence that measures to increase working-class consumption would also foster democratization reflected a real shift from the conventional asceticism of socialist thought. Here Maurice Halbwachs comes back into the picture: in 1933 he brought out a new book on the standard of living of the working classes, revisiting his 1912 work, his views completely changed, he wrote, not just by the time that had elapsed, but also by distance. By that he meant the hugely widened perspective he had gained from his four-month stay in the United States in the autumn of 1930, when he taught at the University of Chicago at the invitation of Robert E. Park, America's most innovative urban sociologist. The qualities that led him to be invited, including his acute sense of "the realities of daily life," his genius for statistics, and his curiosity about racial variety and a "white humanity so different from ours," surely played an important role in making him change his earlier views. But his intermediary was the "precious document" that a leading trade union official pressed on him when he stopped over at the Bureau of Labor in Washington, D.C., on his way home. This was none other than the documentation compiled in Detroit for the notorious Ford-ILO Inquiry.[102]

Upon returning to Paris, Halbwachs pored over the Inquiry's findings as he set about analyzing the best data on living standards available for Europe. These were provided by the German Statistical Office's massive study of 2,036 families undertaken in 1927–28 to take stock of the toll of inflation on ordinary Germans. Reading it through the lens of the U.S. experience, he discerned how differently laborers, white-collar employees, and state officials spent their earnings according to their social standing. Yet now he had been sensitized to the idea that new needs could cause people to jettison fixed hierarchies of wants.[103] "Style of life" was not dependent on "type of labor." The worker made social choices. Conceivably, workers might even display a precocious interest in new consumer habits, provided they had the income, since, unlike the bourgeoisie and lower middle class, they were less invested in the prevailing standards from which society excluded them. To capture these trends, Halbwachs titled his new book *The Evolution of Needs*.

True, Halbwachs had a hard time bringing his colleagues around to his views. When the French Institute of Sociology hosted a discussion attended by his best friend, Simiand, and a handful of other skeptics, their major concern was to discuss the political implications: they wanted their longtime associate to explain how worker consciousness would be affected by the so-called higher standard of living. Were American workers becoming more bourgeois? Did they purchase the products to improve their social standing? Were they forsaking socialism in pursuit of an illusory capitalist well-being? Were not their wants artificial, shaped by advertising? Halbwachs confidently answered that the hoary Marxist distinction between real and false needs was ill posed. Sewing machines, electric irons, washing machines, and kitchen gadgets were not trifles; they deeply altered ways of living, for women especially. Imperturbable, he ignored Marcel Mauss's misogynist crack: "They don't even know what good cooking means. Even women on the farms serve pork and beans from a can." The new consumer habits, he reassured them, were motivated by the desire not to belong to a new class but to engage in a new realm of collective endeavor in which conventional social distinctions no longer mattered. As surely as the new regime of consumption brought forth new freedoms, it would also bring forth new constraints. Therefore, there was need to foresee an end to working-class politics.[104]

Nonetheless, in late 1930s France, after the Popular Front's wage hikes had caused the biggest leap in working-class income in French history, differences in consumption habits increased rather than narrowing, exacerbating rather than reducing status tensions. The only scientific study we have to go on was conducted by Henry Delpech, a conservative jurist at the University of Toulouse who, in his search for data from his hometown, confronted the usual problems, namely that workers kept spotty records, though they were generous about showing them, whereas bourgeois families, though their accounting techniques would do a small firm proud, hid them like their wounded dignity "behind the closed doors of gelid townhouses." Even so, the evidence showed a practically "superstitious," "profound difference of mentality" about what each class regarded as necessary to its well-being. The *rentier* family, faced with declining income, saved on food to keep up appearances; the small functionary who benefited from salary increases spent more, buying more diverse foods; and the manual worker, also with higher earnings, increased his meat consumption, purchasing better cuts.[105]

The opinion that consumers' excesses, encouraged by the Popular Front's wage and leisure policies, directly contributed to the crisis of the Third Republic was widespread in bourgeois opinion. "The standard of living of the people is depending more and more upon the generosity of the State, and less on any real economic foundation," André Siegfried insisted. The French were literally eating themselves into dependency as the rise of food imports shifted the balance of payments from favoring the metropolis to favoring France's colonies.[106] This uncontrolled appetite—for leisure as well as for food—reinforced the conviction, already widely held by conservatives, that the French consumer's nature was irremediably "prodigal," "undisciplined," and "irrational." These behaviors legitimated cutting back on wages as well as calling for experiments with planned consumption such as they saw being undertaken by their ever more formidable neighbor, Germany.[107]

By the late 1930s Nazi Germany had become the model for the most radical experiments in "command consumption." The other major European alternative was the Soviet Union. But the consumer side of Stalin's Five-Year Plans was never viewed with the same awe as the production side. That forced investment in girding the Soviet Union with industry had as its counterpart disinvesting in the most basic necessities—food, shelter, and clothing—for 80 percent of the population, nobody bothered to discuss; nor that the plans required a giant administration to ration scarcity with the aim of differentiating Moscow and Leningrad from the rest of the country and the privileged party bureaucrat and shock-worker from the famished small farmer and labor-camp inmate.[108] By contrast, the Führer publicized his *Volkisch* standard of living in no uncertain terms as the paradigmatic European alternative to the American way of life.

The first practice indispensable to a regime running out of gold and foreign exchange, and dependent on food imports, especially colonial goods and fats, was autarchy. The pressure was on by means of "buy German" campaigns, rationing, and special propaganda directed at the German housewife "against the boundless imports of the postwar period—which seduced our housewives into making demands on the German market disconnected from the soil." Incited by Nazi bureaucrats, German enterprise showed a genius for *ersatz*. Some substitutes were easy, such as German apples for tropical fruits, though they never compensated for the much-lamented loss of bananas; others, like barley malt for coffee, were more deluding from the point of view of taste and stimulation. Finding substitutes for fats was especially difficult, since the country relied on imports, including tons of lard from the United States, and creamed curd, margarine, marmalade, and other sweeteners were not in sufficient supply to compensate. The chemical and plastics industries outdid themselves to find replacements for rubber, wool, and cotton. Propaganda for *ersatz,* recommendations on diet, injunctions to "buy national"—all sensitized German consumers to the nationality of their expenditures.[109]

Command consumption assigned highly visible political value to innovative goods, such as the radio and especially the automobile. No commodity so much as the automobile had marked Germany's backwardness in consumption with respect to the United States, and none had more visibly signaled the difference between the classes. And no other problem related to provisioning engaged the Führer's attention so much. To deliver a low-cost car, he had Austrian-born auto engineer Fernand Porsche visit Detroit, design a new model, and draw up plans for production. Unable to obtain support for production from private capital, notably Opel and Ford, Hitler turned to Robert Ley, head of the Labor Front. Eager to expand his administrative empire, Ley agreed to oversee the Volkswagen project, as well as devising an ingenious plan to fund it out of prepayments from future customers. Within a year 250,000 families joined the plan, contracting to pay 5 RM per week for four years. Consumer confidence must have been dampened when the assembly lines of the huge plant built at Wolfburg in Lower Saxony were retooled to turn out military vehicles. And the plan holders would have received no satisfaction, if they were still alive, when civilian production started up again in 1948. By then their deposits had disappeared into the Soviet zone of occupation, and appeals through the courts to honor their purchase contracts came to naught in 1954, when the final ruling went against the plaintiffs. *Caveat emptor* had a special meaning under totalitarian regimes.[110]

Command consumption also depended on rationing bare necessities like clothing. In 1938, in recognition that three-quarters of all textile fiber was imported, the state speeded plans to produce more ersatz fabrics and to increase flax imports from the USSR. Nonetheless, if the army was to be properly clothed, civilian demand had to drop by 75 percent. Hence drastic rationing plans began to be drawn up in 1939, the capstone of which, set in place after Germany invaded Poland in September, was heralded as a "masterpiece of German thoroughness." This was the

Reich clothing card, whose aim was to "combine a drastic restriction of the individual's total requirement [of] clothing with the freedom to buy what he wants within the theoretical quota assigned to him." Each card entitled the customer to 100 points, which could be used for the purchase of, say, a bathrobe, which cost 60; a wool dress, 20; or stockings, 4. Naturally, consumers had to learn to manage this "freedom" so as not to want for socks or buttons or darning thread. And firm rules stipulated that old overcoats had to be turned in before a buyer could obtain a new one (unless it could be shown that it was being refurbished for a child). Rationing had as its main goal to make it less arbitrary, and perhaps, therefore, less painful, that, with respect to peacetime, the middle classes' purchase of clothing had been reduced by 30 percent, and the working classes' by 40 to 50 percent.[111]

Command consumption also rested on transforming the meaning of standards: no longer necessities accessed by levels of income, standards were determined by the health and dignity of the racial body. Personal fitness, from being the prerogative of the individual who spent on dentists, doctors, or other purchases, a company investment, or a risk to be assumed by the welfare state in the name of the social collective in Nazi Germany, became instead the object of state and party measures in the name of the People's Community. It was consistent with this emphasis on nonmaterial goods that the people should be treated to the cultural goods that had formerly been the monopoly of the cultured bourgeoisie. For Hitler, those in power "should offer the best of all good things to the people," as opposed to "the bourgeois understanding that anything is good enough for the common people." Culture should no longer be "the property right of the rich." There should be food for the soul and spirit as much as for the stomach.[112] The Strength through Joy organization, established on November 27, 1933, though distinctly lowbrow in its offerings, set a new standard for leisure organization, the collective consumption of leisure in some measure compensating for the low levels of individual consumption.[113]

Above all, command consumption set priorities for who should have access to goods. Deciding on who had the right to a rationing card was the simplest way: Aryans did, non-Aryans did not. Then there was the question of how many points should be allowed on individual cards; working men had more, housewives fewer, and children fewer still. Selective standards could also be achieved by commandeering and redirecting supplies, say from urban shoppers to building workers engaged in fortifying the western frontier. At bottom, rationing rested on calculating utility to the People's Community. There were useful mouths and useless ones. The list of the latter kept growing as supplies became scarcer: Jews, the sick and handicapped, old persons, conquered peoples, and, among the forced laborers in labor camps, those who couldn't work or worked listlessly.

In the end, Hitler would return to the blood-and-soil conclusion of his ruminations of 1928: Germany, lacking a territory adequate for its vital existence, required a formal empire. By the late 1930s there was large consensus on this point. The closing up of the world economy from 1931, encouraged by the economic nationalism of other countries with large markets—above all the United States—had convinced even erstwhile internationalists like Carl Duisberg, head of the IG Farben trust, that Germany needed its own regional economic space, a *Grosswirtschaftsraum*; the term was synonymous with *Lebensraum*, with all its racist and pan-Germanic connotations of resettlement, annihilation, and direct rule.[114]

In 1942, at the acme of the Third Reich's conquests, the notion that the New Order would enable a high standard of living acquired surprisingly wide credibility abroad, as well as in Germany. Propaganda promised that the new international division of labor imposed by German rule of the continent would create new economic complementarities, and that Germany itself would renounce some improvements in its own people's standard of living to bring down the costs of production to enable other countries to afford larger quantities of German manufacture.[115] Former pan-Europeanists who saw in Hitler's triumph the fulfillment of their vision of a prosperous, united Europe rallied to the New Order. François Delaisi, the 1930s champion of European integration, was among them. In 1942 he endorsed the "men of the Axis" for their foresight in dividing the world into autonomous "living spaces," each one grouping peoples of the same race and same civilization with the intention of organizing their resources in a complementary fashion so as to improve the standard of living of the greatest number. So a Europe united under German leadership not only would coexist alongside the British Empire and the United States, but would afford the entire region's people a higher measure of economic well-being.[116]

If the peacetime National Socialist standard of living presented itself as the alternative to the American, the wartime version demonstrated that there were just as many individual minima as there are individuals and that from the social point of view there was no bottom: the level of living could be lowered at will, though not too quickly.[117] Systematically, from 1941, with all of the punctiliousness of nineteenth-century Prussia's famously scientific wage and standard of living studies, German state, army, and party offices turned to establishing standards for subminima to eliminate "life not worth living." Planned consumption determined how much food should be extracted, say, from Greece, leaving a quarter of its 4 million people to starve; how many calories should be allocated to the General Governorship over Poland and what specific amount should be set aside for the Warsaw Ghetto. Elaborate calculations broke down into grams, portions, and calories what was the ration for labor camps and what for extermination centers. Everything was itemized: cabbage, potatoes, jam. What was said of Theresienstadt was true for all: "The tables for nutrition in the lager were, intentionally or unintentionally, humbug."[118]

Maurice Halbwachs would have studied this documentation had he carried out the project he was planning for when the war was over. This was a general study of living conditions in Europe. As it turned out, the Gestapo arrested him in July 1944 after he went to Lyons to protest the assassination of his parents-in-law by fascist militia. Deported from the jail at Fresnes, he arrived on August 20 at Buchenwald, where camp doctors, observing he had been stricken by an attack of boils, certified him as unfit to work. His rations reflected this classification: the regular portion of 250 grams of dry bread and three-quarters of a liter of soup were served minus the regulation 12 grams of margarine, and there was no midday break for the nondescript liquid that was called coffee. On that diet, a young, healthy adult housed in the windswept barracks atop the green hillsides of the Ettersberg, where Goethe and Eckermann used to commune with nature, could have survived maybe seven months. Halbwachs was sixty-eight and sick. The talk turned to history and philosophy on Sunday afternoons when his friends were free to gather at Barracks 56, the detention area for invalids a few hundred yards from where Léon Blum was being held in isolation. Bracing him up with an arm around his emaciated shoulders, Jorges Semprun, also a political prisoner, tried to spark his old professor's attention by recalling the course on potlatch he had taught at the Sorbonne. On Sunday, March 15, 1945, his body wasted by dysentery, he died, Semprun whispering, "O mort, vieux capitaine, il est temps, levons l'ancre," verses from Baudelaire.[119]

Halbwachs, an optimistic French socialist by character and culture, whose belief in the civilizing effect of the rising standard of living had been reinforced by his study of the American experience, had no use for the grim predictions of Malthus. What the Third Reich wrought went far beyond the desolation imagined by the austere cleric: its marauding rehearsed the maddest of old-regime scenarios: that the table at nature's feast was overcrowded, and the latecomers, failing to find a place, were cannibalized by their fellow diners.

CHAPTER 3

The Chain Store

How Modern Distribution Dispossessed Commerce

A store is a machine for selling.

EDWARD A. FILENE,
American merchant, 1937

*The structure of retailing is a consequence of historical
causes; it has been retained through habit and custom and
is largely independent of purely economic considerations.*

HERMANN LEVY,
German-British economist, 1947

CONFERENCE ROOM D in the Maison de la Chimie of the Sorbonne, 28
bis rue St. Dominique, had become so stuffy by late afternoon June 26,
1935, that the dozen men seated around the table stretched uneasily to
keep from drowsing off. To absorb the facts and figures from their talk
about commercial practices while still digesting the banquet hosted by
their committee chair earlier in the day at the Hotel George V called for
energies only one among them appeared to possess. That was the diminu-
tive, bright-eyed fellow near the head of the table, the one with the lor-
gnette and bristly white mustache. At every lull in the discussion, he
perked up, a veritable geyser of detail and opinion.

His volubility was not unfamiliar to those who knew him from previous meetings of the International Chamber of Commerce (ICC). They
had all heard his impromptu remarks when their committee met the day
before. At the plenary session earlier that morning they had listened to
ten minutes of his speech, "How Can Our System of Distribution Be Improved?" They had also overheard him inveighing against the undisciplined European who, running on interminably on the topic of "Produc-

tion" in the session before his, had cut short his time. They had seen his good humor return the moment his unflappable assistant, the amiable Mlle. Schoedler, stacked a pile of mimeographed copies of his speech on the hallway table outside the meeting room. She distributed them discreetly as the delegates adjourned for lunch.[1]

Not that anybody needed the whole text. His line of thought was well known by now. The chief economic problem facing the industrial world was to distribute goods in accordance with the now patently inexhaustible capacity to produce them. Not the *overproduction* of merchandise, but its *nondistribution* was the problem to which almost all business troubles could be traced. Indeed, obstacles to finding outlets for consumer goods lay behind the whole current tragic drift toward "unsound radicalism," "general social insecurity," and war. How tedious it was to listen now to his voice syllabize the word *dis-tri-bu-tion,* with its droll Europeanized inflection, as if he were talking to neophytes. And all the more wearisome to hear his latest nostrum—that chain stores be launched everywhere, "machines for selling" that had high turnovers and low, fixed prices "to sell to the masses the things that the masses want." For the hard-nosed younger statisticians in the room such as the Englishman Colin Clark and the Italian Gugliemo Tagliacarne, there was something unseemly about his notion that more efficient commercial techniques were a cure-all for Europe's current overwhelming problems.

Even so, the man was an exciting presence. Ever dapper and communicative, it was hard to believe that he was just two months short of his seventy-fifth birthday. He was reportedly hugely wealthy, notwithstanding his unostentatious habits. He was certainly very deeply committed to the cause of international peace. He was chock full of ideas and projects. One of the most recent, a simultaneous translation system that, he boasted, by using a special translator's booth, electronic broadcasting equipment, and individual headsets solved "the problem of communication" at international conferences (while "saving a minimum of 25% in time and labor costs"), had just been installed in the Sorbonne's Great Auditorium for the opening session of the ICC convention. As the usher accompanied the little man down to the front circle to seat him in the company of President Lebrun and other high French dignitaries, he fairly levitated with self-importance. True, he talked more than he listened, and this volubility effectively concealed how much he really knew about conditions in Europe. More than most Americans, that was safe to say.

The beguiling subject of their ruminations was Edward Albert Filene.

Abroad, he liked to introduce himself as "just a plain businessman" or "a shopkeeper from Boston." This was patently false modesty. For he was one of the United States' richest merchants, a leading philanthropist, a major voice on behalf of world peace, a committed social reformer, and a very effective self-promoter. The second of five children of Clara Ballin, a Bavarian Jew, and her husband, William Filhehne, the son of a Jewish ribbon dealer from Poznan who had emigrated to the United States during the German revolutions of 1848, Edward Albert was born in Salem, Massachusetts, on September 3, 1860. When his father's health failed in 1881, Filene was brought into the family business along with his brother, A. Lincoln, who was five years his junior. Taking over from their father in 1891, by the end of the century they had turned the women's clothing and dry-goods shop, now relocated from Lynn, Massachusetts, to downtown Boston, into the largest specialty department store in the world. Expert in supplying clothing for well-to-do women accustomed to quality merchandise and personal service, the company quickly became renowned for its innovations. The most famous was Filene's Automatic Bargain Basement, established in 1909. Merchandise there had to be sold within thirty business days. The stock was discounted according to a pre-established schedule, 30 percent a week until, on the thirtieth day, the remaindered goods were turned over to local charities. The skill with which buyers selected goods for basement sale from odd lots, manufacturers' surplus, remainders from leading stores, and stocks sold for bankruptcies was such that little remained. It was the American nation's bargain hunters' Mecca.[2]

Even by then the store was earning Filene a fine fortune. A bachelor, living thriftily except on his European tours, he devoted magnanimous sums to the cause of social reform. The most quixotic and self-defeating undertaking came to a climax in 1928, when his effort to strengthen the managerial powers of the employees' cooperative in his own company was scotched by his business partners, including Lincoln, his wiser younger brother. Exasperated, they promoted him president-for-life with all the emoluments due his position. Just as decisively they ousted him from the company's day-to-day operations. Thereafter he merchandised ideas, not clothing, devoting his dextrous mind and fidgety energies to civic causes, both domestic and international. His primary vehicle was the Twentieth Century Fund, which he endowed in 1919. Dedicated "to study and advance the next step forward," it was a smaller, more agile, hands-on philanthropy than the munificently endowed Carnegie and

Rockefeller Foundations, whose patrons, true manufacturing colossi, made Filene's $10–12 million of wealth look piddling. Filene took on personally a yet wider range of projects as well, all related to his profound commitment to making the world safe for consumer democracy. So he backed the international consumer cooperative and credit union movements in the name of raising living standards. Just as ardently he backed the International Chamber of Commerce and other transnational business networks in the interest of liberalizing global trade.

Like most American "one-worlders," Filene was unabashedly Eurocentric, save for a passing curiosity about India. He made a grand tour every year from 1919 to 1937, except in 1934 and 1936, when his busy schedule at home simply didn't allow it. Assuredly, he came for the good living. Though neither an aesthete nor a true *bon vivant*, he appreciated delicious food, taking the baths at Vichy, Aix, or Karlsbad (where he never dallied long), attending a good opera production at the Salzburg Festival, mixing with the chic crowds at the Grand Prix and Longchamps, and visiting with his many expatriate and European friends. He also came to educate himself, using his self-styled "triangulation method" of learning: he canvassed the principal leaders of a country for their opinions on a given situation and then tried to reconcile the different views, going back to some for clarification, then gathering more views from retailers, also from waiters, taxi drivers, news vendors, and other people he met in passing; and after that, he repeated all the same procedures in neighboring countries.[3]

The whole process was a sensible if not exactly scientific way for an American autodidact to make sense of a world whose complexity outstretched his native categories of understanding. In turn, Europe was a good place to try out his own ideas. Not that they were necessarily his own or his homeland's. The credit union idea he had picked up in India. It had been brought in by the British, who had got it from the Germans. Never mind. In Europe, the way Filene pressed it home, it sounded like a wonderfully practical American idea.

Above all, Filene came to promote his agenda for Europe: the Old World had to be peaceful and prosperous if the New World was to have progress and security, and for that, it had to be unified and have a high standard of living. Given that the U.S. government was known after World War I for having turned over many foreign policy tasks to informal diplomats—bankers, former ambassadors, and business magnates—he found a cordial welcome for his efforts. Not that he was ever actually

on official government business. Filene was Wilsonian to the core, and by
the time the Republican administrations of the 1920s gave way to Franklin Roosevelt, whom he ardently supported, he was regarded as too old
and perhaps too undiplomatic for official missions. Nonetheless he behaved as if he were a plenipotentiary, and official Europe treated him accordingly, with red carpets unrolled and the doors through the antecham-
bers of power flung open upon his arrival. Crisscrossing the continent,
plying his schemes as if they were the latest merchandise, he acquired
scores of influential acquaintances. Some were social reformers like Albert Thomas, whom he had warmly welcomed as a guest to his Boston
home upon his first American visit in January 1923, but also business
leaders, economic experts, cabinet ministers, past and current heads of
state, and leading feminists. Through these myriad contacts, he accomplished quite remarkable feats. The European Peace Prize of 100,000
francs, which he funded in 1924, to be awarded for "practical ideas"
only, elicited 15,000 written entries and widely publicized the urgency of
settling the question of Europe's indebtedness to the United States and
other issues outstanding from World War I. The International Management Institute, which he provided with seed money, a program, and personnel in 1926, was central to promoting modern business techniques.
The notorious Ford-ILO Inquiry had been his initiative. He paid for it
and badgered the ILO to finish and publish it. Henry Ford was surely the
best-known businessman in the world; but the fussy, indefatigable Filene
was the best connected.

The irony is that Filene didn't grasp that he, the so-called Apostle of
Distribution, was nudging American capitalism a large further step forward than envisaged by his contemporary, Ford, the so-called Prome-
theus of Production. True, when Filene spoke of efficient distribution
he sounded as if he were merely dotting the *i*'s on the virtuous Fordist
script of mass production, high wages, and mass consumption. What's
more, like several tens of millions of other Americans, Filene revered
Ford, so much so that in 1928 he threw his reputation, money, and connections behind lobbying congressmen, Swedish Academicians, and assorted American media and opinionmakers to award Ford the Nobel
Peace Prize. In Filene's view, the award was perfectly appropriate because
"the principle of high wages—low prices had created a situation in which
both capital and labor were working for lasting peace through ordinary
self-interest, thus enormously increasing the possibility of attaining the
goal." He wasn't deterred in the slightest by hearing that Ford had ob-

tained this result, if at all, by an "unconscious effort," that his accomplishments were due to the selfish pursuit of profit, and that his intractable hostility toward labor unions and abhorrent lapses into anti-Semitism showed anything but a peace-loving disposition. When the Nobel Committee awarded the 1929–30 prize jointly to U.S. Secretary of State Kellogg for the Kellogg-Briand Pact to end war in Europe, and to Nathan Soderblom, archbishop of Uppsala, for convening the world's first ecumenical council of churches, Filene vowed to try again. Fortunately, Edward Bernays, his new public relations consultant, took charge, and the obdurate Filene was persuaded to drop his manifestly futile campaign.[4]

By then "the Age of Production" was sonorously being proclaimed as having given way to the "Distribution Age" or "Age of Merchandising."[5] By contrast with the *mass manufacturer,* who in the person of Ford was the voice of a sellers' market, in which demand looked infinite subject only to supply, the *mass retailer* in the figure of Filene spoke for the new buyers' market, in which distributors and consumers increasingly set the terms of acquisition. Ford believed that if the product was of good quality and priced right it would practically sell itself. Hence it required minimal marketing. By contrast, Filene grasped that consumer demand was not only about price or purchasing power, but also about the constant evolution of needs and desires. Hence mass merchandising called for constant tinkering with every element of exchange that influenced consumer choice, from product design and packaging to salesmanship. In Filene's conceit, "True mass production is not production *of* masses of goods but production *for* masses of people." Ford's major competitor, Alfred Sloan, at General Motors, fully grasped this fundamental change in market conditions created by modern merchandising techniques and more picky consumer behavior. And by committing itself to "style obsolescence" and to offering customers a car for "every purse and purpose," GM sales leaped ahead of Ford's in the early 1920s.[6] Some said that Fordism had thereby given way to Sloanism. More accurately, Fordism had made way for Fileneism, and Sloan had caught on first to the change.

Filene's purchase on the future was sharper than Ford's because he represented with respect to foreign involvements that more forward-looking and sociable element of American capitalism, based in the service, communication, and entertainment economy, which—in tandem with American manufacturing and resolutely backed by the American state—secured U.S. global hegemony down to the 1970s, and which, surpassing the latter in dynamism from the 1980s, spelled the triumph of the U.S.'

"soft" hegemony in the post-Fordist era. As early as 1930, as tariffs rose and U.S. manufacturing abroad retrenched, Ford's voice, once that of a forward-looking industry-led internationalism, was more and more that of a failed industry-led globalism. Though Ford had long endorsed free trade and criticized the United States' perennially high tariffs in the name of the company's worldwide interests, in foreign policy he was an innocent abroad, if not something worse. It was his cockamamie scheme "to get the boys home for Christmas" by sponsoring the Peace Ship to Europe in the first year of the Great War. Always an "America firster," in the 1920s he remained indifferent to the great undertakings of global governance connected to the League and the International Chamber of Commerce except as they narrowly served his company interests, and in the 1930s he went overboard mollycoddling Nazi Germany.

By contrast, Filene's internationalism partook of the salesman's enthusiasm for open markets as importer of goods, eagerness to source supplies abroad, taste for the exotic, and curiosity about other peoples or at least what other peoples had to sell. Filene's service sensibility helped him recognize not just that higher wages were the key to purchasing power, but also that, lacking strong institutional undergirding, economic exchange was vulnerable to the terrible flip-flops the world had witnessed since the disastrous German inflation of 1923. Accordingly, he was outspoken in support of using international networks to establish new rules of procedure and share technological best practice. He set himself squarely against the common opinion that America's high standard of living needed to be defended by high tariffs; U.S. manufacturers had no God-given right to hole themselves up behind protective barriers, waiting for every opportunity to dump their own goods abroad, while fending off foreign companies that wanted to lay their wares before the American public.[7]

Ford's anti-Semitism is not irrelevant here, though Filene would have liked it to be so. True, Filene was pressed to admit that Ford's "judgment and action in matters outside of his field of production" were "often ludicrous and almost always injudicious." But the facts that Ford had been "once led to participate in a lot of silly anti-Semitic propaganda" and had "been misled and hoodwinked in his warfare against the Jew" should be considered immaterial to his great accomplishments.[8] Filene was shortsightedly generous on this score. Ford's anti-Semitism was no mere fluke of his control-freak personality. Belief in the machinations of a "secret international super-capitalist government" infiltrated by Jews was con-

genial to explaining away those elements of unpredictability and complexity of a world that needed to be managed like clockwork over vast
stretches of time and space—as was demanded by the immensely long
commodity chains of global car manufacturing. Fortunately, Ford had
enough business sense when faced with libel suits and consumer boycotts
to disavow his own anti-Semitic outbursts, and the stench of recidivism
befouled his minions instead.[9] So European anti-Semites were not at all
foolish to see Ford as a friendly figure, his disavowals of amity toward
them notwithstanding. Hating Wall Street chicanery, eschewing the ploys
of advertising, he was the heroic pure manufacturer of real things, doing
battle against the speculative capitalist embodied in the financier, the
middleman, and the merchant.

Nor is Filene's Jewishness irrelevant here. Whether abroad Filene was
viewed as anything but a cosmopolitan American is hard to say. Fully assimilated, he regarded himself as an "American of Jewish ancestry" and
did not really gauge the meaning of anti-Semitism until upon his June
1933 visit to Germany he witnessed what he immediately denounced as
"crimes against humanity." However, in the transatlantic world of service capitalism in which he traveled, men of Jewish ancestry stood out as
the movers and shakers, not only because of their connections to merchandising trades—which now counted not just traditional retailing but
also marketing, cinema, and advertising—but also because so many were
immigrants with family connections across the Atlantic, and because they
were experienced in working the pluricultural milieu of their origins in
central Europe, the German-French border regions, and cross-Atlantic
migrations. Thus, Filene's connections with European colleagues were facilitated not just by shared professional interests, but by similar family
roots: like the famous Tietz brothers of Germany, Filene's father had been
born in Poznan. From the perspective of a common Western merchant
culture, these affinities helped to promote the institutionalized amiability
enhancing trust and service in the name of international capitalist exchange. These same bonds, from the point of view of anti-Semites, were
incomprehensible except as the Faustian bargain of Zionist conspirators
with American financial power, soul mates in a vast, secret, nefarious network in quest of global hegemony.

On the occasion of the eighth conference of the International Cham-
ber of Commerce, the event that brought him to Paris in June 1935,
Filene found himself once more in the company of some of his favorite
European interlocutors, two in particular: forty-seven-year-old Pierre

Laguionie, the Distribution Committee's current chair; and this suave Parisian's contemporary, the gregarious Emile Bernheim, an Alsatian-born Belgian, who, in addition to being the deputy chair, headed the International Association of Retailers, a trans-European group. Few men were more prominent in European commercial circles. Laguionie was the very smart son of the self-made Gustave, who from peasant origins had become managing director of France's grandest department store, Au Printemps, in 1905. In 1907, nineteen years old and two years out of l'Ecole de Commerce et Tissage of Lyon, he was named his father's codirector. By the 1920s Laguionie had consecrated his success as a business leader by helping found the Comité d'Action Economique et Douanière, a conservative-liberal lobby familiarly called CAED, established in 1925 in a quixotic effort to lower intra-European tariffs.[10] Bernheim, the son of Jules Bernheim, a Jewish merchant from Mulhouse who in 1897 had founded Belgian's leading department store, À l'Innovation, was the company's owner and general manager. Fluent in English as well as French, German, and Dutch, he had first become acquainted with the United States when during World War I he was sent by his government on a mission to Washington, D.C., to negotiate food shipments for his starving country. His business ambitions far outstretched Belgium's inelastic little home market. And had times been more propitious, he would have fashioned a giant holding company for chain stores covering the whole of western Europe. As it was, Priba, the chain he founded in November 1933, rapidly became Belgium's largest, and after he oversaw its merger with the French chain Prisunic-Uniprix on February 14, 1934, Bernheim sprang loose from his small-pond moorings to hobnob with the merchant magnates of all of Europe's great states.[11]

Like other leading merchants, Bernheim and Laguionie had first made Filene's acquaintance in the mid-1920s as he made a point of meeting regularly with his European colleagues. On the occasion of his European tours, he also visited Georg Wertheim, head of Germany's oldest and largest department store, located on Berlin's Leipzigerplatz; Alfred Leonhard and Gerhard Tietz, owners of the Rhineland branch of the far-flung Tietz family holdings; the ambitious young Max Heilbronn, son-in-law of the Alsatian Théophile Bader, the head of Galeries Lafayette; and Harry Gordon Selfridge, Filene's contemporary, the owner of the giant London department store of the same name. Filene had known "Mile-a-Minute Harry," a midwesterner, from the time he was using his whirlwind managing skills as second-in-command at Marshall Fields to turn the Chicago emporium into the largest department store in the world. That was in 1906, when at age fifty he decided to become his own boss and moved to England. There he would earn his own fortune by twitting "old-fashioned" British merchandising with spectacular "American" retailing techniques. The giant emporium he inaugurated in 1909 on Oxford Street in London's West End shopping district was an instant success.[12]

These men dined with Filene, sometimes at the Savoy, in Paris at the George V or the Crillon, at Berlin's Esplanade, or at other elegant hotels where he habitually resided when he was abroad. They heard out his latest projects, disregarding his boastfulness. They valued his hospitality when they or their associates visited the United States or their sons went there to study. They admired but never quite understood the fussy bachelor's relationship to his indefatigable assistant, traveling companion, and sometime chauffeur, Lillian Schoedler, a Radcliffe graduate, feminist, and Filene's self-styled "right-hand man."[13] They chuckled at his occasional gaucherie, as when he fell under the spell of the fascinating French intellectual and politician Edouard Herriot, a man twelve years Filene's junior, charming and no less susceptible to flattery. Herriot was in dudgeon at the time, as the left cartel he had formed after winning the 1924 elections against the right fell apart in April 1925. Herriot must come to the United States for a couple of years, Filene urged. His spirits would be refreshed. He'd learn English. *And* Filene would pay him $10,000 a year for occasional advice on his European projects. That offer was made to a man who was celebrated for his learned treatises on Diderot, Chateaubriand, and Madame Récamier as well as being mayor of France's second-largest city since 1905. Herriot was neither tempted nor offended. As they parted company, he playfully handed Filene his visitor's card, crossing out his current title, "Mayor of Lyon," and changing it to make it read "Herriot, head employee of Mr. Edward A. Filene."[14]

Not all his contacts regarded him as cordially. Filene's assertive, sometimes manipulative manner grated, as if he were the walking embodiment of the crassness of American society, its do-gooding tinged with self-interest, its know-it-all manner easily overpowering. At first seduced by the *frisson* of excitement engendered by his energy, monies, and networks of talented acquaintances, the objects of his patronage became exasperated by his "unalloyed vanity." By 1930 Albert Thomas, who had once shown real affection for Filene, had come to despise him for his "utterly gauche behavior" in his dealings over the Ford-ILO Inquiry. They broke off relations in 1931 after Filene started to hedge on his financial support for the International Management Institute; the cutoff of that support in 1934 closed the agency down.[15]

The Distribution Revolution

Filene's virtues and flaws, his eagerness and arrogance, the respect shown to him as well as the diffidence were all of a piece with his main commitment in later life, which was to spread the gospel of modern distribution. This term had popped into currency in American English during the 1920s. And its usage became officially sanctioned in 1925 on the occasion of the inaugural National Distribution Conference, convened in Washington, D.C., on January 14–15 at the behest of Secretary of Commerce Herbert Hoover and organized by the U.S. Chamber of Commerce. Distribution was a real "problem," Hoover made clear in his keynote. He and his audience of 250 or so businessmen were not gathered there to "worry on behalf of the lady who wishes to order a cake of yeast by telephone to be delivered by a gold colored automobile."[16] Even so, opinion was divided about what exactly the term signified except for the handling of merchandise after it became a finished commodity. The one certainty was that the venerable word *commerce* no longer described the myriad activities that occurred between the production of goods for final use and their delivery and acceptance by the consumer.

As early as the 1770s, Adam Smith had emphasized that commerce over wide markets was indispensable to the economies of specialized production. But when he wrote that the nailmaker in the Scottish Highlands could turn out "three hundred thousand nails in a year" provided only that he could dispose of them, he could not have known what the terms "division of labor" and "extent of market" implied for mass-consumer-oriented manufacture.[17] According to the traditional view, under the division of labor the manufacturer produced the commodities, the wholesaler, jobber, or middleman carried the stocks, and the retailer sold the packaged goods to the public. However, these distinctions lost their meaning as manufacturers pushed forward to eliminate the middlemen, the retailers pushed backward to source their own supplies, and socialist cooperativists had consumers both buying and selling.

If we consider the "coffin nail," or cigarette, a typical new mass consumer product of the 1920s, the implications are clearer. Distribution started with an effort by upward of thirty-four cigarette manufacturing establishments to gather tobacco from thousands of farms in the United States and abroad by rail and water transport, using the postal services but also the telephone and telegraph. Distribution designated the facilities for shipment and storage as well as the merchandising techniques by which billions of ready-rolled cigarettes were supplied to a million domestic and foreign retail outlets, to be sold to millions of consumers. Distribution also referred to the investment required to create brand recognition as well as the advertising budget dedicated to making the different brands known to the public, the design of the packaging to keep the cigarettes fresh, and the competition among vendors to sell cartons, packets, or single cigarettes. All these steps brought investments in the various new trades that fell under the rubric of distribution, from transport and storage to retail outlets: in 1870 these services had employed 14 percent of the labor force; by 1930 they employed 35 percent. That year, one-fourth of each consumer dollar was calculated as being spent on distribution.[18]

The "problem" of distribution was first identified as a general concern of modern capitalism when in the wake of World War I the prolonged sellers' markets of the late nineteenth-century industrial boom turned into a buyers' market. Organized as big trusts in a protected market, the largest manufacturers seized advantage from the simultaneous growth of transcontinental railroads, large-scale retailing outlets, and national advertising to shorten the lines of communication to consumers. Pushing aside wholesalers, they were pretty much able to set prices as they established their monopoly on new brand-named goods by appealing directly to the consumer over the heads of local retailers. The only way for retailers to resist was to group together to establish new buying organizations or to buy in bulk to sell through mail-order firms or low-overhead five-and-dime variety stores.[19] As manufacturing capacity outstripped demand, it was the retailers' turn to exploit industrial competition and employ their own expertise in merchandising to cater to their customers' desires for variety as well as quantity, low prices, and service.

This new situation created a quandary for retailers. As the businesses closest to the consumer, they could claim to be persuading manufacturers to pay attention to the buyers' priorities rather than simply pressing on the market whatever product suited their plants' capacity. But they could also be blamed for causing the waste, inefficiency, and profiteering that were alleged to push up prices. Even if they weren't responsible, it was left to them to explain why spectacular gains in industrial productivity had no counterpart in distribution.[20] And it was not a simple task to account for why, say, 14 percent was added to the price of sugar between manufacture and sale, 32–35 percent to food and drink, 42–45 percent to clothing, and 76 percent to rubber condoms.[21]

In sum, having won the "competitive struggle for market" with manufacturers, retailers now faced the problem of establishing their legitimacy in the eyes of the consumer, the service sector as a whole, and society more generally. As "purchasing agents of consumers" they had "to discover what customers want, rather than pushing into their hands whatever [they] may happen to have," "wisely place orders to reduce manufacturing fluctuations and factory unemployment," and "eliminate functions which did not add to the intrinsic or intangible value of products in the consumers' view"—and all this while eliminating "waste" "without upsetting the social and political balance" and operating with a heightened "awareness of the interests of the Nation."[22]

In *Next Steps Forward in Retailing* (1937), the *summum* of his thoughts on the matter, Filene recommended three innovations to shoulder that responsibility. The first was to use capital more efficiently by achieving economies of scale in selling, purchasing giant blocks of supplies, and perfecting the handling of inventory. The goal was, simply, "small profits, quick returns." The second was to improve the training, equipment, and organization of the salesforce. Filene, a department-store owner, had in mind the people on store payrolls. But small shopkeepers too could benefit from improved knowledge and networking. The third step was to think about business practice in a new way. Forget "immediate experience as if it were unlimited and therefore important," Filene recommended. "Thinking based on fact finding is more important than tradition and experience."[23] Experience had to be organized by the systematic exchange of information, with each commercial culture challenging the other with its "best practice."

The chain store was the social invention that perfectly embodied these innovations. By concentrating managerial expertise, capital, and decisionmaking capacities in one headquarters, it performed as a "machine for selling." Coordinating information and supplies among tens, but potentially even hundreds or thousands, of widely scattered outlets, it could obtain huge economies by purchasing supplies in bulk from manufacturers, standardizing store layouts, specializing inventory in a relatively small number of items, and simplifying pricing. In turn, it passed the savings along to consumers.

Filene's premise, that merchandising could be organized as rationally and efficiently as manufacturing, was a striking innovation in a world that still idolized the engineer and regarded the industrial entrepreneur as the darling of Western industrial progress. Indeed, over the nineteenth century, as regard for manufacturing had risen, respect for services had been debased. The common view was that the distributive trades, wholesaling in particular, were parasitical excrescences on productive enterprises, beset by monopolies and privileges, tainted by carnival humbug, the chicanery of peddlers, hucksters, speculators, and the other unsavory denizens of "Jewish" capitalism. That in U.S. business culture the merchant should have come to be presented, as Filene did, as a paragon of productive efficiency, much less as at the pinnacle of socially responsible capitalism—to the point of looking out for the well-being of the national economy and caring about the fate of its erstwhile competitors in small business—was a remarkable development.[24]

Modern American retailing was able to advance this notion, and thus establish its hegemony as a model for European practice, for a number of reasons, the first being its hardy economic situation. By being able to draw on a practically inexhaustible pool of urban shoppers, when the department stores faced competition on price from chain stores, mail order, and eventually the supermarket, they could move upscale, using their power to source supplies and their large volume of business to obtain the variety and quality that customers wanted. By offering service and style, as well as assortment, they were able to compete with the specialty stores. They could also expect to find a buying public by moving downscale if necessary. The middle classes in outlying neighborhoods, suburbs, cities, and small towns were so numerous that the pace of store openings across the land surpassed anything comparable in Europe.[25]

Large retailers were also uniquely well placed to dampen the antagonism between big and little, which in Europe was abiding, deep, and recurrently ferocious. In a vast growing urban market, department stores were built and flourished alongside the small dry-goods store, shoe shop, and drugstore instead of displacing them. Aiming at a broad middle class, they competed with each other rather than with the small retailers. Accordingly, the management of Lord & Taylor was not out first and foremost to steamroller the street-level shops, but rather to stiff-arm its counterparts at Altman's, a few blocks down Fifth Avenue. Early twentieth-century American cities were famous for their killer "department store wars." And though American small shopkeepers were at least as vulnerable to economic ups and downs as elsewhere, they had more opportunities to move into other sectors than did their European counterparts. Immigrants in successive waves replenished these entry-level positions before moving on to more lucrative or socially esteemed work, and both they and their children had easier access to salaried employment and wage labor. For that reason, among others, until the Depression the United States was unable to sustain any unified small shopkeepers' movement or any really effective national lobby on their behalf.

Finally, merchants had acquired respect if not honor in the absence of a true aristocratic culture or a bourgeois one that aped its mores. American republican ideology regarded tradesmen less disdainfully than elsewhere, treating them as useful and respected citizens. In the nineteenth century, a lawyer or retired army officer might establish a general store without serious loss of dignity, whereas in Europe the landholding gentry looked down upon wealth accrued in commerce. When occasions for profit arose, American merchants faced fewer hindrances than in continental Europe. American towns having never been the legally privileged sites of commerce, were exempt from the legacy of old regime craft monopolies on the production and sale of certain goods, luxury taxes, and excise stamps on wall posters, newspapers, and other publicity that were the bane of merchandisers on the other side of the Atlantic. Moreover, the anti-Semitism that was still attached to commercial dealings waned as merchandising activities diversified into marketing, advertising, and other new specializations, callings that were just as likely to recruit Protestant ministers' sons with a flair for preaching as the offspring of immigrant Jewish merchandisers with a flair for haggling.

What's more, by the first decade of the century great merchants acquired a strong political voice. Operating in a business culture that rewarded the risktaker—and blew aside the traditionalist—merchant elites early acquired the self-confidence, power, and wealth to attach themselves to Progressive coalitions in alliance with feminist groups, consumer movements, labor organizations, and government that spoke in the name of the customers' interests. As early as 1912 the merchant class showed its political clout nationally by founding the National Retail Dry Goods Association and the U.S. Chamber of Commerce to lobby for their clients' interests in Washington, D.C. In 1917, largely at the Filene brothers' initiative, the Retail Research Association began to pool domestic and foreign merchandising data on behalf of twenty participating stores. Over the next decade the federal government worked marvels from the point of view of fact-finding. The Census on Distribution, authorized by Congress in 1928 to be carried out along with the national population census in 1930, was the first of its kind in the world.

Though the United States was the homeland of big retailing units, it was also rife with efforts first at the state, then at the federal level to regulate in favor of small units by passing chain-store taxes, anti-price-discrimination laws, and anti-loss-leader legislation. Indeed, the Robinson-Patman Act, passed in 1936, looked like a victory for small business in that it barred suppliers operating across state lines from discounting bulk orders with the intent of discriminating against small tradesmen. Its real importance was rather to allow the little guys legal recourse to determine whether it was the economic efficiency of the big unit, or purely its economic muscle, that determined the discount. The greatest good had been established as the consumers' demand for low-priced and varied commodities. The small shop would never be sanctified as it was in contemporary Europe as a social institution valuable in itself, much less invaluable to the American way of life.[26] Far from obstructing the pace of growth of large-scale modern retailing, the American regulations acted like modern forest husbandry, furrowing the wilds of retailing with fire corridors, culling old wood to prevent sparks from lighting on the flammable underbrush that might ignite social conflagrations, and seeding the burnt-over terrain with fast-growing new varietals. The net effect was to accustom business, state policy, and the public to never-ending, head-spinning newness in the retail trades.

The novelty unceasingly pushed by a retail-guided system of distribution thus reinforced that "middleness" that was so distinctive a feature of American consumer culture. Modern retailing spoke with a view to swings in purchasing power, volatility of taste, and physical mobility of that three-fifths of the population that had the income to spend not just on necessaries, but also on extras, occasionally even on luxuries. Middle as in the "middle millions" was also the social self-definition of the growing number of people occupied as employees, managers, and experts in all sorts of merchandising-related services. Middle was the new territorial space occupied by department stores as they spread from the leading East Coast cities and booming Chicago, St. Louis, and Detroit to the Middletowns of the center and West and from the city centers to the fast-growing suburbs. Middle was the business position occupied by the chain store, convenient enough in terms of both price and location to draw the customer away from the upscale department store and from the specialized local dry-goods emporium as well as from miscellaneous small shops. Middle classified the women of diverse social backgrounds who passed through the portals of the same retail outlet to purchase similar goods, thereby reinforcing the sense of social worth of the poorer without impugning the social status of the superior. Middle was the fluctuating halfway point in inventory sales charts according to Filene's "model stock plan." That was the point, as he explained it to European colleagues, at which a good should be introduced, priced, and advertised to maximize the custom of rich and poor, each, it was understood, intending it for a different use. It was the point, to be more precise, "at which women of means will buy a thing for ordinary use, and a woman of little means for best."[27]

Merchant Internationalism in Star-Crossed Times

Could a retail-guided distribution system work in Europe? Filene had no doubts that it would, provided that European merchants banded together. There was no intrinsic reason for them not to, for "there is very little in a department store which is patentable," as the oft-quoted Gordon Selfridge pointed out: "Department store activities take place in the limelight, unlike other kinds of enterprise, where there is secrecy."[28] Therefore it paid for onetime enemies to become best friends. So after the Belgian government sequestered the Leonhard Tietz Company as enemy property during World War I, Bernheim, whose downtown Brussels flagship À l'Innovation was right next door, purchased it at a bargain basement price, then physically incorporated its premises into the art nouveau building that Victor Horta had designed for the firm in 1904. When postwar business resumed across the Rhine River, the two merchants found new grounds for cooperation: Bernheim saw in Tietz the well-capitalized partner to break out of Belgium across the Rhine, and Tietz in Bernheim the well-positioned partner to bring him into lucrative markets westward.

The impulse to band together was also encouraged by the shaky state of European commerce in the wake of the war. The actual destruction of capital was not as lastingly debilitating to trade as the disruption caused by the breakdown of connections, credit, and confidence as monetary fluctuations continued to unsettle commercial transactions, altering the terms of contracts and upsetting predictions about consumer behavior. Moreover, the sellers' market reinforced by war-oriented manufacture lingered on, putting retailers at a disadvantage in a market still divided by cartels, trusts, and special relationships to governments that, to pay off war debts, balance budgets, and cut inflation, admonished their citizens to "produce more, consume less," an injunction that was anathema to retailers. As in the United States, as postwar consumers protested high prices, experts sympathetic to their plight documented the rising costs of distribution as a percentage of the total cost of goods. And similarly, the blame was laid on the most visible elements, namely large retailers or the machinations of the always-suspect if invisible wholesaler, rather than on difficult-to-grasp economic processes.[29]

The bigger countries already had the rudiments of large-scale retail associations, if not something more. At least one was strong and compact, namely the British Retail Distributors' Association, founded in 1920 to represent the interests of the leading West End entrepreneurs. The Germans also had a proven group, the German Department Store Owners' Association. Headed by Oscar Tietz of the Berlin-based chain, it had been founded in 1901 to defend them, in vain, against high tax levies, as well as to assert their voice in a business culture in which every other special interest was organized and vociferous, and at least one, the small retailers' movement, zealously played the anti-Jewish card. By contrast, the great Parisian department stores behaved as powers each unto themselves, at least until 1918, when they were forced to rally together to confront their nemesis, organized labor, who outrageously demanded to unionize, work an eight-hour day, and obtain higher salaries in a show of utter ingratitude for their employers' famously generous company paternalism. Steeled by an "attitude of resistance," the eight largest Parisian employers, Laguionie in the lead, first linked forces to meet as a conference group in 1919.[30]

That the leading European merchants were ripe to go a step further to establish some sort of transnational exchange was evidenced in late June 1926, when Harrods' management invited Filene to be its guest of honor at a London luncheon as he headed back to the United States via Southampton. Harrods was already the only European member of the U.S.-based Retail Research Association, and perhaps at Filene's behest, the firm's directors, the Burbidges, used the occasion to gather nineteen of the North Atlantic's most influential merchants: after touring London's leading department stores, "two billion dollars worth of men," to quote the sensationalist press, were chauffeured to the Savoy Hotel where they dined in its newly renovated banquet room.[31] Over gelatinous hors d'oeuvres they applauded Filene's brief welcoming speech, the gist of which was an insider's tip about how to boost sagging spring sales. This would have had storekeepers recognize that Easter marked the change of seasons when people began to renew their wardrobes and that they must plan ahead for that by fixing their own Easter holiday, say, the second Sunday in April. Now, it is hard to imagine that seasoned West End merchants lacked the knowledge to time special sales. Rather than being dismissed as the ranting of an arrogant fool, Filene's advice has to be interpreted as scoring another point, namely that sound business called for imitating "best practice," and "best practice" called for banding together and sharing stocks of information.

That was the point of Filene's one-on-one meeting with Emile Bernheim, who had just returned from the United States, where he had studied close up how the Retail Research Association operated in order to set up a similar network among European merchants. Filene broached a plan that would give Bernheim a helping hand. His foundation, The Twentieth Century Fund, had been looking for ways to strengthen trans-Atlantic relations by an "exchange of practical services," and this prospect had led Filene in talks begun in late September 1925 with Albert Thomas, Paul Devinat, the ILO's associate director, and a fellow philanthropist, the onetime carton manufacturer Henry Dennison, to establish a European counterpart to the U.S.'s "industrial efficiency bureau."[32] In 1926 Thomas and Filene met once more in the sitting room of the Hotel de Russie in Geneva, this time with Lyndall Urwick, to sign the agreement establishing the International Management Institute. The Twentieth Century Fund, along with the Rockefeller Foundation, would bear the major operating expenses, and the ILO would lend some of the personnel, although it would not have any say in its affairs lest it scare off business cooperation. Reaping credit for the initiative, Filene announced the IMI's debut at the Parisian soirée held in his honor by Mme. Schreiber, daughter of Senator Cremieux and wife of Robert, the founder with his brother, Emile, of *Les Echos,* the first French newspaper wholly dedicated to commercial questions. Emile, by the way, was a dedicated student of American manufacturing technology. This interest evolved into a family vocation. In 1967 his son, Jean-Jacques Servan-Schreiber, would publish *The American Challenge,* the bestselling call to arms to the European Community to defend itself from U.S. domination by emulating its multinational corporations' scale, scope, and investment in research and design.[33]

Though intended to work first with national committees of industrialists to promote scientific management, the IMI found its earliest support
not among nationally rivalrous manufacturers, but among Europe's department-store chiefs. Bernheim and Laguionie recruited P. A. Best, the
head of Schoolbred's of London, and Bernheim's colleague and friend
Ragnar Sachs, of Nordiska Komaniet of Stockholm, and in 1928, with
IMI logistical support, they established the Management Research Group
of Department Stores. In 1931 the group ambitiously enlarged its scope,
renaming itself the International Association of Department Stores and
adding six more members: the western German Leonhard Tietz chain, the
Dutch De Bijenkorf of Amsterdam, the Northern Department Store of
Copenhagen, Italy's La Rinascente, El Siglo of Barcelona, and Harrods of
London. Laguionie was co-opted as the first president. In the face of Europe's growing tribulations, the goals of the organization proved at once
loftier and more elemental than those of its progenitor, the Retail Research Association. Reviewing its meager accomplishments, its mentor,
the American H. S. Persons, the founder of the Taylor Society, spoke of it
kindly as developing "a cluster of principles, rather than a bundle of techniques" and as having shown "wisdom, patience, and grim determination" in sustaining its little network.[34]

Self-organization, assisted by American retailing interests and international agencies inspired by U.S. managerial methods, could not help but
clarify to worried European merchant capitalists the nature of the dilemmas that confronted them. At the same time it immersed them in ways of
thinking about these dilemmas that emphasized modernizing business
practices to the neglect of progressive political alliances; it enabled them
to establish a highly visible position for their enterprises, sustained by in-
fusions of foreign capital and innovation. But it didn't instruct them that
their advanced positions left them more and more exposed to reactionary
forces arising from the old regime of consumption.

The first and most important confrontation of the two retailing cultures, all to the advantage of the American way of thinking about commerce, occurred in June 1931 in Washington, D.C., during the fifth postwar conference of the International Chamber of Commerce. A legacy of
the nineteenth-century Pax Britannica, founded by the great cotton masters of Manchester, the ICC had been refounded in 1920 largely at the
initiative of American businessmen as a harbinger of the twentieth-century Pax Americana.[35] To honor the first decade of this "Businessman's
International" with a display of its refined "diplomacy of technics," the

ICC presented the magnificent seven-volume study it had commissioned on postwar economic trends.[36] The fifth volume, called *Europe–United States of America: Trends in the Organization and Methods of Distribution in the Two Areas,* was a real eye-opener for the Europeans at the conference. Jules Menken, head of the Department of Business Administration of the London School of Economics, spoke for his compatriots when he remembered the report as marking his "first awareness of the signal role of distribution in economic life and social welfare."[37]

That he underscored the word "distribution" is significant, for one effect of the Washington conference was that this neologism, barely five years old in American English, began to circulate in European tongues.[38] And as in the United States, it displaced the word "commerce." However, the New World had no inhibitions about coining new words for new trends or procedures, whereas for the Old World, semantic invention could be wrenching. All the more so since the novel term was intended to expurgate the confusions and paradoxes of meaning the old term had long engendered.

Com mercium! "Together" and "merchandise." Commerce incorporated all the complexity of what men did when "buying and selling together." It reflected the thin line between more or less equal trade and plain piracy that around the ancient Mediterranean had Hermes/Mercury, the god of commerce, figure also as the god of theft. Commerce could denote exchange among men of the various products of nature or industry, as the magisterial *Dictionnaire de la langue française* spelled out, but also the act of purchasing merchandise to resell at a profit, the legal status of those operating that profession, and the name of the profession itself.[39] Unlike distribution, which presented itself as a neutral term, a cluster of techniques, a channel or corridor, indifferent to worries over who gets what, where, and how, commerce conjured up a way of life, one that was clearly based on asymmetries of power but also on the solidarity and trust that induced Adam Smith, like many others, to confide in the civilizing effects of "treaty, barter, and truck."[40]

Yet "distribution" was displacing "commerce" in Europe, much as it had in the United States, and as a result of a similar "economic evolution," one that saw manufacturers shunt aside middlemen "to circulate their production more easily," and cooperatives turn customers into buyers as well as sellers.[41] Since the term sounded French and the modern elements of Francophone merchant culture were in search of a scientific-sounding term in their struggle with the retrograde small "commerçant," it was quickly assimilated in France. In Britain too the new terminology took, at least up to a point: when the Committee on Definitions of the American Marketing Association went a step further in 1940, recommending that "distribution" be discontinued in favor of "marketing," local experts dug in their heels. The problem was the neologism's gender. In British English, "marketing" was what the women did, blowsy in their scarves and aprons, browsing through shops, engaging in old-girl gossip, loading up their bags with provisions—not what men in respected occupations attended to, outfitted in suits with bowler hats, umbrellas, and attaché cases. If a new term was needed, use the venerable word "merchandising."[42] In Germany, by contrast, the Latin-rooted term proved too foreign at a moment when linguistic nationalism was rampant. Anyway, the German language already distinguished between *Handel* (commerce) and *Vertreib* (distribution), and the latter could do perfectly well.[43] But "marketing" was plausibly euphonic, and once the Third Reich had been overthrown and the Federal Republic of Germany became a sponge for Americanisms, it became common coin. The Italians clung to *commercio* down to the 1960s with the specious philological argument that the root words, *commutatio mercium,* were ample enough to embrace "the complex of all such acts of interaction between producers and consumers directed toward effectuating or facilitating the circulation of wealth." Only when professional retailers and marketing specialists displaced humanistically educated professors of statistics as spokesmen for the new field did Italians also start to use the new vocabulary.[44]

"Distribution" was only one semantic blast from this new volcano of volubility. To facilitate communicating the meaning of fearsome new concepts such as "price gouging" and "price crushing," new policies like "resale price maintenance," "deep discount," and "self-service," and new institutions such as the "supermarket," the ICC busily employed multilingual Swiss talent to turn out business dictionaries. With a handful of exceptions, like the 1963 French neologism *hypermarché* to designate an American-size supermarket, the shared words of the new language of merchandising drew on American English.

The 1931 Washington meetings also left an indelible institutional legacy by calling for the establishment of the International Distribution Committee, whose first meeting took place on May 25, 1932. BIPED (Bureau International pour l'Etude de la Distribution), as it was fondly rendered in Francophone culture, like other ICC committees drew on national groups, the first of which, with the French taking the lead, was formed in December 1932 and presided over by Laguionie. With staff and interests overlapping with the International Association of Department Stores, its meetings would be occasions for Filene as well as other Americans to mix with European colleagues in the next several years.

The ICC's volume 5 also made American retailing the measure for judging Europe's progress. Impeccably researched, succinctly written, carefully laid out, it evidenced the redoubtable efforts of its two rapporteurs, one the stalwart British functionary Lyndall Urwick, the other F. P. Valentine, vice-president of the American Telephone and Telegraph Company, a Type-A personality who, before going to Geneva with his results, not only scoured the eastern seaboard for expert advice but organized and published it in all of its plethoric freshness so that it would be available immediately to the American business community.[45] This was not the Ford-ILO Inquiry; nobody explicitly intended for the United States to impose its vision of "the politics of big numbers." Nonetheless, Valentine's earlier published report established the criteria for comparison, its copious data shaped the charts into whose columns the deficient European statistics were slotted, and its optimistic introduction about progress in distribution—moving inexorably from the traditional small to large modern units—was reproduced practically word for word to introduce the volume.[46]

The distribution monster feeds off the fodder of crunched numbers; and no country, not even all the countries of the world put together, had troughs of figures as deep as the Americans'. And that was before the results of the world's first Census on Distribution had become available in 1930; "the fullest, most authoritative piece of market research yet undertaken by a country or an institution," it showed at every stage of the passage of goods from manufacturer to consumer as precisely as possible not only the amounts and kinds of goods that were being handled by every sort of business from mail-order houses to mom-and-pop shops, but also "where the consumers are" and "what quantity of goods they would consume."[47]

By contrast, true to mercantilist traditions that emphasized the value of foreign trade and skimped on domestic consumer markets except as shortages produced riots and rebellions, the figures eked out for Europe were even more catch-as-catch-can than the figures available to study living standards. Before Great Britain, the "nation of shopkeepers," conducted its first general survey of the distributive trades in 1951, it had never bothered to track their vicissitudes. When the Incorporated Association of Retail Distributors undertook its first survey of department-store expenses in 1931 with help from the Bank of England, it did so strictly for the confidential use of its members. France, though armed with excellent statistics on foreign trade, showed a "flagrant insufficiency of statistical data" on domestic commerce in the late 1930s. Figures were still "practically nil" in the 1950s.[48] Not until 1966 did the government undertake the first full-scale "Récensement de la Distribution," whose results were published in 1967. And Italy remained a statistical farrago; its new Central Statistical Office's main obsession was documenting falling birthrates.

Germany alone stood out for its numeracy, as the fetish for numbers of the omnipotent Prussian state, its apparatus of surveillance swinging from military to civilian use, was joined with worry over the parlous condition of small business. Practically single-handedly, Dr. Julius Hirsch, the former state secretary for economics under Walter Rathenau's Ministry of Reconstruction, had used his later lesser position as head of the Research Department on Trade to undertake the Commerce Inquiry of 1926–27. By gathering information from small businesses, especially retailers, Hirsch sought to calculate the costs that distribution added to business in the effort to revive Germany's flagging export economy. Praised by Filene for the thirty-one volumes that resulted, the self-deprecating Berliner cautioned him against being unduly optimistic about retail reform. A Social Democrat, he was a lonely figure in Weimar's archconservative bureaucracy; under Nazi rule, he became an outcast. Fleeing to Denmark in 1937, then finding asylum in the United States, Hirsch took up residence in Cambridge, Massachusetts, where his experience was incorporated into the best practice that had already conferred such significant advantages on U.S. retailing. It was Hirsch who in 1941, working under the auspices of the Boston Conference on Distribution, sponsored by the Harvard Business School, steered to conclusion the world's first study on comparative retailing costs.[49]

The final effect of the ICC's *Trends in Distribution* was to crunch up and flatten out large lumps of data until two large, roughly comparable surfaces took shape, one called America, the other Europe. True, the numbers revealed some inescapably significant discrepancies. For example, in the United States department stores existed wherever the population of a town was large enough to justify it, whereas in Europe, though they were as grand as any in London, Paris, and Berlin, they were virtually absent in sizable centers of central and eastern Europe. Mail order, which was big business in the United States, with its prosperous farm families and well-connected rural postal routes, was in short supply in Europe, where peasant communities, often pauperized and illiterate, remained isolated from the major capitals of consumption by customs barriers, the hazards of rural postal-delivery systems, and the distance between urban and rural ways of living. What most struck the eye was the preponderance of small independent stores, hovering around 97 percent of the total firms in Belgium, Italy, and France, compared to around 80 percent in the United States.

But the thrust of the ICC undertaking was to underscore differing paces of convergence around a common model rather than diverging trajectories. European distribution too, in its effort to satisfy consumer wants by the most direct routes and at lowest costs, was said to be heading inexorably toward large, modern, capitalistically managed, bureaucratic units. That this progress was occurring more slowly than in the United States, and that small firms continued to proliferate, were faults to be blamed on the disruptions of war, the persistence of the sellers' market resulting from heavy military expenditure, and the currently lower per capita income of the European population.

"The ancient European forest, clogged with vines, parasites, and fallen trees, can't be treated like a tidily geometric California field."[50] In these words the ever-quotable cultural conservative André Siegfried advised caution. Later it would seem obvious that unlike in the United States, where retailing grew as frenziedly as manufacturing, in Europe "industry evolves by seismic leaps whereas commerce evolves by sedimentation."[51] Class behaviors, which weighed so heavily on consumers' standards of living, similarly shaped where and how consumers shopped. The plethora of people involved in small commerce regarded themselves not merely as economic units, but as the very pillars of a social order doomed to death if they failed to survive. The price of a good was only one means that customers used to estimate the worth of commodities. Consequently, to "cut" or "crush" prices threatened values. In sum, American "best practice" proved a poor compass for maneuvering amid the tangles and quagmires of the "ancient European forest."

The Double Face of European Retailing

If European commerce was to move to a retail-led system in the American style, it needed more than just intelligent and enterprising leadership; it needed a social revolution in retailing. Instead it witnessed a massive social reaction to any change in the regime of consumption, whose flash-point was the chain store, the very invention that was intended to revolutionize mass retailing.

The fact is that the broad contours of European retailing conformed to the sharp stratifications of bourgeois society generally; its typical institutions—the great department store and the corner shop—were sharply segregated according to the status, wealth, power, and lifestyles of their rich and poor customers. The department store stood at the very pinnacle of the pyramid of commerce. Anchor of the downtown area, provisioner of luxuries and decencies, it epitomized capitalist profit-taking in commerce as it catered to the desire for the novel and appropriate deemed indispensable to keeping up the bourgeois lifestyle. The small shopkeepers formed its wide base. The anchors of sociability of far-flung neighborhoods, drawing their clientele from the poor and the middling classes, these myriad, mostly drab outlets were where the overwhelming majority of European people spent their scant income on food, fuel, and the other basic provisions of life.

True, since the rise of capitalism, commerce had always figured with this double face. No undertaking was more global than merchant capitalism, none more parochial than the face-to-face exchange of small traders. The great capitalist wheels and deals in the world. He makes his fortune betting on the exotic, playing on his access to capital, his command over speed, his access to power, and his capacity to muster force. Often the little storekeeper is hardly capitalist at all, the line between enterprise and household being ill defined. His calculations about costs and income expect no surprises; his position on the market is secured by minimonopolies over local customers who are loyal also because they are immobile. Because he expects exchanges to be more or less predictable, he experiences the vicissitudes of the business cycle viscerally. Of the wider causes of shortages of supplies, fluctuations in prices, or dropoffs in sales, he has no direct knowledge. As if knocking into obstacles in the dark, he dimly perceives whether the origins of his troubles are foreign or native, general to the whole economy or particular to his locality, the result of his own shortsightedness or a downward turn of the wheel of fortune.[52]

The apogee of the department store in Europe coincided with the apogee of bourgeois fortunes at the turn of the century just as twenty years later its crisis stood as the gloomy indicator of their decline. As in the United States, the spread of department stores was bound up not just with sheer urban growth, investment in rapid transport lines, the diffusion of advertising, and more effective sourcing of craft as well as factory-produced goods, but above all with the concentration of prosperous upper classes in the major cities. Around 1930, sales volume overall was less than in the United States: the percentage for department stores of the total retail trade turnover in France was 5 percent; in Germany, 4–5 percent; in Great Britain, 7.5 percent, compared with 10 percent across the Atlantic.[53] But turnover alone was only one measure of commercial capitalism's capacity to innovate. More than simply arising with the bourgeoisie, the department store gave shape and definition to the very notion of a bourgeois way of life.

Accordingly, the location, wealth, and power of the bourgeoisie should be gauged from a map of the stores' spread. Most numerous in northwestern Europe, they dwindled in number and faltered in their fortunes in the center and southern areas.[54] Showing off the physical dominance of the bourgeois classes over old-regime town centers, the new buildings rerouted traffic and displaced myriad small shops, imparting a new profile to the late nineteenth-century cityscape. Alongside the other temples of bourgeois culture, the stock market, the great libraries, the town halls, and the giant train terminals, the "cathedrals of commerce" signaled the segregation of spectacular city centers from the ever more distant, dingy neighborhoods of the working classes.[55]

What's more, by establishing a new mode of selling, the department stores embarked people on a new relationship with the purchase of goods that continues to be revolutionized down to the present. The goods were laid out in tens of departments, each specializing in a range of goods, the most numerous devoted to clothing and dry goods, perfumery, household articles, crafted durables such as carriages—as well as the equipment for the coachman and horses—and eventually fine food products too. The sheer volume of items presented in sumptuous display, each article tagged with a fixed price, emphasized not only immense plenitude but also the uniqueness of single objects. The pricing system had a double virtue for customers: by fixing the article's monetary worth it eliminated the haggling associated with the bazaar or the small store; and by fixing its intrinsic value it evidenced confidence that the store presented only goods that were appropriate to the bourgeois way of life. This image was highly magnified in the full-page ads in the local press.

The department store also reinforced the special place women occupied in the bourgeois regime of consumption. This was the "ladies' paradise," to recall the English-language title of Emile Zola's 1882 bestselling novel *Au bonheur des dames,* conceived both to promote and to protect the circulation of bourgeois women in the quasi-public spaces formed by modern commerce. Thereby it supported a form of emancipation, one that was fully congruous with the subaltern position of women, most of whom had no earning power, no control over their family fortunes, and no real purchasing power of their own. At the same time, by fostering individuality in a context of constraint, it encouraged the peccadilloes of thwarted desire—shoplifting, unauthorized splurges on the husband's credit line, and conspicuous idleness. So long as the elite alone indulged in these pastimes, the problem was simply one of managing the "luxury female."[56]

Finally, the department store expressed Europe's centrality as the crossroads of Western imperial consumption. Department-store buyers were as intrepid as the world was wide. In their search to source goods, they took advantage of the fact that global trade was more and more liberalized, the great powers' colonies more and more secure for prospecting, and the European supply of craft more and more ingenious. Local craft and global exotica thereby mixed to shape what Edmond de Goncourt, himself a prodigious collector of bibelots, called "bric-a-bracomania."[57] The result was that in taste and style, the Belle Epoque bourgeoisie was distinctly orientalist in its obliviousness to the imperial provenance of its goods, but also blessedly indifferent to their national origins, except as they added to their own charm and worth and the sense of Western culture's omnipotence.[58]

It's no surprise, then, that American buyers, who, after circling the European outback to source textiles, carpets, toys, and porcelain wares, upon returning through Europe's capital cities copiously documented the stores' fantastic displays for use back home. Nothing was lost by admitting, as Selfridge did, that behind Marshall Fields there were the spectacular floor layouts of Au Printemps and Bon Marché or that John Wanamaker of Philadelphia found the delectables of the French elite inexhaustibly fruitful status items for Philadelphia's best-heeled citizens to deploy in their contests of pecuniary emulation. At the turn of the century, *vente de blanc* sounded smarter than "white sale," *en vente ici* an improvement over "on sale here," and *choisissez* a refinement on "buy it now."[59] Europe, which is to say Paris, with a doff of the hat to London haberdashery and overstuffed Victorian rooms, lingered on as a taste-setter even when the tide had changed, and in the meantime Europeans were sailing westward to be oriented about the techniques of mass distribution.

Yet the department store, even as it contributed to establishing the bourgeois mode of consumption, inevitably displayed its contradictions, and in the interwar period more and more decisively contributed to its erosion.

First of all, it reinforced status divisions within the bourgeoisie itself. Acquiring vast wealth and power, the great department-store chiefs soared in social rank, no matter how humble their family origins or modest their education. By contrast, shopkeepers, so long as they handled the merchandise themselves, even if their enterprises were purveyors of boots, liquors, or gewgaws to royalty, stayed irrevocably petit bourgeois.[60] Likewise, though the space of the department store was open to all, social distinctions were omnipervasive, and the service relationship reeked of the bonds of servant to master. The floor man was a valet, the shopgirl a lady's maid. The patronage of the parvenu was to be encouraged by all means, but never to the detriment of the *bon ton* of ladies and gentlemen. Staff were drilled to recognize to whom were owed the click of heels, small bow, and deferential curtsy, to whom the cool sizing up and curt brushoff.[61] Not that they needed much instruction. Store employees who were themselves under the tutelage of a cradle-to-grave paternalism to distinguish them from workers or the run-of-the mill service class could be counted on to be as snobbish as the most snobbish customer and at least as expert at sizing up dress, accent, and body language. They were able to discern the social complexion of their customers well before looking at the color of their money.

Second, no matter how successful it was, the department store could not altogether expunge the lingering beliefs that merchandising was morally, if not socially, tainted and that the great merchant was a figure less noble than the manufacturer. Stores of such magnitude, so visible, so profitable, put merchant capitalism back at the center of public life such as had not occurred since the great Atlantic sea empires of the seventeenth century or the great trading Italian city-states of the fifteenth. The leading Parisian *patrons* were sponsors, connoisseurs, and collectors of art on a grand scale, generous in their benefaction, and omnipotent paternalists with respect to their thousands of employees. The same held true of Berlin's Jewish magnates. Oscar Tietz, the president of the German Department Store Owners' Association until his death in 1923, by virtue of the heavy taxation of his wealth was the sole elector of the first class in his home residence, the province of Brandenburg. Since he commanded one-third of the district's total votes, as well as being so prominent in Berlin business circles, the authorities had to treat him as an eminence and consult with him on matters of public interest notwithstanding that he was not only of Jewish origin, but also a religious Jew prominent in the Jewish community.[62]

Pillars of bourgeois civilization, the department-store magnates were nonetheless shaky pillars. In some sense, merchant capitalism was regarded as too pure a form of capitalism, which is too say it was too close to finance capitalism, speculating on the circulation of money. One has only to recall the early nineteenth-century utopian socialist Charles Fourier's invective against commerce—"vampire of obscurantism and cunning, that drop by drop sucks off all the riches"; "vulture of industry." Nor can one forget the deep popular animosity against speculators that sparked the food riots that from the eighteenth through the early twentieth centuries occasionally turned into full-blown insurrections.[63] The other concern, which compounded the anxiety about making money off of money, was that Jewish interests seemed so prominent in the big stores' operation.

The public was right to be puzzled at the mystery that successful businesses could lose money on any single article yet still make a profit on the total. To clear up the matter, Gabriel Cognacq, son of La Samaritaine's founders, forthrightly explained how this was possible.[64] The establishment was indeed first and foremost a banking operation, the central management making loans to department buyers to purchase their stocks and repaying them at interest rates of 3 to 4 percent. As this procedure occurred several times a year, profits accrued before the items were placed on sale, much less sold, especially given the habit of delaying payments to the suppliers. This superprofit was another reason, along with their sheer size, that gave them an unfair edge, critics alleged. And it gave governments in search of revenues a good pretext to levy special taxes on the big stores' sales volumes, setting a precedent for other, more vexatious measures in hard times.

During World War I, distress over capitalist commerce, deeply felt in Prussianized Germany, intimated a wider clash of civilizations. It was the ingenious Werner Sombart's propagandistic conceit to counterpose Germany, a people of *Helden* (heroes), to Great Britain, a people of *Händel* (merchants). Enough of Herbert Spencer's anti-German polemic, which portrayed the British Empire as a peace-loving, progressive power in contrast to Kaiser William II's warmongering feudalism: Great Britain ruled its empire with the harsh logic of the contract whereas Germany was guided by chivalric duty.[65] The Pax Britannica was conceived as a giant merchant's scales, its notions of justice infused with the small-mindedness of the ledger book, whereas the German nation was a model of *Kultur*-civilization, bound by ethical and historical ideals to defend itself against the Entente's materialism. "Heroes" in struggle against "Hagglers": Sombart's antinomy was perfectly calibrated to coalesce a patriotic, reactionary coalition.

In 1929 Sombart returned to his favorite topic, the nature of "high capitalism," to identify the department store as its most consummate expression. Though he was not himself an overt anti-Semite, the pamphleteers who passed as the Nazi Party's experts on commerce lifted sonorous quotes from his writing (for example, "the department store is the legitimate offspring of the age of high capitalism") to give academic validity to a connection they rehashed a thousand times, namely that big commerce was dominated by Jews. Indeed, their own "race research" into the "Jewish trade press" revealed that international finance, operating out of New York, Paris, Amsterdam, and Zurich, was the major force behind the chain-store expansion since 1925. The conspiracy to monopolize German commerce was so flagrant that Galeries Lafayette, notoriously a "Franco-Jewish" firm, flaunted its invasion of German territory by locating its flagship on Potsdamer Platz, the sacrosanct commercial heart of Berlin.[66]

Above all, Europe's great merchants had not resolved their embittered relationship with small retailers, who in no place represented less than 90 percent of local outlets.[67] More important than the percentages, the myriad of small establishments exposed a regime of consumption that however much homogenized nationally, centralized politically, and dislocated by industrialization and urban growth, remained profoundly local, minutely variegated, and continuous with the past. In principle, liberalizing trends in trade enacted across the nineteenth century as governments rescinded guild rights and other special privileges should have produced greater similarity from place to place. But no undertaking was more doggedly conservative yet more adeptly innovative than small commerce. Shops whose undertakings were ruled by accumulations of civic regulations, family lore, craft secrets, and guild custom like the draper's and the ironmonger's, the butcher's and the baker's were interspersed with services for new goods like the umbrella store, the bicycle sales and repair shop, the radio store/repairman, the knitters specialized in darning first silk then nylon stockings, whose operations would in turn be inflected by similar accretions of rules and habits.[68] To explain facts of commercial life that the locals took for granted, such as that the greengrocer couldn't sell dried legumes or a women's dress shop lingerie would have required serious detective work by historians, legal experts, and ethnographers, just to start.

Defying both neoclassical and Marxist calculations about their economic viability, the small units put up resistance to supposedly inexorable economies of scale and scope. Overall, the little guys had the longevity of mayflies, to recall Sombart's disparaging description: if a hundred had set up at the beginning of any decade, only twenty would have survived at its end. Yet barring wholesale urban renewal, though single store owners went under, the shops themselves mostly remained, replenished by the myriad of people in search of occupation in economic systems characterized by chronic agricultural crisis, vast reserves of unemployed labor, low wages, the lack of accident insurance and old age pensions, and the exclusion of women from the paid labor force.[69]

Small commerce also persisted because it was a jewel of customized services, hard though these were to monetize. Clients shopped daily, their purchasing power low and their housing so poor that, in effect, they used the neighborhood shop as a storeroom. From behind the counters, the shopkeepers or their assistants took orders, scooped out supplies from assorted drums, barrels, and large jars, measured and weighed them, and wrapped them in newsprint or brown paper or, if fuel or oil, poured them into the customers' receptacles before totting up the prices. They took cash or gave credit, debiting the sum to the monthly account book. If requested, they also arranged for delivery.

More than that, the shopkeeper was a mediator, balancing his capacity to obtain supplies with his notion of his craft and his knowledge of his clientele. In pricing goods he operated according to the notion of a "just profit," meaning that he marked up most goods with an eye to his survival, which was measured roughly as the standard of living appropriate for a shopkeeper who intended to pass on his shop to his offspring, rather than according to the "market price" which would have involved more precise knowledge about the prices charged by his competitors, expenditures on overhead, and the costs of restocking goods. The goods being familiar, he and his customers haggled over the "just price" of an item, broadly agreeing on its value.[70] In practice, this might mean that the

shopkeeper sweetened prices for Madame's captivating servant girl, musing about her charms and out of deference to Madame herself, who kept
an eagle eye on the household ledger books and constantly threatened to
take her custom elsewhere. Whenever the occasion warranted, he gave
his best customers little gifts, and in turn he received little tokens of their
appreciation. Sometimes he trifled with the sums. No doubt this unequal
treatment made for spats and recrimination. But inequality was a fact of
social life. So long as other alternatives were lacking, unequal treatment
didn't detract from the mutual dependency that bound the local clientele
to their corner grocer.

One needn't idealize the small store as a social institution to understand why small shopkeeper movements could claim to represent all that
was trustworthy, valuable, and solid in society. Over time the shopkeeper
mounted the claim to being the mainstay of the social order by virtue of a
lineage reaching back to the medieval guild, his status as property owner
in a culture that still worshiped immobile wealth, and his performance as
both provider of the goods and mediator of taste in ever-so-subtly differentiated hierarchies of consumption. In Europe when one spoke of the
"metaphor of the middle," it was to signal the precarious status of the
Mittelstand, the lingering power of corporations and guilds, and the pervasive outlooks that saw society as an organic hierarchy, with everybody
in his or her proper place.[71] This concept of the middle resisted displacement by the multilayered idea of "middleness" shaped by U.S. consumer
culture. Likewise, the notion that the economic functions of commerce
could be separated from its political, social, and even moral dimensions
made Filene's dictum that a "store was a machine for selling" both wrong
and reprehensible.

The fault lines within the bourgeois regime of consumption widened
into a chasm during the interwar years as, on the one hand, the department store began to wobble as the standard-bearer of bourgeois consumption and, on the other, small commerce flagged in its claim to represent the sound alternative universe of the middle classes. A third way in
merchandising presented itself, the chain variety store. Though championed by department-store capitalists in Europe, it proved a terribly troubling challenge to both small and big commerce.

The Depression caused European department stores to operate in a far
less mobile market than their U.S. counterparts, reducing their customer
base and weakening their capacity to source goods. When they moved
upscale to recoup clients, by offering more attentive help, refined articles,

and auxiliary services like fashion advisers, fancy imports, or escalators, their costs rose. And as often occurred, their customers, having to cut back on their clothes purchases, turned to specialty shops or home dressmakers, with confidence in their style choices reinforced by fashion magazines, the cinema, or window shopping. If the department stores turned to a lower cut of customers by offering cheaper goods, they risked alienating their old clientele, as well as being unable to locate the appropriate well-made but low-cost item because of manufacturing cartels, weak distribution systems, and rising tariffs. To spread the costs of overhead by branching out in outlying neighborhoods or provincial towns proved too costly given their high standards of equipment and service.[72]

The small shopkeepers too faced new terrible times. The more miserable the economic situation, the more shops proliferated. In Belgium, the country best studied on this matter, one authority spoke of the "cancerous pullulation" of small firms, 25 percent more in 1937 than 1910, many selling only food, plied by suppliers' credit, as much to provision their own families as to serve neighborhood customers.[73] Moreover, small retailers as a group were becoming more and more internally divided as, at one extreme, specialty stores capable of holding their own with respect to the most modern establishments fought to modernize and establish niches of supply and service, while at the other extreme the hand-to-mouth vegetable outlet, unlicensed pushcart peddler, or scrap dealer operated in a gray system in which barter, scavenging, and pilfering all had a place. This divide showed especially sharply in the uneven mechanization of shopkeeping. The first widely sold cash register, the product of the National Cash Register Company of Dayton, Ohio, the precocious discovery of its little dynamo of a founder, John Patterson, and introduced by him into Europe in 1884, revolutionized financial practices. Its mechanical tablets, by calculating accurately and auditing the accounts, saved labor, prevented clerks from pilfering from the open till, and enabled the store client, by reading the posted totals and change, to check on the store's accuracy.[74] By the 1920s NCR had subsidiaries all over Europe. But even in Germany, the most mechanized country, where National Krupp Registrier Kassen did a vigorous business, only half of German retail establishments had cash registers, and only one in four kept regular accounts.[75]

In a machine-driven world, with tried and true shopkeepers representing an ever smaller proportion of the middle classes, it was harder and harder for them to sustain their long-privileged voice as "pillar," "backbone," or "safeguard" of the bourgeois regime of consumption. Workers were now recognized as having a bigger voice as the government legalized collective bargaining, regulated working conditions, and broadened pension rights. Moreover, with the big growth of the cooperative movement from the 1920s, workers were no longer such pliable customers. Not least, the middle classes, who had once claimed to represent the "general interest" of the Third Estate against the special privileges of the aristocrats and church, now had to contend with a new "general interest," that of the consumer. To reaffirm their status, shopkeepers might yet appeal for political protection and lend themselves to being the pet constituency of reactionary politicians. But their best chance, reformers beseeched them, was to quit pretending that they were a *social class,* recognize that they were only an *economic interest,* and, strong in this new identity, ally themselves to the new Third Estate, the mass of impoverished consumers.[76]

The Challenge of the Five-and-Dime

The obstacles to moving in that direction were brought home when the department stores, in an effort to get out of their economic troubles, threw their fortunes behind a foreign invention, the variety chain store. As the big merchants did so, it was far from their intention to change the social relations of consumption underlying their ways of doing business or to promote a new middle-class consumer public, much less to ignite a firestorm of opposition from small retailers.

The new invention, immediately to become the subject of a thousand protests, was colloquially known in the United States as the five-and-dime. In France the new stores were called *prix unique,* or single-price, stores, after the German unitary-price store, or *Einheitpreisgeschäft,* which in turn was a rough equivalent of what was formally called a fixed-price store in the United States and Britain. The name made a virtue of its main characteristic: that all the goods on display were sold at two established units of currency: a nickel and a dime in the United States, 25 and 50 pfennigs in Germany, and 50 centimes and a franc in France. An outgrowth of chain retailing, a form of business ownership set up to manage a number of branches, from only two to as many as hundreds, even thousands, its precursors dated from the second half of the nineteenth century in the British multishop movement, the German *Filialbetriebe,* and the French *succoursales.* Management's goal in Europe, as in the

United States, was to maximize business volume, and branches were often located in smaller towns where rents were low. Almost all specialized in bulk-buying nonperishable packaged goods that were sometimes described as colonial wares for their association with imports from European empires, notably tea, spices, coffee, condiments, and jams. In Europe, the best-known if smaller counterparts to the United States' A & P included Great Britain's Thomas Lipton, J. Lyons, and Hunters the Teamen; the French chains Dock Remois and Felix Potin; Belgium's Delhaize Le Lion; Latscha in Germany; and Julius Meinl in the Austro-Hungarian Empire.[77]

The chief characteristic of the five-and-dime or variety chain in addition to its pricing policy was its wide assortment of goods and reduced service to purchase them. Though its offering of 2,500 to 4,000 items was smaller than the department store's, which might offer as many as 200,000, inventory turned over eight to ten times a year, and all the goods, no matter what they were, were arrayed across fifteen to twenty departments on the basis of their price. Customers made their selections, then the clerk—a poorly paid, unskilled, usually female worker—rang up the price, collected the money, and bagged the goods. There was no delivery and no returns. The prices represented a savings of 6–12 percent over comparable goods at department stores and specialty shops.[78]

Frank Woolworth's giant chain was to the invention of the five-and-dime what the Model T was to mass mobility, Rotary to men's service clubs, Coca-Cola to soft drinks, and McDonald's to fast food. An oversized general store, first successful in Lancaster, the prosperous center of the Pennsylvania Dutch country, the enterprise spread so rapidly that by the turn of the century it showed that mass retailing could make as heady a profit as manufacturing. Beginning in 1912 Woolworth was registered on the stock exchange, demonstrating that retailing could also attract outside capital. By 1929 the company's 1,825 U.S. subsidiaries did a $303 million-a-year business, making it second only to General Electric Corporation in total turnover. That year it paid out a 7.7 percent dividend to its shareholders. Headquarters were located at 233 Broadway in the fantastic fifty-four-story Gothic structure with flying buttresses topped by a tiaralike spire designed by Cass Gilbert. Built in 1913 with no mortgage, inaugurated by President Wilson, who from the White House on April 24, 1913, flipped the switch to turn on the lights with a tap of a telegraph signal, the Woolworth building was the tallest in the world until 1920, when it was overtaken by 40 Wall Street and the

The Woolworth Building, the world's tallest building when it was inaugurated in 1913. In 1879–1929, Fifty Years of Woolworth *(New York: F. W. Woolworth, 1929).* Courtesy of the Thomas J. Watson Business and Economics Library, Columbia University.

Chrysler Building. Its twenty-fourth-floor executive suite was copied from Napoleon's campaign headquarters at Compiègne; the portrait of the emperor was later replaced by one of Frank Woolworth himself. The gimmicky statistics the company publicists churned out couldn't but impress Europeans: that in 1918 one billion persons entered Woolworth stores, 820,000,000 of whom bought something; in 1920 every town in the United States with over 8,000 people had a "Red-Front," and in 1929, on average, every American made twenty-five purchases at the stores.[79]

In 1909 Woolworth established its first overseas branch, a three-and-sixpence store in Liverpool. Taking a jumbo lead over the competition, mainly Marks & Spencer and British Home Stores, it had opened 400 branches by 1930. As the continent's economy stabilized in 1925, the parent company planned to move across the Channel. Its main interest

Immense Woolworth warehouse, Sonneberg, Germany.
Courtesy of the Thomas J. Watson Business and Economics Library,
Columbia University.

was Germany, where before the war Frank Woolworth had mass-pur-
chased Christmas ornaments, marbles, dolls, and other crafts, had huge
warehouses built in Bavaria and Thuringia to supply the U.S. stores, and
would have opened up local outlets but for the outbreak of the war. This
plan was finally authorized on November 2, 1926, seven years after
Woolworth's death in 1919. On Saturday July 30, 1927, all the appropriate licenses in hand, the German-speaking manager, Ivan W. Keffer,
grandly staged the opening of the first 25-and-50-pfennig store in the
port city of Bremen, a perfect location as its economy picked up with the
return of international trade. Twenty-three more stores opened in 1928,
including establishments in Düsseldorf, Wiesbaden, Bochum, and Berlin,
their glass and steel storefronts exactly the same as the red-and-gold
design of the American stores. Sensitive to the antiforeign climate, the
company heavily publicized that the branch managers were all Germans,
likewise its 4,000 employees; it purchased 98 percent of its goods in Germany; and, lest anybody accuse it of benefiting from occult financial favors, it paid cash for bulk purchases from its suppliers. Opening new 25-
and-50-pfennig stores as fast as it could find appropriate locations, at
a rate of two or three a month, it was operating eighty-two stores, fourteen in Berlin alone, by 1932. That was when the Brüning government,
shaken by Nazi-led shopkeeper protests, passed legislation to curb further chain-store expansion. Woolworth's German operations remained

Müllerstrasse, Berlin, Store

Universal "Red Front Store," Berlin, 1929. Courtesy of the Thomas
J. Watson Business and Economics Library, Columbia University.

handsomely profitable nonetheless. In 1939, when F. W. Woolworth Co.
was forced to write off its initial $10 million investment after the Nazi re-
gime banned the reexport of profits, it was valued at four times the original capitalization of $7.5 million and employed 6,500 people.[80]

As early as 1925, in anticipation that Woolworth was about "invade"
the continent, European retailers organized to defend themselves. The
German department-store heads were especially pained at Woolworth's
plans to capture two new market segments that had previously been ignored, namely Germany's pauperized middle classes and its relatively
prospering unionized workforce. Filene's daylong meetings with the Cologne Tietz Company management on July 6, 1925, surely occurred after
Alfred Leonhard Tietz had already decided to establish his own chain.
However, his management took to heart two of Filene's points. The first
emphasized "Mr. Woolworth's aggressiveness" in contracting with manufacturers to buy out their entire stock run, his policy being to pay them
six cents an item. Manufacturers could be persuaded that this was a good
arrangement by having it pointed out that it was a sure deal and certain
to cut costs for advertising, middlemen, and bookkeeping. Filene's second point emphasized studying the cheapest full line, which meant the
lowest price an article could be sold at yet still be of good enough quality
that the customer would buy it again.[81] In other words, mass retailers
had to rethink the relationship of price to quality to satisfy the maxi-

mum number of customers. Whether or not Filene's advice was superfluous, it didn't hurt Tietz to know that his own business strategies had
been practiced beforehand in the United States or that American capital
was available for investment. In January 1926 he opened the first 11
branches of Ehape (or Atktiengesellschaft für Einheitspreise), in 1927
another 20. In 1926 the Berliner Rudolf Karstadt launched his own
new line of stores, also with backing from American banks. Called Epa,
it soon became Germany's largest. Karstadt was followed by another
Berlin-based chain, Epawe, and by the Leipzig-based Wolhwert, a chain
of independent stores grouping together to purchase supplies. In 1931,
after five years of rapid-fire growth, 15 variety chains were operating 400
new stores.[82]

Following the Germans' lead, French, Belgian, and eventually even
Italian department stores backed one-price chains. In cautious France
the first venture was undertaken only in 1927 and at the initiative of
outsiders, the Audiberts. The Cinq et Dix, on the unfashionable 4 Rue
Chauchat, near the Porte d'Orléans, used 45,000 francs from Madame
Audibert, a onetime fashion house promoter, as the initial capital. The
idea had occurred to the couple on their trip to New York, and they
avowed that it was an outright imitation of Woolworth. As evidence, Mr.
Audibert pointed to the sign *"servir"* posted by the checkout counters;
the gramophone music, which purportedly increased sales by a third the
day it was installed; and the popularity of the store, which led them to establish two more, on Avenues de Clichy and Barbès, in November–December 1929. Nonetheless, he himself admitted that the prices were not
equivalently cheap. Instead of 1.50 and 3 francs, they ranged from 5 to
10. The problem was sourcing. The structure of French industries didn't
lend itself to producing quantity and quality at discounted prices. Indeed,
that was the reason Woolworth cited for not going into France: whereas
its German subsidiaries obtained 98 percent of their goods locally and
the British stores 80 percent, for France at least 50 percent would have to
be brought in from abroad, with all kinds of complications, from import
regulations to nationalism, in addition to the prohibitively high costs.[83]

The success of French upstarts, together with the success of the German and Britain chains, disposed Parisian department-store managements to view the chain-store idea more favorably. Jean Milhaud, Filene's
erstwhile "Boy Friday," later famous for founding CEGOS, the first
French business consulting firm, had a hand here by promoting what he
aptly called "technical tourism." In 1929, capitalizing on Filene's old

idea to organize discount transatlantic travel packages for management, he founded TRANSAT out of his office on Rue Miessine. The first "voyage expérience," organized in 1930 to study U.S. chain stores, offered "a stimulus to an entire industry" in Milhaud's immodest view, the participants concurring at their return that "American procedures might be applied with all due caution." Cross-Channel visits to London's Woolworth and Marks & Spencer reinforced this disposition.[84] As early as 1928 the Nouvelles Galeries de Paris with backing from Laguionie's Printemps and Karstadt set up Uniprix. Subsequently the latter two founded a second chain, Prisunic. In 1932 the venerable Bon Marché allied itself to the upstart Boka, a Luxembourg food chain, to launch Priminime. In turn, Galeries Lafayette allied with Felix Potin to set up Monoprix. If the ever-restless Emile Bernheim had had his way in his never-ending quest to break out of Belgium, he would have organized a European-wide department-store trust along the lines of the American Federation of Department Stores, which Filene's own Boston firm had joined in 1929. Though his old partners, the Cologne Tietzes, were willing to take the risk, since they operated the biggest conglomerate on the continent, Harrods demurred on the grounds that such a venture would ruin its princely image; and Prisunic, Printemps, and De Bijenkorf, though interested in principle, were loath to relinquish their autonomy of action. Faced with competition from the upstart Sarma chain, Bernheim set aside his family's longtime rivalry with the Vexalaire department-store dynasty. The profits from the new Priba chain, formed in alliance with the Vexalaires' Bon Marché, soon outstripped the parent companies'.[85]

By the middle of the 1930s, counting Great Britain, the variety chain stores numbered 12,000 in all of Europe. Whereas in the United States they accounted for about 23 percent of retail turnover and in Britain for about 7 percent, in Germany they amounted to only 1.5 percent, in France 1.3 percent, and in Italy perhaps .3 percent. Though the latter figures seem minute, a closer look shows that they, rather than the grand bourgeois department store, now stood "on the cutting edge of society."[86]

The chain store's challenge to the old regime of consumption is better appreciated in terms of its location, pricing system, and the people who patronized it. For the first time, the chain store moved large-scale retailing from the city centers to outlying urban neighborhoods and towns with populations under 100,000. Department stores had traditionally favored places where the circulation of people was intense, mainly the city centers, whereas chain stores thrived where habitation was dense. In

Paris the new retail outlets pushed out from the center toward the north
on Avenue de Clichy, Faubourg du Temple, Avenue d'Orléans, Place de la
République, and to the west and south of Bon Marché on the left bank,
Rue de Rennes, and Rue de Vaugirard. In Berlin the department stores
were around the Potsdamer Platz, whereas the variety stores were located
on Leipzigerstrasse. In Rome La Rinascente was on the elegant Corso,
whereas the first Upim stores occupied the populous Via del Tritone and
Via Nazionale. The length of the blocks that separated the two types of
stores looked short. But the social distance that separated the coming and
going of the new clientele of the one-price stores from the well-worn
paths trod by the well-shod feet of department-store customers was significant. Mass retailing was now available to the masses as it pressed into
residential neighborhoods amid small shops that had not hitherto had
to contend with major competition. Whereas the department store presented itself as a unique place, the chains by multiplying so rapidly imparted a sense of mobility and omnipresence. True, France had only one
five-and-dime for every 269,000 inhabitants (compared with one for every 80,000 residents in Germany and one for every 20,000 in the United
States). That Paris alone should have thirty new glass-and-metal neon-lit
enterprises could be absorbed, more or less; likewise that downtown Lyons and Marseilles would acquire respectively four and three. However,
that towns like Amiens and Dijon, with populations of just over 50,000,
had one, the slow-paced Alsatian town of Mulhouse had three, and each
of twenty-four towns with 20,000 to 50,000 residents had one, together
with twenty towns with populations under 20,000, including out-of-the-
way Hayange and the sleepy Savoyard town of Montbeliard (both of
which acquired two), visibly enlivened the local scene.[87]

The second effect of the chain store was to revolutionize pricing. The
department store, though it boasted high turnover and low profit margins and periodically held great sales at which it discounted prices, never
provided attractive convenience goods at low fixed prices. The individual
pricing of thousands of articles made it look as if they had an intrinsic
worth that the buyers and salespeople knew and the customer became acquainted with as she appraised and purchased the article.[88] In contrast,
by fixing prices at one of only five or six sums management conveyed the
impression (not necessarily correct) that the chain store offered its stock,
if not at the lowest possible price, at the lowest price consistent with its
quality. Trust in the pricing system thus came from factors that were extrinsic to the item, such as the knowledge that stores bought in bulk, the

functional look of the store layout, with its clean, rectangular spaces, orderly counters, bright, uniform light, and the modest-looking clerks. Trust grew in proportion to the customer's capacity to move freely about the store, comparing articles that were arranged in different departments yet counter by counter were all marked as costing the same amount. Trust also developed from the feeling that customers were all being treated equally: there were no cheeky clerks or sour-looking salesgirls standing around sizing up purchasing power or questioning their taste and judgment as they fingered an item and nervously inquired about its cost.

In effect, by establishing a price system based on comparison of items priced as equal but otherwise incommensurate, entrepreneurs not only enhanced customers' capacity to exercise their purchasing power but also encouraged them to practice their purchasing skills.[89] Faced with a clutter of new goods and a limited budget, having purchased the staples and lacking other product information, customers worked backward from the price to estimate the article's utility: whether the goal was to purchase cheap tinware for kitchen use, solid flatware for family dining, or a silver-plated service for special occasions, the goal was to get good value for one's money. This more fluid "American" notion of value would have crossed the Atlantic far faster had European chain-store managers had their way. For Max Heilbronn, chief of Galeries Lafayette, as well as the moving force behind its new chain, the Monoprix, the French notion of *valeur* referred to the rarity, beauty, objective utility, and craftsmanship of an object. Pricing reflected this value, and the price paid demonstrated that, indeed, the article was "of great value." By contrast, when Americans spoke of "*a* great value," they intended qualities that were pertinent to the article itself, such as taste, shape, solidity, and convenience, but also qualities that the consumer saw in it, such as ease of acquisition, the range of choices available, and factors such as delivery, maintenance, and service.[90] In sum, as a bourgeois connoisseur Heilbronn cherished *valeur;* as a chain-store entrepreneur he promoted "value."

Finally, the chain stores spelled a social revolution by attracting a socially mixed clientele. Thereby they lessened the gap in purchasing habits between the bourgeoisie and the middle classes broadly intended, and in some places between the lower-middle and working classes. The attractiveness of the stores, the novelties they offered, the increase of brand names advertised in the women's magazines, the fact that they were open at lunchtime attracted the custom of more socially favored lei-

sured women from outside the neighborhood. After a fashion, they also
connected women consumers to women workers: Marks & Spencer, as it
advertised itself, was the store that "introduces the girl who makes the
stockings to the girl who wears them."[91]

Since the 1880s, whenever there was significant change in the scale and
style of retailing, small-shopkeeper movements had burst out with a familiar litany of protests: large-scale retailing sapped money from the
community, destroyed opportunities for independent employment, exploited labor with lower wages, practiced unfair competition, tended toward monopoly, and drove healthy family-run stores out of business.
These recriminations acquired a new resonance beginning in the late
1920s as small retailers faced competitors that could more plausibly be
denounced as foreign and customers who were more and more inclined
to attach themselves to new models of consumption.

To survive, small retailers had exercised power over both price and
taste. Improving profit margins proved more and more difficult. But it
also proved harder and harder for them to control taste in view of the
chain stores' contention that consumers should be free to determine quality, on the basis of the use they intended for the item. Shopkeepers could
claim, of course, that customers were paying for the quality of the services they offered. But how to prove it? If they told customers to shop
around, they too would become part of the cash nexus.[92] They also faced
the risk that as consumers became increasingly aware of alternative uses
of money, they would become more independent of the shopkeeper as ar-
biter of social taste.

Inevitably American market culture was implicated in the anxiety over
changing values. From any point of view, American society was a money
society: divorces were settled with huge alimony payments; mergers and
takeovers occurred, the public interest and the little guy be damned; the
United States behaved dishonorably, like a despicable usurer on the matter of war debts; greedy financiers of Wall Street, their own speculative
racket out of control, had caused the banks to crack in Europe, precipi-
tating the Depression. Uncle Sam = Uncle Shylock: so many of the conventions of thinking about money that were imputed to outsiders, to the
Jews mainly but also to the Huguenots, were imputed to the United
States. This habit of thought ran deep, especially among the cultured
classes, who connected the loss of value of objects they held especially
precious to the perception that the Old World's wealth was being si-
phoned off by crapulous American millionaires.

By the 1920s Americans clearly experienced their relationship to money more flexibly than Europeans. More and more Americans were used to managing credit, as well as new kinds of currency in the form of postal money orders (1864), travelers' checks (1891), and credit cards (1914), as well as omnipresent installment buying and other time-payment plans, not to mention the precociously established fixed-price stores. Accordingly, the sphere of what Charles H. Cooley aptly called "pecuniary valuation" widened. "Our line of progress," wrote this sage midwestern reformer, "lies . . . not over commercialism but through it; the dollar is to be reformed rather than suppressed." Skills in using money, meaning skills in differentiating among its uses, thus came to be regarded as a sign of personal competence and mastery of the social environment.[93] Capital in America was a form of earning power rather than, as in Europe, a form of property yielding income, making the timing of investment and profit-taking all-important and the "hustle" in economic transactions a way of life. The result was a paradox, nicely captured by Geoffrey Gorer, that "Americans talk far more about money than Europeans and generally value it far less."[94]

If, then, pushing value, understood as prices, to a minimum came into conflict with preserving values, meaning taste, culture, and civilization, reformers were faced with an awful quandary: How to calculate the social price of commerce while calculating the costs of making the system more efficient? Liberalism could not provide the answer, at least not liberalism as traditionally conceived, wrote Halbwachs's onetime colleague the Alsatian legal scholar Henri Laufenberger. Commerce needed to be protected as a measure on behalf of "public order," especially "at a time when the nations of old Europe are experiencing not only economic but also so-called social dumping of certain new and young countries." A prominent member of the French technocratic reform group, X Crise, Laufenberger advocated modernizing distribution networks. But to squeeze retail prices to the bare minimum would be "to regard commerce as simply a technical organ of industry, responsible for the placement of goods."[95] And that would spell the end of the civilization based on "sweet commerce."

Filene's Last Tour

Filene was due to visit Europe in the summer of 1937. Normally, he went every year. And he had never yet failed to attend the ICC's Distribution

Committee meeting, which was scheduled for July. He felt under particular obligation to go, since he was the vice-president, and he had not met with the group since their June 1935 meeting in Paris. Moreover, his *Next Steps in Retailing* had just come out, and his prestige, he was told, was greater than ever and his presence all the more valued. The situation in Europe had become "so dangerous," his assistant Percy Brown urged him, that this year's ICC convention presented itself as an "especially important opportunity to contribute toward doing away with the barriers and obstacles to trade . . . which, with the alarming burdens of increasing armaments, threaten revolution and war unless remedies are found quickly."[96]

However, the ICC intended to hold its meetings in Berlin, and aside from having heavy responsibilities at home, Filene emphatically opposed any initiative that gave credibility to Hitler's regime. Arguments to the effect that Emile Bernheim was going, as well as the greatly esteemed Alberto Pirelli, an Italian of Jewish background, or that he would be considered a "kicker" if he didn't show up, were to naught. He stood by his June 1933 judgment that "the situation in Germany is not a matter merely of the persecution or the acts against the Jews, but is a crime against civilization and ought to be approached and regarded by the outside world as such."[97]

In the event, there was a world of difference between 1935, when Filene spoke in Paris, holding out his vision of the chain store as the solution to the tribulations of trade, and 1937, when all European countries except Britain and Sweden had passed legislation aimed to obstruct their spread. The discussions in Berlin indicated that the ICC was oblivious to the reactionary turnaround. Most speakers issued paeans to the new age of scientific distribution. Only a couple spoke of the need to recognize what the German representative called the "human element" in retailing, a code word for solidarity with the small retailer.

In effect, the two forms of commerce—the chain store and the small shop—did not have to be counterposed. Arguments for a middle way could be made: that the big and the little could coexist, that both were indispensable economically as well as socially, that any project that disregarded the latter's existence risked exacerbating their resistance. Filene, faced with criticism, always reiterated the point he had made in Paris in June 1935: the small must not cease to exist, but must cease to be small. The little store had to join with others in voluntary chains for purchasing, exchanging information, even advertising. Voluntary chains like the one he had seen in the United States, one composed of fully 6,000 individually owned member stores, could make it. "European business leadership," he exhorted, "must organize these shopkeepers, for many of them are in no position to take the necessary initiatives." Indeed, with the small shops organized in voluntary chains, retailing would take a step in the "right direction," namely "selling to the masses the things that the masses want":

> Not merely food, shelter and clothing. Not merely the little comforts but the great satisfactions and many even of the luxuries of modern life. Beautiful homes. Beautiful household furniture. Electric appliances. Electric refrigeration. Modern plumbing. Radio Sets. Good automobiles. Hundreds of things.[98]

This flight of rhetoric sat incongruously with Filene's own fitful observations on the groundswell of opposition to the chains and departments in Germany in the wake of the Nazi seizure of power. The chain stores were "better machines to sell better goods for less price than the enormous number of little stores, with very limited trade and at an incredibly big expense." But the German government had capitulated to the latter "because there are so many of them that their total is an almost compelling force politically in their contact with their customers and their neighbors."[99] Whether Filene would have at least listened to exponents of a "third way" in retailing remains a moot question. In the ever-so-bright and conscientious German-born British economist Hermann Levy he would have found an interlocutor of the first order. In those very years, Levy was researching the book that he would limpidly call *The Shops of Britain,* finding in their "social utility" and "economies of locality" intangibles such as community goodwill and services such as store credit, repair work, and advice that were especially important to neophyte consumers and to operating new durables such as radios and household electric appliances.[100] In his effort to reconnect craft and customers by improving the quality and range of goods and the services the stores offered, Levy recognized that the small, independent store was a social institution, not a machine for selling, no more and no less than the department store was a social institution, or for that matter the chain store too.

However, the conditions for taking Filene's "next step forward" proved lacking on the continent. In many circles, to speak positively of the chain stores implied consorting with left-wing cooperatives, unfettered big business, and the cosmopolitan outlooks identified with the

United States and international Jewry. To speak of "rationalizing" retailing was to unleash blind market forces and elicit unbridled consumption. Faced with the choice between allying themselves to new retailing and a new middle-class constellation and consolidating their base in old retailing backed by a reactionary political coalition, most governments chose the latter.

One immediate effect was legislation to stop chain-store expansion. This took the form of retail price maintenance, discriminatory taxes, restrictions on store services, and outright curbs on new establishments. With Austria and Germany in the lead, most of the countries of continental Europe restricted the expansion of variety chain stores and other large-scale retail operations.[101]

Behind this legislation lay the struggle between two outlooks on the modern market. One was sociable: originating in American commercial capitalism, it foresaw a whole new nexus of institutions to manage modern market forces, emphasizing low per-unit costs, standardized goods, high turnover, and consumer choice. It sent a mixed message about values. In principle, the chain store had none: it was a "machine for selling." In reality, it valued choice, freedom from want, and the right to comfort. In the best of circumstances, in recognition that competition was "imperfect," it found a compromise by legislating measures to negotiate fair prices through legal channels.[102] Modern distribution was perhaps no less costly, but the costs were spread differently, and they were regarded as a legitimate condition for the changeability, variety, and choice typical of mass consumer society.

The solidaristic outlook, in contrast, advocated protected markets and spoke of "just profits" and "just prices." It explicitly treated distribution as a social question: goods embodied values, as determined by their cost and craftsmanship, and crushing prices risked not only wiping out small retailers but also destroying the solidity of the communities they served; or worse, it exposed the nation to being overwhelmed by alien values. Based not just on the conventions of needs of the neighborhood, but on the worth of a whole way of life, the "just price" was a cost that customers had to bear.

Even though Filene had decided not to attend the International Chamber of Commerce meeting, so much was happening in Europe that when his schedule suddenly opened up, a cabin was reserved for him on short notice, and on July 14 he embarked on the S. S. *Normandie*. His sworn purpose was to take the cure at Karlsbad, but his visit turned into the usual "semibusiness" trips from the spa town to Prague to visit with the Czech president Eduard Benes and to speak at the Rotary club, then four days in Vienna where, among a dozen other appointments, he met at length with his friend the beleaguered Austrian Chancellor Dollfuss to urge him to steel himself against Hitler's pressures.

Looping down into Italy before heading through the Alps toward France, Filene made a quick detour to Zurich, where, at the warm recommendation of his old friend Julius Hirsch, he finally met the notorious Gottlieb Duttweiler, known as the most militant price buster in all Europe. An emigré to Brazil, where his foray into the coffee business had failed, rebuffed at his return from finding employment in the local cooperatives because of his bad credit rating, at thirty-seven years old he had rustled together five used Ford pickup trucks to found Migros. Offering heavily discounted foodstuffs, the spiffed-up vehicles circulated among the small towns and outlying villages of Bern Canton, rapidly building up an enthusiastic clientele. Despite ferocious opposition from small retailers, Duttweiler's fleet of trucks soon operated throughout Switzerland. Visiting Duttweiler's simple but attractive home in Rüschlikon above Lake Zurich and meeting his wife and helpmate, Adele Duttweiler-Bertschi, before they all went down to the city to dine, Filene heard a story of heroic entrepreneurship. First, there were the magnificent 20–30 percent discounts Duttweiler offered and the ferocious legal obstacles he had to battle to be able to "crush prices." He spoke warmly of his staunchest allies, Swiss homemakers whose demonstration of worldly-wise knowledge about goods and prices made him outspokenly advocate the right of women to vote (which continued to be regularly denied). To buck the opposition, he had done what no other entrepreneurs of his time did, which was to go into politics himself. In 1935 he founded his own populist political party, one of many eccentric movements of a decade in which men with causes went straight to the people. Though Duttweiler never exerted as much influence on his fellow Europeans as the Americans did, the Swiss simply not having the same clout even when they did come up with an ingenious idea, Filene recognized in him a fellow "apostle of distribution." Thirty years younger than Filene, he still had a lot to accomplish. When he died in June 1962 at age seventy-three, 30 percent of Swiss families were served by his enterprises. By then, all opposition overcome, they encompassed every stage in the progress in food retailing since the 1920s, from the traveling outlets, cooperatives, and self-service shops to thirty-eight supermarkets.[103]

Paris was Filene's ultimate goal. His two-week stay was like old times. Once he had acquitted his primary engagement, which was to represent the United States at the International Cooperative Congress, he consulted with the usual round of public figures, including Minister of Finance Bonnet, attended receptions, and lunched with old acquaintances, including Laguionie and Heilbronn. On September 18 he left by car for the Boulogne–Folkstone Channel crossing, from where he was to go to London and then to Southampton to sail to New York on the *Queen Mary*. Arriving at Boulogne at dusk, he was overcome by wracking chills and a high fever. At the American Hospital at Neuilly, the doctors diagnosed him as suffering from a recurrence of the virulent pneumonia he had contracted two years earlier in Moscow, and notwithstanding the fact that his brother mobilized prodigious medical expertise and paraphernalia, on September 26 he died in an oxygen tent. Encircled by floral tributes, his body lay in the private chapel of the hospital grounds before being cremated at Père Lachaise. The ashes were to go back to Boston to be thrown into the Charles River. Bernheim's wreath, accompanied by an affectionate note, was notably magnificent.[104]

Whether in the course of his conversations with Pierre Laguionie and Max Heilbronn, with whom he dined the week before, Filene had absorbed what French department-store owners were up to at the time is unclear, nor is it clear whether he could have grasped the diverging paths that their world was taking from the only one he really understood, which was the American. Filene had never grasped how conservative the Paris department-store group was; or if he did, he overlooked its flagrantly reactionary political positions as injudicious but irrelevant, much as he had treated Henry Ford's anti-Semitism. Starting in 1928, the Department Store Study Group subsidized right-wing, paramilitary leader Pierre Taittinger's Ligue des Patriots, whose goal, as propagandists for the cause delicately phrased it, was to "reinforce the executive power" of government. It also doled out sums to various profascist leagues proliferating around the city. At a time when trade unions had begun to be accepted as an inevitability of modern society, the leading department stores' managements intransigently opposed unionization drives in their own enterprises. Their employees, they dreamed, were happily segregated from proletarian degeneracy by the bourgeois style of living provided by their employers, who claimed to act out of paternalistic kindness. So in the early 1930s the department-store managements augmented expenditures on orphanages, professional schools, kindergar-

Nazi Storm Troopers picketing a Berlin Woolworth store,
March 9, 1933. By permission of the Associated Press.

tens, and old-age homes, as well as indulging their employees with numerous other tokens of fatherly care, even as they sliced away at their salaries. When, on June 3, 1936, department-store employees went on strike
for the first time, their bosses were stunned. Learning nothing from this
experience, they justified their opposition to the 1936 Matignon Accords,
which called for the eight-hour day, salary increases, and expanded employee representation, as just and proper resistance to the insatiable appetites of workers already "gorged with legalized leisure time." In October 1939, as the left opposition weakened, they made a last-ditch effort
to roll back salaries by one-third. If their move had not been so untimely,
taken at the very moment the men were being drafted for military duty,
they might have got away with it. As it was, the minister of labor, Charles
Pomaret, blocked the effort as unpatriotic given the sacrifices the call-up
was imposing on French working families.[105]

No matter how prescient Filene was in condemning Nazism, nothing
would have prepared him for its viciousness toward Jewish commerce,
so much in the public eye, thus so easily the butt of boycotts and incite-

ments to violence that culminated in the pogroms of November 8 and 9, 1938. At the Königstrasse Woolworth store in Berlin, he would have seen the broken glass left after the rampage, as well as the revolting slogans slopped on the façade: "If you're a true German, you won't buy from the Jews." He would have heard from his longtime acquaintance, the U.S. commercial attaché Douglas Miller, of the squalid legal measures the Nazi government enacted in the wake of Crystal Night to complete the ruin of Jewish store owners. The first, dated November 12, which called for the "restoration of storefronts by Jewish businessmen," stipulated that all damages caused by the "indignation of the German people in the previous days, such as smashed shop windows, wrecked store fixtures, etc., had to be repaired immediately." Another proviso specified that the costs of said repairs had to be borne entirely by the shop owners themselves. If the insurance companies made good on any claims, the state had the right to confiscate the premiums. He would have seen that the measures worked as intended. Three or so weeks later, the storefronts on the downtown thoroughfares looked in good repair, with all the glass windows, doors, and fixtures remounted. But few of the old establishments had resumed business, and those that had were all operating under Aryan management.[106]

Of course the Nazis had bigger fish to fry, namely the chiefs of the big department and chain stores. However, much as they denounced these operations as the acme of price-breaking, speculative Judeo-capitalism, they had to conclude that they were indispensable to efficient retailing. All that had to be done to transform them into models of rational enterprise was to Aryanize their management. That done, the great German Jewish merchants were wise to use their connections and whatever of their wealth they managed to secure abroad to leave their homeland as expeditiously as possible. Jewish merchants elsewhere experienced the anti-Semitic persecution later. Max Heilbronn, at the fall of France to the Germans, went into the Resistance and, captured as a partisan, was fortunate to end up at Dachau, classified as a partisan rather than a Jew, before being transported to Buchenwald, where he survived until his liberation in April 1945. Emile Bernheim, fleeing Belgium just ahead of the German invasion in June 1940, first sought sanctuary in Vichy France. From there he made his way first to Dakar, then to the Philippines before finally, in 1941, obtaining entry into the United States. In October 1948 he would turn up in Paris for the first postwar convention of the International Chamber of Commerce, where, as feisty as ever, he hammered away at his old message: "Distribution is today in every country without exception the strangulation point of the economy."[107] By then the heyday of the great bourgeois department store was over. Leadership no longer lay in the hands of great merchants, unless they converted to new systems—which Bernheim did on the basis of his prolonged U.S. experience—but rather in the plans of government experts, pressure from American advisers to the European recovery programs, and the profit-seeking of new cohorts of chain-store and supermarket operators.

By the spring of 1940 Germany's main shopping streets showed the effects of the war economy even though the Third Reich had not yet engaged in combat its main Western European enemies. Believing that consumer outlooks offered a good gauge of public opinion toward Hitler's regime, the U.S. commercial consul in Berlin took a shopping tour of downtown Berlin, Leipzig, and Dresden. People were still window shopping. But rationing and shortages were visible in the store displays. Candy and liquor store windows were ornamented with empty bottles, pretty packages, and decorative cartons. In department stores, floor articles were displayed, but no stock was available for sale. To avoid accusations of fraud, law-abiding store managers attached inconspicuous signs to the effect that the "exhibited articles are not for sale" or that the contents were "decoys." The authorities tolerated these subterfuges, if not encouraging them outright; anything to cheer up people demoralized by the sight of the pitifully depleted store windows. Only when customers became infuriated at the sham were these ruses banned as dishonest commerce. As the ban took effect, the better shops of the downtown commercial districts showed their inventiveness by filling their show windows with the bric-a-brac of refined interior decoration—gloriously plush Persian rugs, exquisitely framed paintings, and polychrome vases with silk flower bouquets.[108] Bourgeois taste was still intact, even if the means to satisfy it had been pauperized.

Hardly four weeks later an event occurred on the other side of the Atlantic that went into the annals as a new first: namely the "greatest bargain basement crush in history."[109] As the German Panzer units advanced on Paris in early June 1940, ending the Phony War, Filene's buyers scooted around the fashion district from Coco Chanel's atelier to Schiapparelli's and Mainbocher's buying up hundreds of outfits designed by Paris's best-known couturiers. The "distressed goods" were shipped back to Boston, where they were placed on sale in Filene's Automatic Bargain Basement, none marked over forty-nine dollars. War terminology was becoming all the fad, as the description tells. Fifteen thousand women, some from as far away as Chicago, "blitzkrieged the Basement" just after the doors opened at 8:00 A M In less than a minute the plain pipe racks were stripped bare. No woman in the United States was "gun shy" when it came to getting a great deal on the dress of her dreams.

CHAPTER 4

Big-Brand Goods

How Marketing Outmaneuvered the Marketplace

*They have better art maybe over there, more history, more
of the finesse or savoir vivre, but less of the comforts of life,
the real aids to living . . . Let them have their past; we'll
take care of the future, and cash in on it as well as the
present.*

> DAVID LESLIE BROWN,
> business manager, Goodyear Tire
> and Rubber Export Company, 1929

*Now, from America, empty indifferent things crowd over to
us, counterfeit things, the veriest dummies . . . The lives and
living things, the things that share our thoughts, these are
on the decline and can no more be replaced.*

> RAINER MARIA RILKE,
> poet, 1925

"WHERE IS THE FAIR?" American dealers would ask when they had
wandered as far as Brühlstrasse, a few minutes away from Leipzig's
grand Central Train Station. "The fair is everywhere," sly Leipzigers
liked to answer, poking fun at the newcomers' disorientation. Waved in
the direction of the inner city, the innocents plunged into the narrow
streets, where the wall-to-wall crowds nudged them toward the Market Square. There, if they missed the information booths and couldn't
make sense of the crazy quilt of signs, helpful policemen and English-
speaking guides pointed out the entranceway into the seven-story Ring-
Messehaus, Europe's largest fair building, or walked them over to the

ramp leading down into the newly built subterranean fairground, the largest anywhere in the world.

Thereafter they were on their own. A sizable number of the display stands were to be found in the rationally laid-out spaces of the Petershof or the brand-new Grassi Textile Palace. Other exhibitions had them venturing through dank passageways and courtyards to reach the rabbit warren of rooms cut out of the princely merchant warehouses that lined the streets back from the Market Square. Moving from building to building, weaving amid the pavilions showing the wares of thousands of exhibitors, pressed by the mobs of dealers fingering the objects and turning them over to check their specifications, distracted by the hubbub of sales pitches spoken in myriad foreign tongues, they guessed at the worth of products laid out side by side, one display case after another. Ordered according to an unfamiliar taxonomy, they included arts and crafts, furniture and wickerware, haberdashery and fancy goods, leather goods and luggage, notions, novelties, and giftware, and so on to include another fifteen categories. Only a few score could be identified by familiar brand names.

These American neophytes may have been disoriented. But for scores of thousands of people from Europe, the Middle East, and Asia the Great Fair of Leipzig was a well-known event. Seven centuries old, uninterrupted in war or peace, it took place for one week twice a year as regularly as clockwork: the Spring Fair always started the Sunday before the first Monday in March; the Autumn Fair, the last Sunday in August. Offering circus processions, stunt-flying airplanes, modernist advertising displays, and other hoopla during the day, afternoon lectures by distinguished visitors, and evening café concerts in the passageways, scabrous back-alley cabarets, Bach organ chorales at St. Thomas and the Nikolai Church, and Mendelssohn, Haydn, and Brahms at the Gewandhaus, the Leipzig Fair was that wonderful alloy of commerce mixed with carnival turbulence and cultural refinement peculiar to Old World merchandising at its apogee. Around 1930, with its 8,000 display stands, 20,000 registered exhibitors, 180,000 or so accredited visitors from forty-five countries, uncounted thousands of sightseers, and incalculable numbers of samples, it was the world's largest single commercial event.[1]

Though the fair looked quaintly different from what self-absorbed Americans and their still scanty European emulators archly spoke of as "modern merchandising methods," the institution the Americans visited around 1930 was not an anachronism. At Leipzig, Europe's ancient merchant culture had developed a strategy to respond to the same problems that had ultimately brought American marketing strategies to focus on building up brand recognition. These problems included how to get goods from suppliers to customers in the face of fast-moving railroad, road, and steamship transport and telegraph and telephone communication; how to accommodate wider, more volatile international markets; how to pick and choose among the inexhaustible variety of supply of commodities; how to explain new product specifications; and, finally, how to respond to rapid-fire shifts in consumer tastes.

For the Americans, the solution was to create brand-name recognition, which involved new product development, intense scrutiny of consumer habits by means of psychological and social profiling based on opinion polls and statistical surveys, and a giant apparatus of salesmanship backed by favorable state and international regulation. All were designed to move brand-name goods from their original manufacturers to their final consumers, securing their loyalty no matter how physically distant they were and diverse in culture.

The Great Fair had taken a decidedly different route: to offer a gigantic display of samples, one that brought suppliers, wholesalers, and retailers together amidst the frenzied buzz of the marketplace; and to encourage knowledge and trust by means of its regular occurrence in a central location. That location was in Germany, true, but as its foundation long predated the foundation of the modern state of Germany, and it acted like a free port from the point of view of commercial regulations, it could rightly insist on its identity as a world institution and as the chief site evoking Europe's thousand-year-old tradition of commerce. The sheer volume of traffic showed the great vitality in this alternative way of moving commodities. At the turn of the 1930s, a half-billion dollars' worth of goods were sold annually at the Leipzig Fair.

The phenomenon of the fair raises several questions, the first being how dissimilar the Leipzig market was to American marketing. More generally, we want to turn back to a question at the heart of this book: How did American salesmanship take stock of European commerce, and in particular of this, the most venerable of all of forms of merchandising? The heart of the answer lies in the development of another of the great social inventions of American consumer culture, brand recognition. Though this was not a specifically American invention at all, by the early 1920s American consumer culture was becoming known in Europe for several score of high-profile consumer goods, whose commonality lay in the way they were marketed. It is a paradox of the commercial confrontation between America and Europe that the victory of brand-name marketing bypassed the Great Fair and, in the process, contributed to rendering it obsolescent.

The Fair in the Light of the Morning

In the early twentieth century, lore about the fair's seven-hundred-year-old history reinforced a commercial ethic that still sought trust in the longevity of contacts and the solidarity of face-to-face contacts. Although it is difficult to distinguish fact from legend, the Leipzig fair did indeed have ancient roots, going back to the mid-eleventh century, when merchants started to congregate periodically on the grassy low-lying plain just outside Urbs Libzi, a fortified center of a few hundred inhabitants at the confluence of the Pleisse, Weisse Elster, and Parthe Rivers. In 1165 the margrave of Meissen, Otto the Rich, granted the townsmen a charter establishing their monopoly over the traffic occurring just outside the city walls; and as a further mark of favor he banned any other transactions in the vicinity while the fair was in progress. A century later, Dietrich I, margrave of Leipzig, gave his solemn word, written on parchment and sealed with his ring, that traders could pass through western Saxony on fair days without fear for their lives, limbs, and property. This promise would hold even if he should be at war with the traders' rulers, which in this bitterly contested region was often the case. Under the Holy Roman Empire, as commerce flourished where the Via Regia crossed the Via Imperii and the wealth from the silver mines of the Arch Mountains was exchanged for the rich wares from the long-distance trade routes stretching from the Atlantic to the Baltic, the fair became a regular event, with both Kaiser Maximilian I in 1497 and Pope Leo X in 1511 reaffirming the town's privileges. By the seventeenth century Leipzig had become one of the great hubs of old-regime commerce, a full-fledged commodity or merchandise fair. On fair days, merchants arrived from all over, hauling their goods to the display areas, where they stashed them in makeshift tents, pavilions, and depots until their sale had been negotiated and the goods had been consigned to their purchasers, who paid on the spot and arranged for their transport. All said, the Great Fair at Leipzig was the most precious of Europe's "wheels of commerce" by means of which preindustrial capitalism circulated far and wide a remarkable abundance of goods.[2]

In the second half of the nineteenth century, in the face of trends toward free trade that reduced the need for a specially protected, toll-free space, and with more efficient rail and boat transport, which made it possible for goods to be shipped directly from factories to outlets, the fair's management, a private corporation, undertook to transform the old fair for commodities into a fair for samples. The year this transformation became official, 1895, was a propitious moment. German industrial hegemony was reaching its apogee, and the "sea" of Saxony surrounding the "inland port" of Leipzig had become the continental heartland of consumer-oriented manufacture, as well as Europe's leading producer of machinery. Since workmanship was the major selling point for both kinds of goods, and since it could not be rendered simply by a picture or a description, buyers came to inspect their quality, as well as to size up the competition and to learn of coming innovations. The moldering warehouses that had once stored piles of merchant stocks were transformed into attractive display areas where dealers checked specifications, negotiated prices, and made out orders to be executed at the contracted time, the merchandise to be dispatched from seller to buyer without passing through the locality of the fair.

Thus reborn, the fair thrived, especially during wartime as the Entente's sea blockade cut off Germany and buyers and dealers converged from as far west as the Rhineland and Westphalia and from Austria-Hungary and Turkey.[3] Goods previously not admitted were brought for display such as foodstuffs, textiles, raw materials, and ersatz products, chiefly in the domain of scarce food and textiles. As peace returned and the economy picked up in the mid-1920s, the fair management added new trading palaces in the downtown area, then put up seventeen massive halls to house the Great Engineering and Technical Fair, ten minutes by tram from the city center, the last stop before the pharaonic Monument to the Battle of the Nations. By 1930 the forty-eight buildings dedicated wholly to fair activities embraced a total exhibition space of more than a million square feet.

Honored as the "spiritual mother" of all the sample fairs springing up across the continent, Leipzig's only rival was the "Queen of the West," the Great Fair of Lyons, relaunched on March 1, 1916, by Edouard Herriot, the mayor-potentate of France's second-largest city, to reinforce the Entente's blockade of their enemy and to strengthen the "economic offensive" by redirecting business to their own venue.[4] The rebirth of Lyons and the revival of sample fairs as prominent fixtures of European merchandising recalled the conditions under which the medieval fairs had first flourished, namely to ensure safe passage and free zones, offsetting the vexatious tolls, piracy, and other perils to which long-distance commerce was prey. In the 1920s, in recognition that world trade had not returned to its mid-nineteenth-century openness, Europe's fairs flourished as "a natural reaction of private interests against the narrow rigorism of official tariff policies."[5] Thereby business enterprises, especially relatively small craft manufacturers, with sponsorship from state and city governments, connected local trade enclaves to international traffic by facilitating travel discounts, visa arrangements, export licenses, and currency exchanges. "When economic life moved ahead," Fernand Braudel observes, "fairs were like old clocks that would never catch up; but if it was sluggish, they came into their own."[6]

Still, the Great Leipzig Fair was more a novel mechanism than an antiquated time piece. New exhibits kept pace with product innovation, new spaces opening up in turn for the sports equipment, foodstuffs, office appliances, photographic equipment, motion picture machinery, and the packaging and advertising arts. As German export trade recovered in the second half of 1920s, the number of foreign buyers and exhibitors rose sharply, so that at fair time Leipzig looked like the center of global commerce. Czechoslovakia and Austria, the two nations depending most on trade with Germany, built permanent fair houses of their own, while Italy, France, Great Britain, South Africa, and Chile regularly sponsored their own stands. British dealers also established an Association of British Exhibitors entirely dedicated to managing their empire's interests at the fair. By the early 1930s the Soviets too, desperate for trade opportunities abroad, made their pavilion a showcase of socialist production, the stands piled high with bear furs and other pelts drawing some of the biggest crowds much as had been true under the czars. Japan's exhibition stand, once mainly known for its displays of mechanical toys, exquisitely painted celluloid dolls with blinking eyes, and precious Kyoto porcelain, by the 1930s was showing bicycles at a mere twelve Reich Marks apiece and automobile tires at eight, prices that no Western economy could possibly beat.[7] Significantly, the years that saw sample fairs boom in Europe saw no such development in the United States. For every twenty European fairs of any magnitude, there was only one in the United States. And none were true sample fairs, with practically every sort of merchandise. Rather they were trade shows, specialized, say, in shoes, livestock, or farm machinery, though all on a grand scale, given the giant output of

*Leipzig: Central Fair Palace on Main Market Square, circa
1930.* By permission of the Stadtarchiv Leipzig.

leading sectors of agriculture and manufacturing and the intensity and
breadth of competition.[8] The only American event comparable in fame to
Leipzig was the Iowa State Fair. But what a different occasion it was,
with its farm-belt arts and crafts, homey 4-H club competitions, rodeo
roundups, and endless wooden enclosures crowded with the sleekest,
most nutrition-stuffed animals anywhere.[9] The distance from Des Moines

to Leipzig was as wide as the plains and seas separating Duluth's Babbitts from the bourgeois Rotarians of Dresden.

At the high point of the boom in 1929, relatively few Americans attended the Leipzig Fair; maybe 2,100 registered, compared with 35,000 or so other foreigners. In 1931 only fifty American firms had displays of some sort, a skimpy figure considering that the number of firms then operating in Germany alone was thirty times that.[10] What's more, the U.S. government had no official presence, much less a permanent stand. The only time officialdom showed up in force was in 1925, when the U.S. Department of Agriculture sponsored a pavilion to exhibit American farm produce and foodstuffs. If commercial attachés came from Berlin, only an hour from Leipzig, they came on their own initiative, having caught on that the fair offered the best occasion to size up German commerce and perhaps engage in some industrial espionage. Back at the home office of the Bureau of Foreign and Domestic Commerce, in Washington, D.C., there was an entire room specialized in analyzing foreign inventions, and its staff especially welcomed information on German inventions, best if accompanied by a drawing. If it looked useful, they passed it along to American firms, which might commercialize it or at least reassure themselves that their own technologies would hold up to the competition.

To the degree that Americans were present, it was most often as buyers, often sons of emigrants and fluent in German, come to seek out novelties for department stores and chains. In that respect the commerce recalled the prewar years, when Europe was such an important source of craft-made consumer goods. The articles contracted for delivery would be shipped through Hamburg or Bremen, the European terminus of the United States Lines fleet. In their bizarre variety, they made the walrus's tale of shoes and ships and sealing wax in *Alice in Wonderland* seem monotonous—holds filled with granite stones, copper and brass household and plumbing fixtures, cutlery, pelican-shaped sewing scissors, draperies, statuary, hosiery, underwear, silk handkerchiefs and scarves, buckles, gloves, hats, jewelry, multicolored glass and lead Christmas ornaments from Lauscha, polychrome embossed postcards, and crates of singing canaries from the Harz Mountains, ordered by the thousands for sale in Woolworth's, Kresge's, and other five-and-dimes. The latter were accompanied by trained attendants who cared for their delicate cargo and kept strict inventory of their stock by returning to the senders the heads of those that perished during the Atlantic passage.[11]

From the point of view of American sellers, the Great Fair was a more

The power behind rising hegemony: unloading Chevrolets in Antwerp, 1930. By permission of the J. Walter Thompson Company.

problematic arena. It had never been set up to handle what still formed the bulk of American exports to Europe, namely staple goods. Though the United States had ceased to be an economic annex of Europe during the Great War, its quasi-colonial relationship lingered on in the crude and semimanufactured goods that still made up the largest part of its exports. Down to the 1930s, at least 40 percent of U.S. exports still consisted of farm products, about 90 percent of which were shipped to Europe.[12] Trade in raw cotton, wheat, and tobacco, pork products and hides, copper, petroleum, and lumber continued to be carried out on the basis of samples. Having cleared customs at dockside, the goods were warehoused before being shipped to local processors or prepared for transshipment by barge or rail to other countries. Their ultimate destination, much less the purpose that led to their purchase, was basically irrelevant to their American sellers. Consequently, they could see no point in paying for anything more than minimal representation abroad. In turn, by the time staples were processed, manufactured, and distributed, European consumers would have had little inkling of their U.S. origin. Cheap American wheat and hogs had huge effects on local agricultural politics by driving down prices. But around the table, bread was bread whether the flour was made from grain from the Russian steppes, East Elban flatlands, or American prairies.

Yet by 1930 U.S. goods had begun to emerge from anonymity as the proportion of finished manufactures and packaged or canned foodstuffs rose rapidly with respect to crude materials and semi- and unfinished goods. By 1930 the amount of commodities ready to be sold to their ultimate consumers in the form in which they arrived had quadrupled in value. As a result selling became a much more complicated transaction. All the problems that the American producer engaged with when he tried to get consumers at home to buy, namely the stimulation of wants, the grasp of national psychology, the spread of mass purchasing power, and the rendering of service after sales, now had to be addressed to sell on the European market.[13] To deal with these issues, the American businessman or his trusted delegate needed to be on the spot. That was why more and more Americans showed up at the Leipzig fair.

Even so, American manufactures did not necessarily show to best advantage at the fair, not even when they were displayed right alongside European models, even when by various criteria they would have been regarded as technically superior, as was true for office equipment, especially typewriters. By 1930 the United States supplied 80 percent of world

*The power behind declining hegemony: the Leipzig railroad
station, Europe's largest, circa 1930.* Courtesy of the Thomas J.
Watson Business and Economics Library, Columbia University.

demand for the machines, whereas Germany, its main competitor, sold
less than 20 percent. Sure enough, all the leading U.S. firms were represented at the fair: Underwood-Elliot-Fisher, Remington-Rand, Royal,
and L. C. Smith and Corona. But they were eclipsed by the sheer number
of machines offered by European companies, especially by the Germans.
At least twenty German companies sent samples.[14] From the displays
alone, dealers, much less the public, would not have known that all the
German firms that manufactured typewriters also produced other equipment—bicycles, sewing machines, precision instruments, even firearms.
As a result of this diversification they could not invest as much in research, design, and marketing as the American firms did, and their line of
models was more limited.

Dealers who checked the specifications of the latest Remington and
Underwood models could verify that the machines were practically noise-
less and that the keyboard responded to the lightest pressure of the finger.
But what information would lead them to make a value of "noiseless-
ness" and "light touch," or weigh those qualities against the high costs
when they could count on the heavy discounts offered by the German
dealers? Though their workmanship was clearly solid, if not superior, not

even close physical inspection of the machine could effectively convey the satisfaction derived from their proper operation and care, the ample guarantees on repairs and parts, indeed, the whole vision of modern rational office culture, which—as advertising spreads in contemporary magazines detailed with so much example and illustration—would be satisfied not merely by purchasing the single Underwood or Smith-Corona typewriter, but by investing in the whole battery of American-style office equipment, from the adding machines supplied by Ellis, Dalton and Comptometer, and the Mimeograph and Multigraph copiers, to the Kardex, Hollerith, and IBM information and filing systems. The hard sell favored in the United States typically pushed a whole package of inducements to convince clients not just that the products were novel, but that they were well worth their premium price.

A similar story could be told for writing instruments. The 1920s opened a golden age for fountain pens, and many of the dealers and visitors crowded into the exhibition room simply to admire them. Rapid innovations in synthetic materials, ink storage and loading devices, designs, and colors showed visibly in the samples displayed by the leading U.S. firms, namely Parker, Schaeffer, Wahl Eversharp, and Waterman, which, long rivals on the American market, had moved their fierce struggle for market shares into Europe before World War I. During the 1920s this competition led them to invest millions more dollars in research and development, as well as marketing. The celluloid the Schaeffer Company developed from plant fibers, though still a costly process, permitted the intricate patterns and bright primary colors characteristic of art deco motifs. Latching on to the process, the Parker Company launched its Duofold in Lacquer Red, Mandarin Yellow, and Lapis Lazuli Blue. Its top of the line, the Duofold de Luxe, also manufactured in Silvery Pearl and Black, promoted for its automatic pumping mechanism, was twice as thick as any other pen on display, its plumpness signaling the unique patented double-barrel ink storage, which with just one filling could write 6,000 words. When the company launched it in Europe in 1926 with the costliest advertising campaign ever mounted for a writing instrument, it shook up the sector from top to bottom.[15]

Even so, the dozen or so American products couldn't stand a chance against the sheer numbers of European- and especially German-made instruments. Scores of the pens on display were the little-known but serviceable local brands in the drab black color of instruments fashioned out of hard rubber vulcanite or ebonite that was commonly used before the shinier but far more costly celluloid came into use. The real competition came from the Pelikan Company, the venerable Hanover artists' materials firm founded in the 1830s. It had broken into the high-end market for pens only in 1929 with the Pelikan 100, the model with the heart-shaped breather hole in the nib. But it had also done very well with the efficient-looking, economically priced Rappen, a more obvious choice for the traveling salesman facing hard times. The other crowd pleaser was the stand displaying the Montblanc line. Its producer, Simplo of Berlin, advertised itself as being the first European company to free itself from relying on gold nibs imported from the United States. Its cachet was enhanced by its brand mark, the fetching white star on the pen cap. One didn't have to be a connoisseur to recognize the fabulous Meisterstück. When Montblanc first brought it onto the market in 1924, its lustrous carmine color, its fabulous price of over twenty Reichsmarks, and its life-time guarantee put it at the very top of the social pecking order of writing instruments. To draw the Meisterstück from one's inside jacket pocket or pen case was tantamount to announcing: "Behold, I am a truly modern gentleman." The sleek if self-effacing advertising by the Bauhaus-trained Grete Gross suited it just perfectly. Gre-gro, as this chic Berliner was known in avant-garde graphic design circles, the head of Simplo's advertising department, produced the modernist display signs for the exposition. It was she who had devised the giant Montblanc banner rigged on the fuselage of the small plane that looped lazily over the fairgrounds at midday.[16]

What fairgoers were not seeing among the displays was exactly what U.S. manufacturing was becoming fabled for, namely high-profile branded products. These were the consumer durables, the convenience items, the comfort goods—the utility car, household appliances, perfumed toiletries, and packaged foodstuffs—that critics cited when they deplored the American "invasion" and that European marketing agents cited as of exemplary interest when they scrutinized U.S. techniques of salesmanship. These were the goods that were spectacularly magnified on outsize advertising billboards in the city centers. They gleamed in the automobile showrooms and home appliance dealerships on the Champs-Elysées, the Kurfürstendamm, and Piccadilly Circus. They were piled up under brilliantly colored display cards on the pharmacist's counter and in shop window displays. They flashed across the screen in Hollywood movies. They stood out in half- or full-page ads in magazines and the mass press. They enthralled bourgeois customers and were excoriated by cultural critics. For the most part, these wares were the so-called first movers in their sector.

These articles arrived on the market intended to establish new standards for product attributes and consumer satisfaction in order to create the large demand that was required to offset the high costs of their promotion. General Motors' Frigidaire was one preeminent example: it made a value of food being fresh and cold and guaranteed that the food would stay so. Gillette was another: its ads for its safety razors deplored beards and stubble as unhygienic, damaging to one's appearance—and it guaranteed a smooth shave. Kellogg's Corn Flakes set the standard for a breakfast food: it prescribed wholesome instant morning meals for vigorous health, and promised to deliver it to anybody who purchased the crackly, shredded-up maize paste packaged for freshness in the black-lettered white, green, and red boxes. Coca-Cola opened the way for carbonated sugared beverages: it invented thirst at the same time as it promised to quench it. All of these goods, not just because they were new, but because they established new categories of values for objects, fitted uneasily into the taxonomy of goods established under the auspices of the bourgeois merchandise fair.

Foodstuffs, America's forte, likewise fell between the taxonomic cracks. The profusion of canned goods, including Gloria Milk, Campbell's soups, and Dole sliced syruped peaches, may have been comparable to local brands, all less widely known. Not so the pineapple canned by Libby, Del Monte creamed corn, French-cut beans, and beets; or the luminously printed carton packages of Sun Maid prunes and raisins from the cornucopia of California's central valleys; or Royal Baking Powder, the first industrially produced packaged leavening powder for homemade breads and cakes; or the Camels, Chesterfields, or Lucky Strikes made from American-grown blond tobacco; or Wrigley's chewing gum, originating in the chicle milk extracted from the Yucatán's sapodilla trees. The banana too was a novelty: officially introduced at the 1876 Philadelphia Centennial Exhibition, where each banana was sold wrapped in foil for ten cents, it had begun to be commercialized on a mass scale in Europe only after World War I. By 1926 the thirty-four refrigerated steamships belonging to Elder and Fyffes, United Fruit Company's European agent, were delivering 5 million bunches to England and Germany alone.[17] Marketed as Blue Label from 1929, before being renamed Chiquita in the 1940s, it was the first fruit to be brand-named in Europe, and it was far more widely distributed than any domestic pro-

duce. The guarantee of its quality was the trademarked paper band. According to the sales agreement, the retailer was obliged to remove it as
soon as the yellow peel began to mottle and the flesh bruised and turned
mushy. By so doing he sealed the foreign, faraway suppliers' arduously
pursued, intense, costly relationship with the local consumer. Not unexpectedly, the brand-named banana had no place at the fair.

Famously at the outset of *Das Kapital*, Marx wrote: "A commodity
appears, at first sight, a very trivial thing, and easily understood." The
rest of the volume was dedicated to showing the impossibility of understanding a thing in itself, disembedded from its social context. The commodity form conceals the sweat and skill of the workers who made it and
whose labor the capitalist expropriates; presented for sale, it belies its un-
adorned use-value, as a thing to nourish, sit down upon, or write at; it re-
fuses to divulge its exchange value, meaning its value as determined by
qualities extrinsic to it, such as its scarcity, its usefulness as compared to
other goods, and its status value. Commodities play yet another trick on
the collective imagination: they appear to go to market under their own
power and to make exchanges on their own account. That is where, as
Marx said, "their guardians, who are also their owners," come into view,
as "they place themselves in relation to one another."[18]

If we step away from the crowded precincts of the Leipzig Fair and
think of markets "not as a place, but as masses of people spread over
space," the radically new character of brand-based marketing becomes
clear.[19] Old World merchandising emphasized the character of the product, highlighting qualities that could be said to be intrinsic to it and
closely related to the environment in which it was produced. The New
World's marketing emphasized the product's personality, highlighting
outward charms that compensated the consumer for not knowing its
place of origin or its intrinsic qualities. Goods made in small batches,
craft wares, and customized products showed to best effect at Leipzig.
They were familiar and thrived in one another's company. It is true they
competed after a fashion. But by being grouped all together, the specifications particular to each were enhanced, at least to the expert eye of the
dealer. Though similar in kind, each was customized for a particular clientele. Each had its little niche. None could be substituted for another.
And because they offered themselves as unique, they commanded high
prices. Given that the articles were turned out in small batches and on order, their manufacturers and middlemen needed high markups to make
sufficient profit.

*Goods that travel alone: Palmolive Shaving Cream gathers
a crowd.* Transatlantic Trade, *September 1931.* Courtesy of the
New York Public Library.

By contrast, the mass-manufactured brand-name good thrived on traveling solo. Or, better, it moved about in the company of a very costly retinue of salesmen, marketing experts, and advertisers. Outdoor signs, advertising displays, and dealers brashly presented it as unique when in fact
it was exactly like the tens of thousands of other standardized articles
moving off the same assembly-line conveyors. It commanded high prices
not because it was scarce, but because it set itself as the standard of novelty and usefulness that other products had to catch up to.

Whereas craft goods in a local market had an air of familiarity and
needed no added words to sell them, the mass good needed the verbiage
of high-pressure salesmanship to instruct about its usefulness and desir-
ability. Lacking the aura of the original artifact, Walter Benjamin would
have said, the mass-manufactured good was devoid of the charm of au-
thorship, artistic genius, or craft skill.[20] In turn, lacking authenticity, it
was imbued with charisma, in the very sense that Max Weber used the
term to describe a quasi-religious style of leadership bursting out of the
confines of bureaucratic systems. Accordingly, the brand-name object

Goods that travel together: dolls being individually handled by exhibitors, Leipzig Fair, 1936. Courtesy of the Thomas J. Watson Business and Economics Library, Columbia University.

stood apart from the crowds of homey crafts and bourgeois bibelots; it presented itself as an abrupt break with established norms and with the institutions that sanctioned them; its legitimacy came from being the object of the worshipful attentions of the entourage of salesmanship; its authority derived from its self-avowed capacity to minister to the needs of its devotees.[21] In the eyes of the purchaser the standardized mass good could thereby acquire as distinctive an appearance of individuality and familiarity as the customized crafted object.

This difference showed in the self-presentation of the two contenders. The Leipzig Fair, queen of the marketplace, and U.S. salesmanship, the genie of modern marketing, represented their role in buying and selling. The fair was a miracle of compactness, its method of merchandising "the maximum business with the minimum expense, in the minimum of time, over the minimum of space."[22] The Trade Fair Office advertised itself not just as the hub of European commercial traffic, but as the locus of a worldwide economic exchange. It offered whatever was necessary to cultivate face-to-face relations; its lifeblood was whatever stimulated trade; it promised every convenience, comfort, and protection for its customers, from travel discounts, import-export permits, and bookings for the the-

They spent $288,072 in EUROPE *in one month*

and were not even there!

How would you like to buy $288,072 worth of European advertising in one month *as easily as this?*

The client sent instructions in two cables and one letter. Our European offices handled the campaign.

It appeared in 677 publications — in 16 languages — in 21 countries of Europe. Think what a labyrinth of detail that would mean! Yet the campaign went through to flawless completion. *And not an executive of the client's company left his American headquarters.*

It takes *experience* to do such a job as that. Erwin, Wasey & Company has the oldest experience of any American advertising agency on the European continent.

It takes *size* as well.

This Company maintains eleven thoroughly qualified and competent organizations of its own in eleven European countries.

We believe there is something here of vital interest to American manufacturers — and to their American advertising agents. For both, we provide a sure and easy means of successful advertising in foreign markets — with the fullest economy of your executive time.

If you come to Berlin for the I. A. A. convention, come to our Berlin office, where you can talk with men who look upon European advertising problems with the viewpoint of two continents...Thus only can you get a true conception of the European situation in American terms. You will be welcome.

11 foreign offices in 11 foreign countries with 11 years' experience.

ERWIN, WASEY and COMPANY, *Ltd.*

Offices:
CHICAGO
NEW YORK
LONDON
BERLIN
PARIS
STOCKHOLM
BRUSSELS
ROTTERDAM
HELSINGFORS
MILAN
COPENHAGEN
ZURICH
BARCELONA

*American representative of European offices Graybar Building New York City

Marketing big brands: one impersonal touch of the telegraph button to advertise goods. Printers' Ink, *July 25, 1929.*
Courtesy of the Thomas J. Watson Business and Economics Library,
Columbia University.

ater and other entertainment, to moneychanging, general information on fair business, and, finally, arrangements for travel home. The fair presented itself as the pure social relationship of the market, making no reference to the sovereign authority that licensed it, which was the German state.

In contrast, American salesmanship is well represented in U.S. Commerce Department maps showing the European "sales territories" as a crisscross of lines in search of customers spread over space.[23] The hubs were scattered, selected for their concentrations of population, the links between them measured by hours of travel, indifferent to geographic par-

Promoting the Fair: A personal invitation to advertisers.
Gebrauchsgraphik, *September 1927.* Courtesy of the
New York Public Library.

ticulars such as water, mountains, or national frontiers. So Bari was a
straight line to Durrës, eight and a half hours across the Adriatic by boat.
A properly ambitious dealer could add to his route Constanţa on the
Black Sea, only five hours by train from Bucharest; Cernăuti, another Romanian backwater, twelve and a half hours away; and Chişinău, yet another—via Iaşi—fully thirteen. In 1930 the lines of traffic pushed right up
to the borders of the Soviet Union, beyond which only the most intrepid
and well-introduced capitalist passed.

Behind the presentation of the fair as the hub of all traffic was the railroad, the tracks of the German Empire's prodigious system converging in
Leipzig, which, with the inauguration of the city's Central Station in
1923, became the largest railroad terminus in Europe. Behind the American map, by contrast, were the speed of the telegraph and telephone, the
instantaneity of radio transmission, and the capacity to reproduce identical advertising copy using rotogravure press equipment to appear simultaneously in a score of different languages. Behind the Leipzig sample
fair there were the productive power of the region of Europe richest in
small and medium firms and village handicrafts and the give-and-take of

Decentering the marketplace: the U.S. Department of Commerce maps new sales terrain, 1933. Courtesy of the Thomas J. Watson Business and Economics Library, Columbia University.

wholesalers and retailers. Behind U.S. mass merchandising there were the huge economies of scale and scope of American mass-production industries, reinforced by the ambition of U.S. advertising agencies to position themselves as masters of the global market. Erwin, Wasey and Company's muscular advertisement for itself touted the power of modern telecommunications indispensable to the marketing revolution. In the eleven years since the Armistice, when the New York agency had established its first overseas offices in London, it had implanted eleven foreign offices in eleven countries. Now, riding the economic boom of the late 1920s, the firm could boast of being able to launch an advertising campaign covering the whole continent from its offices in the Graybar Building on Lexington Avenue. Paying no heed to the labyrinth of detail, without being physically anywhere in the vicinity, the modern advertising agency could

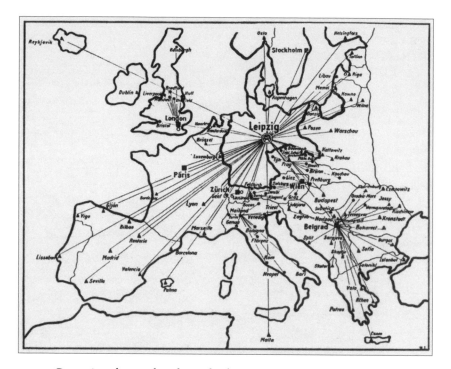

*Centering the marketplace: the fair management points the way
to Leipzig, 1933.* Courtesy of the Thomas J. Watson Business and
Economics Library, Columbia University.

place copy in 677 publications, composed in sixteen languages, to appear
in twenty-one European countries. The effect was like alchemy. One
press of the button produced dollars out of thin air, $288,072 worth of
advertising: "And not an executive of the client's company left his American headquarters."[24]

Minute in quantity relative to the total number of goods in circulation—no more than a few dozen compared to countless tens of thousands of locally known trademarked or unmarked goods circulating in
European countries during the interwar years—the high-profile branded
goods of America's marketing system loomed disproportionately large in
the imagination. Moving promiscuously through space rather than dis-
cretely tied to place, transnational instead of local, they established a new
standard for what it meant for goods to go to market. Whereas the fair's
abundance was condensed into a single spot in the midst of a desert of
scarcity, mass merchandising marked the whole territory with signs of
corporate manufacturers' huge prolificity.[25] Products once regarded as

unique because they were available only seasonally or in particular locations or specific outlets now became available year-round, easier to handle, more standardized, and, above all, more visible. Whether they in fact reached a mass audience, which was not likely initially, given their high cost, they gave the appearance of accessibility. And because trademarks and advertising made them so visible, people could observe their trajectories—where they were sold and bought, and who purchased them, one's own sort or not.

Building Brand Recognition

If American jobbers relaxing at the Café Felsche or the Bauer or another of the beerhouses around Leipzig's Market Square had been asked why Americans were taking the lead in branded consumer goods, they might have shrugged and answered, "Yankee ingenuity." It was the superior quality of the goods and their sheer usefulness that made them move. The English had believed the same of themselves in the early nineteenth century, the Germans likewise, well into the twentieth. More accurately, American manufacturing was commercializing a large variety of standardized consumer goods after 1900, generating hundreds of thousands of patents around basic innovations.[26] For example, the vacuum tube, which was indispensable to control devices such as elevator landings, train switches, and continuous-process production, was refitted for the radio, loudspeakers, the electric phonograph, picture telegraphy, and television. The hot electric coil, first invented in 1892, was then applied to every variety of clothes iron, curling machines, hair-waving apparatus, heaters, fireless cookstoves, kettles, and warming pads. Chemical inventions, say, in the field of cellulose nitrates, produced rayon, quick-drying colorful varnishes and plastics, as well as the materials used in camera film, phonograph records, fountain pens, eyeglass frames, later the ballpoint pen, and after that the many throwaways.

The large scale of operation of consumer-oriented industries offers one reason for the range of new products coming on the market. By 1910 it was economic to apply mass-production techniques to cigarettes, matches, cereals, soap, and a wide variety of canned goods. It was also profitable for purposes of keeping continuous-process systems at work and maintaining control over supplies of raw material to develop complementary products. For example, if the main product was petroleum, perhaps some use could be found for the gummy paraffinlike residue that built up on oil pumps. That was the calculation made by Robert Augustus Chesebrough, a rig owner in eastern Pennsylvania, when he patented Vaseline petroleum jelly in 1878. Thereafter marketing invented a range of uses for this lubricant, from smoothing skin and curing small wounds to polishing furniture and cleaning shoes. For a large firm producing soap, whose basic ingredient was cottonseed oil, it was profitable to control the whole supply. To use the excess, Procter & Gamble's researchers and designers invented Crisco, an utterly smooth, pure white fat, substitutable in cooking for lard and olive oil. As an automotive producer, General Motors specialized in engine-building, metalworking, and assembling parts into useful and complex products; like the automobile, the refrigerator required an electrical system and a compressor for the cooling system. That was the logic behind mass producing the Model A—not the car, but the first Frigidaire. The Armour Food Company, Swift Foods, and other firms engaged in meat processing used the whole hog: hams, bacon, and hocks for human food; bristles for brushes; fats for lard, soaps, and every kind of emollient; hides for shoes and gloves; hooves for glue; innards for animal feed; "everything," it was said, "but the oink."[27]

To amortize the costs linked to developing new products, big firms invested heavily in marketing. Marketing in turn became a burgeoning industry in its own right. Developed at first as professionally managed sales departments, it split off into specialized offshoots such as advertising firms, opinion research outfits, and marketing agencies. All of these had powerful interests in promoting themselves as indispensable to placing goods with the final consumer. In turn this specialized apparatus of salesmanship intensified the commercialization of new inventions by providing feedback from consumers. It didn't take science, superadvanced technology, an especially educated managerial force, or some peculiar native genius to collect information on new needs and to experiment to develop new products that could potentially serve them. Within ever more specialized industries, competition for markets conceived with the mass consumer as target mightily concentrated the collective entrepreneurial mind to turn out more and more inventions of a second order of ingenuity. These were the hallmarks of the United States' fabulous consumer market.[28]

Naturally, new goods were inconceivable—and would not have been salable no matter how much they were promoted—without new social trends, in particular new eating habits, standards of household equipment, physical norms, and leisure use. Generally, many of the new U.S. inventions were labor-saving, whereas in Europe they were resource-saving; the former were applied to households, the latter to manufacture. Increased household expenditure was entirely legitimate in a society that put a high premium on women's labor (servants being in short supply), houses were often large, home ownership was widespread, and notions of women's rights—at the very least their right to perform their housekeeping duties to the best of their ability—were pervasive. Inventions around food processing were also related to reducing work: the rapid and vast innovations in canning, freezing, and packaging, all capitalizing on the United States' greatest resource, agriculture, joined with various ideologies about uplift, hygiene, and health as well as real needs for easily prepared food in view of the long hours of work, mobile immigrant populations, and makeshift urban housing. Then there were the inventions targeted toward beauty and physical well-being, variously called personal products or toiletries; such were shaving equipment, makeup, creams, perfumes, and tooth-care items, including brushes, pastes, and mouthwashes. Rapid commercialization exploited their use not just for hygiene and saving labor but also for democratizing bodies by making them look more alike. Mass-marketed hygienic articles and cosmetics, like mass-produced clothing, exploited the possibilities of self-transformation; they encouraged shared notions of cleanliness and the making-up, making-over mentality of a fluid society. Above all, inventions targeted the communication needs of a mobile society: automobile transport was a huge generator of inventions; likewise entertainment, as attested by the bountiful innovations in radio, recording, film equipment, and photography.[29]

Whether products were altogether new or substitutes for old, branding made them appear utterly novel. In principle, to brand a product is nothing more than to imprint it with the identity of the producer, and brands in one form or another had existed since antiquity. Branding was common everywhere there was manufacturing, and by the turn of the twentieth century all leading countries had legislation protecting brand names from infringement. European enterprises produced novel goods with trademarks, and there were big brands associated with the baker's dozen of continental multinationals with highly visible names, signally Unilever; the Dutch electronics firm Philips; the Swiss food corporation Nestlé; the Swedish home appliances corporation Electrolux; the brands of German AEG Works for lightbulbs, irons, and toasters; and the

Czechoslovak firm Bata's shoes. And all countries had a handful of well-known national brands. In Germany, for example, most urban bourgeois families would have recognized Kaffee Hag, Persil wash soap, and Lingner's Odol. However, in keeping with the smaller scale of European firms, the more restricted purchasing power of the multitude of people, and the conventional habits of expenditure of the bourgeoisie, the most familiar transnational brands were sweets like Sarotti, Van Houten chocolates, and Horlick's malt powder; taste intensifiers such as Bovril, Maggi, or Liebig broth cubes; and liquors, notably Cointreau, Martell, Prunier, Pernod, Campari, and Martini vermouths. These were goods that even the most provincial and down-at-heels bourgeois families would contemplate buying, at the very least to mark festive occasions.[30]

However, the United States' expanding, mobile market made brand marketing central to merchandising. Promoting the brand was not just a defensive weapon to induce retailers to stock the item, but an offensive weapon to establish tight control over market shares, pricing, and the meaning of new goods. If the qualities of a particular commodity could be condensed into a single name or emblem so that people would buy the good because they recognized it, the company could establish what was in effect a monopoly and thereby prevent price alone from being the chief reason for buying its product. If it had to compete with other firms with similar kinds of products, it could do so not by slicing away at already minute price margins, but by promoting the brand name. Typically, promoters of new product categories also had to sell the category itself. If they succeeded, the payoffs were huge. And because new brands stood for both a cluster of particular attributes and the general qualities of a whole class of items, they could appeal across established social-status hierarchies to redefine the line between luxury and necessity, orienting customers' attention to qualities they hadn't contemplated before, at least not in so many terms, such as hygiene, cleanliness, convenience, appearance, texture, disposability, odor, instantaneity, shininess, and speed.[31] It is significant how many of the American brands turned into generics in Europe. Thus a sewing machine was a Singer, a vacuum cleaner a Hoover, Ford stood for cars, the self-shaving razor with disposable blades was by antonomasia a Gillette, Kodak was the universal name for cameras (and Kodakism for the mania for photography), Frigidaire the archetype for cold storage, Xerox the equivalent of photocopying, and McDonald's the fountainhead of fast food.

And if the United States was not itself the terrain of the invention, often an item became a generic after its patent was picked up and marketed by American-based firms. It was the English rubber manufacturer Frederick Walton who in 1863 first patented linoleum, the floor material made from oxidized linseed oil mixed with pulverized wood and coloring matter. However, the marketing strategies of the American plants built in 1872 widely popularized it. A German company first patented Thermos, though after 1918 the American Thermos Bottle Company made it a household name. By the 1920s the United States far surpassed Europe when it came to the so-called dilution of brand names. Thereby first movers became generic names for products: the pianola, the gramophone, the dictaphone, and vinyl were just a few. American marketers also surpassed Europeans in establishing new categories—instant coffee, breakfast cereals, blue jeans, leisure clothes, sanitary products, pet food. In sum, first movers both defined the needs and provided for their satisfaction; they set the terms of the equation and they stood to profit from the solution, hugely and often for decades continuing down to the present.

Over time brand names acquired a remarkable asset, namely goodwill. This concept treated property as a person "with a standing in public opinion which it receives from constant or habitual customers, on account of its local position, or common celebrity, or reputation."[32] Legally, goodwill signified the power that customers came to exercise in response to this property. In theory, they could choose other wares of their own free will. But they had settled on that particular item. In principle, goodwill was intangible. Yet it was also a capital asset and a legal property whose price tag could be calculated separately from sales profits. By the late 1920s goodwill could pump up the value of a company to as much as sixteen times the annual earnings: the American people's passion for Jell-O was bought for $35 million in 1925; the Maxwell House Coffee habit went for $42 million in 1928.[33] Through this remarkable system giant corporations could establish "reputations and relations with consumers as surely as the corner grocer did through personal contact and personality."[34]

Moving into New Sales Territory

The determination of U.S. corporations to establish equally intense relationships with customers in foreign lands fired the decision of leading American consumer-goods manufacturers to move abroad earlier in the product cycle than caution would dictate, when kinks in manufacture and product design were still being worked out and the home market was not near saturation.[35]

Company histories tell adventurous stories of the moment their founders discovered the Old World as sales territory. It was a historic moment for National Cash Register when in 1885 plucky little John Patterson, barely a year after founding his company in Dayton, Ohio, set off to establish European outlets.[36] On August 14, 1914, ten days after the start of the war in Europe, Thomas Pelham, Gillette's general manager, declared his own "war against all previous Sales Records," and in the spring of 1915 he set sail with a cargo of razors and blades to repair the commercial disaster to the firm wrought by the European conflict.[37] For Waterman, the moment came when Frank D. Lewis, nephew of the founder, was sent to represent the company at the Paris Exposition of 1900, where the ultralarge No. 20 pen won the gold medal for excellence; it was a pity that he made the ill-conceived move of selling the distribution and manufacturing rights to L. G. Sloan of London.[38]

Short of digging into company records, it is impossible to know, much less rank, all the calculations that prompted company decisions, first to export, and later to establish manufacturing plants abroad. One sure reason was to outflank rivals at home. Another was to lift sagging profits with new markets. The gold-rush mindset of the 1920s reinforced the consensus that to stake a claim in the European sales area testified to entrepreneurial dynamism. So it was that once one firm made the move, others in the same line of business followed, each slyly eyeing the other and all keenly sizing up the European competition. All told, many went over, though only a few succeeded.[39]

The confidence to move abroad was supported by accumulated profits, as well as signs of the softening of home markets. But the collective idea that American products represented a material civilization that was universally extendable, only more advanced than others, also played a role. One-worldism thrived on the belief, well expressed by the J. Walter Thompson Berlin bureau chief, Clement Watson, that "the habits, customs, traditions and living conditions of people are important to know and understand." But "people are fundamentally alike the world over. Except for a few fanatics, all peoples seek protection, seek betterment of living conditions, seek added comfort, seek greater enjoyment of life."[40] Nobody spoke up against what critics of affluence would decry as consumer waste, more specifically the waste that is engendered when what is considered necessary in a rich society becomes the organizing principle of a more impoverished, or at least differently organized, one. Sinclair Lewis, who deplored America's philistine materialism at home, regarded it as civilizing abroad. Main Street in Zenith, Minnesota, was embodied in the petty-minded physicality of the real estate agent George Babbitt, who furtively disposes of his throwaway razor blades by hiding them on top of the bathroom cabinet. But when Main Street went to Paris in the figure of another son of Zenith, it became a force for good. As the manufacturer of Revelation Automobiles, Sam Dodsworth, dedicates himself to building prefabricated housing to supply the needs of the world's people for shelter, he gives himself the courage to ditch his bored, vacuous wife; thereby he also sets a moral example by besting the pseudo-aristocratic French lounge lizards who have seduced her fickle fantasy.[41]

Going abroad, U.S. manufacturers bet that even if the selling climate at home had not yet evolved, it would do so quickly enough, building on the common needs latent in all humankind and pushed by the heavy promotional effort that was permitted to U.S. firms by virtue of having tested their product in the home market, their superior technologies of merchandising, and their large cash reserves. The decision to move production abroad by setting up branch plants or subsidiary concerns, sometimes by buying out foreign competitors, was obviously a more complicated and costly decision than merely to export. Thomas Pelham himself acknowledged that until 1913, Gillette had followed "the lazy man's route," simply consigning the merchandise to its European distributors and letting them handle local sales.[42] And this continued perforce to be the path pursued by hundreds, if not thousands, of small firms. However, large U.S. companies had been installing European-based subsidiaries as far back as the 1870s. There were numerous reasons to do so: to lower freight costs, to exploit cheaper labor, to obtain the lower tax rates gained by local incorporation, to outwit domestic rivals, to take on European competitors in their home base, and not least to circumvent tariff barriers.[43]

In the 1920s American firms were also determined to defeat European competitors who operated with the advantage of proximity to the market and exploited the fact that trademark protection was generally weak in order to appropriate American innovations and adapt them to local tastes. With a few finishing touches on the original U.S. product, firms that were generally small in size, working with short runs and customizing their products, could put them on the market themselves at an equal or lower price, taking advantage of the fact that labor was cheaper in Europe, they didn't need to pay duties, there were no extra transportation charges, and, above all, that they were on familiar, even personal terms with the circuits of wholesalers and retailer chains that ultimately put the goods in customers' hands. The Germans were regarded as especially worrisome competitors on this score.

Marketing the brand thus became a way to neutralize the Europeans' monopolies over circuits of local knowledge. Given that the normal European customer base was regional rather than national and rarely transnational, if the American firms set their sights on the whole territory as they had in the United States, they could take advantage of the fact that Europe was a sellers' market, as it was in the 1920s, without becoming entrapped in the notoriously perilous quagmires of European retailing. Local production also offered the advantage of circumventing hidden tariff barriers, not just government purchasing policies, say, for military hardware or heavy equipment purchases, which quite logically discriminated against nonnational firms, but also regional and national taste cultures. Being on the ground made it possible to go a step further, namely, to customize products for finicky bourgeois clienteles.[44]

Almost invariably American firms trusted in three big advantages. First of all, they were well supplied with capital. Consequently, they were able to offset initial losses on the accumulated profits from the home market. Second, they were working with a product that had been perfected at high cost in a mass market and that they were convinced presented exceptional advantages in terms of design. Finally, their business was conducted flexibly in one important domain. American entrepreneurs were keenly interested in, on the one hand, inveigling consumers to experiment with new goods and, on the other, to adjusting to their needs, to the best of their corporate capacity and in keeping with the bottom line. Unfamiliarity with the difficulties of a world of multiple jurisdictions and with what was repeatedly decried as "legal and linguistic chaos" made American entrepreneurs often appear stupidly innocent as they made their way. However, ignorance of their own limitations could also prove an advantage by furnishing them with an optimistic inventiveness that enabled them to brave difficulties that a more informed entrepreneurship might not have wished to confront. All else being equal, the myopia of manufacturers, wide-eyed in their search for final consumers and oblivious to the obstacles strewn across their path, could be a blessing in disguise.

That said, U.S. enterprise abroad had a visibly helping hand in the form of the U.S. government. By World War I, no peacetime government was doing more to promote its export economy than the federal bureaucracy in Washington, D.C. Convinced that American exporters were late starters and operating with a handicap with respect to European manufacturers, it emulated what were viewed as European practices, lending strong state support to business abroad. These measures included special tax breaks on corporate income made abroad and the Webb-Pomerene Act of 1919, which exempted cartels engaged in foreign business from U.S. antitrust law. It also afforded just the sort of skeptical, yet informed and often upbeat information that tempted companies to risk marketing consumer goods in unknown places.[45]

No government initiative was more important to exporting American consumer culture than the Bureau of Foreign and Domestic Commerce. Founded in 1912, it came into its own at the outset of Herbert Hoover's tenure as secretary of commerce from 1921 to 1928. He immediately signaled the BFDC's flagship role by appointing Julius Klein, the Harvard-trained economist and historian, as its head. Acting on the belief that the function of government is to chart the channels of foreign trade and keep them open, Klein brought to foreign trade promotion not just his patriotic fervor, but also the expertise developed in the home market "to break down all barriers between the consumers and commodities." Lobbied by Klein, Congress increased its appropriation to the BFDC from $100,000 to $8 million. By the time Hoover was elected president, an office with a staff of 100 had grown into a full-fledged agency of 2,500.[46]

True, other countries, notably Great Britain, with its seasoned Department of Overseas Trade, reported on the state of foreign markets. But no other country turned out reports that "reflect to the same degree, the practical needs of their national distributors or the attitude towards market information of a scientifically-minded man of business"; and no other was so successful at "integrating the official and private standpoints in business questions."[47] They were authored by the foreign commercial consular attachés, who were invariably white Protestant men, educated at Yale, Princeton, or Dartmouth. Well supervised and well disciplined, they proved astute informants about native practices and were eager to exploit them in the interests of American enterprise, and not inclined to tolerate foolish entrepreneurship that would spoil the environment for other firms. During a typical week in 1932, the Berlin commercial attaché met with the sales representative from the Burston Knitting Company of

Rockford, Illinois, who complained that he wasn't getting enough official help to locate a German distributor; he prepared the paperwork to obtain more favorable tariff classifications for the Heinz Company of Pittsburgh's imports of tomato ketchup, tomato chutney, and tomato juice; and he scoured the trade press for the information on markets for toiletry preparations, automotive parts, and American movies requested by the home office.[48]

Like any other good, an American import to Europe was first and foremost a commodity. It had no intrinsic identity. Nationality is an invention in the best of circumstances; for a commodity it is a fiction. A product was American according to the interests of its master. Sometimes companies changed the name for trademarking purposes, often to make it easier to pronounce. Carnation, the canned milk, was linguistically less chameleon than Ford, Coca-Cola, or Kodak, and it was patented in European countries under the name Gloria. Sometimes goods called American, like American Baking Powder, were not made in the United States at all. The genuine article was Royal Baking Powder. The so-called American product was a German facsimile. Other wares were known as American not because advertising called attention to that fact, but because of qualities attributed to the original products. Hence cigarettes packaged in glossy paper and using blond tobacco, finer blends, and, later, filter tips, were generically American even though they were produced in Italy, Turkey, or France. The utilities that advertising slogans made salable in promoting Camels, Chesterfields, or Lucky Strikes—finer filter, finer flavor, king size—were assimilated into local advertising lingos: "fine filter," "long format," "light taste," "full aroma," "at long last an American cigarette."

Laws did not help much to clarify national origin. Few European governments required that a good be stamped with the mark of the country of origin, and then only if it was a branded product. France was an exception in that the government specified that all imported goods had to be clearly marked not "Made in U.S.A.," which, imprinted in English, suggested brand advertising, but *Fabriqué aux Etats-Unis d'Amérique du Nord.*[49] Where, as happened in Germany, foreign raw materials, capital, or semifinished articles went into manufacturing goods locally, the law delegated the determination of nationality to the civil courts. Guided by the German Unfair Competition Act of June 7, 1909, the courts constantly wavered as to whether German-made meant goods produced by German-owned manufacturers or manufactured with German raw materials, or actually made by German workers and distributed by German retailers. The more contentious the issue became, the more the courts leaned to calling German manufacture any good made in Germany. Accordingly in 1928 the sewing machines produced locally by Singer, which had been introduced by the Hamburg merchant George Neidlinger in 1865 and had been manufactured since the turn of the century at a giant factory complex at Wittenberge, were finally certified as national.[50] After the Nazis came to power, foreign firms were banned from calling themselves *Deutsch,* as in Deutsch Royal Backpulver-GmbH, a practice used by about 3,800 companies, many American, to distinguish their local subsidiaries from the parent companies. The remedy was simple enough, to find a new name, which most of them did, assuming they could behave like local firms, which meant accepting currency-export restrictions, abiding by raw-materials quotas, and purging their non-Aryan employees. Thereupon they acquired all the rights accorded any other firm in the national economy. So from 1934 on, the automobiles that Ford manufactured locally were officially classified as German products. To advertise the degree of their Germanness the Berlin sales offices on Unter den Linden put a Ford chassis on display with a large *D* (as in Deutschland) stamped on all the parts manufactured locally, which was practically every piece visible.[51] If its professions of Germanness weren't enough for Ford to gain the contract to produce the new German national car, the Volkswagen, the company wasn't discriminated against for other kinds of government procurement. After obtaining a generous contract to build convoy trucks in 1938, it built a whole new assembly plant at Berlin. By the middle of 1939, together with Adam Opel (which had been taken over by General Motors a decade earlier), Ford had become Germany's largest producer of armored tanks.[52]

The issue of a product's nationality became more and more complicated by the late 1930s, as, on the one hand, multinationals internationalized brand names and, on the other hand, states tried to nationalize consumer preferences at the same time favoring one country's goods over another in terms of tariffs, quotas, and clearing arrangements. To find agreement, the International Chamber of Commerce's Committee on Customs Techniques recommended that the country of origin that appeared on labels should be either the place where the entire manufacturing process took place or, if it took place in more than one country, the place where the last substantial change had occurred.[53]

Such an agreement could not of course settle how consumers responded to this knowledge. "Made in ——" could be an incentive or a deterrent, depending on the connotation of the place of manufacture. So it was discovered in Great Britain during World War I that, after the government had ordered its arch enemy's goods stamped "Made in Germany," British people actually went out of their way to shop for them because of their reputation for superior quality.[54] A neutral solution could be to stamp goods as not produced locally, as in "Not German Made." Whether "buy national" campaigns were effective was not at all self-evident, even if government joined with prominent businesses to mobilize support from the widest range of political and civic institutions. Faced with the flood of American imports, German nationalists in alliance with some key manufacturers had taken strong stands on the *Überfremdung,* or overforeignization, of national industry. At Adam Opel, salesmen were warned not to show up at the plant driving foreign vehicles. And company marketing showed a flair for elegant nationalism in the slogan "The car you purchase doesn't have to be an Opel, but it has to be German."[55] After General Motors took over in 1929, Opel advertising still played the nationalist card; it was the genuine German product, as opposed to Ford, its major competitor—which merely assembled its cars in Germany! Diehard nationalists may have responded to "buy national" campaigns. However, advertisers doubted that, all things being equal, the prosperous, urbane younger customers who were their main targets made an issue of national origin.

So there was no hard-and-fast rule whether to emphasize the Americanness of a product or conceal it. Down to World War II, the Gillette Company operated in the conviction that "Made in America" was a powerful selling point. One reason was to fend off competition from German blades using Swiss trademarks, which were practically indistinguishable down to the design of the blade wrappers, which bore the likeness of a Teutonic-looking King Camp Gillette. Other companies spoke to the nationality of the brand, as advertising often does, to provide additional arguments to reassure customers that they had made the politically correct choice after they had already made it on other grounds such as cost, style, and prestige. Everybody in Britain knew more or less that Ford was an American car, and its reputation for quality derived from that knowledge. But local Ford advertising emphasized that its cars were made in Britain, which was true, and in the mid-1920s it added a new color to its palette, namely Imperial Grey.[56]

By the same token, to emphasize that the brand was universal was not necessarily to renounce nationality. Kodak had been operating in Eu-

rope since before the turn of the century, and its name had become synonymous with photography. Metonymy for the modern, it was everywhere, but from nowhere. That made it American, though not in so
many words. What was important was for crossnational advertising to
reiterate the same message. So if the French edition of *Vogue,* read in
Rome, told an Italian woman the same thing about a product as her daily
copy of the *Corriere della sera,* she was far more likely to buy the product
than if the publications told her different, perhaps conflicting, things
about it. And if a German, taking his holiday in Switzerland, read in the
local papers what he had already learned from the German press, he too
was more likely to become a loyal customer.[57] Ultimately goods went native quickly, especially once they began to be produced locally. If there
was a commonality to U.S. goods, once their marketers no longer saw a
virtue in advertising them as American, it came from the way in which
they first appeared on the scene, solo, the apparatus behind their arrival
the hugely costly, complicated, and circumspect alliance of international
capital and national government. As Douglas Miller, the commercial adviser attached to the U.S. embassy in Berlin, remarked, "one of the most
valuable commodities we have to export is American merchandising and
distribution technique."[58] In sum, the commonality of American commodities in Europe was the way they were merchandised: with a doff to
Marshall McLuhan, the new medium in which they moved was marketing. And marketing was the message.

Building Brand Recognition in 1930s Europe

Given the huge impetus behind it, American big-brand salesmanship had
an influence in Europe far in excess of the volume of sales of any single
object or the number of U.S. consumer brands actually being marketed—
which still added up to only a few score down to World War II. Still, a basic law of merchandising is that when one company in a sector starts to
brand its products, the others follow suit.[59] So branding might start with
a certain fabric, and then spread like wildfire to dresses, hats, trimmings,
lingerie, silks, ribbons, jerseys, rugs, covers, umbrellas, handkerchiefs,
shirts, and detachable cuffs and collars. Subsequently it would spread to
other types of goods such as drinking glasses, electric fans, and pots. Before long it would be the turn of sewing notions, paper goods, sports
equipment, even children's toys and board games. In sum, brand names
bred branding.

Yet to launch a brand in the American style was no simple affair. After all, the practice in the United States was bound up not just with the large size of consumer-oriented firms, business strategies calculated with an eye to mass merchandising, and the existence of a specialized apparatus of selling, including the advertising agency itself. It also reflected a whole way of envisioning material life, notably the way that customers themselves identified their individuality with the satisfactions the brand name promised.

How, for example, could a perfectly respectable European manufacturer of razor blades take on the Gillette Company when, by the 1920s, the latter's name was practically synonymous with disposable blades? Gillette had been founded in 1904 in South Boston, and its sales had grown steadily until the war, when they soared after the U.S. government was successfully lobbied to issue Gillette safety-razor kits to the entire armed forces. Meanwhile the company brought the self-shaving gospel to Europe. There too it prospered on army contracts and reaped publicity from the widespread use by soldiers. Eventually even the French soldier, the *poilu* (fuzzy-faced), was converted; pillaged shaving kits from abandoned enemy positions were as gratifying booty as the shoes, pistols, or knives stripped from abandoned cadavers. Expanding its manufacturing plants from England and France to subsidiaries in Belgium, Switzerland, Spain, Denmark, and Italy, Gillette dominated 60 percent of continental sales by the late 1920s. Everywhere the clean-shaven look for men triumphed over facial hair. In Italy, Gillette gained the imprimatur of Il Duce, who, in battle against the beards and mustaches of liberal gerontocrats, declared Fascism anti-whiskers. Hirsute faces were decadent. The proof lay in the marble statuary of the Roman Republic and early Empire in the portraits of smooth-cheeked Caesars.[60]

Whether any French firm, even the most venerable and well run, could find a niche in this market was the problem that students at Paris's Business Training Center (Centre de Préparation aux Affaires) pondered over several class periods in 1934. Founded by the Chamber of Commerce of Paris in 1930, the CPA had revolutionized French marketing studies by adopting the Harvard Case Method.[61] No course of study could have been less European: to take real-life business cases, examine all the alternatives the firm faced, and, at the end, provide management with a practical recommendation. Case number 310, supplemented with 316, was just one of the hundreds that students studied from 1930 to 1941. But it was a classic, for it dealt with the absolutely respectable Perrot works, a firm of early date, famous for its fine cutlery, which though well managed and having spent one million francs on advertising its new product, after three years had still not obtained a toehold in the French razor blade market. It is true that the medium-scale firm was up against a multinational with a record of remarkable accomplishments. On the continent, Gillette's only competitors had been German firms. These it confronted head-on in April 1926 by purchasing a controlling interest in the Berlin-based Roth-Büchner Company. King of the European nonbranded blade market, it had produced blades sold under 250 different private labels. Thereafter Gillette practically dominated the "Gillette-type" blade business of the world.[62]

The most obvious way for Perrot to start was simply to throw its venerable hat into the ring: "Perrot launches a razor blade, you owe Perrot a try." The trouble was that Perrot was known mainly for its cutlery, and it was interested in producing razors only as a way of finding a use for waste steel laminate. For consumers, the connection of shaving implements with knives was discomfiting. Moreover, cutlery was normally sold through hardware stores or specialty shops, whereas razors were sold in pharmacies, five-and-tens, or cosmetics stores. What would happen, the students asked, if David sold his goods cheaply to undercut expensive Goliath? This strategy too was unworkable, they concluded, since high price was associated with high quality. With no sales apparatus of its own, Perrot would have to work through wholesalers, and these had no particular incentive to place Perrot's blades as opposed to those of one or another competitor. Forget the retailers: they were completely under Goliath's sway, having been barraged by display materials and offers of special discounts from its special sales representatives, as well as by requests from consumers, who had become acquainted with Goliath's product from press and other advertising.

The solution the students came up with was for David to avoid Goliath altogether. Perrot should give up on developing its own brand and use a wholesaler to sell its blades as private brands to barbers and sundry retailers. Meanwhile it should use its reputation and connections in government to lobby for tariff increases against foreign-made blades![63] Not that this strategy would hurt a hair on Goliath's head, for by the early 1930s Gillette had established a wholly-owned subsidiary in France. Thenceforth it benefited from any protection or incentive the French state offered local companies. In 1953, in the wake of handsome incentives from the French state to move production from the Paris region to the provinces, Gillette opened up a giant, fully automated plant in Annecy. Its hold on the French market stronger than ever, it resisted developing the long-lasting stainless-steel blade on which it held a sleeping patent so long as it made good profits on its less durable carbon-steel one. Only in 1961, when the British firm Wilkinson Sword Ltd. made plans to market stainless-steel blades, the U.S. American Safety Razor Co. and Schick promised to follow suit, and Gillette's share of the European market began to be eroded, did it preemptively put its long-lasting Extra-Blue into production. With means that no other firm could match, it launched a marketing campaign unparalleled in French history, culminating in fall 1961, when it distributed 3 million sample blades to French households.[64]

And what happened if brands did come on the market but lacked the requisite distinction, character, and goodwill to make them stand out from the mass of generic goods? If lacking the appropriate introduction, they would cause ambiguity about the new needs they were to satisfy, or worse, the class of people they were intended to please. The awful result would be that they undercut the solidarities of familiar craft goods without establishing a new hierarchy of taste, without contributing anything to the sense of the richness of life that was nurtured by the high quality and craft with which Europe's goods were identified to contrast them with the standardized, mass-produced items that were called "American."

This was the prospect that Hanns W. Brose, the German advertising pioneer, bewailed with Wagnerian pomposity as the "Götterdämmerung des Markenartikels"—"The Apocalypse of the Brand-Name Good." This was the *cri de coeur* of the post–World War I bourgeoisie, who, immersed in the old canons of quality, wanted new goods, but wanted them to have that "cultivation," or *Bildung,* that would impart distinction, yet who lacked the purchasing power individually and collectively to give a proper tone to mass goods. Brose would have called himself typical in this sense. Born in 1899, the son of a prosperous West Prussian dry-goods store owner, he had grown up surrounded by the mass-produced yet luxury-quality brands of his epoch: his childhood madeleines were his father's Waldorf-Astoria cigarettes, his mother's Kaffee Hag and Riquet chocolates, and the fine Salamander footwear with which the entire family was shod. Well-read but no student, though he professed to love Goethe, he had the good luck, after the small factory he inherited failed, to be able to turn his snobbery into a metier by finding a position at the Berlin offices of Erwin, Wasey and Company. There, under the spell of the American profession, he completed his self-styled "almost 'romantic journey'" from German literary studies to advertising. This was reconsecrated in a wholly German milieu when he joined the in-house staff of Karl August Ligner's Dresden firm. There he dedicated himself to campaigns for Odol, Europe's best-known brand of mouthwash, some of the immense profits from which the industrialist-philanthropist Ligner devoted to building Dresden's renowned Hygiene Museum, the first in the world to be dedicated to eugenics. Writing advertising text for Odol, sitting at the antique desk in the studio of his villa on Hochuferstrasse in Dresden-Blasewitz with a view from the terrace across the Elbe to the three Albert palaces, of which Ligner had inherited one (a second belonged to the von Mayenburg family, which owned the Chlorodont factory), Brose came to the realization that the "the genius and vision of the entrepreneur" were one with "the imagination of the artist," and "the world of the brand-name good was hardly less symbolic and cultural-laden than the world of Goethe." The "respect for quality," and the sense of "certainty and direction" that this new world of marketing inspired in him, combined with a robust sense of business opportunity and political opportunism to carry him successfully from the Weimar Republic through the Third Reich to the boom years of the Federal Republic, his professional reputation unbesmirched and his livelihood intact.[65]

Brose's sense of revulsion toward the new branded goods derived not from the process of branding itself. He was not nostalgic for unlabeled craftsmanship. What he abhorred was the proliferation of cheap brands to the detriment of the status of the celebrated ones. Brose blamed Chancellor Brüning for trying to drive down prices. Inevitably "a poor land must be a cheap one." Desperate to market their products, small firms resorted to advertising, and to do so they had to devise a brand image. The result was that bad brands drove out the good ones: the market for the output of marginal and failing firms was not the discriminating bourgeoisie, but the masses of destitute lower-middle classes and workers.

The solution lay in what Brose called "collective advertising" *(Gemeinschaftswerbung)*. His version of it was to promote goods by sector or by category, a practice that was not at all uncommon elsewhere: fruit or rice growers, milk producers, and banana importers combined their respective advertising resources to promote consumption, the increase overall redounding to the interests of the sector as a whole. The ideal brand should be able not only to show off its "utilities," but also to display a meaningful "collective ideology" *(Gemeinschaftsideologie)*.

So ambitious a project could never have been contemplated had not

the clever Brose linked his fortunes to the Society for Consumption Research, or Gesellschaft für Konsumforschung (GfK). Founded in 1934 at
Nuremberg by Professor Wilhelm Vershofen, whom Brose would exalt as
"sociologist, philosopher, and poet," the GfK was famous as Germany's
first market research organization. Working with 750 correspondents
each in contact with twenty clients, it was well known for its bulletin,
Die Deutsche Fertigware (German Household Goods), which in 1938
changed its name to *Markt und Verbrauch* (Market and Consumption).
It is also renowned for having had as an up-and-coming associate the
young economist Dr. Ludwig Erhard, later celebrated as the father of
the postwar German economic miracle and the foremost ideologue of
1950s West German consumer culture.[66] It was Brose's unique contribution to join the *Ding an sich*—the aestheticized "thing in itself"—with
a very practical and profit-oriented notion of branding. The modern marketer's duty was to get bourgeois consumers to relinquish their paralyzing nostalgia for so-called authentic goods by creating brands that were
useful, tasteful, and sensitive to preserving social hierarchy.[67]

The Fair at Dusk

The power of big-brand marketing began to be felt in perverse ways even
at Leipzig, where the fair flourished despite the Nazis' initial disfavor.
Cosmopolitan, liberal, a place of international truck and trade, it was,
according to the first Nazi plans, to be revived as a "Brown Fair" (as in
Brown Shirt) under the slogan "Think German—Sell German—Buy German." In keeping with this chauvinistic and parochial view, the Great
Fair would be recreated as a "department store of middle-class industry
where only goods of German origin [would be] allowed to be displayed,"
and customers would be enticed off the streets to search for bargains.[68]
However, the fair had been badly battered in 1934 by foreign boycotts to
protest the regime's anti-Semitism, as well as by the deepening depression
in international trade. Hence those who were better advised on the fair's
centrality to foreign trade insisted on restoring the fair to its original purposes. The regime acquiesced, after ousting the fair's director, Paul Voss,
who was suspect as a liberal and a Rotarian. With Nazi flags fluttering
from all the fair buildings, Goebbels himself demonstrated the new government favor by inaugurating the 1934 fall season.
    In the hothouse economy of the Third Reich, the fair as an institution

flowered like gorgeous blooms out of season. Avid to capture trade for their little fiefdoms, the Nazi *Gauleiters,* like the tyrants of yore, each trying to bring trade under their power, swelled the number of fairs to 634 by the end of the 1934, only to have the government step in, aware of the chaos and waste, to cut back on their number. On October 29, 1936, the government ordered that only four places could be designated as international fairs, namely Königsberg, Breslau, Cologne, and Leipzig. On December 20, 1937, the Saxon *Gauleiter* Mutschmann celebrated Leipzig's anointment as an official State exhibition center, or *Reichsmessestadt.* Reflecting its exalted position in the Third Reich, the fair was more and more a showcase for German industry. And increasingly it also reflected the Reich's colonial ambitions in the region, with more and more buyers and sellers coming from southeastern Europe, where the Nazi New Order intended to expand its *Lebensraum.* The tougher environment in which to find export markets increased pressure to brand products. If industrial firms did not, it was conceived that the fair itself could do so, by awarding seals of approval that would vouchsafe for the quality of the goods. The fair, then, would act as the supreme guarantor of the craft culture of the German nation, giving its stamp of approval to the individual good in the name of the general interest of Germany's economy and people. This was not a capitalist contract, unlike the bond of goodwill established by the brand between manufacturer and consumer. It was a bond of social trust, underwritten collectively by the age-old solidarities of the guild, the venerable merchant traditions of the fair, the aesthetic of the poet, the craft of the manufacturer, the skill of the publicist, and, of course, the refined taste of the public. Ultimately under the sovereign protection of Hitler's Reich against the marketing monopolies of an unspecified foreign capitalism, the Leipzig Fair was "a place where competitor can meet competitor in fair and open combat for the world's custom."[69]

In October 1941 plans were formalized to build a Commemorative Hall in honor of "the creative German" on the site of the Technical Fair. This would be to the Labor Front what the vast stadium of Nuremberg was to the Nazi party. Plans were also drawn up to double the exposition space in the city center over the next decade by constructing fourteen new buildings. As German armies invaded all Europe, the fair's seven-century history was revisited to recall its survival through the thick and thin of the Thirty Years' War, the Seven Years' War, and the Continental Blockade by the Corsican general, whose army, it was never forgotten, had

Leipzig Fair buildings at the war's end, 1945. By permission of the
Sächsisches Staatsarchiv, Leipzig.

been routed in 1813 when the people of Leipzig themselves had seized
arms and rushed to the battlefields. It was forgotten that so long as the
then-independent kingdom of Saxony was allied with Napoleon, it had
flourished, the fair providing an outlet for two-thirds of Lyons' silk production. During World War II the fair continued to flourish, at least until
Allied bombing started, as commercial traffic quickened with the annex-
ation of Poland and the Third Reich extended its power southeastward
into Hungary and the Balkans. It flourished too because the government
wanted to sustain the flow of consumer goods, in the knowledge that
consumer tastes change more abruptly and unpredictably in wartime
than in peacetime.[70]

   The expectation that the Great Fair of Leipzig would thrive in the New
Order was junked as tons of bombs began to be dropped on the city on
December 4, 1943. On April 18, 1945, American military forces occupied Leipzig as they pressed forward to meet up with the Soviet forces
at Torgau on the Elbe, just thirty miles to the northeast. This occurred
on April 27. However, long-standing accords between the U.S. and Soviet high commands put the city under Soviet occupation. On July 2,

1945, dejected bystanders saw the first Soviet troops straggle into the city's war-ruined, rain-soaked shambles of a downtown, the men ragged and famished, mostly on foot, the officers in dilapidated Jeeps, the sick and wounded on trucks and farm carts harnessed to oxen and mules. By the spring of 1945, 80 percent of the fair buildings had been destroyed. That season, for the first time in centuries, the fair didn't open in Leipzig.

CHAPTER 5

Corporate Advertising

How the Science of Publicity Subverted the Arts of Commerce

The skills and talents we offer to advertisers throughout the world . . . are rooted in our experience and perseverance in gathering more and more information into our library of knowledge . . . Our goals can be attained only by demonstration that we can deliver more for the money than anyone else.

SAM MEEK,
American advertising man, 1952

What sadness would be conveyed by streets, squares, stations, subways, palaces, dance clubs, dining cars, travel, automobile routes, nature, without the innumerable posters, without display windows . . . ? Yes, truly, advertising is the most beautiful expression of our era, the greatest innovation of the day, an Art.

BLAISE CENDRARS,
French writer, 1927

THE FIAT SPIDER was the first car ever seen in the village. Scrambling up the mule path, motor whirring, dust spurting from under the chassis as it skidded back and forth, it burst into the dilapidated public square and jolted to a stop. The driver and his companion, urbane young men with slicked-back hair, jacquard vests, and snappy shoes, pulled themselves out, stretching and laughing after their hell-raising ride. After inspecting the place for a few minutes, pausing at the village pump to splash some water into a tin they pulled from their sack, they stood in front of the whitewashed wall by the church. This, they agreed, offered the perfect emplacement. As the villagers coming out of Sunday mass stopped to look, one fellow took a wicker brush and smeared the stucco with glue paste while his companion carefully unfolded a large square of glossy paper. Smoothed down, the poster hung at eye level. A bottle-green chimera leaped from a bright-white background to entwine itself around a checkered can and imbibe its contents. The lettering said "Best-Oil, the Favorite Lubricant."

This event, purported to have occurred in the Apennine hills of Emilia-Romagna in Italy in 1932, was used by the expert who told about it to reflect on the excesses of modern advertising. His main point was twofold. First, the craze for publicity had lately got out of hand. And, second, the mania for costly poster campaigns was particularly ill conceived. Engine oil was a superfluous item in the unnamed place we shall call Colibrì. The village had no tractors or any other motorized farm equipment. Up to that moment, there had been no automobiles either. Hand-held coffee grinders and pedal sewing machines were the only machines in need of lubrication. And there was plenty of gasoline and olive oil for that. What purpose then could advertising serve here? His answer, in brief: none whatsoever. Advertising should not be about bravado. It was a serious profession, a science whose goal was to sell goods.[1]

If indeed the aim of publicity were only to sell the goods being advertised, then we might concur with the expert, Dr. Brunazzi. However, advertisers themselves would have been the first to acknowledge that it is difficult if not impossible to determine exactly the impact of their message on the public. The joking adage that "fifty percent of all advertising dollars is wasted; we simply don't know which fifty percent," sometimes attributed to Albert Lasker, the self-assured chief of Lord & Young, had become a cliché by the 1930s, at least in the United States. By that time much had been written about the significance of advertising as a language of goods. For marketing campaigns clearly not only introduced the qualities of commodities, but also illustrated the needs they satisfied, often with new concepts and phrases. They highlighted their availability while reassuring customers that the choices they had made were wise ones. Moreover, advertising accustomed people to speak about the things they appeared to have in common, enriching with visual images and idiomatic expressions their conversation about what they held dear or despised about the world in which they lived.[2]

As a matter of fact in Colibrì on that early autumn Sunday nothing was sold or bought. An automobile arrived with an announcement, and the announcement told people not yet familiar with, much less desiring, an automobile that it had its own needs, first and foremost for motor oil. As it turns out, the latent desire that the publicity event stimulated was not for lubricants or even for that marvelous object, the car. If anything, it promoted another utility, one that cars were invented to satisfy, namely automobility. Now for the people of Colibrì to satisfy that basic want, which might in turn excite the desire for automobiles, which in turn would create the need for motor oil, first of all they needed a road. And so it happened that the village priest, the community's activist, having seen from the drivers of the car that came to advertise the motor oil that the old cart path could accommodate traffic, convinced the local authorities (behind whom stood a dictator who championed such public works) to upgrade the ancient roadbed. On the assumption that Colibrì's history is like that of many similar European villages in the 1930s, with the road smoothed, widened, and cobbled, it soon became the destination for the occasional Sunday tourist. In turn the villagers more easily made their way down the hillside on market days to bring back supplies—canned goods, flypaper, knitting wool, hairpins, tin pots, perhaps even a radio. At least one enterprising resident would have spent the savings accumulated from the sacrifices of a life of emigration on a used Ford to provide a van service. Eventually the village youth would have drifted down to the plain to seek paid employment, settle in the money economy, and partake of urban consumer routines.

To be sure, this is an extreme case of publicity as *primum mobile*. Its point is to underscore that as a social invention, contemporary advertising was more than a specific technique or form, the age-old graffiti, a handout, or poster, the press insert, radio ditty, television spot, or website pop-up. From the start it was, as it still is, a complicated dialogue about goods, one mediated by specialists with diverse interests to balance. Advertisers themselves hankered after professional dignity, social status, and income, and these acquisitions depended perforce on cultivating good business relations with their clients. In turn they had to gain the confidence of the public, whose mutable tastes and own growing expertise they were under constant pressure to probe, test, and master, and whose responses they knew only by reflex, by what was said to it and about it.

Like other inventions of twentieth-century consumer culture, advertising was initially a culturally bound phenomenon, the local idiom developing out of close-knit communities of consumption. There was no universal language of commerce. Publicity could be oral, as in the peddler's cry, the merchant's cajoling, or the broadcaster's jingle. Or it could be visual, taking the form of stunning wall posters, colorful handbills, densely worded advertising copy, the animated tv commercial. The problem here is to understand how the practices of one milieu of marketing, the American, were propelled into another milieu, the European, on the road to becoming a global phenomenon. In other words: How was a system of publicizing commodities which had begun to regard its practices as universally valid assimilated into a declining commercial civilization, one that Europeans themselves regarded as failing in the skills of persuasion demanded of modern marketing? American advertisers posed their goal as promoting a science in the name of corporate profits; Europeans often claimed to be defending an art, in the name of a community of feeling about the familiar brands, pastimes, and places of local material life. Here the clash between the new and the old regime of consumption occurred over which advertising language to use to address a mass public.

In the first quarter of the century, American advertising industry stood out not just in terms of its gigantic size, revenues, and the fat sums it added to the costs of distribution compared with all other countries of the world, but also for its growing legitimacy as a public vernacular.[3] American advertising invoked new social authorities to testify to the worth of freshly invented goods even while fostering faddish notions about the basic needs that new goods could satisfy: such were refreshment, dryness, softness, coolness, clear complexion, toasted taste, restful lighting, fresh breath, staving off nighttime hunger, and so on, ad infinitum. The American advertising industry brought with it systematic and costly procedures that claimed to be universal even as it exploited these ostensibly universal practices to impugn local knowledge and taste.

Above all, American advertising carved out a new domain in public space, one that was shared by the intrusive chain stores, big-brand marketing, and the Hollywood-led cinema industry. This is what we might call the commercial cultural sphere as distinct from the political cultural domain, which, under the pressure of U.S. ad techniques, was now stretched beyond the turn-of-the-century publicists' imagination to include all of the press, even the most political, roadways, radio, cinema, and eventually television, shopping malls, and the Internet. Thereby commercial space cut into the public space that had been carved out of eighteenth-century absolutist regimes and in the nineteenth century was grafted onto every tissue of city centers—at well-trafficked crossroads, the sidewalks of boulevards, public squares, at subway, tram, and bus stops, around train stations—in sum, in all the places where people crossed paths with one another and congregated more or less freely. Moreover, by drawing on the commonsense appeal of everyday experience, American advertising self-consciously blurred the distinction between arguments made on behalf of political claims and the rationales used for making consumer choices. In turn, the rationale behind selling goods could be redeployed to make social claims as well. This slippage was especially troubling under systems of exchange in which commercial messages overflowed with provocative sensuality and psychological excitement, yet the main thrusts of development were to differentiate the needs of one social class from another and to restrain consumer desire from expressing itself through the untrammeled coveting of material goods.

If Dr. Brunazzi, as he denounced the futility of postering at Colibrì, had been asked what kind of publicity he recommended, he would have warmly endorsed what at the time was becoming familiar as the "American style," which for him as for other self-styled "modern" experts meant the carefully studied advertising copy published in the mass-circulation press. The poster, by contrast, he regarded as an artifact of the past, an aesthetically pleasing gimmick perhaps, but unsuited to the dynamism of modern marketing.

From the Frontiers of Our Far-Flung Empire

That the poster pasted up at Colibrì publicized engine oil is not accidental. Advertising for automobiles stood at the cutting edge of commercial promotion in the 1920s, reflecting the rapid globalization of the industry after World War I and the intense marketing of the various fuels, lubricants, tires, axles, spark plugs, batteries, tools, pumps, paints, synthetic leathers, and the myriad of other accessories, auxiliary industries, and services connected to the purchase and use of cars.[4]

It took the great advance abroad by the world's two largest automotive firms, Ford and General Motors, to catapult the leading U.S. advertising agencies into Europe. Before the mid-1920s the prospects for selling significant quantities of cars in Europe, where there were already well-established manufacturers, had not looked especially promising compared with prospects in Canada, Argentina, Brazil, and Australia, where there were no native industries. American-made cars could not expect to obtain more than a 10–20 percent share of the transatlantic market given their relatively high prices, stiff tariffs, heavy government taxes on horsepower, their low fuel efficiency, and the conspicuous evidence they gave of great wealth that might expose their owners to unwanted scrutiny from state tax collectors. Nonetheless, by 1926–27 the Big Two, in the process of extending their domestic rivalry, determined to take on the European competition, especially as they saw renascent French, British, German, and Italian carmakers bidding for foreign markets. A strong presence in Europe also mattered for purposes of international prestige. Ford's star billing in London resonated in Johannesburg, Delhi, and other stretches of the British Empire. Showing the new models at the annual October Salon de l'Automobile at the Grand Palais in Paris, "the shop window of the world," as well as opening spectacular display rooms on the Champs-Elysées, was still the best conduit to Arab princes, scions of Turkish merchant families, Romanian great estate holders, as well as the prosperous Luxembourg engineer or Belgian industrialist who was disdainful about the quality of French automobiles yet for political reasons would never purchase a German model. As GM and Ford competed with each other for market share in Europe, with Chrysler coming in a distant third, they upped the ante on advertising expenditure. In turn, as leading European automobile manufacturers Fordized their manufacturing processes to compete with U.S. industry, they took a lesson from American marketing practices by boosting their advertising budgets. France's own Big Three, Citroën, Peugeot, and Renault, took this step, likewise Italy's Fiat. The largest and most German of automobile manufacturers, Adam Opel, did so after it was acquired by General Motors in 1928 and had its advertising account turned over to the H. K. McCann Company.[5]

Late January 1927 was the moment that American advertising could truly be said to have arrived in Europe. That was when the giant J. Walter Thompson Company sent its first "expedition" abroad after reaching an agreement with General Motors, the world's biggest spender on advertising after Unilever. The pact required that JWT open an office in every country where GM had a manufacturing or assembly plant. Accordingly, the firm rushed to open outposts in Berlin, Copenhagen, Stockholm, Madrid, and Alexandria, Egypt. In 1928 it moved to The Hague, Paris, and Port Elizabeth, South Africa. The following year it set up an office in Warsaw. By 1932, just as GM began to cut back, JWT established outposts in Bucharest and Barcelona. As each office opened, the staff sought to obtain the local accounts for the other major brands the company promoted back home. By 1930 JWT's continental European offices also managed the overseas accounts of a baker's dozen of prestigious brands, namely Pond's soap, Kodak, J. B. Williams toiletries, Kellogg's cereals, Coca-Cola, Gillette, Frigidaire, Listerine mouthwash, Wrigley chewing gum, Horlick's malted milk, Royal Baking Powder, Odorono deodorants, and Fleischmann's yeast.[6]

In the meantime, others among the big firms that had begun to cluster around Madison Avenue made the leap as well. The United States' third-largest advertising firm, the Philadelphia-based N. W. Ayer and Son, though tempted to go abroad at the behest of the California Prune Growers Association, did so only in 1927, after it had also obtained the lucrative Ford account. H. K. McCann, the fifth largest, launched itself with the account from the Standard Oil Company of New Jersey, and the upstart twelfth-ranked Erwin, Wasey and Company set up a main office in Paris, smaller shops in Milan and Berlin, and eventually ten or so other local agencies after winning the Goodyear Tire account.[7] By the early 1930s international billings had pushed J. Walter Thompson well ahead of its leading rivals, N. W. Ayer and Lord & Thomas, to make it the world's largest advertising firm. It held this position for most of the years down to the millennium.

True, Europeans had been curious about American advertising methods long before 1927, and they would learn about them from other sources after the arrival of JWT and other U.S. agencies. After all, advertising is a form of culture, and its movement could never be demarcated by the movement of a single industry. By the 1920s American techniques were being documented through at least a score of dynamic local publications: in France, by *Vendre, La Publicité, Réussir,* and *Mon bureau,* to name just four; in Germany, by *Die Reklame, Gebrauchsgraphik,* and *Die Deutsche Werbung;* in Italy, by *Pugno nell'occhio, Commercio,* in which Dr. Brunazzi wrote about Colibrì, and, later, in the gorgeously produced *Pubblicità d'Italia.* Typographers and graphic designers were familiar with the most venerable of U.S. trade journals, *Printers' Ink,* founded in 1895. "How-to" books appeared in translation, the most widely circulated being Claude Hopkins's *My Life in Advertising,* which after its translation by the journalist Louis Angé was heavily promoted as its bible by the fledgling French firm Jep and Carré. With its homilies and recipes for business success, it could be likened to Henry Ford's self-promotional memoirs. The story Hopkins told Europeans was that a mere craftsman, a onetime reclusive copywriter at Lord & Thomas, had made himself a lucrative career by discovering the "plague" of tooth plaque while dutifully researching the dental hygiene literature to find the information indispensable to writing convincing advertising copy for a new tooth cleanser. Once he had dug out this knowledge, Hopkins could authoritatively explain how "cloudy film" accumulated on teeth as well as the "reason why" his product, Pepsodent, could eliminate it. This knowledge also gave him such unwavering confidence in his product that he invested his small savings in its manufacture. The company's success made him one of the first advertising copywriters to become rich.[8]

In their own array of distinguished national theorists, Europeans would more easily have found high-minded divagations on crowd psychology than crass considerations of profit or nostrums about best practice. These figures—one thinks of Victor Mataja, Rudolph Seyffert, Girolamo Bevinetto, Octave-Jacques Gérin—were intellectuals in the traditional sense; sometimes they were quite distinguished academicians.[9] Though distant in formation, spirit, and method from the prevailing American paradigms, sooner or later they too had to engage with them, and their views on the matter were in turn widely studied and cited. Inevitably European advertisers also found more and more occasion to meet their American counterparts in the decade after the war. Sometimes these meetings occurred in the course of the technical tourism that brought groups of advertising men to visit the famous sites of American productivity, only their mecca was Times Square and its jumble of illuminated signs rather than Detroit and its implacable assembly lines. Sometimes individuals set off alone to apprentice in a U.S. firm in order to return with an edge to advance their own careers. On other occasions groups from both sides of the Atlantic, organized in their respective national associations (initiated after studying American prototypes), converged at international congresses (the first of which, convened in 1904, was strictly an American affair). Lively events these were, where advertising men, gregarious sorts, scrutinized one another's practices and exchanged gossip about the state of the art.

Consequently, to say that the mere physical presence of American advertising agencies on European soil made all the difference would grossly exaggerate. What it did do was to make the Americans themselves more aware of the distinctiveness of their own practices with respect to the Europeans'. In the short term, this discovery made them more aggressive about their superiority with respect to the local craft they denigrated as "backward" and "undeveloped." Over the long term, it made them more calculating about how to outmaneuver local businesses and prospect large-scale challenges—when to pull back, as during the 1930s Depression; when to advance, as happened with the emergence of the Common Market at the turn of the 1960s. In turn, the American presence put pressure on Europeans to become more self-conscious about their own peculiarities. So, as they set about updating indigenous practices, American standards were in their mind's eye. Even if after local ways were assessed and it was determined that, after all, they were the best suited to local environments (with some tweaks and adjustments), they could never again be justified as universally valid as the Americans claimed theirs to be. Rather they were to be cultivated as appropriate to "our selling environment," in keeping with "national traditions," or, more parochially, as "our way" not "theirs." In this roundabout way, too, American best practice established itself as the norm.

By all measures, J. Walter Thompson was as formidable a corporate beast as could be imagined. Headquarters for its world operations were in the thirty-one-story Graybar Building on Lexington Avenue, which, when occupied by its staff of several hundred in 1927, made JWT the largest tenant of what was then the largest office space in the world. Under the leadership of Stanley Resor, the amounts the agency billed its clients tripled in the 1920s, the first boom time of U.S. advertising. Tops in billing, it emerged as the standard setter for an industry that, overall, had doubled in value since 1890, represented 3 percent of the gross national product in 1929, and accounted for fully 15 percent of the very high cost of distributing goods in the United States.[10]

By then, advertising had been industrializing for over half a century, and J. Walter Thompson, first the man and then his firm, marked its every moment of advance. Thompson himself, though born in Massachusetts in 1847, shared with several other industry pioneers the fundamentalist Protestant culture of self-transformation of the small-town Midwest where he grew up. After serving in the Civil War he went to New York City, where in 1868 he found work as a bookkeeper and assistant in the two-man office of Carleton and Smith. Just a few years later, with entrepreneurial intuition unfazed by social snobbery, Thompson realized that mass-circulation magazines, especially those genteel illustrated monthlies favored by women and gentlemen of substance, could be a valuable medium for publicizing branded goods. Assuring their publishers that their reputation would suffer no damage from vile truck with the advertising trade, he obtained exclusive contracts to place ads in a list of twenty-five, then thirty of them. In 1878, well before this operation was concluded, he was able to buy out his longtime employer.

Over the next three decades Thompson turned his business into the prototype of the full-service agency, grouping under one roof all the personnel and equipment needed to carry out advertising on a "scientific" basis. Science in this sense meant coupling studies of market, product development, and packaging with consumer surveys, carefully pitched compositions, and ad placement. On this basis, JWT obtained accounts from leading consumer manufacturers, notably Procter & Gamble and the American subsidiaries of Unilever. Under immense pressure to maintain their market shares while turning out new products, these giants were willing to pay richly for the specialized services the agency offered. Picking up on cross-Atlantic trade opportunities, Thompson set up a small office in London in 1899 and only five years later could make the astoundingly grandiose claim (one that eventually proved true) that his agency had "annexe[d] the entire British domain to the advertising realm of the ambitious American manufacturer who sighs for more worlds to conquer."[11] In 1908, as JWT expanded to Cincinnati, Chicago, and Detroit to be near booming midwestern markets, Thompson brought in a cohort of collaborators three decades younger, notably Stanley Burnet Resor, who would stay with the firm until he retired in 1955 at age eighty. In turn, Resor hired a former coworker, Helen Lansdowne. Even then she showed the compositional skills, taste, and intuition about pleasing other advertisers and company clients that would make her the doyenne of copywriters. Business boomed, and in 1916 the couple, together with several other partners, bought out the old man. From there they proceeded to shed their smaller accounts, pinning their fortunes on the billings from a score or so of premium national corporations. The next year Resor and Lansdowne consolidated their own efficient, affectionate, and richly profitable relationship by marrying.[12]

By virtue of their talent, education, and business strategies, as well as the unique division of labor between the two—with Stanley as president in charge of oversight and Helen as chief of the creative aspects—the Resors transformed JWT into a major corporate power. In so doing they defined several features of American advertising that made it stand out on the world scene. The first feature was the industry's image as a business, one that in its own terms could be counted to be as productive and profitable as manufacturing; the second was its vast authority to counsel the political elite on matters of state; and the last, its pervasive influence upon public language. The upper-middle-class Yale-educated Resor, backed by two scores of vice-presidents of similarly elite Anglo-Protestant backgrounds, could not have been more distant from the huckster peddlers with their razzle-dazzle nostrums who personified nineteenth-century advertising. Statesmanlike and with a quiet sagacity and rectitude that led contemporaries to compare him to Woodrow Wilson, he was so alien from the rat race of big-city life that commuting on a daily basis to the Graybar Building from his home in leafy, luxurious Greenwich, Connecticut, by cutting through Grand Central Station's Graybar tunnel, his feet only fleetingly touched the vile sidewalks of Gotham.[13] Under sterling leadership, the firm set the standard for solidity, probity, and continuity that distanced the memory of the early industry's disreputable fly-by-night operations and gave the lie to Madison Avenue's modern reputation as "ulcer gulch," Western capitalism's most sordid, fatuous, and volatile redoubt.

The same rigor and commitment Resor brought to his own firm, he brought to organizing the profession as a whole. Like other industry leaders, he recognized that internal restraints and corporate self-organization were indispensable not only to reassure the public, which deeply distrusted advertising, but also to ward off threats of state regulation. For that purpose, he and other agency leaders gathered in 1917 to found the American Association of Advertising Agencies, the so-called 4-As. Its code of standards, which he authored, was designed to encourage transparency in business dealings by promoting "truth in advertising," publicizing accurate newspaper circulation figures and rates on space, and trumpeting the high ethical conduct expected of the profession's members. By the mid-1920s the president of the United States, if not yet fully a skeptical public, solemnly rejoiced in the profession's service to the nation. In attendance at the 4-As' annual convention in the fall of 1926, Calvin Coolidge volubly commended the advertising profession for uplifting U.S. citizenship, ennobling the commercial world, and preventing future business downturns.[14]

JWT was in the forefront of turning advertising into a model practice, as if it were a social science, at the moment the social sciences were becoming the American academy's nostrum for solving society's social ills. The staff of this "University of Advertising" as Resor liked to describe it, was populated by young men and a few women with B.A.'s and doctoral degrees from elite colleges in the effort to bring to the subject "precision and rationality." "Consumption is no longer a thing of needs, but a matter of choices freely exercised," according to Paul Cherington, a former professor at Harvard Business School, who in 1920 was hired to head the new Research Department. To determine scientifically how these were formed, two years later Resor brought in the well-known behavioral psychologist John B. Watson, who had taught at Johns Hopkins University before a scandalous divorce and polemical temper propelled him out of the backbiting puritanism of the ivory tower into the ethical jungle of the business world, where he thrived.[15]

In turn, the training of copywriters and artists entailed that they go out into the field to meet housewives, customers, and tradesmen in order to obtain a feel for retail problems and consumer tastes. They were also drilled in the so-called T-Square. These were the five questions indispensable to developing any advertising campaign on a sound basis: What are we selling? To whom are we selling? Where are we selling? When are we selling? How are we selling? Practically speaking, these queries were no different from the emphatic "who, what, where, how, when" dear to post–World War II American behavioral scientists. In pursuit of answers, no company was as dedicated as JWT to statistical research and opinion polling, compiling impeccably laid-out charts of population, income, and patterns of ownership of key goods and services, such as electricity, telephones, and cars, and relying on dealer surveys, consumer panels, and door-to-door interviews (on both sides of the tracks). At the same time, no firm was more convinced of its capacity to tap into a "universal psychology." "After all," John B. Watson averred, "it is the emotional factor in our lives that touches off and activates our social behavior whether it is buying a cannon, a sword or a plowshare—and love, fear and rage are the same in Italy, Abyssinia and Canada."[16]

The company also stood out for its contribution to the universal vernacular of consumer culture, meaning the common language derived from talking about goods and divorced from conventional ceremonial, regional, or class address.[17] Admittedly, JWT was only one of a score of leading (not to mention the myriad little) firms engaged in developing this shared language; JWT itself might even be characterized as among the most staid in terms of linguistic and visual inventiveness. Not for it the crass jingle or forgettably vulgar jargon of so much contemporary ad copy. The Creative Department's hallmark was literate prolixity, and the style of its ad copy was widely influential. It was the master of the specious argument delivered with well-modulated rhetoric, the editorial voice castigating bad habits and enjoining new virtues, and the invidious comparison sweetened by the scientific factoid. "Laboratory tests show that 455 out of 660 toilet tissues contain harmful acids" (but not Scott Tissue, Thompson client in 1932). Or "Science says coffee is a wonderful stimulant—drink it to sharpen your wits as well as to pep up your muscles—but never drink STALE coffee." (JWT had discovered that stale coffee contained rancid oils—but not Chase and Sanborn's dated coffee, an advertisement from 1933.)[18] Given its international vocation, rather than merely changing "the word-currency of one language into the word-currency of another" the aim was "to reproduce the pith and point of the original advertisement." And this meant "to take to pieces the word structure of American English and re-erect it in a form suited to people of different tastes and different temperaments."[19] So the lingua franca of early twentieth-century America's commodity culture was conceived on the way to becoming a universal vernacular. Advertising, as the French conservative litterateur Georges Duhamel reproached, sold not only the goods but also the adjectives to talk about them.[20] The capacity to change the terms of conversation about life's basic needs was an immense power.

Most important, JWT stood in the forefront of the agencies whose power derived not just from having become intimate advisers to the fickle, suggestible, and inexperienced new masses of economically enfranchised consumers, but from giving wise counsel to their public leaders.[21] Inserting itself into the ideological void left wide open by the lack of permanently mobilized political parties, advertising emerged as the medium for getting across strong messages. It was a newspaperman, George Creel, who convinced President Woodrow Wilson to give free hand to a newly created Committee on Public Information to publicize the United States' engagement in World War I. JWT's second-in-command, James Webb Young, was among the first advertising men whom Creel enlisted for his Foreign Section. The task assigned him in the course of the "world's greatest adventure in advertising" was to convince Germans on the Western Front of the "inevitability of defeat" and to "put gloom and despair into the heart of every person in the German Empire." How this was to be done was unclear, given that Webb knew next to no German and nothing about German psychology except silly stereotypes he had picked up about his hometown Cincinnati's moody German-speaking community.[22] What mattered were tunnel vision and soaring ambition. Wartime advertising, *Printers' Ink* later concluded, showed that "it is possible to sway the ideas of whole populations, change their habits of life, create belief, practically universal in any policy or idea." And it gave advertising men "an opportunity not only to render a valuable patriotic service . . . but to reveal to a wide circle of influential men . . . the real character of advertising and the important function which it performs."[23] In turn, the American state acknowledged the special place advertising occupied in the conduct of foreign affairs. Whereas other countries employed propaganda in pursuit of their interests, by means of heavy-handed government sloganeering, America employed publicity in pursuit of its global mission, using essentially private means, the skillfully nuanced counsel of its mass-communication industries. And whereas other countries propagated ideology, the American nation professed ideals.

From the onset of World War I, then, no firm would be more imbued with the consular mentality of the conscientious empire-builder than JWT. In post–World War II Europe the company emerged as the leading consultant for Europe's makeover under the Marshall Plan. It was advertising's job to explain the significance to enduring peace of a "socially-conscious capitalism" and to impress Europeans with the pay-offs from "engineered markets" and "Trade not Aid."[24] As the senior member of the Advertising Council, which first gathered during the war to advise President Roosevelt, J. Walter Thompson took charge of publicity for NATO during the delicate period from 1956 to 1959 when the North Atlantic Treaty Organization underwent an "identity crisis" as U.S. taxpayers protested against the costs of defending Europe and Europeans began to protest against U.S. imperialism. JWT's recommendation was that this "shield of freedom" called for a new image, one that in view of NATO's upcoming tenth anniversary, 1959, would refashion the "alliance" into a "community." So advertising would "make clear to the world the striking superiority, as much moral as material, of the Western conception of Man and his dignity." The NATO Birthday, NATO Song, and NATO promotional slogans such as "Good night—sleep tight—NATO stands on guard," "N.A.T.O—four letters that spell peace," and "Since NATO, not an inch of territory lost" would work "to forge a history of community and tradition."[25]

Not just as seller of products, then, but as merchandiser of ideas and institutions, JWT established its first outposts on the continent in 1927–28. With the arrogance of true believers, its agents found that "by our own standards, the great mass of German advertising is bad," and store displays "atrocious." In German press advertising, "Mechanics receive more attention than the 'message' with attention to so-called 'clever' art and eye-catching typography, emphasizing the unusual, with the effect of reducing the amount, importance, and quality of the copy."[26] In Sweden and Denmark, they found that "this complex mixture of art and craft that we know as advertising is simply beyond the range of Scandinavian thought. We can explain our technical methods, for example, to prospective writers or printers or artists, or even to the Danish agents of our clients, and we get usually nothing more than a half-hearted 'yes, yes.' The most careful discussion is largely wasted. It's like talking of the fourth dimension: the background, the *belief* in the thing is not there."[27] More generally, they determined that little could be accomplished where there was still a culture of haggling, as in Poland, for selling brands through local retailers called for rigorously fixed prices. In eastern Europe it proved "impossible to keep prices uniform . . . with shrewd Polish Jews carrying on most of the mercantile trade, and Jews forming a large part of the buying population." Sweden was simple by comparison, largely because the retailer was a "pure bred Swede" and not "a foreigner or of an objectionable race."[28] Stereotyping is indispensable to the advertising trade. And these images were not surprising in an industry that until the 1960s was dominated by white Protestant elites, rife with racial prejudice, and insouciantly anti-Semitic.

One measure of JWT's self-importance was its high cost. Its fee of 15, later 17.65 percent on the net expenditures for a campaign was nonnegotiable. This commission was advanced in a milieu in which clients were accustomed to commissions of 5 or 10 percent and fees were almost always sweetened by secret rebates from the media where the ads were placed. The primary purpose was to establish the value of a full-service agency—a value that couldn't be ascertained on the basis of sales alone. The high cost also reflected the monopoly price these services could command once they were accepted as valuable. That for several decades its pricing policy deterred the company from obtaining local accounts was beside the point. The prestige attached to it added to its aura. And eventually it made for great success. Not in the 1920s or the 1930s, but certainly by the 1960s, JWT established the benchmark for the high fees charged by leading local agencies for services whose efficacy was always hard to gauge. In doing so, the company also jump-started the concept that the more of a country's gross national product was spent on advertising, rising upward to 7–8 percent, the better it was launched on the road to development.

Above all, JWT took pride in improving the milieu in which it operated. The success of its London office was its pride and joy, as well as be-

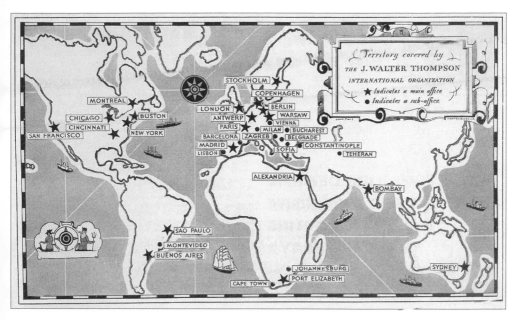

The new world of scientific advertising: the full-service agency in its global reach. Fortune, *March 1930.* By permission of the J. Walter Thompson Company.

ing useful to its later continental operations. When the office had first opened, it operated for the purpose of placing British products like Pear's soap and Peter's chocolate on the American market, as well as serving as a stopping-off place for the peripatetic Mr. Thompson. However, it wouldn't flourish until the terms of trade had changed between the United States and Great Britain and the London office began to acquire important American corporate accounts on its own. The first came in 1924, when Libby, McNeill and Libby advanced $100,000 to break into the British markets for canned food. After Sun Maid Raisins started to advertise on a big scale and Lever Brothers, the U.S. subsidiary of Unilever, hired the agency to promote its new bar soap, Lux, JWT moved ahead of the venerable Crawford Company to become Britain's largest advertising firm. By 1930 the company occupied the nine-story Bush House, a quasi-skyscraper, the first in London to be built with American money. It also boasted of being the biggest user of color in the British Isles. In 1924 it became the first firm to have its own market research department. And in 1933 it established the British Market Research Bureau, the first facility to offer to prepare consumer studies for non-clients.[29]

As the decade closed, reports back to the home office from what the agents abroad teasingly called "our far-flung empire" took the measure of the company's success. The Paris director recalled that when he had arrived eighteen months before, "all we knew about the French . . . was that they used a great many gestures and frequently uttered 'impossible.'" Persevering, the Paris operation made rapid progress. The offices had since moved to Place Vendôme from a two-room fourth-floor walk-up at 16 Rue de Gramont on the outer boulevards, and the staff increased from three to fourteen. Meanwhile "all France had been divided into eight marketing areas" on the basis of newspaper circulation figures that "we know are reliable." The bureau had conducted twelve consumer investigations entailing more than 3,000 interviews. Each month it placed 206 different advertisements composed in four languages in the press of ten countries. In Germany, agents boasted of having acquired more information on press circulation and advertising rates than the continent's largest publishing firm, Berlin's House of Ullstein. This feat was made possible only by the doggedness of U.S. government commercial consuls who went city by city, checking the circulation rates, political outlook, and social composition of the readership of hundreds of newspapers and magazines. Thus armed with local knowledge, U.S. government support, and big capital, JWT broke into the German press cartel, no mean feat. In Spain, with "native help," Arthur Hartzell, the Madrid head of office, was conducting first-time-ever door-to-door surveys on behalf of Frigidaire and mulling over how to breach the cloistered domesticity of Spanish grandes dames. In Belgium, the Antwerp subsidiary introduced the Thompson Index, a chart of purchasing power based on totaling per-capita automobile and telephone ownership and levels of income tax by province.[30] True, most of the accounts the company handled were American. For firms with little prospect of moving beyond their current clientele, the services JWT offered were extravagant and the fees exorbitant. But that fact didn't impede curiosity about the firm's operations or the local perception that for better or worse American ad agencies represented the future of the business.

Revolutionizing the Grammar of Advertising

As always, claims of accomplishment presented as claims of superiority should be treated with skepticism. "Backwardness" was first and foremost in the eyes of the beholder. As well as being a potent psychological bludgeon against contenders, such claims gave a tidy psychological boost to the "invaders" or "colonizers," as the Americans jocularly styled themselves. Anyway, bluster was part and parcel of a profession that put a huge premium on novelty and image. European advertising men went along. They accepted or rejected the Americans' bluff depending on whether it helped or hindered their own designs. So the pragmatic, garrulous Marcel Bleustein-Blanchet, founder of Publicis, later France's leading advertising agency, flaunted French anti-Americanism but saw himself conceding nothing to American power when he boasted that he visited "the States regularly to recharge my batteries and cultivate my 'rage to persuade,' and I have never been disappointed. Each time, I leave newly enthusiastic, taking with me an innovation, a project or a fresh angle."[31] In the first of several memoirs, he recalled the hospitality of the people at J. Walter Thompson and the McCann Company on his maiden trip in 1929, as well as his marvel at the high technical quality of their services. Returning again in 1933, he took in more information on his forte, radio advertising; and upon his return he established his own Radio Cité (after Radio City Music Hall), the first private station in France to broadcast from 6:00 A.M. to midnight and the first to offer contests, commercial jingles, talent searches, and on-the-scene news reporting. In 1938, on yet another visit, he made the acquaintance of David Sarnoff, the president of RCA, who in turn introduced him to George Gallup, from whom he learned of the use of opinion polls not only to promote sales but also to predict political outcomes.[32] To Bleustein-Blanchet's regret, it would not be until 1954 that in the Radical party leader Pierre Mendès-France he found a candidate willing to try them out. Meanwhile, marching to the beat of U.S. innovations, he wholeheartedly endorsed Ernst Dichter's psychological motivation studies and established the Prénatal chain to supply French women with the ready-to-wear fashions worn by pregnant American women. In 1958 he turned the ground floor of his headquarters on the Champs Elysées into Le Drugstore: open eighteen hours a day, with its chic late-night clientele, magazine and book section, "pic-nic" delicatessen, gift shop, and restaurant, this elegant emporium resembled not at all the U.S. soda fountain that had inspired its name yet did bring Peoria closer to Paris if only by flouting prevailing conventions of French retailing.[33] In the decade following, Bleustein-Blanchet introduced the concept of "social marketing," a form of advertising then being heavily promoted by JWT and Young & Rubicam to take "a long-run public-interest perspective" rather than focusing exclusively on "the consumer's short-term satisfaction." Naturally none of these innovations would have turned Publicis into post–World War II France's leading firm had not this astute, if rudimentarily educated son of Jewish furniture dealers on the Boulevard Barbès not had a remarkable sense of timing, considerable charm, drawn warm support from his own tight-knit family network, and gained access to government favors through the connections he forged while fighting with Charles de Gaulle's Free French forces during the Liberation.[34]

The conventional story, the one that Bleustein-Blanchet tells, is that advertising in post–World War I Europe resembled the American industry but was several decades behind. When in May 1927, as a twenty-year-old with no formal training, he set up shop, it is true that Paris was home to only three other agencies of the American kind, namely Jep et Carré, Dam, and Elvinger. And it was in that three-room second-floor walkup apartment off a dumpy back courtyard on the Rue de Faubourg-Montmartre that the imaginative novice wrote his first ad copy for Le Comptoir Cardiner, a gift shop belonging to friends of his mother, then for two other Jewish-owned businesses, Brunswick, "the furrier who causes a furor," and André, the "shoemaker who knows how to shoe." Common practice at the time had the copy picked up by brokers who brought it around to a placement agency. In France, the chances are that the broker would have been Havas, which was greatly expanding its domestic advertising services as its role as a world news agency, like Britain's Reuters, declined in the face of the United States' Associated Press. Neither the broker nor the advertising agent, much less the advertiser, necessarily knew the actual rates being charged or the circulation figures.

What was sure was that the ad copy, when published, was massed together in the back pages, the jumbled layout and eccentric typefaces depending on the whim of the chief compositor according to what pleased his tired eye and the fonts that happened to be left unused after the rest of the newspaper had been set. The advertisements themselves, framed in minute boxes, were mostly for goods that would have had no market if not heavily publicized: "pseudo-pharmaceutical remedies . . . full of aggression and impudence [that] took pride of place," interspersed with "veiled ads for bordellos and abortion services." The ads exhausted the supply of "bad advertising superlatives"—"superb," "magnificent," "astounding," "luxurious," "sensational," "can't be beat," "incomparable," "unheard of," "the only one," "the best." One ad promised a "'sewing machine' for a few cents, then sent you a needle when you mailed in your payment!"[35] The reigning theorists of advertising, even the most eminently sensible like Octave-Jacques Gérin, were inspired by theories of psychic suggestion. Advertising was a form of hypnosis, as Gérin, known as the "father of French advertising," explained in his often-quoted *La publicité suggestive* (1911); effective advertising worked by dint of subliminal appeals.[36]

Yet, rather than considering it "backward" or "behind," European advertising should be regarded as working off of a basically different set of economic resources, cultural traditions, and aesthetic principles from the American. Like European distribution generally, advertising pivoted around the major capitals of consumption and their mainly bourgeois clientele. Trendsetters could thus rely on what Edward Bernays called the "innate social-fashion-taste planning" of European elites.[37] Given that manufacturers, stores, and places of entertainment—the main advertisers—had well-established relations with their clients, there was no necessary reason to jettison seasoned typographic and pictorial conventions in the interest of building up sales.

This "innate planning" common to still homogeneous commercial cultures was greatly reinforced by the rich design resources available for publicity in the neighborhood clusters of graphic design shops, book producers, type foundries, and lithographic industries that found in the city centers the perfect backdrops for the superb production of luminous book covers, intricate decorative labels, and the elaborate shop-window displays that were the handiwork of the artists and craftsmen they employed. Major advances in lithography, the chemical-based printing process invented by German Aloys Senefelder in 1797, had so refined the craft of postermaking that as early as 1848 it was possible to print sheets in large batches by slathering ink on grease-etched limestone to bring the colored regions into relief, retouching the design, and stamping the images on large paper leaves. By the turn of the century, gorgeous posters plastered city surfaces of every kind, from train tunnels to street urinals.

In reality, government authorities closely monitored public spaces to prevent commercial signposting from running riot. This was the intention of a French law of 1881: by making it a crime to violate the areas marked "Defénse d'afficher" with commercial clutter, it reiterated the liberal principle of freedom of expression, but defended the official "posting places" allocated for electoral and official notices from signposting and graffiti. To keep commercial notices under surveillance, but especially to earn revenue, municipal governments required a tax stamp

The humanistic old world of postering: kiosk with pedestrians on a Berlin street. Die Reklame, *September 1924.* Courtesy of the New York Public Library.

to indicate that the item had been registered, its content deemed appropriate, and a fee paid according to its size. In post-1848 Prussia, the institution of the kiosk or Litfass column was likewise intended to discipline the chaos of wall postings that ensued once political censorship ended. The inventor of the specially designed columns, the soon-to-be-rich typographer Ernst Litfass, was also contracted by the city of Berlin to maintain them.[38] Unlike in the United States and Britain, where billboards and other postings were unlicensed, and advertising notices showed up practically everywhere, political authorities on the continent saw the powers of persuasion of advertising as a rival force to the degree that they encroached on public space.

The bias against commercial expression had the paradoxical effect of turning new experiments in advertising, as the spectacularly crafted U.S. corporate advertising was judged to be, into an appealingly iconoclastic medium, one that was initially far more attractive to European cultural vanguards than to corporate elites. So with some titillation, it was discovered that nothing was sacred before the American juggernaut: not the privacy of the body, not death, certainly not religious sentiment. The earnest professional who upon his return from the United States reported excitedly about the boosts that would come to his metier's legitimacy from polished ad copy, audits to verify newspaper circulation and copy rates, and Better Business Bureaus to denounce plagiarism, check for faulty products, and more generally solicit public confidence in the profession's probity, cringed at the memory of some of the excesses he had seen. By any criterion the publicity showed awful taste that pictured Christ on the Cross and a Roman soldier offering him gall to quaff his thirst with apologies that it wasn't Vinegar X.[39] The last thing that a not-yet-legitimate profession wanted to risk was to associate itself with anticlerical Europe's own hearty strains of blasphemy.

So it proved an unexpected blessing for the emerging profession that government law and church censorship, not to mention bourgeois niceties, restrained the locals' sacrilegious temperament from erupting into the commercial domain, at least until the cultural revolution of the late 1960s, when European laicity would firmly bond with American commercialism. Thereafter, from the point of view of sacrilege, Vinegar X couldn't hold a candle to European impiety. Oliviero Toscani, later to become world-notorious for his Benetton campaign posters, set the pace as early as 1972, when on behalf of the upstart Italian company Jesus Jeans he made an outsize street poster featuring a female model in jeans the campaign centerpiece. The legends on her backside, "You will have no other Jeans but me" and "He who loves me will follow me," incited just that flash of notoriety which advertising feeds on, especially after they were condemned by Italian bishops and intermittently banned by Italian public authorities. Notoriety turned into sales, and Jesus Jeans successfully carved out a tidy market niche between the U.S. giants Wranglers and Levi's.[40]

In the 1920s, however, the craze for advertising was at first mainly an aesthetic plaything for intellectual elites, its stripped-down language, mass appeal, and zinging business tempos bespeaking the new bridges between art and everyday life—and between people and things—so important to the politically engaged aesthetic experimentation of the postwar decade.[41] "Advertising is all-powerful; it adorns the world with fresh raiment," wrote Jacques Jongert, the Dutch postermaker, in those years. "Advertisement is the desire for growth that is in us all, the desire for continually different development and ever more perfect form in society."[42] In Leipzig in the spring of 1922 the fair fathers commissioned Peter Behrens to build Ad City (Reklameburg), a task the modernist architect tucked into by planting a gaudy citadel right in the middle of the central Market Square, its three-story-high corner turrets set over jagged-edged expressionist advertising kiosks, the whole magnificent jumble bestrewn with blown-up trademarks, giant-lettered brand names, and oversized papier-maché icons—an upended grand piano, a beer bottle, a coffee grinder. For the city's cultural avant-garde, it was exuberant critique; for local cultural conservatives, it was "an abomination, the likes of which the world ha[d] never before witnessed."[43]

In Berlin prominent writers including Frank Wedekind, Kurt Schmitters, Carl Zuckmayer, and Bertolt Brecht hired out their talent to write advertising copy, to the embarrassment of critics of the new wave of commercialism. Remembering his visit from Vienna, where his politically correct tastes had been cultivated in the circles that sat in worship of the irascible Karl Kraus, Elias Canetti recalled his excitement at being introduced to his idol Brecht, a fixture at Schlichter's Café, on a warm summer evening. Looking for a conversational entrée, the twenty-year-old "railed against the advertisements contaminating Berlin," assuming that the stick-thin poet-playwright, then thirty and grubbily dressed like an unemployed proletarian, would share his sober cultural predilections. Not at all: Brecht's reply was crushingly dismissive: "They did not bother him; on the contrary, he said, advertisements had their good points; he had written a ditty for Steyr automobiles and been given a car for it. For me, these were words from the devil's own mouth. His boastful confession floored me." Ibby Gordon, a common friend, tried to comfort the crestfallen purist in sweetly gendered terms: "He flatters his car even now. He talks about it as if were his girlfriend. Why shouldn't he flatter it *beforehand* in order to get it?"[44]

Even the most sensational advertising, that which the casual observer would have described as epitomizing "American methods," took a different tack from what U.S. experts intended when they spoke reverentially of the "science of marketing." Take the case of André Citroën, the upstart car manufacturer, surely the most Americanizing industrialist in all of Europe. He visited Detroit repeatedly, purchased U.S. machines for his assembly lines on Paris' Quai de Javel, built company sports, recreational, and health facilities for his workers following American designs, at one moment even had his whole staff learn English, established a sales-training school for his dealers, obtained American backing for SOVAC, the first credit company to finance major consumer appliances and office equipment, and was rarely quoted in the press without a nod to Henry Ford. As the first European carmaker to mass-produce automobiles, Citroën counted on generating a mass outlet by advertising: "publicité technique," he insisted, not "publicité héroïque," and he paid for it richly as the first A-1 rolled off the assembly line in 1919 by taking out big loans. Yet Citroën never undertook a market study until 1935. And that was only after the firm, burdened by heavy debt, depressed markets, and aged equipment, went bankrupt in 1934, its founder died soon afterward at only fifty-seven, and its management was taken over and reorganized by the Michelin Tire Company.

Around the same time that General Motors was hiring J. Walter Thompson to mastermind its global accounts, André Citroën was tinkering with a marketing strategy designed to turn himself into a globally recognized brand name much as Ford had done without any direct advertising in the decade before GM became a significant competitor. The focus was not on the corporate logo or the particular model car, but on the man Citroën, the Napoleon of carmakers. The strategy had its logic, and was certainly congenial to the industrialist's grandiose style of entrepreneurship. Faced with a public suspicious of newcomers, especially newcomers who were Parisians, Jews, and without any particular experience in car manufacture, and having as his main rivals Renault, France's first well-established car producer, and Peugeot, the staid family firm from the Jura long familiar to French households for having produced hoop skirts, umbrellas, and bicycles, Citroën needed to push his way into the public eye by associating his name with the phenomenon of modern motoring.[45] Taking Paris as his commercial backdrop, the "Henry Ford of France" took a cue from Detroit by opening his factories in the Grenelle quarter of the city to visitors, the only manufacturer in all Europe to do so, and he located his showrooms on the Place de l'Opéra, the busiest commercial space in the world. He made sure that his name appeared in every possible venue—in cartoonists' vignettes, on banners towed through the sky, on toy cars, taxi fleets, and tour buses, and on the vehicles in the Paris-to-Timbuktu car rallies, which were carried out in the spirit of Napoleon's Egyptian campaign with similar claims for their usefulness to identify commercial traffic routes across Africa and to collect scientific information. The *summum* was to commandeer the Eiffel Tower. First rented in 1925 on the occasion of the Exposition of Decorative Arts, it offered a structure for the Franco-Italian engineer Fernand Jacopazzi to spell out C-I-T-R-O-E-N. The first year the name was set out in 200,000 lights in the shape of a constellation, surrounded by stars, comets, and signs of the zodiac; the second, amid four fountains of light that spurted up and down; and in 1927, surrounded by thunderbolts flashing from heaven to earth.[46]

The public enjoyed such spectacles but remained distrustful of advertising as a guide to purchasing goods. When Bleustein-Blanchet started, he recalled, he faced "the scorn of decent people." Advertisers were caught in a vicious circle: "Charlatans made French consumers distrust advertising and this distrust made manufacturers unwilling to spend money on it."[47] Customers could afford to distrust advertising, for they still engaged in a type of shopping in which traditional tastemakers such as small shopkeepers, family members, or Mme. Colouche, Frau Brühl, or Signora Boldini next door had greater authority than the impersonal processes of giving advice supplied by advertising. To earn that trust, advertisers, unused to speaking to any but a narrow bourgeois public, would have to take two different steps at the same time: to earn the confidence of other bourgeois professions so they wouldn't be suspected of crass slumming, and to experiment with new vernaculars that afforded some guarantee of communicating with a mass public.

The Crisis of the Poster

What powers would be gained by appropriating the new vernacular of advertising? What lost? The stakes involved in forsaking one medium of commercial communication for another come to the fore in "the crisis" of the poster, also called "art on the street."

In its most elementary form, the crisis centered on whether to pursue the editorializing copy style familiar to readers of the American mass-circulation press or to prefer the design aesthetic associated with European postermaking traditions. The textual style promised profits and new professional dignity, whereas the visual representation of goods identified with poster design promised to preserve artistic autonomy and defend local aesthetic traditions. Those who staked their future on the new argued that goods be portrayed realistically to highlight what they did for the consumer, as American practice recommended. Those who wanted to stay with the prevailing styles of representation argued that goods should be animated by symbolic, evocative pictorial traditions, using subliminal references and psychological suggestion to activate latent desire. Back and forth: publicity worked best once the consumer understood the "reason why"; no, it was most effective if it made an emotional indent with a visual "punch in the eye."[48]

Behind these conflicting postures, publicists were arguing about the fundamentals of their practice: whether they should stand by their familiar bourgeois public and notions of bourgeois vocation or instead embrace a vernacular accessible to these voracious new publics, whoever they were; whether they should remain linked to the structure of the craft world, poor, but mindful of the individual and the deep meaning of Art, or turn to promoting big brands and succumb to becoming cogs in the wheel of corporate capitalism. In sum, fears about the fate of the world of the poster were magnified by American competition, though at bottom they reflected real, if incompletely grasped, changes that European society itself had been undergoing since the war, changes for which there were no easy solutions. "The cry of the posters from the concrete walls / Proclaims a fairyland that we have lost": aching words from 1927 by the Dadaist poet Richard Hülsenbeck, recalling the good old days of the Belle Epoque.[49]

Whether or not the prewar years were good times, placarding city surfaces with posters had been the dominant practice in pre–World War I advertising. By the turn of the century, the three-stone lithographic process enabled artists to achieve every conceivable color, yielding nuances and intensity impossible in other media. Paper was relatively cheap, and the ability to combine images with a memorable line of well-chosen words in a format so magnificent and economical turned urban streets into veritable corridors of commercial design. As posters gave value to commerce, they in turn acquired commercial value, becoming collectors' items as exhibitions, galleries, and magazines celebrated their creators, and dealers and connoisseurs trafficked in their purchase and sale.[50]

The poster's worth increased too because the growing volume of merchandising put a premium on inventive advertising. The merchant wanting to market a special article to the bourgeois trade, say, silverware with mother-of-pearl handles, looked for a motif that stood out from the all-purpose designs that lithographic companies normally stocked. He knew that the public easily became bored with cookie-cutter images, the only variation among them a slogan or phrase to identify the good being promoted; and he didn't want the image he had purchased to show up on posters advertising café concerts, patent medicines, or worse. In search of artistic originality and refinement, manufacturers and merchants bestirred themselves to seek out and hire commercial artists. As men of culture in societies that regarded instruction in design as part and parcel of learning the trade, they prided themselves on being knowledgeable patrons of the local art scene. With their backing, poster art experienced a high tide of experimentation, involving intensely local schools. There was art nouveau in Paris and its equivalent, the Jugendstil in Vienna, both renowned for their vibrant expression. The British Arts and Crafts movement, the Glasgow School, and the Dutch Sloalie flourished in the belief that commercial art also had a social mission to perform. This same commitment inspired the effort of the Munich Secession of 1893, the Viennese Secession of 1897, the Wiener Werkstatt founded in 1903, the German Deutscher Werkbund established in 1907, and the postwar foundation of the Bauhaus—all were rebellions against art for its own sake with the goal to infuse craft objects with social meaning, eliminate the barriers between artists and crafts people, and bring about collaboration among artist, manufacturer, merchant, and customer.

Like their markets, poster publicity was local, even if some leading postermakers were becoming known as artists to international connoisseurs. The prodigious talents of French postermasters Henri de Toulouse Lautrec, Alphonse Mucha, a Czech who worked in Paris, and Jules Chéret were mainly known locally, and among them the gallant Chéret best of all for his omnipresent charmingly festive orange, blue, and green music-hall posters and firm-handed management of Imprimerie Chaix, the printing house for René Péan, Lucien Lefèvre, Georges Meunier, and other masters of the exuberant snaky-haired female figures, curvy lines,

European "Thing in Itself" poster, Lucian Bernhard,
circa 1908. Gebrauchsgraphik, *April 1927.*
Courtesy of the New York Public Library.

and floral curlicues familiar to fin-de-siècle France's spectacular visual culture. Parisians were unfamiliar with the output of Hollerbaum & Schmidt, the Imprimerie Chaix's Berlin counterpart, which under the advertising expert Ernst Growald cultivated the so-called Berlin School, whose circle of modernist graphic artists included Lucian Bernhard, the inventor of the so-called *Sachplakat,* or "Object-Poster." To be known across national borders, like Leonetto Cappiello (1875–1942), famous throughout Latin Europe for the luminously brightly colored sprites and other wild creatures springing out of opaque brown-black backgrounds, designed for the scores of treats and cures familiar to the bourgeois public—including Cinzano, Bitter Campari, Chocolat Klaus, and Thermogène—required that the artist be both peripatetic and superproductive. Cappiello turned out 3,000 posters in the first quarter of the century as he moved between his native Italy, Spain, and his adopted home, Paris.

Several perils were said to account for the poster's "decline" or "decay" as a medium of commercial value. First, it was accused of degenerating into a partisan form of expression as the line between publicity and propaganda, never very clear, disappeared, and the poster became in turn the medium that government used to mobilize civilians during the war, left-wing street politics used to rally comrades during the 1918–1920 revolutions, and antagonistic parties used to fight bitterly contested elections. Then, the consensus of what made for good taste broke down. Beset by inflation and hectically changing markets, businessmen lost their ability to judge which pictorial conventions were best suited to selling their wares and services. Finally, commercial artists were so knocked about by unemployment and competition that they lost confidence in their craft, especially in its capacity to earn them a living.

To reestablish the poster's standing as a means of selling goods was no simple matter. Though postwar artistic experimentation greatly increased new varieties of figurative and pictorial motifs, commerce was increasingly conducted on too large a scale to permit regular contact between businessmen and the milieu of graphic artists. Forced to take up their portfolios in search of clients, commercial designers cast their personal idiosyncrasies in crasser forms. And when they were executed, the designs had too much personality. Which was another way of saying that they reflected the artist's own vision too strongly and too little that of the public's—which was harder and harder to intuit. At the same time, the old formulas, so successful in the prewar period, such as Lucian Bernhard's "Object" poster, with its intensely angular rendering of the commodity, intriguing lettering, and thick saturations of bright color from new inks that neither faded nor ran, lent themselves to tedious imitations. So the effects for which he was famed in posters for Pelikan pencils, Stiller ladies' shoes, and Manoli cigarettes began to look passé.

Even when young artists developed innovative styles that were commercially attractive as well as salable, it was only to discover that their work could be easily plagiarized. This loss of aura, in this case by sheer piracy, was the condition not only of graphic arts but of art in general in what Walter Benjamin famously called the "age of mechanical reproduction." Modern capitalism portended the "dismantling of the artist in his present form," as Georg Gross and Wieland Herzfelde warned in *Art in Danger* (1925). The commercial artist, the sources of his creative labor choked off, like all other artists now had to face up to the alternatives: "he could merge into industry as a designer or advertising man or else he must become a propagandist for the revolution."[51]

In turn, merchandisers and promoters suspected that the poster was becoming an anachronism, at least for their purposes. The 1920s had brought major shifts in distribution with new products coming on the

market, new clienteles in the lower-middle and working classes, the revamping of urban space, and economic crisis. As big-city populations
soared, local governments redistricted the commercial downtowns to facilitate the flow of motor traffic, cleaning out the clutter of poster emplacements, and built new subway lines and tramcar systems to whizz
passengers through the congested commercial centers to outlying districts. At the same time, the cost of poster campaigns soared as the price
of supplies and labor rose with inflation and city governments, strapped
for revenues, raised fees and imposed stiff fines to curb the clutter of posters, painted advertisements, enamel signs, and illuminated displays.
These levies were not reinvested in maintenance, including the repair of
hoardings vandalized by poor people who ripped out chunks of the glue-
laden paper as fuel for heating and cooking.[52]

With so much speed and so many new stimuli, the worry was that people had neither the time nor the taste to appreciate the old, if gorgeous,
styles of signaling products and events. Were the harried salaried "little
men" of Hans Falada's 1929 novel *What Now, Little Man?* as inclined to
appreciate their qualities as the slow-paced bourgeois clientele for whom
they were originally designed? Or Siegfried Kracauer's "little shop girls,"
their thoughts distracted by the movies? Could the poster still work its
magic if it followed its onetime customers into the beflowered but empty
streets of garden suburbs? Could poster campaigns be organized to differentiate one class of customer from another? Close tracking of commuting patterns offered one solution, Berlin experts calculated, given
that the 950,000 people who on an average workday mobbed the station
platforms on their way to and from work were in an ideal "subjective
state" to be impressed by advertising messages. Once promoters had
gauged the class character of this crowd, they could act accordingly. So
they would appeal to the workers crowded onto U-Bahn lines going eastward with posters for soap, cheap furniture, tobacco, clothing, and food
products. And for the better-off middle classes traveling the lines westward, they would poster for luxury wares, including furs, electric appliances, bathing suits, and record players.[53] As the rage for "rationalization" swept mid-1920s Europe, Parisian experts spoke of the need for an
accurate "reconnoitering" of emplacements to calculate the appropriate
"dosage" and "productivity" for posters. New indices of visibility were
drawn up, taking into account the number of passersby as well as the
length of daylight. "Sixteen hours of action" could be predicted for a
bright summer day, but only half that around the winter solstice, when

the sun rose around 8:00 A.M. and set at 4:00 P.M. and the air was sodden with pollution and drizzle.[54]

With attention spans shorter, product turnover more rapid, art styles more transient, and the struggle for space among competing claims more and more ferocious, the poster ceased to be the point of orientation it once was, good not just for days or months but even years. It still had its Andy Warhol moment of celebrity: "A successful poster immortalizes for twenty-four hours" was a Berlin advertising man's soulful joke.[55] The truth was rather that under the stress of the outpouring of announcements brought by Germany's postwar economic upheavals, Ernst Litfass' ingenious device to bring visual order to public space broke down, boding the destruction of the bourgeois commercial sphere. "The principal space" was now occupied by "the movie poster with its pernicious excrescences and high-sounding titles calculated to appeal to cooks and kitchen maids." It pressed down onto "the numerous announcements of offices for the buying and selling of gold and jewels, advertisements of pleasure resorts, 'beauty dances,' go-go girls, etc." These in turn were interspersed with "red placards topped with fabulous sums in millions of marks for this or that criminal." Betwixt and between, "small and modest like the agonized sighs of a man being suffocated, [there were] official state announcements for the benefit of people who, in reality, were no longer to be regarded as part of the economic life of the nation."[56]

Faced with dire predictions about the death of the poster, lively coalitions formed to engage in two distinctly different strategies in defense of European design traditions. One preached diehard resistance, mounted by joining the postermaker to regional markets and emphasizing the unique and local character of the poster as an idiom of commercial expression. This posture was especially visible in the segmented markets of southern Europe, notably Italy but in France as well. The other spoke to reform by developing a more varied aesthetic idiom and wider marketing appeal, and it was most eloquently practiced in Germany, drawing on its traditions of modernist artistic experimentation and the dynamism of its export-oriented economy.

The strategy of resistance was embodied by the Italian Giuseppe Magagnoli (1878–1933), the founder and director of the poster workshop Maga. A former salesman for the celebrated French poster concern Vercasson, Magagnoli set up his own atelier in his native Bologna in 1920, with showrooms centrally located in Milan and Paris and business connections as far away as Buenos Aires. Criticized as "old school" by proponents of the new advertising and overly invested in postering,

European "Punch in the Eye" poster, Achille-Lucien Mauzan,
1927. By permission of the Mirande Carnévalé-Mauzan Collection.

the firm went bankrupt in 1932, and the following year the choleric
Magagnoli died of heart failure.[57]

In its prime, however, Maga was a glorious undertaking, employing
the leading talents of French and Italian poster craft, notably Cappiello,
the French-born Achille-Lucien Mauzan, Mario and Severo Pezzati,
Marcello Nizzoli, Sinopico, and Pozzati (Sepo), as well as lesser-known
and often unnamed figures who worked in the house style. From the plat-
form of "Punch in the Eye" (*Pugno nell'occhio,* or *Pan dans l'oeil*), his
company newsletter, the excitable Magagnoli ranted against "all the old,
rancid, and idiotic systems used up to now." He especially despised the
purported scientificity and staid design of American corporate advertising, with its "difficult phraseology" and "cabalistic" formulas, whose
sole aims were to "boost the self-image of the speaker" and to impress
an "audience of imbeciles." In contrast, Maga's posters "materialized
ideas," aiming to "take audiences by surprise." As enlarged trademarks,
they "firmly fix the name of the product in their minds."[58]

Maga's international reputation rested on the prodigious output of

Mauzan (1883–1952), a virtuoso designer as well as inventive lithographer. Drawing directly on the stone or zinc, he could turn out daily two press-ready posters 140 by 140 centimeters worked in four colors; in his twenty-three years of peak activity he produced approximately 3,200 works. In keeping with the house style, Mauzan played on quick visual wit, the cunning of the gimmick *(la trovata)*, the odd juxtaposition, the animation of the inanimate object, the stereotype. On a poster for Berkel scales, the bright red scale stood at the forefront, with a Solomonic black-robed judge, his finger raised in admonition, under the words "Not all weights are equal"; for Radiotilina, a radium-based pep-up tonic, Judas was shown rising from the dead, enveloped in a shroud of sparkling yellow; for Augea metal cleaner, a pop-eyed Jewish pawnbroker feverishly polished his little mounds of coins. For Mauzan, a sensualist, a craftsman, advertising was a carnival of exotic imagery in rebellion against the rhetoric of restraint and reasonable consensus called for by corporate business advertising. The poster, like a circus barker, clamored for attention (and Clamor, fittingly, was Mauzan's first Italian undertaking, later to become the first Italian road sign company). In Italy, commented a British expert on publicity, "you have to increase the sound of your voice—to be heard."[59] The poster was also an "announcing machine," according to A.-M. Cassandre: it represented an animistic world, not a fearsomely commodified one in which "things ride in the saddle" (to recall Ralph Waldo Emerson's anxious image). People and objects interacted, as if useful to one other, their mutual attraction rehumanizing market exchanges. When the poster went up, the performance started, the visual effects multiplying to what ultimate effect nobody could tell. This was the bravado that had brought the youth from Bologna to Colibrì in 1932. Maybe Maga had sent them.

By contrast, the reform movement exemplified in German commercial art of the late 1920s was based in Berlin and was largely identified with the figure of Professor H. K. Frenzel, the founder and editor of *Gebrauchsgraphik*. Started in 1924 to promote "artistic publicity," the intellectually rich, exquisitely designed monthly enlarged its ambitions in 1928 to promote "international advertising art." Its goal was to update European commercial art by keeping abreast of design innovations all over the world, including Japan, but mainly the West, and especially the United States.[60]

In Germany itself it was impossible to speak of a single style, except to the degree that poster art resonated with the legacy of Johannes

Updated European "Thing in Itself" poster, Walter Nehmer,
circa 1926. Gebrauchsgraphik, *April 1927.*
Courtesy of the New York Public Library.

Gutenberg in its marvelous experimentation with lettering and typefaces, play of heraldic symbols, and tense engagement with modernity. At one extreme there was the "objectness" of the Berlin School of Lucian Bernhard, which in the postwar years fed into the modernist abstraction of internationalist design. Good advertising, by mustering symbolic representations, such as a crowing cock for early morning, an arrow for speed, a bird for flight, could yield a universal language. Form and function went hand in hand in a progressive, cosmopolitan, experimental, and artistically rigorous commercial design that seemed in every way a positive alternative to America's corporate advertising.[61]

At the other extreme there was the "amiable and soliciting" pictorial style identified with the Bavarian artist Ludwig Hohlwein, whose "expressive sentimentality" combined an unerring sense of color with a superb capacity of line. For subject matter he drew on the local traditions of genre painting—animals, landscapes, and still lives—as well as the vigorous local craft culture. And he had no qualms about deriving his subjects from photographs and "swipes" from magazines, including the *Saturday Evening Post*. At once elegant and populist, his work was widely popular in Germany. The same could not be said for Bernhard, who, as well as being Jewish, was regarded as too abstract for conventional middle-class taste. In the United States too, Holhwein was regarded as a kinsman of American commercial realism, albeit with perhaps too strong an aesthetic personality.[62]

The strategy of opening up to the world, becoming more responsive to commercial pressures, and deprovincializing local styles, which in practice involved mounting extravagant and beautiful expositions, partaking in international congresses, and studying *Gebrauchsgraphik* and likeminded trade publications, had two paradoxical effects.[63] One was to encourage a keen appreciation of the artistic conventions underlying local German schools, which perhaps contributed to sharpening regional idiosyncrasies, especially the contrast between Berlin's modernism and Munich's traditionalism respectively embodied by Bernhard and Hohlwein. The other was to suck individual German artists into the voracious gristmill of the American advertising industry, thereby adding to the United States' ever-accumulating mountain of cultural capital.

In February 1926 Lucian Bernhard could be found working in the design studio that Adolph Ochs, the owner of the *New York Times,* had provided for him in the Times Annex Building just off Times Square. When Otto Hahn stopped by to interview him on behalf of readers of

Gebrauchsgraphik, he paused to explain the tradeoffs between working in the United States and working in Germany. True, he had been flush with commissions since his arrival. But their execution required "a distinct departure" from the work that had made his reputation at home. Anybody who leafed through the *Saturday Evening Post* could see that "the guardians of the entire advertising world in America, that is the powerful advertising agencies, are much more concerned with maintaining a general level than with any soaring or jumping out of the ranks." As much as American advertising agencies plagiarized from German designs, they regarded most as "too brutal and extravagant" for local taste. Everything had to be toned down. At the moment, he had no difficulty finding a balance. He earned good fees in New York but kept a creative foothold in his workshop in Berlin, which his fellow poster master, Fritz Rosen, managed in his absence.[64] When, after the Nazis took power, he was expelled from his post in the German school system and his workshop was closed down, his move to the United States became permanent; another blow to the head of Old World commercial art.[65]

Bernhard's forced departure coincided with a more general drift in poster art that reduced its role as a medium of commerce even more, yet raised its public visibility. Its major sponsor had ceased being the department-store magnate, manufacturer, and entertainment impresario and had become instead the interventionist state of the Great Depression, political parties, interest groups sponsoring collective advertising campaigns, as well as the well-established firm whose reputation was so well known that it could benefit from patronizing important artists for the sake of "reminder value." That is the context for the Franco-Russian A.-M. Cassandre's man-in-movement posters for Dubonnet's Paris subway promotions as well as his looming prows for Compagnie Générale Transatlantique, Charles Loupot's whizzing cars for Peugeot, and Jean Carlu's smiling blue monster ingratiatingly holding out his soap cake for Monsavon. That context too explains the London City Council's commission of E. McKnight Kauffer's advertising series for the London Underground. It also explains Marcel Dudovich's turn from composing delicious art nouveau ladies shopping in the Rinascente department stores to designing faceless pillar-of-salt mothers for the Fascist regime's women's and children's organization.

Standing away from the hurly-burly of commerce, the posters of the 1930s promoted social messages. They appealed to the public—as opposed to the consumer—to purchase items beneficial to public health like milk or useful to the national economy such as bananas, rice, and beer, or, as in autarchic Italy and Germany, ersatz goods like synthetic wools and malt coffee. In so doing, postermakers allied themselves with the public space of politics rather than the commercial public space and with state power and organized interests in the name of mobilizing public interest rather than inviting individual consumption. True, the line between publicity—as belonging to the private sector—and propaganda—as belonging to the state, public sphere, and politics—had always been more porous in Europe than in the United States, where the separation between the two was cherished in theory, if not in practice.[66] It is also true that the poster could be at the service of the left or the right: of progressive regimes like Léon Blum's Popular Front or the fascist dictatorships. The point is that the poster now tended to represent commodities as icons of scarcity. True, to conserve a sense of the object was also to preserve the fiction of solidarity between artist, artifact, and public that delighted Mauzan. In fact it also celebrated holding at bay the alternative, which was to find a language to speak to mass publics about shared consumer wants. Roger-Louis Dupuy, who advertised his long-lived agency as an alternative to Americanizing trends, made the point in no uncertain terms: "No need to construct a scenario: the object, the object alone, the object-king, just solicit it, it will tell its own story."[67] Lacking a new scenario and with no new script, the commercial poster told the same old story: about scarce goods and narrowly self-referential social circuits.

Capitalist Populism: Texts in New Contexts

Its "crisis" was magnified as the poster was counterposed to what was ever more regarded as a commercially effective alternative, namely the carefully composed, tastefully arranged ad inserts circulated by means of the mass press. True, print advertising was already widely in use for publicity purposes in Europe. However, ad placement was hard to manage so long as rates and formats were not standardized and publishers kept circulation figures a secret. Moreover, most newspapers were openly affiliated with distinct social strata, particular political constituencies, and specific localities, so that ads had to be placed very widely, making national campaigns arduous and costly. In 1927 Germany, Europe's most literate country, a decent-size campaign called for inserts in 135 newspapers, adapting them to 127 different column sizes ranging in width from six to twelve centimeters. If a campaign for washing soap wanted to

American "Reason Why" advertisement. Saturday Evening Post,
May 11, 1929. By permission of General Electric.

reach every single housewife in Germany, it would have had to be placed
in 1,000 different newspapers.[68] Once printed, ad copy had to jostle for
space with a myriad of other announcements, most of which simply
named the product, without giving any information about it. It was as if

the newspaper itself were being treated as an emplacement, and the ad as a miniature poster, using only heavy black on white, emphatic with a single word, displaying the name of the article advertised in as large a typeface as was available. With no decoration or illustration whatsoever, it looked as if it had been composed "to deliver as hard as possible a blow between the eyes through the medium of printer's ink."[69]

In reality, the means of communication tending to displace the poster was not the press insert in itself but a specific kind, namely the carefully argued, meticulously designed, sometimes multicolor text advertisement that was becoming more and more conspicuous in mass-circulation magazines of the interwar years, in particular the *Ladies' Home Journal, Saturday Evening Post, Good Housekeeping,* and *Life* magazine. Exposed to this artifact by the marketing campaigns of J. Walter Thompson and other American companies in Europe or by studying the ad copy in American magazines and newspapers, European advertisers saw Americanness in its lengthy, densely packed text, well-crafted composition replete with titles, decoration, drawings, photography, and forthright way of addressing the public.

In fact American text advertising was a highly contrived artifact. In order to compose persuasive copy, seasoned staff labored for weeks, having pretested the market for the product and developed enough of a familiarity with the product's qualities to evince a strong if temporary dose of empathy for the consumer. Whatever the convention chosen—whether the advertisement offered a "testimonial" by a "social leader," a "before" and "after" contrast, or a cartoon vignette with recommendations from Aunt Jane or Uncle Henry—the copy aimed at giving the "reason why" such-and-such a product was being endorsed by setting out the good's characteristics and explaining how consumers could use it. Accordingly, the advertisement "sold the benefit instead of the product: illumination instead of lighting fixtures, prestige instead of automobiles, sex appeal instead of mere soap."[70] Playing on the fluidity of these novel categories of needs, text advertising created new openings for advertisers. By presenting goods as "collections of utilities rather than the thing in itself," Canadian sociologist William Leiss observed, "the utilities themselves [began to be] juggled about." In turn, "previous categories of need dissolve[d], new ones form[ed], [and] the constant re-division and recombination [made] it harder for individuals to develop coherent sets of objects and thus make judgements about the suitability of particular goods."[71] As a form of public address, well-articulated advertising texts blended "characteristics of formal-public and informal-private styles" to develop a colloquial language that, though it mimicked the popular, was by virtue of what it included and left out distinctly of corporate and commercial origin.[72] Authoritative but never academic, intimate in tone yet not condescending, this new vernacular was inflected with a democratic sensibility as if it were a universal tongue, spoken by promoter and public alike. This was the style that Michael Schudson felicitously calls "capitalist realism"—in contrast to "socialist realism" and which I shall call here "capitalist populism" to underscore the democratic affect implicit in its sociable address.[73]

Like medieval miniatures, text ads were chock-full of visual clichés and moral postulates, illuminating parables of virtue and vice. For their goal was not primarily to change brand preferences so much as to establish clear criteria for making choices. With her refined compositions, JWT's Helen Lansdowne Resor was undoubtedly the old master of the genre. From her ad copy there emanated the calm reassurance that the scale of contemporary life entailed no loss of intimacy, the publicness of needs no loss of privacy, standardization of products no loss of individuality; and the authorities who were being introduced, however distant from family and neighbors, were as trustworthy as the community doctor, church pastor, or grade-school teacher. Imitating the look and layout of the medium in which it was printed, mainly illustrated magazines and newspapers, it played on the lack of differentiation between "real" reading matter and editorializing for consumer products. Quickly perused, it could then be reread in the calm of the evening before being handed on to other family members, neighbors, and friends. All said and done, it appeared to render "the common understanding of its audience."[74]

To account for the difference of the American text style with respect to their own advertising vernacular, Europeans offered explanations that, if sometimes fanciful, never lacked some kernel of truth. So it was said that American advertising worked by evocation and the European by seduction. The American text style was puritan whereas the European poster was pagan. Americans worshiped the word, reading advertising texts as if they were the Bible, with some of the same fundamentalist fervor and belief in self-conversion. By contrast, Europeans worshiped multiple idols, bowing before the intense visual power of the poster with its ornamental sensuality and iconic rendering of the god-commodity.[75] American graphic designers were interested in the "reproduction" of things, commented one French poster master after viewing an exposition of

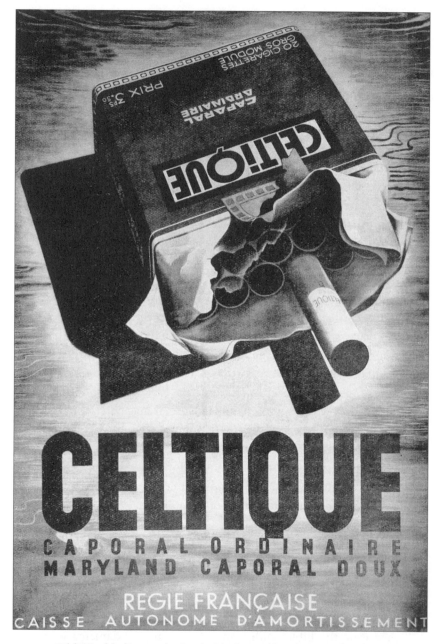

Old World elite aesthetic: A.-M. Cassandre draws "the object alone, the object-king" for Celtique. La Publicité, October 1937.
Courtesy of the New York Public Library.

American poster art, whereas their French counterparts were interested in their "translation." If the European was advertising a cigarette, he would focus attention on the object itself by showing the smoker's lips gripping a cigarette or a giant package with two or three poking out. The American, by contrast, would treat the cigarette as it appeared in reality, showing a satisfied smoker while the text set out the reasons for his contentment.[76] This layman's intuition uncannily anticipated the distinction that the French sociologist Pierre Bourdieu would draw a half-century later between the "popular aesthetic" and the "aesthetic of elites." On the one hand, there were the people, who, "dominated by ordinary interests and urgencies . . . reluctantly accept abstraction not just from lack of familiarity but from a deep-rooted demand for participation, which formal experiment systematically disappoints." On the other hand, there were cultural elites, who "believe in the representation . . . more than in the things represented" because they experience the world "freed from urgency and through the practice of activities which are an end in themselves." To the repugnance of aesthetic elites, American commercialism accentuated the divide by siding with those "dominated by ordinary interests and urgencies," with a "deep-rooted demand for participation."[77]

Capitalist populism enabled American corporate advertising to fill that vacuum of advice for a public in need of broad guidance, not just about product attributes but also about taste, social correctness, and psychological satisfactions. Even though the public it was addressing was by no means infinite, perhaps 70 percent in total, it had to stretch its vocabulary to embrace the cross-class mass of customers who were regarded as its main targets. In particular, it had to address the least well known public, namely the female. The "little lady" of the household had been J. Walter Thompson's first target when he originally sized up the profits to be had from the monopoly on placing ad placement in women's magazines. By the 1920s it was a cliché that women were the "purchasing agents" for their families, and that 85 percent of all consumer spending was done by women. Accordingly, the stretch to reach women and formalize the language by which they might be engaged revolutionized the medium and vocabulary of commodity exchange. "The proper study of mankind is Man," according to *Printers' Ink,* "but the proper study of markets is Woman."[78]

However limited this audience actually was in the United States, it was incomparably wider than anywhere in Europe. Limited to the middle classes, wealthy peasants, and the highest-paid industrial working-class families, the public for advertising might have amounted to 30 percent of the people in Great Britain and northwestern Europe, 15 or 20 percent in France and Germany, and perhaps 5 or 10 percent in Italy. Spain could be regarded as a worst case: JWT's local agent Arthur Hartzell found nothing by which even to begin to gauge "purchasing power"; telephones, a usual measure, numbered only 185,000 among a population of 22 million, and an electrically wired home for the most part meant a single line attached to a lightbulb illegally spliced into the municipal electric grid. Not being able to chart purchasing power with the usual categories of revenue from A to D, he likened the market to "a chocolate layer cake: the icing would represent class AA (the wealth aristocracy whose wealth is something no one can estimate), the top layer would represent Class A and the center layer (which is almost invisible to the human eye) would represent class B. Classes C and D represent the thick soggy mass which is at the bottom. In other words, there is an enormous number of people in Spain which make up a market that is of no interest whatsoever to the American manufacturer."[79]

Facing far smaller publics, with fewer resources and little pressure from clients, European advertisers had good reasons not to appropriate a language of communication that many of their own set regarded as being pretentiously didactic, grossly literal, technically ill adapted to presentation in the European press, and difficult to understand for anybody not fully literate.[80] Yet they also had compelling reasons to experiment with American methods, in addition to reacting to the obvious drawbacks of postering and roughshod printed texts: one was to legitimate their claim to having real expertise in advertising in order to obtain client accounts, and the other was to legitimate new forms of mass address whose development had been inhibited locally by social diffidence and the incapacity to recognize, much less communicate with, emerging communities of consumption.

By the 1930s this groping for accounts had led to a striking transformation in the style and address of European advertising. As the insider Bleustein-Blanchet concluded, the logic had been accepted: "to sell well, you must reverse the communication process. The route is no longer from product to consumer but from consumer to product."[81] The risk-takers were first and foremost the new full-service agencies as well as large firms' in-house publicity departments, perhaps two score of them, counting Great Britain and the continent. American models were their primary inspiration, and a good half-dozen were founded by personnel shed by J. Walter Thompson, Erwin, Wasey, and other U.S. firms as they retrenched in the early 1930s. They found clients in manufacturers who, faced with volatile markets, were uncertain whether to cut marketing costs or to increase them. The latter view prevailed as it was recognized that advertising offered a means not simply to attract customers, but to publicize prices so that retailers wouldn't overcharge or offer discounts, to establish qualities with which the retailer was unfamiliar, and to appeal to consumers to keep up pressure on the retailer, who otherwise might not want to risk stocking a novel item. In sum, the advertising industry was a welcome invention for a time of economic disorder, allying itself in turn with the new demand and the old supply sides of the economic equation. What had become clear, as Maurice Halbwachs cautiously observed, was that in Europe "advertising [was] no longer a means subordinated to the ends of enterprise, but an end in itself . . . in search of profits."[82]

In turn, ad agencies pressed to make the mass-circulation press a more pliable outlet for publicity. JWT-ers had often posed the questions "What are your rates per thousands of readers?" and "What is your effective circulation?" Often they couldn't get an answer. Germany's House of Ullstein was the exception, having started to have its circulation figures notarized in 1926—lest anybody doubt that its flagship, the *Berliner Illustrierte,* selling 1.9 million copies a week, was far and away the largest circulating advertising medium in the country. Indeed, Ullstein's management boasted that its whole great stable of magazines was "quite American in their advertising sections: the announcements are calculated to catch the eye, and in short well-worded sentences contain a description of the characteristics of the advertised product."[83] By the mid-1930s the bureaus of audit founded in most Western countries required that the press register circulation rates, and, in the interest of attracting advertising income, most newspapers and magazines were willing to comply. Advertising also provided an incentive to improving quality of reproduction, consistency of layout, and standardization of page formats and column sizes, an improvement facilitated by investment in giant new rotary presses and new rotogravure techniques often imported from the United States, which by the end of the 1920s had displaced Germany as the world's foremost exporter of typographic equipment.

The press itself was more disposed to welcome advertising in an effort to offset fast-rising costs not covered by circulation. Given a choice, advertisers preferred independent, middle-class dailies like the Parisian

L'Intransigeant or Milan's *L'Ambrosiano*. The public of the nationalist press might be well heeled, but it was not usually receptive to new products, especially not if they were foreign-made. Party newspapers were not off-limits, especially as they too began to welcome advertising to cover their costs. French advertisers appreciated that the socialist readership of *Le Populaire* lived mainly in the Paris area and, as workers went, were prudent consumers, well-enough off to save for radios, purchase small household items, and indulge in a late-day drink, as the name "Le Popu," a favorite brand, testified. After the Nazi party made its giant electoral breakthrough in 1932, the party newspaper, the *Völkischer Beobachter,* advertised itself in *Die Reklame* as the ideal medium to reach Germany's new middle classes. *VB* wasn't interested in publicity only to earn revenue. Publicity inserts gave its layout a modern look, making it seem legitimate, mainstream, even transcending politics, and that effect was desirable for a movement eager to please still-wary conservatives. As in the United States, magazines devoted the most space to advertising, especially magazines for women. Even so, no newspaper or journal came close to dedicating 40 percent of its space to advertising as *Life* magazine did. This excess was the prerogative of a society in which paper was cheap, advertising accounts fat, and readers more and more dis-habituated from differentiating the images and editorial voice of ad inserts from reportage and real fiction.[84]

The most significant pressure to shift to American-style text advertising was also the most complicated, namely to enable the advertiser to communicate with his public. As early as the late 1920s, European experts began to highlight the need to address women, though how that should occur was not immediately apparent. "Most money spent passes through the hands of women," wrote Hanns Korpff, who, with Edward Bernays's brother-in-law Bruno W. Randolph, had authored Germany's first widely circulated marketing manual. That trend was stating the obvious. The problem was that because women "relate everything directly to their appearance, their happiness, their sympathies," "the majority of marketers find it very difficult to write advertisements for women." They "think in terms that are too complicated, too masculine . . . They frequently use expressions that mean something entirely different to women, that lead to misunderstanding, indeed, that often offend them." Taking a page from American marketing, which Korpff knew intimately, from having started his professional career under Bernays's tutelage, he advised: "Make goods seem that they will make her life easier, more pleasant, and nicer. Text is important, likewise the picture illustrations . . . Women see things with their eyes—nothing can move them to read an ad that, for some reason or other, does not appeal to them on first sight."[85]

But whole groups of consumers, male as well as female, were open to being influenced by what was commonly called the New Living Culture. Siegfried Kracauer spoke of the "spiritual homelessness of the commodity world of the new class" as "the house of bourgeois ideas and feelings in which they previously lived . . . collapsed because of the erosion of its foundations, brought on by economic development," so they were living "at present without a doctrine to which they can look up, without a goal to guide them."[86] In some measure, various and sundry magazine advertisements—"for Koh-i-noor pencils, beds, crepe soles, white teeth, rejuvenation treatments, coffee consumption, dictaphones, quality pianos on weekly installments, as well as cures for hemorrhoids, hair loss, writer's cramp, and trembling, particularly in the presence of others, etc."—provided new axes of identity. But it was unclear whether in the face of this "spiritual homelessness" identity politics that rested on market messages was persuasive enough to reestablish social bearings; nor was it evident that advertisers were socially self-confident enough to adopt the empathetic posture required to communicate with masses of whom they had no way of having firsthand knowledge. Plainly, an advertising agent could no longer simply "Ask Jules," the majordomo, or question one's chauffeur for information about the tastes of "the cooks and kitchen maids." Nor was it useful advice to couch one's appeal according to banal distinctions of sex, as in "Seduce the Ladies," "Instruct the Gents."

Consider the problem of speaking with an authoritative voice: For the testimonial ad, a J. Walter Thompson favorite, American advertisers would enact scenarios with some degree of verisimilitude simply by telephoning the appropriate agency and describing what was desired. The agency would then check in its Rolodex and come up with an unemployed actor or other individual who, when properly outfitted, had the dignity to pass, say, as a trusted local bank president, loyal family doctor, or beloved grandfather. Within a few days the photographs would arrive. In Europe, by contrast, the advertiser who wanted, say, to produce photographic copy for an ad for watches that had a doting man of means bestowing a gold wristwatch on his daughter for her twentieth birthday, would have had to turn to his circle of acquaintances to find somebody to pose for it. When all of them would have begged off, he might have persuaded one of his more distinguished-looking retainers to dress up for the part, only to have the young lady decline to pose with the servants.[87] The royalty, stars, and socialites that J. Walter Thompson lined up for its advertisements had no equivalents in Europe, except perhaps in Scandinavia. From Berlin JWT's correspondent Julius Watkins reported that at the House of Ullstein they had no notion of what "I was talking about" when he spoke of testimonial advertising: there was no universally accepted "smart set" in Weimar Germany, and the "old Royalist Crowd of course, would have a very narrow hearing." Neither were actresses "regarded in the same way as starlets in America as persons to be admired and imitated."[88]

Short of speaking in a wholly foreign vernacular, European advertisers would have to invent one that was authentically their own. However, for that to happen, as the observant Swiss advertising expert Adolf Guggenbühl insisted, they had to reach out to the public; "they had to stop saying, 'I' and 'we' want, and start saying 'you.'" They had to stop believing that mass consumption meant an end to their own individuality, which also meant ceasing to end every conversation on the subject with "Thanks be to God that I am not like them over there . . . that I'm still an individual person, not a standardized mass product!" "Culture means community," Guggenbühl insisted: "We'll progress spiritually and economically if we stress commonalities more than differences." Better to "live in a standardized house with a boiler, central heating, and a bathroom than a personalized, individual, and original house with no warm water, tile-stove-heated rooms, and a zinc tub in the cellar." The notion of originality was just a bourgeois excuse for inaction: "during the greatest artistic eras, such as the Gothic Age, the originality of individual artists was of such minor significance that today in many cases, we are able recognize them only by their schools rather than as individual artists."[89] In sum, the bourgeois advertising man need not renounce good taste, but he had to cease being a snob.

The pressure to incorporate, even sometimes to plagiarize, American text styles came from leading enterprises and showed up particularly vividly in the ever-more-massive advertising for food, drink, and toiletries that was spurred by the introduction of American brands, national industries in search of mass markets, and new standards of diet and hygiene.

In interwar France, no advertising was more familiar than Cadum's, and no image more familiar than Bébé Cadum, the endearingly curly-haired, chubby-faced, rosy-colored infant that was Cadum toilet soap's brand symbol. The image was so prominent, so controversial, and so commercially successful that when the company changed its marketing campaigns in the 1930s the public—as well as the advertising profession—took notice.[90] True, the company had been a big advertiser since 1912, when its founders, the American manufacturer Michael Winburg, the founder of the Omega Chemical Company, and the French distributor, the pharmacist Louis Nathan, showed "great temerity" by spending 350,000 francs for publicity on a volume of business of 75,000 francs to launch its perfumed toilet soap. By the third year the company was turning a profit, and by the 1920s the product was distributed in pharmacies nationwide, a market that was wide but not deep. By that time the brand had become completely identified with Baby Cadum, and most of the advertising budget was spent on store displays, posters, and giant billboards overlooking the squares of Clichy, Pigalle, and Bastille—perennially the object of conversation over their artistic merits and intrusiveness—which was only to the good from the point of view of publicity.

In the 1930s, after a change of guard in the wake of Winburg's death in 1930, the company faced new competition from Unilever, which in 1929 had merged with the Dutch firm Jurgens and launched Sunlight soap on the French market. The incoming head, the soap producer Jean Landais, assisted by a new head of publicity, Mery Van Minden, a member of the modernizing Groupement des Chefs de Publicité, revamped marketing techniques to invest more in press advertising to distinguish the brand, and less on postering, also because Baby Cadum's image had started to tarnish. This strategy was reinforced in 1935 after Colgate, the producer of Palmolive soap, took it over and hired Lord & Thomas as its advertising agency. Thereafter the company upped its advertising budget to 10–12 percent of its costs, of which 50 percent went to the press, 25 percent for radio publicity, and 25 percent for posters, shop displays, and illuminated signs.[91]

As more monies were budgeted for press advertisement, the whole pitch changed from "presentation" *(entretien)* to "reason why" *(argumentation)*. Just as in the United States, the text aimed first at establishing a value, namely a "Cadum complexion," rosy, clear, and bright. The goal—to be beautiful—was not just desirable, but imperative, and it could be achieved, as the text explained, only by a "rigorously pure and neutral soap," in contradistinction to the commonly used Marseilles soap. Appeals to social authorities and science made claims for the product sound reasonable and convincing: "Cadum gives a marvelous complexion." Why? Because its superabundant suds "cleanse in depth." The

American-style advertising with a French touch: "Reason Why" text, spot for Cadum Variety Hour, and cameo of Baby Cadum. Advertising World, *May 1937.* Courtesy of the New York Public Library.

originally sedate ads became a three-ring circus, embellished with comic strips, photographs, advertisements for the Cadum Variety Show, and ornate with the multiple eclectic typefaces common to American publicity. Running two campaigns annually that placed ads in fourteen or fifteen major newspapers and half as many leading women's magazines, in addition to the Tuesday evening weekly broadcast on national radio and numerous spots on local stations, the company consolidated a 10 percent share of the market.[92]

The problem yet to be faced was what to do with Baby Cadum. Initially the thought had been to suppress him, as an illuminated billboard cost upward of 20,000 francs a month. However, by the mid-1930s Baby Cadum had become what Pierre Nora calls a "site of memory," an em-

blem not so much of the soap itself, but of nostalgia for the previous decade: "Who doesn't remember that eternally present Baby Cadum whose
lovely skin and delightful smile could be observed everywhere?" For experts, that the company preserved his image, usually as a tiny cameo
amid a half-dozen other themes, was taken as a sign of the "Europeanization of the American Spirit." Expertly, advertising based "on a purely
American idea" dangled a Proustian madeleine to its French clientele.[93]

A New Order in Advertising

It was the boast of German advertisers and the opinion of authoritative
American advertising men that by the late 1930s Nazi Germany offered
the most propitious environment for American-style advertising in all Europe. This is a nasty paradox that can be explained at least in part by the
decision of Hitler's government, upon coming to power, to act decisively—as it did in other domains—to end the "chaotic conditions" alleged to have prevailed and to "set up standards of practice which might
well serve as a model in many countries." Well versed in techniques of
propaganda and persuasion, as well as ferocious to establish control over
all the media, the new regime immediately issued a one-page diktat requiring that newspapers publish accurate circulation figures, state their
advertising rates, and outlaw rebates to space brokers. It also banned
publicity that promised premiums, prizes, and gifts, and it curbed outdoor advertising to preserve the landscape. In the name of "truth in
advertising," it barred invidious comparisons with other products, un-
founded claims, and the use of any testimonials that did not identify the
person giving the endorsement, quote the full sense, give the date, and
guarantee that no payment had been made. Finally, it established the Advertising Council to the German Economy (Werberat der deutsches Wirtschaft), composed of a committee of sixty to seventy experts from all
branches of industry, working in collaboration with the long-standing
German Association of Advertisers, but responsible to Goebbels's Ministry of Public Enlightenment and Propaganda. It was intended to assure
that the advertisements be German in thought and expression, avoid foreign words, and use good taste; whenever possible, ads were to talk
about what one's own product could do rather than what one's competitor's could not. Subsequent decrees banned all radio publicity, standardized newspaper formats and rates, and set strict standards about posting
commercial notices in public places. Experts abroad as well as in Ger-

many concurred that the new laws made advertising under the Third Reich a model for European practice.[94]

Eliminating any fine distinction between publicity and propaganda, the Nazi regime was seizing back the friable ground of commercial space and subordinating it to the political sphere. By its vigorous action, it purged commerce of unethical practices and unfit agents, making it worthy of a people of heroes not hagglers. More realistically, it changed the course of advertising. On the one hand, the crisis of consumer industries, faced with shortages, the growth of large cartels dividing up the markets—so as to make advertising unnecessary—the suppression of 1,200 newspapers and 800 magazines, and the establishment of strict regulations against billboards and over the amount of space that kiosks could devote to commercial notices, reduced the volume of advertising. On the other hand, publicity for new substitute products, often carried out on a collective basis, increased it. So did the fact that many business firms that would not have spent on advertising were obliged to do so when solicited by the *Völkischer Beobachter* or Field Marshal Göring's luxuriously laid-out journal *The Four Year Plan*.[95]

The most remarkable change was in the medium of advertising itself: once known as the homeland of the stripped-down, experimental poster, in the late 1930s Germany became the homeland of the world's most plethoric text advertising. By 1937 the amount of advertising budgets devoted to print had risen to 87 percent, a higher share than in the United States, whereas the amount devoted to commercial postering had dropped to 3 percent. The poster was banned except for official propaganda and advertising for collective goods, and the idiom in which it was drawn had to be some variant on populist realism. Under these circumstances, the amiable style of Holhwein, hardened in the face of the tasks of the new Reich, came to predominate: aesthetically it was the preferred style to the ruin of the various Bernhards, Rosens, and Bayers who sooner or later went into exile. At the same time, the experimental typography that had yielded Bernhard Kursiv, Locarno, Ultra Bodoni, Memphis, Beton, Neuland, Prisma Capitals, and Futura was destroyed by the ban on non-Gothic typefaces—to the benefit of the more conventionally eclectic American use of fonts.[96]

In turn, advertising texts outdid each other in prolixity, the reasoning about the product becoming more and more of a morality tale, more and more distant from the motivations of crass commerce, and more and more suffused with the authority of the advertiser as advice counselor,

Increasingly prolix advertising, 1927–1937: Carnival Time:
"Kupferberg Gold—The Good Old German Brand." Advertising
World, *May 1927.* Courtesy of the New York Public Library.

product expert, and author. Advertising for the sparkling wine produced by the eighty-year-old Mainz firm C. A. Kupferberg, a great favorite for genteel occasions, highlights this evolution. Copy from the mid-1920s shows a light, Americanizing touch, with a good pinch of anti-French sentiment, as jazz-dancing carnival celebrants turn down "watery wine"

"Troubles in Paradise": Christian Kupferberg himself guarantees his drink's socially therapeutic qualities. Die Woche, *November 3, 1937.* Courtesy of the New York Public Library.

and "cheap Champagne" to toast with Kupferberg Gold, "the good old German brand." Copy from the early 1930s shows the absent expert asking "Is your marriage happy?" And the advice is that the young wife alone at home should "combat the burdens and responsibilities of everyday life and its unvarying monotony" with "a little party" complete with a chilled bottle of Kupferberg Gold: "As soon as the exquisite golden liquid bubbles in the glasses, the festive spirit takes over." Copy from the late 1930s shows the head of the firm, Christian Adalbert Kupferberg himself, who was also a leading member of the Advertising Council, pitching his advice to consume sparkling wine in prose of short-story length, whose theme is healing a bourgeois marriage. "Cloudlets Darkening Marriage Bliss?" Truth in advertising under the Third Reich called for the voice of authority not just to be present, but to be visible in a totalizing way—as owner of the firm, adviser on affairs of the heart, one-time suitor, expert on fermentation processes, propagandist for sparkling wines in general, and man of letters who could cite "the poets" when they "declaim little champagne sprites are at work and make us men, even hardened married ones, into attentive lovers."[97]

No consumer-related undertaking was more cowed than the advertising business by the uncertainty and distress brought on by armies on the march. On June 7, 1940, three days before the Germans occupied Paris, Marcel Bleustein closed his office to rejoin his military unit, only to see it disband after the French government surrendered. In the next four months, after his business was confiscated under the law of October 3, 1940, ordering the seizure of Jewish properties, he moved south to Marseilles in the so-called Unoccupied Zone to join his family. Later he recalled trying to support them by marketing a toothpaste his father-in-law had invented, an undertaking that failed uncharacteristically but not unsurprisingly given the times. Under threat of arrest for his activities in the Vie-Lucien resistance group in 1942–43, he obtained fake papers under the name of Blanchet that enabled him to escape over the Pyrenees to Spain, and from there travel to Gibraltar, whence he left for England. Once there, having established contact with the Gaullist forces, he became press officer to General Pierre Koenig, head of the Free French Forces in France. Entering Paris at the Liberation, he discovered that his radio station had been blown up by the retreating Germans. In his memoirs he claimed he had to start all over. That claim was only relative. By 1945 there was an advertising industry. What's more, by then he himself had two decades of experience, his Gaullist political credentials were impeccable, and by hyphenating his Jewish name with his gentile *nom de guerre,* he gave his social standing a smoother veneer. Bleustein-Blanchet had also accumulated enough capital to acquire the palatial building on the Champs-Elysées that had been used as Allied headquarters. This became his own new corporate headquarters. Having come out of the working-class neighborhood of Rue de Faubourg-Montmartre, with stopovers at 62 Boulevard de Strasbourg and a handsome building at number one Boulevard Haussmann, he came to occupy one of the most prestigious business addresses in Paris. Drawing advantage from the breakup of the collaborationist Havas firm to set up his own ad placement firm, Regie-Presse, and obtaining the accounts of Colgate-Palmolive, Singer, and Shell, together with the state-owned Renault firm, soon to become France's biggest advertiser, Publicis rapidly emerged as France's premier advertising agency. All this happened to the chagrin of American companies, JWT in the lead, which, despite their wish to head off competition, awaited political stabilization, economic recovery, and the return of American manufacturing enterprise to pump new resources into their local offices.[98]

Anyway, JWT had no office in France by 1945. When the Germans occupied Paris in 1940, the staff of Agence Thompson fled south. Idled on the Côte d'Azur while waiting for an exit visa for his wife, "Deke" (Lloyd Ring) Coleman, who had been JWT's man in Paris from 1932 until the German occupation, could not "imagine a place where there is less to do. No dancing, no night life, no libraries, no interesting magazines and newspapers, everybody you meet (mostly Jews) depressed and dull." A favorite way to while away the time was to compose experimental copy for new products: the most obvious need, Coleman decided, was for a "tonic pick-me-up" given the "privations of the war plus the nerve strain plus the absence of cheap, high-powered aperitifs . . . something with iron and vitamins and a high-powered stimulant such as cola." "We can handle the advertising if it gets started." On a more realistic and high-sounding note, he had to confess that an "honest company," if it were to embark on an advertising campaign now, "would have to do it to reduce consumption."[99]

The tiny Belgian outpost in Antwerp, founded in 1929, was the only JWT office to pull through the war more or less intact, thanks to the foresight of the local staff, which over the previous decade had put their "heart and soul" into its well-being. Though the office never turned

The New Order Diet: Myron Cerny's ironic ad in the J. Walter Thompson house style, 1945. By permission of the J. Walter Thompson Company.

much of a profit, it prided itself on having undertaken exhaustive market research that was useful not only to its own operations but "to everybody who wants to rationalize their sales efforts in Belgium."[100] Under the German occupation, unbeknownst to headquarters, its local director, J. H. (Myron) Cerny, a Czech national, used the office as a front for the underground Resistance. It was Cerny who in the fall of 1946 happily reported that business was getting back to normal. The stores were once more stocked with food. And though the Belgian Labor party had won the first postwar elections, the Communists had made a poor showing, and nonparty experts had been appointed to the Ministries of the Treasury and Commerce. With the paper shortage over and newspapers beginning to solicit advertising, old clients had started to reopen their accounts, and new clients were coming on board. The first big shipments of Kellogg's Corn Flakes were due to arrive in November, and the promotion campaign would start the first week of December.

This announcement was Cerny's way of informing clients that the company was once more open for business. Using the house style, he developed an incisively phrased, cleanly composed testimonial ad, portraying himself in the conventional format of the satisfied consumer— "before" his diet and "after." It was an macabre conceit to treat the starvation politics of the New Order as a successful if drastic "regime," with the recommendation that those who underwent it avoid "dangerous drugs and strenuous exercise." It was especially odd given that it had left Cerny himself permanently disabled. But Cerny had become a true believer: there should be only one point in a text advertisement; the contents should offend no one, as his certainly did not with its gentle reference to those who had made the "cure" possible by "living quietly." In sum, nothing about this repackaging of the New Order as a diet would have caused disturbance. If there was any cause of perplexity at the home office, it was that their frumpy employee had the makings of a war hero. But then the home office wasn't always the best judge of the politics of its European staff. The suave expertise of Henri de la Chassaigne, the former administrator of JWT's Paris office, continued to be so well regarded that the New York office toyed with the idea of rehiring him even after being informed that as a Vichy government official he had extorted a fortune by ousting French Jews from the cinema business and overseeing their deportation. Before they reached a final decision, *Reader's Digest,* the world's biggest circulation advertising medium, snatched him up to

manage the office of its first European beachhead, a newly leased headquarters located in a faded mansion on Boulevard Saint Germain.[101]

When Bleustein-Blanchet recalled the interwar years, he compared advertising to his favorite hobby, flying: "like aviation in those days: we
could fly farther than before, and with greater safety, but flying still relied
on sight—we did not have radar, automatic pilots, or all-weather landings. Those would come later."[102] We would add that since the sales territory was still largely unreconnoitered, the flight charts were supplied by
American experiences, the compasses as well. As for the objective—a
higher standard of living—which was also fuel for his enterprise, that
concept would be embraced by Publicis' chief only at the turn of the
1950s.

CHAPTER 6

The Star System

How Hollywood Turned Cinema Culture
into Entertainment Value

*The Americans do not understand that if cinema is 20% art
and 80% industry, we—Europe—have that 20%. That's
our strength and that's how we will win.*

VLADMIR WENGEROFF,
founder of Westi Films, 1926

*We dominate world screens not because of armies, bayo-
nets, or nuclear bombs, but because what we are exhibiting
on foreign screens is what the people of those countries
want to see.*

JACK VALENTI,
president, Motion Picture Association
of America, 1977

THE WAY FRITZ LANG told the story, the inspiration for *Metropolis*
came to him on the deck of the S.S. *Deutschland* as it docked on October
12, 1924, and he got his first glimpse of the Manhattan skyline. The director was no stranger to modernist phantasmagorias. He was a Berliner.
But looking up, he saw New York City standing there "completely new
and nearly fairy-tale like for a European," the buildings like a "vertical
veil, shimmering, almost weightless . . . the night streets lit as if in full
daylight by neon signs and topping them oversized luminous advertisements, moving, turning, flashing on and off, spiraling," the dreadfully
hot downtown "a crater of blind confused human forces pushing together and grinding upon each other, motivated by greed." "I knew then
that I had to make a film about all of these sensations." Over the years,
he repeated the story time and again.[1]

Lang's story is a fabrication. In this sense: even before he embarked at Hamburg, he was considering making an epic about the awe and might of modern industrialism. He had spoken about it early that year in the final days of filming *The Nibelungen,* the medieval Norse-German saga based on the Siegfried epic, the Viennese-born director's riveting tribute to his new homeland's patriotic myths. And in July–August, before he left for the United States, while on vacation at Salzkammergut in the Austrian Alps with the well-known writer and movie scenarist Thea von Harbou, his wife, she had started work on a script set in a futuristic city about the apocalyptic consequences of machine civilization.[2]

Still, Lang's insistence that the Brave New World of Manhattan was his inspiration is truthful. It was his prideful way of saying that he, the outsider, a European, could render the creativity and catastrophic destructiveness of capitalist modernity in a way Hollywood could not "because it lives inside of it."[3] It resonated with the ambition common to the best filmmakers of his time, namely to keep abreast of the U.S. cinema's visual innovations by embracing the newness and potency of the society that lay behind them. It conveyed the belief of this cultivated, cosmopolitan artist, a onetime painter and cartoonist, that film, his chosen medium, had "an advantage over all other expressive forms in its freedom from space, time, and place."[4]

In fact there was no happy ending here, no perfect synergy arising out of fusing the New World's visual spectacle with the Old World's epic vision. Reality cut in during the three years between the conception of the project in 1924, the actual filming, which went on for sixteen months, from May 1925 to October 1926, at UFA's Berlin-Neubabelsberg studios, and the picture's dazzling Berlin premiere on January 10, 1927, at the UFA-Palast am Zoo.

First, there was the crass reality that the accounts didn't add up. The undertaking cost 5.3 million marks, the most that had ever been spent in Europe for a film. Indulged by Erich Pommer, head of production at UFA, Germany's biggest and best-equipped motion picture company, Lang, the autocratic perfectionist, had been granted practically his every request. These included a cast of about 38,000 extras; the monumental sets and stunning optical tricks to create *Metropolis*'s surface of speedways and jutting skyscrapers and underground hellhole of giant machinery, evil slums, creepy catacombs, and biblical tribulations; and the movie crews, cash, and food required to shoot for 310 days and sixty nights. Notoriously, Hollywood blockbusters often ran over budget, only to be bailed out by their bankers within the studio system and by their flush Wall

Street backers. UFA was undercapitalized under any circumstances. And by the time filming was under way, the revalued mark, soaring costs, and slumping export market had revamped the whole economy of movie-making. Instead of recouping UFA's fortunes, *Metropolis* was running it into bankruptcy.[5]

Then there was the vexed reality of distributing the film. True, UFA was practically unique in Europe in that it was vertically integrated like the leading American film producers: it owned outright a chain of about thirty big-city theaters and controlled 3,000 other smaller exhibition spaces into which it could feed its several hundred annual releases. To celebrate the prosperous times, its gorgeous flagship in central Berlin, the UFA-Palast am Zoo, had been completely renovated in 1925 at the hands of Sam Rachman, in the ornate, kitschy purple-and-yellow decor familiar to Broadway show houses. However, the German audience for movie tickets, though Europe's largest, amounted to barely a quarter of the United States' film spectatorship. Not even a runaway success could recoup more than half of the costs on the home market, no matter how many theaters UFA controlled. Therefore exports were indispensable to recoup costs. But by 1924–25 Hollywood movies had begun to cut deeply into Germany's markets abroad and make inroads into its outlets at home. Moreover, the proud UFA had proved powerless to get the major American studios to honor the distribution agreement they had concluded as part of a loan to bail out the German firm. Worse, to fend off UFA's rumored takeover by foreign, namely U.S., interests, in March 1927 Alfred Hugenberg, the Rupert Murdoch of the Weimar Republic, moved to buy it out. Even before the final takeover, the new head of the board, Hugenberg's ally Ludwig Klitzsch, ordered spending cuts, including the fat budget allotted to promote *Metropolis*.[6]

Finally, the reality of the film's ambiguous if not inchoate message made marketing it a complicated proposition even under the best of circumstances. True, *Metropolis* dealt with the universal themes that made films popular, namely awful exploitation and redeeming love. But the film reeked of the acrid ambivalence for which the Weimar Republic's intellectual culture was notorious, whether technology emancipated or dehumanized, exploited workers were justly rebellious or unjustly rampaging rabble, entrepreneurial power was creative genius or pure tyranny, the heroine a saintly virgin or demonic whore, and the son and heir a slow-witted playboy or ingenuous idealist. Even know-it-all Berliners, the only people to see the director's cut in its entire three-hour-plus length, left the theater puzzled by its larger meaning. What did the final intertitle mean? "Between the mind [read: entrepreneurial genius] and the hands [read: laborers], the heart [read: Christianized femininity] must mediate" could be read by the ever-fearful right as presaging the victory of some Communistic ideal of fraternity or on the left more accurately as Lang's or perhaps Thea von Harbou's capitulation to romantic reactionary piffle. The imagery was marvelously experimental. But it lacked "real, tangible, distinct, and empirically grounded life," one critic noted, "the real concerns, the real longings, the really burning existential questions."[7]

On March 10, 1927, when Paramount premiered it at New York City's Rialto, the original sixteen reels had been cut to ten. Moreover, in the hands of Channing Pollock, the American playwright hired by the studio's national booking agent Walter Wanger to crack down on the symbolism run riot and give the American release greater continuity and clarity of plot, the story line of the chopped-down film had been completely reshaped. Pollock's "adaption" told a simpler story: "A greedy employer hoped to grow rich by hiring an inventor to create hundreds of robot workmen. These proved to be perfect, except that they could not be endowed with souls, and the result was catastrophic." And the new ending was unambiguously positive, the workers making peace with the boss, the boy reunited with the girl. With that, the "Monumental Film" created in order to express the synergy of Old and New World visions of modernity as well as conquer the American market for films made in Germany ceased to exist. The best that could be said, commented a well-disposed *New York Times* reviewer, was that *Metropolis* was a "technical marvel with feet of clay."[8]

The three years marked by the making of *Metropolis* thus saw the end of illusions about creating a dynamic interface between European and American filmmaking. Down to the mid-1920s, the Germans, especially those employed at the marvel of an enterprise that was UFA, were supremely confident that they had the resources, talent, and cinema culture to measure themselves against the very best films coming from the United States. American experts also believed so, even as they observed that other places that in previous times had produced major films, notably France, Italy, and Denmark, were suffering piteously from the rapid inroads of Hollywood products. But by 1926 the German cinema industry too showed wide fissures. Lacking capital, leached of some of its most talented personnel, losing its cosmopolitan vision, it was increasingly prey to pressures to revamp itself as a national, "German" cinema and to gesturing toward the establishment of a not easily defined "European" cinema, one that was capable of countering the streams of capital, techniques, and films flowing out of Hollywood.

How "Hollywood"—by which we mean the mass-produced, classically narrated feature film mainly fashioned in the giant studio systems of southern California—challenged European commercial civilization is the subject of this chapter. No American industry was more self-consciously rivalrous about its role in shaping international cultural trends, none more engaged in reaching out, responding to, and shaping consumer tastes abroad, none more aggressive in taking on the barriers and obstacles to its installation in other societies. Economically, motion pictures were far and away the most remunerative cultural export. By the late 1930s they ranked fourth in value among all goods sold abroad. And geographically, American film was the United States' most widely circulated commodity, second only to Gillette razor blades and Ford cars. Since 1945 there have been periods of expansion and of retraction depending on the creativity of local cinemas, Hollywood's own capacity for renewal, and global economic conditions. At the turn of the twenty-first century, the largest film companies in Europe were not European but American multinationals. Hollywood's market share of European film receipts was 80–90 percent. For every dollar of film Europe exported to the United States, the United States exported 1,500 to Europe.[9]

Abroad, in turn, no single American commodity presented itself as more disruptive. The upset was never simply economic, that which an industry of huge scale and scope equipped with enormous marketing skills, vast control over distribution networks, and deep financial backing generated in the face of relatively small units, shaped by craft traditions, drawing on theatrical traditions, whose financing was often fly-by-night. It was also disquieting culturally. As a good that presented itself at one and the same time as commodity and cultural artifact, it overrode national boundaries, eluded political controls, infiltrated local community, insinuated itself into private lives, and was suspected even of penetrating into the unconscious, especially of the most vulnerable individuals, namely women, young people, and children. Communicating in the language of a new vernacular, one that was visual, animated, and eventually spoken as well, the American cinema trespassed the hard-bound lines that in Europe still divided the high and academic from popular and mass cultures. In sum, no medium more effectively shaped the prevailing notion, only to challenge it, that a country needed to have its own entertainment establishment and to express its national identity in order to exercise full sovereignty over its territory.

Yet from the perspective of the first decade of the twentieth century, this American predominance was by no means a foregone conclusion. In its plasticity, the silent film was practically anational, its turn-of-the-century producers tossed and turned by the wild traffic crisscrossing both continents and penetrating the rest of the globe. On one side of the Atlantic and on the other, dispersed industries whose patents and copyrights on inventions were little respected generated widely diverse genres that were not viewed as clear-cut brands, and were often marketed in pirated or duped versions through jobbers and middlemen. The places in which they were viewed could be circus tents, music halls, and outdoor theaters—wherever a crowd could be gathered by a small-time entrepreneur with a projector and a reel of film. The sources of inspiration could be whimsical tales, amazing events like volcano explosions, or imaginary travels—to the moon, to Polynesia, around the world, to the land of Cockaigne. Gathering confidence and capital circa 1905, moviemakers produced longer and longer films. At first the state of the art favored Europe, exploiting the area's rich melodramatic traditions, ingenious optical techniques, the sensational realism of serialized novels, and the rich resources of theaters with their skilled craftsmen and stage actors. Around 1910 France, Italy, and Denmark were the leading exporters.[10] Consequently, when the locus of innovation moved to the western shore of North America after two decades of having been well entrenched on European shores, it proved a mighty turnabout not only for film producers, but for the whole myriad of interests and identities invested in the earlier order of entertainment.

If a single person embodied the versatile skills, mental dexterity, and local knowledge to keep his balance amid this sea change, it was Erich Pommer, who, with his wife and helpmate Gertrud (née Levy), was photographed at the ship's rail arm-in-arm with Fritz Lang as the S. S. *Deutschland* berthed after its ten-day crossing. The chief of production at UFA, Pommer was already well known for having backed a whole run of wonderfully captivating silent films, including *The Cabinet of Dr. Caligari* (1919), *Destiny* (1921), *Dr. Mabuse* (1922), *The Nibelungen* (1924), and *The Last Laugh* (1925). It was he who had organized the monthlong trip in the first place, whose first stop was to be New York City to inspect UFA's newly opened American offices and, after a brief stay in Chicago, had as its final destination Los Angeles, where the two men were to be introduced around Hollywood. Pommer's own background was not dissimilar to that of the larger-than-life moguls of the Hollywood studio system, although his candor, flexibility, and complicated destiny made him an altogether more humane figure. Born in 1887 in Hildesheim to Frau Anna Pommer and her husband, the prosperous textile merchant Gosta, he had started in merchandising like numerous other producers of Jewish ancestry. His first job was as a salesclerk for Machol & Lewin, the fashionable Berlin men's store. In 1907 at age twenty he discovered his true vocation as a "film man" after being hired as a factotum by the Berlin subsidiary of Gaumont, France's second-largest movie firm. Over the next three years he learned good French and "all the cinema secrets of the time" and was promoted to head of operations at Gaumont's Viennese subsidiary. From there he moved to Eclair, Gaumont's chief rival, where in the same capacity he mastered the tricks of the distribution trade for the whole confounding Austro-Hungarian Empire as well as for the more transparent markets of Denmark, Sweden, and Norway. This was his first love, he later said, being on the road all the time, all over the continent, breaking into new markets. Still, to move into the pressure-filled business of production was a logical next step. There was a real need to fill the insatiable demand for new stock with a reliable supply of releases; whence in 1913 his undertaking with Eclair's head, Marcel Vandel, to found Viennese Authors' Film. Hardly thirty years old, Pommer was already an old hand when, near the end of his third year of war duty, which he was serving in the Balkans after being wounded on the Western Front, the Picture and Film Office (Bufa or Bild und Film-Amt), the German Supreme Command's new film unit, tapped him to make documentaries. Before that, in February 1915, while back in Berlin on furlough, he had arranged for the assets of Eclair, now declared an enemy firm, to be preserved within a new German company, Decla (D[eutsch] Ecla[ir]) Filmgesellschaft. In 1921, a year after his feisty little firm had merged with Germany's oldest film producer, the Bioscop Company, Decla-Bioscop was bought out by the four-year-old government-subsidized Universum-Film AG. The deal was that in this fast-growing baby giant, better known by its famous logo UFA, Pommer would become head of production.[11]

Now recognized as a true film producer as well as a film manufacturer, Pommer plunged into the "creative hocus-pocus" of postwar Berlin. He worked "eighteen hours a day, four or five films in work at the same time," his coworker Billy Wilder recalled; "skinny, sensitive, and ner-vous," he chainsmoked and "drove everybody relentlessly."[12] Always pragmatic, though never to the detriment of his craft, he well grasped the stringent pressures to update production imposed by the ever more strenuous cross-Atlantic competition. A cinema that succeeded, whatever else it did, kept a sharp eye on the box office. For Germany, given its narrow home market, this meant making films for export. Pommer accomplished this superbly well, working with leading filmmakers, notably Ludwig Berger, Robert Wiene, F. M. Murnau, and Joe May, as well as Fritz Lang, drawing from them some of their most distinguished work. In recognition of this success, Hollywood vied with UFA for his expertise, as did film studios in Great Britain and France. Posthumously he would be recognized along with Alexander Korda as the only European producer equal in stature to the great studio heads of the classic era, Selznick, Zanuck, Warner, Wanger, Thalberg, and Mayer. For George Canty, the American government official most expert on European film matters at the time, Pommer was, very simply, "the most versatile film man in the world."[13]

Pommer's zigzag career illuminates both the internationalism of a cross-Atlantic cinema whose human talent was as mobile as every other form of capital and the growing nationalism that time and again compelled him, a man capable and desirous of working across cinematic cultures, to suffer the pain of exile, loss of work, and ostracism from his metier. Called upon not just to be a producer, but also to represent the film establishments in whose employ he was working, Pommer experienced firsthand every major turn in the struggle for hegemony across the North Atlantic: he was in Berlin in the early 1920s, when the Weimar Republic's movie industry still grasped at being a major global player; in Hollywood in 1925 and 1926 as the Hollywood majors entrenched their power on the continent; and back in Germany at the turn of the 1930s to assist UFA's first experiments with sound in the effort to recoup its European leadership. In exile in Paris, London, and Hollywood while the Nazi-led industry battled to build a German-dominated European cinema, in 1946 he returned to Berlin, where, at the head of the U.S. Army film task force, his assignment was to dismantle once and for all the obstreperous, Nazified German "entertainment empire."

That the alternative establishment to the American film establishment proved to be the German is not surprising, nor that Lang, a native of Vienna, together with scores of other directors, producers, cameramen, writers, actors, and technicians from central Europe, many of them of

Jewish ancestry, made Berlin their first destination. German commercial culture in this domain, as in others, arduously emerged as the chief rival of the American cinema. Subsequently, under Nazi rule, it more and more aggressively presented itself as the European alternative to the Hollywood studio system. This was not only the effect of having in the giant UFA an enterprise of such scale and scope as to exercise European-wide influence, or a reflection of Germany's powerful export-oriented economy with its fierce grip on the markets of a half-dozen fragile east-central European nations. It was also the outcome of German nationalists' effort to reestablish the cultural hegemony that had been lost in World War I. One avenue was to seize the opportunity that was opening up as the visual mass media replaced print culture and to capitalize on German culture's centrality, especially as the encroaching Soviet Union was pushed back from central Europe after 1920. The pioneers of Gutenberg's revolution, Germans' preeminence in print culture still showed in the profusion of writing, theatrical pieces, and pictorial experimentation that yielded deep and quirky veins of fantasy and talent as well as antipathy to screen images as plebeian and trashy.[14] Indeed, the very power of German print culture initially discouraged the growth of the film industry, so that around 1910, 85 percent of the releases on the German market were foreign-made, mainly French, Swedish, and Danish. However, during the war years military and political elites recognized that film offered a signally important medium of communication and that the German state, the Supreme Command taking the lead, needed to encourage its development for the sake of propaganda and education, if not entertainment.[15]

In the war's wake, German nationalists came around to recognizing the cinema as a building block of national power. This view was reinforced by the recognition that the German-speaking public was only partly located in the national territory; the rest, not counting the millions of German origin in the United States, were minorities in the new east-central European national states whose markets German businessmen expected to reclaim. However, to realize this potential required shaking off the disdain elites felt for a type of entertainment that had hitherto been regarded as *Schmutz* (trash). It also involved addressing the larger conundrum: namely that economic factors dictated that the cinema should have a strong enough national identity to secure the home market, yet that this identity not preclude spectators in other lands. This major problem of mass cultural industry—to produce a commodity imbued with national cultural values yet having international entertainment appeal—was not only a European one.[16] The Americans experienced it as well. And the solution they gave to it established their global leadership.

Pearl White's "Almost Ferocious Smile"

Not by chance, American-made motion pictures were first interpreted as being "American" when they suddenly showed up on the European home fronts during World War I. In Paris, Philippe Soupault, the futurist poet, remembered their arrival as the first event in a veritable revolution in the mass media. "Then one day we saw hanging on the walls great posters as long as serpents. At every street-corner a man, his face covered with a red handkerchief, leveled a revolver at the peaceful passers by . . . We rushed into the cinemas and realized immediately that everything had changed." Pearl White's "almost ferocious smile" flickering in the dark announced "the revolution, the beginning of a new world."[17] The moment must have been mid-1916. For it was then that U.S. motion picture exports to Europe leaped, taking advantage of the slowing of local production and the calculation that, though prey to German U-boats, the North Atlantic shipping lanes were still open. All of a sudden, the screens showed the series featuring the grinning, swaggering, cane-poking "Little Tramp" produced by Charles Chaplin for the Mutual Company. There was Cecil B. De Mille's titillatingly racist melodrama, *The Cheat,* playing the Japanese-American star Sessue Hayakawa as the suave white slaver, who burns his brand into the white shoulder of the vulnerable lady of good society as if she were simply another of his oriental trinkets. There were the death-defying, acrobatic, girl-in-jeopardy cliffhangers of Pearl White. That the habit-forming installments featuring the brittle blonde trouper from Greenridge, Missouri, were mostly produced by Pathé clearly made them no less American to French viewers.[18] By August 1918, when the Armistice ended the fighting, American releases could be found practically everywhere there was a moviehouse, the big exception being Germany, where they had been both embargoed by the Entente and barred by government regulations.

Careful studies show that from the 1890s onward, the cinema boom consequent upon the industrialization of staged entertainment with the invention of what was variously called the cinematograph, vitagraph, kinetoscope, and so on occurred more or less simultaneously on both sides of the Atlantic, with several inventors in as many countries claiming credit. On the supply side, experiments in cinema-related technology turned a medium indulging in light shows, trick optics, and other genial improvisations into a highly organized, ever more concentrated industry. On the demand side, fast-growing wage-earning urban populations in search of small pleasures avidly consumed the automated live entertainment that the movies provided. The potential public was immense, as urban audiences had a seemingly insatiable taste for ever more sophisticated novelty, stimulated by the high standards of amusement set by regular theaters. At the turn of the twentieth century before audiences of several thousand, the London Hippodrome staged melodramas with the capacity, say, to simulate typhoon waves tossing about beleaguered ships and hapless heroines, the water churned by motors installed in enormous tanks. The feeries or fantasy plays of the theater district around Paris's Boulevard du Temple relied on painted *trompes l'oeil* to stunning effect, mechanized props to produce the rising and setting of stars, sun, and moon, the illusion of flight with hoists and cables, even galloping horses hitched to steam-driven lines to keep them in place.[19]

At the outset, then, moving pictures added only one more tasty ingredient to the already rich cake of popular entertainment. The clear leader in the industrialization of wonder at the outset of the century was France, the world's most prolific producer of motion pictures. Building on the technologies of the Lumière brothers and the fantasy of Georges Méliès, French firms with Pathé Frères in the lead capitalized on the large, lively public provided by its big cities, wealthy investors, huge empire, and conditions of free trade to establish worldwide distribution networks, set up production companies that readily absorbed motifs and techniques from other nations' cinemas, and install plants on the booming American East Coast to manufacture and service equipment. At their peak, circa 1907, 40 percent of the total film receipts from the U.S. territory went to French firms.[20]

More generally, the U.S. market, the world's fastest growing and most competitive, voraciously consumed releases of any provenance. The typical small theaters that began to proliferate in the first decade of the century packed in 199 places (200 required a theater license), used ordinary chairs for seats rather than rows bolted to the floor, sometimes came equipped with a piano for musical accompaniment, and cost a dime or nickel, whence the name nickelodeon. Open year round, renting films rather than buying them, showing them twelve to eighteen times a day, and changing their three-film sequence about three times a week, a "theaterlet" could require 450 titles a year. With 4,000 to 5,000 of them around 1907, demand soared. Where the films were actually made nobody really cared, certainly not a public consisting mostly of working-class immigrants, ethnically mixed and plurilingual, whose tastes for pantomime might be just as happily satisfied by playlets or full-fledged dramas made in Naples, Italy, home of the first diva movies, as by the eccentric pictures (e.g., collapsing buildings, rushing locomotives), slapstick comedies, and action stories filmed at the Biograph, Edison, or Vitagraph Studios in New York City and northern New Jersey, the chief centers of U.S. motion picture production at the time.[21]

The spectators' nonchalant ecumenism about film nationality was eroded by the American industry's precocious cultural chauvinism. Its origins in this domain can be traced to developments in U.S. consumer culture manifested in other areas of innovation, namely businesses' efforts to create the appropriate selling environment to promote brand loyalty and, in this instance, to mold new standards of taste in film among several million recent immigrants.

Starting around 1907, local film industries created a national oligopoly out of the violently feuding interests among cinema patent holders, equipment manufacturers, producers, and distributors. The chief mover on this matter was the Edison Company, which had seen its lawsuits against competitors for patent infringements on its motion picture cameras, projectors, and film stock incessantly contested through the courts, flouted by outright piracy, and otherwise resisted by shifting combinations of firms allied to secure preferential licensing agreements. These conflicts had been ruinous, enlarging the opportunities for film importers. Starting in 1908, however, the Edison company, in collaboration with American Mutoscope and Biograph finally succeeded in establishing the Motion Picture Patents Company to collect fees on a regular basis. Though this monopoly would be repeatedly challenged by coalitions of independent firms and the MPPC was brought to court, tried, and eventually convicted of breaking the Sherman Anti-Trust Laws, it survived.

Not only did the MPPC survive; it shaped the future organization of the whole industry. Its licensing arrangements, by closely linking production, distribution, and exhibition, encouraged the vertical organization behind the Hollywood studio system and permitted it to tighten its control at all levels of the entertainment industry. By treating films like any other standardized commodity, it established distribution systems that determined rental costs by the brand name and reel footage irrespective of contents. By its intimidatory treatment of competitors, it proclaimed that as a business depending on so many interlocking interests yet promoting a product whose shelf life was evanescent, it had a right to ride roughshod over recalcitrants, especially foreign ones. In the effort to establish its monopoly, the MPPC had barred foreign firms from its licensing cartels, all except those too powerful to be excluded, which were the leading French firms Pathé Frères, Méliès, and Gaumont. To oust the French, it pursued yet another strategy, which might be called "the cultural defense."

The nickelodeon revolution had already called the attention of that oddball coalition of civic forces that typically coalesced in support of American xenophobia, notably Progressive reformers, social feminists, labor leaders, religious bigots, and cultural commentators of various ilks, to the proliferating venues of cheap amusements. And the outrage was great at the degenerate effect these unwholesome places had on the heterogeneous public that found amusement therein: children, women, and multitudes of racially mixed and foreign immigrants, mostly illiterate in English, economically disenfranchised, physically unkempt, socially marginal, and politically suspect.[22] To fend off criticism that the motion picture industry itself was responsible for this social spectacle, the industry made itself an ally of the cause of moral regeneration. By means of the usual trade magazines and newspaper columns dedicated to film, but also through the fervor of Progressive Era associational life, it engaged spectators in a cacophonous debate over the style and content of movies. The solution to the vexed issue of how to distinguish healthy films from insalubrious ones was found in formalized new canons of judgment that in turn called for everybody to agree on new aesthetic categories. Given that the United States was a country of immigrants and practically everyone was sensitive to who and what were foreign or native, evaluating films turned upon differentiating the style, look, and message of indigenous films from motion pictures being produced abroad.

The case was made by taking on Pathé, the biggest firm in the world, headquartered in Paris, but with important subsidiaries in the United States. A Pathé film was easily recognized by its trademark, a strutting Gallic cock, especially since the quality and quantity of Pathé's film stock had largely guaranteed the supply and novelty behind the nickelodeon revolution. Purchased outright or circulating in pirated versions, Pathé "actualities" like the frightful February 1902 explosion of Mount Pelée in Martinique, fantasy films, and film stories such as *Sleeping Beauty, The*

Life of Louis XIV, Faust and Marguerite, Puss-in-Boots (advertised as very good for children), and *The Strike* (a "sensational film," one of the "greatest headlines since the *Great Train Robbery*"), set industry standards during the first years of the century and were highly popular among "the little people."[23]

It was exactly these "little people" whom the trade press wanted to convert to national film values. One means was to obsess about the tints used by Pathé productions to enliven viewing pleasure, a process developed in 1903–04 using assembly lines of women workers to hand-color each release print to highlight emotionally evocative items such as flowers or female accessories like umbrellas, hats, and dresses. The U.S. trade press stigmatized the effect as frivolous, decadent, and fake. True Americans should prefer high-contrast blacks and whites, for these were the colors of solid realism (at least until Technicolor came along, whereupon European neorealist black and white was dismissed as backward and alien). Foreign films featuring Grand Guignol melodrama had previously been applauded for their capacity to render the pathos of human suffering. Now critics excoriated the genre as lacking moral fiber. True Americans would prefer a narrative style affirming strong characters, exuding optimism that "tomorrow will be a better day," and having a happy end. "Let's cater more to the happy side of life," the recently emigrated Carl Laemmle, the founder of Universal, enjoined in praise of the new morality: "There's enough of the seamy side without exposing it to further view."[24]

It took the popularization of a new genre, the Western, to root Americanness in film culture. Naturally, Pathé rushed to turn out its own cowboy-and-Indian pictures to respond to growing demand. But American critics denounced Pathé for hijacking the national landscape and being inauthentic. The Indians gave it away: any red-blooded American could distinguish a genuine "Redskin," meaning a befeathered, well-muscled white stunt man in brownface playing at ambushing settlers on sets in the southern California desert, from a fake, meaning a flaccid pony-riding horseman galloping around locations in the Camargues, but more likely in "inauthentic" New Jersey or Los Angeles, where so many of the American genre were produced.[25] Naturally, nobody wanted to be accused of "Pathémentia," the social pathology so alien, effeminate, morbid, and otherwise reprehensible as to merit censorship. Cut out of licensing deals as well as excluded on cultural grounds, Pathé Frères' share of the market dropped rapidly after 1907. Thenceforth, as immigrant publics were domesticated, the nickelodeons were turned into reliable outlets for an increasingly standardized national product.

With the U.S. market thus permanently captured for national producers by a system of protectionism exercising power over both distribution and taste, motion picture manufacturers set to fighting with one another over the quality of their output. The outcome, coinciding with the first two years of the Great War, was the foundation of the classical Hollywood system. The standard for programming became the big-budget feature film, designed for mass audiences, running as long as five reels and renting for a percentage of box-office receipts. Product branding took the form of the star system. As the studios recognized that the faces and figures of popular actors rather than their own names guaranteed customer loyalty, they put actors under contract for a succession of films, then cranked up interest in their personas, much as J. Walter Thompson and other advertising agencies marketed the product "personalities" of Crisco shortening, Pond's soap, or Kodak cameras. This undertaking involved substantial investments in salaries, retinues, and promotion, and could be accomplished only with the economies of large-scale production. It also required that stars be willing to see themselves as outsize individuals, ready to sacrifice bourgeois privacy and to conceal the eccentric lifestyle typical of the artist-as-genius in order to promote their celebrity. In terms of labor, the motion picture industry specialized tasks, using the scenario to plan for efficiency. Continuity editing devices established guidelines for constructing the narrative. Innovative camerawork and artificial lighting gave films a polished veneer unknown in the prewar period. In sum, coming out of World War I, the Hollywood studio system was to the standardized, mass-produced, internationally marketed cultural commodity what Fordism was to the global consumer durable trade.

Above all, the American motion picture business came out of the war geared up to expand abroad. Like J. Walter Thompson and the burgeoning advertising industry, Hollywood had linked up with the Creel Committee, which in the last year of the war established a special Division of Films. This was not only dedicated to making propaganda films, but also promised in the framework of American war aims to assist the U.S. motion picture industry to undercut its European competitors. Bullish patriotism and business pragmatism thus went hand in glove as the cinema establishment, eager to be assimilated into the American consensus, embraced President Wilson's vision of the cinema as "the very highest me-

dium for the dissemination of public intelligence, and since it speaks
a universal language, it lends itself importantly to the presentation of
America's plans and purposes."[26]

The cinema industry's economic capacity to carry out this mission
was powerfully assisted when Congress passed the Webb-Pomerene Act
in 1918. Designed to back U.S. firms in their competition against foreign, especially German, cartel arrangements, the bill exempted export
associations from antitrust regulation, permitting them to form cartels,
fix prices, and engage in other anticompetitive practices abroad that
were barred at home by the Sherman Anti-Trust Laws. Since the 1920s
the American movie industry has been the bill's greatest beneficiary and
remains its most affectionate supporter. "Without the embrace of the
Webb-Pomerene," as Jack Valenti, the movie trade association chief, remarked, "the U.S. film and television industry would have been seriously,
perhaps fatally, crippled in its efforts to win the admiration and the patronage of foreign audiences."[27]

The industry might not have benefited from such generous state support had it not already revamped itself for that purpose. Its major trade
association, the Motion Picture Producers and Distributors of America,
was established in 1922 to solidify its control over the industry, improve
its awful public image by self-policing, and promote better business practices. But under the leadership of the amiable autocrat Will H. Hays, the
MPPDA, also known as the Hays Office, immediately showed its strong
international vocation. It was quick to latch onto Commerce Department
slogans to the effect that "trade follows the film," motion pictures supplied "an animated catalogue for ideas of dress, living, and comfort,"
and "a dollar was earned for every foot of film sent abroad." By 1926 it
had wheedled a substantial congressional appropriation to pay for a special Motion Picture Section with its own fulltime staff, which in 1930 became a full-fledged division.[28] The Hays Office also established its own
"Foreign Division," which communicated daily with the State Department as well as with the Bureau of Foreign and Domestic Commerce section. It even operated its own overseas headquarters in Paris, under the
supervision of Hays's brother-in-law, who was in constant touch with the
U.S. embassy.

But Hollywood's most valuable contact with the European scene was
George R. Canty, the BFDC Film Division's chief emissary from 1926 to
1939. A naturalized American born in County Cork, smart, gregarious,
and unflappable, he could "so coolly, calmly, and soberly" size up the

state of local business and political affairs that Europeans themselves regularly plied him for information about their own and competing film establishments.[29] His diplomatic skills were well honed from negotiating with European governments as well as calming his own conationals, who often turned stubborn trade issues into diplomatic standoffs. He also saw it as part of his job to organize the Americans to keep a united front in foreign negotiations, though nothing was harder than "getting the boys together and keeping them in line." When foreign resistance to American film showed itself specially intractable, Hays himself intervened, and the U.S. government trade emissary stepped out of the way. "Czar" at home, "ambassador" abroad, Hays conducted private business as if it were an affair of state, personally negotiating quota arrangements with foreign heads of state, a private-sector plenipotentiary officially authorized, should negotiations fail, to punish offending states with devastating trade boycotts.[30]

Securely cushioned by such firm support and rich with capital, the U.S. cinema industry invested heavily abroad beginning in the 1920s, multiplying direct-sales offices, insinuating itself into the cinema establishments of other nations, wooing talent to come to Hollywood, and engaging in sharp marketing practices such as block booking, which entailed requiring local exhibitors to take the whole offer of the distributor, duds and all, not just the one or two releases that they regarded as appropriate to their markets. More important, these myriad connections backed the industry's capacity to create a transnational taste culture much in the way it had created an all-American movie culture. As Hollywood bookkeeping made it standard practice to calculate foreign income as part of estimating profit margins at the end of World War I, the industry showed more and more solicitude for the opinions of foreign audiences—or for those who might restrain them by censorship, criticism, or boycotts. Just as it had to persuade the public on its home terrain that its goods were harmless if not morally sound, it had to convince foreign governments, censorship boards, Catholic and other religious groups, together with various and sundry political and civic institutions abroad, that its products were morally inoffensive and ideologically neutral.[31] Acting on the basis of local knowledge, with an eye to national and religious censorship dictates, sometimes enlisting paid foreign consultants, it adjusted the content of films to ensure their welcome. From the mid-1920s on, the MPPDA put more and more pressure on all who were involved in filmmaking, regardless of individual studios' styles, to conform to more and more comprehensive censorship guidelines. Thereby it deflected threats of government censorship, which would be the norm everywhere else in the world. This unique exercise in aesthetic and moral self-policing, which offered a less rigid but smarter and more intrusive instrument of regulation than state censorship boards, crystallized in 1930 when the Hays Office published its Production Codes.[32]

Before that silent movies had proved malleable subjects on the score of censorship, as alterations could be made at a half-dozen or more points without the film's becoming totally incoherent—in the editing room itself before the official release, by the exporter, at the office of the censor, even by the local projectionist, who might snip out a piece here and there at the command of the parish priest. Sound films called for more intervention at the point of production. Here the Production Codes Administration guided the studios with expert advice. It was positive to play up universal themes such as love of home, family, and children, devotion to a supreme being, pleasure in play and sport, and loyalty to one's country. It was offensive to dwell exaggeratedly on sexual play, white slavery, or other commercialized vice. Similarly, it was repugnant to indulge in themes that made virtue look odious and vice attractive, weakened the authority of the law, offended religious beliefs, or induced the morally feeble to commit crime. Self-censorship by those in the know, who judged not so much by the plot or its intent as by subjective reactions, was recognizably superior to the heavy-handed literalism of public censorship, wherever it originated. As the irascible sex reformer and avant-garde film promoter the Honorable Ivor Montagu noted, the British Censorship Board was farcical in its efforts to uphold public morals: it gave its stamp of approval to a film like Fred Niblow's *Two Lovers* (1928), which showed Ronald Colman vigorously wooing Wilma Banky (and gave at least one charlady "sensations she had been waiting for all her life"), yet banned "representations of the copulation of snails, and even the ejection of sperm into water by an echinoderm."[33]

Whether the Catholic Church or the Hollywood Code was more effective at managing the emancipationist tendencies of movie culture is hard to say. Each acknowledged and applauded the contribution of the other. The Hays Office, headed by a Republican who was a practicing Presbyterian responsible to Jewish studio heads, delegated to the Catholics of the Legion of Decency the formulation of the industry codes. In turn, when Pope Pius XI promulgated his encyclical *Vigilanti Cura* on June 29, 1936, warning the faithful against the dangers of modern-day entertainment, the grim pontiff treated sin as existing in the eyes, mind, and soul of the viewer and recommended self-control as the best remedy. The ideal model was not the meddling censorship of Caesar's state, but rather American civil society's sinuous system of moral self-vigilance.[34]

The result of such constant, subtle interference was an international product replete with paradox. Hollywood had absorbed an important lesson, namely to play down the American cinema as the vanguard of a new mass culture while playing up its superior entertainment value. The process made for the remarkable tension between American movie-making's conformism, intended to broaden spectatorship, and the experimentation intended to stimulate viewers to go to the cinema and to cement their loyalty.[35] The outcome of this often contentious dialogue was a vernacular of universal currency whose grammar was always being renegotiated. This was especially visible in the strongly positive response to slapstick comedy, a European favorite across classes. "One has to hand it to the Americans," reflected Siegfried Kracauer, the cultural critic, observing the rapturous hilarity of his fellow Berliners at the harsh facts of modern life the American films presented—the oppressive technologies of work, the puritanical moralism, heavy-handed policing of everyday life—and the uproarious nonsense performed by Buster Keaton, Harold Lloyd, and Charlie Chaplin in rebellion against them: the Americans' cinema produced a "reality" by which "they subject the world to an often unbearable discipline," but which in turn "dismantles this self-imposed order."[36]

Cinema vernacular was literally a language, in the case of Britain strategically adapted to reinforce working-class girls' peer culture. The "new woman" of the 1930s was the maid Elsie of Winifred Holtby's novel *South Riding*, who, "like most of her generation and locality . . . was trilingual. She talked BBC English to her employer, Cinema American to her contemporaries and Yorkshire dialect to old milkmen."[37] The wisecracks, jive talk, and slang ("scram," "Don't strain the brain, Jane," "Cut the steam, dream") was used to shock parents. It offered a supply of practices—"little tricks," as one young woman characterized them, "such as curling my boyfriend's hair with my fingers, or stroking his face, or closing my eyes when being kissed," important to changing sexual manners. After seeing polished lovers on the screen, women wanted something better than the local boys.[38] It was not a one-way street. In gritty Longwy, a coal town of the Lorraine on the border of Belgium, Luxembourg, and France, male spectators, second-generation Italian workers, were in awe of Humphrey Bogart, a real *barbeau* (ladykiller), so self-confident yet no great physical specimen. For the least socially privileged, who were also the most socially awkward, he offered a model of savoir-faire.[39] Across national frontiers, gender roles were bent just as much as they were reinforced. No role was better remembered by women and men than Greta Garbo's crossdressing portrayal of the star-crossed young ruler in *Queen Christina*.

American film introduced a world of sensory speedup, jam-packed with the props of everyday life. There were no artificial conventions that excluded the common object—cans of corned beef, tins of shoe polish, or the telephone, which in 1930s Italian cinema was picked up to characterize a whole new genre of sentimental comedy, the "white telephone." Whether these objects were the playthings of the superrich, the guns and speeding cars of gangsters, the proverbial Western bar with its thousand liquor bottles waiting to be overturned with cascades of breakage and spills, the elaborately draped, seamed, and fastened outfits of Adrian (for MGM) or Edith Head (Paramount), they were far in excess of what was needed for the narrative of the film. The point is not that so bountiful a vision created a desire for those goods, as American trade officials claimed, as if advertisements merely sold goods by showing them. But they did reinforce a new economy of desire for more details, more sights, more movies with similar excess. In that sense, the attraction to the American movie was akin to the pleasure taken in the literalism of American advertising, the spectacularity of goods mounted on supermarket shelves, and the literary realism used to vivify the average man's way of life that won the Nobel Prize for Sinclair Lewis in 1930.

What a challenge, then, Hollywood was shaping up to be: its economic power based on control over a vast domestic market, its vertically integrated organization backed by big capital and by a government whose leaders were convinced of its utility and worth. It posed as the protector of universal values even while it dismissed as mere quibbles the debate over whether the cinema was a commodity or a cultural good, an industrial product or an art form. It produced a new vernacular offering new strategies of communication that undermined the old barriers of culture and deference, all the while promising cooperation to contain the excesses of mass culture.

The Cultural Defense

How could the motion picture industries of Europe defend themselves against this system's onslaught? There had been no self-consciously national cinemas to speak of until the challenge of American cinema presented itself in the form of Hollywood, much as in the United States there had initially been no American cinema. To pursue the United States' strategy in post–World War I Europe was a far more complicated matter, especially since by the 1920s Hollywood had clearly established itself as the first mover, defining what was intended by a "good" film as well as asserting control over the all-important channels of distribution.

The motion picture industries of Europe fitted into a far more complicated cultural order than in the United States. As late as the 1920s, European elites were divided on how to regard the functions of the cinema: whether as entertainment, art, education, or propaganda. It was still unclear what a powerful movie industry—or a weak one—meant for national prestige, whose traditional measures were high culture, extent of empire, strength of weaponry, or outputs of coal and steel. Having been classified as popular entertainment at birth, emerging motion picture industries had often been subjected to legislation that discredited them as cultural trash, hence the object of special censorship and police surveillance. Or they were treated as luxuries, hence subject to heavy taxation. And because they attracted Jewish entrepreneurs and artists, not unlike other new service and entertainment industries, distaste for them was tinged with anti-Semitism.

True, the U.S. business had faced similar obstacles before becoming legitimate. That the bulk of production moved from the cement lots of the East Coast to the flowering deserts of fast-growing southern California was a big help: in an environment far distant from the traditional cultural establishment, motion picture elites acquired a legitimacy all their own, their brilliant talent, beautiful people, and wealth of a million Mycenaes offsetting prejudices against the crass commercialism, Jewish domination, lurid sex crimes, and plain vulgar manners for which they were stigmatized. In Europe, by contrast, the motion picture industries were never more than a stone's throw from the great capitals—Paris, Berlin, Rome, Vienna, Budapest, London—and they always felt the uneasy tug of established intellectual elites. In the best of cases, this proximity made available to the cinema the intense intellectual life of the café and salon, the political engagement of social movements, and the stock of versatile talent from the theater and artistic avant-gardes. European cinema culture resonated closely with contemporary movements in other artistic media, notably expressionism, surrealism, and neorealism. In the worst of cases, this proximity subjected struggling industries to political hounding, anti-Semitism, and the vagaries of intellectual fashion, which had the effect of distancing them from far-flung provincial domestic audiences and draw-ing the latter closer to Hollywood.

The fact remained that moviegoing audiences of Europe represented a far smaller percentage of the public than in the United States. In 1930 the United States had 18,000 moviehouses, compared with 2,400 in France, 3,730 in Germany, and about 3,000 in Great Britain.[40] True, audiences leaped in size in the 1920s, spurred by American releases, much as the United States' nickelodeon revolution had been stimulated by the films of Pathé and other foreign firms. Consequently, the first films people viewed were more often than not Hollywood films introduced into circulation by exhibitors who, avid for any stock they could get their hands on, con-cluded deals with American-supplied distributors. As local industries be-gan to revive and export, they bumped into the newly entrenched Ameri-can-dominated exhibition systems. And when quotas or tariffs began to be enacted in 1925 to protect home markets, first in Germany, then al-most everywhere else, they were more likely to obstruct films being im-ported from other European countries than the American releases, whose distributors fast acquired the local resources, know-how, and political clout to circumvent them.

The sensitivities generated by the cultural issue were keenest in France, partly because the global position of the French enterprises making films had experienced such a devastating turnaround. In 1910 Pathé and Gaumont had been the world's leading producers; fifteen years later, in the *annus horribilis* 1925, American releases outnumbered French-pro-duced motion pictures 577 to 68.[41] Worse, after the war, as soon as Pathé and Gaumont sized up the American advantage, both abandoned feature production to invest in a far more lucrative trade, namely distributing films. And whose releases were most reliably supplied and profitable? American ones. Thereafter, feature filmmaking was handled by three types of enterprise. The first was that rara avis, the dynamic medium-size firm epitomized by Aubert and Albatros.[42] The second was the big-time Hollywood-style studio with its own local moguls, two of whom stood out from the small pack that included Adolphe Osso, Jacques Haik, Diamant-Berger, and Henri Louis Nalpas, namely Jean Sapène, the high-living editor of the Parisian daily *Le Matin* and founder of Cinéromans, and Bernard Natan, the much-defamed Romanian-born business vision-ary, founder of Rapid-Film. Before launching their own undertakings, each tried his hand at reshaping Pathé along the lines of a Hollywood major studio, only to fail for lack of sufficient capital.[43] Then there was the proliferation of small-scale, often one-shot independents congenial to the French business landscape; whatever their virtues as artists and craftsmen, they were not easily organized as a sector, and their power was zero on the distribution circuit.

However, official concern was first stirred not so much by the economic predicament of French motion picture producers as by their problematic cultural status. Legally, film was still ruled by laws generated out of the panic that swept the old regime in the belief that the theater and other entertainments, once freed from absolutist rule, would foment civic disorder. The postrevolutionary order was left with a heavy legacy of licensing, censorship, and exorbitant taxes on amusement that began to be undone only in the middle of the nineteenth century, notably in 1864, when theaters were reclassified as normal business enterprises, and thus freed from the most vexatious regulations. This change did not redound to the benefit of motion picture exhibitors, however, because when they began their undertakings around the turn of the century the law treated them as itinerant and impermanent fair barkers. Consequently, their licenses had to be renewed yearly, and they could be revoked by the authorities at any moment on grounds of violating public order. Motion pictures were also subject to special censorship rules, administered by the minister of justice until 1919 and by a central film commission thereafter. In addition, they were subject to heavy taxation on the grounds that entertainment was a luxury and should be tithed to the benefit of public charity. As state welfare burdens grew during World War I, taxes on tickets rose steeply. The fact that upward of 30 percent of the price of tickets went to the state was a strong disincentive to invest in the motion picture industry.[44]

In this context, it made sense to speak of the cinema as a national art, which to be properly defended economically needed to be upgraded in the cultural hierarchy. At very least, the cinema should be dignified with the same tax breaks, censorship codes, and subsidies as the theater. French intellectuals also began to draw on France's own deep well of imperialist topoi and stereotypes to speak of their own "colonization," and the term "imperialism," which previously had been reserved for economic monopolies, came to be used to characterize cultural domination, as in "American cultural imperialism." Against it, in addition to protection for the film industry, regulations were passed to copyright the French national cultural patrimony so as to prevent foreign (meaning U.S.) film companies from exploiting as set backgrounds familiar national monuments like the Arc de Triomphe, the Opéra, and Notre-Dame.[45]

In 1926 the French government finally took up the issue of defining a "national cinema" largely thanks to the action of Edouard Herriot, founder of the Fair of Lyons, friendly host to Edward Filene, and perennial mayor of his hometown. At the time the fifty-year-old statesman was serving as minister of instruction in Raymond Poincaré's cabinet, in which capacity he also directed the Fine Arts Section, which had jurisdiction over the cinema. Recognizing that this sector was outside his ken, he responded to the clamor of complaints about the parlous state of the industry by appointing a fifty-person investigative committee. Convening over the next several months, the so-called Herriot Commission took up two issues. One was to tender the cinema the same legal rights enjoyed by theater, which in effect meant to declare motion pictures an art. The other was to provide the cinema the same level of state protection it had started to garner elsewhere in Europe, notably in Germany.

Herriot, as an old-fashioned liberal and man of letters, dealt more easily with the former issue than with the latter. Indeed, having to deal with both put him in an uncomfortable position. For although he was dedicated to protecting high culture, he was also a devoted pan-Europeanist committed to free trade. No undertaking as much as the cinema highlighted that commerce and art were pulling in different directions, all to the benefit of Hollywood—which was indifferent to, if not dismissive of, the distinction.

This tension was nowhere more visible than in the outcome of the first international film conference, which was held at Paris from September 27 to October 2, 1926, just three months after Herriot took office. The initiative for the gathering had come from the French branch of the Institute of Intellectual and Cultural Cooperation, an advisory body to the League of Nations, whose leading figures were men much like Herriot himself, cultivated, cosmopolitan professionals distant from the truck of commercial interests except when it came to promoting their own ideas. Their larger mission was to find some cure to the "Magic Mountain syndrome," whose symptoms, according to Thomas Mann's catastrophic diagnosis of Europe's tubercular culture, might be characterized as the fading of bourgeois cosmopolitanism under the weight of jingoist nationalism, the fatuous chatter of feminized idle classes, the decline of standards, and the spread of mass entertainment, specifically "the Hollywood invasion." The Paris agenda specified that the conference would deal with aesthetic and educational questions exclusively, although practitioners, which is to say film producers, were expected to use the occasion to make business contacts. American movie men were welcome. How-

ever, because the United States wasn't a member of the League, it didn't
send any official representative. And the Hays Office refused to go on the
grounds that to treat film as art and education rather than as an industry was implicitly critical of the American posture. Moreover, with the
war-debt question still roiling public opinion, it held that "the Conference might easily develop into an anti-American affair if we took part in
it." Conference participants tried to brush the American absence aside:
"If the Americans see practical results they will come next year."[46] As
it turned out, American business lost nothing by not being there. The
conference concluded with a roster of platitudinous good intentions:
"the usual nonsense about raising the moral and intellectual standard of
films," as the British press described them; "platonic wishes," wrote the
French. The response to a subsequent meeting held in Berlin the next year
was so tepid that there was no followup.[47]

Nonetheless, the engagement of European intellectuals combined with
pressure from French producers reinforced Herriot's belief that the cinema was a valuable tool of national pedagogy. There was loud applause
for his brilliant oratory when in early December 1926 he spoke of the
"cinema" before the Chamber of Deputies: "an endless lesson with unbounded possibilities," it was "the best means to show the world to
children." True, "bad" films, meaning "romances based on vulgar love
stories," might "sow bad ideas in the minds of youth." But the representatives of the French people could rest assured: against this menace "I,
the guardian of the children of the nation, intend to protect them." Digging down into the old regime of consumption's bag of cures, Herriot
pulled out two homely remedies. One was more policing: educational authorities had to supervise closely the motion pictures attended by school
youth. The other was more education: measures had to be taken to "replace the romantic conception which only results in the transcribing of
poor novels for the screen." Having "studied the question very thoroughly" the venerable minister of instruction intended to provide France
with "something that she does not have," namely "an institute of pedagogy" where "we can investigate the possibilities of instruction by motion pictures," promote educational films, develop a "film professoriate,
and support and guarantee artistic freedom."[48]

With the cinema now elevated to the status of art, the knottier problem was to provide for its economic support. In the conviction that
if safeguarded with a mild *régime de protection* France's motion picture industry would find "unity within itself" and thereby reestablish its

prestige, on February 18, 1928, Herriot instructed his commission to deliver its long-studied resolutions. Predictably, it recommended that cinema be accorded the same fiscal and censorship rules as the theater. More controversially, it called for a quota system on foreign films along with the creation of a new office in charge of arranging contingency agreements. This would require foreign firms that wanted to distribute their films in France to arrange to exhibit French films of the same worth in their home markets. The import quota, specifying that four foreign films could be released for exhibition for every one made locally, was hardly draconian. And no provision was made to end the practice of producing "quota quickies," the low-budget films paid for by U.S. companies to fill requirements that a certain percentage of movies distributed annually be locally made, yet so deliberately slipshod that they offered no competition to Hollywood-made productions.

In fact the changes proposed by the Herriot decree resonated more with the open-trade sentiment favored by small-time exhibitors, Herriot's constituents, than with the protectionist clamor favored by big-time producers whom the minister of instruction disdained for cutting special deals with American capital and turning out Hollywood-inspired "romantic films." Even then, the internationalist Herriot, a dedicated supporter of a united Europe, not especially anti-American though his own culture was very distant, had not calculated on the virulence of the American response.

On March 28, 1928, Will Hays himself embarked for France. His grand purpose, he told the press at his arrival in Paris on April 4, was "to make it possible for the motion picture to play worthily the great part which is reserved for it in the world of today . . . For it is today the greatest single expression of the world, and it has it within its power to foster and strengthen those common ties which must ultimately triumph in the peace and brotherhood of the world."[49] On April 9 he met with Herriot, who candidly reiterated his belief that his government was operating within the terms of the Geneva Convention on free trade, and was acting only to preserve the French industry's survival. Hays was not mollified, and on April 20, just as Herriot was about to board the train home for the elections scheduled for April 22 and 29, he delivered his ultimatum. The MPDDA could not operate under the new regulations. Unless the decree was repealed or held in abeyance subject to further study, the association intended to continue its boycott of the French market. To restart the negotiations, Hays proposed to eliminate any scenes in films deemed offensive to French national feelings, study ways by which the French and American industries could cooperate to mutual advantage, arrange for representatives of the French film industry to come to Hollywood to study American production techniques, and favor the circulation in U.S. markets of any French film considered suitable for world distribution.

Meanwhile the French were warned not to disregard the effects of the boycott: no U.S. films had been contracted for sale since March 1, and as moviehouses started to close down as they ran out of stock, 8,000 to 10,000 French people would be out of work. That prospect provoked rapid reconsideration of the matter. On May 4, after discussion before the Commission for the Control of Cinema, chaired by the founder of French cinema, Louis Lumière, the Third Republic statesman reached a new agreement with Hollywood's chief lobbyist. France would allow the release of seven foreign films for every film produced locally. U.S. companies would be under no obligation to purchase French films. The Americans could distribute up to 60 percent of the movies they had exhibited the previous year in addition to those allowed by the quota. In sum, the agreements ratified the prevailing market ratio. In turn, Will Hays showed his solicitude for French cultural sensibilities by arranging for the French literary critic Victor Mandelstamm to go to Hollywood to advise the Hays office on the standards appropriate for French spectators. That wasn't the last word. When the accords were reconfirmed in 1932, Minister of Commerce Georges Bonnet wangled one additional concession from U.S. trade negotiators, namely to lower American tariffs on champagne, a humiliating reminder of the terms of exchange then prevailing in Franco-American trade.[50]

The Economic Defense

The more obvious defense was economic, but only Germany had the capacity to wage it. The German motion picture industry came out of the war with unusual advantages: it was mostly new, centralized, big, and had government support. The Entente's blockade convinced the German High Command and leading industrialists that the nation needed its own nationally oriented, centrally controlled motion picture output. In July 1917 government and private interests put together the capital to found UFA, whose civilian directors, after experimenting briefly with the High Command's notion that it should concentrate on patriotic and propa-

ganda themes, set about responding to the long-suffering public's demand for entertainment films. By the end of the war, benefiting from the
lack of competition, state favors, technological prowess, and nearly un-
quenchable demand, UFA had staked a commanding position in the German motion picture industry that would last until 1945. By the early
1920s it had built its own distribution system and mounted the biggest
and best-equipped studios in Europe. The Neubabelsberg studio was
"tremendous," Alfred Hitchcock marveled after working there as an assistant director in 1924, better than the lots he later worked on at United
Artists.[51] Thriving in a business culture that favored concentration, industrial cartels, state protection, and developing strategies for export, the
German film industry was uniquely able to develop economic counter-
strategies with respect to Hollywood.

Even more important than its economic prowess was its capacity to develop genres expressive of German culture yet possessing a transnational
appeal. "A people has to know where their Niagara, their inimitable,
lies," Erich Pommer once remarked.[52] Whereas the Americans were at
their best with Westerns, social drama, and slapstick, the Germans ex-
celled at the highly stylized expressionist features, the somber realism of
theater-inspired dramas, the harsh street films, and films of legends and
myths characterized by their historical authenticity, psychological texture, and a good eye for the macabre, uncanny, and bizarre.[53] Pommer
himself had fostered these qualities at UFA after becoming chief of production in 1921. But it was also a keen nose for niches in the international market that encouraged producers to turn the peculiarities of German filmmaking—including its theatrical traditions, talented writers, and
stock of fine actors—into a marketing strength against Hollywood's standardized products.

In turn, Hollywood filmmakers kept a close eye on the German cinema's progress, to appropriate whatever elements could profit local
scriptwriters, hire talent to make the "American art industry . . . more
truly universal," and block its competition, especially in France and east-
central Europe, Turkey, and Palestine.[54] As soon as Germany's export
boom ended in 1924, the American industry flooded Germany with new
releases. From that moment on, the major studios recruited some major
producers, directors, and stars by offering them high salaries, the promise
of stimulating if frenetic work conditions, and relative freedom from the
penny-pinching pressures to which UFA had succumbed. In 1926 all
three inducements brought Erich Pommer to southern California to work

under B. P. Schulberg at Paramount. Meanwhile American capital floated the industry: in 1925–26 UFA turned to Paramount-MGM for a 17 million Reichsmark loan at 7.5 percent interest. Many smaller firms concluded similar deals. By 1927, 75 percent of German film production was financed by American capital.[55]

The year 1927 marked the high point of the U.S. industry's attempts to buy into and thereby weaken its strongest competitor. Thereafter nationalist entrepreneurs moved in with state support and no squeamishness about exploiting the new medium's popular appeal. After Alfred Hugenberg's multimedia conglomerate, the Deulig Corporation, acquired a majority share in UFA by buying out American interests with help from the Foreign Ministry and the minister of the economy, it moved to consolidate UFA's position in the market by rationalizing production schedules, branching out into equipment manufacture, and broadening exports by redoubling the company's efforts to break into the American market. Conceding that UFA films would have to take into account "the mentality of the American public," UFA recalled Erich Pommer, who, having completed two successful films for Paramount, had shown his skill in producing "international features." As an incentive, UFA's new managing director, Ludwig Klitzsch, who had known Pommer from their war days on the Balkan front, in addition to offering him a good salary by European standards, set him up with his own production unit, Erich Pommer Produktion der UFA.[56]

As he prepared to assume leadership in the German industry, Pommer openly professed that his Hollywood experience now inclined him toward an "Americanized or democratic production view for the domestic and world markets, emphasizing purely materialistic concerns." At Paramount he had "trained in an entirely different school." From his new training he had learned how to invest potentially divisive subjects like the Great War with broad appeal: both *Hotel Imperial,* a tale of love between a wounded Austrian officer and a Polish hotel maid, and *Barbed Wire,* about a German prisoner of war and a French peasant girl, were set at one remove from the front and blended suspense, romance, and anxiety over feminine virtue. Of Hollywood, he recalled the sheer size of the facilities, the opportunity to move from one set to another without dismantling the previous one, and the superiority of American lighting—which led him to ship back "one of every kind of light" upon his return to Berlin. He also appreciated that America's studios operated with "the mechanical precision of any other great industry and the commercial side is equally efficient, that business first is the motto followed and respected by not only the operative side, but by stars, directors, and writers."[57]

In the end Pommer fell back on the now conventional distinction that had been established by counterposing culture against entertainment. Accordingly, he distinguished the art film from the crowd-pleaser, the former being suited to audiences with "demanding views," the latter for "tired masses." Given the necessity of a tradeoff, it was better that "a film is too light than that it is too heavy." American films commanded the market because "the mentality of the American film . . . apparently comes closest to the taste of the international movie audience, despite all criticisms to the contrary." Since the "mentality" drew on specific structures, namely the star, the slickness of advanced technology, the standardization of narrative, the happy ending, he was implicitly endorsing a whole ship's list of qualities. This appreciation, he explained, was "not intended as a value judgment at all, neither in an artistic nor in a technical sense." Now there was simply "another category by which to measure worth." No matter how much critics lambasted the so-called naiveté of American films, it was "this lack of complexity that made it a winner on the international market," that gave it "entertainment value."[58]

Sound and Sovereignty

The coming of sound films at the turn of the 1930s once more showed the American studio system setting the rhythm of European developments. For several years after October 1927, when the enterprising Warner Company premiered *The Jazz Singer,* the first film to have a recorded dialogue, Hollywood precipitated a process of competitive innovation that transformed every aspect of the motion picture business from production techniques and distribution down to the very smallest details of promotion, including giveaways, fan clubs, and beauty contests.

As usually happened at such junctures, the American motion picture business made the best of its lead, which in the case of sound was very narrow, the technology having developed pretty much simultaneously on both sides of the Atlantic. For market leaders such as the German-Dutch sound equipment combine Tobis-Klangfilm-Küchenmeister, inventor of the T-Ergon sound film process, the changeover meant quick, sure, and big profits. UFA, naturally, was the first German company to convert to sound production. Erich Pommer had been shooting a silent film about a down-at-heels hussar who, to pay for a horse, persuades his peasant lover

"What's up? Is the Al Capone gang at it again?"
"No, it's the Western Electric Company having a friendly
negotiation with the management of the Barberini Cinema."
Kines, *June 7, 1931.* Courtesy of the Biblioteca "Luigi Chiarini," Centro
Sperimentale di Cinematografia, Rome.

to prostitute herself, when he received a cable from Ludwig Klitzsch ordering him to reshoot with sound. At the time Klitzsch was on a visit to Hollywood, where he realized how firmly American business had embraced the new system. The struggle against "vassalage to the Americans" was on. Racing the clock, Pommer worked with "obstinate, primitive equipment" to finish, edit, and premier *Melody of the Heart* before Warner's second sound release, *The Singing Fool,* debuted in Berlin. To use the new medium to best effect, Pommer had his lead, the popular actor Willy Fritsch, sing in four languages—French, English, German, and Hungarian—and punctuated the narrative with choruses and dance numbers. In the process he invented a new genre, the operetta film, which by combining Hapsburg scenery, Austro-Hungarian musical tastes, and Old World gallantry with German sound technology, was destined to garner considerable success in Mitteleuropean milieus.

Nonetheless Hollywood won the race. On June 3, 1929, Warner Brothers rushed *The Singing Fool* onto the Berlin screen through its local distributor, National Film, a German company, in which it was majority stockholder. The premiere took place at the Gloria Palast, which had been converted to sound using Western-Vitaphone systems in open disregard of the court injunction enjoining it from infringing German sound patents. It was not until half a year later, on December 16, that *Melody of the Heart* premiered at the UFA-Palast am Zoo.[59]

The prevailing belief in Europe was that as "Hollywood's American identity became audible," national-language audiences could easily be reclaimed for local industries, and European nations would reestablish sovereignty over their cinema establishments. Few spectators outside England could comprehend American-language productions, and no audiences would long tolerate dim subtitles or crude dubbing. In sum, the opportunity was finally at hand for film to become national.[60] The producers for big European language areas, Germany in the lead, imagined that they would have an advantage not only in their own language markets, but in smaller nations with linguistic similarities like Sweden and Denmark, whose own high-quality products had hitherto occupied tidy little niches in the international silent film market.

However, Hollywood was prepared for the conversion to sound in ways that the motion picture industries in Europe could not be. The investments involved to convert from silent to sound production were huge, for they required not only retooling studios but also refitting theaters with new projectors and allocating bigger budgets for marketing as audience tastes and incomes became more and more unpredictable during the Depression. In Europe the demand for silent movies was still expanding. To hurry the shift when thousands of rural outposts had barely installed silent projectors, and when rich profits were still to be made from satisfying this demand, represented a real loss in Europe. Filmmaking in Europe still had a big investment in the art traditions that treated film as an essentially visual medium. "Noise yes, words no." The "talkie," it was feared, would break the "complicity of silence" and cause filmmakers to forsake the montage techniques peculiar to silent films for the banal panning effects favored on sound sets.[61] In the United States, if there were similar doubts, they were overwhelmed by a capitalism in the habit of crushing yesterday's brilliant innovation, junking obsolescent equipment, and wiping out the careers of those whose talents were unsuited to the new technologies.

In the face of doubts whether national-language cinemas would sub-stantially damage their interests, the Hollywood majors resolved to re-fasten their grip on European markets. One way to do this was to run subtitle translations of the English dialogue. Another was to make origi-nal language versions of every release. By opening new production facili-ties at Joinville outside Paris in 1930, Paramount brought to continental Europe the most advanced division of labor ever seen in movie manufac-ture. Geared to assembly-line rhythms, production simply repeated takes of the same scene in different languages, changing the stars, moving scen-ery, adapting the music, and, if necessary, retouching the script.[62] Dub-bing proved a more logical course, though it too was expensive and re-quired sharp sensitivity to render the tone of voice, as well as the proper class accent and regional inflection. In some countries, like Italy, new laws were enacted to force dubbing to be done locally, thereby creating a new if subaltern cottage industry. People acquired careers, if minor ones, speaking the voice of Ronald Colman, Cary Grant, Greta Garbo, or Joan Crawford. At the same time, the promise that sound pictures would gen-erate a national audience, coinciding with the economic crisis and rising nationalism, raised demands from the cinema business, as well as from government officials and political leaders, for more decisive state inter-vention.

In France by the early 1930s, the cinema had been consolidated as a national "art," as well as being recognized as an important industry in its own right. That the French motion picture business had become the country's fastest-growing business was good news for the industry, though reflecting poorly on the stagnant condition of other sectors. The giants who in the early 1920s had retreated from production to exhi-bition merged with other companies to return to making films. How-ever, Gaumont-Franco-Aubert Films went bankrupt in 1934, and Pathé-Natan, sapped by financial scandal, failed in 1936. Time and again, parliamentary inquiries pressed for the sector to discipline itself, only to acknowledge by default that the vitality of French filmmaking might lie in the proliferation of independent, one-film enterprises.[63] They operated by renting equipment and studio space from Pathé, Gaumont, or Eclair, and it was they who accounted for the growing number of releases in the late 1930s, as well as for their quality, which was greatly enhanced by the social commitment of Popular Front artists and the influx of talented refugees from the Nazified German industry.

In Italy the Fascist regime decided to build its own "Hollywood on the

Tiber" under two influences, the desire to exploit sound technologies and the need to widen the dictatorship's political base. For various coteries of young intellectuals, including the Roman circles to which Mussolini's oldest son, Vittorio, belonged, the cinema was the ideal medium to bridge the gap between elite and mass cultures. Most were realistic enough to recognize that the industry had been practically wiped out in the 1920s by foreign competition, misinvested capital, and worn-out genres. And even though production had picked up slightly, Italy still produced only one of every nine releases; practically all the others came from the United States. Consequently it was unthinkable to stop imports. Indeed, after being advised by an authoritative study released in 1934 that Italy was at least five years behind other leading movie-making countries, the Duce himself was convinced the country had to remain open to foreign experiences.[64] If his son's advice were followed, the Italian cinema would favor America's "technical virtuosity and fluid narrative styles" over "heavy-handed German trauma" and the "trite farce and double entendre" of the French: "once we have appropriated the solid commercial structure and narrative style 'made in the USA,' then we can begin to talk about Fascist cinema."[65]

The dictatorship had clear priorities. In 1925, to forestall the invasion of Fox newsreels, it had secured control over information by founding the Istituto Luce. But nine years passed before it established a general Directorate of Cinematography responsible to the undersecretary of press and propaganda (later the minister of popular culture) to draw up a plan for state intervention in the film sector. After a monthlong visit to Hollywood, its new chief, Luigi Freddi, a former editor of Mussolini's newspaper *Popolo d' Italia,* proposed to build a state-run equivalent to MGM. Ideally this would be powerful enough to integrate production, distribution, and exhibition, yet free of day-to-day political interference. This boondoggle promised to move forward as it obtained enthusiastic support from Mussolini's son-in-law, Galeazzo Ciano, as well as from Mr. John McBride, the bright-faced young American trade consul who corralled representatives of the Hollywood majors to attend various high-power meetings until the BFDC home office ordered him to stop. It was one thing to assist U.S. enterprise abroad, another to involve American government offices in building a foreign film establishment.[66]

Wiser counsels prevailed anyway. State control over feature film-making promised box-office failure. One example was enough: in 1934 the Istituto Luce had spent 4 million lire (about $550,000) to make

Giovacchino Forzano's propaganda-art epic *Camicia nera (Black Shirt)*. The result was a risible flop, infuriating Mussolini.[67] Interest shifted instead to plans for a state monopoly over the distribution of films as opposed to their production. As in France and elsewhere, it was the large measure of American control over the circuits of exhibition that favored U.S. releases. And these circuits concentrated on the prosperous areas so that many outlying urban areas, not to mention small towns or villages, lacked sound-equipped theaters. This huge lacuna showed when Charlie Chaplin's *Gold Rush* was released onto the Italian market in 1934. It sold 4.5 million tickets, the largest number for any film ever shown in Italy. Yet 4.5 million tickets represented just over 10 percent of the Italian people. Fascist Italy, government officials estimated, should be capable of turning out 25 million spectators and raising the number of exhibition spaces from the miserably low number of 1,800 to 4,000, which would be a respectable number by European standards.[68]

Accordingly, production was left in private hands. Which is to say, the dictatorship funneled bountiful state subsidies into the hands of a single wealthy entrepreneur, the industrial engineer Carlo Roncoroni, who in 1935 had purchased the bankrupt Cines studios, formerly Italy's only major motion picture producer, from the national holding company IRI (Istituto per la Ricostruzione Industriale). With state monies, Roncoroni in turn oversaw the construction on Via Tuscolana on Rome's eastern outskirts of a 36,000-square-meter complex of studios designed to replace the old Cines works on Via Veio, which had providentially burnt to the ground just nine months after this prescient entrepreneur had purchased them. Inaugurated by Mussolini on April 28, 1937, the enterprise combined a craft-based organization with the most technologically advanced equipment available in Europe, the whole operation efficiently supervised by a Hollywood-trained Italian engineer. The Alfieri Law of June 16, 1938, gave yet another handout to movie producers. Any film whose script had been passed by censorship regardless of its artistic or other merits was granted an automatic bonus equal to 12–25 percent of its gross receipts.

To establish a state monopoly to distribute films meant confronting the American majors. After Will Hays paid a personal visit to the Duce in Rome in November 1936, Mussolini lifted a previous order to curb imports. Not that the order was incomprehensible: imperial Italy was struggling with a terrible balance-of-payments deficit, which was exacerbated by the fact that in 1935 around 70 percent of the gross earnings on new film releases was being remitted to U.S. companies. However, as soon as Cinecittà started to generate a supply of films, the state went ahead with its decision to set up a state monopoly over the distribution of films. In principle, the Ente Nazionale Industrie Cinematografiche, or ENIC, was not intended to drive American distributors out. And various overtures were made to mollify the majors. But by the end of 1938, faced with its arcane directives and drops in profits, the leading U.S. firms withdrew from the Italian market.

With no competition from Hollywood, Fascist Italy was turned into a motion picture investor's paradise. The conditions provided were ideal: from state-financed production studios (which at Roncoroni's death in 1939 passed into government hands) and a national distribution cartel to allocate markets, to big bonuses that were awarded for quantity rather than quality on the basis of box-office receipts rather than for artistic merits or cinematic professions of political faith. At their nadir in 1927, Italian producers turned out 31 features; in 1942 they made 119.[69] Best of all, Italian motion picture producers acquired confidence that the loss of Hollywood stars and genres did not inhibit moviegoing. Italian cinéastes developed their own take on American genres, such as the "white telephone" films and musicals, as well their own star system, in addition to embarking on new directions that would flourish after the war, notably neorealism. Deprived of Hollywood, it was feared that spectators would desert the theaters. Not at all: moviegoing had become a habit stronger than allegiance to any single star or style. Ticket sales leaped from 348 million lire annually in 1938 to 477 million in 1942.[70]

The Nazi Entertainment Empire

The Third Reich stands out for its success not just at building a national cinema but also at establishing a cross-European alliance against Hollywood. This success was partly the result of circumstances the Nazi regime inherited, namely Germany's giant, relatively cohesive cinema establishment and strong export economy. Hitler's dictatorship used its power to curb interfirm rivalries, cut costs, deepen its home markets, and increase exports. To a surprising degree, it also encouraged new ways of conceiving entertainment films, building on the UFA tradition, at the cost of distancing Germany's cinema culture from Weimar's modernist experimentation and bringing it closer to Hollywood.[71]

The Nazis came to power with the anticipation that the movement would express its *Völkisch* nature through the movie medium. Within the Nazi movement, however, there were always diverse positions on how this should occur. The extremist-populist wing favored movies with an explicitly political or propagandistic content. It also wanted to help out small and independent theater owners, notable numbers of whom were Nazi stalwarts and were suffering from dropping attendance, high rental prices, inadequate supply, and the expense of remodeling for sound. Their anti-Semitism was ferocious, accentuated by their dependence on distributors, many of whom were Jewish. At Hitler's appointment and with party support, they had immediately launched boycotts against Jewish distributors of American films.[72]

By contrast, the institutional wing, including the Third Reich's new minister for public enlightenment and propaganda, Joseph Goebbels, an informed and zealous movie fan, contended that economic soundness and artistic merit should be guiding precepts and that state policy should be oriented toward streamlining and developing existing industrial practices. In his first major address to the film guild at the Hotel Kaiserhof, Wednesday evening, March 28, 1933, he proclaimed that "Art is free, however it must conform to certain norms." He set a high if eclectic standard by listing his all-time favorites: Sergei Eisenstein's *Potemkin* ("a perfect artistic picture, although with Bolshevist tendencies"), the classical montage artist Vladimir Gardin's *Anna Karenina* (1914), Lang's *The Nibelungen,* and the contemporary German Luis Trenker's *The Rebel* (1932), the story of Andreas Hofer, the south Tyrolese student who led the 1809 rebellion against the French occupation. "Parades and trumpet fanfares" weren't sufficient to make a film "national," Goebbels intoned. "New ideas" were needed, the subjects for which "could easily be found in everyday life on the streets." The only thing sure was that "the public's taste and psychology are not such as a Jewish director imagines them to be. In order to have a true picture of what the German people want and like, one must be German."[73] Had he revisited his rambling speech, he might have noted that Jews had directed three of his four favorites.

This convenient blind spot made Goebbels sensitive to UFA's effort to keep Pommer, who was recognized as the force behind the success of German "talking" features in east-central Europe to the detriment of Hollywood. In 1931, largely because of the popularity of Pommer's *Congress Dances,* a grand-scale operetta about a romance between the czar of Russia and a poor glovemaker set at the Congress of Vienna and starring Lilian Harvey, Willy Fritsch, and Conrad Veidt as Prince Metternich,

UFA had paid out a dividend of 6 percent.[74] To sidestep the fact that UFA rescinded his contract on March 29, 1933, the day after Goebbels's speech, fumbling gestures were made to exempt him from the anti-Jewish decrees on the grounds of his honorable military record. These overtures were cut short by Pommer after he learned that his son was to be barred from the annual May Day students' parade. His only request was that while he considered the proposal Goebbels show his good faith by not letting his passport be stamped with a "J." In late April 1933, he used it to leave Germany with his family, first to go to Paris where he was already under contract with Fox's French subsidiary and where he produced two films, then, in 1934, to return to Hollywood.[75] Goebbels made similar overtures to Fritz Lang, whose *Metropolis* both he and Hitler greatly admired. But two days after Goebbels's cinema speech, the censorship board banned *The Testament of Dr. Mabuse* as Communistic and dangerous to public order and safety, which it probably was in view of its uncanny portrayal of the paranoid doctor plotting from the lunatic asylum to plunge the world into an "abyss of terror." This ban caused a 200,000-Reichsmark loss to Universal Pictures, which had purchased the distribution rights for Germany.[76] It also reinforced Lang's inclination to leave his homeland as soon as possible; he too departed for Paris, where he directed *Liliom* for Pommer before also moving on to Hollywood.

The *auto-da-fé* of the German film industry, by causing a mass exodus from the highest positions—company executives, producers, directors, sales managers, screen artists, musical composers, and so on—and the huge boon to Hollywood that resulted, make the eventual success of the Nazi's investment in the cinema all the more remarkable. Its first step was to take over the film industry's major organization, the German Film Industry Trade Organization (Spitzenorganisation der deutschen Film Industrie, or SPIO). This had been founded at Erich Pommer's initiative in 1923 with the idea that it would function like Will Hays's vertically integrated MPPDA, bringing together producers with distributors and exhibitors. But it was only in the early 1930s, under UFA chief executive Klitzsch's leadership, that the SPIO become a notably compact interest group, all the more so in late 1932, when all the American interests joined it in the hope of strengthening their hand against the new regime, as well as to conceal their foreignness. Recognizing how useful the SPIO was to its own "coordination" of German institutions, the Nazi regime removed Klitzsch, purged its numerous Jewish members, renamed it the Reich Film Chamber, and reopened it for business in its usual offices with a new mandate, namely "to cooperate with the decisions of leaders, to eliminate waste and lost motion, unqualified and otherwise undesirable elements in the trade, and, in sum, to aid in a general regeneration of the industry."[77] The Americans would have liked to stay involved, given their significant investments. But many of their personnel were Jewish. And business as usual could not tolerate incidents like that which befell the inoffensive Max Friedland, a German national, the continental manager for Universal, as well as the company president Carl Laemmle's favorite nephew, who during the week of April 15 had been pulled out of his bed at his home in Laupheim, hustled off to the jail, where he was held for five hours with no explanation, and had his passport confiscated.[78] Haltingly, having to believe the worst because, more than other industries, so many of their personnel were hit by anti-Semitism, the American firms withdrew or quietly reinvested in Aryanized businesses.

The more complicated issue of reconciling commercial appeal with a specifically Nazi cinema style arose as the industry's profits slumped in 1936–37. Partly this crisis resulted from rising costs. Some ensued from the high expenses related to making sound features. Others arose from the giant salaries commanded by German stars in the face of competition from Paris and Hollywood. The anti-Jewish decrees of 1933 had, in effect, depleted the supply. The dropoff in exports, exacerbated after 1933 by foreign boycotts to protest German anti-Semitism, put further pressure on profits. Whereas in 1932–33 the industry could recoup 40 percent of the costs of making movies from exports, in 1936–37 it recovered only 6–7 percent.[79]

The response to this crisis was fourfold. First, the industry was subjected to another round of concentration and cost-cutting. By removing Hugenberg as head of UFA's board, the dictatorship brought the company directly under government control. It then forced the three other leading film producers to coordinate their operations with UFA so that by 1939, as a state-run combine, its capital greatly augmented by the newly founded FilmKredit Bank, the company produced 75 percent of all German feature films. Next the government sought to build up home consumption. It did this by essentially political as opposed to commercial means. In other words, rather than the fan club, movie magazines, giveaways, and other promotions typical of U.S. marketing campaigns, which were widely imitated elsewhere in Europe, the Nazi regime mobilized the party and trade union apparatus. The sprawling afterwork organization Strength through Joy was especially active, offering discount tickets, sponsoring UFA "revivals," and promoting traveling cinemas. As the country went to war, going to the cinema was a distracting and sociable, as well as warm, relief. By the third year of the war, the number of moviehouses had increased from 5,071 to 7,042, and yearly ticket sales had practically quintupled, from 245 million to 1.1 billion.[80] Meanwhile the regime enhanced UFA's entertainment value by cultivating German stars in place of Hollywood favorites and closely imitating American genres. "At least until the grass takes deep enough root to squeeze out the weeds": that, according to one Berlin producer, was the reason why gangster films were still being made on studio lots in the spring of 1939, complete with pleasant-looking policemen and clerks in shirtsleeves, telephone-studded desks, and skyscraper backdrops.[81] Finally, the regime broadened its export market, at first by peaceable means, through bilateral distribution and coproduction arrangements with Italy, Austria, Hungary, and France, and then by force, by annexing Austria and Czechoslovakia and by the subsequent conquest of continental Europe.

The results were rapid and far-reaching. From 1937 to 1939 production increased to about eighty features per year, studio use expanded, and innovations in sound technology and color (UFA- and AGFA-color) began to be applied to production. At the same time, American releases dropped from sixty-four in 1933—accounting for 31 percent of the film releases while German productions amounted to 57 percent—to twenty in 1939, or 20 percent.[82] One reason for this decline was stricter quotas. More important, the Contingent Office, which licensed imports, banned many American films on the ground that the film's cast, director, or scenario writers were unacceptable to the Ministry of Enlightenment and Propaganda on racial, political, or other grounds, and also that they were artistically inferior, morally offensive, or otherwise inappropriate. It was said that Goebbels wanted to exclude American releases altogether on cultural as well as economic grounds, but that Hermann Göring, his great rival as minister of industry, urged that there be no such ban on the grounds that the competition stimulated better domestic productions; it would also reveal Goebbels's incompetence in matters regarding an industry that in 1939 still did not produce enough releases to meet national demand. Their rivalry also opened some space for debate over the merits of American films, Goebbels having banned press criticism of domestic productions as well as cowardly "laugh critics" who made their views heard in the dark of the theater. In large cities, where the public was sophisticated and critics more easily escaped the eye of vengeful party hacks, film notices could be favorable to U.S. releases, if only to draw invidious comparisons with German films they disliked. In the provinces, by contrast, the minister of public enlightenment and propaganda's injunctions that "film art" was a "serious affair" that needed "to take serious things seriously" had wider resonance. Anything that wasn't understood was put down as "incomprehensible nonsense," another example of "decadent Jewish influence," or reeking of "Hollywood philosophy."[83] To the degree that American releases remained popular it was in Berlin, where in 1939, among the eight top box-office draws were two Hollywood films: MGM's *The Girl of the Golden West,* playing at the UFA Tzt; and Paramount's *Spawn of the North,* at Marmor Haus.[84] It was not until 1940 that the Nazi regime, using Anatole Litvak's *Confessions of a Nazi Spy* as a pretext, banned U.S. film imports altogether.[85] Ultimately the disruption of markets by total war was perhaps a more effective means of stopping the circulation of American releases than Nazi-Fascist policing.

Simultaneously the Third Reich addressed the prospect, much bruited in the second half of the 1920s, of building a cross-European counterweight to Hollywood. The initial effect of sound had been to splinter efforts to unify European cinema establishments. At the same time, the German industry had promoted unity in some very concrete ways. It had fostered a flourishing Mitteleuropean cinema culture by drawing on Berlin directors, actors, and technicians from Austria, Hungary, Czechoslovakia, Poland, and Romania, as well as from Soviet Russia. It also helped put French firms back into the European market. For example, in 1930, by entering into accords with Klangfilm and UFA, the Gaumont-Franco-Aubert conglomerate had been able to participate in European distribution cartels; and by working out a trust relationship with Tobis-Küchenmeister, it had entered the sound equipment market. In their effort to obtain support for a cross-European cartel, German industrialists had long encouraged their potential partners, first and foremost in France, to establish a vertically organized lobby like their own SPIO in order to end their internal squabbles and exercise more effective political power. An alliance of like-minded organizations offered the best means of facing down the influence of the American majors concentrated in the MPPDA.[86] In 1935, at German instigation, the representatives of various European film establishments present at the Venice Film Festival took a step in this direction by signing an accord to found the International Film Chamber, or IFC. A cosmopolitan effort, its twenty-four members included representatives from Japan and India, each of which produced far more films per year than all the European countries combined, but did not, of course, compete with European interests.[87]

The International Film Chamber's main interest was to organize the continental European market: its first president, Fritz Scheuemann, was also president of the National Film Chamber, a recent Nazi invention; its vice-president was the Italian industrial magnate Count Giuseppe Volpi di Misurata, founder of the Venice Film Festival and the behind-the-scenes promoter of Italy's quest for "vital space" in the Balkans. The IFC wooed the French by holding its second meeting in Paris in 1937, a move that entailed offering a Frenchman the next turn in the presidency. There was no anti-U.S. bias intended in the IFC, the Italians feigned, worried about offending the Americans so long as their own cinema economy relied so heavily on American imports. This fiction did not convince American trade representatives, who, with their British allies, were always on guard against any new German-dominated entente. The Anglo-Americans boycotted not only the Paris meeting of the IFC but all its subsequent undertakings as well on the grounds that they were tools of a German-led, anti-American bloc.[88]

To the degree that a European cinema culture had begun to evolve, its focus was that sophisticated social event the Venice Film Festival. Conceived in 1932 as the "First Exposition of Cinematographic Art" under the auspices of the XVIII Venice Biennale Art Show, its middle-Europe location on the Adriatic Sea, Fascist sponsorship, and tasteful pomp gave it a cachet that no American gathering could possibly yield. Becoming an annual event in 1934, it was distinguished not so much by the films it previewed and prized, which included numerous Hollywood features, so much as its distinctively European style. From the seaside terrace of the Excelsior Hotel to the light shows and evening festivities, it was as the Fascist cultural bureaucracy intended it to be, a showcase of openness, at which Hollywood, but also European stars, famous directors, and powerful producers mixed with rich and worldly tourists, dapper Fascist officials, and well-known artists and intellectuals. The juries were selected for their sagacity and good taste. The acme of this mythical Europeanism was 1936. Italy had just become an empire; the Axis looked like a healthy counterweight to Franco-British-American plutocracy; the prizes were divided up with an eye to the cinematic virtues of the continental film industry: Augusto Genina's *White Squadron,* a colonial war film, won the

Mussolini Trophy; *The King of Kalifornia,* by Luis Trenker, the prize for best foreign film; Paul Muni was best actor, Annabella best actress, and Jacques Feyder best director.[89]

However, as the Rome-Berlin Axis was consolidated after 1937, this cosmopolitan cultural multiplicity gave way to reactionary political correctness. Beginning in 1937, the prize for best foreign film was regularly won by a German feature, and that year the jury was warned away from awarding any major prize to the obvious choice, Jean Renoir's *Grand Illusion,* an antiwar paean to German-French reconciliation. In 1940 Viet Harlan's *Jud Süss,* that nasty *chef d'oeuvre* of Nazi anti-Semitism, made its world premiere at the film festival. Thereafter the event was renamed the Italo-Germanic Film Exposition (Manifestazione Cinematografica Italo-Germanica) to seal the dictators' wartime alliance. The tenth and final event, dedicated to "The Armed Forces" and inaugurated on August 30, 1942, by Goebbels and his Italian counterpart, Alessandro Pavolini, the Fascist minister of popular culture, included only the Axis powers, together with their numerous satellites, puppets, and fellow travelers. They put their cultural common front on display by all showing films with an anti-Bolshevik theme.[90]

Without the forcible exclusion of U.S. films from continental Europe, which was possible only under wartime conditions, the success of this German-dominated European bloc would have been inconceivable. In 1939, purely in terms of numbers, Hollywood produced 527 feature films, whereas the combined total for Germany and Italy was around 160.[91] The Hollywood film was a package, part and parcel of a whole cinema culture, the sun in the firmament of a globalizing cinema culture to which all other cinemas made more or less explicit reference. The same system that produced the film for export supplied a wide set of parameters to define the context for its reception, whether through the promotional hoopla of exhibitors, the attention of critics, or the buzz of conversation. The system also conditioned the whole configuration of local production, whether it sought to compete head-on with Hollywood's costly entertainment features, looked for alternatives in popular local genres, or steered some path in between.

Neither state protectionism, government supports, censorship, nor outright political coercion halted the seemingly irresistible movement of American cinema models through international markets. At the time of the French Popular Front, MGM's *Voice of the Lion* was rallying thousands of little children in Laurel-Hardiste fan clubs, and in Civil War

Spain MGM's sound-equipped advertising trucks showed no partisanship; they toured behind both the loyalists' and the rebels' lines. In 1937, as Mussolini's regime was drawing up plans to close out the U.S. majors, the Duce's own son, Vittorio, was in Hollywood to conclude a deal with Hal Roach to film Italian operas. Not even the most self-isolating system was impervious: in the autarchic Germany of the early 1940s, actresses drove about in their cream-colored Phaetons and directors drew moviemogul salaries while Goebbels was exhorting UFI producers to make quality entertainment for the Reich's captive audiences by studying the standardized plot lines and happy endings of Hollywood.

Ultimately the "unitary order" imposed by the Nazis depended on extramarket pressures. These included the political exactions made possible by conquest, namely army censorship, confiscations (especially of extensive Jewish properties), rigid regulation of news sources, and strict rationing of scarce resources, notably film stock. The expansion of the German industry got its first big boost when, following the Nazi takeover of Austria, the Reich seized control of the local film industry. The fate of Czechoslovakia, which Germany occupied in March 1939, was more punitive. The republic had been remarkably successful in fighting off the rival hegemonies of Hollywood and Germany by means of contingents, quotas, and an effective export campaign. In retaliation, the occupiers reduced Czech production to 20 percent of its prewar level, expropriating Prague's excellently equipped Barrandov studios from their majority owner, Milos Havel, and turning them over to the Reich, which in turn handed them over to German producers. The Polish cinema was virtually obliterated, and the ebullient Yiddish-language culture of eastern European Jewry, whose talents had nurtured practically every Western film industry in one form or another, was eradicated by the annihilation of Jewish communities. In turn, the German New Order fostered the cinema establishments of its allies, collaborators, and puppet regimes once they had been purged of their Jewish and nonconforming elements. Accordingly, the German film cartel sponsored the birth of Croatian, Slovenian, Slovakian, Bulgarian, and Romanian national cinemas; it greatly boosted the vitality of the Italian and French cinemas; and it took the Hungarian cinema under its wing as a junior partner in the conquest of the Balkans.[92]

In January 1942 the New Order in the domain of the European cinema was consolidated by the establishment of the giant UFI holding company, whose purpose was to combine the assets of all major firms involved in motion pictures, including UFA. The dimensions of its continental market made it equal to the U.S. domestic market. Distribution accords gave it about 16,000 outlets by the early 1940s. Its technical accomplishments made it a peer of Hollywood. It even had its own equivalent of Hollywood flair, the so-called UFA style.

But not until the war was well under way and racial laws were being widely applied did voices outside Germany chime in to specify the ethnic-political nature of the New Order's European cinema culture. For Vittorio Mussolini, the Duce's son and man-about-Cinecittà, the cinema had been "snatched from the hands of judaic finance and its masonic minions." "Once remolded by European civility," it had been "detoxified of judaic poison, [which was] subtly falsifying of history, morally lax, licentious in habits, [and] deliberately confusing about interpreting bad and good."[93] The new cinema order, reinforced by anti-Semitism, provided an outlet for those who in the past had speculated that Hollywood control was a facet of the world-Zionist conspiracy. In France, Maurice Bardèche and Robert Brasillach's *Histoire du cinéma,* published in 1935, was packed with allusions to the malefic and vulgar influence of "foreigners" who "denationalized" the cinema and turned it into crass mediocrity. The notion that the cinema had become a "Jewish art" echoed Sombart's argument about why Jewish merchants were so prominent in modern retailing, namely that Jews were "obligatory mediators of the future" given their "experience of internationalism" and their "freedom from local loyalties" such as religion and the idea of the fatherland.[94] That the publication of Bardèche and Brasillach's book coincided with the bankruptcy proceedings against Pathé-Natan, and that Natan was accused of ruinous and unethical business practices, reinforced the belief that the French industry, a particularly precious national cultural source, was being run into the ground by Jewish influence. By 1941 most Jewish filmmakers, a variable but never inconspicuous percentage of the people involved in the cinema industries of Europe, had been purged even in countries like Hungary and Italy that had not yet been occupied by German forces. In France, if the fascist press can be believed, the business lost 50 percent of its directors and 80 percent of its producers.[95] Bernard Natan, who after his disgrace in 1935 had continued making films on a small scale with his brother, Louis, figured prominently in the "Despoilers of the Screen" section of the national exhibit "The Jew and France," which opened on September 12, 1941, at the Berlitz Palace in central Paris. Stripped of his French citizenship in 1941, he was interned at the

Drancy concentration camp before being turned over to the Gestapo, who deported him to Auschwitz on September 25, 1942, where he died a few weeks later.[96]

The French wartime experience is better remembered not for these anti-Semitic depredations, which were conveniently ignored, but for the long-awaited renascence of the French cinema. Under the German occupation, French production blossomed. In the four years of occupation, the industry, reorganized according to the centralized Italian model under the protection of the UFI cartel and generously infused with German capital, produced 220 feature films. At the outset, German planners equivocated about how French cinema culture should fit into the New Order: one option, in keeping with German stereotypes, was that French directors should be assigned to making mediocre, as Goebbels put it, "light, frothy and if possible corny pictures" for home consumption.[97] But business, artistic, and political considerations prompted a more versatile use of French resources, namely to supply the UFI international cartel with high-quality releases for export. Naturally, the success of this decision depended on the exclusion of the U.S. industry. It also rested on the expropriation of distribution chains from their non-Aryan proprietors. By 1942 the French industry had finally realized the reforms sought for two decades. The 410 out-of-control units of 1939 had been reduced to a more or less disciplined coterie of 42 firms. Capitalizing on the availability of cheap labor, the ban on showing double features (which resulted in increased ticket sales), the lack of alternative amusements, which sent movie attendance soaring, and a lax German-run censorship system, a national cinema was finally born and the humiliation by Hollywood lived down.

However, all efforts to envision, much less sustain, a trans-European cinematic New Order were incorrigibly flawed. The Nazis were determined simultaneously to produce a widely marketable commodity and to find a way to promote a "nationalistic"—as opposed simply to a "national"—cinema. Though keenly knowledgeable about the sources of Hollywood's power, the New Order's cinema was unable to replicate it. The U.S. motion picture industry still had the advantage of complete control over its home market. It also knew how to tap into and commercialize its multicultural sources so as to produce a commodity that was salable in a wide range of cultural and social venues. With a keen eye to what pleased its complicated home public as well as foreign audiences, Hollywood had to all effects "denationalized" its products. Never having made any pretense of being *Kultur,* Hollywood was never embarrassed to call its output a commodity whose value was unabashedly measured by business balance sheets and box-office receipts. It was not just committed to entertainment value; it prided itself on having invented the notion.

Much more self-consciously, Nazi Germany moved to make German cinema widely salable abroad. To keep abreast of the American competition, Goebbels fully grasped that captive audiences too had to be turned into eager consumers. As American releases became scarcer and scarcer, he used his offices to procure films and hold biweekly showings to instruct German filmmakers in the art of producing films for entertainment value, and his diaries and conferences proliferated with jejune and ponderous object lessons about how Hollywood exercised its hegemony. Based on observing U.S. relations with neighboring Canadian and South American markets, the lesson for Germany was to cultivate indigenous producers rather than extirpate them. This conciliatory approach assumed, of course, that their only aim was to express their cultural existence in a local way and that they had no pretensions to move outside their own little market niches. Under no circumstances should they be allowed to develop an autonomous commercial base of their own.

The second lesson was drawn from observing Americans' capacity to create new genres. They were "masters," Goebbels noted, at taking their own (admittedly scarce) "cultural stock" and freeing it of "political ballast." Thereby they were able to make it palatable to a mass public.[98] How a result that involved such a fine-tuned interplay between market forces, repressive tolerance, and state support, not to mention the large freedom of action of big-time Jewish entrepreneurship, could have been achieved in a racist, closed system ruled by military force is hard to imagine. It is true that the cartel of multinational cinemas organized under UFI tolerated a wide exchange of cinema experiences; and the positions opened up by the purge of Jews and politically nonconformist film personnel were soon filled by bright new talent, often graduated from professional cinema schools rather than coming from theater, classical music, or other artistic movements, hence better trained technically, and representing a younger generation dedicated first and foremost to motion picture production. Under the pressure of scarce labor and raw materials, they were pushed to make fewer, better-capitalized, higher-quality movies, with the expectation that each would be seen by a far bigger audience than before. Now more explicitly than ever, it was considered advisable to avoid films with a political content and endeavor instead to "discipline distraction," "engineer emotion," and foster fantasies of escape while holding audiences in a tight ideological embrace.[99]

From early 1942 Goebbels reaffirmed the cinema industry's commitment to producing entertainment cinema, or *Unterhaltungsfilm*. For 1945, sixty-four of the seventy-two motion picture features commissioned from UFI were conceived in this general style, and numerous of these were supposed to be "cheerful" films, meaning lighthearted musicals and comedies.[100]

The film that was dearest to Goebbels, the costliest, and the most widely promoted of that epoch epitomizes the effort to create a new European cosmopolitanism at once expressive of German culture and appealing to international audiences. This was the extravagant *Baron of Münchhausen*. Commissioned in 1941, when it looked as though the New Order had prevailed in Europe, with an eye to the 1943 celebration of UFA's twenty-fifth anniversary and the tenth since the Nazi "renascence" of the German cinema, the production was intended to show that the German motion picture industry could equal contemporary Hollywood epics. The competition was *Gone with the Wind* (1939), which Goebbels had viewed in private after the German navy had procured a print, but which had been barred from release although Margaret Mitchell's novel had sold the most copies of any book in Nazi Germany after Hitler's *Mein Kampf*. With a budget authorized at 4.57 million Reichsmarks (later increased to 6.5), Goebbels entrusted the *Münchhausen* project to the reliable forty-one-year-old Josef von Baky, a talented, apolitical Hungarian who after moving to Berlin in 1927 was known for a couple of anodyne operetta films, *Intermezzo* and *Menschen vom Varieté*. For the screenplay he turned to the well-known novelist Erich Kästner, who was half-Jewish, but very talented, Goebbels admitted. The screenplay was a pastiche of the tales popularly attributed to the fictitious eighteenth-century Saxon libertine, a contemporary and sometime sidekick of Cagliostro, who like him and other similarly fictitious eighteenth-century heroes—Casanova, Dr. Faustus, Don Giovanni, and the Baron of Crac—was notorious for his wit and skulduggery. Imperturbably adventurous, supplied with magic powers acquired from Cagliostro, including the gift of immortality, the Baron, played by Hans Albers, the supple embodiment of Aryan masculinity, effortlessly transits time and frontiers: a roué when courting the Great Catherine of Russia, a kindly despot toward his faithful valet Kuchenreuther, implacably cunning to escape the Sultan at Constantinople, a refined lover at the behest of the Princess d'Este. With fantastic trick photography—of the cannonball flight to Constantinople, the Montgolfier trip to the moon, the lunar flora—UFA responded to Alexander Korda and Walt Disney (whose films Goebbels reportedly procured to assist von Baky). The medium was dazzling Agfa-color, Germany's answer to Technicolor.[101]

Between the time the film was conceived, in 1941, at the acme of the Nazi New Order, and March 1943, when the film had its gala premiere at the UFA-Palast am Zoo, everything had changed. Downtown Berlin was enshrouded in sulfurous dust from the Allied bombing only three days earlier, and public opinion was still under the pall of the news, scarcely a month old, that the Sixth Army had been annihilated at Stalingrad and Field Marshal von Paulus had surrendered to the Red Army. Promoted heavily, the film was popular beyond expectations. It was a marvelous work of distraction. Yet it could also have been viewed as spent power in search of the security of quiet domesticity. After the Baron's razzle-dazzle romp across the vast playground of a Eurolandia whose heartland is Saxony and whose far reaches are St. Petersburg, the Caliphate, Venice, and the Moon, he is shown in the closing scene, his own Aryan hair silvery smooth instead of covered by a powdered wig, his dress an elegant suit instead of eighteenth-century frippery. As attentive young people listen to him finish, his story becomes a flashback, and he, a latter-day aristocrat, confesses to having renounced the Faustian inquietude of eternal youth to age in peaceably bourgeois style with his long-suffering wife. Far distant from the cranky experimentation of the UFA in the early years of the Weimar Republic, its spectacular artifice pumped up to rival Hollywood's, the *Baron of Münchhausen* showed German cinema transcending the boundaries of national-state culture to appeal to a trans-European public. That it did so in this splendidly crafted work by counterposing to Hollywood's modern myths the archaic fantasies of a domesticated eighteenth-century cosmopolitanism suggests that the Nazis had lost out to the competition even as they verged on losing the war.

While UFI was marshaling its last forces to consolidate the Nazi "empire of the imagination," the Hollywood industry advanced its pretensions to exercise an even greater voice in the postwar exercise of U.S. global power. On the eve of the war, the needs of the U.S. entertainment industry had begun to contribute a new rationale to "why we fight." States with closed economies were by their nature inferior culturally because their culture could not be tested by the market of public opinion. Hence it was legitimate on both cultural and economic grounds to muster the vast power of the U.S. entertainment industry to end the thralldom of the consumer to inferior products that resulted from subsidies, cartels, and other forms of protection imposed by foreign states to block access to their markets. "Persistently and adroitly, we must make the foreign movie goer acutely conscious that the American picture is a product of decidedly superior quality—of rich and varied artistry, of entertainment value unmatchable in the run of the mill output of our competitors abroad." So wrote the head of the BFDC's Movie Division in 1939: "We must make this high quality factor so universally recognized that local audiences abroad will have no desire to see inferior films that owe their existence simply to some government legislation or subsidy."[102] During the war, faced with the decline in exports to Europe, the industry diversified its markets, making further inroads into the British Empire and Latin America. By pitching in to support the military effort, it won enormous public recognition and government gratitude. Postwar Hollywood promised to be of value not only to the economy but also to "familiarizing foreign publics with American ways of life." For Walter Wanger, now head of his own studio, who as national booking agent for Paramount, in 1926 had been responsible for editing Lang's *Metropolis* out of existence, the Hollywood film industry was a "veritable celluloid Athens," "with its array of statesmen and humanitarians like Walt Disney, John Ford . . . Donald Duck as World Diplomat!" It was these figures, real and imaginary, that would make Hollywood the capital of a "Marshall Plan of ideas."[103]

As the Allied forces occupied Berlin in April 1945, Hollywood made it clear that according to its agenda the "war had been waged to win back the European film market."[104] A new cartel, the Motion Picture Export Association, was set up to negotiate with distributors to prevent the thousands of American films backed up after years of exclusion from undercutting each other by overwhelming the European markets with a tidal wave of releases. Setting up offices in all the European capitals, including Warsaw, Prague, Budapest, Bucharest, and Sofia, the MPEA arranged to work with the occupation forces, the State Department, and local governments to return to the previous status quo. Although Germany was devastated and occupied, its film industry was still regarded as a dangerous competitor. At least one studio head, Jack Warner, advocated a "cinematic Morgenthau plan" to splinter the UFI empire into a thousand impotent units. "If it is true, as others have stated, that 'films are as strong as bullets,' and if the Allies will not permit Germans to remount the munitions industry, they should not be permitted for any reason, even if temporary, to rebuild a motion picture industry."[105]

For the purpose of ending its occupation and restoring civilian government, the American military government proposed another agenda. As soon as possible, film production should be placed in the hands of the Germans themselves, and the new German cinema reformed as a medium of democratic education. True, the new structure should not contemplate any form of concentration, much less a new version of the state-run UFI. Capital for new production should come from the private sector. And the substance of the new films should be "propaganda through entertainment," to quote the pat recommendation of Billy Wilder, who was back in Berlin advising the Division of Information Control. Steering a middle course between the Office of the U.S. Military Governor Film Division's effort to revive production and Hollywood's desire to shut it down led to some notable missteps in the effort to raise capital to restart production. When the Film Division undertook to release reels of 1930s UFA films for export in order to obtain currency to buy film stock, MPEA lobbyists accused it of trying to revive the Nazi entertainment empire.[106]

These not small complications, set against the background of the rapid revival of production in the Soviet Zone, where the bulk of UFI assets, including the Neubabelsberg studios, were located, accelerated the search for a "specialist." The job description wanted somebody: "born in Germany, [who] speaks German like a native; and [has] a precise knowledge of the German film industry and the persons active in it up to at least 1937." The position also called for "first hand knowledge of all stages of film production, preferably a recognized producer or director from Hollywood."[107] It sounded as if it had been drawn up with somebody already in mind. That would have been Erich Pommer, who, now aged fifty-nine, after a series of grave illnesses and career missteps that had reduced him and his wife to working in a California porcelain factory, had been naturalized as an American citizen in May 1944 and was now ready to come out of semiretirement.

Returning to Berlin as film production control officer in July 1946, Eric Pommer, as he now spelled his name, wore the uniform of a U.S. army officer and was armed with the powers of a Roman proconsul. As it turned out, he was caught between hell and high water. On the one hand, Hollywood interests, suspecting him of being pro-German with designs to resuscitate the UFA cinema empire, undermined him at every turn; on the other hand, his onetime colleagues, who had eagerly awaited his arrival "as sailors look to a polestar," saw him as a dupe of Hollywood and disparaged him as "the father of de-cartelization." The effect of his stay, if not the intention, was the latter. The remnants of UFI in the Allied zone were broken up into independent units for production, distribution, and exhibition, and once the lots were cleared of American Army surplus, the main site of West German motion picture production was moved to the onetime Emelka Studios at Geiselgassteig, outside Munich. By 1949, 70 percent of the releases in the U.S. zone were Hollywood-made. Thus began the shriveling of the old world of German cinema that would lead the young upstarts of Germany's new cinema to announce in 1962 that "Dad's cinema is dead." Today the brand name UFA stands for an entertainment distribution company that also produces some television programming.[108]

Recalling the extraordinary burst of creativity following Germany's defeat in the previous world war, Pommer, ever a flexible, candid, and hopeful man, saw the opportunity for a new start, one drawing on a "rich tradition of poverty and ingenuity." The gritty realism of the rubble-strewn city favored filmmaking in the style of Italian neorealism rather than the studio tradition that had become his forte wherever he worked, whether in Europe or Hollywood. "The reality of our ruins is dearer to us than a film castle on the moon . . . There would be no stars, no glitz." "Poverty can have a productive effect," within limits of course. "Authors need first of all cigarettes and coffee. As long as I can't give them something to smoke or something stimulating to drink everything is hopeless."[109] In reality, there was no going back to Weimar days. For the forseeable future, to create a successful national cinema meant finding a niche within the Hollywood system.

CHAPTER 7

The Consumer-Citizen

How Europeans Traded Rights for Goods

In Alsace in 1945, a German spy disguised as a GI blew his cover when he picked up an old cigarette butt. Everybody knows that the Americans don't pick up old cigarette butts.
ROBERT GUÉRIN,
French wit, 1955

Consumer sovereignty and the liberal system . . . stand or fall together.
GEORGE H. HILDEBRAND,
American economist, 1951

SPAIN WAS THE ONLY COUNTRY in all Europe excluded from the Marshall Plan. Until Stalin turned down the offer of aid, even the Soviet Union was eligible for the grants, credits, and supplies that the U.S. government started sending abroad in June 1948 under the terms of the European Recovery Program. Spain was barred because Francisco Franco's dictatorship, now firmly ensconced, continued to be regarded as a "squalid offshoot of Nazism."[1] To include this pariah among nations along with the fifteen other countries finally declared eligible, President Harry S Truman determined, was "not only a bad credit risk" but "a moral risk" as well.[2]

In Spain's exclusion lies the plot of a whole movie, titled with self-evident irony *¡Bienvenido Mister Marshall!* Made in 1952 by the gifted young director Luis Garcia Berlanga, the film was loosely based on an actual event. This was the mission of U.S. Army Major General James W. Spry, conducted from August to November 1951 at the head of a survey team of ninety, to reconnoiter the country for Cold War military bases. Mixing the fond populism of contemporary Italian neorealism with the Spanish taste for grotesque caricature, Berlanga satirized official Spain's subservient quest for handouts. Belatedly, under the terms of the Mutual Security Act of 1951 in recognition of Spain's newfound usefulness as an ally, the dictatorship began to collect the aid it had been begging for since 1949.

Welcome Mr. Marshall! slyly succeeds, where written records fail, in telling of a Europe coming face to face with this behemoth of well-being: of the fanciful expectations the Marshall Plan aroused that Europeans would soon enjoy American standards of living; of new alliances formed in the name of the consumer, dynamized by Cold War politics and smoothed by U.S. economic and cultural capital; but also of the travailed journey most people took over the next two decades from the ruins of the bourgeois regime of consumption to the jerry-built foundations of what in Europe too by 1960 was known as "the mass consumer society."

Berlanga's film opens as a rundown Castilian village rouses itself from its secular slumber at the early-morning news that the Americans are due to visit. The mayor prepares to welcome this "Mr. Marshall" in the time-honored fashion with toasts of lemonade and sangria, only to be persuaded by a passing entertainment agent that Villar del Rio as it really is—with its dried-up fountain, broken-down town clock, scrawny animals, black-shrouded women, and listless men "sitting around the central square dreaming about harvests they'd never planted"—will never attract the Americans' benefaction. The whole world knows, Manolo the flashy impresario argues, that people need to package themselves properly to become the objects of America's generosity.[3] With an alacrity that confounds the deadbeat local elite, the townspeople transform their desiccated flat land into an enticing Andalusian stage set, of the kind familiar to aficionados of *Carmen* and to American tourists with a picture-postcard image of Spain. As the full-dress rehearsal of their new identity reaches its climax, the sun-bleached cow patch now a sun-drenched Potemkin Village of chorale-singing school children, Flamenco-dancing women, and bull-fighting men, the Yankee cavalcade whizzes through. It doesn't even slow down enough to register the town's existence, much less respond to its ingratiating display of creativity.

Hollywood condemned the film as anti-American when it was shown at the Cannes Festival in 1953 (where it was acclaimed for its humor).[4] The industry's dour emissary, Edward G. Robinson, missed its point—

which was not at all to castigate U.S. indifference, but to chide public illusions about quick fixes. The film showed the people who had formerly stood in the shadows of back-street doorways stepping into the foreground, raggedly lining up in the central square to voice their hodgepodge of wants. It showed the town intellectual petitioning for a telescope to enable him to see further; an old peasant lady, prodded to make her choice, screeching out "chocolate," the ancient craving of the poor; and two working women squabbling over whether both can list a mass-produced good, the sewing machine. The peasant Juan's longing for a tractor is shown consummated in a dream sequence that has the machine delivered from an airplane, its bearers, the Three Magi, bearded like Santa Claus and mustached like Stalin, parachuting it to earth, where Juan, smiling seraphically like a Five-Year Plan hero, throws it into gear and speeds off to plow his hardscrabble lands.

All fantasies to naught: The final scene shows the chastened villagers straggling into the central square to pay for their frilly costumes, paper garlands, potted plants, and other props—not with money, for they have none, but with trussed-up chickens, candlesticks, mirrors, copper water jugs, and the other bric-a-brac of humble lives. The last to arrive, the stiff-legged old Hidalgo, obliges by donating his rusted sword, emblem of his own onetime grip over Villar del Rio and his conquistador ancestors' long-lost hegemony over the American "cannibals." Silly deluded ones, the omniscient narrator gently chides them: change, when it comes, will occur at your own tempo, through your own resources, and be in your own image.

How much and what should the people of Europe be getting in the wake of World War II? Any study of the challenge of American consumer culture to European commercial civilization has to consider the Marshall Plan, as it really was, as central to the answer. Not as enlightened benefaction, but as bearer of new ways of thinking about producing affluence. Not as a gift propagated with glossy images of giant dockside forklifts in Southamptom, Rotterdam, and Antwerp unloading countless tons of cotton, grain, coal, and corn to feed people, provide animal fodder, and supply voracious industries, mammoth turbines destined to generate hydroelectric power, or immense steel presses to stamp out automobile parts, but the staging ground for a more austere scenario. This promised all the abundance that a revved-up capitalist war economy could deliver. But its price was to suppress the cornucopias of populist tradition, cut back on necessaries, and inculcate the discipline to satisfy wants in an orderly sequence.

The fact is that the Marshall Plan was neither the first nor the only response to defining the standard of living appropriate for postwar Europeans. There were new alternatives; for the vexed problem began to be revived in terms now utterly altered with respect to the past as reformist coalitions took shape across Europe to proclaim the right to a decent standard of living.

At its publication in December 1942, the Beveridge Report was the earliest indicator of this profound change in expectations. Drawn up at the behest of Winston Churchill's wartime cabinet to rally public support as German planes bombed British cities, it launched the first comprehensive scheme for what contemporaries eloquently spoke of as the *welfare* as opposed to the *warfare* state. Authored by Sir William Beveridge, the liberal reformer, the report detailed the five giant "social evils"—illness, ignorance, disease, squalor, and want—that beset the British people. In extraordinary amplitude, it also set forth the remedies: nothing less than national health care for all, then full employment, universal secondary education, subsidized housing, and state insurance against sickness, unemployment, and old age. The 300 pages of bureaucratic prose presented such a powerful statement of the well-being that the Allied victory would bring to Europe that Nazi propagandists mobilized to vilify it as "humbug," nothing of which would remain once the war was over except government sops for "veterinary aid to cats and dogs." As it turned out, the Beveridge Report inspired the governing ethos of both Labourites and Conservatives for the next three decades. If "the name of a man" did not become the "the name of a way of life, not only for Britain, but for the whole civilized world," as Sir William immodestly hoped, it was only because the United States pressed forward a more persuasive alternative in its prescriptions for the "American way of life."[5]

Positions in sympathy with the Beveridge Report, if less comprehensively acted on, could be found across the political spectrum. The new Italian constitution put into effect on January 1, 1948, asserted in its article 2 that "it is the duty of the Republic to remove all economic and social obstacles that, by limiting the freedom and equality of citizens, prevent the full development of the individual and the participation of all workers in the political, economic, and social organization of the country." As he made his farewell speech before the French parliament on November 21, 1947, Léon Blum finally saw the wide support to "improve the working-class condition and accordingly the real purchasing power of income and salaries up to the very limits of the current possibilities of the French economy."[6] The "modern day economy" would be "neither a free-market system of liberalized buccaneering" nor the "free interplay of forces," the Christian Democrat Ludwig Erhard reasoned in 1948 on the way to becoming the German Federal Republic's first minister of economic affairs; it would be "a socially committed market economy conferring the deserved rewards on achievement."[7]

In the United States, too, raising the standard of living had become the official watchword for postwar global reconstruction. "Freedom from want" numbered first among the "Four Freedoms"—followed by freedom of religion, freedom of speech, and freedom from fear—that President Roosevelt set out on January 6, 1941, to press Congress to send Lend-Lease aid to the alliance of nations already at war against the Axis. Following Roosevelt's death, as the New Deal gave way to the Fair Deal, Truman made the "standard of living" a central motif of successive State of the Union speeches. Under American influence, the signatories of the United Nations Charter of 1945 subscribed to article 55 affirming the global objective "to promote higher standards of living." And article 25 of the UN's 1948 Universal Declaration of Human Rights specified in perhaps greater detail than Washington would have liked that "everyone has the right to a standard of living adequate for the health and well-being of himself and of his family, including food, clothing, housing, and medical care and necessary social services, and the right to security in the event of unemployment, sickness, disability, widowhood, old age, or other lack of livelihood in circumstances beyond his control."[8] In the Point Four program presented to Congress on June 24, 1949, Truman expanded the United States' goal "to assist the people of economically underdeveloped areas to raise their standard of living."[9]

As the issue of "raising the living standard" turned up on one political agenda after another, it stirred up a wasps nest of contention over who should be getting what, where, why, and when. Beware those "careless habits" of mind that confuse the current "planes of living" with new "standards of consumption," castigated Joseph Davis, the newly elected president of the powerful American Economic Association in February 1945. Years of depression and war had shown that the "marked disparity . . . between what [people] had and what they urgently wanted and felt they had reason to expect" yielded "bitter frustration" and could provoke "social disaster." Yes, it was positive news that "we are now in the throes of change in the standards of living of the community of nations . . . Our own national interests are deeply involved in translating this possibility into actual fact." But to introduce "external standards" would "only court disillusionment and frustration" given that "nothing like the full potentialities can be realized within calculable time."[10]

Professor Davis's considerations, advanced when the war in Europe was not yet over, reflected liberal common sense. Their premise was simple: as war ruins were repaired, markets opened up, government regulations were lifted, industrial output rose, and wages increased, the average European's standard of living would slowly rise to the same norm as the average American's. Meanwhile the cart of expectations couldn't go before the horse of productivity. Yet conventional liberalism had never had a good grip on the obstacles to changing the European standard of living. And it had not yet imagined the political leverage that the Market Empire could bring to bear to eliminate them—once its "national interests" showed that this was necessary.

Having seen how recalcitrant ways of life are to change, it should be no surprise that the Allied victory notwithstanding, levels of living were still stratified by social inequality, encoded in radically divided political outlooks about the meaning of the good life, and subject to all nature of government and private checks and controls. True, people everywhere chafed at impositions from wartime, especially the rationing of food, clothes, and fuel, which in many places lasted as late as 1951. In England sweets were rationed until 1953. However, nowhere was it automatic that the multitude of people, if faced with the choice between minimal guarantees of social security and new streams of consumer goods, would automatically select the latter. And nowhere could it be taken for granted that governments, if faced with the alternative between providing social guarantees at the cost of slower economic growth and deregulating markets and structural reforms at the risk of public protest would choose the latter. In sum, the war had dislodged the old regime of consumption. But it had not at all cleared the way for a civilization of creature comforts on the American model, with its overweening confidence in technology, raucous commercialism, and tolerance for social wreckage as the price paid for progress.

Indeed, social reformism, which had now triumphed in western Europe with the defeat of the reactionary right and narrow-minded liberalism, continued to work from a different legacy from the American. The solidaristic impulse, from having shown its most reactionary profile under the Nazi New Order, now revealed its largely progressive face. The issue of the breadth and depth of the market was still there. And since no single country nor Europe as a whole yielded a domestic market on the scale of the American, most government leaders resolved to address it as Keynes had advised, using the national state to promote economic recovery with full employment by priming demand within protected markets. The problem of dreadful inequality still existed. Now they intended to address it by embracing the new social orthodoxy, namely that the market could not be trusted to be egalitarian and that government had to intervene to equalize their citizens' purchasing power. Thereby European societies had come around to embracing the right to "social citizenship," in the absence of which the majority of their people had been kept from exercising the political rights and opportunities for personal development promised by liberal rule.[11]

To acknowledge that a "minimum existence" was a right, hence no longer the subject of "doctrinal disputes," marked a big step forward. If nothing else, it opened the way for a new consensus, namely that everybody could agree to disagree about the specific sets of goods and services that added up to an adequate "minimum."[12] In negotiations for new labor contracts, for example, having to include the cost of shelter, what calculations should be made about the size, not to mention the quality, of housing? In mid-May 1950, when hard-nosed delegates of the French industrial employers sat down with their equally tough-minded trade union counterparts to negotiate the details of France's new "minimum vital," rent, they agreed, was a necessary item. But employers wouldn't concede that the two rooms plus a kitchen that were right for a worker with a family were also right for one who was single. One room would do. To that, the exasperated General Confederation of Labor delegates responded: Fine, if it is one room only, make it the kitchen![13] Not yet imagining how fast minimums could change, nobody at the time foresaw that hardly a decade later the standard of shelter for workers would include not just newly built low-rent housing, but a kitchen with running water and a battery of shiny new appliances, an indoor toilet, a common living area, and a bedroom, or even two or three if the household included several children.

Driving the stunningly rapid change in consumption standards that Europeans would experience starting in the early 1950s was the conflict between the European vision of the social citizen and the American notion of the sovereign consumer. Each of these models rested on very different justifications for pressing for a higher standard of living, defining the bundle of goods and services that could satisfy it, and determining the means by which these would be attained. The former claimed higher standards as a social right, looked to the state to reduce inequalities among consumers, and was strongly influenced by the shared values of still intact political, religious, and community subcultures. The latter rode on the economic boom of the "miracle years" of the 1950s and 1960s, confided in the market to deliver goods, and embraced the profusion of new identities associated with U.S. consumer cultural goods and practices. The European *citizen-consumers* who evolved from this conflict were hybrids. "The children of Marx and Coca-Cola," as Jean-Luc Godard famously described them, the first huge cohort of them, born in the decade after the war, came of age in the 1960s.[14] At once discomfited and indulged by the explosion of consumer gratifications, they were torn between social struggles for higher wages and more public goods and individual striving after private satisfactions. Contended for by left and right, they turned uneasily between state and market, and between the security promised by the European welfare state and the freedoms promised by American consumer culture.

This contentious development makes better sense if it is set within the framework of the renewed confrontation between American consumer culture and European market civilization, though now on a very different plane and with new frontiers. On the one hand, the post–World War II American model, more self-confident, clear-cut, and aggressive than ever before, advanced with more direction on the part of policymakers in Washington, D.C., and with better synchronization between the national government, international corporations, and foreign policy aims. It held that the consumer was sovereign and the people, like the economy generally, prospered from the free play of market forces, rising output, and growing demand. If markets functioned as they should, people should be able to satisfy their "legitimate aspirations" for physical comfort and personal self-fulfillment. Hence there was no innate need for the state to step in to provide goods or step up its delivery of services. In the best of possible worlds, consumer freedom was the most basic of all freedoms. The skills, habits of mind, and desires exercised by consumers in their daily transactions sharpened their capacity as citizens to influence the political system by calculating and weighing their choices in the voting booth. In the struggle with totalitarianism, liberal political theory anguished over the capacity of individuals to make free choices. In consumer freedoms it saw the potential for society to develop people who were not only economically wise but also politically rational and ethically good. In sum, "consumer sovereignty and the liberal system . . . stand or fall together."[15]

By contrast, European principles of social citizenship conceived of people as requiring a certain minimum to belong to society. This was a "right" as opposed to a "legitimate aspiration" or "claim." If this standard was wanting, collective services, also called social consumption, had to be introduced. Not the market, then, but the political process shaped by ideals of equality and justice and culminating in the vote determined what these would be. In turn the state was duty-bound to intervene should market forces, in the course of generating new habits of consumption, also create new inequalities among citizens. In principle, more and more egalitarian consumer habits would be accompanied by more widespread political democracy, social justice, the satisfaction of basic needs for decencies, and the wider dissemination of European traditions of high culture to strengthen national identity. All in all, getting consumer goods was an important means of achieving the good society. But never could it be the end-all.

That this latter position arose out of collective ideas of community needs, now largely identified with reformist socialism, Marxist ideology, and Soviet-type planning, transformed the differences on either side of the Atlantic from a tug-of-war over policies into a major front of the conflict between the superpowers. In the first half of the century, the struggle between the ascendant U.S. market culture and the declining European bourgeois commercial civilization mostly treated the Soviet experiment as irrelevant, except for two key moments: in 1918–1921, when the Soviet revolution threatened to spill over into western Europe, and during the 1930s, when the mighty Five-Year Plans of Stalin's dictatorship presented themselves as an alternative to the sick-unto-death Western capitalism of the Great Depression. Now the line traced by the "Iron Curtain" from "Stettin on the Baltic to Trieste on the Adriatic" became a long front of struggle over which system more effectively satisfied standards for the good life, with each spelling out, in opposition to the other, a definition of mass consumption suited to its resources and legacy of development. On material cultural grounds, the two worlds were as distant as Duluth was from Dresden at the outset of the century.

Yet Joseph Stalin too had spoken about the "standard of living" when, in his first major speech to the Soviet electors on February 9, 1946, he reviewed the successes of the war against fascism. Wanting to downplay the "enormous achievements" of the Red Army, whose leadership appeared dangerously competitive with his own, he underscored that "above all, it was our Soviet social system that triumphed. The war showed that our Soviet social system is a truly popular system." As for the future: "We will pay particular attention to increasing production of consumer goods, to raising the standard of living of workers, by progressively reducing the cost of goods and by creating all sorts of scientific research institutes."[16]

Observers, not only on the left, took very seriously the Soviet system's capacity to accomplish this. Given the high growth rates reported for the Five-Year Plans of the 1930s and the Soviet Army's remarkable mobilization of the country's resources to defeat the Nazis, it was generally expected that centrally planned economies would rebuild quickly and that investment in producer industries would rapidly give way to turning out the basic consumer goods that European workers generally lacked, meaning adequate food, proper clothing, decent shelter, and collective services such as education, health care, and leisuretime pursuits. This illusion persisted well into the mid-1970s: until China's feats of the 1990s, no country delivered more refrigerators, television sets, or washing machines per capita in a ten-year period than the USSR in the decade from 1970 to 1980.[17] And even later the Soviet bloc still presented itself—and was regarded by a substantial chunk of the western European left—as the only viable model for the impoverished postcolonial world. What's more, many European intellectuals continued to admire socialist Europe's high standards of cultural consumption, contrasting its patronage of the arts, egalitarian education systems, and heavily subsidized books, records, and theater tickets to the squalid pulp culture alleged to be propagated by America's invasive imperialism. True, the main terrain of armed conflict between the United States and the USSR took place outside Europe. But the main theater of the battle over living standards was western Europe.

Welcome Mr. Marshall!

Seen as a keystone of Europe's travailed development as a consumer society, the Marshall Plan acquires new meaning, for its imprint lies not so much in its financial contribution to European reconstruction as in the conditions that were demanded to disburse the aid. All told, the actual sums expended in Europe in the form of credits, grants, and supplies are now regarded as small with respect to indigenous investment, representing perhaps 5 percent of the total capital formation during the years of recovery down to 1950. Working in close collaboration with like-minded western Europeans, U.S. planners, aid officials, and business leaders aimed to prevent political leaders, with the memory of the great depression and wartime economic administration still fresh in their minds, from being tempted to fall back on state intervention, centralized planning, and closed economies. Accordingly, the goal of the European Cooperation Agency (ECA) set up to administer the European Recovery Program was to coordinate cross-European arrangements. Operating out of headquarters in Paris under the direction of Paul G. Hoffman, the former president of the Studebaker Company, it worked through local country missions to establish the aid guidelines. These aimed at building a self-sustaining industrialized Europe, one that thrived by intraregional trade yet was firmly inserted into the American-dominated world economy.[18]

Though often regarded as the starting point for western Europe's postwar boom, the Marshall Plan was not at all conceived to create a consumers' Europe. Its first consideration was to address the dollar shortage that prevented European suppliers from purchasing U.S. goods and risked bringing recovery to a standstill. This shortfall was blamed on the trade gap between the two areas, which in turn was blamed on Europe's perennially flagging economic output. Consequently the first priority of aid was to boost productivity by investing in industrial retooling and infrastructure such as power stations, electric grids, port facilities, and railroad bridges. For the time being, national levels of consumption were not to exceed the prewar benchmark of 1938. Accordingly no aid was to be released to refurbish ragged wardrobes, replenish war-ravaged homes with household crockery and furnishings, pay for pensions, much less raise wages. Even food assistance was doled out parsimoniously—only in cases where it was absolutely necessary politically—as in western Germany in 1948, to relieve malnutrition, offset the worst shortages, and enable governments to push ahead with recovery without stirring up furious protests from people who were famished. Given these aims, the Beveridge Plan was the Marshall Plan's bête noir: ECA officials were furious that Britain's Labour government took American aid only to pour it down the bottomless pit of welfare state spending.[19]

More fundamentally, western Europeans had to be persuaded to accept what Charles S. Maier has concisely called the "politics of productivity."[20] For this to happen, business had to let go of its Malthusian belief that all-out production, based on introducing Fordist principles and the latest American technology and machinery, would bring about oversupply and depression. The more difficult proposition was to persuade labor to relinquish its resistance, for revamping production systems called for layoffs as well as intensifying the vexatious time-and-motion studies, clocking, speedups, and piecework systems that workers loathed. In the past labor had rarely benefited from increasing output, and nothing new was in store in the late 1940s. The pressure was on to revive exports—which was indispensable if European manufacturing was to re-enter global trade circuits more and more dominated by U.S. international corporations. All signs pointed to exploiting Europe's cheap labor force, if possible even to cut wages, though the prices of food, clothing, and housing, swelled by shortages and inflation, showed no signs of dropping.

True, the "high standard of living" of "Joe Smith, America's average worker"—with his sturdy build, tidy home, clean blue-jean overalls, shiny tools, and car—was the showpiece of campaigns to persuade European wage earners to work harder, accept unemployment, and defer consumption for the sake of investment. But the unspoken price was curbing autonomous trade union power and restoring managerial hierarchies. As a condition for obtaining aid, American officials not only pressed for the more or less legal ouster of the left from governing coalitions, but with help from missions of U.S. labor union officials to Europe, it sought to repress labor radicalism by splitting the trade union movements and turning a blind eye to firing militant workers and Communist union delegates.[21]

For a mass market to be established as the basis for intra-European cooperation, which, as propaganda insisted, would in turn promote peace and a higher standard of living, huge power was applied and consumer expectations of higher standards not only postponed, but emphatically lowered. Hence the "striking contrast" between U.S. and western European levels of consumption around 1950: whereas western Europeans were consuming only 3 percent more than in 1938, even though industrial output was up fully 50 percent, American consumption levels had risen 70 percent. Moreover, pricing practices remained "monstrous," notably in France, the fault of the "megalomania" of producers, the inefficiencies of distributors, and the disorientation of consumers in the face of inflation and shortages. Duly considering the different legacies of distribution of wealth, the terrible war damage inflicted on eastern Europe, and the very unequal sets of resources available to each to rebuild, the investment priorities set for the Atlantic Community by the Marshall Plan turned out to be as harsh on lower-class consumers as those imposed within the Soviet bloc by the various Five-Year Plans.[22]

Yet there was a world of difference. For the ultimate intention was to promote a cross-Atlantic, western European–wide alliance to grow consumption rather than to revive the anticonsumption coalitions of the prewar era. Hostility to higher norms of consumption was intended to be temporary. And so it happened that around 1951, as inflation was reduced, basic industries took off, trade recovered, and labor protests began to burst out across western Europe, American ECA officials reminded their allies that the Marshall Plan had originally been conceived to fight Communists, hence the funds now needed to be disbursed more generously for housing, hospitals, schools, tourist facilities, and the like. Employers too, if they were not to appear like the politically reactionary, economically retrograde bourgeois industrialists of the continent's unhappy past, should share their profits from productivity gains with the "little people of Europe."[23]

Meanwhile, to convince western European publics that the long-term benefits of this new market culture offset the short-term costs, the ECA engaged in mass marketing. As a onetime company executive, Paul Hoffman regarded it as self-evident that for the local missions to function without a "strong information arm" would be "as futile as trying to conduct a major business without sales, advertising, and customer relations."[24] A half-century's practice at selling products and public policy had taught that information imparted in nonideological language offered the most effective means of convincing people to trust new social calculations. Hence the Marshall Plan should emphasize best practice, not politics, the "American assembly line," not "the communist party line," the "full dinner pail," not the "free lunch."[25] Any well-managed U.S. corporation at the time spent 5 percent of the costs of a new product launch on marketing: that was the exact percentage Hoffman ordered the local missions to spend on education and information.

A generous part of the monies went to the ECA's Film Unit, which in the hands of talented teams of European filmmakers produced about 200 documentary-style movies from 1949 to 1953. Sober realism was their leitmotif rather than populist reveries. The scripts called for trusting in slow progress rather than expecting instant gratification, focusing on concrete needs rather than embracing utopian schemes, and confiding in European traditions rather than imitating social makeovers of foreign provenance.[26]

That was the carefully calibrated message of *The Story of Koula,* one of a handful of films dedicated to the reconstruction of Greece, where the

United States was involved in an arduous, eventually successful operation to restore the conservative monarchy in the face of Communist-led republican insurgents. Filmed in 1951 (the same year Berlanga conceived his feature), Charles (aka Vittorio) Gallo's pseudodocumentary was similarly focused on the fate of a rural backwater.[27] As the camera moves amid the stone hovels, olive trees, and dry-as-dust fields of Filavia, a mountain village of Xanthi in northern Thrace, to show the futile labors of the old men, boys, and women in the absence of adult males (victims, it is implied, of the Communist-fomented civil war), the narrator speaks in stentorian tones of the people's inveterate struggle for subsistence. Their biggest need, as he diagnoses it, is powerful draft animals to furrow the rebarbatively rocky soil.

The story of Filavia's redemption then unfolds. Fatalistic and diffident, the old people ignore the official notice to register to be eligible for aid. Were it not for the enterprising spirit of a single lad, nobody would have applied. When the date of consignment comes due, with his old Papu in tow, Kyriakos hitches up the oxcart for the two-day trip down to the port of Kavala. Normally aid was stamped "For European Recovery—Supplied by the United States of America." But for live Missouri mules, that label was inappropriate: not that the rodeo atmosphere at the dockside or the Roman-lettered "Texas" branded on the animals' glossy haunches left any doubt about their provenance. As the older men futilely try to domesticate the braying animals with kicks and slaps, Kyriakos shows that persuasion works better than force: animals, like humans, work more efficiently if treated as individuals, called by name, and cajoled into new routines, rather than like anonymous beasts of burden, cursed, beaten, and starved into submission. Even so, democratic manners won't tolerate the high-spirited Koula's insubordinate bucking when he is finally harnessed to work. There is no place at Filavia for an unproductive animal, especially not one with his scale of appetite. Now Old World common sense comes into play. Kyriakos hitches the massive mule to his spindly female donkey, and the main message comes through: individuals resolved to choose a better future, combining new machinery with age-old practice and prowess with patience, "work together for a little more productivity, a little bit more well-being." So the villagers of Filavia get the message right. The Marshall Plan is intended to produce not the high standard of living in itself, but rather the technologies, procedures, and information about how to achieve "a little bit more well-being." Expectations for the future draw on sound traditions, and none should be so grandiose as to confound the current planes of living with the "external standards" that the United States' own example threatened to introduce.

Fighting the Nylon Wars

The great predicament facing the Market Empire as its great former enemy, European merchant civilization, capitulated, and as it geared up militarily and ideologically to fight the Cold War against its new enemy, Soviet collectivism, was whether a mighty power could be sustained on the basis of the humdrum principles of material betterment. No matter how much faith the Americans reposed in the belief that their standard of living was superior, and that the alternatives to freedom of choice, the high standard of living, and democracy were coercion, deprivation, and dictatorship, there was something problematic, even contradictory, about resting such huge power on such a labile basis as the satisfaction derived from mass consumer goods. Historically, the capacity to make war had been associated with the aptitude for sacrifice. Yet from the turn of the 1950s, the U.S. corporate elite promised a "people's capitalism," a system that could mount a full-fledged war effort even while guaranteeing higher and higher levels of consumption. Unlike old Europe, the United States had the industrial capabilities to deliver both guns and butter.

Still, discomfiting questions abounded. Was Western civilization (as the North Atlantic area was now regularly described), based on the dulling comforts of mass consumption, also a society worth fighting for in terms of values? How could it be shown that Soviet claims to be catching up by means that guaranteed both equality and well-being were meaningless when large parts of Europe, as well as the globe, were not just not catching up with standards of living proposed by the West but were being left further and further behind? How could it be demonstrated that the so-called sovereign consumer was truly sovereign, and that mass-consumption society was not paralyzing to the political skills and critical capacities of its citizenry? "Between nations, a certain equality of condition . . . is necessary for understanding and frankness." Writing about Europeans' growing estrangement from the United States in the early 1950s, the philosopher Hannah Arendt's point about the misrecognition begotten by extreme disparities of living conditions could have been taken straight from Woodrow Wilson.[28]

In "The Nylon Wars" (1951) the sociologist David Riesman captured the dilemma of a nation whose hegemony rested on the plumped-up cushion of material affluence. At first reading, his short satirical essay sounds like a paean to peaceable conflict resolution. The U.S. military is commended for the "inspired" decision to bombard the Soviet Union with consumer goods in the belief that "if allowed to sample the riches of America, the Russian people would not long tolerate masters who gave them tanks and spies instead of vacuum cleaners and beauty parlors."[29] Under the code name Operation Abundance, the first raids pound the Soviet people with 200,000 pairs of nylon hose, 4 million packs of cigarettes, 35,000 Toni permanent-wave kits, 20,000 yo-yos, 10,000 wristwatches, and a barrage of odds and ends from Army PX overstock. The Soviets retaliate with their own "aggressive generosity": tins of caviar, ill-fitting fur coats, and copies of Stalin's speeches on the minorities question. Saturation bombing culminates when American forces make a massive drop of two-way radios. Armed with these gadgets, private Soviet citizens are in turn able to command drops of goods as if they were ordering from a Sears Roebuck catalogue. Succumbing to American strategic cunning, the Soviets ingloriously scramble around gathering up capitalist junk, the electrical supply collapses under overloaded circuits, and, the American victory proclaimed, totalitarian government turns from producing guns to turning out butter.

The goods-poor USSR was an easy butt of ridicule, and Hollywood films and newspaper columnists often indulged in an attitude that Riesman himself later disavowed as encouraging "a way of life racism."[30] In fact his satire cut two ways. Though Riesman was unimpeachably anti-Soviet, he worried that Americans' obsession with war materiel was the other face of their growing fixation on consumer material. By treating bombardments with commodities as real combat, he expanded on an idea first set out in his famous book, *The Lonely Crowd*, namely that the American middle classes, who had once been a wholesome "inner-directed" people guided by an internal moral gyroscope, under the corrupting influence of mass consumption had degenerated into an "other-directed" people guided by the external radar of conformist impulses. This pliability left them susceptible to the militaristic posturing incited by the mass media. Peer pressure had turned them into Cold War fanatics. If war it be, better then that it be acted out through the play of Operation Abundance than by dallying on the brink of nuclear holocaust.[31] Accordingly, "The Nylon Wars" closes with a double victory: as the Soviet dictatorship turns its resources from armaments to the accouterments of mass consumption, the American people abandon their nuclear saber-rattling for a more innocuous war-games fantasy.

More concretely, official America rose to the challenge of resting mighty power on the bases of consumer democracy by developing a number of strategies, none altogether new with respect to the past, but all far better coordinated. The most fundamental move was to contrast the consumer freedoms and affluence of the Atlantic Community with the closed economies and low standards of living of collectivist societies. Fusing the right to a higher standard of living with the two other fundamental values of the anticommunist crusade, democracy and freedom, propaganda declared that the Soviet Union was the archenemy not only because it was totalitarian and anticapitalist, but also because the lack of consumer choice was the purest evidence of the absence of freedom. If there was no consumer choice, there could be no human development, however big the leaps in gross national product.

Even so, the USSR's sheer economic capacity drew begrudging admiration, and American officials closely followed every move the Soviets embarked upon after Stalin's death to compete around the standard of living. One result was totally to reverse the official attitude toward trade fairs, for the planned economy's strong suit was the collective display of its productive might and confidence in the future. Indeed, it so happened that as Leipzig had fallen into the Soviet Zone in the last days of the war, when the Great Fair reopened in May 1946, the first "Freedom Fair" became a showcase of economic planning: first for the rapidly reviving industries of Saxony and Thuringia, then for the output of the Five-Year Plans of the Soviet bloc. Under the management of the German People's Republic, more and more energy went into the Machine Fair, its displays of dynamos, tractors, and hydraulic equipment, dominated by giant statues of Stalin and Mao Tse-tung, greatly eclipsing in size and visibility the venerable Sample Fair with its characteristic displays of porcelain dolls, photographic equipment, office machinery, and fountain pens. Moreover, western European buyers had not lost the habit of going to Saxony for machine goods, as well as for fine finished products—Leica cameras, musical instruments, and toys. At the Fall 1954 fair they mingled with 670,000 visitors.[32] This was a worrisome development. For one thing, the buyers brought back glowing news of the achievements of socialist reconstruction. Worse, the contacts created opportunities for trafficking in Western technological secrets, which was illegal according to National Security Council Order 68 of April 14, 1950, which barred

American allies from trade in strategic materials with Communist-bloc countries.

Political concerns as much as trade interests thus strengthened the Eisenhower administration's determination to build an alternative fair system. In August 1954, with monies drawn from the presidential emergency fund earmarked for cultural programs, it launched "immediate and vigorous action to demonstrate the superiority of the products and cultural values of our system of free enterprise." Drawing on "a national network of volunteers dedicated to the twin principles of decentralization and voluntarism," government departments collaborated with national business associations like the Advertising Council to solicit donations of manpower, equipment, and money. Whereas the Soviet fairs showcased the power of planning, focusing on monster machinery, technological advances, and scientific discoveries as stepping-stones to universal progress, the American fairs showcased the eclectic material democracy of the here and now: at one time or another, the exposition grounds mounted with Buckminster Fuller's geodesic domes and other modernist follies hosted full-replica self-service stores and ranch homes, exhibitions of abstract art, jazz concerts, Cinerama spectacles showing snippets from everyday life, and fashion runways. In 1960, six years into the program, the Commerce Department's recently established Office of International Trade Fairs ran ninety-seven official exhibits in twenty-nine countries, exposing more than 60 million people to the way of life of a nation in which government seemed practically nonexistent and liberty was shown not as some abstract right but as exposure to the concrete freedom of making choices by selecting among a myriad of spectacles and artifacts.[33]

The U.S. government also took in hand the elaboration of statistics to demonstrate the superiority of the American Standard of Living. Responding to "insistent public demand for comparative wage and price data," the Bureau of Labor Statistics, guided by the economist Irving Kravitz, constructed new indices to calculate the purchasing power of hourly earnings.[34] By cutting through the muddle of estimates about local costs, currency, and wage differentials that had plagued the ILO-Ford Inquiry and caused the breakdown of crossnational comparisons in the 1930s, they facilitated the comparison of standards from country to country. Practically any medium could cite these figures, and any consumer could grasp the sense. When it was learned that, on average, American workers had to labor for 6 minutes to buy a pound of bread, 27 minutes for a dozen eggs, and 32 minutes for a pound of butter, whereas their Soviet counterparts had to work respectively 25, 158, and 542 minutes for the same items, the case for which system was superior seemed open and shut.

In reality these indices suffered from many of the same drawbacks as the Ford-ILO inquiry, insofar as they assumed that the standard of living was based on individual income and the price consumers paid for single items. They indulged the habit of ignoring the contribution to individual welfare of government services (like tax discounts on mortgages) or price supports (such as big highways and cheap fuel). And they made no determination about what goods people really wanted. Nor did they offer any way of measuring the value of goods acquired through informal exchanges or gray markets—which in centrally planned economies went along with the terrain. Nor did they reflect the human and other costs of the high productivity that resulted in higher income, as well as lower prices, but also more intense and longer work time. Though these indices could have been applied to practically any reality, which was their virtue, they were almost invariably used to contrast the hardest to compare, namely market-driven and planned economies with their wholly different systems of pricing and supply. Rarely were the figures used to make historical comparisons, as between the postwar era and prewar times. Nor, more instructively, were they used to compare the ever more prosperous core areas of western Europe and the emerging Third World countries or its own ever more marginal periphery, notably Spain, Portugal, southern Italy, and Greece; nor did they compare the tenor of life in the latter countries with the rising standards in fast-industrializing Poland, Yugoslavia, and Hungary.

As such comparisons became the norm, workers too were solicited to voice their opinions about relative standards of living. And as this happened, they too learned to explain their opinions on material grounds rather than according to ideological beliefs. So in 1955, when 1,000-plus French workers were asked to rank countries according to where they thought workers lived the best, the majority ranked their homeland France the highest, the United States second, and neighboring Italy last. They were completely split about the Soviet Union, with a quarter marking it the best place and a slightly larger group the worst. Left-wing union members were similarly split. Half thought that American workers lived best, on the basis of what they heard about American workers' owning cars, televisions, refrigerators, and washing machines, dressing well, and having more amusements and fun. Half said that Soviet workers lived best, on the basis of their belief that Soviet society was more egalitarian and workers were engaged in the pursuit of social justice, labored for the collectivity rather than for the bosses, and got more respect.[35] As polling became more professionalized, questions about best and worst would be reframed as questions about the quality of life as determined by goods and services. It was implicit that the answers should be based on individual satisfactions framed in terms of the choices being offered, and not on collective beliefs about the relative merits of alternative political systems.

Above all, American policy pressed for the areas the U.S. armies had occupied after the war, Japan, but especially Germany, to become showcases of consumer democracy. That was a more problematic strategy with respect to Japan: that everything about living conditions, from the tiny scale of shelter to the semiotics of diet, was so distant from the Western consumer experience made it hard to agree on benchmarks for consumer progress. Anyway, in the larger scheme of geoeconomics, it was more important for Japan to be turned to producing consumer goods than to consuming them.[36] In western Europe, by contrast, the impatience for Europe to lift its standards was great, especially as the argument that low standards of living had caused fascism was adapted to explain the popularity of Communism. Turning Europe into an area of high consumption also made more and more sense from the point of view of rationalizing the division of labor within the Atlantic Alliance. Because of its "inability to resist militarily," western Europe "has to compensate economically." To do this, the region had to keep pace with Soviet rates of growth. Thereby it could "weaken if not destroy the appeal of communism to its workers and intellectuals." In turn, "its rising standard of living would give the lie to communist propaganda about the decadence of the West" and have "a magnetic effect on the satellite peoples."[37] It was an unspoken aim that as European elites accepted this new division of labor, they would surrender the galling snobbery that Europe stood for true culture whereas the United States stood for crass civilization.[38]

For western Europe to become the showcase for consumer democracy three conditions had to be fulfilled. The first was that it renounce irrevocably the region's mercantilist traditions, opening up its markets. This was indeed occurring under American pressure and with the core western European states' own steps toward establishing the Common Market beginning in the early 1950s. The second condition was for the imperial powers—France, Great Britain, Belgium, Holland, and Portugal—to distance themselves from, if not renounce, their colonies. This meant renouncing the special economic ties that were under pressure anyway in the face of anticolonial movements and changing terms of trade that favored the United States. It also meant renouncing a major pillar of the old regime of consumption, namely the colonial way of life, which had justified to colonialists the rightness of their civilizing mission, differentiated the peoples of each empire from one another, and reinforced their ties to the hierarchies of distinction of the metropolis. Tying their standards to American society, some western Europeans expressed regret at the distance that this would create with respect to their former colonies. The leaders of the nonaligned world, meeting in Bandung, Indonesia, in April 1955, recognized as much. As a "Third World" in the making, they took stock both of their outcast status under the old bourgeois regime of consumption and of the unattainable heights of the new American standards, seeking in Soviet-type strategies of collective provisioning some new alternative. Thereby western European states were more firmly joined to the White Atlantic, and more inclined to the appropriate vocation of a second-order power, namely to guarantee the material improvement of their own citizens. Henceforth competition among them was no longer measured in terms of the power of arms, size of colonial territories, or wealth of empire, but within the framework of comparative data on gross national product, inflation rates, index figures for expenditure on health and leisure, and diffusion curves for indoor plumbing, automobiles, washing machines, and television sets.

On the other hand, Europeans too had widely come around to accepting that Europe's perennial state of war in the twentieth century had been the major obstacle to raising living standards, hence that enduring peace alone could guarantee that prosperity would persist, and even grow. This turnabout in thinking made the possibility of armed conflict between superpowers on European soil, with the threat of nuclear annihilation, all the more terrifying. Consequently, America's western allies had little trouble finding majorities convinced that economic security could not be achieved without military security, and that this could best be achieved under the American nuclear umbrella. This was all the more true as it became evident that such a commitment not only did not interfere with, but in fact greatly enhanced, the share of the national product available for consumer goods and services.

Without the "birth of the mass market," however, these conditions would have been harder, if not impossible, to secure. This auspicious event took place in 1953, as Howard Whidden, foreign editor of *Business*

Week, expertly wrote, when "a sudden spurt in personal consumption" made it appear that "the long-neglected consumer will play an increasingly important role in the European economy." Sharply rising demand had the effect of reorienting the distribution system to the "one-class market" that had enabled American manufacturers to commit to mass-production systems in the early twentieth century. By so doing, it broke the monopoly of "manufacturers who in their domestic sales were too exclusively concerned with service to a limited, almost custom-tailored, high quality market." By the end of the decade, Whidden predicted, "an American style consumer market will be quite fully developed in Britain and some other continental countries, while in the rest of Western Europe it will be well on the way."[39] This optimism was borne out as early as 1954, when the recession that hit the United States with the end of the Korean War left the European economies pretty much unscathed.

This "one-class market," which many had yearned for but nobody expected to appear so suddenly, came from four sources. The first was fuller employment. The second was an upward nudge in real wages for workers, which resulted from higher output. The third was the decline of income differentials between the wealthiest and the lower income groups as a result of war losses, inflation, and the introduction of income taxes. The fourth was the rise in social benefits associated with welfare statism, including rent control, housing subsidies, pensions, and family allowances. Government programs imparted a sense of security as well as giving heft to purchasing power for household goods when wages were still very low. By setting priorities with an eye to the succession of developments in American society, government also fostered a sense of the sets of goods people could expect to obtain in the near future.

The one factor missing from this account was war, namely the Korean War, which unlike the two earlier global wars fought in the twentieth century was blessedly distant from European territory. Lasting from June 1950 to July 1953, the conflict had many of the same profitable effects for European manufacturers and consumers that European wars had had for the Americans earlier in the century. The demand for armaments exceeded the capacity of the main belligerent, the United States, and the urgency of satisfying this need, as well as the demands for consumer goods in countries not engaged on the war fronts, generated higher employment. In turn, higher employment generated greater purchasing power. Meanwhile, in the belief that Korea was a diversion and that the main attack from the USSR would still come from the east, the United States poured millions of dollars more into Europe, mainly in the form of army procurement. As the number of well-cared-for U.S. divisions deployed by NATO rose from one to six, and the troop levels from 81,000 to 260,800, compared with the 238,600 Americans stationed in Korea, their host regions boomed.[40]

Moreover, by pressing its European allies to contribute materiel to the war effort, the United States gave a nice stimulus to the European economy. The Allies' old enemy, Germany, was the biggest beneficiary. Whereas other western European states threw resources into military production at the expense of the civilian sector, the German Federal Republic had been banned from producing for military purposes. Consequently, West German enterprises were left to concentrate on capital and consumer goods. Initially these goods were destined for export. But as business picked up and employment and wages rose, leftover capacity began to be used to manufacture for home consumption as well. For the first time, not just the trade unions but also government and business conceived of the nation as having markets that were deep at home as well as expansive abroad. With full employment and rising wages, West German industrial workers began to be treated as full-fledged consumers.

During the Korean War, West Germany was more firmly drawn into the western European trading area, bringing the region one step closer to having the breadth of market indispensable to the economies of scale and scope of American-style mass production. If left to their own devices, German enterprises would have sought this breadth of market outside its borders to the east, as it had in the past, returning to its old markets in central Europe. But American strategic interests barred this tendency. Forced by Cold War politics into the more competitive environment of Atlantic Europe, West German enterprises came under more and more pressure to curb their cartels, introduce American techniques of mass production, and be more receptive to the mass-marketing methods indispensable to establishing themselves in new sales territories.[41]

Thus the rump state of the great German Empire, the sole power that in the first decades of the century had been capable of anchoring a European-based, continentwide market at the same time as generating a notion of market culture that presented itself as an alternative to the American, was integrated into the western area, to become the powerhouse of the crossnational export trade indispensable to the development of a regional mass market. Its cultural pretensions reduced, the chastened western area of the German nation embraced the basics of consumer well-being with remarkable equanimity. Ludwig Erhard, economics minister under Konrad Adenauer from 1949 to 1963 and chancellor in his own right for the three years following, was especially eloquent in endorsing the "basic democratic right of consumer freedom," which he defined as "first and foremost the freedom of all citizens to shape their lives in a form adequate to the personal wishes and conceptions of the individual, within the framework of the financial means at their disposal." However, for Erhard—as a Catholic, a onetime member of the circle around Wilhelm Vershofen's Society for Consumer Research at Nuremberg, and a firm, if subdued, critic of the Nazi command economy before the Anglo-American forces appointed him economic adviser for their occupation zone—consumer well-being was never an absolute good, as current American ideology held. Consumers acted in their own and society's best interest when they were properly guided by carefully negotiated national labor contracts, a tight money supply, and conservative good taste.[42]

Practically speaking, by the turn of the 1960s West Germans were no longer either heroes or hagglers; they were becoming known as affluent Europeans with high rates of expenditure on kitchens, automobiles, and holidays. So the west of the nation, once the least hospitable to the idea of consumer sovereignty, had now became the most open, albeit within the constraints of stolid middle-class virtue and the protections advised by the social market economy. It was in 1959 that for the first time a German spoke of "our consumer society."[43] The proclamation wasn't without ambiguity. It expressed the immense self-satisfaction at the progress made since 1945, when Germans were scrounging cigarette butts from American GIs, as well as pride at being the showcase of the Western way of life against the collectivist vision being showcased on the other side of the Brandenburg Gate. But this new self-definition was also mixed with the anxiety to assert that "our consumer society" was not exactly identical with the American version, castigated for its excess of materialism and degenerate youth culture, and to paper over a well-known secret, that many older people remembered the last good times as the peaceful late 1930s before Germany had been led into war.

Breaking through Barriers, Leveling Differences

What did the advance of the mass consumer society mean in view of European society's history of contentious politics? Had affluence begun to make the publics of Germany, France, or Italy into a "people of plenty,"

as David Potter characterized contemporary Americans?[44] In the early
1960s the French sociologist Pierre Bourdieu was among the first to pose
the question: What impact did consumption have on class? And in the
next decade his main research would be dedicated to mapping the new
social "distinctions" generated by the redistribution of "cultural capital"
as consumers made choices among an ever more abundant and disparate
array of goods and services.[45] Clearly, there were no easy answers. A
quarter of a century later, a Bourdieu protégé dedicated to answering the
same query would respond: "the figure of the consumer has to be conceived in relation to an ensemble of changes that are not purely of an economic order, even if, indisputably, its development is coterminous with
the growth in quantity and diversity of consumer goods as well as access
by new social groups to goods and services hitherto reserved to a nar-
rower section of the public."[46]

By the mid-1960s western Europe's occupational profile was acquiring
some traits common to the United States as, everywhere if very unevenly,
peasants became scarcer, the number of capitalists and independent professionals declined, and the proportion of salaried executives, white-collar employees, and factory workers rose. Still, to speak of the growth of
"middle classes," as if to imply that social inequality had declined or political power was effectively democratized, was open to challenge by any
number of studies that showed the persistence of "inequality of access to
nearly all of the rewards of the socio-economic system."[47] For good reason, most Europeans continued to emphasize the glass half empty, rather
than the glass half full.

Nonetheless, western Europe had begun to move away from the castelike hierarchies of the pre–World War II era as the sheer increase in the
proportion of salaried people in the total population made it possible for
more and more of them to make new choices about using their income.

The choices becoming available to people from increased income as
early as the first half of the 1950s were the focus of the first consumer
survey ever in France, and the first to be undertaken by any government
in Europe. This was conducted in 1954 under the auspices of the General
Commissariat of Planning as the government prepared to launch France's
second Four-Year Plan. Shifting investment priorities from capital goods
to consumer equipment, the plan calculated that family income would increase at an annual average of 4–5 percent. This was a spectacular sum
compared with the 3 percent increase for the entire period 1938–1950,
not to mention the paltry 5.5 percent overall gain by western Europeans
for the period 1913–1929.

"You earn 20 percent more; what are you going to do with it?" That was the shockingly direct question that the commissariat hired the Institut Français d'Opinion Publique, or IFOP, to ask. It was the first time that French citizens—or any European people—were asked what they would do if they had more income. Moreover, the pollster, Jean Stoetzel, a longtime collaborator of George Gallup, built his sample of "urban salaried people" to include not only skilled wage earners, unskilled laborers, and pensioners, but also managers. In the past they would have been regarded as too diverse in their "aspirations and desires" to be comparable. Now, however, the supposition was that there was no intrinsic difference. To account for differences in their wants, the statisticians studied variables such as family size, place of residence, and disposable income instead of assuming different needs for different classes.[48]

A preliminary look at the responses shows how remarkably inegalitarian and uncomfortable a place urban France still was in terms of basic necessities: 76 percent of all households had no running hot water, 90 percent no washing machine, and 91 percent no refrigerator. Only 5 percent of the men who worked went by automobile, compared with the 85 percent who used public transportation, rode bicycles, or went on foot. French salaried people, no matter how large their income, were still parsimonious: 57 percent had never used credit. Most were familiar with the new commodities they could purchase with more income and looked forward to the time they might take a vacation, buy kitchen appliances, or purchase an automobile. But large numbers of manual workers and pensioners intended to spend any additional income on food, especially meat and vegetables. And when managers and office heads spoke of making "important purchases," they were referring to what we would regard as basics, such as clothing, home improvements, and household equipment. If mass-consumption society was being "born," it was an excruciating slow labor: two-thirds of the cadres said their standard of living had improved since 1950, but only one-third of the office employees and skilled workers, and less than a sixth of the unskilled. That the old regime of consumption still cast a long shadow over social relations is underscored by the quaint class stereotypes that the IFOP's bright young statisticians used to illustrate their findings. Social standing may have begun to be regarded as mattering less when it came to spending income. Nonetheless the little diagrams still emphasized social distinctions based on education, dress, work tools, and body language: the office manager was shown suited seated at his desk, the supervisor flourishing his telephone to bark out commands, the clerk clutching his dossier of papers, the

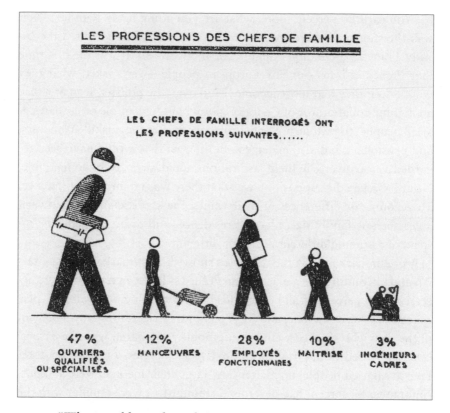

LES PROFESSIONS DES CHEFS DE FAMILLE

LES CHEFS DE FAMILLE INTERROGÉS ONT
LES PROFESSIONS SUIVANTES......

47%
OUVRIERS
QUALIFIÉS
OU SPÉCIALISÉS

12%
MANŒUVRES

28%
EMPLOYÉS
FONCTIONNAIRES

10%
MAITRISE

3%
INGÉNIEURS
CADRES

"What would you do with 20% more income?" Occupational
stereotypes are still being used to characterize consumer wants,
1955. Courtesy of the Bibliothèque de Sciences Po.

skilled worker brandishing his toolbox, and the unskilled laborer bent
over his wheelbarrow.

At least another decade passed before these differences were eclipsed
by a new world of reference outside the traditional status hierarchies of
class, work, and education. As nonworking time increased, income rose,
and exposure to the mass media became more and more intense, especially as a result of the jump in television ownership, the commercial-
cultural sphere that we saw pressing into the political sphere even under
authoritarian regimes established itself as an unrelenting font of new cultural models for millions of urbanized peasants, emigrant laborers, and
women entering the labor force, not to mention the young. It was a signally important font for new elites of managers and executives, who, in
the values of efficiency, relaxation, and democratic manners or the habit

of the "week-end," the "barbecue," or Saturday supermarket shopping, established their social visibility and legitimacy with respect to traditional bourgeois conventions of distinction. It was no less important for young people who, in their quest to establish their identity as a "generation," drew on the music, dress, and other paraphernalia of cross-Atlantic youth culture. Now fully transatlantic in scope, the commercial-cultural sphere offered an endlessly rich repertoire of commodities and customs, from rock and roll and blue jeans to dating and the pill; it made for the biggest break between one age cohort and another experienced in the twentieth or any other century.[49]

Unlike the traditional political-economic or cultural leadership, the new elite of celebrity fashioned by mass consumption and spectatorship lacked decisionmaking power, yet were "objects of discussion, interest, admiration, imitation, and collective affection." As "celebrities," Franco Alberoni, the Italian sociologist, presciently observed in the early 1960s, they did not stand at the apex of society in any conventional sense. Thus they could engage attention without provoking the class envy, resentment, or hierarchical patterns of emulation typically stimulated by the old elites. In sum, they were a resource like other commodities, offering new models of social belonging.[50] What is more, their origin could be just as easily international as national. The celebrity could be European—the Italian pop singer Mina, the French crooners Jonny Halliday and Sylvie Vartain, or the Beatles—or from the United States like Bill Haley, Elvis Presley, James Dean, Natalie Wood, or any number of other Hollywood stars. By the 1950s the distinction between the autochthonous and the alien was becoming ever harder to draw; the commercial-cultural sphere already existed wide and deep in the United States, and for decades it had been intermixing with that which existed in European societies. Only now the connections were more intense and politicized, and the points of contact between the two sides of the Atlantic more numerous, clearly drawn, and pervasive.

As had occurred in the United States far earlier, the consumer market began to yield a brand-new social scientific visualization of consumers, assisted by American marketing and polling agencies, with George Gallup and the Nielsen Company in the lead.[51] The images it produced in turn blurred, then eventually obliterated the figures that were emblematic of the old categories of social stratification—the parsimonious worker, the self-sacrificing housewife, the disoriented, fascist-leaning salaried man, the conservative *bürgerlich* man of culture—to make way

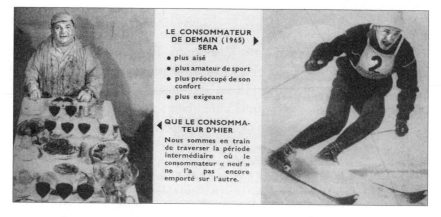

LE CONSOMMATEUR
DE DEMAIN (1965) ▶
SERA

● plus aisé
● plus amateur de sport
● plus préoccupé de son
  confort

● plus exigeant

◀ QUE LE CONSOMMA-
  TEUR D'HIER
Nous sommes en train
de traverser la période
intermédiaire où le
consommateur « neuf »
ne l'a pas encore
emporté sur l'autre.

Changing stereotypes, 1961: yesterday's gluttonous, sedentary
worker becomes tomorrow's sleek, comfort-minded consumer.
Entreprise, *February 1961.* Courtesy of the Thomas J. Watson Business
and Economics Library, Columbia University.

for new figures—the middle-of-the-road managerial cadre, the discern-
ing Mrs. Consumer, the blue-jeaned, "ye-ye" teenager, the "affluent
worker"—followed, in the 1970s and 1980s, by the proliferation of so-
called lifestyle identities like the Huppé, the French equivalent of the
Yuppie, the working wife, the Gay, or the *paninaro* who hung out in the
fast-food shops of Rome and Milan.

As in the United States earlier in the century, marketing spoke as if the
mass market existed. True, the structure of demand was changing. Beginning in the 1960s, statistics picked up on a phenomenon that American
consumer markets had experienced as early as the 1920s. People with
higher incomes were the first to purchase new goods like automobiles or
refrigerators when they came on the market. But those with lower incomes caught up on novelties more and more quickly. In 1954, when
color television came on the market in France, 5,000 units were sold; in
1965, 4.2 million. The well-off bourgeois family may have been the first
to experiment with new goods around 1960, but around 1970 it was the
middle-level manager's household or even the decently paid young working-class family tuned into advertising and willing to buy on credit.[52]
Class distinctions were known to be sturdy, and real social power remained vested in old elites. Even so, business found that for purposes of
marketing, it worked to divide all of western European society into four
categories of revenue from A to D, and to plot marketing strategies accordingly. It was especially exciting for them to observe the emergence of

a new mass-middle, in the big movement of lowest-level D earners to the striving middling C.[53]

For mass consumption to become the material basis of a "new civilization," to recall Simon Patten's phrase, people of different backgrounds had to recognize each other with respect to shared norms of living, even if they accepted that not all citizens, sometimes even hardly any of them, could attain the most prestigious items. With remarkable rapidity as western Europe passed from an "era of scarcity" to an "era of abundance," ideologues of European consumer society began to speak of the new "civilization" of consumption without the dread of out-of-control desires that the prospect of mass consumption had sparked among the bourgeoisie in the first half of the century. The French sociologist Jean Fourastié, the Candide of the *trente glorieuses*, or the Thirty Glory Years, 1945 to 1975, was particularly eloquent on the subject. Like Patten, he envisaged consumption as having civilizing effects: "a new genre of life should normally create a new civilization," he hazarded as early as 1947.[54] When Fourastié returned to the subject of the "civilization of consumers" two decades later, far from fearing that modern consumption standards would destroy the old way of life, he welcomed that spending less on food and drink and more on leisure, health, and education would prolong as well as improve life—for everybody.[55] Accordingly, primitive consumption would give way to civilizing consumption. Henceforth the physically unhealthy and socially immobile proletariat that conservatives often reproved for spending wage increases on food was treated as capable of becoming upwardly mobile. So the obtuse, obese worker fixed to the table, gobbling down platefuls of food would be transmogrified into a sleek, quick-witted sportsman slaloming down the ski slopes. Even so, the image that was given to illustrate this radical change in the 1961 issue of *Entreprise*, the bimonthly of French managerial elites, is so ambiguous that it is hard to tell whether it was intended as parody about personal self-transformation, a prescription for upward mobility, or an ugly stereotyping of the worker, a still physically repugnant social antagonist.

Building a European Community around Consumption

The figure of the consumer-citizen took a further step away from the past with the establishment of the Common Market in 1957. Article 2 of the Treaty of Rome affirmed that the European Economic Community's main social objective was "to promote to the highest degree the satisfaction of needs of the Europeans." In reality, only one article, number 39, actually used the term "consumer," in referring to agricultural policy as a means to "secure reasonable prices for delivery to consumers." Nevertheless, the whole framework was inspired by the neoliberal faith that the enlarged market area would improve the international division of labor, relieve the obstructions to the passage of goods, and lend itself to economies of scale and scope, such that consumers would benefit from increased productivity, higher incomes, new variety, and lower prices. In the euphoria that accompanied the first steps to implement the treaty, Jean Monnet predicted flatly that Europeans would achieve "the standard of American living within fifteen years."[56]

Europe's "founding father" wasn't so far off the mark if we consider the advances made down to 1973–74. Each year the gross national product of France, Germany, Italy, and the Benelux countries grew on average 3.5 percent a year compared with 2.1 percent in the United States, and per capita consumption grew 4.6 percent, compared with the latter's 2.9 percent. More important, disposable income practically doubled for wage and salary earners, and the volume of trade within the area tripled, quadrupling for automobiles, with visible results on purchasing habits.[57] As tariffs dropped, the Dutch, inhabitants of a pancake-flat country with no significant auto manufacture, discarded their bicycles to move around by car. Belgian families, who had been cut off from household amenities by high tariffs and inefficient distribution, were suddenly exposed to Italian refrigerators, German washing machines, and German, Dutch, and Japanese radios. Even West Germany, though the largest exporter of household appliances, was also an importer of lower-range refrigerators, washing machines, and radios, as well as the shoes, underwear, and food products that we would expect from sharing markets with its partners, France and Italy.[58]

The excited perception that European markets were becoming homogenized to the benefit of the consumer contained a large measure of wishful thinking, which was greatly reinforced by the first marketing surveys. The very first was conducted in 1963 under the auspices of the *Reader's Digest*, the United States' premier advertising medium, which, after installing its headquarters at Paris in 1945, had immediately become a European fixture, translating its pablum, liberally interspersed with advertisements, in all of Europe's leading language areas. Interpreting the gloriously illustrated graphs and charts, which were based on interviews

conducted by six independent consumer research companies of a sample
of 12,500 people, the economist U. W. Kitzinger concluded: "the countries of Western Europe, Britain and the Six (if we except Central and
South Italy) now really look substantially alike. The homes of the Dutch
have much of the same durable goods as the homes of the North West
Italians, the homes of the Germans have much the same amenities as
those of the Dutch."[59] This finding did not preclude myriad tiny differences, especially in eating habits, that plugs and outlets were rarely compatible from country to country, that pharmaceuticals like birth control
pills that were licensed in one place were banned in another. Nor did it
preclude huge price differentials for the same or similar goods, which
common value-added taxes sought to diminish starting in the early
1970s, only to be thwarted by leaps and dives in currency rates from one
country to another. But then the notion of a European consumer, like the
American consumer or, for that matter, the French, German, or Italian
one, was in large measure a marketers' fiction in the face of the cleavages
of class, locality, and ethnic background internal to every nation, as well
as leaving out half of Europe. It was a convenient fiction, nonetheless, for
investors, marketers, and public officials. The discovery of common consumer habits—which consumers themselves would still have been hard
pressed to recognize—redounded politically to the success of the emerging European Community, taking into account that its first aim was to
motivate investment and thereby secure greater economic integration.

Official Europe had envisaged that the Common Market would reinforce ties with the United States, just as official America envisaged that it
would reinforce U.S. ties to Europe.[60] But nobody anticipated the degree
to which fast-footed American corporations moved in, or the degree to
which they were capable, far more than before the war, of leaving their
mark on entire sectors of economic activity, including those that had once
seemed especially resistant to American corporate inroads, like food and
retailing. Down until 1958–59, unless they already had substantial experience in the region, like Kodak, Coca-Cola, or the big automakers, most
companies stayed clear of continental Europe, scared off by the regulations, fearful of labor unrest, and dismayed by anti-American animosity.
For high returns from direct investment abroad, they preferred Latin
America or their special favorite, Anglophone Canada, where by 1960
U.S. companies owned 43 percent of the capital invested in manufacturing.[61] However, as regulations began to be lifted, and as profits on standardized goods sagged in the United States, while consumer spending in

Europe promised to continue to rise, U.S. enterprises became excitedly bullish about investing in the Common Market, especially since they were advantaged by the overvalued dollar. Accordingly the old firms redoubled their efforts, and new companies rushed in. Whereas American capital contributed perhaps 2 percent to fixed capital formation in 1950, it amounted to 5.2 percent in 1965.[62] Moreover, the effects far exceeded the overall volume of investment, for it was directed toward highly visible industries, notably food, cosmetics, and household appliances, all of which were characterized by rapid growth, high profits, and heavy marketing. Capitalizing on a scale of operations that was used to continent-size markets, European-wide distribution networks, and well-oiled marketing departments, American companies were well positioned to be the first to offer novelties or low-cost models. Such was well known to be the case of the Ford Taunus, which, as it set about "its conquest of Europe," forced European car manufacturers, the French in particular, to bring down the price of their low-cylinder models. In view of the aim of the Common Market to offer consumers more choices and lower prices, American corporations proved "more European than the Europeans."[63]

It was practically impossible to escape the new logic of competition established by American multinational capitalism. Charles de Gaulle, the austere president of the Fifth Republic, regarded U.S. multinationals as the long arm of American imperialism, and like the millions of other readers of Jean-Jacques Servan-Schreiber's celebrated book *The American Challenge* (1967), he was scandalized to discover that the biggest single economy in the new Europe was not any European nation, but the total output of American corporations operating within the Common Market. It was Servan-Schreiber's prescient recommendation that European companies organize across national lines in the image of their U.S. counterparts. Their capacity to mobilize capital and knowledge was especially important in the arena of telecommunications and information, to compete with American firms in the onrushing next phase of investment and innovation.[64]

Not being able to eliminate U.S. manufacturing, de Gaulle's government tried to bend it to the advantage of the French economy. This was the thinking behind the Gaullist revolution in the perfume industry. As standards of hygiene changed and income rose, a huge export market was opening up for the scents created by the centuries-old industry centered at Grasse, a lovely medieval hilltop town of Provence surrounded by fields of tuberose, lavender, roses, and jasmine. However, like many other craft-based consumer industries, it was not inclined to budge from old routines: perfume oil was obtained by enfleurage, which involved collecting and steaming blossoms and roots in huge copper vats with chemical solvents, then tamping their extracts with tallow. Slow and costly, the process was also limited by shortages of raw materials. And it produced an unstable product with an unpredictable shelf life, which put a crimp on adopting novel marketing strategies. In the 1950s, though Grasse's perfume industry still controlled 95 percent of the West's trade in natural raw aromatic materials, it had little chance to compete abroad, much less to satisfy growing demand on home markets. Increasingly, it had to face the challenge of expensively marketed American synthetic scents imported by Estée Lauder, Revlon, Elizabeth Arden, and Harriet Hubbard Ayer, which in turn had built not just on marketing skills but on the fact that the United States had come out of the war with a cutting-edge chemical industry, thanks in part to the presence of foreign chemists, notably Germans and Jews. Consequently, when the U.S. firm Universal Oil Products, which had developed synthetic scents by tapping into the concentrated know-how generated around the petro-chemical works of northern New Jersey's marshlands, presented itself on the scene, the French state welcomed it. In 1966 it licensed the company to purchase a majority share in Chiris, the biggest French producer. In return the French industry obtained access to U.S. patents and international markets—including the largest and hardest to enter, the American. By 1970 American firms had taken over eleven of France's fifteen leading perfume companies, and the whole sector had been revamped. Parisian connoisseurs may have noted the difference, but not perhaps wealthy Park Avenue matrons, much less new masses of fragrantly scented consumers. In the next years, Grasse would diversify, becoming as well known for its production of food-flavoring additives and other synthetic odors as for its perfume fragrances.[65]

As the Common Market transformed local, delimited, and familiar groups of clients into transnational, unlimited, and unknown masses of consumers, the moment was ripe for American marketing to reappear on the scene.[66] Like U.S. corporations generally, advertising agencies had reduced their European investments to a trickle after the war in anticipation of more secure times. J. Walter Thompson was typical in this respect, cautiously reopening its Paris office at the turn of the 1950s and setting up a one-room, two-man office in Frankfurt in 1952. As the Treaty of Rome was concluded, the New York office put its European agents on notice to "keep ahead of developments in the Common Market and be flexible enough to take advantage of every opportunity."[67] So they would.

The completely rebuilt sky-scrapered city of Frankfurt, not London or Paris, was the center of JWT's new continental realm. Under the direction of the Silesian-born Peter Gilgow, who, in the void left by the war and the Allied occupation, was largely American trained, the company flourished. By 1964 JWT's staff of 470 filled a five-story mansion alongside the consular buildings on Bockenheimer Landstrasse and was handling accounts for 117 products and services, including the German-made Ford Taunus, Kraft, Pepsi-Cola, Triumph women's undergarments, Unilever soaps and detergents, Maggi bouillon cubes, Findus frozen foods, De Beers diamonds, Jacobs (Germany's largest coffee manufacturer), and the Deutsche Bank. As in the 1920s, its equipment set the new standard for full-service agencies. In addition to having its own photographic film editing with Moviola, sound-recording studios, a projection theater with closed-circuit television, and a research library with current magazines and newspapers from all over the world, it installed its own gleaming industrial kitchen to test products and packaging.[68]

As earlier, JWT thrived on the extracurricular interests that it regarded as indispensable to marketing in a service-oriented society. Cross-European markets were indeed more homogeneous. But as the U.S. experience taught that large-scale marketing campaigns called for "a high degree of flexibility based on local knowledge," JWT backed the foundation of ESOMAR, the European Society for Marketing and Opinion Research.[69] The company also played a central role in establishing the new German Association of Full-Service Advertising Agencies (Gesellschaft Werbeagenturen, or GW), which, like the "Four A's," or American Association of Advertising Agencies, was to improve and promote the profession. One of its first initiatives was to lobby to roll back the competition-inhibiting legislation that the Nazis had passed to moralize the advertising industry. JWT was also the foremost local advocate of the "social advertising" advocated at home by the Advertising Council to deflect the public criticism of the industry incited by the crusading writing of Vance Packard and Ralph Nader. Working under the auspices of the GW, it campaigned for Community Spirit in Action (Aktion Gemeinsinn), a volunteer corps whose honorary president was Wilhelmine Lübke, the wife of the Federal Republic's president. Its four-year goal was "to educate the West German to a democratic way of life by influencing him to become active in public affairs." JWT was responsible for the slo-

gan "The government cannot do everything, it should not do everything—the citizen must play his part in public affairs," as well as for its
bugaboo: Herr Öhnemichel (Mr. Indifference).[70]

By joining American sociability with European social solidarity in the
name of an emerging service-oriented society free from state interference,
JWT was on the same wavelength as West Germany's renascent Rotary
clubs. By the end of the 1960s the Federal Republic of Germany offered
the ideal economic, political, and cultural humus for a fresh bloom of
clubs. A quiet few recalled the clubs' tormented effort to conform to the
Nazi regime. But the prevalent belief was that the prewar circles were
cradles of liberalism, which, after they were forced to dissolve by the dictatorship, hung on as "Clubs of Friends" harassed by the Gestapo. That
they survived was the result of bonds of friendship and heroic acts of sub-
terfuge by means of which they preserved the club regalia in the face of
Nazi terror. As the American forces occupied Germany, the surviving circles sought to regroup. When twenty-seven-year-old Captain Don Sheldon, a Rotarian from Prescott, Arizona, occupied Munich in the name of
the Fifth Army on April 30, 1945, he developed an immediate affinity
with Karl Scharnagl, a bread manufacturer, former mayor, and onetime
dining companion of Thomas Mann at the Monday Rotary gatherings.
Right after the troops' arrival, old Scharnagl had gone around to city hall
to introduce himself as a Rotarian—the proof his blue-gold enamel lapel
pin nestled in its little box, which he had kept hidden away in his vest
pocket all the time he was imprisoned at Dachau. (An unlikely story,
sniffed Rotary International's Swiss liaison, when he heard it. If he had
really had it with him and he really had been at Dachau he would have
been dead. But that was easy enough to say for somebody who had sat
tight as a tick in Zurich throughout the war.) Anyway Preston treated
the pin as Rotarians intended: as a badge of rectitude and mutual recognition. AMGOT, the American occupation forces, needed a new lord
mayor for Munich, and although the officer in command of reeduca-
tion programs (a Rotarian from Tuscaloosa, Alabama) would later judge
Scharnagl "not so hot as an Oberbürgermeister in this day and age," he
was duly sworn in, his enamel Rotary lapel pin the only decoration
adorning his lank, threadbare dress suit. The times, if not a new spirit of
service, had him out with the people in the next terrible months, a gaunt-
cheeked, snaggle-toothed old gentleman, taking his turn at the shovel to
dig out the rubble left by seventy Allied bombing runs.[71]

Rotary International had wanted to hold off reorganizing the German

clubs for at least five years—until Germany had its own government, local applicants, like everybody else, could pass through denazification
procedures, and the Belgians, and other peoples who had suffered under
the Nazi occupation, were pacified. However, the Americans saw the
clubs as contributing to defending the West against Soviet aggression. So
Rotary was back in Germany by 1949, earlier than anybody expected,
except onetime German Rotarians. With the aristocratic members fled or
dead, the Jewish bourgeoisie extinguished, and the professionals and
business elites scrabbling to deal with the material cares of everyday life
having little time for cultural self-contemplation, the German club members promised to be model international citizens. Assiduous about measuring itself against international norms—for strict attendance, recruiting
younger members, increasing contacts with foreigners, and sponsoring
community service programs—the movement spread rapidly during the
1960s, especially in the prospering industrial and commercial centers of
the Rhine and Ruhr. In Cologne, where Max Adenauer, the founding father and Konrad's son, was the president in 1969–70, fully three Rotary
clubs had been established to meet the needs of the growing middle
classes of the sprawling city; that year 320 were active in the German
Federal Republic, organized in seven districts with 11,500 members. Service, translated simply as *Dienst* or *Dienstleistung,* had become a familiar
concept, and the club was regarded as a model of both social and international service. Adenauer was reportedly very busy as town supervisor, yet
he personally oversaw the club activities. Over the previous two years he
had spearheaded the efforts to commemorate the fortieth anniversary of
the club's foundation by raising monies to purchase a Volkswagen van
for a school for mentally and physically handicapped students. In addition to funding fellowships for university students and sending emergency relief abroad in cases of natural disasters, Cologne's Rotary clubs
often joined forces with the Lions Club and other volunteer associations.
In Frankfurt Peter Gilow, head of JWT, though not a member himself,
frequently attended the weekly Rotary luncheons.[72]

What did this changed sensibility toward serving citizens as consumers mean for consumer rights? At the outset, the European Community
lacked any concept of the representation of consumers. Article 193 of the
1957 Treaty of Rome called for an "Economic and Social Committee,"
one of whose functions was to "represent the different categories of economic and social life," specifically named as "producers, agriculturalists,
distributors, workers, retailers, artisans, the liberal professions, and the
general interest."[73] "Consumers" weren't mentioned. There were high

hopes nonetheless, as a spokeswoman for France's Women's Civic and Social Union recalled: "The European housewife will gain from having the whole of Europe for household furnishings! Television will erase what remains of commercial frontiers." Though consumers did indeed experience greater choice, prices were rarely lower, except in the fiercely competitive automobile and refrigerator markets. What the Women's Union wanted from consumer-citizenship was active representation, that consumers be protagonists rather than passive subjects whose desires were left to the interpretive whims of private enterprise. Many had experienced disorientation, if not damage, from rapidly changing material habits. Marketers had stepped in where public planners feared to tread. "All affirmations to the contrary, the wish seems to be to turn us into the typical consumer of the consumer society, whose model is exactly present-day American society."[74]

"The affluent society banks the fires of indignation," Raymond Aron famously observed in 1957.[75] The governing consensus was that, as in the United States, left "religions" would die off with the consolidation of the consumer society, following to their graves the reactionary Catholic and nationalistic ideologies of the 1930s. It was popular to misquote Werner Sombart to the effect that in America "socialism broke apart on shoals of roast beef and apple." Thereafter European political systems would steer a decidedly centrist course, more and more resembling America's "non-ideological" alternation of political parties. That Americanization would result in the suppression of left-wing politics was a consoling prospect for conservative elites. That European cultural values might suffer, if not be extinguished in the process, understandably caused some anguish. Pierre Massé, the grand old man of French planning, spoke to this predicament just after the French parliament passed the Fourth Plan in February 1962 with practically no debate. He recognized this event as a real turning point, for the goal of planning was no longer measures on behalf of the economic modernization and minimum well-being regarded as indispensable to the salvation of the French nation; it was higher and higher levels of individual consumption pure and simple. Far be it from him to "reproach the consumer" or philosophize about the "fluid frontier between need and desire." Yet "the consumer society" had to take responsibility for "collective goods" against the "perverse effects" of the "cult of growth rates" that resulted in "a less limited idea of mankind." And consumers had the duty to enlighten themselves to their true needs and to exercise their power to curb the excesses perpetrated in their name.[76]

The fact that conservative and center-right political coalitions had been

the main beneficiaries of relative well-being had originally only reinforced the left's view that mass consumption was politically numbing.
However, in recognition that consumer goods were still very unevenly
distributed and that their constituents wanted higher standards of living,
the social democratic and Communist left pressed for higher pay packets,
accepting the tradeoff, namely speedups, physical exhaustion, even the
loss of political voice. To reinforce social solidarity, they also pressed for
more social infrastructure, public transport, and collective programs for
leisure, endeavors that more often than not were frustrated or waylaid.
The first heyday of individualist mass consumption—the 1960s—was
also the high point of modest national and municipal Communist and social Catholic forms of collective social and cultural undertakings—outing
clubs, local governmental vacations for children and pensioners, public
theater, alternative movie circuits, and so on. Wondering about the political effects of these projects, critics within the left asked whether the "collectivization of consumption" was really "synonymous with democratization." The answer, "nothing enables us to say so," garnered a wide
consensus. To increase "the quantity and quality of consumer goods and
services" only yielded the "appearance" of democracy, so long as the "users" possessed significantly different "aptitudes to use them."[77]

These issues came to a head in the vast protest movement of students
and workers in 1968–69, now generally seen as a double movement. One
was identified with young workers especially, expressing outrage at inequality of access to mass consumer society. The other identified with
students expressing outrage at the accumulation of problems that mass-
consumer society not only had not solved, but in effect had exacerbated—the loss of a sense of the authenticity of material life associated
with old kinds of labor, craft, and neighborhoods and the closing off of a
sense of future in the substitution of grand projects of social redemption
by the humdrum of small increments of material change.[78]

One outcome was that official Europe began to recognize the consumer as an organized interest. After rejecting the need for a specific
consumer policy in 1967, in 1975 the European Economic Community
launched its own "consumer protection and information policy."[79] This
recognized five rights: to the protection of health and safety, to the safe-
guarding of economic interests, to redress, to advice and guidance, and to
representation. In May of the next year the EEC carried out its first *Study
of European Consumers: Their Interests, Aspirations and Knowledge of
Consumer Affairs.* This showed that lots of people had indeed come to

identify themselves as consumers, but not first and foremost. Party loyalty still mattered. But many of those interviewed felt that the political parties in general did not concern themselves at all effectively with their problems as consumers.[80] Given that the consumer interest was likely to become increasingly better articulated, this finding did not bode well for the solidity of party allegiances.

The very ambiguity of this metamorphosis spoke to the openness of possibilities, but also to the confusion and conflict of interests competing in the so-called new Europe of the 1960s: a "Europe of 221,750,000 consumers."[81] Whereas "oxcart Europe," to recall François Delaisi's expression, had mostly fallen under the Soviet sphere of influence, "horsepower Europe" was ever more visibly spanned by the long hand of American corporate enterprises and by the neocalvinist ethic of service capitalism of a reborn, rapidly spreading Rotary club movement, the revamping of mass distribution systems, the proliferation of full-service advertising, marketing, and polling agencies, the renewed triumph of Hollywood films, and the circulation of yet more new social inventions—the self-service supermarket, the all-equipped consumer household, and the endlessly proliferating lifestyles shaped by fast-changing consumer industries of the last quarter of the twentieth century.

CHAPTER 8

Supermarketing

How Big-Time Merchandisers Leapfrogged over Local Grocers

A supermarket can outweigh a lot of 'isms.
RICHARD W. BOOGAART,
American capitalist, 1958

*Everywhere that small merchants set up shop, struggling
day in day out, dealing with every sort of difficulty, today a
supermarket maneuvers its way in, knocking out the whole
lot. Progress can't be conceived this way.*
GIULIO MONTELATICI,
Communist city council member,
Florence, 1961

HE WAS TALL AND BROAD, with large hands and feet, and his slow gestures and pleasant face exuded quiet self-confidence. They would have
guessed that he was American even if he hadn't been wearing a cowboy
hat against the raw February drizzle. At the sight of a vacant lot, an
empty garage, or an abandoned moviehouse, he and his friend would lin-
ger, confabulate, take measurements, and jot down notes. Sometimes
the big one simply looked around as if sizing up the people passing on
the street, estimating the height of apartment buildings, or surveying the
comings and goings at the neighborhood food outlets—the butcher, the
fruit and vegetable lady, the bakery, the fish vendor, the dry-goods grocery, the delicatessen, the oil and wine concession, the café, the kiosk selling salt, cigarettes, and matches, the tripe stand, the candy shop, the milk
outlet, the Sicilian with the flowercart, not to mention the score of stalls
on market day overflowing with fresh produce, cheeses, meat, and every

other God's good. Sometimes he would stop passing women to ask directions, and they would gesture carefully to make certain he understood. He seemed to. Then he would lean down and say, "Mille grazie, Signora," his mouth widening in a toothy grin just like the Americans in the movies.

Richard W. Boogaart was the American crisscrossing the back streets of Milan in the late winter of 1957, a Kansas entrepreneur in search of spaces in which to build the city's first supermarkets. At the end of six weeks, after walking throughout the city and circling around it four more times in a Fiat 600 with the guidance of a large street map, he still had not found exactly what he was looking for: a commercial space of roughly 7,000–8,000 square feet, the size of an average American self-service operation. It was not just that the cost of land was prohibitive and zoning laws blocked the commercial use of many of the vacant lots left from wartime bombing, but that most local buildings were constructed of reinforced concrete, and the multiple posts jutting up through the ground floors prevented the installation of wide-aisle stores. In the end, Boogaart had turned up only seven possibilities, five garages and two theaters, though the price being asked for the most desirable of them was preposterous. Still, from all that he saw of the prosperity, industriousness, courtesy, and open-mindedness of the people, his optimistic first impressions were confirmed: this was a city where the food business could profitably operate thirty, even fifty supermarkets.[1]

Boogaart's tour of Milan marked the opening of a capitalist adventure story, so vivid and successful from a first reading of his animated reports to his home office in New York City, the enthusiastic accounts of contemporary press, and the excited behavior of the new stores' patrons that it could have been scripted in Hollywood and filmed against the radiant backdrop of north-central Italy during the turn-of-the-1960s boom. Boogaart would play the lead role. But the story's real star was an enterprise, Supermarkets Italiani Inc., a subsidiary of Nelson A. Rockefeller's International Basic Economy Corporation. A potent and genial expression of postwar America's globalizing corporate entrepreneurship, IBEC had been founded by the Rockefeller brothers in 1948 to export capital, management, and technology. Investing in housing construction, food processing, and distribution, it embodied postwar American capitalism's crusading effort to combine what Nelson Rockefeller called "social objectives and capitalistic incentives" by promising simultaneously "to raise living standards and earn substantial profits."[2] IBEC first forayed into food marketing in Maracaibo in 1949. By the mid-1950s, in addition to its substantial other holdings, the company operated ten supermarkets in Peru, Puerto Rico, and Venezuela.[3]

Going into northern Italy in 1956, IBEC showed American multinational capitalism at its most self-confident. Until then its terrain had been the U.S.-colonized Southern Hemisphere, where the Rockefeller family had amassed huge holdings and where Nelson himself had acquired economic expertise and political clout, first in his capacity as coordinator of inter-American affairs in the State Department, then in 1944 as assistant secretary of state for Latin America to help implement Roosevelt's "Good Neighbor" policy. Having served the Truman administration as chairman of the International Development Advisory Board on aid to underdeveloped countries, and having advised President Eisenhower on foreign affairs after serving as his undersecretary of the Department of Health, Education and Welfare, Rockefeller had the knowledge and connections that prepared him to take risks that few other U.S. business leaders were willing to run. In Europe, in particular, IBEC's Board of Directors was eager to show that "it is hard to be a Communist with a full belly" and that a well-managed supermarket chain could maneuver around the secular encrustation of laws and regulations weighing down European commerce.[4] When Supermarkets Italiani made its debut in Milan in November 1957, it was the only U.S. retailing company in all of Europe to underscore its American credentials, and the first to be a majority stockholder in a European-based commercial undertaking.

Boogaart, the managing director, wore a Stetson, drove a Cadillac, had a wife named named Marg with two blond children in tow, and described himself with self-deprecating candor as a "Kansas hayseed" with his "feet on the ground." The owner of a successful supermarket supply company and a fifteen-store supermarket chain based in Concordia, where he had been introduced to the trade by his grocer father, Boogaart had operated the first supermarket chain in Mexico City from 1946 to 1949 before joining IBEC to revive its flagging Venezuelan operations. It was there that he met Nelson Rockefeller, and it was Rockefeller himself who contacted him in 1956 to ask him to take on the European project. He accepted, "because I am not against money, but more important, I admired Nelson's motives, and the challenge was damned appealing."[5] In Italy he was accompanied by two sidekicks: a boyhood friend, Roland H. Hood, his expediter and construction specialist; and his meat man, Duane B. Horney, formerly manager of the midwestern chain Save-a-Nickel King, whose mission it was to train Italian butchers to standardize cuts. A business visionary who dreamed of putting a mass-produced chicken in every Italian pot and teaching Italians to eat ice cream in winter, Boogaart was also the impeccable bottom line man. Relentless in his command over inventory, he brought in the latest IBM punch-card control systems, and he was endlessly patient at checking the manual calculations made to cut waste, negotiating with suppliers, and setting snares to catch pilferers, the bane of self-service operations everywhere.

In sum, he was a model American capitalist of his times, his commitment to the service ethic infused with the good-natured populism that came from his Cold War convictions that America was right and his experience that championing the customers' interests fruited handsome profits. After three years of daunting bureaucratic trials, tales of devious Communist tricks, and blunt confessions of failure, following several triumphant months in the black in 1960, Boogaart moved on to new challenges in Buenos Aires. He left behind relatively satisfied Italian investors, many thousands of faithful customers, and a chain of supermarkets that would grow to twenty-six by the mid-1960s. By that time IBEC's initial stake of $425,000 had been sold to its Italian partners, and the $2.7 million of profit from the sale was withdrawn from Italy to pay off investments gone bad in the housing market of the Shah's Iran and to underwrite IBEC's new supermarket operations in Argentina. In the next decade Supermarkets Italiani would be renamed Esselunga (the Long S), after the elongated modernist S of Max Huber's elegant logo. Ever since then it has stood out as one of Italy's largest and most innovative grocery chains. Currently it has 110 outlets, and no one recalls its foreign origins.

The story of Supermarkets Italiani sounds straightforward enough. It is the story of a purposeful, consumer-oriented globalizing capitalism. It tells of a forceful entrepreneur working with an expert staff to forge a new social alliance between foreign capitalism and local consumer interests by endorsing a high-volume, low per-unit-cost operation. By skipping over middlemen to pass the savings along to consumers, Supermarkets Italiani cut the cost of living while providing more variety and higher quality. As it adapted and responded to Italian consumers while teaching stubbornly backward-looking local shopkeepers some lessons about modern retailing, it sowed the seeds of modern distribution.

However, revolutions never speak with a single voice, and certainly not revolutions in commerce, which involve the overturning of entrenched interests, carry heavy risks, and provoke tumultuous changes in the steadiest habits of daily life.

To take the measure of Boogaart's ambitions, we should recall that the defeat of the Nazi New Order spelled the eventual doom of practically every system with which it was intimately associated—not least reactionary retailing systems. During the war, traditional distribution systems began to be revamped in the name of rationing and military procurement policies even in Nazi Germany. As the war brought more and more ruin, commerce generally was disrupted by the destruction of cities, transportation systems, and communication lines, the ruin of Jewish merchants, the creep of black markets, and the ruinous impact of out-of-control inflation. Even years after the war, people remembered their dealings with commerce as a time of degradation. Their own pathetic opportunism as consumers was exposed; defeated and hungry, they were reduced to being the grubbing materialists that apologists for the New Order excoriated in the name of a renascent Europe: "all stomach, no spirit." But the shopkeeper was the truly blameworthy figure, epitomizing the cheating, political collaboration, and apathy endemic under the Nazi occupation.

This dreadful complicity is the stuff of Jean Dutourd's cynical novel *Au bonne beurre* (1952), the story of "ten years in the life" of Mme. and M. Poissonard, owners of a small Parisian creamery, whose loyalties shifted at every change in the political wind while they profiteered from ration cards, played favorites among the customers, and adulterated their foodstuffs by watering down the milk, cutting the butter with margarine, and sifting milt into the flour.[6] Against this social dyad—the ill-served, obsequious customer and the tradition-bound, high-handed provisioner—progressive influences were expected to prevail. There could be no return to the *pauperisme* of the prewar period, the Belgian scholar Jacques Dansette concluded as he put the last touch on his meticulous tome, *The Modern Forms of Distribution*. That occurred on August 2, 1944, at Woluwe-St.-Lambert while the Allied armies broke through the German resistance in Normandy to advance toward his homeland. Henceforth, to enhance "purchasing power" to the greatest degree possible, the public authorities would undertake "rational," "massive" efforts to reform the circuits of distribution.[7]

For Europeans, but for Americans too, food provisioning could not but emerge as a central item on the agenda of reconstruction. Food had to be distributed on an emergency basis to famished civilians, and food aid was part and parcel of the Marshall Plan. But over the longer term, something had to be done about the obvious disparity between the productivity of American agriculture and that of continental Europe, for it was at least as wide as the gap between American and European industry and far harder to bridge. The United States presented itself on world markets with awesome farm surpluses; Europe was dependent on imports, its own output stunted by traditional agricultural techniques, antiquated processing methods, the availability of cheap colonial imports, and archaic distribution circuits. If industry was to recover and the economy to turn to the production of consumer goods and services, the cost of food had to be brought down to levels closer to the American. An average European worker's family spent around 50–60 percent of its budget on food. Its American counterpart spent less than half that. In the margin between the two lay the difference between a population that had only enough for the basics and a population that was not only better nourished, but also left with extra income to spend on other items, including new varieties of food. American farmers were eager for European prosperity, as was American agricultural business. During the war the latter had developed a massive capacity to package, can, and export foodstuffs. As military procurement came to a halt, it anxiously sought new outlets abroad.[8]

The Self-Service Revolution

This cluster of concerns focused attention on the self-service supermarket, the most important invention in retailing over the previous two decades. *Supermarket, Spectacular Exponent of Mass Distribution* is the eye-catching title of the 1935 book by the United States' leading expert on the subject, Max Zimmerman, editor and publisher of *Super Market Merchandising* and founder of the Super Market Institute, a trade organization that started in 1937 by recruiting 35 members and by 1950 counted 7,000. A self-avowed admirer of the Schumpeterian entrepreneur, the Massachusetts-born Zimmerman identified himself with "individuals of resourcefulness and pioneering spirit, even if sometimes simple hucksters or grocers or distributors who knew when to step out of the conventional pattern of food retailing to venture into new forms." His European acquaintance would have seen in him some of Filene's abrasively self-promotional zeal and keen sense of mission, if none of his cultural refinement or political vision.[9] Unlike Filene, Zimmerman had no particular familiarity with European conditions. But his multiplying contacts with European entrepreneurs passing through the New York offices of the Super Market Institute convinced the U.S. government to send him on a mission in 1947. The outcome was a handy little booklet called *Surveying Europe's Food Picture*. The six-week trip, which began on November 18, 1949, with Zimmerman and his wife crossing the Atlantic by Stratocruiser, took him around Europe to study the "high spots of self-service activity" and to meet with the chief executives of Emile Bernheim's Priba and Duttweiler's Migros, as well as Tesco, Great Britain's leading chain. His conclusion was that the world was ready for an international network among entrepreneurs in what was newly being called "the food business."[10]

The First International Congress of Food Distribution was the outcome. Inaugurated in Paris on June 20, 1950, it brought 1,000 delegates from twenty-two countries to meetings at the Maison de la Chimie, the very place where fifteen years before Europeans had skeptically listened to Edward Filene's pleas on behalf of the "chain store revolution." Now, however, the response to innovation was excited and quick. Paris's venerable Center for Commercial Studies endorsed the event, and Jacques Lacour-Gayet, the gray eminence of French commerce in his capacity as honorary president of the organizing committee, welcomed innovation as inevitable to bring down the cost of living. The real sponsor was Paridoc, France's leading self-service food chain. Founded in 1930, it had in its president, Henry Toulouse, a fervent exponent of American retailing technologies who had first visited the United States in 1938 to study retail food distribution and returned once more in 1947—when he met Zimmerman—before establishing his own first self-service outlet in Paris in 1948. By the time the convention met, he had pulled together an organization of thirty chain-store groups counting 7,000 local outlets, 70 of which were modern self-service stores managed by Paridoc itself. Toulouse's effort to promote self-service stores had seen a big boost in May after the first French "Distribution Mission," which was backed by Marshall Plan monies, returned from its American tour thunderstruck. As he was inaugurated as the new organization's first president, Toulouse graciously recognized Zimmerman as its "spiritual father."[11]

Toulouse's opening words alerted all who were involved in the food business to "work along with the community of Western nations . . . to resist disintegrating forces." They had a common role and interest, namely to guarantee "the welfare of the people, who know that their security and happiness depends on their liberty and democratic rights." Wanting to find a symbol for their undertaking, Toulouse invoked the Atlantic Alliance only to discard its conventional figures—Truman, Queen Juliana, King George, President Auriol—in favor of a new standard-bearer. This was the consumer. *She,* Toulouse emphasized, was "a young woman . . . of no particular nationality" who, guided by her "strong personality, knows how to pick and choose in view of her family's needs and budget" and possessed "the spirit and soul to dream about the future." "Give us the means to subsist honorably if you want us to think freely," she pleaded.[12] It was at once gallant and progressive to offer self-service to this Marianne of the marketplace, or *libre-service,* as Paridoc's Jacques Pictet smartly translated the term. The new technique of merchandising involved not just individual choice, but *free* choice, as in *liberté, libération.*

Indeed, from Zimmerman's account of the history of supermarket, this latest "revolution in distribution" had a more explicitly democratic impulse than the earlier chain-store movement and none of its fussy scientific pretensions. Single entrepreneurs, often outsiders to retailing, had taken the initiative by starting up outlets, mainly for food, outside the old urban centers, retooling old freight houses, lofts, and plants vacated by Depression bankruptcies. Attesting to the importance of automobility for this new American undertaking, they employed their utility trucks to comb the countryside in search of cheap fresh produce and discounted canned and packaged goods, and they could afford to set up their establishments in semirural areas in the expectation that their customers would drive their cars to them.[13] Expert hawkers of merchandise, they embellished the populist rhetoric of the New Deal era with the commercial hoopla associated with the movie industry publicity mill— "super," "colossal," "unprecedented." The first of them, King Cullen, who founded his store in 1930, called himself "the world's greatest price wrecker," spoke of dealing "death blows to profiteers," and proclaimed his unswerving dedication to his constituents, "the public," "my boss, my judge, my jury."[14]

Since the supermarket was first and foremost identified with a necessity, food, it was more publicly and unequivocally associated with women than either the chain or department store. In turn, U.S. women, many of whom had worked during the war and were savoring their independence, automobility, and higher incomes, treated self-service as a time-saving convenience rather than a cutting back on service that offloaded labor and equipment costs onto the housewife.[15]

By the 1940s, as a result of wartime labor shortages, one-stop, self-service shopping had made speedy progress. It was to the advantage of its promoters to characterize themselves as constituting a whole "new industry." Zimmerman and men like him dedicated themselves to clarifying their special mission. The most widely accepted technical definition was that the supermarket was a highly departmentalized retail establishment, wholly owned or operated as a concession and built to offer adequate parking space. At the very least, the grocery department operated on a self-service basis. Although at first profits could be made from abandoned buildings, depressed land values, and discounted agricultural produce, very quickly the operations required more and more specialized and costly equipment such as vast refrigeration units, air-conditioning, neon lighting, and security systems. Then there were the innumerable minor inventions required by self-service shopping, notably the turnstile entries, basket carriers and carts, frozen food units, display gondolas, and checkout stands with registers designed to itemize, add, and print out purchases. Altogether they required huge capital investments. But the monies were there. American financial markets had long been accustomed to investing in retailing, and well-capitalized chain stores like the oldest and biggest, A & P, together with Safeway, Grand Union, and the Jewel Tea Company, were prompt to regear their outlets to the new methods.[16]

As the United States converted to peacetime, the supermarket was cheered as the hallmark of the American system of free enterprise. The wartime experience had taught "that the common good is best serviced by producing and distributing goods in high volume and at low unit cost," to quote the letter of salutation Harry Truman sent to Chicago in 1946 to greet the first postwar national convention of supermarket promoters.[17] By 1958 Americans spent 95 percent of their food money in self-service stores and 70 percent of it in supermarkets. The U.S. family's one-time weekly grocery shopping, the cart spilling over with cartons, cans, and every other good, had become a symbol of the American way of life.

For Europeans, the supermarket offered a new model of industrial beauty: the shadow-free luminosity of neon lights, the constant temperatures of air-conditioned spaces, the vast glass-and-steel refrigeration units, the rows of brightly colored cans and packages, the mounds of fresh produce graded in string sacks or cellophane-wrapped containers. The most astonishing change of all was that the product sold itself: the seller had gone completely incognito; the merchandise on display was the star.[18]

When Italian entrepreneur Quirino Pedrazzoli petitioned the prefect of Milan for a license to open his supermarket in January 1949, and he was asked to spell out how it differed from the department store, his response conveyed the novelty:

The buyer once inside the supermarket and having deposited all bags and packages at the checkout stand is provided with a cart mounted with a basket, which he circulates around the store. As he goes, he comes across numerous shelves, but with no clerks, on which the most varied merchandise is displayed, all appropriately packaged . . . above all foodstuffs, each with a special sticker showing its price.

The customer is free to pick whatever he wants and place it in the cart. Once the rounds are finished he brings the cart to a checker, who, after adding up the stickers, calculates the total bill. Thereafter the cart with the goods goes to the outstation while the customer goes to the cashier to pay, whereupon he retrieves his goods or arranges for home delivery.[19]

The invention seemed simple enough, and it promised to cater to what Zimmerman expounded as unimpeachable fact, namely that "universally, families wanted to spend as little money as possible on their groceries."[20] However, people's ways of provisioning are deeply embedded in all kinds of institutions, values, and beliefs, and these could pose formidable obstacles to this particular innovation. The successful implantation of a supermarket, even on a smaller scale than that commonly found in fast-growing U.S. suburbs, depended on a total transformation in the environment of buying and selling, reaching back to the suppliers—to change agricultural techniques, processing, and packaging—and moving forward to the customers—to change their household equipment, finances, and food habits.[21]

On the one hand, self-service assumes that before the goods reach retailers, they are weighed, counted, packaged, and marked for price, as well as advertised. Packaging required a packaging industry. Branding assumed a marketing industry. The goods, especially if produce, had to be constantly available and as uniform as possible in appearance, size, and quality; and that assumed sustained relations with the source, whether they were local farmers and processors or importers. On the other hand, self-service presumes that the customer is capable of selecting goods, recognizing symbols, and calculating expenditure, as well as carting goods away, storing them, and knowing how to prepare them. In either direction, for those who had never before tried out the system, there were all sorts of unexpected challenges—from the obstructive behavior of farmers, pressed to deliver new kinds of goods and furious as they learned how much they were marked up by the time they reached the consumer, to the recalcitrance of consumers, who were generally quiescent about the old system, barring penury, inflation, or revolution, so long as they knew no other, but who when introduced to the new systems were full of complaints until habit made them compliant.

The pioneers found the path laid with snares. From France came news of the crash of Casino's first undertaking: the old family firm from Saint-Etienne, founded in 1898, with a grocery chain of 785 outlets in south-western France, launched a *libre-service* in its hometown on October 27, 1948, to the great excitement of the locals, only to see the crowds melt away once the novelty had disappeared. Pierre Guichard, the grandson of the founder, was frank about the troubles they faced, and his diagnosis, echoed by others who did not suffer his painful experience, was that Europeans did not yet have the wherewithal to make the supermarket a going concern. The environment was mainly to blame: French families lacked refrigerators to hold foodstocks, not to mention automobiles to carry them home. In addition, their purchasing power was three to four times lower than that of the average American family. And the store was unable to slash prices with respect to the local shops, in part because the public was used to an attractive selling environment, in part because it couldn't squeeze labor costs any lower, since they already were minimal, equal to only 6–7 percent of the gross expenditure, compared with 15 percent in the United States. The last straw was the disappearance of the figure of the shopkeeper, who was supposed to be hovering around the store, standing at the checkout counter, chatting with customers, or tidying up the shelves. From customer complaints, it seemed that self-service was just another trick in commerce's ever-evolving repertoire.[22]

La Formica of Milan offered other early object lessons—ones that Richard Boogaart would take to heart a half-dozen years later when, over Sunday lunch, he quizzed Quirino Pedrazzoli about why his store had failed in 1949. A seasoned international buyer for the Rinascente department-store chain, Pedrazzoli had learned about the supermarket revolution in 1939, when he met a Mr. Smith from "Carolina" at the Leipzig Fair who, upon his return to the United States, sent him miscellaneous pamphlets on the subject. With this knowledge and a rich capital of 150 million lire (about $245,000) from an incautious backer, Pedrazzoli opened "The Ant—store without clerks," in central Milan in December 1949. Located on the chic Via Torino, it occupied 1,600 square meters, its eccentric design adapted to the two-story space it occupied in the old palace, with the space created by the back courtyard ingeniously used to house the circular staircase designed to move people from one floor to the other. Against all convention, Pedrazzoli had customers come in on the second floor, where he located the high-profit departments, meaning wines and liquors, sweets, and fresh-baked pastries. From there they went to the first floor, where they found the staples, bread, rice, meat, oil, and so on. That the store went bankrupt after only seven months was blamed on women shoppers. They were alleged to have an "aversion to cans and boxes," hostility to "the idea that time is rationed," making it necessary to "sacrifice their own aesthetic and gastronomical preferences to what is practical and fast," and disdain for the puffed-up claims of packaging and publicity.[23] The view that "national character" had undone the experiment was probably wrong, for the store's customers numbered around 25,000 weekly. More likely, poor inventory methods couldn't keep track of supplies, demand outstripped supply, and the capitalization was insufficient to carry the store through its first difficult months. Facing ruin, Pedrazzoli had tried to open two additional stores to expand his volume of business and to attract more capital, but he was stalled from doing so by state licensing regulations.[24]

These spectacular failures recommended caution. European retailers who studied American commerce in the course of missions sponsored by the European Productivity Administration advised a gradualist approach: "present-day business heads" could derive "numerous perspectives of progress" from "across the Atlantic," but they should be applied "without brutal subversion."[25] Accordingly, the main investment was in self-service equipment designed for operations over a relatively small area, chiefly in city neighborhoods—what the Americans called "superettes." From 1950 to 1960 western Europe saw the number of such enterprises rise spectacularly from 1,200 to 45,500.[26]

Even so, to launch a full-fledged supermarket in Europe was regarded as a risky business in the mid-1950s, especially for outsiders. In 1956 the Treaty of Rome founding the Common Market was still only a glint in the eye of its framers, and if the "economic miracle" was already being called such, nobody was certain that it might not vanish. Consequently, IBEC's decision to enter Europe has to be regarded as motivated not merely by economic considerations, though calculated with an eye to the economic risks. Political considerations stood in the background: Communism was apparently making headway in western Europe, and for Rockefeller, "lower food prices represent the same thing as an increase in wages." If the venture proved successful, the reasoning went, other supermarkets would follow. This development would in turn "pressure suppliers into lowering prices" and "force the suppliers and manufacturers to re-organize more efficiently, modernize, etc."[27]

To determine more precisely where such an operation might work, in the spring of 1956 Boogaart was contracted to conduct a survey, which he carried out in May and June. Starting in France (which gave him a very "dim view of Europe") and ending in Italy, he found "obstacles in all the countries." These consisted of "high taxes, low incomes, short store hours, limited availability of merchandise, strong cartels and guilds, government controls and licensing restrictions, few automobiles, shortage of building sites and materials and many others."[28] However, prospects were decidedly worst in England, Germany, and Switzerland. England was already "a country of chain stores," and self-service stores and supermarkets were becoming well established by the giant Lever, which owned the Colonial and Lipton chains, by Sainsbury, and by Express Dairy, as well as by working-class cooperatives, which were rapidly modernizing their retailing techniques. Moreover, the British economy was in deep recession, and it was difficult to import equipment up to U.S. standards. West Germany was promising from the point of view of food processing. General Foods, Kellogg's, Kraft, Corn Products, and the Container Corporation had set up business there. However, the Germans were "getting into the supermarket business at a fast pace and competitors from outside were at a disadvantage with respect to capable local operators." "Charming" Switzerland was a place simply to visit as a tourist, for Gottlieb Duttweiler's fame was now known far and wide, and his cooperatively run Migros set a high standard, which in turn was reflected in the excellence of its competitors. The prospects for the Netherlands were poor, for any foreign enterprise would have to respect strict government regulations on labor, land use, and construction. France was discounted outright given the lack of new housing development, the strong position of local merchants, and government controls and import regulations on equipment and processed foods. There was no comment on the exploits of the grocer-turned-political-militant Pierre Poujade, but Boogaart could not have ignored the international press coverage of the populist grocer's march on Paris at the head of 250,000 small merchants to protest their declining fortunes, or his remarkable success in the national elections of January 1956, when he won 2.3 million votes.[29]

As it turned out, the two countries that might have been regarded as the poorest prospects, in view of their sizable number of small shopkeepers and antiquated laws, turned out to be the most promising, namely Belgium and Italy. The former offered a small, densely packed, and prosperous population, and its government was eager for foreign investment. Antwerp had many sites suitable for construction, costs were comparable to those in the United States, the labor climate was good, several leading U.S. food processing companies had set up headquarters there, and the location was accessible to the rest of western Europe. Best of all, "there are no teeth" in the "Chain law" *(Loi du Cadenas)* blocking chain-store expansion, which was finally allowed to lapse in 1959. The one drawback could be competition from the Priba and Sarma food chains.

The latter country, Italy, would have seemed even less promising, in view of heavy state regulation, the relative backwardness of most consumer indicators, and the restiveness of labor organized in trade unions that reminded Boogaart of the large state-controlled labor movements of Venezuela and Mexico. However, Boogaart had in mind northern Italy, specifically the city of Milan, with its relatively prosperous 1.5 million residents; one in three Milanese families had refrigerators, compared with one in twenty for the country as a whole; and they had similarly high rates of automobile ownership. The city was also ideal from the point of view of IBEC's "do-gooder" motives. Prices had been sharply rising, making it one of the West's most expensive cities, and Italy had the largest Communist party outside eastern Europe.[30] A businessman could also appreciate Italy's recently passed foreign investment legislation, the most favorable in Europe with respect to repatriating profits. In sum, Italy looked like the right place to start, assuming that the company could be guaranteed the many licenses and permits it needed.

The decision to recommend Italy was also influenced by the jamboree of excitement generated at the installation of the "American Way Supermarket" at Rome's EUR's Congress Palace on the occasion of the Third International Congress of Food Distribution in June 1956. Though the Food Congress organization operated out of Paris and was nominally under French tutelage, it was the Americans who took charge of the exposition, starting in 1950, when the National Cash Register Company had mounted a full-scale self-service store. For the 1956 meetings, the U.S. Department of Agriculture with support from the State Department prevailed upon the National Association of Food Chains to set up a state-of-the-art supermarket capable of displaying 2,500 food items. Before the exhibit closed on July 1, 450,000 visitors had passed through its portals and circulated through the aisles: merchants, members of parliament, notables, members of the press and media during the day, the general public in the evening. At the exposition held in Zagreb the following year, the operation reached the acme of perfection as the National Association of Food Chains, U.S. government offices, and hundreds of American companies set up a supermarket pavilion that enabled Yugoslav visitors not simply to look at the goods on display but to walk in, take a cart, and practice shopping. By then national goals could be said to be "so deeply embedded within commercial products that propaganda slogans were totally redundant."[31]

Breaking into the Market

The most remarkable aspect about IBEC's leap was its surefooted landing. This was cushioned by its prior business experience acquired in the midwestern heartland of U.S. mass consumption and in Latin America and by large capital resources. However, it would never have made the jump had not friendly figures reassured it that local rules could be bent to obtain the myriad licenses and permissions to operate. In Rome IBEC's men could count on U.S. Ambassador Clare Booth Luce, a personal friend of Rockefeller, who introduced them to potential backers, as well as her successor, James Zellerbach, the former head of the European Cooperation Agency's Italian mission.[32] In Milan they could also count on the Angleton family. James Hugh, the longtime head of the Italian subsidiary of National Cash Register Company, was president of the American Chamber of Commerce (as well as a leading Rotarian), in addition to being engaged in assorted useful side interests, including poultry farming. His son, James Jesus, also known as "Junior," knew practically everybody. Head of OSS counterespionage for Italy from 1944 to 1947 and formerly the chief conduit for American funding to local anticommunist campaigns, currently he was at the acme of his influence in the CIA.

The expectation that IBEC would gain official support to operate locally was nourished by the spectacular success of the "American Way" supermarket exhibit. True, everything was written in English, the products were not selected for Italian tastes, the measures were in pounds and ounces, and the prices were in dollars and cents.[33] Still, the word on the street was that supermarkets were a must for a modern nation. So it seemed certain that the center-right government would back initiatives in that direction. That at least was the calculation of Amadeo Malfatti, the brother of the secretary of the ruling Christian Democratic party, who in partnership with Franco Palma, Squibb's managing director in Italy, purchased the entire equipment of the exposition, including the IBM inventory system, sent an operative to the United States for six months to learn the supermarket business, and opened three pilot stores in Rome, the first of which made its debut on the well-trafficked Viale Libia in February 1957.

IBEC was above such political cronyism and small-time risk-taking. Its initial concern was rather to explore the terms of its alliance with Italian capitalism. It had no trouble finding contacts; "our association with the Rockefeller name worked almost like magic—prospective partners looked us up," Boogaart crowed.[34] For local knowledge, it would be wise to work with the venerable Rinascente or La Standa, the leading Italian five-and-dime chain, both of which wanted to go into food retailing and made overtures to work with IBEC. However, these firms "would probably want controlling interest and a voice in management and all sorts of things."[35] Another possibility was to go with a potential supplier with good knowledge about distribution like the Motta company, with its chain of baked goods, candy, twelve or so restaurants and twenty stores around the country, which already worked as distributor for the National Biscuit Company. However, this course risked making IBEC too dependent on existing business networks. Yet another prospect was Gaetano Marzotto, "a good textile man and very wealthy." But he was regarded as "a poor merchandising man," and he too would want a controlling interest as well as the exclusive for his soaps, wines, and so on.[36]

All things considered, IBEC wanted three things from its partners in addition to capital, namely freedom of action, political clout, and transparency—which is to say one set of books rather than the two that were common practice in Italy, one for internal inventory and the other for the state tax authorities. Those objectives led it to the summit of Italian industrial capitalism in the figures of the Lombard textile magnate Mario Crespi and his retinue. Crespi, whom some described as the Italian Rockefeller, and who had intermarried with the Agnellis of Fiat, was known for his probity. The retinue also consisted of Marco Brunelli, the scion of a wealthy family of antique dealers, and the two Caprotti brothers, Mario and Bernardo, who were important textile manufacturers familiar with the United States as well as being considered broad-minded and efficient. That the Crespi family also owned Italy's leading daily newspaper, *Corriere della sera*, offered at least two advantages: favorable reporting and discounts on advertising rates.[37] Moreover, the Italian group was satisfied to enter as minority partners with a 49 percent share. And it not just welcomed but insisted that the management be strictly American. "They did not want our stores to be influenced by any Italian people. They wanted the stores to be run and look exactly like they do in the United States," reported Boogaart. They also wanted the American reference clear in the name, thus "Supermarkets," with "Italiani" added as a happy compromise.[38]

If there was a big unknown, a factor absent from IBEC's experience in Latin America, it was the vast, pullulating world of small merchandisers. Milan alone, a city of 1.5 million people, was estimated to have 31,500 stores in addition to 10,000 street vendors. Altogether 14,000 outlets sold some kind of food product. The Americans were dismissive about the power of these small-timers to compete economically. They were organized under the leadership of the Merchants' Union and collectively, adding up their families and relatives, they represented a sizable constituency. If they were organized, they might become worrisome. All the political parties, from the Christian Democrats to the Communists, seemed to be vying for their favor.[39]

The key to success was to make a speedy entry and offer stunningly effective service. The stores would open for business so quickly and perform so efficiently that public officials, starting with the mayor, would grant them the licenses to operate. Faced with lower food prices and eager to respond to customer enthusiasm, they would gather ever greater support, and the licenses needed to open additional stores would be granted. Within a matter of weeks the company mobilized technique, knowledge, capital, equipment, and supplies to establish a monopoly over the modern circuitry of food distribution.[40]

The goal was a completely self-contained system of equipment and supply, with accordingly large investments in plants, warehousing, trucking, and inventory systems, including IBM punch-card accounting machinery. To supply variety, it imported canned fruits and vegetables from South Africa, processed cheese from Denmark, and frozen fish from England. To supply staples such as pasta and bread products in the volume and quality required, and to provide products that had hitherto been prohibitively costly, such as eggs, chickens, and coffee, or in only seasonal use like ice cream, it built its own plants. To provide equipment, it started by importing its own, then turned to Italian manufacturers listed at the Milan Trade Fair, placing orders with them for goods built to Supermarkets Italiani's specifications, holding out the prospect that they would readily find export markets for their well-designed, low-cost shopping carts, food counters, and checkout stands.

The bakery was the most pressing undertaking, for it was discovered that the average Milanese family of five consumed twelve kilos of bread per week—in addition to two of rice, three of pasta, and two of pota-toes.[41] It was out of the question that any Milanese bakery could supply the quantity Supermarkets Italiani required, at least not according to management's specifications. A visit to the Baker Perkins Company of London to study its bulk bread production taught that whereas Italians obtained 115 loaves from 100 pounds of flour, the British got 143. The trick was not to use lard or sugar, and to inject large quantities of moisture, even more than the amounts used in American mass-manufactured bread.[42] As management consolidated the bakery operations in Florence in 1960, it brought in the former chief baker for the U.S. armed forces, a German, who had previously served in the Wehrmacht. The final set of recipes found a middle way between Anglo-American Wonder Bread and Italian craft loaves by offering a wide range—from packets of standard-ized breadsticks *(grissini),* a favorite in middle-class homes, and the soft white bread packaged as Peter Pan, to the loaves familiar in appearance to those provided by local bakers, except that they cost 25 percent less.[43]

Notwithstanding management's remarkable alacrity and skill in re-sponding to all the unknowns of a new operation, the company ran into two formidable impediments. The first seems obvious in retrospect. Notwithstanding all reassurances, obtaining the appropriate licenses ran into ferocious opposition. Before the supermarket invasion, food store li-censes were issued solely by the municipal authorities under Law 2174 of December 16, 1926, governing small shops. But by 1959 the National Merchants' Union had successfully pressured the government to change the ground rules by having supermarkets reclassified as fixed-price chain and department stores. This change made them subject to Law 1468 of July 21, 1938, which granted licensing power to the prefect, the national government's local representative, on the grounds he had a better view of the situation. But he too was supposed to consult with the local chamber of commerce before granting the permissions. In effect the new store had to gain approval from future competitors. And this was the likely out-come. However, there was always recourse if the license was turned down: to appeal to the Ministry of Industry and Commerce in Rome. But if the ministry approved, then local merchants could appeal. "This is a country," Boogaart acknowledged amid his bureaucratic travails, "in which even an American can become confused."[44]

Consequently, the goal of opening five stores in rapid succession to carry the heavy load of overhead from a practically enclosed system was frustrated. The first licenses squeaked through, while the others were in the offing. Meanwhile Supermarkets Italiani went ahead and commissioned Gio Ponti, the Milanese architect famous for the glimmering glass Pirelli Tower, Italy's first true skyscraper, to build a graceful blue-brown-tile construction for its fourth site on Viale Zara. The store was completely stocked and ready to open when, under pressure from the local Merchants' Union, which represented 15,000 food-shop operators, the government delayed issuing the license. By the time it was finally granted, $250,000 in capital had been idle for eight months. Even thereafter, notwithstanding the huge crowds at the new store, volume at the first three stores remained lower than expected, so low that, as Boogaart admitted, "we weren't even breaking even."[45]

Indeed, Supermarkets Italiani might have met the fate of La Formica had not IBEC in early May 1959 become the recipient of a low-interest, easy-term $1 million loan (650 million lire) from the recently established Export-Import Bank of Washington. The bank's funds, the fruit of the Agricultural Trade Development and Assistance Act, were generated out of the proceeds in local currencies from the sale of U.S. agricultural surpluses abroad. It was the first such loan authorized for Europe. With the understanding that it would contribute to the development of southern Italy, the Italian Treasury and Agricultural Departments signed off on it. Paying 7 percent interest per annum (a half-percentage point lower than local bank rates), repayable over an eight-year period starting two and a half years after withdrawal, it was so generous that to spend it the company would be propelled to expand elsewhere.[46]

The second big hitch remained volume. It was expected, following the U.S. experience, that low prices, combined with the bright and attractive atmosphere, self-service, and cash and carry, would immediately attract a large clientele. Prices from 5–25 percent below the city average, together with the sheer abundance of products, immediately attracted mobs of city residents to the stores. However, many of the people were "sightseers." Purchases per capita, the key to retailing volume, remained low by U.S. standards: the average was calculated at $2.50 per visit, compared with $7.50 in the United States.[47] Management discovered—and rushed

Opening day, Supermarket Italiani, Via Milanese, Florence,
February 1961. By permission of Foto Locchi.

to correct—the numerous problems that might account for customer dis-
satisfaction.

It was discovered that packages were too large for people used to shopping on a daily basis and with low incomes. Frozen meat didn't sell in
spite of excellent quality and low price even after lights had been installed
to diminish its discolored look. Italians hadn't formed "the can-opener
habit" or a taste for frozen foods. There was no market at all for pre-
cooked items and little for prepared cake mixes. Shoppers were suspicious of the prelabeled weights and measures, and they needed more advice on the floor to orient themselves. The huge size of the shopping carts
imported from the United States only worsened the problem; a rueful
Boogaart remarked that "we asked the Italians to push a Cadillac when
they are unable to even buy a Fiat."[48]

With the top management itself virtually always on the job—sack-
ing vegetables, cutting meat, stocking shelves, even working like carry-
out boys—the company was able to respond rapidly. Accordingly, it put
more shopgirls on the floor to provide advice. It provided scales to check
weights. It laid out more produce and fewer canned goods, and in smaller
packages. It cut prices on the chief purchases—pasta, flour, and wine—
even if doing so meant taking losses, as on sugar, which was a state oli-

Opening day: fur-coated types mingle with the middle-class masses. By permission of Foto Locchi.

gopoly, or well-known brand-named pasta and canned tomatoes like Barilla and Cirio, which refused to discount even large orders. It offered its own ice cream concocted with margarine rather than cow's milk at 250 lire a liter instead of at the going rate of 750.[49] Exasperated by the fussiness of the clientele, Boogaart joked that Supermarkets had practically been turned into a "market for specialities": "we fry fish for them all day Thursday so they don't have to fry it themselves. We take produce and put it in a bag so they just have enough for one meal. We cut their bunches of celery in two parts for them so they can buy a half bunch, we divide a cabbage head in two or three parts and sometimes four. We make a mixed package of vegetables for them with a bit of everything in it. We make mixes of fruits so they have a bit of all kinds in it."[50]

With flyers straightforwardly listing products and their prices distributed apartment block by apartment block in the areas surrounding the stores, the occasional full-page advertisement in *Corriere della sera* listing the prices at the store in one column and the city average in the other, and balloons for the children, Supermarkets Italiani courted the consumer-housewives. "We almost kiss every lady's hand who enters the store." Boogaart reported. "I think our personality is very good."[51]

A Model for Emulation

Whatever Supermarkets Italiani's startup problems, they were well con
cealed from outsiders, so much so that even before it began to show
profits in 1960, it came to be regarded as a superbly managed operation.
Several offers were made to purchase the whole company, and many to
obtain stock. The Milan stores were the subject of a three-day field trip
for students at IPSOA, the prestigious management school in Turin.[52]
And its managers were sought out as consultants on a range of undertakings, from a two-store operation at Padua to La Rinascente's new acquisition in Rome, Malfatti's and Palma's Supermarket chain, which, as
Boogaart had predicted, went bankrupt and was grabbed up by the expanding department-store giant. News of Supermarkets Italiani's "calming" effects on prices spread beyond the city when on April 9, 1959,
at the behest of the central government, *Corriere della sera* published
a full-page advertisement comparing Supermarkets' prices with the Milan average as determined by the city's Office of Statistics. Women in
Padua, Verona, and other towns reportedly brought the page to their
own grocers, demanded price reductions, and harried local officials to set
up similar operations. Government authorities involved in modernizing
the Mezzogiorno sought out advice about what produce the south of Italy could supply to the new chains; the answer—sweet potatoes, yams,
peanuts, avocados—surely more closely reflected the ecology of IBEC's
Latin American colonies than that of Sicily.[53] The signal that Supermarkets Italiani had arrived socially came when the Milan Rotary recognized
supermarketing as a respectable new category of enterprise by inviting
Marco Brunelli, the congenial thirty-two-year-old head of the board, to
join its circle.

The most important evidence of success was that supermarket operators elsewhere in western Europe were eager to exchange their experiences with the American managers. By the early 1960s supermarkets had
begun to be at home as they had not been only a half-decade before. The
sudden surge of firsts—the first discount store at Audergham, Belgium
(1961); the first hypermarket, Carrefour's at Sainte Geneviève-des-Bois
(1963); the first shopping center at Frankfurt Taunus (1964) attested to
the stunningly rapid changes that went under the name of the auto-fridge
revolution. These entailed remarkable transformations not only in demand and supply, but in the whole environment in which provisioning
was shaped. An upheaval was occurring: the expansion of traffic in food-

stuffs and equipment with the consolidation of the European Economic Community, the loosening of legal impediments to new commercial establishments, the big population movements with large-scale urbanization, women leaving the household for work in factories and offices, and the spread of improved standards of family nutrition.

In this context, Supermarkets Italiani represented the power condensed in American consumer culture both to accelerate and to shape material standards in Europe. A model, a catalyst, and a sustained presence, it drew on deep pockets of capital, knowledge, and the strategic use of political influence, as well as collateral cultural capital. Things American were everywhere the rage in Italy. Nineteen-fifty-eight was the year the Neapolitan singer Renato Carosone produced the hit song "Tu vuo fa l'Americano"—"You wanna act like an American." It was addressed to the swaggering twenty-year-old of the city streets "who loves rock 'n' roll and baseball but can't hold his whiskey and soda." Boogaart's Milanese high society spoke of the United States as "the only place and where they would all like to live."[54] Rockefeller himself was being introduced to a mass public as a benevolent democratic figure in early 1959 as all the women's magazines dedicated pages of gossip to the marriage of Steven, Nelson Rockefeller's introspective son, to the young Norwegian Anne-Marie Rasmussen, formerly the family's kitchenmaid.

With so many forces converging to make it notorious, Supermarkets Italiani was clearly exceptional. Yet its installation was connected with three trends visible to a greater or lesser degree everywhere in Europe that made American power immeasurably significant in the commercial revolution. First, it showed European capitalists that investments in food retailing could harvest excellent profits. Second, it set a clear standard for procedure and equipment. And, third, it lent support to a new alliance, forged among big capital, new local entrepreneurship, government, and consumers. This alliance was indispensable to revising laws and changing customs so as to establish the supermarket as the main reference point for making calculations about provisioning.

Outside Italy, American retail capital found the most hospitable reception in Belgium, as Boogaart had foreseen in his 1956 survey. There the initiative came from the Belgians themselves. Indeed, it came from the two conjoined family dynasties, the Bernheims and the Vexelaires, with their vast holdings in department stores and the Priba food chain. In 1960 they had turned to the Jewel Tea Company of Melrose, Illinois, for support to launch a new company, S. A. Superbazar, a combination food store and discount outlet.[55] The United States' sixth-largest chain, founded in 1916 and managing 323 American outlets, Jewel Tea could be relied on by its new partners for "its long and dynamic experience in self-service."[56]

In any case, Jewel's Belgian partners were primed for the risk. Keyed up by the prospects of expanding through the Benelux region, then going into northern France, with Paris itself as the final goal, they had made the obligatory "pilgrimage" to Dayton, Ohio, where the "Pope of Super-marketing," Bernardo Trujillo, chief of National Cash Register's merchandising seminars, held court. Starting in 1956, NCR not only organized its Modern Merchandising Methods (MMM) clubs abroad, with their hub at Paris, but also established its own school at its main center of production in Dayton.[57] There the Belgians were exposed to Trujillo's shouts and swagger, his voice becoming a raucous bellow as he led them through his weeklong seminar for 135 or so foreigners, a dozen of whom would have been French-speaking (given that more than 1,500 French nationals registered to attend from 1958 to 1964). Putatively the son of a wealthy Colombian family that had gone bankrupt, Trujillo was said to have studied at the Sorbonne, which accounted for his genius in languages, before being hired as a youth by NCR to translate the firm's self-service brochures. It was the courses organized under the slogan MMM that brought him fame:

> Modern Merchandising Method
> Move More Merchandise
> Make More Money

And nobody who went through them forgot his slogans: "Islands of Loss, Oceans of Profit"; "No Parking, No Business"; "The Only Sure Thing Is Change."[58] With big stashes of American expertise and capital, the Belgians regarded themselves as embarking on nothing less than a seachange of civilizations, from the fixity of the city center to the mobility of suburban space. Anticipating trends that were just beginning to be palpable—urban flight, the decay of the city center, the surge in automobile ownership, the willingness to change food habits—the scion of the conservative Vexelaire dynasty had become synchronized to the new beat of business ideology: "We firmly believe that in this universe in which everything evolves following our vertiginous rhythm, there is no place for those who do not think and act at the same time as the others."[59]

Reflecting the decline of center-city retailing, speculative investment also significantly accelerated it: no western European city would experience more dreadful blows to its magnificent commercial architectural legacy than Brussels. The grand co-operative of the Socialist party, failing to modernize, fell on hard times, and in 1964 the building that housed it, Horty's art nouveau monument, was sold, then demolished to make way for a nondescript government building. Bernheim's own flagship, À L'Innovation, likewise a Horty building, was dealt an even more terrible blow: on May 22, 1967, a fire swept through it, killing 235 customers. This event occurred amid the big promotion of American merchandise inaugurated in the presence of the U.S. ambassador, which was the target of anti-American protests tied to opposition to the Vietnam War. Suspicions that the fire was set were never confirmed.[60]

Bernheim's ambition to create "a Europe of retailing" now promised to bear fruit, this time with the generous fertilizer of American capital and know-how. The venture was the establishment of Inno-Paris. The huge store, occupying the bottom two floors of the venerable Belle Jardinière department store, just off the Pont Neuf, with food on one floor and sundry wares on the other, opened on March 22, 1962, but only after the French government finally threw its weight behind the "heretics of distribution" and overrode the objections of traditional French commerce. In an effort to rally public opinion—and to overcome skepticism in retailing circles that a supermarket could make profits in the heart of Paris—Inno's executive director, Henry Weill, laid out the three factors that would guarantee the victory of his "war on high overhead": the first was "the dynamic, competent and at the same time experienced team, that had completed various trips to the United States to study the new type of organization they want to develop in France"; the second, "the methods, studied in the United States but transformed according to the French taste and the particularities of life in France"; and the third, "financial power."[61] The last was especially significant, for the Belgian-American consortium had finally enlisted French capital, including the Edmond de Rothschild Group, the Banque de l'Union Parisienne, the Banque Commerciale de Paris, and the Compagnie Continentale d'Importation.

In this respect, the debut of Inno-Paris marked a sea change in the outlook of the financial world toward investing in local as well as cross-European retailing. On June 1, 1962, the prestigious Credit Suisse of Zurich announced the establishment of its Intershop Holding, a 250 million Swiss franc consortium organized to buy stock in existing companies and to develop new outlets in the retail trade, particularly in the form of shopping centers, supermarkets, and self-service stores. The first European-scale shopping center enterprise was founded in 1962 in Luxembourg. Called General Shopping SA, it would eventually hold stock in national enterprises like Neckermann, the Sears Roebuck of Germany. Its own capital drew widely from Europe, especially from funds repatriated from onetime colonial holdings such as the Bank of Indochina, the Compagnie Française de l'Afrique Occidentale, and Distilleries d'Indochine, but also from American sources such as the Morgan Guaranty Trust's International Finance Corporation.[62]

This influx of capital made it possible to surmount obstacles posed by the high cost of land, construction, and equipment. It was estimated that in the early 1960s it cost three times as much to open a supermarket in western Europe as it did in the United States; and since the pressure was mounting to emulate the state-of-the-art American model, even if the potential volume of such stores did not warrant it, a different course evolved. Many entrepreneurs set up larger and frillier stores than they might have otherwise, and dedicated the increased space to nonfood items on which they could obtain higher profit margins. The result was a hybrid, with only 15–25 percent of the space and 40–45 percent of the volume of sales taken up by food, and the prices on food, contrary to publicity, not at all low by comparison with more traditional stores. The most glamorous example, Inno of Paris, was a well-stocked supermarket and discount department store with brand items selling at about 15 percent below list price. As it turned out, the mix didn't work. Relatively high prices, combined with supply problems caused by boycotts by French distributors to protest the practice of discounting brands, together with the unusually high pilferage rate—estimated at 7 percent as opposed to the normal 1–2 percent—incurred huge losses. Scarcely two years after its inauguration the Belgian-American holding company was forced to sell the store to Galeries Lafayette.[63]

Provisioning, Italian Style

The problem, then, for the supermarkets was not just to break into the system, but to make their procedures part and parcel of the normal calculus of daily life. This process was protracted and fraught.

Supermarkets Italiani always assumed that it would expand, its initial goal being ten stores in Milan, each with a volume of business similar to that of an American outlet, with new undertakings in other prosperous northern cities, namely Turin, Bergamo, and Bologna. However, saddled with high overhead, slowed by the impediments to licensing, suffering from low volume, and, last but not least, faced with the need to invest the Export-Import Bank loan, it had to expand further. Consequently it welcomed an invitation from the prefect of Florence to establish stores there, especially after he promised not only to deliver several licenses, but also to help locate appropriate lots for construction, arrange for financing the land purchases, and contribute to the costs of construction. On inspection, Florence had all the right ingredients: the highest cost of living in Italy, partly because of the pressure of the tourist trade; a large foreign resident population, accounting for 25,000 of the 400,000 residents, mainly British and Americans, who would use the stores; and a vociferous left, which, though not in power, could do with a good tweaking.

Even more than in Milan, powerful political forces smoothed the way. From mid-1957, when the national government decided that factional splits made the city incapable of self-rule, until mid-February 1961, the city was virtually a dictatorship, governed by the prefect, Francesco Adami, and his special commissioner, Count Lorenzo Salazar. The man who was in line to become mayor, Giorgio La Pira, was a Christian Democratic mystic with strong internationalist sympathies, who would never have welcomed big capital to Florence, much less issued zoning variations or quelled small shopkeeper protests. Salazar, by contrast, a debonair authoritarian, prided himself on maintaining public order, which, in the Spanish-Neapolitan traditions that were his family's, meant cheap food and some occasional circus. In that spirit, the public authorities invited Supermarkets Italiani to Florence. Not beholden to any political constituency because they were not elected, these officials could ignore public demonstrations, such as those that were immediately mounted by small tradesmen under the leadership of the Merchants' Union to protest the opening of the first Supermarket in Via Milanesi. "If there was any blame to place for this revolution," the prefect reportedly told the Rotary club at its Monday gathering on March 6, 1961, "he would accept it as it was he who had started it by asking [them] here."[64] By mid-March, when La Pira was finally sworn in as mayor and the city council convened to begin to debate the occurrence, protests were faltering, and the new center-left coalition ran circles around the Communist opposition.[65]

In fact the opening of the first of the five supermarkets IBEC planned for Florence on February 13, 1961, was to all appearances a successful

public event. That Saturday, 15,000 people passed through the doors.
The chief of the fifteen policemen on duty to control the crowds and to
keep back hecklers recalled that "during the war, when people were half
starved and had to line up for handouts, they hadn't acted in so unruly
a way.[66] Over the next three weeks the city continued to be shaken by
protests as small merchants went on strike, demonstrators tried to boycott the stores, and the local newspapers opened their columns to reportage and readers' letters. The brouhaha precipitated in this dull town
only caused more crowds to show up. For management, the high circus
reached its culmination when a hospice brought seven blind men to "see"
the store. Management exulted: "You would think everything was for
free the way they stampede. We could raise prices on everything in the
store and never slow them down. It just seems to be what they have been
waiting for."[67]

The claims of the American entrepreneurs in Italy were so forthright
about their pursuit of lower prices in the interest of making profits, so observant in their analysis of the customers' wants, that they did indeed
seem to give the people what they wanted. Yet retailing statistics for 1971
suggest another story. A decade later, Italians still spent only 2 percent of
their expenditure on food in supermarkets, in contrast to the 14 percent
spent by the French, the 32 percent spent by West Germans, and the 70
percent spent by Americans.[68] Although figures for individual localities
are lacking, in the cities of the north-center, where most of the supermarkets were concentrated, including Milan and Florence, the patronage was
well above this measly national average. However, the national figure
alone provides reason to reflect on the self-doubts that Boogaart expressed when the operation was still running a big deficit. At the time he
was puzzled to discover that residents in the zones lying just around his
Milanese stores spent only 6–10 percent of their food budgets there.
"Knowing that saving money is the most important thing a low income
family could want to do, I can only say that we have a problem that isn't
operation or prices; it is a resistance to our stores for their size, the manner we sell, or it is the 33% which I mentioned the other day."[69] He was
referring to the 33 percent combined vote of the left. Elsewhere, to explain the low volume to his board of directors, he mused: "if I were a psy-
cho-analyst, I would say they had some kind of a quirk which we can't
locate."[70]

The quirks that eluded this skillful capitalist have eluded historians as
well. The commonest way to explain the slowness of supermarkets to

take hold is to call attention to the resistance of so-called traditional retailing. Accordingly, Italian commerce was backward, much like Italian
society generally. Traditional commerce mounted a strong lobby, and
conservative interests had a political interest in pandering to it in order to
keep voter support. Even if this went against consumer interests, it didn't
matter, since these weren't organized.[71]

A more nuanced view holds that there was a general political consensus that small commerce performed indispensable functions, the principal one being to absorb unemployment.[72] This consensus prevailed despite the fact that throughout the 1960s a number of bills to liberalize
commerce came before parliament, and all parties seemed to concur that
such legislation was both an important and an inevitable step to modernizing the country. The project that was finally agreed upon in 1971, the
so-called Helfer Plan, was originally intended to speed the reform of
commerce. Instead, it had the effect of further restricting it by moving the
power to grant licenses from the prefect down to the municipal level.
Parties from the left to the right supported it for different reasons, even if
it flagrantly contradicted the professed aim of modernizing distribution.
It was a tacit admission that Italy gave the little guys nowhere else to go.
On the one hand there was large-scale capitalism, which hired relatively
few new workers; on the other hand, there was the proliferation of small
firms in commerce as well as craft. With the rural world in fragments,
how could it not be tolerated that enterprising immigrants set up some
kind of small service to tide themselves over?

This consensus made Italy's retail trade look more and more anoma-
lous during the boom years. In 1971 Italy counted 538 supermarkets
(compared with 2,000 in West Germany, 1,833 in France, and 400 in Belgium) and none of the new "hypermarkets" (whereas West Germany had
451, France 151, and Belgium 16). For every supermarket there were
101,585 inhabitants, compared with one for 23,000–25,000 in the other
three countries. Everyplace else, the little shops were on the wane, but in
Italy their numbers rose staggeringly, from 316,304 in 1951 to 468,169
in 1971, including the swarms of stores that each year had succumbed
like mayflies. Moreover, relatively few stores made the effort to become
modern retailers. At the beginning of the 1970s only 4.2 percent of
northern Italian retailers had introduced self-service, one-third operated
without a telephone, just 11 percent used a cash register (though 26 percent were handy with adding machines), 73 percent had never bothered to
run an inventory check, and 41 percent didn't keep systematic accounts.[73]

In March 1961, after Florence's center-left coalition took power, the

The old-time butcher still holds on to his power, Florence, 1963.
By permission of Foto Locchi.

supermarket question finally appeared on the city council's order of business. Municipal politics was still conceived as the fiery heart of Italy's incandescent political-public sphere, and the chambers in the Palazzo Vecchio were the stage where politicians grandstanded on international issues. Before taking up this most pressing of local issues, the council's first act had been to telegraph its condolences to the widow of Patrice Lumumba, the Congo's first prime minister, who had been murdered the previous January at the behest of the Belgians with the support of the CIA. In anticipation of a showdown, the supermarkets' management had primed the Christian Democrats with arguments and packed the gallery with supporters. It helped too that the majority whip, Giovanni Ciabatti, was its main attorney.[74] Faced on the one hand with protesters shouting that their livelihood was in jeopardy, and on the other with snide comments from fellow councilmen, like Christian Democrat delegate Gugliemo Bacci, who accused the opposition of hypocrisy, since when he had visited East Germany he had seen "all department stores, only run by the state, not by private enterprise," the Communists argued that the plight of the small shopkeepers reflected the social costs of Italy's jaggedly uneven development. In Florence as elsewhere, struggling small enterprises supplied the jobs for the masses of people unable to find other employment because they were new to the city, lacked skills, or needed flexible work to fulfill other obligations like housework.[75]

To make a compelling argument that supermarkets should therefore be banned was hardly simple, though Giulio Montelatici, a used-bookstore owner and Resistance hero, did his best. True, local commerce was remarkable for its "pulverization." But Florence lacked "industrial lungs" to provide other kinds of work. And the supermarkets would jeopardize the business of 12,000 groceries, upon which the livelihood of perhaps 50,000 citizens depended. True, supermarkets offered the one-stop shopping that working women needed. But they also creamed off the best clients, those who paid in cash, leaving the poor customers, those who paid on credit, to the small shopkeepers, a result that only made them poorer.[76] True, supermarkets offered cheaper prices; but given their monopolistic position, they would soon behave like any other monopolistic enterprise, raising prices as it became convenient, unobstructed by competition or public power. But with all this said, the best the left could do, pending a thorough study of the situation, was to urge small shopkeepers to get on board the train of modernization, form consortia and cooperatives, and thereby become more competitive. Ideology wasn't going to stop a soul from patronizing the new stores, concluded Mario Leone, the representative of Florence's minute Radical party: "In the end, socialists and communists, when they are acting in their role as consumers, will patronize the supermarket too, for human instinct is to buy at the lowest price possible, or at least to think [they are doing] so, and the reality is that at the supermarket there are long lines of consumers."[77]

But was that so? When the Americans spoke empathetically about the desires and needs of their Italian customers, when they championed the housewives of Milan as "the type of woman capable to judge and choose by herself without the friendly suggestions of the shopkeepers (which sometimes are selfish ones),"[78] they had the American Mrs. Household Consumer in mind. Portrayed as a sovereign individual, majestically maneuvering her loaded cart through the aisles, she was fully empowered with the household income to pick and choose from among the 4,000 or so goods on display that originated in forty-two countries. Mrs. Consumer would be experienced at calculating purchases on the basis of comparison shopping, would trust the store's pricing systems (and if that trust was broken, she would have had the self-confidence to protest prices, outright or by going elsewhere), and would confidently weigh the value of her labor and time against money. She lacked any specific class connotation, though of course her family might have greater or lesser in-

*Superfrutta, a knock-off of Supermarkets Italiani, Viale dei Mille,
Florence, 1963.* By permission of Foto Locchi.

come at its disposal. The main point was that she was figured as acting
without constraints of a political, social, or cultural nature on her calculations about what was a good buy.

Mrs. Household Consumer, however, had no exact counterpart in the
European housewife of the 1960s. The Italian housewife, the *massaia,*
was hardly classless. True, the supermarket offered the impression of a
place where everybody was treated equally, its emplacement often established in zones that straddled neighborhoods, closer to the middle-class
housing but accessible by public transport to the more popular quarters.
Ideally it would cater to women's common interest in putting food on the
table. However, class lines were still sharply drawn, as Boogaart saw to
his surprise when he glimpsed some of his first Milanese customers. The
first time some of the chic bourgeois women showed up, they came into
the store with their chauffeurs and handed them the packages to carry. It
was only later that they waited in the car, while the women themselves
did the picking and choosing. Management still hadn't understood the
class standing of their clientele until July of their first year of operation,
when all the well-off families left the sweltering city and "our fur coat
customers changed into the peon class." Even when the store made up
smaller packages and dropped prices, this new clientele averaged no

more than 500 lire per visit.[79] In Florence too in the first year, business was suddenly becalmed in the third week of June. That year it happened that the last week before payday for wage earners coincided with the moment just after the Festival of St. John, the city's patron saint, when "the idle rich and nobility" departed for their summer residences.[80]

That upper-class women welcomed supermarket shopping is not surprising, given their greater physical mobility, more abundant leisure, and keener sense of the other ways available to spend money originally earmarked for food. From women's magazines, they learned of the satisfactions it could offer in convenience, as well as in high standards of hygiene. Cleanliness was an obsession in those years, and revulsion at the dirtiness of small stores, often of recent vintage and operated by newcomers, especially southern Italians, added a quasi-racial edge to the epithet "robber."[81] That the upper classes were the first customers at his no-frills discount stores was a phenomenon that the French discount king Edouard Leclerc had also remarked upon. Having to make new calculations about improving their standard of living, they were willing to shop around for the best prices in order to cut costs on food in favor of mortgage payments, installments on automobiles, vacations, and health care.[82] As for store decor, "They couldn't give a hoot. They don't go into a store to dream, to be blown away. They have what they need at home. The neon lights, music, chrome, [and] mirrors of variety stores are good for dazzling people who live in slums." However, it was only a matter of time before the latter too would change their outlook: "as soon as unskilled workers and agricultural laborers have to pay car installments at the start of the month, they too will learn that 'a sou is a sou,' that it's far better to shop at the discount center, ugly though it is, than to pay for the smiles and shop windows at the corner grocer's."[83]

For lower-class women, income was a real but not the only impediment to turning to the new systems of retailing. The problem for workers was not only that they had little income, but that it often came in irregularly. Housewives generally received no fixed sum for food. Having to lay out as much as half of the budget on it, they often resorted to using store credit, which they paid off on a monthly basis. They were thereby as much bound to their local stores as their storekeepers were bound to them.[84]

The second impediment to going elsewhere was tradition. Standards of living were in flux, but far less fluid in poor families. Low income was an obstacle to experimentation, as were family traditions, the norms of the neighborhood, and the range of choice offered by the local shopkeeper. Food items were just starting to be advertised widely in the early 1960s. In any case, women were not just free to choose new brands off the shelf. With crowded housing and extended families, choices often involved not just the mother, but also the mother-in-law and other female relatives. To change shopping habits called for some form of collective authorization, validated by the male head of the household. Notoriously, the supermarket encouraged impulse buying. It was not just the new item, but the unexpected expense: the managers themselves calculated that as a rule customers spent 20 percent more than they'd intended to. In Florence it was not uncommon, management said, to witness families outside the stores spreading out the groceries, incredulous at the total, checking each item against the cash-register receipt.[85]

The housewives' relationship to pricing was different from that of their U.S. counterparts. In small stores, prices could vary substantially from store to store on the same item. Moreover, because shopkeepers didn't often calculate the costs of replacing goods, they might drop prices if customers haggled or, as happened in Milan and Florence, compete with the prices advertised by the new supermarkets. They would absorb the cost of fixed-price merchandise in order to undersell the supermarkets. But they might also raise prices on other items. More generally, shopkeepers and customers continued to behave according to the notion of a "just price," which is to say that the cost of certain staples followed a customary rhythm: if it shouldn't be raised, neither should it be slashed or "broken." This customary valuation went hand in hand with the notion of "just profit." Customers lived cheek by jowl with shopkeepers, whom they regarded like other working people as needing enough income to support their families, according to local standards. When the merchants at the outdoor market on Via Giovanni Lami, near the Via Milanesi Supermarket, cut their prices, their old customers returned.[86] However, local people kept a sharp eye on the spending habits of storekeepers: the thought that the latters' sons, with money from Papà, could afford a bright-red Giulietta Sprint while their clients had to sacrifice to purchase a Fiat 600 or NSU Prinz was a motive to complain and gossip, if not to go elsewhere.

Figuring in the housewife's calculations was also a wide range of services offered by the local stores—not just credit, but also repairs, advice, and gossip. These fall under the rubric of what students of retailing call "economies of locality" or "economies of convenience." The latter terms are used rather generally to explain the success of the minimonopolies established by small shopkeepers in their neighborhood: they explain why, even if items cost 15–20 percent higher than at the supermarket, housewives are still willing to patronize the store and pay these prices. The women make a rough calculation of the value of their time, labor, and service, and the costs even out.[87]

Even if housewives had shopped around, comparing prices, what estimation would they have made of their own time and labor in the process? The 1950s and 1960s marked the cusp of the new calculations about the relative worth of women's labor in the home. More and more women were entering the labor force, and they gave enormous weight to alternative uses of their time. One reason for getting a job was to generate the income that was required to live in an increasingly money-mediated urban environment. But the stretch to reallocate income for new housing and other needs called for a more effective use of household labor and more efficient systems of provisioning. More and more, women's magazines and advertising publicized new models of household economics, underscoring the value of time saving as well as exercising new choices to improve the nutrition, comfort, or pleasure of family members. After the weekly laundry, provisioning took the most labor. The argument for one-stop, self-service shopping strengthened. By contrast, supermarkets stinted on advice about products. Since the vast range of choices was disorienting, shopping proved not only time-consuming as housewives figured out quality, prices, and weights, but also costly if they made mistakes. Only after consumers repeatedly complained that they needed more advice did Supermarkets Italiani temporarily put more shop assistants on the floor. Even then, shoppers made their selections cautiously, sticking to well-known items. Except for cleaned vegetables, they were loath to purchase the relatively few preprepared items, and the preprepared items in common use—tripe, codfish, chickpeas, olives in barrels—were not available. It would take higher incomes and more practice, as well as the ease of experimentation that one might expect from experienced bourgeois customers (who could afford mistakes), to encourage more adventuresome shopping.

The other service that was missing was delivery. This service was almost invariably offered "free" by small shopkeepers. Which is to say, it was provided by unpaid help that was unavailable to the supermarket (which had to use unionized labor)—the dim-witted nephew, unemployable poor, or school-age children. Boogaart recognized that "a lot of peo-

ple resent carrying their groceries home." But he felt that "this will correct itself in time."[88] A self-service society equalizes the workload for
certain types of women's labor. Upper-class women would not have been
caught carrying groceries; that was the maid's job, or the chauffeur's.
And working-class women would not have had cars and would have
been deterred from going a great distance unless public transportation
was handy.

Clients of the local stores would also have been making calculations
about what we might call "neighborhood overhead." With changes occurring so rapidly in the 1950s and 1960s, the local store was a reposi-
tory of neighborliness. Women were especially attached to this clustering
of services, since under normal circumstances they did not go outside the
perimeter established by local shops and their children's schools. Accordingly, even if the markups were noticeably high, they paid them because
they saw no alternative, but also out of fear that otherwise local storekeepers might go out of business at grave cost to neighborhood interests.

That the supermarket represented a social-cultural as much as economic rupture is suggested by the gender of the earliest clients. There was
the unanticipated presence of numerous men in the company of their
wives or alone; in Milan, over a third of the customers were male.[89] Several reasons might account for their presence. Men were needed to help
carry the groceries, and women were timid about venturing outside the
neighborhood without company. They did not want to risk succumbing
to impulse buying, which could easily raise the bill 15–20 percent, unless
their husbands were present to legitimate it. All the hullabaloo about
modern shopping impressed male opinion that food shopping at the supermarket fell under the category not of antiquated female drudgery but
rather of modern leisure. Food shopping started to be considered a family
enterprise.

What then was the effect of the pressure exerted by shopkeepers on
their customers to stay with them when they were offered the alternative
of the supermarket? It was said in Milan that politics was a dividing line,
that political solidarity with the left acted as a deterrent to militant families. The situation was less clear in Florence, as the left-wing town councilmen themselves admitted. The small shopkeepers had only recently begun to look to the Communist party for protection, and historically,
small shopkeepers as a category were suspect, not merely because they
were archetypal petit bourgeoisie, but because in Florence they were notorious for their support for the Fascist regime. The strikes did little to

improve the reputation of the small merchants. And their appeals to the public about the dangers posed by this new extension of "finance capitalism" and the "illusory well-being it promised" fell on deaf ears. But in the end they too wanted to join in the new progress, with demands for easier terms of credit to renovate their stores and protests against the unfairness in the distribution of licenses, which prevented them from expanding the services they offered.

Very quickly their voice became only one in the din of debate as the "consumer" was conjured into being, by Supermarkets Italiani's management but also by new organizations: the League of Consumers scheduled its first public meeting on February 26, 1961, at the Pastorini Gym at the same time as the first general convocation of the General Merchants' Union; a local branch of the National Union of Consumers was founded a week later.[90] Still, being the best organized, capitalized, and focused, Supermarkets presented itself as the consumer's most effective advocate. Far from just doing business, management pushed into the community: it sent out 40,000 letters to local residents explaining why the butchers were mistaken to protest the special status that enabled Supermarkets to sell meat on Thursdays while they had to close. Management also donated food to the Catholic parish in the Giannotti area, in exchange for which the local priest encouraged his flock to lobby for the store's opening. Finally, it sent numerous embassies to Rome, including at least two members of the city council who were on its payroll. In sum, Roland Hood boasted, Supermarkets Italiani had "used every possible angle except force."[91]

Faced with this battle, one can well imagine that the housewife, given her priorities, regarded Supermarkets Italiani with sympathy. And she viewed with antipathy the protests against it as acts of coercion with regard to her own capacity to value and judge. That was the gist of the Signora Tosca Mazzi's letter to the *Giornale del mattino*. A resident of Via delle Ruote, a modest street near the train station, who would have reached the Via Milanesi store by a several-block street-car ride, she wanted to know on behalf of "a group of shoppers who get by on a miserable fixed income . . . what is it that the shopkeepers don't like? We would like to know why it is that the shopkeepers never complained when the price of basic necessities went up . . . making Florence one of the most expensive cities in Italy while family allocations are among the lowest." Perhaps, she went on, "for these shopkeepers the privileges they benefited from are about to stop, or perhaps they don't like the end of all

Self-service takes hold: now men love to do the shopping, 1963.
By permission of Foto Locchi.

of those types who crowded around a product and raised its price from 2 lira at the farmer to 200 lire at the retailer. 'Not a lira less, or better that it rot,' they used to say, and they all agreed. Let them all survive, but at least let all the customers have the possibility of purchasing wherever they want to."[92]

As purchasers, meaning housewives or "consumers," as some rather tentatively began to call themselves, began to express their demands, calculations started to look different. Certainly they had good reasons to patronize the supermarket. But there were also good reasons to go to the smaller stores in the neighborhood. Consumers basically had a choice between two kinds of retailers, each trying to establish a kind of monopoly. Supermarkets had a monopoly on the big brands, and once they clinched their hold over the neighborhood by driving out competition, they could raise their prices because there was no real alternative. In turn, the little stores could play on their minimonopoly based on their proximity to customers, provided they showed some willingness to reach out to those customers. And so it happened that those who succeeded best quickly changed their outlook, lowering prices and stocking some of the goods offered by supermarkets. To their gratification, customers in Florence observed that "more and more, the client is becoming a precious and contended creature; every store is trying to secure his or her loyalty, offering discounts and favors and proffering smiles."[93]

True, the competition was unequal: the supermarket set the pace of innovation. It established the new alliance of consumer and big capital. Nevertheless, the solidarity that allied the interests of the householder to those of the small shopkeeper could still be as persuasive as the personable if impersonal economy of the supermarket. In Braudel's imperturbable words, "The preserve of the few, capitalism is unthinkable without society's active complicity."[94] In the middle term, the rupture produced by IBEC fostered complicity on behalf of small commerce even as the capitalism of the supermarket was assimilated into local exchanges. With the passage of time, the calculations that made the supermarket more and more central to local shopping were assimilated into material life. Small stores introduced self-service, the freezer units with the frozen fish and peas, and the metal shelves with the canned pineapple, kernel corn, asparagus, and salmon. And they began to fill the shelves with standard brands, the products of General Foods, Procter & Gamble, Nestlé, Campbell's, and Heinz Foods. Their owners also put on display the services they could offer: the family touch, the element of local color, and perhaps advice, delivery, and credit. Meanwhile the supermarket itself was assimilated into the wider perimeter of the neighborhood as new housing was built up around it, advertising and habit made it a familiar presence, and the acquisition of a small-cylinder car or scooter made it accessible. The next generation of shoppers would see it as a local fixture, operating amid the small shops and open-air market, its relative weight and its meanings in their customs very much changed, the children of neighborhood shopkeepers employed in its operations, its exogenous origins forgotten.

This popular inclination to "go slow" was not out of line with the outlooks of planners, state officials, and the modernizing small and middle-size retailers of the city centers. The more contact European observers had with the furious pace of change in U.S. retailing, the more they reflected on the devastation that accompanied it. Nowhere was this more striking than in American cities of the 1960s, and nowhere more catastrophic than in the capital of modern retailing, namely Dayton, Ohio. By the early 1960s, European visitors found a shell of a city. National Cash Register Company still had its headquarters there, though most of its employees had relocated to the suburbs. Trains had used to arrive thirty times a day; now they arrived scarcely a half-dozen times. The venerable Woolworth's had closed down, and Main Street had become a parking lot for churchgoers and customers at the desolate-looking Horn and Hardart's self-service restaurant. American retailing's new lesson was that the commerce of town centers needed protection lest the European urban landscape suffer the fate of the American city. It was a lesson that Europeans, recalling that commerce was a social institution, were in a good position to grasp, if not to improve upon.

CHAPTER 9

A Model Mrs. Consumer

How Mass Commodities Settled into Hearth and Home

*Give us cars, refrigerators, and above all, give us peace,
and you will see that European housewives will act just like
American ones!*

> Dr. Elsa Gasser,
> economic adviser to Migros, 1950

*A missile in the garden is better than a Russian in the
kitchen.*

> Slogan,
> Dutch pro–cruise missile movement,
> early 1980s

Around 1968 a housewife living at Sarcelles, the largest and loneliest
of the housing tracts that had proliferated around Paris since the mid-
1950s, would have wondered at hearing her door buzzer ring in the late
morning. It was unlikely that the caller was a neighbor, much less a relative. So few people were around during the day. More likely it was a
salesman. But if it had been March or April 1968, it might very well have
been a door-to-door canvasser. For March was "D-Day" for the start of
the biggest marketing launch that had ever occurred on French soil. Over
the next several weeks, every French domicile in every town with more
than 2,000 residents was to be visited by the hundreds of women hired by
Procter & Gamble, the leading U.S. household products manufacturer
and the world's biggest corporate advertiser. Their job was to promote
Ariel, "the world's first washing machine detergent with enzymes."[1]

Leaving off her tasks, her toddler underfoot, Madame Martin, as she was known to marketing experts, would have smoothed her housecoat, turned down the radio, and given her hair a fluff before she half-opened the door; whereupon a marketing *pas de deux* rehearsed a million times would have taken place. With a show of respect for the household's privacy, the canvassers would have stood back a pace or so from the threshold. But mindful too that their supervisors were waiting at the curb and scores of interviews had to be done to fulfill their daily quota, they would have rushed their questions and dashed down the answers. Did Madame have a washing machine? If so, what make? And what was her preferred soap brand? Her favorite radio program? Someone was soliciting her opinion, and that someone was also offering a suspiciously generous sample of detergent, 600 grams! It was nicely boxed too, the brisk red letters *A-R-I-E-L* set against fresh green, the logo a blue sprite whirling in whiteness like an atom in orbit. Madame Martin was nobody's fool. She'd try it, of course, though the one she used worked well enough. Anyway, nothing would convince her that detergents weren't all basically the same, except maybe in their price, packaging, color, and scent.

This episode or some similar event would have occurred countless times in the sixteen years from 1952, when Unilever launched Omo, to 1968, when western Europe experienced its last, costliest, and most prolonged mobilization of marketing resources before public television opened its channels to advertising spots at the turn of the decade. The broad context was the "laundry revolution," a term coined by some journalist, fusing the hyperbolic lingo of American-style marketing with one of the key words of Western politics to capture the tumultuous upheavals in material life of those years. Brought to bear on the age-old problem of doing the family wash, this bombast usefully underscored the myriad of small-magnitude changes in the technology of housework, in the conduct of household routines, and in the prestige of the housewife—that, together with other well-documented trends such as the rapidly growing numbers of women employed outside the home, new shopping routines introduced by self-service shops and supermarkets, and more equal treatment of women in society, dealt the death blow to the household organization behind the old regime of consumption.

Though concealed from systematic public comparisons in its layout, furnishings, management, and the meaning it had to its dwellers, no institution so much as the household distilled the profound differences of lifestyle and family fortune that had characterized respectively bourgeoisie and working-class domiciles and set apart rural abodes as especially bleak. The working-class household had appeared relatively open, with its vast back courtyards, garrulous doorway chatter, neighborly barter of goods and services, and frequent comings and goings. But there had been no home there in the modern consumer sense, its development having been stunted by the precariousness of the lease, the miserable state of the dwelling, the occupants' poverty, and the withered expectations about what paper doilies, filigree curtains, a shabby rug, or fake flowers could possibly do to improve their surroundings. By contrast, the bourgeois household had been turned inward, its largely self-sufficient operations staffed by servants under the mistress of the household, the decorum of its conduct as fixed as its furnishings by the conformist conventions of the bourgeois lifestyle. But even the bourgeois household had been a backwater with respect to labor-saving equipment. This fact had nowhere been more visible than in the dank quarters, windowless backrooms, basement washtubs, sludgy hearths, and back landings and stairways opening onto squalid courtyards that, in lieu of a true kitchen area, were commonly the places improvised with the use of badly paid servants to prepare meals, wash up, launder, and clean.

The modern consumer household, by contrast, as it emerged in post–World War II Europe, was inspired by a common, public, indeed Western-wide standard of equipment. Against the class-divided, regionally segmented, highly localized living styles of the past, government, business, tastemakers, and consumers converged in envisaging a mass-middle standard of household consumption. This common standard was favored on economic grounds to accommodate the large-scale output of mass-production industries. It was favored for social purposes as cross-class norms of living provided a stronger sense of national cohesion. It was favored on grounds of gender politics to demonstrate that women's work in the home was treated on a par with other kinds of labor in society. And it was favored for cultural ends as well. For common standards of equipment communicated far and wide the comforting notion that in certain basic essentials like the need for indoor plumbing, warmth, stove-cooked food, refrigeration, and radio and television, people's lives were basically similar, no matter how distant they were socially or geographically.

The new household's center of operations was the kitchen. Here the battery of machinery was located—the set defined from the mid-1950s and 1960s as the stove, refrigerator, washing machine, vacuum cleaner, together with assorted automatic mixers, blenders, and coffee grinders; from the 1970s it included dishwashers and television sets as well; and from the 1980s microwave ovens, toasters, and electric steamers and fryers. The kitchen's manager was the modern homemaker, a Mrs. Consumer who worked solo or with her "electric servants." Her most important task was to balance the competing needs weighing on the family budget as it was buffeted by the cascades of innovative goods pouring onto the market.[2]

The laundry revolution could be conceived as having three dimensions. First, it involved a remarkable change in the technologies applied to cleaning clothes. Doing the laundry had previously been the most tedious, time-consuming, and unhealthy of household tasks. A *corvée*, the French called it, recalling the levies of labor imposed on peasants under the *ancien régime* to haul quarry stones, build fortifications, and fill in the muddy ruts along the king's highways. It involved hand-washing woolens, lace collars and cuffs, and other delicate garments while household linens and work clothes were steeped in tubs of boiling water, percolated through a chemical-laden rinse, rubbed against a washboard, then rinsed and squeezed through a hand-wringer before being hung out on lines to dry, gathered up, repaired and mended, and then given a last pass with a hefty stove-heated iron. The laundry revolution brought first semi- then fully automatic machines that heated the water to the appropriate temperature and leached out dirt with detergents. The tumbler mechanism wrung out the excess water, dryers eliminated the clothesline, and thermostats regulated the heat on electric irons.[3]

More important, the laundry revolution gave new significance to women's labor in the household by showing that it could be substituted by machinery and therefore valued in new ways. With the time once spent on laundry, women could earn cash in the workplace. They could improve other household services like keeping the house tidier, spending more time on children's homework, or staying on top of paperwork and visits to obtain health, educational, social security, and other benefits from public services. True, the homemaker was thereby subject to more and more claims on her time and skills: she needed to select, manage, and, if necessary, repair, the equipment that replaced her labor, respond to new standards of household management, and, if she had any free time to speak of, learn how to occupy it in useful pursuits.[4] In the process she acquired qualities that were widely regarded as indispensable to a well-functioning consumer economy such as good taste, expertise, and foresight, in addition to the ability to measure her family's well-being with respect to her neighbors', her community's, and national conventions of consumption. The purported lack of these qualities earlier in the century was often cited as a good reason to curb lower-class consumption.

The well-managed consumer household not only stimulated industrial demand, turned warmaking technologies to everyday applications, and reinforced family togetherness, but also gave a cozy domestic texture to western Europe's newly cherished culture of security. Security thus came to be valued on multiple levels: on the individual family front in the form of that decent standard of living that diminished the precariousness of daily existence; at the national level in the shape of the welfare state, which lessened the risks of living in industrial society; and in the international arena in the solid ties of the Atlantic Community, which would prevent the recurrence of warmaking on European territory. So the assimilation of the catastrophic language of militarism and revolution—of launches, D-Days, mobilizations, and battles for market shares—into the banal lexicon of transatlantic consumer culture gave semantic proof that the bad past was exorcized. What's more, as the well-managed consumer household was consolidated as a common acquisition, it promised to safeguard families against the reckless standoffs of the superpowers and the incessant novelty identified with America's restless commercialism.[5]

The Detergent Wars

The so-called detergent wars expressed the marketing profession's own awe at the mammoth resources spent by giant multinational corporations as they battled over the consumer market for detergents. Paic, the first detergent marketed in France, in 1948, had "the effect of a bombshell."[6] However, the real "war" was first joined in the early 1950s, when the world's three leading detergent producers, Unilever, Procter & Gamble, and Colgate-Palmolive, unleashed their competition to expand and divide the booming market for detergents on the European continent. The opening sally came from Unilever, which in 1949, after adding bleaching agents to Persil, the venerable soap powder first developed by the German company Henkel in 1907, relaunched it as the first all-purpose cleaning powder under the slogan "Persil washes whiter than white." In October 1952 the giant British-Dutch conglomerate was again the pioneer in launching the first synthetic all-purpose detergent, Omo, spending a billion old francs on the marketing campaign, only by the end of 1953 to have to contend with Tide, the product of its major competitor, the century-and-a-quarter-old U.S. firm Procter & Gamble. Famous since

1879 for having invented Ivory, "the soap that floats," the company prided itself on attacking where the competition was already searing hot. Under the slogan *"Toujours en avance d'un progrès,"* Procter & Gamble constructed a vast glass-and-steel research center at Amiens while installing its main production facilities at Marseilles, the soap capital of the continent. From there it allied itself with the distinguished old firm Fournier-Ferrier, manufacturer of Le Chat and Catox laundry soaps, to distribute Tide nationally.[7]

In 1956 French stores carried only four nationally advertised brands of synthetic laundry soap; by 1970, no less than thirty. Consumers could choose liquids, powders, or flakes; boxes, sacks, plastic bottles, or cardboard drums. If they wanted nonsudsing soap for their washing machines, they could choose Skip or Dash or the low-sudsing Dinamo, Persil, Skip, Supercroix, X-tra; if they wanted all-purpose regular powders, there were Comète, Dixan, Omo, Bonus, and Tide. If they switched to the "biological generation" using enzymes, first there was Ariel, then Axion, Crio, Genie, Lava, Bio-Ajax, Omo Scientific, and Super Tide. For "safe-for-the-hands" lingerie and delicate fabrics, they could buy Paic, Coral, Mir, and Dato. Then there was the proliferation of additives such as Calgon to eliminate calcareous deposits, the perfumed softeners Soupline, Lenor, Comfort, and Silan, not to mention two scores of nationally branded household cleansers like Mr. Propre (Mr. Clean) and Spic, the detergent for car surfaces. With sales rates growing at 4–5 percent per year, by the turn of the 1970s detergents had become as indispensable to household operations as gasoline was to cars. Like the market for petroleum products generally, the market for detergents was highly concentrated. The leading three manufacturers controlled about 80 percent of the continental market; in France, 85 to 90 percent.[8]

Detergents are uncommonly useful commodities for reflecting upon larger processes, here nothing less than the decline and rise of great powers. Surface surfactants, the two-part molecules that pull greasy dirt from clothing and suspend it until it can be rinsed away, were first developed during periods of warmaking under the auspices of German and Anglo-American military-oriented research laboratories. But their first commercialization occurred in peacetime in the hands of Anglo-American consumer-oriented oligopolies. Blockaded by the Entente in World War I, German chemical industries efficiently set to developing petroleum-based soaps in an effort to find substitutes for cleansers based on natural oils and fats. Chronic shortages of animal fats and the lack of peanut, palm, vegetable, and other oils from colonies that were available to countries with overseas empires encouraged further research for ersatz products under the Third Reich. But because the costs to produce detergent for commercial use were still high relative to the cost for old-fashioned soaps, before World War II, except for Dreft and Drene, which Procter & Gamble marketed in 1930s America, the main use for the substance was as a wetting agent in the textile industry to prepare fabrics for dyeing.

World War II renewed the competition among the belligerents, with German laboratories trying to synthesize hydrocarbon derivatives to launder army uniforms while the United States and Great Britain searched for washing agents suitable for their navies to use in cold, salty seawater. The war over, the great corporations cornered the patents for peacetime use—for laundry use, but also as household cleansers and for personal hygiene. The match was pure marketing genius: they had easy access to the basic raw material, petroleum, and plenty of capital to spend on research and design; they already had a century of experience promoting soaps, a fine art calling for carefully designed packaging, aggressive distribution, and massive advertising. Moreover, the need for the substance, if new standards of equipment and hygiene prevailed, was practically limitless.[9]

Thus began a rapid succession of innovations that turned synthetic cleansers into ever more versatile and widely used household washing agents. Technologically, they were vastly superior to fat-based soaps. They reduced scrubbing and wringing by leaching out dirt; they whitened and softened fabrics even in cold water; and they left no scummy residues. As the big three battled over market shares, pressed by competition from handfuls of smaller producers like Henkel in West Germany and Mira Lanza and Scala in Italy, prices plummeted and washing products occupied a more and more conspicuous space on the shelves of supermarkets, self-service outlets, and neighborhood shops. Within two decades they had largely replaced the ashes, soap, and caustic substances that women had used for centuries to launder and clean.

Like any product sold on the basis of brand recognition, marketing was indispensable and carried out ferociously, scientifically, and at humongous costs. By the 1960s, Unilever, Procter & Gamble, and Colgate-Palmolive spent more on press advertising than any other company in France except Renault, the nationalized automobile works, whose luscious plum of an account Marcel Bleustein-Blanchet had plucked for Publicis in 1946.[10] By the end of the 1960s the big three had at one time

The detergent line, French supermarket, circa 1970. Courtesy of
the Chambre de Commerce et d'Industrie de Paris.

or another employed every one of the twenty-two techniques known to
contemporary salesmanship, from the two-for-ones and giveaways to
contests with much-coveted prizes, like the trip for two to the American Far West sponsored by Omo in 1964. For advertising counsel, they
turned to the firms experienced in American-style promotions—J. Walter
Thompson and Publicis first and foremost, then Elvinger, Dupuy-
Compton, and, for Lever, its house agency, Lintas. They paid handsomely
for the consumer polls and panels supplied by Gallup, Nielsen,
STAFECO, IFOP, SECODIP, CECODIS, and other recently formed public opinion surveyors. They filled the airwaves with advertising spots,
broadcasting from off-territory transmitters, notably Radio Valleys of
Andorra, Europa 1, Radio Luxembourg, and Radio Monaco. They fat-
tened the proliferating numbers of women's magazines with full-page
color ads, spelling out their slogans and setting new standards for attractive layout. Their display lines crowded out the foodstuffs and sundries
on the shelves of mom-and-pop stores. In supermarkets, they occupied an
entire aisle, for detergents were the perfect loss leader, meaning that man-

agement bought in bulk and marked down its price near to cost so that the consumer would buy it in large quantities; whatever was lost in low profit margins would be recouped as she purchased canned goods, ice cream, and other products with high markups.

With every product launched, the multinational corporations stepped over the thresholds of more and more European households. After public television was licensed to show publicity spots, an event that occurred in France in June 1969, they made themselves right at home. By then detergents had became the most meaningful symbol of the new regime of consumption. For French cultural critic Roland Barthes, detergents exemplified the process by which trends in consumer society that are not at all natural are regarded as "it goes without saying," such that nobody recalls whence they came into being.[11] So advertising established that detergents produced different degrees of whiteness, and on that basis the housewife could gauge her laundry's hygiene and cleanliness and others her housewifely zeal. It was grist for Barthes's mill that in turn-of-the-1950s West Germany, *Persilscheine,* literally "Persil-clean," had became the colloquial expression for the certificate of good conduct that citizens obtained in the course of de-Nazification procedures. If investigators turned up any dirt, the family doctor or minister could vouch for your clear conscience: "Persil makes it like new"; "Persil washes even Nazi brown shirts white."

Brought face to face with an object that was so obviously insubstantial yet so clearly indispensable to household routines, radical social critics were slowly clued into the inadequacy of their grasp of the mundane practices of consumer societies—and of the growing divide that split women, whose day-to-day task was to manage this new world of gadgetry, from men, whose world-historic role was to design grand progressive utopias. Observing the social effects of detergents, the philosopher Jean Baudrillard was at first convinced that the Marxist dialectic persuasively explained that, at the outset, a new consumer product created a wide if inauthentic sense of community among its users, only to turn them inward into an atomized, intensely private, depoliticized world. Later, having observed that mass marketing completely saturated public space with its own self-referential language, he abandoned Marxism as inadequate to decipher the signs and signifiers of this new "hyperreality."[12] For the maverick Marxist, the philosopher Henri Lefebvre, detergent revealed that scientific materialism had yet to evolve any systematic project for studying the practices of everyday life. From the late

1940s on, he had intuited the need for such a study. But nothing clicked until "a woman to whom—detail without much importance—I was married, happened in [my] presence, apropos of some detergent, to utter these simple words: 'This is a really excellent product.' With an authoritative tone." In their "triviality" these words crystallized for him the concept and embarked him on his "critique of daily life." By the early 1960s his university lectures were dedicated to developing the notion of the "bureaucratic society of managed consumption," which, it has to be said, never addressed the gender dimensions of the practices of everyday life, or reflected on the oddity that whether or not she was his wife, it was a woman who uttered that seminal triviality. By the end of the 1960s his students, like the rest of their cohort, spoke with familiarity and scorn of the diffuse powers of the "consumer society." In so doing, they demonstrated a keen grasp of its semiotics, but indifference to its complicated historical genesis, much less the agency of a new historical protagonist, the housewife-as-consumer.[13]

By the end of the 1960s detergent could be a metaphor for radical change as well as for reactionary coverup. "Self-transformation washes whiter than revolution," read one memorable graffito scrawled on the walls of Paris's Latin Quarter during the May 1968 student rebellions. It is a remarkable slogan, insofar as it attests that the notions of individual makeover proliferating out of the commercial-public sphere were now refashioning models of collective political action. It also testifies unwittingly to a dispiriting paradox: namely that at the very moment, spring 1968, when hundreds of thousands of young activists were on strike, mounting the barricades, demonstrating, and occupying factories to protest the Vietnam War, to revolt against government, school, military, church, and other authoritarian bureaucracies, and to condemn the artifice, waste, and alienation of consumer society, a whole other and far vaster mobilization was going on under the slogans of multinational corporations; its main constituency millions of householders, its ramparts the home, its utopia neatly folded piles of fresh-smelling laundry.

The Ambassadors

By their lead in marketing detergents, not to mention any number of other innovative products for household use—from fly spray with DDT, teflon pans, aluminum foil, and linoleum to state-of-the-art refrigerators and air conditioners—American corporate capitalism played an indis-

pensable role in the creation of a cross-Atlantic consumer household—
succeeding, finally, at what it had long endeavored to do, to step over the
family threshold into the privacy of daily life. Over several decades,
American housewares had made a huge impression at France's annual Salon of Household Arts. Started in 1923 as the Salon of Household Appliances, the exposition displayed all the ingenuity of its founder, Jules-
Louis Breton, a chemist-inventor, France's undersecretary of state for inventions during World War I, and the founder and director of the National Research and Inventions Ministry in its wake. A dedicated socialist
with an anarchist tinge who practiced what he preached, Breton, a father
of five, wanting to end slavery in the home, had his own home furnished
with all the modern conveniences and then wanted to convert the French
nation to the same vision. Three of his sons joined him in the project. The
three-week-long exposition at the Grand Palais, falling in the slow period from late January to mid-February and accompanied by voluminous
press coverage, department-store displays, home economics conferences
and publications, focused national attention on the progress of home
equipment. The last year before the war, 608,000 people attended. Reopening in 1948, the Salon reached its acme in the mid-1950s with 1.4
million visitors. After it was moved from central Paris to the outskirts
at La Défense in 1961, the Salon became more and more a place for manufacturers' sales representatives and dealers, and from the mid-1970s it
reduced the number of days it was open for individual consumers. By
the early 1980s the Salon became superfluous as it became clear that in
the domain of household technology widespread advertising had rendered most commodities familiar, discount distribution networks made
the goods more accessible and cheaper, and the public's craving for the
basic equipment had been saturated. In 1983 the venerable institution
was unceremoniously closed and its staff dismissed.[14]

From the first year, American manufacturers were there, showing a
score or so of chrome-and-white-enamel refrigerators and washing machines. Thereafter they never missed the event. In 1924 they sponsored
fourteen stands, the most of any foreign country, and in 1925, the "year
of the washing machine," they dominated the show. The first overall impression of the United States' preeminence in household convenience was
imparted in 1926, thanks to "a most unusual ambassador." This was a
ten-room, two-story, shingled house furnished in the colonial style and
equipped in "the last word in modern comfort and labor saving devices,"
meaning running hot and cold water, gas and electric service, four bath-

rooms (and five toilets), and "a place for every labor-saving and comfort-providing device used in American homes throughout the country." Naturally, that contention was greatly exaggerated. Most American women still did their household chores by hand. Even so, the consortium of thirty manufacturers who first assembled the house in Brooklyn showed characteristic promotional verve in conceiving of such a display, vaunting its value at $10,000 (2.5 million francs), and shipping it over in 375 crates. With practically every element that would define what the "modern" house was over the next century (except air-conditioning, microwave ovens, home entertainment areas, and Internet connections), it promised to provoke another French Revolution, said Albert Broisat, the general commissioner of the Salon's American section, this one a "revolution in the household." "The French housewife who still does her washing, ironing, cooking, sewing, scrubbing and cleaning with her own hands (and for whom electricity is used almost exclusively for lights) has much to learn from the American woman who uses little electrical servants for such work."[15]

In successive fairs, visitors would equally "rub their eyes in amazement" at the run-of-the-mill gadgetry—can openers, electric eggbeaters, potato peelers, but especially the imposing white-enamel refrigerators, stoves, and washing machines. The last set the pace in terms of automation: as early as 1926, Maytag presented an electrically powered machine; in 1948 Whirlpool exhibited its fully automatic "Jeep"; in 1949 Bendix dominated the show. As its giant self-operating machines hit the spin cycle, flinging the multicolored clothes around in demonic whirls, passersby seated themselves in the chairs lined up three aisles deep, gasping and giggling at the sight as if it were a Charlie Chaplin gag. Whether such machines were appropriate for French consumers was another issue: aside from brusquely agitating the wash instead of alternating rotation with a leisurely soak, they could cost a hefty 200,000 francs, which at very least called for installment payments. And these were not yet customary. They also called for ample water pressure, heavy-duty electrical wiring, good drainage systems, and homes large enough to accommodate their bulk. Even so, for middle-class women a few turns of the dial and a press on the button offered the appealing prospect of ending considerable drudgery, and for the men who saw the show, the logical, solid machinery satisfied the dream of automated utopias of work-free gadgetry.[16]

Yet to speak of Europe's clothes-washing revolution or any other change in the practices of daily life as largely the effect of a new technology or the marketing of new brands, whether these were of American or some other provenance, would be deeply misleading. Nothing is more fixed in habit and place than a household. Changes in clothes washing, like changes in other habits of private life—eating, childrearing, sexual conduct, leisure pursuits—are finely sieved through the mesh of national, local, and especially family traditions, accumulate at a slow, uneven pace, and are shaped in unpredictable ways by multiple, diverse, and subtly circuitous pressures.[17] That said, cleanliness, comfort, privacy, and communication with the world were indispensable to living a modern life, and the housewife-consumer promised to show the way. The invention of a European equivalent to Mrs. American Consumer underscored the fact that a high standard of living meant new norms of household equipment, efficiency, and comfort. It reaffirmed that the "proper study of markets is woman." And it brought home the fact that the military security afforded by the Pax Americana was bound up with security in the most intimate sense, meaning that European householders could calculate their fortunes and futures free from the destitution and war that so many of them had experienced over the previous half-century.

Following the circuitous ways by which American models of household and housewifery settled into European homes calls for some brief considerations of the gender dimensions of America's global mission and the characteristic division of labor between men and women on which it rested in the United States.

In the tradition of Woodrow Wilson's empathetic imperialism, it was men who by their vocations as diplomat-salesmen spread America's vision of prosperity and freedom. That American men proved such convincing ambassadors of goodwill resulted from the robust good order of their homeland, which in turn was entirely due to the solidity of the American home and the exceptional social capacities of the Republic's women. Emancipated, well educated, and habituated to managing their families in accordance with the standards afforded by a decent family income, they had oriented national norms of consumption to spend less on food and clothing and more on household equipment, education, health, and leisure pursuits.

In some measure, this happy sexual division of labor shaped all the social inventions of mass consumer culture. Accordingly, the Rotary clubs had incorporated female touches like the ethos of community service and the friendly manners that facilitated face-to-face diplomacy to consolidate their global networks. The sciences of merchandising, advertising, and marketing first practiced their appeals by trying to address the hardest-to-know customers, namely women. The Hollywood system turned around the charisma of female stars. The end result was that, first by recognizing the consumer as foremost social actor, then by identifying consumers as female, the Market Empire established a special alliance with women abroad. The harbinger of "life-style feminism," it spoke to young women in particular of relief from household drudgery, romantic love, expressive goods like nylon stockings, makeup, and blue jeans, and the technologies of birth control.[18]

Yet as much as American consumer culture acted as a force of disruption, it also offered a means to contain disruption. Hence the propaganda that accompanied the Marshall Plan underscored not only the industrial productivity measures that ensured a high standard of living for "Joe Smith," but also the benefits accruing from anchoring the household to his mate, the typical American housewife. Mrs. Consumer was a distinctly middle-class figure, with her tall, lean body, stylishly upswept hair, and light self-mockery about her housewifely condition. Europeans were familiar with her from travel, as well as from the visits of American businessmen and diplomats, who invariably, as at Rotary congresses, were accompanied by the wife-consort, a second-order ambassador, whose competence, tranquil demeanor, and alacrity at settling in and getting a handle on local minutiae to shop and take care of other family necessities was held to outshine her culturally bound, ham-handed, slow-moving spouse's. That she accompanied him nonetheless offered prima facie evidence of his power. They also knew her from television: in the figure of the dizzy but down-to-earth, very funny Lucille Ball of *I Love Lucy,* the primly self-confident Betty Furness, hostess of *The Westinghouse Hour,* and the tediously long-suffering Harriet Nelson of *Ozzie and Harriet,* anchors of family television viewing in 1950s America and widely rebroadcast on European channels.

From the point of view of western European men, this uxorious coupledom might have passed without comment had not American consumer culture sparked sexual panic from the very moment it trespassed European frontiers in the 1920s. Unlike the female figures of the oriental Other, who could be held at a decent distance, the female creatures of the New World, with their "puritan minds and pagan bodies," were physically extruded into the European imaginary space. Forty-five years before Federico Fellini's episode of *Boccaccio '70* (1962) had the archetypal "American" star Anita Ekberg lean down from a giant roadsign, her magnificent bosom spilling out of her dress as she exhorted Italians to "drink more milk," sophisticated Parisian men like Philippe Soupault had been smitten by Pearl White's "ferocious smile" or seduced, like the novelist Louis-Ferdinand Céline in *Journey to the End of Night* (1932), by the American Expeditionary Force nurses' swinging gait. In the mid-1920s the synchronized kick-lines of the Tiller Girls had mesmerized Berlin cabaretgoers while inspiring reflection on what that observant social critic, Siegfried Kracauer, called the "mass ornament," the kaleido-scope pattern of gorgeously gyrating women, expressing both the strait-jacket of technology and the irrepressible vivacity of female humanity.[19] With her feral energy, feigned submissiveness, and technical virtuosity, at once female, exotic, and American, Josephine Baker, the black jazz singer, demonstrated the impossibility of quarantining this sexual danger.[20] In 1946 the cinema goddess Rita Hayworth, star of the film *Gilda,* had her poster plastered on dilapidated billboards throughout western Europe; the story of the fraud, betrayal, and corruption among expatriate Americans was so cynical, and Gilda's own vixen character so feckless, that it was banned by the Catholic censorship system, the same that Pius XI had modeled on the Hollywood production code devised by the League of Decency and the Hays Office.

Whether in the form of the priapic legs of precision-line dancers, the outsize posters of precocious Hollywood stars, or the curiously dressed woman-tourist wandering about solo, the American female figured as a symptom of the disruption that was occurring everywhere as the "new women" abandoned the privacy of the home in quest of freedom, un-leashing an innate female proclivity for change.[21] If anything, American female eros had become more and more disquieting as manly power could no longer be regained on the parade grounds of militarism. For Denis de Rougement, one of Switzerland's handful of renowned writers, the defeat of gallant love was of a piece with Europe's catastrophic de-cline. Coming home after seven years in the United States, his return painfully delayed by World War II, de Rougement regretted that in pres-ent times the cult of love-as-passion had given way to love-as-romance, aristocratic sensibility to vulgar sensationalism, and the grand epics of troubadours, poets, and playwrights to Hollywood's scripted myths. So courtly love had given way to "Celtic corporeality." And the tragedy of passion, consummated by Tristan and Isolde in death's embrace, had been forsaken for the gushy feelings of shopgirls and gangly adolescents who flirted, petted, and dreamed that their starry-eyed infatuations would be requited in the bonds of marriage. Marriage itself, a contract, signed, sealed, and sanctified by settling down in a well-equipped household, marked the death of passion. Europeans had learned to live with this disillusionment by means of little subterfuges and with a refined sense of sin and forgiveness. Americans sought transparent solutions. The most common one was to divorce, after which individuals once more set out to rediscover passion in the perfect love object, remarry, and reestablish a new existence anchored in their material investment in home and household.[22]

That the sexual bargain which sustained the family unit offered a key to understanding the relations between the sexes in the United States—and, by extension, some insight into the character of American coupledom, market culture, and the sexual dangers that awaited Europe from Americanization—had long been the subject of comment. With his usual perspicacity Alexis de Tocqueville had incisively addressed the subject in the 1840s. American girls—and young people generally—benefited from the free ways that came from the constant overturning of customs; there was always a new youth culture in the making. But this same turmoil forced them, as they became wives and mothers, to focus all their forces on the family to safeguard its fortunes. As women and men joined themselves in marriage to secure their future, they negotiated each other's functions with contractlike precision as if in a business partnership, each bringing equal but different capital to the family enterprise. The resulting bond subjected the married woman to unusual constraints yet conferred on her a status such that "nowhere does she enjoy a higher station." In this "superiority of their women," Tocqueville concluded, lay "the chief cause of the extraordinary prosperity and growing power of this nation."[23]

Although it is unlikely that they had read Tocqueville on this or any other point, a wide range of European male reformers—and women feminists as well—saw in the American household an ally on behalf of a well-ordered consumer society. So on the one hand, the United States was viewed as the main source of the explosion of female emancipation, gross displays of sexuality, and crass romance, while on the other it was regarded as the model of a new domesticity resting on smaller families, greater distance from relatives, constantly updated technical knowledge, significant equipment whether the household was rented or owned, and the expert Mrs. Consumer as its mainstay.

The open-armed welcome extended to the European woman-as-consumer by the speakers at the First Congress on Food Distribution at Paris in 1950 sounded remarkably fresh compared to the tired nods of appreciation for the rational, efficient, patriotic housewife common in prewar rhetoric. Women, the assembly agreed, represented the interests of the family in the marketplace, and smart business had to respond to their demands in order to be profitable. Mary Bailey MacLane, director of economic research for Swift and Company and one of three or four American woman who spoke at the meeting, was categorical that no self-respecting food store management "speaks to a male clientele . . . The housewife, the mistress of the household, is sovereign in alimentary democracy, which she exercises directly or delegates to salaried help"; "the man only has an advisory role."[24]

That MacLane would make such a provocative assertion surely reflected not just her high position at the world's second-largest canned-meat corporation as well as her conviction that Europe was very backward, but also the belief, sacrosanct to marketers ever since the Model T came off the line, that the homemaker was indispensable to managing the high-wage, mass-production economy. Indirectly, Henry Ford had recognized her function by pressuring his five-dollar men to turn their paychecks straight over to their wives, who, in full command of the budget, would know how to spend less on food, shelter, and clothes, and more on consumer durables, health, and leisure-time pursuits. Dissatisfied American women needed no lessons from Henry Ford on this point. In 1913, the year before the five-dollar day was adopted, author Christine Frederick published *The New House Keeping*. There she set out the latest dogma in the Fordist credo, namely that the efficiency "methods which were applicable to organized industries, like shoe manufacturing or iron foundries, [could be] applied to my group of very unorganized industries—the home." True, movements to relieve household drudgery and improve hygiene had been around for at least a half-century, favored by leading nineteenth-century feminists, notably Catherine Beecher and her sister Harriet Beecher Stowe. But the popularity of industrial efficiency as a panacea for all social ills, combined with the deluge of new equipment, renewed their impetus. So did the growing frustration of emancipated women, who, though barraged with advice on how to be dutiful consumers, were excluded from the very professions that made marketing to women their business. After being shunted into the dreary routines of suburban housewifery, Christine Frederick discovered a new vocation in the "gospel of home economics" and acquired national celebrity and eventually fame abroad as spokeswoman on behalf of the "new international face of home efficiency."[25]

The less-well-known but more novel aspect of her project, developed in the 1920s, was to see women as protagonists of the "free-spending, creative wasting policy" that was largely responsible for raising wages and standards of living. The publication of Frederick's *Selling Mrs. Consumer* in 1929 was targeted first and foremost at the advertising industry. Unlike the tradition-bound American man, the American woman embodied a "volatile" "new race-mixture without fixed social roots or tradition in a new and democratic country." The American woman was a visionary who looked to "a larger end, beyond the draining of the last bit of utility," unlike "merchandise hoarders, clinging as do the Europeans to tradition and the antiquated." Mrs. Consumer's free-spending, uninhibited, perhaps unpredictable behavior needed no apologies. That is what gave merchandisers a livelihood. Shrewd as well as suggestible, she expected from advertising the "intelligent invitation to compare values." She also expected "seduction, wiles, and fun."[26]

By the 1920s it was a settled matter for American marketing experts that the family unit was central to mass consumption, that women were the busy bees of innovative family oriented shopping, and that family love was a ubiquitous and fundamental bond that salesmanship could exploit for profit. Expose the family's needs, get the message through to the woman of the household, and even the most physically distant and ideologically intractable customers could be touched. "In all this turmoil, what human emotions remain?" That question summed up advertising copywriter Helen Lansdowne Resor's curiosity about the state of the Soviet Union during the early 1930s. It was directed to the celebrated photographer Margaret Bourke-White, who had been invited to brief the J. Walter Thompson staff following her January 1933 visit to the land of Stalin in the throes of the Second Five-Year Plan, the purges, and agricultural collectivization. "I mean, what would we appeal to if we were advertising to them?" That was Lansdowne Resor's question. "There is still the small family, isn't there?"[27]

The "small family" really meant a place, whether an apartment or house, headed by a white, heterosexual couple with two or three dependent children living on the husband's income. Advertising catered to this image; so did government statistical inquiries and the home efficiency movements. Good management of the family held out the promise that the American Standard of Living would continue to improve not just because wages rose, credit abounded, and the relationship of wages to prices remained steady, but because American women were becoming more and more adept at converting wages into goods and services. The "art of spending" was notoriously "backward," as American economist Wesley Clair Mitchell famously formulated the problem in 1912. "Ignorance of qualities, uncertainty of taste, lack of accounting, and carelessness about prices—faults which would ruin a merchant—prevail in our housekeeping." And so it would be until "well-schooled citizens of a Money Economy" learned to "plan for their outgoes no less carefully than for their incomes."[28]

This, more or less, is what happened as the American public accepted a novel idea, namely that the sovereign consumer was not the *acquisitive individual,* as posited in classical political economy, but the *acquisitive household.* If advertisers targeted all the members of the household and each responded according to his or her whim, a possibility raised by the 1920s boom, all plans to steer buyers to equip themselves with standard sets of consumer durables would be dashed by waves of erratic purchasing behavior and founder on shoals of superfluous goods. To hold in check the irrationality of the consumer economy, the modern household had to be envisaged not as a single entity, observed *Middletown, U.S.A*'s author Robert Lynd, but as a "cluster" of related people. "Setting out together in the face of the exotic wonderland of productive capacity," they easily parted ways in the "adventure of buying a living."[29] Behind the apparent simplicity of the single household stood three interlocking institutions: first, there was the physical plant, which was constantly in the process of being upgraded as new standards of equipment and service were introduced; then the family, intended as the sum of its single members' needs and desires; and last, the plant manager, who took stock of individual needs and calculated overall spending according to the limits set by the budget. Given the pressing competition for shares of the family's income as new products came on the market, whoever was the manager needed a strong hand, precise knowledge about the plant, intimate familiarity with individual wants, and sensitivity to new consumer norms, as well as a proven capacity to control his own psychic impulses and quirks. There could be no doubt: the person in charge could "only be the woman head of the household."[30]

In effect, early twentieth-century American consumer society called for replacing *Homo oeconomicus* with the better-socialized "Economic Woman." Economic man had evolved far enough as an individual to calculate the marginal utility of, say, eggs, meaning the price he would pay if he only had one dollar and desired to purchase a half-dozen of them in preference to some other good. Economic woman, in the figure of Mrs. Consumer, personified what economists came to call the "family utility function": in making choices she behaved as if she knew the wants of her husband and children as well as she knew her own, plus those of her neighbor Mrs. Jones, who similarly represented her own family's wants.

Mrs. Consumer had a European counterpart in the figures of the French *ménagère*, the German *Hausfrau,* and the Italian *massaia.* Associations organized by women to represent women's interests spoke earnestly about her investment in the well-being of the family and nation. The state appealed to her in times of penury and wartime to scrimp, save, and sacrifice. Pioneers in the marketing professions spoke about her volubly but abstractly, endlessly repeating the commonplace that women were in charge of 80 percent of all spending. The left spoke of her as a free individual whose social awareness would expand as she entered the labor force and her household duties were collectivized or at very least mechanized. In reality, household reform was a halting project; just as there could be no precise equivalent to Fordism in the European factory, there could be no exact equivalent to Fordism in the household. In this context, household "rationalization," as it was called in Europe, promised to preserve a style of life that in its institutions, amenities, and ambitions reinforced the separation of bourgeois households from their working-class counterparts and perpetuated the traditional metier of the housewife, with its emphasis on parsimony, intense labor, and making do.[31]

The American model twinkled like a lodestar for European feminists, their attraction to it subsiding only as the Depression debunked ideas that home economy could substantially change family routines and rising nationalism discouraged feminists from traveling to international women's conferences. The French feminist Madeleine Cazamian expressed typical views for the times. After visiting various American homes where she observed the conduct of family members at mealtimes, she concluded that Americans had done away with "natural roles"; everybody gave a hand as if the family had contracted to divide up labor, assigning each member the most appropriate task—the mother to prepare and serve, the children to fetch while eating, the father and children to wash up. Domestic appliances promised to turn the daily drudgery of household work into a more efficient home management, regardless of whether the tasks were being done by the middle-class mistress of the house, the servant, or the double-burdened working-class woman. Reorganized according to American models, the backward private space of domesticity handled by women would no longer be partitioned off from the modern, public domain ruled by men. In sum, in one part of the world, America, women had been liberated from "the inveterate bonds of female self-abnegation."[32]

Whatever the hopes, the distance between the prospects for innovation in American and European households appeared as great as the difference in the life trajectories of Christine Frederick, the incandescent star of the American household efficiency movement, and Paulette Bernège, the no-nonsense doyenne of the continental European movement. Christine MacGaffey, born in Boston in 1883, the child of divorced parents, raised eccentrically, superbright, a graduate of Northwestern University, where her gifts as a communicator were already recognized, was the consummate middle-class striver. Setting aside her own career after she married J. George Frederick, then an up-and-coming employee of J. Walter Thompson, she bore four children before beginning a series of remarkable self-transformations that enabled her to reconcile the gospel of household efficiency with Hollywood optimism about women's freedom to love and live freely. So she founded the National Housewives' League and the Women's Advertising League. Adapting to the country's fast-paced commercialism in the 1920s, she became the bestselling author of manuals about home economics, sought-after contributor to leading women's magazines, well-paid consultant to the advertising industry, and earnest consumer advocate testifying before congressional committees.[33]

Bernège, a decade younger, the daughter of Lyonnais bourgeoisie from the same solid cloth as Edouard Herriot, was smart, educated, unmarried, and undaunted by the defeat of the women's suffrage movement. She was also a prodigious institution builder. Adviser to Jules-Louis Breton at the Salon, founder of her own limping movement, the League of Household Efficiency, she was also the sometimes grating pivot of a whole network of political reformers, teachers, engineers, architects, and doctors with similar concerns about the backward state of the French household. A prolific publicist as well, she founded and edited *Mon chez moi* (My Home), a magazine designed to promote the "practical and rational spirit," whose wellspring was American innovations, and which enjoyed a decent distribution after Hachette agreed to distribute it in newspaper kiosks and railroad stations. Her *De la méthode ménagère* (1926), which combined Christine Frederick's manic appeals to housewifely efficiency with a pixie-dust coating of Cartesian rationalism, went through forty editions, the last appearing in 1969. Priding herself as a theorist, with self-important nods to Xenophon, Descartes, and F. W. Taylor of time-and-motion studies fame, Bernège was also a finger-wagging authoritarian, her buzzwords "order, carefulness, and plan ahead" spoken with the same scolding tone as the high school home-economics instructor finger-wagging her students with the adage: "A place for everything and everything in its place." Faced with having to wash dishes 1,095 times a year, what was "best practice"? Women's freedom wasn't about consumer choice, certainly not about shopping around, and there was very little about installing labor-saving equipment; it was about efficient motion, concentration, scheduling, and elbow grease. Even the best-organized woman could plan on a thirteen-hour day, on the move from seven in the morning till eight in the evening. After that she could count on quality time with her family, doing accounts, reading, and thinking.[34]

At the optimistic zenith of the movement at the end of the 1920s, the two women met and became mutual admirers, if not friends. Bernège toured the United States, and Frederick, who spoke passable French, traveled around England and the continent, giving keynotes at international conferences and lecturing before various housewives' groups. Her talks were distinctly patriotic: Americans had solved the servant problem by simplifying housekeeping through labor-saving devices, and no self-respecting American woman would move into an old-fashioned house or apartment until it had been brought up to date. That Europe needed to catch up was all the more reason for her to be admiring of the great strides European women were making, especially under the influence of her "brilliant, self-sacrificing" friend Bernège and her "small but brave" movement.[35] The war over, during which Benèrge acquitted herself badly as a reactionary, return-to-the-soil nationalist obsessing about population growth, she was still regarded as the most obvious person to turn to for the woman's voice on consumer affairs. From her place of honor at the International Food Congress of 1950, she strongly commended the supermarket for its time-saving virtues. But she did so with the admonition that no French housewife should settle for the convenience of sliced cheese and white bread. They should follow her engaging suggestion to pressure entrepreneurs to choose even only 200 from among France's 6,000 regional dishes, standardize the ingredients, and package them for mass distribution.[36] That same year, Christine Frederick, now sixty-seven years old, having experienced all the booms and busts of the first half of the century, was making a new life for herself in Laguna Beach, California. Long estranged from her spouse and with no social security benefits, since all her work had been classified as freelance, she dedicated the next twenty years of her life to a new career, interior decorating, and to an absorbing new hobby, the study of the occult.[37]

Bringing the Kitchen out of the Closet

Like other social inventions whose adoption marked the passage from the old regime of bourgeois commerce to the new regime of mass consumption, the discovery of the "New Household" passed through the throes of postwar reconstruction. The war over, plans for recovery revealed a monstrous if well-known inequity. The housing that had sheltered the vast majority of Europeans for decades was squalidly backward, and the tools available to the housewife were relics of preindustrial times. Suddenly, the standard of living was no longer only about wages and increasing them to provide for the basic necessities. Now it embraced the norms of comfort identified with modernizing household plant and equipment. In 1948 IFOP, the newly founded polling service headed by Jean Stoetzel, the George Gallup of France, sounded a wake-up call by putting a scientific face on the shortcomings of contemporary French housing. As if hit by a bolt from the blue, the French elite was stunned to find that 96.2 percent of France's 39 million people lived in habitations lacking "modern elementary comfort," defined as meaning indoor toilets, running water, heat, electricity, and piped gas. That finding was compared with the only 23 percent of U.S. households in that condition. In Paris, 18 percent of households had a bathroom to wash up in, as distinct from the water closet common to French housing, compared with the 90 percent of households in large American cities that had both. That America now set the standard for all of Europe was taken for granted; that France didn't come even near to meeting that standard was "absolutely unworthy of a great nation which has contributed so largely to the scientific advance and technical progress of the modern era."[38]

So too others cited women's emancipation as cause to support the new standards. A sensitive conservative, Bertrand de Jouvenal, gave perhaps the most profound rationale for eliminating the backwardness of the household. It was not just that the heavy burden of household labor diminished the capacity of women to exercise their rights as citizens, rights that had finally been formally recognized when the 1946 constitution gave them the vote. In France as elsewhere in Europe, manual labor continued to be regarded as debasing and mechanization as the wellspring of civility. Consequently, so long as women were "subservient to physical tasks" they would not be regarded as men's equals. Even the worker, who was himself finally being liberated by machinery from degrading, filthy, exhausting tasks, would not "treat his wife as an equal so long as she remained a species of unskilled laborer." No real social equality could be achieved either so long as the "wives of some were provided with service by servants while the wives of others were nothing but servants." De Jouvenal concluded: "the greatest rapprochement possible in social conditions will be procured by the rapprochement of women's [domestic] occupations."[39]

Suddenly the rural world too discovered the new world of urban household comforts. For the sixty-five delegates from the General Confederation of Agriculture, whom the European Cooperation Agency sponsored to tour the United States in early 1952, the visit to a midwestern farm family was a "veritable revelation." Peasants themselves, members of the National Youth Circle, they faced the problem common in many rural areas of Europe, that the men could no longer find brides short of importing them from even more desolate regions such as Piedmontese hilltowns, southern Italian villages, or rural Spain and Portugal. With jobs opening up in urban areas, rural women gave vent to their revulsion at the servitude and filth of country homesteads by emigrating en masse. A peasant woman didn't have to be a feminist "to want mirrors, running water, and an indoor toilet."[40]

In 1947, when the Salon of Household Arts reopened for the first time since 1939, and 800,000 people passed into the exposition halls, the solution no longer lay in the grand display of equipment and gadgetry. As the Salon's organizers conducted their first survey of the visitors' social composition, they discovered that "everybody" did not attend: 90 percent of the visitors were middle class, mostly from the Paris area. The question was posed: What would it cost an average working-class family to equip its household with the basics, assuming a large and stable enough lodging, running water, and enough amperage to run major appliances? Just counting the basics, meaning a water heater, stove, pressure cooker, washing machine, refrigerator, vacuum cleaner, an iron with a thermostat, and, for a family with several children, a sewing machine and various and sundry kitchen machinery like an automatic vegetable

Madame is served: her "electric servants" are introduced at the
Housekeeping Salon, 1955. Marie-Claire, *March 1955.*
By permission of the Société des Amis de la
Bibliothèque Forney.

cleaner, blender, coffee grinder, and mayonnaise mixer, the amount approached a half-million old francs. Calculating that a French worker's guaranteed minimum wage was 18,500 francs per month, and that most workers brought home less than 50,000 francs, counting the government payments for children, on the score of costs alone it became clear that the working class was pretty much excluded from the new household consumption.[41]

Yet over the next decade and a half the Salon's standard became the national standard; by the mid-1970s it had spanned western Europe; and by the mid-1980s the standard was being advanced in eastern Europe as well. The reasons are multiple, complex, and intertwined. Perhaps the most fundamental was that the enormous pent-up demand for housing began more or less to be satisfied by massive construction of new units that both required and could accommodate new equipment. But

Madame is served: stove being installed at Marcelle Verhaegue's home in 1954. The intention of Électricité de France was to bring Bourg Achard, population 1,200, up to a standard "almost as comfortable as the United States' average." Elle, February 22, 1954. By permission of the Société des Amis de la Bibliothèque Forney.

other trends also played a role. The purchasing power of workers' wages rose as pay packets grew, inflation was curbed, and equipment prices dropped. A greater number of working women earned wages in factories or service jobs. Credit became available and acceptable to purchase consumer durables. A new and irrepressible conviction spread across the European region that *not* to possess the goods universally defined as indispensable to living according to the minimum standard of comfort stigmatized whoever lacked them.

The surge in housing construction starting in the mid-1950s and the renovation of old stock that took off in the late 1960s was crucial. Europe's record of sheltering its population had been appalling over the previous century, and the chronic shortfalls that came from fast-growing urban populations had been exacerbated by war, depression, the speculative housing market, and sheer decrepitude.[42] Down to the 1970s, at least, finding decent housing entailed long waits, frustration, and often disappointment. And what appeared at the time to be a utopian solution, the rapidly built concrete high-rise projects built on city edges, much coveted by hundreds of thousands of urban slum and shanty-town tenants, would in their turn fall into decrepitude only three decades or so later. Nevertheless, the new housing developments conformed more or less to new national building codes, which called for a separate bathroom and a kitchen equipped with heating, piped hot and cold water, electricity, and, later, gas lines.

To obtain one of the new flats was like a dream come true; hence it was not an uncommon theme of European film and fiction of the postwar decades. For Jo, the fifteen-year-old narrator of Christine Rochefort's 1961 novel, *Les Petits enfants du siècle,* the eldest of a gaggle of children who reside with their parents in a squalid three-room tenement on Paris's southwestern edge, to live at Sarcelles is to consummate her every desire. Sarcelles was the mother of the so-called Grands Ensembles. Rising out of the farmlands where the Oise River meets the Seine, its 170 hectares made it the biggest construction site in all France from 1955 to 1965; when its blocks of concrete-and-glass housing, interspersed with social services and wide green spaces, were finished, they housed about 50,000 new residents. For the urban planners, sociologists, social workers, and marketers who converged upon these residents as they moved in, they were prototypes of the new mass consumer-citizen. Studies of the first 20,000 to 30,000 inhabitants found them to be well equipped with the basics—refrigerators, washing machines, cars, and televisions—yet often beset by depression. The symptoms, for which the comfort of their new domiciles offered little surcease, lent themselves to no precise diagnosis, though common sense said the cause was the stress caused as decent, sim ple people tried to adjust to so much that was new. The syndrome was familiarly known as "Sarcellitis."

As consumers pressed the market, the cost of equipment was forced down, mainly by foreign competitors—American in the high range, but most effectively German, and by the Italian producers Zanussi, Indesit, and Candy. Exploiting their own very cheap labor and Fordized factory systems, employers in Italy maneuvered around France's lazy distribution systems and high-priced manufacturers as the Common Market brought down trade barriers. Before the French state itself put pressure on the proliferation of small French firms to merge, adopt new equipment, and cut prices, unnerved local manufacturers were granted one last reprieve, a six-month tariff to hold off foreign competition. Thereafter the concentration and transformation of the sector speeded up: as the output of washing machines jumped from 217,000 in 1949 to 839,000 in 1964, and to 2 million in 1974, prices would gradually be halved. The number of households with washing machines rose from 8 percent in 1954, the first year statistics were gathered, to 27 percent in 1961, 57 percent in 1971, and 80 percent in 1980.[43]

Washing machines were regarded as one of those "inelastic" goods, meaning that families were likely to purchase them even if they had low incomes because they were regarded as necessary. Being able to buy on the installment plan helped. Credit, once prohibitively expensive and socially unacceptable, became a commonplace from the mid-1950s. Manufacturers wanted it. As in the United States, where the credit revolution had started in the 1910s–1920s, it helped smooth out costly seasonal fluctuations by facilitating the movement of inventory from supplier to dealers. The supply of credit was encouraged by new enterprises, notably Cetelam, which, after its management visited the United States in 1953, sponsored by the Federation of Electrical Industries, improved the terms offered to electric equipment dealers as well as to their customers. Unlike those in the United States, French consumers had to be pushed to believe that credit was not sinful or socially disgraceful. This became easier as large strata of people brought home regular salaries and could thus anticipate being able to pay their bills. Women's magazines made the case that installment purchases were not at all "déclassé" or "almost synonymous with poverty." It wasn't like going to the pawnshop or to the backrooms of "Auntie" and "Uncle" for a loan. Americans, they said, regarded installment purchases as rational, discreet, smart, conservative family decisionmaking; "credit, far from diminishing increases your standing, enhances it."[44] Consumer advocates were naturally more circumspect. As the Women's Civil and Social Union admonished: "Know how to think it over . . . calculate, and be informed." It was bad to use credit for daily necessities, much less anything superfluous. But the mother of a small-town family with nine children whose father earned only 350 francs monthly, a sum that rose to 1,200 when the family allocations were included, might consider it entirely appropriate to purchase a washing machine on credit. Signing for a loan from the Family Allocations Fund, she might arrange to pay back 66 francs per month for eighteen months; the 20 percent that would be taken from the monthly paycheck was heavy but "ever so worthwhile." And so it was that, faced with competing demands and in view of rising income, wage and salary earners introduced this costly as well as risky undertaking into their calculations. By the early 1960s a third of the washing machines bought by workers and employees were purchased on credit, well above the national average for other goods; the rate of installment purchases of televisions was even higher. Just as usury went with misery and penury, installment credit went hand in hand with consumer affluence.[45]

Drawing on American models, the women's press, the leading source for women for information about consumer standards, boomed. Though some magazines dated back to the late 1930s, the late 1940s and early 1950s saw them proliferate. By the 1960s at least 200 journals targeted practically every sector of the highly diverse female public. Their basic message was clear enough: that the "ideal kitchen" was a "veritable factory inside the home" within which "the woman exercises her profession . . . Her work can be hard, or easy, bothersome or agreeable, all depends on the way in which her kitchen is organized."[46] Practical advice, as it was called, was so much in demand that in 1958 two new magazines debuted specifically for that purpose: *Femme pratique,* advertised as the first "technical journal for the woman in the home," quickly reached a circulation of 250, 000 readers; *Madame express,* the "review for household enterprises," 450,000.[47] That they found such a receptive audience so rapidly testifies to the degree to which household equipment had become the first measure of comfort, status, and convenient living, and how curious yet uncertain this first generation of mass consumers was about the specifications required to operate in the new regime.

By the 1960s the working class could be expected to share the same basic equipment as the bourgeoisie. Working-class purchasing power doubled from 1948 to 1970, taking a big leap in 1968–69.[48] The process of accumulating household equipment was systematic, only far slower, and for big families it was certainly aided by government family allowances. For the family of Jo, Christine de Rochefort's fictional working-class consumers, General de Gaulle's 1945 appeal for "twelve million beautiful babies" to repopulate the nation was irrelevant to their decisions about having one child after another. Rather, one kind of commodity was being produced to get another. Each child brought an additional family allocation from the government. And each increase was used to improve the family's stock of equipment. Jo's father never forgot the first sign of her recalcitrant character, that her late delivery had caused her parents to miss the birth bonus they had expected had she been born within two years of their marriage. Thereafter, "Thanks to Nicolas we could get the washing machine repaired and that was a good thing, otherwise diapers . . . we could get back the TV, and with that back, there was lots more peace . . . After that, with a little luck, we could maybe think about a car. That was what they had their eye on now, more than the fridge, Mom would have wanted a fridge, but Pop said that it was his turn this time to have some comfort, not always his wife's."[49]

By the turn of the 1970s the community of belief that the new standard of living was based on the full stock of household equipment included not only all classes, but also regions formerly excluded from any national notion of norms of comfort. No region in France had been more castigated for its barbaric rural ways than Brittany. In 1961, six years after the start of the boom, it appeared to be falling behind again. Yet barely a decade later a young sociologist from Rennes, after subjecting the local population to a battery of questionnaires about their possessions, processing the answers through a run of econometric tests, and illustrating his findings with the supply-and-demand curves that were *de rigueur* for American-style consumer economic studies, triumphantly proclaimed "truly spectacular progress in the principal elements of comfort" thanks to a "deep structural and moral transformation." Because of its new spending habits, Brittany had overcome the "great part of its handicap with respect to the national community." Its capacity for "catching up" was also the result of efforts by local officials, who had pressed the national government to invest one-fifth of the total of the Fund for Economic and Social Development in local industry and housing, and the monies spilled over into jobs, new households, and modern household furnishings: whereas in 1962, about 11 percent of the Bretons had washing machines, in 1968 41 percent, and the prediction for 1974 was 64 percent. One index of improvement was even more fateful: Brittany was outstripping the national average in television acquisition: in 1962, 6 percent of the households had one; in 1968, 55 percent; and practically all townspeople owned one.[50] With television, there was no longer any reason for Brittany to fall behind in terms of the latest information on consumer goods and styles. And that indeed proved to be the case.

So by the 1970s, Brittany was "catching up" to the whole of France, and France in turn was moving up to the levels of equipment of northern Europe and Switzerland, while Italy was pushing ahead to match France on the score of washing machines, levels that Spain and other poor European states would approach by the end of the 1980s.[51] Thereafter one could well argue that from nation to nation and region to region, these goods had different meanings. But the narrative of how household goods came to be possessed—technological change, rise in family incomes, and revolution in outlooks, all sanctioned and pushed by a new cross-Atlantic standard of living—was in large measure indifferent to variations in class, local cultures, and history.

Making Choices

From the perspective of the early 1950s, the consumer was a skeptical creature: not yet living in a commercialized civic culture, she made "her choices on the basis of advice from parents or friends inasmuch as she [wouldn't] take on faith the one-sided arguments of salesmen or commercial advertising."[52] Naturally, all who had some stake in mass marketing strove to put a face on the elusive person whom French marketers called Madame Martin. Indeed they practically forced her into existence, so that sooner and more obstreperously than anticipated, women consumers began to organize themselves as voices in the market place. As editor of *Elle,* Françoise Giroud, the restless Pygmalion of France's new managerial elites, was dedicated to putting a face on this anonymous creature, for the sake of France's image as a progressive nation as well as to promote her magazine's readership. The archetype she had in mind was the Gallic equivalent of Betty Furness, modest as a film actress, but a soothing, competent presence as television hostess for *The Westinghouse Hour,* where she became America's best-known homemaker. To identify a single figure as an idol in mid-1950s France was still greatly complicated by the country's diversity, especially by the still great gap between the cities and the provinces. French women were famous for showing off their differences in taste, especially in their refractoriness to advertising slogans. If a brand of stocking was advertised as solid and economical, a provincial might be persuaded, but the Parisian would scoff. If it was promoted as having "sex appeal" or being the "favorite of the stars," the solid middle class would dismiss it as a product for loose women. If marketed as the "one true French brand," there were always those who argued that "everything made abroad is better." And if advertised as "Made in America," others would gripe: "But, really, don't they make perfectly good stockings in France any more?" Giroud's solution was to champion a single average housewife consumer, "Madame from Angoulême." Emerging out of France's heartland, she was ingenuous but intrepid, a restless Madame Bovary in her consumer desires: she needed good counsel about "doing the wash without effort," but also advice about organizing the "wonderful Sunday outing." Naturally, she was first and foremost interested in outfitting her home, but she was also fashion conscious and ever so curious about the new makes of scooters and cars. Whether there was any correspondence between this figure and *Elle*'s readership is dubious, given the cultural distance that around 1960 still prevailed between the provinces and Paris, where most of *Elle*'s million readers wanted to live if they weren't already there.[53]

The J. Walter Thompson agency could be expected to be more scientific about identifying the characteristics of the "new housewife." In 1964, when it conducted the first survey in Europe of the young women "who each year set up home and set out upon a lifetime of running it, keeping it clean, cooking, shopping, and having children and caring for them," it expressed the urgency of knowing this "primary target group" for household products, as they were in the process of "learning and forming habits which may last for a considerable time."[54] From its sample of 1,000 young British women, aged sixteen to thirty-four, JWT learned that even if they were still living with their parents, they had high expectations of having their own home. From advertising and other media, they had acquired a vividly detailed optimism that "this home must be the best one can get, as the family will live there almost indefinitely." Their "training to shop" was based on their own experience, although working-class young women tended to inherit their mothers' preferences even though they were not always up to date on what they were. The most satisfying result was to know that both working- and middle-class women read advertisements and were very receptive to new products, the latter perhaps more than the former, not only because they had more income, but because on average they lived farther away from their parents.

In sum, Mrs. Consumer was in the making, though the experience of working-class women at Sarcelles throws into relief how many obstacles she had to overcome. For the young working-class couple of the Paris region, Sarcelles offering housing that was the "best one can get." But down until the mid-1960s, if not later, this suburb was also a consumer desert, with little of the lively street commerce that poor urban dwellers were used to. In 1962 only seventy stores served 20,000–30,000 people, and there were only three bakers, so that on some evenings, when commuters returned home, they faced lines of thirty to forty similarly worn-out customers.[55] However, the working-class homemaker's worst enemy was often her own family, her husband in particular, especially if on payday he drank and hung out with his buddies. Acting like a good consumer, scrimping, planning, tidying up, scolding, and indulging her own carefully regulated desires for knickknacks to prettify the bureau tops and windows, she was accused of becoming "bourgeois," and "lent herself to flack and heavy-handed ribbing and sometimes (which was far worse) the vague suspicion of conservatism." The effort to persevere was nonetheless so determined, so clearly patterned, and occurring on such a wide front that there was good basis for describing her struggle as having the quality of a "social movement," though the manner of its development could not have been "more diffuse, spontaneous, or elusive."[56]

Mass marketing acted as an important catalyst of this "social movement." When Procter & Gamble decided to launch a "new generation of products with enzymes" in 1968, it planned for the biggest marketing campaign ever conducted, and the last, it turned out, to be based on door-to-door canvassing. Calculating the costs at 30 percent of the first year's gross sales, 20–30 million new francs, the company spent ten months surveying test markets, using every technique of consumer polling available before its scheduled launch. The strategy was the classic one, namely to leap over local retailers to meet face-to-face with the *ménagères,* thereby capturing their interest in the product. In turn, the housewives would look for it in the stores they patronized; and if they didn't find it on the shelves, they would go straight to the manager and pressure him to supply it. To encourage this action, the canvassers handed out discount coupons to 9.3 million households. To keep up the pressure, six months later they made another sweep of the rural areas, handing out another set of one-franc coupons.

For the company, clearly, the bottom line was sales. Marketing executives could calculate their growth, but little was known about exactly which single tactic, factor, or attitude accounted for it. The more intense the advertising, the stronger the give-and-take between corporation and consumer, and the more the consumer matured her skills—though not necessarily to the benefit of loyalty to the brand. Once detergents with enzymes had been launched and were no longer a novelty, it was hard to distinguish the properties of one brand from another. In retrospect, marketers wondered whether they might have done better to appeal to consumers' intelligence: if they had called attention to Ariel's active ingredients, linear alkyl benzine sulfonate, sodium carbonate, and high solubility alkyl, would they have more convincingly explained why the cleaning properties of the brand were so special and indispensable?[57]

The more marketing campaigns labored for brand recognition, the more consumers treated detergents as "natural" products, which is to say they regarded the product as if it were salt, milk, or flour, having involved no special work to develop it. Diffident of advertising claims short of proof of real innovation, they shopped for price, just as they did for other basics like bread, milk, beef, string beans, and new potatoes. Shopping around, consumers were likely to find the best prices at supermarkets and discount centers, sometimes as much as 25 percent lower. And unlike at the neighborhood shop, the checkout clerks made no fuss about honoring the discount coupons.[58]

"The great seducers of our age are no longer called Don Juan or Casanova; they bear the names of detergents, insecticides, and toothpastes," Françoise Giroud commented in 1953.[59] Fifteen years later, marketing strategists were still "seducers," but they had also been "seduced by their strategy." They had introduced housewives to all the techniques of salesmanship: box size, weight, pricing, packaging. And their customers had become indifferent, unpredictable, and, worse, voracious in their desire for giveaways, special offers, and rebates.[60]

This surging consumer self-assurance showed up in the new images concocted by advertising campaigns to appeal to consumers. In 1972 the Ariel account was held by the R.-L. Dupuy firm, which had recently merged with the British Compton Agency. When Dupuy founded his firm in the late 1920s, he had positioned himself as the proud anti-

Americanizer, though that position had not prevented the elegant old fox from swiping from American publicity. His witty testimonials for Blanco-Completo soap powder, one an admonition from the archetypal busy-body Parisian concierge, the other from a lace-bonneted Breton house-wife, had already demonstrated the firm's taste for inventing strong female types. The campaign for Ariel introduced an altogether new figure, Madame Monique Pérignon, a doe-eyed working-class wife and mother, who with her hands firmly on the shopping cart spoke for her family as her casually dressed husband, their toddler in arms, looked on. Armed with experience, she brusquely turned away the salesman who was trying to violate the family's interests with his manipulative two-for-one offer. No longer the sociologist's subject, the efficiency expert's ward, or the ad-man's dupe, she didn't even entirely confide in her own mother. Explaining her choice, she announced that she had purchased her first washing machine only the year before. Before that, her mother had washed the diapers by hand. Mother said Ariel was the best. But she wouldn't accept that on faith. She had to judge for herself. So she tested the product on splotches of carrot, milk, and egg on little Laurent's overalls. Her decision was final and categorical: against the salesman's wiles, she would "stay true to Ariel." "Cleanliness, like Ariel, that can't be traded away."[61]

Now brand loyalty, however it was justified, was exactly what the giant corporations were battling for. The trouble was that familiarity could also result in brand disloyalty: consumer confidence turning into skepticism then diffidence about advertising puffery, costly packaging, and pseudoscientific explanations about the product's prowess, leading the consumer to decide on the basis of price. Something was clearly amiss in the early 1970s as economic growth slowed and the rate of growth of detergent sales dropped from the previous decade's 5 percent per year to around 2.5 percent. It was at this point that Carrefour, France's leading hypermarket, faced with stiff competition from Auchan, Mammouth, and other big chains, as well as from Leclerc's and Intermarché's discount outlets, took the decision to sell detergents under its own name. Management recalled hearing enthusiastic reports about the success of so-called private brands from consumer activist Esther Peterson, President John Kennedy's adviser on consumer affairs, who, as consultant to Giant, the leading local supermarket chain, had overseen their introduction in the Washington, D.C., area. The one major obstacle to introducing their own *produits drapeaux* was that the Institut de Liaison et d'Etudes des Industries de Consommation, organized at the initiative of U.S. multinationals in 1960 to prevent price-cutting by local outlets, would take action to

"Je n'en veux pas de votre échange.
Je reste fidèle à Ariel."

Madame Monique Pérignon, deux enfants, a récemment refusé d'échanger le baril d'Ariel qu'elle venait d'acheter contre deux barils d'autres lessives. Voici ce qu'elle nous a dit :

"Avant l'année dernière, je n'avais pas de machine, alors ma mère lavait les couches. Elle m'a dit, c'est Ariel qui est le mieux. J'en ai essayé une ou deux autres mais ça n'a jamais été ça. Avec Laurent, il y a des taches de carottes, du lait, des œufs, enfin de tout. Je n'utilise qu'Ariel, c'est toujours propre".

Une propreté comme celle d'Ariel,
ça ne s'échange pas.

Consumer power: young working-class housewife resists marketer's pressure and stays faithful to Ariel Detergent. Femme pratique, October 1972. Courtesy of the Bibliothèque Nationale de France.

boycott "aggressive" distributors. But by the early 1970s France's national distribution chains were well enough established for Carrefour, with support from the others, to force the multinationals to back off. As many of the chains brought out private-label products—Carrefour advertised its as "free products," as in "free choice"—price competition reduced the cost of detergents, consumers shopped around for the best price, and the sales of detergents in supermarket chains soared.[62]

Champions of consumer freedoms often made the point that the habit of exercising consumer choice would reinforce the exercise of choice in other domains, mainly politics. That prospect left the cultural conservatives to worry that choice might also be exercised in other areas, such as sexuality and cultural taste. Indeed, the connections were there—and marketers were among the first to make them. Fearless about women's exercise of freedom of opinion, indeed welcoming it, they assumed it would be malleable. From the 1930s, cinema fan magazines like *Cinémiroir* had advocated a local version of "life-style feminism," declaring the self-assertiveness, sports-mindedness, and lack of inhibitions of Hollywood stars worthy of emulation. *Cinémonde* strongly backed the vote for women on the shaky grounds that if they voted, homely middle-of-the-road candidates like Joseph Paul-Boncour and Pierre Laval would never be elected. After French women obtained the vote in 1946, advertisers simulated electoral contests as marketing ploys. Publicity for Omo appealed to the mass vote under the banner "Omo has been elected," backing up the slogan with the testimonial from the mechanic's wife challenging family tradition: "My mother said if you don't like dirt, don't marry a mechanic. You can see she didn't know about Omo." In the 1960s the leading French household appliance firm proclaimed: "Moulinex liberates women."

In the 1970s, however, freedom of choice began to be translated into the political freedom not to choose. The UN declared 1975 "Women's International Year" in the wake of the fast advance of women's liberation movements in the West. That was also the year that in France the feminist movement decided to contest what it saw as the leading symbol of conventional housewifery, the Household Arts Salon. "Moulinex doesn't liberate women." "No to household gadgetry; Yes to collective equipment" were the slogans that demonstrators from the Women's Liberation Movement and the Movement for the Right to Abortion and Contraception shouted when Françoise Giroud, whom President of the Republic Valéry Giscard d'Estaing had appointed undersecretary of state for women's affairs, arrived for a tour. Earlier, the visit of another of his new appointees, the first undersecretary of state for consumption, Christiane Scrivener, had passed unnoticed. By the same year a half-dozen national consumer organizations were regularly attending the Salon. Most were of the conservative, family-oriented variety, worried about price and product quality. But there were also more militant organizations like Que Choisir: the Federal Union for Consumption. By mistake, the Salon organizers had let it set up its stand near the entryway, where it leafleted visitors against the exhibitors' highway robbery.[63]

The Cold War in the Kitchen

By the 1970s the right to a kitchen had become the goal of family savings, the reason for women to enter the labor force and for men to work overtime, a cause of indebtedness, and the subject of national and international surveys. The supplies to equip it had brought about the consolidation of dispersed consumer-durables industries and streamlined national distribution systems. So logical had a kitchen in every home become as a goal, so obvious was it as a desirable standard, that there was no longer any need to cite exogenous examples, certainly not the American-style kitchen. Quite to the contrary, the kitchen acquired local meaning. The different qualities of the equipment and the different ways in which households organized them heightened a sense of participating in new national standards. They became elements of commonplaces about national identity, of how, say, daily life in France differed from that in Germany, or the Danes' sense of hygiene could be distinguished from the Swedes', hence the subject of stereotypes, ironic comment, and ethnographic research.[64]

For American global politics, however, this detachment represented a loss, one that was not immediately visible. Through the mid-1960s the kitchen had been mobilized as an icon of the Western way of life, whose main pace-setter and protector was the United States. The Pax Americana stood for making life comfortable for women, and government propaganda about the American way of life dovetailed nicely with publicity from America's giant appliance corporations as they battled for shares in western Europe's emerging markets. At the 1957 Household Arts Salon, the General Motors kitchen, costing 300,000 francs, foretold the innovations housewives could expect for the twenty-first century: infrared heating, ultrasonic dishwashers, and 360-degree television screens flashing recipes fed by an IBM machine using punch cards and linked with a telescripter to order supplies. At the 1958 Milan Samples Fair, the RCA Whirlpool "kitchen of the future," playing to the American exhibitors' common theme of "technology for a better living," made such an impact on the public that it was remounted at thirty-two other exhibitions around the world with not a hint of self-consciousness about its utter incongruity in most places. At the sight of the bewildered women timidly passing through the kitchen at the International Agricultural Fair at Delhi in 1961 with their bare-bottomed babies slung in their bangled arms, Daniel Boorstin worried that so much was being invested in image, so little in ideals.[65]

The so-called Kitchen Debate, when Soviet Premier Nikita Khrushchev and Vice President Richard Nixon confronted each other at the June 1959 Moscow Trade Fair, was the occasion for these ideals to be spelled out. The fair itself was the outcome of agreements the two superpowers had signed on September 10, 1958, to host expositions in each other's countries, the Soviets at the New York Coliseum, the Americans at Moscow's Sokolniki Park. The exchange was a gesture toward peaceful coexistence: the focus was the development of "science, technology," with "political content . . . to be avoided by both sides." Naturally, each envisaged the occasion for its own ends: the Soviets, to break out of their isolation and impress Americans with the progress the country had made over the previous eight years as its gross national product grew at 7.1 percent annually, twice the rate of the United States'; the Americans, to confirm their belief that the more Soviet people knew about the United States, the friendlier they would be. The moment was not good from the American point of view: during the preceding two years the Eisenhower administration had been stunned by the Soviet launch of Sputnik; the failure of its own program, which Democrats chidingly called "Flopnik"; an anti-American uprising in Lebanon; and Fidel Castro's offensive against Fulgencio Batista. At the same time, however, Khrushchev was eager to cut a deal on Berlin, the major outstanding issue in the European area, and welcomed détente more generally so that the Soviets could spend less on armaments and more on investment to raise domestic consumption.[66]

But nothing had prepared Soviet officials for the exhibit the United States mounted in Sokolniki Park. What they had expected was machinery, science, and technology, much like the Soviets themselves had put on display the previous year at the Coliseum, where they had shown the latest advances in space exploration, including full-size models of the three Sputniks, advances in agricultural technology, peaceful uses of atomic energy, and their latest-model automobiles. Only as an afterthought, and with doubts about whether it would dumb down the dynamism of the rest of the exposition, did they add a couple of "way of life" touches, a fashion show and a kitchen. By contrast, the U.S. exhibit was entirely

dedicated to the American way of life. The 50,000-square-foot main exhibition hall, enveloped by a fan-shaped aluminum roof, was divided into
two areas: "the house of culture," with a diorama of American life; and a
"house of items," chock-full of consumer goods. Between one exhibition
and another, the fair included three kitchens, the one set up by General
Foods and General Mills to prepare ready-made cakes, frozen, and other
convenience foods; Whirlpool's Miracle Kitchen; and the color-coordinated kitchen that was the center of the three-bedroom ranch house, jok-
ingly called "Splitnik" to call attention to the walkway that enabled visitors to cut across its interior. This kitchen, sponsored by General Electric,
was the setting for the famous last repartee of the debate.

Since the Soviets regarded what they called the "standard of science"
as a far superior measure of the worth of a civilization to the "standard
of living," they regarded the American exposition, on the whole, as a second order of invention. The model house attracted particular criticism
since the U.S. organizers presented it as a typical working-class home, a
facsimile of the tract housing built by All State Properties in Long Island,
fitted out by Macy's with $5,000 worth of equipment and furnishings, in-
cluding built-in appliances and wall-to wall blue carpeting. State Department officials warned Nixon that since the previous March, the Soviet
press had been ridiculing the house: it was no more typical of the abodes
of American workers than the Taj Mahal was of housing for Bombay textile workers or Buckingham Palace for British miners. Given that the purpose of Nixon's visit was to publicize his presidential qualities in anticipation of the 1960 elections, he was primed to use the house as an
arguing point and a backdrop.

As Nixon conducted Khrushchev around the fairgrounds, the two
started their banter. Nixon admitted that the Soviets might be ahead in
rockets, but the United States was ahead in other things—"color television, for instance." As they walked through the model house, William
Safire, who at the time was a Westinghouse publicist, pulled them aside
to pose them in front of the washing machine. The move prompted
Nixon to say, "Anything that makes women work less is good," to which
Khrushchev replied, "You want to keep your women in the kitchen.
We don't think of women in those terms. We think better of them." In
turn, Nixon extolled the virtues of the model house, which he said cost
$14,000 and was easily within reach of American workers. To which
Khrushchev replied: his society provided for all, regardless of income,
and houses in the USSR were built to last, not to become obsolescent.

Nixon's final point was "we don't have one decision made at the top by one government office . . . We have many different manufacturers and many different kinds of washing machines so that the housewives have a choice . . . Would it not be better to compete in the relative merits of washing machines than in the strength of rockets?" To which Khrushchev responded, "Yes, but your generals say, 'We want to compete in rockets.' We can beat you."

The most pressing issue, so far as the western European press was concerned, was whether this person-to-person diplomacy would relax tensions over Berlin.[67] By the end of the 1950s it was clear that the United States had won hands-down on the scorecard of standard of living. True, the left press, as well as a wide band of public opinion, would have agreed that in the United States there were no social safeguards for workers: as Khrushchev was quoted, "if you don't have the money, you sleep on the street." But whatever the defects, the USSR was becoming irrelevant as offering an alternative vision of collective well-being.

"We won't thrust it upon you," Nixon said in June 1959, speaking to Khrushchev of the American way of life. But, he predicted, "your grandchildren will see it." At the time of the exhibition, there was little sign that the model kitchens were a particular attraction. At the secret ballot box, where Soviet fairgoers were urged to vote for their favorite exhibit, the model house ranked only thirteenth out of the fifteen choices: Cinerama and jazz were at the top and the "miracle kitchen" at the very bottom.[68] The color-coordinated "kitchen of the future" was as irrelevant to Moscow standards of living as it was to most of the world's. Even so, the capacity to supply consumer goods had already emerged as a giant political issue. Three days before the American exhibit opened, the Soviets inaugurated a goods fair at nearby Luzhniki where visitors could obtain hard-to-get consumer items ranging from foodstuffs like eggs to cameras and tape recorders. By the time the Sokolniki Park affair opened seventy-two hours later, it had attracted 350,000 people.[69]

By the mid-1970s, when western Europe was becoming saturated with basic household equipment, eastern Europe had begun to deliver washing machines, stoves, and black-and-white television on a new mass scale—in addition to elements of social consumption in the form of heavily subsidized housing, food, education, medicine, and cultural goods. However, the troubles of the 1980s are more familiar, partly because they were so often predicted in Western analyses of the Soviet bloc. Shortages, combined with the incapacity to deliver the next levels of goods, were inherent in systems with no market feedback. In the USSR, more investment in both production goods and consumer goods was obstructed by the military-industrial-party complex. There was little point in trying to increase output by making workers labor more intensively, since money incentives didn't work so long as there was little to spend them on. As it was, wages often went into the flourishing gray market or, in East Germany, into a booming business across the border with West Germany. Government efforts to import consumer goods in response to lengthening queues greatly increased indebtedness to Western nations. The more televisions and radios circulated, and the more vacationers traveled westward, the more familiarity there was with western European habits of consumption. The more these habits were officially denounced as "capitalist offal," the more their appeal grew. The worse the provision of social services, the less "really existing" socialism was a real alternative to capitalist market economies.

When the Soviet bloc crumbled apart in 1989–90, its demise came to be accepted as inevitable. For the emergent women's movement, the regimes' failures could be laid to their failure to produce the comforts identified with the well-being of women and the family. The feminist Slavenka Drakulic, then a citizen of Yugoslavia, recalls that as the Soviet bloc dissolved, what she and other women wanted to know about first and foremost was "the small everyday things of the West: how people ate and dressed and talked, where they lived. Could they buy detergent? Why was there so much rubbish all over the streets?" Their preoccupation was not the fray of politics, but the basics of material comfort: "Sitting in their kitchens—because that was always the warmest room in their poorly heated apartments, cooking, talking, drinking coffee, talking about men and children, about how they hoped to buy a new refrigerator or a new stove or a new car."[70]

Conclusion

How the Slow Movement Put Perspective on the Fast Life

A firm defense of quiet material pleasure is the only way to oppose the universal folly of the Fast Life.

MANIFESTO,
Slow Food Movement, 1989

Despite everything, America as an idea, as a brand, still works wonders.

JACK TROUT,
global marketing consultant, 2004

TWO EVENTS FROM THE FINAL tumultuous months of 1989 mark the close of this history. One is epochmaking and familiar, the breaching of the Berlin Wall on November 9. The opening up of frontiers, followed by the collapse of state socialism, the breakup of the Soviet empire, and the imposition of devastating free-market policies, signaled the end of the so-cialist resistance to the Market Empire much as the defeat of the Nazi New Order in 1945 had signaled the end of the conservative and reac-tionary opposition.

That said, the debacle of socialism raised new questions about the via-bility of the American model of consumer society: Could there not be an alternative that was less devastating in its free-market megalomania and claims on global resources, and more appropriate to the needs and sensi-bilities of peoples distant from the material civilization spanning the North Atlantic? True, the vexed old issue of the standard of living now sounded tiresomely old-leftish. Liberty was now widely interpreted as meaning freedom to choose among lifestyles rather than promoting social equality or participatory democracy. How then to address the ever more conspicuous gap between the new rich and the new poor of post-socialist societies or between the haughtily affluent regions of the world and the humiliatingly poor? The American model of consumer society had thrived by setting itself up as the democratic, comfortable, equitable alternative to repressive, goods-scarce, and unjust ways of life. With no enemy to challenge it, would it retain its irresistible power?

The other late 1989 event, trivial by comparison, occurred a month after the fall of the Berlin Wall. On December 9 activists from seventeen nations gathered in the foyer of the Opéra Comique in Paris to endorse the protocol founding the International Slow Food Movement, after which they made champagne toasts and sat down to a banquet for 500. The occasion marked the start of a "delicious revolution," in the conceit of its founder, the Italian Carlo Petrini, one whose distant origins lay in the aftermath of 1789, when the palace cooks of the *ancien régime* recycled themselves as innkeepers, inventing modern gastronomy to nourish and entertain their new bourgeois clientele. Critical of the "Fast Food Nation" but also of the old left's ascetic outlooks, these latter-day revolutionaries recognized their cause in the cacophony of social movements whose leitmotifs are anxiety about globalization, the mobilization of cross-national networks in the name of peace, environmental issues, and world community, and fears about mad cow disease, genetic engineering, and other degenerations in the food culture.

Likewise, the Slow Food Movement posed new questions for the first world of consumption, challenging the false binaries that had previously organized resistance to the Market Empire. Turning away from the alternative between free markets and state protectionism, it affirmed a "virtuous" vision of globalization, one that would end regulation that discriminated against small producers and use the Internet to connect them to informed consumers. It sought a third way between the superficial sociability promoted by brand recognition and the defensive solidarities favored by the closed communities of traditional protest movements. Slow Food also embraced capitalist commerce in recognition that the movement needed a sound financial basis to thrive and that for lack of effective marketing strategies, the hostelries and traditional foods that were its hallmark would succumb to multinational agribusiness, fast-food chains, and supermarket convenience fare. Finally, Slow Food presented its vision as universal and not anti-American. True, America was the homeland of its nemesis, fast food. But as its membership grew to over

100,000 by 2004, America was also home to the largest and fastest-growing contingent outside Italy.[1]

Flexible computer-based production systems, rapid-response distribution methods, hectically changing consumer lifestyles, dynamic new regional economies—the pace of all of these continued to be marked by American developments. Yet one of the outcomes was the consolidation of western Europe as a consumer's paradise. Another was the prospect that the whole world would be pulled into the orbit of Western consumer society. The strangest consequence of all was that as mass consumer models became universalized, the grounds for American hegemony became less evident.

The disorientingly rapid development of the information technologies that in the 1990s evolved into the Internet contributed to the uncertainty about American leadership. Spearheaded in the 1960s by the Rand Corporation, the foremost Cold War think tank, the initial goal had been to invent a system that would enable government authorities to communicate in the event that a Soviet nuclear attack knocked out centralized networks. From the 1980s the United States and its new rival, Japan, were in the forefront of applying the new information technologies to consumer-oriented manufacturing processes. However, the capacity of western European enterprise to ride the waves of business innovation across the North Atlantic had now been consolidated. And from the mid-1980s, as western European firms joined cybertechnologies with flexible management styles, they adeptly exploited their local knowledge to cater to highly diverse markets, disperse their manufacturing into smaller, more diverse units closer to sources of cheap labor, and enable the just-in-time production that turned their distribution outlets into sources of continual feedback about customer demand.[2]

By the 1980s Ford had ceased to be a household name; Ikea took its place. At around the same time, the Age of Filene gave way to the Age of Benetton. In the mid-1980s, exploiting decades of adeptness in adjusting to cross-border commerce, fleet-footed European merchandisers came to challenge superannuated American chains on their own turf. The upscale French hypermarket chain Carrefour brought "boutique-ization" to affluent American suburbs. The same years saw the all-but-unknown German deep-discounter Aldi take over the Jewel Tea Company of Illinois, Emile Bernheim's onetime American backer, a move that taught it to improve profits in blighted urban neighborhoods by cutting inventory, service, and decor to the bone. As Woolworth's teetered on the brink of in-

Woolworth's, Berlin, 2004, a wholly German discount chain.
By permission of the author.

solvency, finally closing all its American stores in July 1997—to leave only its German and Australian outlets intact—the giant Kmarts and Wal-Marts, combining nonunion U.S. labor and cheap Asian goods with American-size economies of scale, rumbled into Europe, bringing "deep discounting" on a mammoth scale. Here the opposition it faced was less vociferous than the opposition mounted in small Vermont towns. To speak of the "Europeanization of American retailing" indicated that European merchandisers had now not only learned the American game but become full-fledged global players.[3]

Uncertainty about whether American power was waxing or waning was also encouraged by uncertainty about how national states would bear up under the pressures of global competition. If the "Washington Consensus" prevailed, governments everywhere would create a capital-friendly environment by tightening budgets, reducing debt, and opening their markets to foreign investment. The result, critics argued, would be a world of hapless "Kmart" states. Like the American discount chain store that had become notorious in the 1980s for its nonunion work-force, no-frills service, and trashy stock, the Kmart state stood for government on the cheap, one that pandered to finicky global investors by

cracking down on labor unions, stripping away Keynesian cushions protecting against high unemployment rates, and paring social services.[4] The
Kmart state also stood for governments with diminished sovereignty over
national culture, making the stock of local cultural goods vulnerable to
the American information and entertainment conglomerates that were
the hallmarks of the new global economy.

But the Kmart phenomenon had a way of backfiring. European Union
states had now accepted that more national-level regulation would stran-
gle their capacity to withstand global competition: there had to be deeper
and wider coordination among them. If the goals of the 1992 Maastricht
Treaty were achieved by the early twenty-first century, Europe would
present a single market for capital and labor, complete with its own coin-
age; it would be unified in some measure politically and would be establishing a unique cultural identity. Naturally, the prospect of operating
in the richest market in the world caused U.S. firms to increase their investments by the end of the 1980s, especially as saturated home markets sagged. For marketing purposes, they were tempted to exploit their
brands' Americanness. To use America as a signifier and to export American lifestyles was perhaps acceptable, and in any case familiar, just so
long as the product wasn't closely identified with America's bristling military, political, or economic might. This unease grew as the United States
became more closely identified as the chief manager and beneficiary of
economic globalization.

Uncertainty about American leadership was also fed by the fact that
the United States was no longer regarded as the world's foremost advocate of the right to a decent standard of living. Down to the 1960s, American policymakers had treated efforts to raise the standard of living as the
centerpiece of the global movement for human rights. And the American
"standard package" of goods was held up as a model to prod western Europe to develop its own concept of "citizenship goods" and pressure Soviet Europe to dedicate more resources to consumer investment. But from
the 1970s on, official America backed away from asserting any universal
right to a high standard of living. And by the 1980s, on the score of
health care, leisure time, diet, social security, and numerous other indicators of the good life, the average western European enjoyed a higher standard of living than the average American.

The 1975 Helsinki Accords marked the watershed on this issue, emphasizing liberty as opposed to equality, and individual rights to freedom
over collective rights to subsistence. Implicitly, the thirty-five signatories

recognized a notion of universal rights compatible with the precepts of a democracy of consumption by emphasizing freedom of choice, movement, and expression while condemning states that provided the basics yet prevented their consumers from using them freely for personal expression. Though the Soviet Union was a signatory, the premises were distinctly anticommunist: given that global wealth was sufficient to satisfy material needs, it was no longer imperative to reiterate the need for a universal benchmark or to postpone democracy in the name of development. Knowing that its major antagonist, the USSR, competed with it on the score of who could best promote social equality, the United States was particularly insistent that freedom of choice rather than guarantees of basic material needs was the first and most fundamental human right.[5]

This shift in emphasis occurred just as the high postwar growth rates of the West began to slow, wages began to fan apart, standards of collective provisioning became more uneven, and the basket of goods and services that defined the necessary started to look more and more varied. The average spenders were no longer Joe Smith and his consort, Mrs. Consumer, nor their European counterparts, the office manager or union worker married to Madame Martin. From the late 1970s on, multinational marketers, faced with slowdowns in sales, discovered that earlier target audiences, such as the fulltime homemaker, blue-jeaned youth, or Americanizing manager, were not just unresponsive and unpredictable, but perhaps no longer even existed. New marketing strategies focused on identifying lifestyles, meaning the choices consumers themselves revealed in their efforts to fashion self-identities in the face of proliferating goods and disquieting times. To identify new trend-setters, marketers expanded their target fields to include "work-wives," "gays," "yuppies," and "preteens," not to mention the "preschool" and "pet" markets. It had taken a half-century for European marketers to recategorize a class-stratified population according to the famous revenue bands, A to D; life-style categories were taken on board instantaneously. And with Marxist analyses of social status fallen into disrepute and the left having abruptly bade farewell to the working class, European social science too latched onto the notion of life-style segments to classify, if not predict, public opinion.[6]

By the close of the century, then, Europe was as much a consumer society as the United States. Indeed, as multinational firms of both cross-Atlantic and European provenance competed for shares of a widening European market, and batteries of governmental, European Union, and

*Florence's first mall: Esselunga, once a Rockefeller enterprise, is
still breaking new ground in the twenty-first century.*
By permission of the author.

private survey research institutes generated consumer profiles, the multiplicity of lifestyles appeared to be as great as, if not greater than, those in
the United States. Here, at the world crossroads of culture and commerce, diversity generated a kaleidoscope of "Euro-styles": marketers
could latch on to the myriad of regional cultures and the proliferation of
minority identities; they could also draw on the revival and recombination of status symbols inherited from the bourgeois regime of consumption and, in eastern Europe, on nostalgia for the simple gadgetry, garden plots, and social security enjoyed under the People's Democratic
Republics.

In this framework, the issue of Europe's culture returned in a very different guise from early in the century, when elitist *Kultur* had been
counterposed to crass materialist civilization. European advocates of the
human rights agenda of the post-Helsinki era were especially emphatic
that destroying a community's cultural heritage could be as devastating as crushing its political rights; not that this "right to culture" should
then be used as a pretext by the state or any other self-styled spokesman
to infringe on the rights of others in the name of protecting it. Much to
be debated, of course, was the violence done to this right by market

Big brands on the move: Pampers embarks for Sicily, 2004.
By permission of Nancy Goldring.

forces. This notion of culture as a valuable social resource emerged as the sticking point as the Uruguay round of the talks toward the General Agreement on Tariffs and Trade that began in 1986 moved to a conclusion in 1993. For American trade negotiators, GATT's goal was to negotiate away remaining commercial barriers, especially those designed to curb open traffic in cinema and other media goods. Only after European Union officials insisted that audiovisual products be treated as the "cultural exception" to free trade principles did they grudgingly capitulate; EU member states could keep quotas on television programming, though only for the time being. On this score, the American concession differed little from positions taken in the past: the compromise deliberately avoided discussion of principles, especially over whether audiovisual products were commodities or culture, much less over whether protecting culture from market exchange should be treated as a form of free expression, hence protected as a basic human right. Time was on their side, the U.S. negotiators told themselves: time and the new satellite and digital technologies that American businesses were expected to dominate and which would render local media quotas meaningless.[7]

A New Dialectic of Consumption

By the 1980s Europe's old left did not have a consumer leg to stand on. Much had been said throughout the century about the false conscious-

ness of false needs. But by the early 1980s it was clear that every movement to build "an insurmountable barrier against the invasion of false
needs" had failed; the "Maginot line of austerity" had been "circum-
vented at the demand of consumers themselves."[8] Those who believed
that new consumer advocacy movements could coalesce the "dispersed
interests" of consumers into a strong and effective political lobby were
equally disillusioned.[9] Acting in their interests as consumers, Europeans
proved as agilely opportunistic as Americans, choosing exit, by going to
another store or not buying at all, rather than voice, by mounting meaningful protests over the injuries of mass consumption. Well before the
collapse of the Soviet bloc, there was consensus, if a deeply disconsolate
one, that with the exhaustion of "alternative scenarios" the consumer society had to be recognized as "our only future."[10]

Over the next decade, this realization spurred salutary reflection about
how the expressive elements of American consumer capitalism could be
reconciled with European ways of living, while honing the capacity to
critique its regulatory and standardizing effects and minimalist notion of
democratic participation. For the cohorts that had partaken of "Americanism from below" during the 1960s in the form of rock 'n' roll, the free
speech movement, and sexual liberation, regarding it as powerfully sub-
versive of bureaucratic and patriarchal regimes, consumption could even
be regarded as a realm of freedom and the basis for new kinds of resistance. This was even more the case for youth growing up in the 1970s
and 1980s as the old left disappeared. By the mid-1990s European scholars too had launched themselves into studying the history of European
consumer society, and social activists inspired by Naderite, Green, and
various and sundry no-global movements were engaged in promoting
"critical consumption."[11]

Italy offered an especially fertile terrain for the latter movements. From
the second half of the 1980s, critiques of consumer society fed off of the
playful hedonism of a lay culture in rebellion against Catholic prohibi-
tions and socialist puritanism, the persistence of traditionalist local and
regional cultures, and the general rethinking of repertoires of social protest caused by the crisis of the old left. Though the Italian Communist
Party (PCI), the largest outside the socialist bloc, had never used the word
"consumer" in any programmatic way, it had made huge advances as the
mass consumer's party in the 1960s and 1970s by pressing for higher
wages, responding to social needs at the head of some of the best-admin-
istered towns in Europe, and backing cooperatives, leisure organizations,

and other consumer-related groupings. Though not at all the leadership's intention, the PCI's constituents moved into the mainstream of consumer society. This development registered for the first time in the early autumn of 1986, when the PCI's National Festival of Unity was mounted in Milan, Italy's fashion capital. At Italy's most popular annual fair, hundreds of thousands could see that the book displays, realist cinema, lotteries, Chilean folksingers, oom-pa-pa bands, and down-home meals of pasta with Bolognese sauce, bountiful meat, and local wine had made way for video rock shows, nonstop fashion displays, how-to encounters with Communist entrepreneurs, and eateries offering Italian "new cuisine." Onetime Marxist cultural theorists seized the occasion to celebrate a postmodern "eclectic hedonism." No longer were commodities inherently either good or bad: the issue was to learn how to consume "productively." Therein lay all the difference between supporting a progressively conceived "right to pleasure" and succumbing to the reactionary self-indulgence facetiously known as "Reagan hedonism."[12]

This shift was more permanently registered at the grass roots when ARCI (Associazione Ricreativo Culturale Italiana), the left's several-hundred-thousand-strong recreational movement, began to split up into life-style segments. By the end of the 1990s this onetime bedrock of solidaristic working-class subculture had been transformed into a national federation overseeing sections for consumers, environmentalists, and women's interests, ARCI-Kids, ARCI-Gay, ARCI-Caccia, the hunters' group with its creaky-kneed contingents of ex-partisans, and, not least, ARCI-Gola, or the "glutton's" movement.[13] The precursor of Slow Food had its roots in Bra, a South Piedmontese town in the Langhe, a district known for its wine, truffles, and cheese, which in the 1970s after years of depopulation had become a port of return for dispirited jobless from nearby Turin, as well as for former student militants eager to distance themselves from Communist bureaucrats and far-left terrorists. That was where Carlo Petrini, together with local comrades, founded "The Free and Praiseworthy Association of the Friends of Barolo," its members bonding over good food and drink, running a local cooperative, and using the old ARCI network to fraternize with like-minded groups across the center-north. One such outing in 1983 took them to the Tuscan hill town of Montalcino, where after being served a "revolting meal" by the comrades at the local Casa del Popolo, Petrini decided to make a political issue of the left's self-denying culture of consumption: How, in good faith, could it press for a higher standard of living through the cash economy when it condoned the low quality of life evidenced by the sodden pasta and rotgut wines of proletarian production? The movement took off, finding support in *Il Manifesto*, *Gambero rosso* (Red Shrimp), and other leftist publications with columns dedicated to food and wine, as well as in the Rabelaisian underside of popular culture, whose obstreperous voice had last resonated a full century earlier in Paul Lafargue's *Right to Laziness*. Pleasure was not a bourgeois monopoly or a sin. So was launched the quirky and intelligent movement that in 1986, after picketing the opening of an oversize McDonald's in the baroque heart of Rome by parading in front of it with bowls of hot pasta, emerged as a high-profile international protest against the "fast life."[14]

The fact that Slow Food became a full-fledged movement by confronting McDonald's suggests that the Market Empire still marked the pace of change in material culture. Indeed, the advance of the last of the mighty inventions of twentieth-century American consumer culture recapitulates the advance of earlier inventions we have studied here. Fruit of the entrepreneurial genius of Ray Kroc, a fiftyish milkshake-machine salesman from Oak Grove, Illinois, who in 1954 bought the rights to franchise a quick-order hamburger outlet operated by two brothers, the McDonalds, in San Bernardino, California, the company could be regarded as the last great heir to Fordism. Making its appearance on the most universal of terrains—what, how, and where people eat—McDonald's management brought to the service industries all the hallmarks of standardized production and marketing, from its uniform product line—hamburger, fries, and Coke—routinized procedures for preparation, and minimally trained, maximally efficient labor with their tidy uniforms, jaunty caps, and bright "service smiles," to the relentless advertising and minutely calculated control over customers by means of the location of outlets and the determination of menus, pricing, seating, and decor. Headquartered in Kroc's hometown, with its "Hamburger University" set up at nearby Elk Grove to teach the rules of the business, it expanded by selling local franchises to small entrepreneurs with the promise that they could duplicate them profitably in practically any environment. Operating on that double register of regulation and freedom—of disenchanting the world with procedures and reenchanting it with small pleasures—that doubleness which observers of American mass culture had remarked upon since the 1920s, in the 1980s McDonald's wrought yet another sea change in the consumer culture of Europe.[15] In this sense, it played much the same role on the plane of eating that Hollywood cinema had played in terms of visual culture in the 1920s, and the chain store and supermarket played with respect to self-service shopping during the 1930s and 1960s.

Also like earlier social inventions, the intrusion of McDonald's was interwoven with local trends. Coming into continental Europe in 1971, it was not notably profitable until the same conditions that had given rise to it in United States spread in western Europe, namely commuting, the continuous work day, the habit of using convenience foods and eating out as more and more women worked, increasingly differentiated tastes in diet, ever more exposure to advertising images, and ever more pandering to children's desires as consumers. Until 1984 it stayed clear of Italy, out of fear of terrorism, inflation, strikes, and labor laws, which until they were changed in 1982 barred the use of the part-time employees, youth at their first jobs, who were McDonald's signature workforce. Consequently, it fell to local entrepreneurs to satisfy the new need for public catering. At first, café owners simply improvised by supplying sandwiches at stand-up bars. Then, in February 1982, acting on information about American developments, a home-grown operation, Burghy, debuted in Milan with a menu consisting of hamburgers and french fries. By the time McDonald's opened its first outlets in Italy three years later, many of the words suggestive of the fast-food lifestyle—sandwich shop *(paninoteca)*, snack *(fermino)*, and eat and run *(mordi e fuggi)*—were already in circulation. The Milanese Burghy outlets were also notorious as youth hangouts for scruffy bands of "Punks" and Timberland-shod, down-vested "Sandwichees" *(paninari)*.[16]

Just around the time McDonald's was to open in Italy, the Italian cooperatives were negotiating with Soviet officials in the spirit of Glasnost to open the first "new food" outlet just off Red Square, capitalizing on the fame of food "made in Italy," their flexible management style, and, of course, their political access. Looking to time the debut in conjunction with the opening of the 1986 congress of the Communist party of the Soviet Union, the New Food Trade Company's president, Marco Minella, undertook a hurried mission to the United States "to learn about collective catering" and to "try to translate it into an international language." In this spirit, Italian "new food" intended to serve 800,000 Muscovites a day, its menu offering chicken and pizza but no hamburgers, which local authorities had rejected out of hand as "symbols of capitalism and imperialism."[17]

The McDonald's opened in 1986 by Rome's Spanish Steps was at the time the largest in the world, with 450 places, and because of heavy tour-

Authenticating fast food: entryway plaque marking McDonald's founding in Italy, 1986, adjacent to Roman mosaics, circa 200 A.D. By permission of Livia A. J. Paggi.

ist traffic in the area, it stood out as the company's largest single money-maker for several years. Within a year there were at least twenty copy-cats in the vicinity—Benny Burger, Big Burg, Best Burger, Golden Burger, and so on—and McDonald's services had generated a whole new vocabulary: *frappé* had become "milkshake," "fryers" stood at the "grill," and "cleaners" washed and swept up at closing. By the late 1980s, as part of a general overseas expansion as U.S. markets slowed and the project to strengthen the European Union became clear, McDonald's announced a plan to open fifty more franchises in Italy. Specifically, it wanted to undercut Italy's leading chain, Burghy, which in the meantime had changed hands and was buying up its domestic competitors. In the next decade, McDonald's bought out Burghy, then fended off Burger King, which had entered the Italian market in a joint venture with Autogrill, the next leading Italian chain. The food at McDonald's was a matter of indifference. It was the cultural associations that made for its appeal: the bright lights and noise; the milling of tourists and other outsiders; colorful employee uniforms; the absence of adult mediators like waiters; the self-service and open seating; the tie-ins with familiar Disney cartoons and Coca-Cola; the familiarity of the company mascot, the red-haired clown Ronald Mc-Donald, said to be the world's most widely known figure after Jesus; and the small toys handed out free to the children.[18]

Italian "New Food" had barely got a toehold in Red Square before the Kremlin was forced to end its political monopoly over markets. Less than three months after the fall of the Berlin Wall, on January 28, 1990, Mc-Donald's opened its first franchise on the corner of Pushkin Place. Already well established in West Germany, it pushed into the former German Democratic Republic as well. In the early spring of 1990, it installed a mobile cart in the down-at-the-heels center of Dresden, before opening its first franchise in the tatty old textile town of Plauen; the entrepreneurship of local franchisers, onetime socialist strivers who had formerly operated the town's Konsum Services, brings to mind the intrepid spirit of precommunist Plauen's business elites, who in 1929 had successfully made a special plea in view of the town's small size to establish their own Rotary club.[19]

By 1990, however, American entrepreneurship's heady expansion eastward sought not the conquest of all Europe but "global realization." The Moscow McDonald's broke Rome's record for size and customer volume. The Beijing McDonald's, inaugurated in 1992 and built to seat 950 people, outstripped both. In January 1993, to catch the pilgrimage trade, a McDonald's franchise opened in Mecca. By 2000 there were 30,000 outlets worldwide.[20]

As fast food advanced so did Slow Food, albeit on a different trajectory. The movement was emphatic that it would not become hostage to McDonald's by making it the whipping boy for nasty eating habits or a symbol of the depredations of capitalist globalization. On this point, it wanted to distance itself from the French farm activist José Bové, a respected leader of the international no-global movement who in 1992 became a national hero by bulldozing a half-built McDonald's in his hometown of Millau. Slow Food, its leaders affirmed with neohumanistic solemnity, was "not born to defeat, subordinate, or obstruct, but as an instrument of knowledge." The local chapters were linked to the international movement not by rules, but by shared experiences, on the premise that conviviality should remain a cultural good rather than becoming commodified. One important weapon was irreverence. The perky snail, the movement's symbol, is slow, cautious, but also edible; *Homo sapiens* exists to know, but also to *savor* life, first of all food. The task of the new association was to combine styles and notions that were hitherto thought incompatible: quality and affordable prices, enjoyment and social awareness, quickness and lazy rhythms; the aim, a social movement that was "open, democratic, and uncontaminated by particular interests, and would avoid making itself ridiculous with rites, protocols, and trappings."[21]

Slow Food flourished because of its good commercial instincts. Reaping excellent profits from its widely distributed Italian gastronomic and wine guides, it also plays host to the annual Taste Fair (Salone del Gusto), Italy's largest food show, whose hundreds of stalls, dispersed through Fiat's Lingotto factory, the onetime cradle of Italian Fordism now converted into a postmodern exposition hall, provide an international market for hundreds of small food producers whose goods, until recently, rarely left their locality. Inevitably, it has to address the accusation that it is an elitist operation for food snobs in search of the perfect pork sausage or aged Parmigiano Reggiano, and thus only reproduces the hierarchies of distinction between the elite and the masses, quantity and quality, and taste and convenience that in the past undergirded bourgeois culture and justified resisting the American standard of living in the name of the European way of life. In response, it would underscore that there is a more elemental issue at stake: namely that in the contemporary world, access to decent food has reemerged as a class question, dividing those with the income, knowledge, and time to afford decent nutrition from those without and who therefore suffer from lack of choice, food manipulation, and nutritional diseases, signally obesity. What's more, the capacity for food production marks the huge divide between the protected, subsidized agriculture of the First World and the subsistence agriculture of poor nations. Accordingly, the ambitions of the Slow Movement expanded: from promoting eating, drinking, discussing food matters, to organizing programs like edible schoolyards to teach children to eat less and eat better and bringing farmers' markets to urban neighborhoods.

In larger perspective, the movement recognized that if globalization had the homogenizing effect of allowing multinational corporations to extend their reach to virtually every corner of the world, it could also aid the small producers, using the Internet to open up niches to help them to survive. Much as biodiversity turns attention to plants and animals in risk of extinction, eco-gastronomy would embrace programs for the survival of endangered foods. From this premise came the decision to award

"Nobel" prizes for biodiversity, establish Slow Food presidia or for-
tresses to preserve endangered species, and build a symbolic Ark of Taste
to rescue farmhouse cheeses, barley wine, or prize Piedmontese steer at
risk of extinction as a result of the deluge of agricultural standardization.
Going to international bodies like the World Trade Organization, delegates lobby for liberalizing commerce in agriculture, though in terms that
would deter giant multinationals from dumping genetically modified and
subsidized food on countries like Mali, where an imported baguette ends
up costing less than a kilo of locally produced sorghum or millet.[22] In
sum, Slow Food would treat agricultural commodities much like cultural
goods, reviving the occasions of their production and use, and lobbying
for their protection as if they were cultural goods protected by a form of
intellectual property rights, their geographical names or indications, or
GI in trade parlance, becoming the exclusive property of the villages, regions, or countries where they originate. Hence the right to the name
Dijon, though sold by Kraft as a type of mustard, would revert to producers from the French city. Likewise, Vidalia onions would revert to
growers in Vidalia, Georgia. For the movement's impresario Petrini, the
United States is "natural Slow Food territory," and one of Slow Food's
fondest missions would be to reinstate the food traditions that made the
United States known all over the world for the plenitude of its food products, and not for McDonald's.[23]

America's Turn

This confrontation over food cultures might be treated as merely of ethnographic interest, another dimension of the cross-Atlantic "food fight"
among well-nourished populations with similarly high standards of living, were it not for the decisive turn in the politics of American empire
from the early 1990s on.

   The collapse of the Soviet bloc in 1990 caused policymakers to think
again about Woodrow Wilson's legacy, especially whether the free-market, democratic values that had purportedly triumphed with the collapse
of the USSR could be the basis for establishing a new, American-led,
global order. Lacking any effective military-political enemy, could not
U.S. hegemony be refounded on a different mix of force and persuasion?
As local cultures converged more and more around a single global model,
could not the "soft power" resources accumulated over previous decades
be exercised more persuasively to allow for a cutting back on the costly

"hard" or military dimensions of U.S. power? The exact meaning of "soft power" was left vague as some blend of diplomacy, public image, and cultural values that would make "others want what you want."[24] Absent from this formulation was Wilson's empathetic notion of serving the world as evidenced in his salesmanly imperative of 1916 to "consider what they desire, not you desire." Nonetheless, the soft-power scenario had some initial plausibility. U.S. telecommunications and media networks appeared poised for ever greater dominance as the forces of globalization caused patterns of material life to converge as never before.[25] It was also plausible in light of the apparent earlier success of U.S. consumer cultural models in helping to reconstruct western Europe as a place of peace and to have discredited Soviet totalitarianism along the way. However, this scenario overlooked the dispersive nature of contemporary commodity movements. And it failed to detect the sense of hopelessness and antipathy generated by the barrage of newness that caused Western models of materialism to be identified with the United States as objects of revulsion and repudiation. Nor was it aware enough of the violence growing out of the "clash of civilizations" earlier in the twentieth century to imagine the violence that might be unleashed at the turn of the twenty-first century, albeit inspired by a different fundamentalist message and employing a far different arsenal of weapons.[26]

In the wake of the Al Qaeda attacks against the United States on September 11, 2001, salesmanship promised to overhaul the bad image of the Market Empire. Could it be that Islamic terrorism was the consequence of some basic incomprehension of American motives? That the global marketing machine that had advertised the habits and goods typical of the American way of life had fueled deep miscommunication about the positive values inherent in Western material culture? Around the time it launched its first military response in Afghanistan, on October 2, 2001, the Bush administration named Charlotte Beers, celebrated in the public relations demi-monde as the "Queen of Branding," to a recently created State Department position, undersecretary for public diplomacy and public affairs. With skills honed as former chief executive at J. Walter Thompson and a billion dollars in government appropriations, Beers set about mounting the most expensive public relations campaign ever. Its purpose, simply put, was to take "market shares away from Jihad" by targeting "disaffected populations," especially in the Middle East and South Asia, "where a poor perception of U.S. leads to unrest, and unrest has proven to be a threat to our national and international security."[27] At the same time, the Office of the President established its own rival Office of Global Communications to "disseminate truthful, accurate, and effective messages about the American people and their government," whose purpose was "to prevent misunderstanding and conflict, build support for and among United States coalition partners, and better inform international audiences," especially about the administration's "non-negotiable demands of human dignity" as "a framework for more listening and greater dialogue around the globe."[28] In March 2003, as the Bush administration mounted its war against Iraq, Beers resigned for health reasons. Her "shared values" campaign had failed. Testifying before the Senate Foreign Relations Committee a week before leaving office, she concluded: "The gap between who we are and how we wish to be seen, and how we are in fact seen, is frighteningly wide." In December 2003 a global poll conducted by the Pew Research Center for the People and Press showed that favorable ratings of the United States had plummeted, even among its allies.[29]

Though there was nothing new about "selling America," this effort marked a significant departure from the operations of the Market Empire at its Cold War apogee. At the turn of the 1960s, the promise of the consumer revolution was backed up abroad by government agencies and private enterprise with the active cooperation of grass-roots movements. The American model promised a high standard of living and set out procedures to achieve them. Cultural diplomacy went hand in hand with $13 billion of Marshall Plan aid, carefully targeted to rebuild western Europe as a wide, deep, regional market. While the State Department hosted trade fairs with model homes and supermarkets, the U.S. government provided massive amounts of development aid; Rotary International almost doubled the number of its service clubs globally, from 340,000 (1950) to 650,000 (1970); and American multinationals launched themselves into the European Community, setting standards for the consumer good life as well as competing to drive down the price of consumer equipment. Above all, in Europe the Market Empire presented itself as peaceable, and in this respect it distanced itself from the warmongering traditions of Old World militarism.

For much of the twentieth century, American consumer culture acted as a revolutionary force, its social inventions and message about the right to comfort as powerful a solvent of old ties as any political revolution. But no revolutions are permanent. They change course. They peter out. Or their principles and institutions become so diffuse that they are no longer identified with their originators. New forces come into play; the solutions of the past turn into the problems of the present. Though the United States may still be the single most dynamic force behind to-day's now global consumer culture, it no longer exercises a sufficient technological edge to monopolize innovations in either production or consumption. Ultimately, the efforts of the national government to take upon itself the task of salesmanship have ended only by exposing that salesmanship has become not an instrument of statecraft, but a substitute for it.

So the Market Empire has lost its impetus to other regions. Today 80 percent of Europe's 519 million people use supermarkets, and 85 per-cent of the United States' 280 million. Yet over the last several years, the region that invented supermarkets has done the least to spread them globally. In the last decade, Carrefour has been the main innovator in Latin America. In China, with a potential market of 2.2 billion people, where already 30 percent of the volume passes through supermarkets, Carrefour was the first Western firm to enter Beijing in 1994, and still nudges out Wal-Mart, the world's largest retailer, in competition that be-came no-holds-barred in December 2004, when protection against for-eign retailing ended. Both Western firms are second to the leading Chi-nese conglomerates, which in only twenty years have mastered the latest standards of international distribution; and both face competition not only with one another and from other Western firms, but also from Hy-Mart and Trust-Mart and Lotus, the Taiwanese giants, and from Lotus, the leading Thai retailer.[30]

As multinationals have gone global, nothing now prevents the pio-neers of multinationalism from themselves falling prey to global preda-tors. In 1987 J. Walter Thompson was taken over in a hostile bid by the British-based firm Wire & Plastic Products. WPP's chief executive, Mar-tin Sorrell, had been the "third brother" at the London-based Saatchi & Saatchi until 1987, when, after acquiring WPP, he used its assets to take over first JWT, then two other of New York City's most prestigious old firms, Ogilvy & Mather and Young & Rubicam. Today they are cogs in the wheel of the London-based marketing service that operates forty companies in eighty-three nations.[31] In Europe, only Publicis is bigger.

Amidst the uncertainties of global public opinion, U.S. corporations vacillate about whether to link selling their products with selling the American nation. Though some marketing experts advise that "consum-ers can disapprove of Bush's cowboy image while still identifying them-selves with the Marlboro Man," public relations campaigns spending hundreds of millions of dollars a year are averse to risks.[32] Coca-Cola, still the world's leading brand in value and recognition, has become one with the landscape, even in far corners of rural China. It is present more surreptitiously through its longtime practice of buying up any carbonated beverage with a local customer base; currently, the parent company markets 300 other brands in 200 countries.[33] Procter & Gamble's Ariel still prospers by preserving its anonymity about national origin, the same strategy that won it a big share of market in the 1960s European "detergent wars." Relative newcomers on the European market like Anheuser-Busch, maker of Budweiser, differentiate their pitch according to the sensitivities of local consumers: in Germany the beer is marketed as Anheuser-Busch Budweiser with a strong gesture to the Germanness of its emigrant founder, in postsocialist Hungary as American Bud, and as plain Bud in 15 other countries. "We are not multi-national, we are multi-domestic," says McDonald's management after several years of brand backlash, as its outlets came under attack as the U.S. government's local surrogate and metonym for the violence perpetrated by the fast-track globalization of Western models of development. To the skepticism of experts who say that "a brand can only become so global before it is left with nothing," McDonald's has embarked on a campaign to connect all its markets and reach out to people of all ages. The Golden Arches have become smaller; the interiors are keyed to the local ambience with theme formats—Music, McDo Generation, Mountain; mascot Ronald McDonald now wears low-slung cargo pants and a loose-fitting shirt instead of a goofy worker coverall. In the Old World, a new menu promises to "get healthy for Europe" by adding salads to the core of burgers and french fries. The universal slogan "I'm loving it" hopes to reaffirm an emotional bond with consumers. There is huge potential there, as currently, for better or worse, people everywhere evince strong emotions about America.[34]

In the end, mass consumer culture is such an ephemeral form of material life that the great ruptures that formed it are easily lost to sight. As interest in its history grows and U.S. hegemony is discredited, the temptation will be strong to downplay the role that American social inventions played in local developments. The Rotary sign is posted once more in Dresden; and not just one, the first, posted in 1991 at the entrance to the newly opened Dresden Hilton, but two others, which serve the city's outlying districts and a less prestigious if broader membership. But today members more readily recall the vicissitudes of the 1930s than its American origins.[35] And their current concerns as a club root them very much in local realities, namely to find a balance between the "Ossies" of the former DDR and the "Wessies" of the Federal Republic, as well as to keep the small number of women members from dwindling below three. They are hard pressed to undertake significant service obligations at the international level when at home the incipient high-tech economy has still not brought local unemployment rates much below 20 percent and so much is yet to be done to rebuild the city from the last war. One of their first local initiatives was to help restore the nineteenth-century Semper Synagogue. The goal was not restitution, but to reassure religious Jews from the former Soviet Union that if they accepted contracts as first violinists in the city's orchestras, which have to compete with Stuttgart, Bonn, and other cultural upstarts, they would be guaranteed an appropriate place to worship. Though no longer as cosmopolitan a club as it was under the Von Frenkells, Arnholds, and Kühnes, its members thrive in a global world. In June 2004 club president Horst Jehmlich, a fifth-generation manufacturer of organs, was absent on a trip to Texas to install one of the family firm's giant instruments in the First Presbyterian Church of Kerrville, population 20,000. The club still regularly welcomes out-of-town visitors. At its luncheon in the Europe Room of the Hilton on June 9, three guests listened to the service subcommittee's report on the club's hard-fought effort to get international backing for local reconstruction projects, enjoyed an elegant if rapidly eaten three-course lunch, and heard Herbert Süss, chief executive of the East Saxony Savings Bank, speak about savings rates and local investment. One guest was a businessman from Dortmund, Germany, another a businessman from Patakuranga, New Zealand, and the third a historian from New York City; the historian's reasons for being there were both scientific and sentimental: she wanted to catch up on what had become of the club since September 1937.

Hardly a few decades will pass before it will take a sensitive archaeological eye to discern the traces left by the advance of the Market Empire in the stratifications of material culture deposited in the European area over the twentieth century. Then it will be discovered that the most ancient layers of debris, circa 1900–1915, reveal extremely rich artifacts. Their variety, quantity, and sheer craft imply an astonishing refinement in the styles of living, but also castelike differences among its peoples. The layers of a middle period, circa 1915–1945, reveal great swirls of conflict. Shards of tin and green glass, dented movie canisters, and fragments of pulp magazines abounding in sites across northwestern to central and

Toasting traditions: the Rotary of Dresden luncheon, Hilton Hotel, June 9, 2004. Courtesy of the Rotary Club of Dresden.

southern Europe suggest heavier and heavier contact with the western shores of the Atlantic, only to be pushed back, then propelled forward by the forces of war. Only a decade and a half later, circa 1960, the north-central area appears to be overrun with artifacts and buildings of cross-Atlantic influence. Everywhere the upper layers reveal a material life in upheaval. Even in regions known for their slow-changing ways the bones of oxen are mingled with Deere tractor pistons, and junked village well pumps are interlayered with steel fittings for ceramic toilets, 40-watt bulbs, discarded radio tubes, and carcasses of television sets. When central Paris is excavated, the remains of Le Drug Store seems to offer incontrovertible evidence of the triumph of a syncretic new material civilization, one linking Zenith, Capital of the Unsalted Seas, to the City of Light. The last decade of the twentieth century yields similar patterns of sedimentation accumulating on the banks of the Elbe; by the first years of the twenty-first century, the shopping malls, street life, and youth culture of the new high-tech center of Dresden don't look remarkably different from downtown Duluth's. The Hilton where Dresden's Rotary meets on alternate Wednesdays is only a little more polished than the Radisson where Duluth's gathers every other Thursday. Less than a century has passed, but American hegemony has left traces as distinctive if not as permanent as the Roman Empire left over a span of four centuries. Like Latin, classical aesthetics, Judeo-Christianity, legal codes, and the "urban package" of aqueducts, town fortifications, and colossea, these residues have become the bricks and mortar that local people will find, use, and have to make sense of in order to grasp the irresistible rise and inexorable decline of the Market Empire.

Notes
Bibliographic Essay
Acknowledgments
Index

Notes

INTRODUCTION

1. Woodrow Wilson, "Fighting Is the Slow Way to Peace," Address before the Salesmanship Congress, Detroit, July 10, 1916, *Congressional Record,* 64th Cong., 1st sess., app., 1480–82, reprinted in *The New Democracy,* vol. 4 of *The Public Papers of Woodrow Wilson,* ed. Ray Stannard Baker and William E. Dodd (New York: Harper and Brothers, 1926), 232–233; *Detroit News,* July 10, 1916, 1; *New York Times,* July 11, 1916, 1, 7. On the milieu in which Wilson was speaking, see Walter A. Friedman *Birth of a Salesman: The Transformation of Selling in America* (Cambridge, Mass.: Harvard University Press, 2004).

2. Geir Lundestad, "'Empire by Invitation' in the American Century," *Diplomatic History* 23 (spring 1999): 189–217; idem, *"Empire" by Integration: The United States and European Integration, 1945–1997* (Oxford: Oxford University Press, 1998); John Gaddis, "The Emerging Post-Revisionist Synthesis on the Origins of the Cold War," *Diplomatic History* 7 (summer 1983): 171–190. See also the various terms contemplated by Charles S. Maier, "The Politics of Productivity: Foundations of American International Economic Policy after World War II," in *The Cold War in Europe: Era of a Divided Continent,* ed. Maier (Princeton: Markus Weiner, 1996), 193; idem, "Alliance and Autonomy: European Identity and U.S. Foreign Policy Objectives in the Truman Years," in *The Truman Presidency,* ed. Michael J. Lacey (Washington, D.C., and New York: Woodrow Wilson International Center for Scholars and Cambridge University Press, 1989), 273–298; Reinhold Wagnleitner, "The Empire of the Fun, or Talkin' Soviet Union Blues," *Diplomatic History* 23 (spring 1999): 499–524.

3. Michel Foucault, *The History of Sexuality,* vol. 1: *An Introduction,* trans. Robert J. Hurley (New York: Pantheon, 1978), 95–96.

4. Paul Rabinow, ed., *The Foucault Reader* (New York: Pantheon, 1984), 376.

1. THE SERVICE ETHIC

Epigraphs: Sinclair Lewis, *Babbitt* (1922; reprint, New York: New American Library, 1961), 72; André Siegfried, *Europe's Crisis,* trans. H. H. Hemming and Doris Hemming (New York: John Wiley and Sons, 1935), 127.

1. On Dresden, see Erich Haenel, *Das alte Dresden: Bilder und Dokumente aus zwei Jahrhunderten* (Leipzig: H. Schmidt & C. Gunther, 1934); Eugen Kalkschmidt, *Dresden: Geschichte der Stadt in Wort und Bild* (Berlin: Deutscher Verlag der Wissenschaften, 1984); Elizabeth A. Ten Dyke, *Dresden: Paradoxes of Memory in History* (London: Routledge, 2001).

2. On Duluth, see Edith E. Nyman, comp., *Scrapbook of Duluth, 1930–1933* (Duluth: n.p., 1930–1933); John Flanagan, "The Minnesota Backgrounds of Sinclair Lewis' Fiction," *Minnesota History* 37 (1960): 1–13; Glenn N. Sandvik, *Duluth: An Illustrated History of the Zenith City* (Woodland Hills, Calif.: Windsor, 1983).

3. Michael W. Fedo, *"They Was Just Niggers"* (Ontario, Calif.: Brasch and Brasch, 1979).

4. George Killough, "Sinclair Lewis—Minnesota Rustic," *Sinclair Lewis Society Newsletter* 7 (fall 1998): 1, 9, 11, 12–13; see also Flanagan, "Minnesota Backgrounds."

5. Kjell Espmark, *The Nobel Prize in Literature: A Study of the Criteria behind the Choices* (Boston: G. K. Hall, 1986), 61.

6. Fredrik Böök, "Presentation Address," in *Nobel Prize Library: Published under the Sponsorship of the Nobel Foundation and the Swedish Academy,* ed. Alex Gregory (New York: CRM, 1971), 222; see also 52.

7. Thomas Mann, "Acceptance Speech," in Gregory, *Nobel Prize Library,* 226–227; Donald Prater, *Thomas Mann: A Life* (Oxford: Oxford University Press, 1995), 180. On the circumstances surrounding the award, see Kjell Strömberg, "The 1929 Prize," in Gregory, *Nobel Prize Library,* 391–394.

8. *Why Sinclair Lewis Got the Nobel Prize: Address by Erik Axel Karlfeldt, Permanent Secretary of the Swedish Academy, at the Nobel Festival, December 10, 1930; and Address by Sinclair Lewis before the Swedish Academy, December 12, 1930, on the Occasion of the Award of the Nobel Prize* (New York: Harcourt Brace, 1931); Glen A. Love, *Babbitt: An American Life* (New York: Twayne, 1993), 70; Richard R. Lingeman, *Sinclair Lewis: Rebel from Main Street* (New York: Random House, 2002), 351–359.

9. Sinclair Lewis, *Main Street* (1920; reprint, New York: Harcourt, Brace and World, 1948), 267.

10. Norbert Elias, *The History of Manners: The Civilizing Process* (1931), trans. Edmund Jephcott, vol. 1 (Oxford: Blackwell, 1994), esp. 3–28; idem, *The Germans: Power Struggles and the Development of Habitus in the Nineteenth and Twentieth Centuries,* trans. Eric Dunning and Stephen Mennel (New York: Columbia University Press, 1996).

11. Most eloquently and at length in Thomas Mann, *Reflections of a Nonpolitical Man* (1918), trans. Walter D. Morris (New York: F. Ungar, 1983), esp. 121–122, 264.

12. H. L. Mencken, "Portrait of an American Citizen," *Smart Set* 69 (October 1922): 37–40; reprinted in Martin Bucco, ed., *Critical Essays on Sinclair Lewis* (Boston: G. K. Hall, 1986), 138–140.

13. "Report of Special Commissioner T. C. Thomsen," October 1, 1928, Dresden file, European Office box (hereafter EO), Archive of Rotary International, Chicago Office, Rotary International, Evanston, Ill. (hereafter RIE); "Rotary Club Dresden (in Gründung)," October 16, 1928, ibid.;

Roster List of Charter Members, Rotary Club of Dresden, ibid.; Friedrich Von Wilpert, *Rotary in Deutschland: Ein Ausschnitt aus Deutschem Schicksal* (Bonn: Behrendt, 1991), 11–12.

14. Prater, *Thomas Mann,* 165; *Wochenbericht* Rotary Club München (hereafter RCM) 1/2 (October 9, 1928), Rotary Collection, Deutsche Bücherei, Leipzig (hereafter RCDB); "Mitglieder-Liste des 'Rotary Club of Munich,'" n.d. [October 1928–May 1929], Rotary International European Office, Zurich (hereafter RIZ). More generally, see Paul L. Unschuld, *Chronik des Rotary Club* (Munich: Cygnus Verlag, 2003), 13–47.

15. "Rotary Club München (in Gründung)," *Wochenbericht* RCM 1/2 (October 9, 1928), 1/5 (October 30, 1928), 2/20 (February 26, 1929), 2/21 (March 5, 1929), 2/23 (March 21, 1929), 2/32 (21 May 1929), all RCDB; Wilpert, *Rotary in Deutschland,* pp. 12–13.

16. Mann, "Acceptance Speech," 225; *Wochenbericht* RCM 3/21 (November 11, 1930), RCDB; Wilpert, *Rotary in Deutschland,* 26. For an example of Mann's talks, see "Mein Sommerhaus: Vortrag von Rot. Thomas Mann im RC München am 1 Dezember 1931," *Wochenbericht* RCM 4/22 (December 1, 1931), RCDB. On Mann's receipt of the Nobel Prize, see *Wochenbericht* RCM 2/21 (November 19, 1929), RCDB. On Mann's reported absence from the club, see *Wochenbericht* RCM 5/38 (March 3, 1933), RCDB; Unschuld, *Chronik,* 83–90.

17. "Das Problem der Freiheit," Mann's 1939 lecture, was reworked into "Krieg und Demokratie" (1940) and then into "How to Win the Peace" (1942), following the U.S. entry into the war. This last speech was presented to the Rotary Club of Los Angeles on February 12, 1942; S. Volkmar Hansen and Gert Heine, eds., *Frage und Antwort: Interviews mit Thomas Mann 1909–1955* (Hamburg: Knaus, 1983), 285 ff.; Prater, *Thomas Mann,* 311, 316–317, 339.

18. Quoted in Barbara J. Drake, *The Rotary Club of Gloucester: A History, 1920–1990* (Gloucester, U.K.: Orchard and Ind, 1990), 1. More generally, on Rotary in the United States, see Charles F. Marden: *Rotary and Its Brothers: An Analysis and Interpretation of the Men's Service Club* (Princeton: Princeton University Press, 1935); Jeffrey A. Charles, *Service Clubs in American Society: Rotary, Kiwanis, and Lions* (Urbana: University of Illinois Press, 1993); David Shelley Nicholl, *The Golden Wheel: The Story of Rotary 1905 to the Present* (London: Macdonald and Evans, 1984).

19. Georg Simmel, *The Philosophy of Money* (1900; trans. Tom Bottomore and David Frisby, London: Routledge and Kegan Paul, 1978), 476; Mary Ann Clawson, *Constructing Brotherhood: Class, Gender, and Fraternalism* (Princeton: Princeton University Press, 1989), 264.

20. Charles A. Beard and Mary Beard, *The Rise of American Civilization* (1927) (New York: Macmillan, 1930), 730–731.

21. Robert and Helen Merrell Lynd, *Middletown* (1929; reprint, New York: Harcourt, Brace and World, 1956), 301–309.

22. University of Chicago, Social Science Survey Committee, *Rotary? A University Group Looks at the Rotary Club of Chicago* (Chicago: University of Chicago Press, 1934), 55–62.

23. Robert Putnam, *Bowling Alone: The Collapse and Revival of American Community* (New York: Simon and Schuster, 2001).

24. Alexis de Tocqueville, *Democracy in America* (1835–1840), trans. George Lawrence, ed. J. P. Mayer (Garden City, N.Y.: Anchor, 1969), 509–517.

25. Johan Huizinga, quoted in Herbert H. Rowen, ed., *America: A Dutch Historian's Vision—From Afar and Near* (New York: Harper and Row, 1972), 236–237.

26. Lewis, *Babbitt*, 151.

27. Tocqueville, *Democracy in America*, 514, 521.

28. C. R. Hewitt, *Towards My Neighbour: The Social Influence of the Rotary Club Movement in Great Britain and Ireland* (New York: Longmans, Green, 1950), 132–138 ff.; University of Chicago, *Rotary?* 122.

29. Charles Perrow, "A Framework for the Comparative Analysis of Organizations," *American Sociological Review* 32 (1967): 194–208; Clawson, *Constructing Brotherhood*, 240.

30. Quoted in *60 Jahre Rotary Club Saarbrücken, 1930–1990: Beständigkeit im Wandel* (Saarbrücken: Rotary Club, 1990), 10.

31. "Manual of Procedure: The Rotary Name and Emblem and Their Uses," *Proceedings of the 12th Annual Rotary Convention* (Chicago: International Association of Rotary Clubs, 1921), 509; Carl Andrew Zapffe, *Rotary! An Historical, Sociological, and Philosophical Study Based upon the Half-Century Experience of One of the Larger Rotary Clubs* (Baltimore: Rotary Club of Baltimore, 1963), 9–11; also University of Chicago, *Rotary?* 10.

32. Marden, *Rotary and Its Brothers*, 38 ff.

33. "Duluth Plays Unique Part in Rotary Annals," *Duluth News Tribune*, May 18, 1936, 4. See also *An Introduction to Rotary International and the Rotary Club of Duluth* (Duluth: Rotary Club of Duluth, 1993).

34. Charles Haddon Nabers, *When Rotary Hosts Trek Eastward* (Charlotte, N.C.: Presbyterian Standard, 1928), introduction.

35. T. C. Thomsen, "What Can Rotary Do for Europe?" 69–70, 74, Proceedings of the 1927 Rotary Convention, Ostend, Session of Tuesday morning, June 7, 1927, RIE.

36. J. Anton E. Verkade, "The Extension of Rotary in Europe," 78, ibid.

37. F. W. Teele to Chesley R. Perry, November 22, 1927, 3, European Convention file, box 3, General Affairs, RIZ; see also Zurich 1926, ibid.; "Feuille de Quinzaine du Rotary Club de Paris," September 22, 1926, France 49th District, 1926–27 file, ibid.

38. Zurich 1926, European Convention file, ibid.; Marcel Franck, "Admission de l'Allemagne dans le Rotary International, discours de Marcel Franck, Gouverneur 49ème District," 5-page speech in typescript, n.d., France 49th district, 1926–27 file, ibid.; Conference of leaders of 49th District in Paris, October 14, 1926, ibid.

39. "Wilhelm Cuno, Response to Welcome," 78–79, Proceedings of the 1928 Rotary Convention in Minneapolis, Session of Tuesday morning, June 19, RIE.

40. Fred Warren Teele, Corresponding Secretary, Rotary International, to Governor Willems, November 11, 1927, Extension file, European Advisory Committee (hereafter EAC), RIZ; Fred Warren Teele to Chester R. Perry, November 22, 1927, box 3, General Affairs, RIZ; Meeting, Zurich, November 19, 1927, ibid.

41. "T. C. Thomsen," *Kraks Blaa Bog* (Copenhagen: Kraks Legat, 1963), 1538.
42. Report of Special Commissioner T. C. Thomsen, October 1, 1928, Dresden file, EO, RIE; see also Wilpert, *Rotary in Deutschland*, 11–12.
43. Edgar A. Mowrer, *This American World* (London: Faber and Gwyer, 1928), 157. The power exercised by the images and models of Americanism on interwar Germany has been much studied. For persuasive introductions for the 1920s period, see Mary Nolan, *Visions of Modernity: American Business and the Modernization of Germany* (Oxford: Oxford University Press, 1994); on the 1930s, see Hans-Dietrich Schäfer, "Amerikanismus im Dritten Reich," in *Nationalsozialismus und Modernisierung,* ed. Michael Prinz and Rainer Zitelman (Darmstadt: Wissenschafliche Buchgesellschaft, 1991). For a more general introduction, see Frank Trommler and Elliott Shore, eds., *German-American Encounter: Conflict and Cooperation between Two Cultures, 1800–2000* (New York: Berghahn, 2001).
44. "Gedicht von Dr. Krüger für Nov 6, 1928," Dresden file, EO, RIE.
45. Wilpert, *Rotary in Deutschland*, 11.
46. *60 Jahre Rotary Club Saarbrücken,* 12.
47. Simone Lässig, "Nationalsozialistische Judenpolitik und jüdische Selbstbehauptung vor dem Novemberpogrom. Das Beispiel der Dresdner Bankiersfamilie Arnhold," in *Dresden unterm Hakenkreuz,* ed. Reiner Pommerin (Cologne: Bohlau Verlag, 1998), 129–191; Simone Lässig, "Juden und Mazenatentum in Deutschland," *Zeitschrift für Geschichtswissenschaft* 46 (1998): 211–236.
48. Zapffe, *Rotary!* 117; "Meeting of the EAC," Prague, March 3–4–5, 1933, 2, box 2, EAC, RIZ.
49. Peter Gay, *Weimar Culture: The Outsider as Insider* (New York: Harper and Row, 1968), 23.
50. Committee on Elections of Clubs, December 5, 1928, EO, RIE; Secretariat at Chicago, excerpt of letter from Alex Potter to Rotary International, Chicago Secretariat, October 8, 1931, RIE.
51. Benjamin Lapp, "Der Aufsteig des Nationalsozialismus in Sachsen," in Pommerin, *Dresden,* 1–24; also idem, *Revolution from the Right: Politics, Class, and the Rise of Nazism in Saxony, 1919–1933* (Atlantic Highlands, N.J.: Humanities Press, 1997), esp. chaps. 6–8.
52. Ferdinand Tönnies, *Gemeinschaft und Gesellschaft* (1887), in *Community and Civil Society,* trans. Harris Hollis and Margaret Hollis, ed. José Harris (Cambridge: Cambridge University Press, 2001), 102.
53. Niebyl, "Kant und Rotary," *Beilage zum Wochenbericht* (Baden-Baden) 34 (1934–1935): 1, RCDB.
54. Eugen Kahn and Rudolf Forschner, "Zur Einführung," *Der Rotarier für Deutschland und Österreich* 1 (October 1929): 2. One mark of of this self-referential behavior was the systematic collection of all Rotary publications, however ephemeral they might be. In his capacity as director of the Deutsche Bücherei at Leipzig, Rotarian Uhlendal at Von Frenckell's suggestion established a special German Rotary Archive, the only one of its kind, with 17,400 items by 1935, almost all in the German language.
55. Thomas Mann, "Vom schönen Zimmer," *Der Rotarier* 1 (October 1929):

24–25; more generally, W. H. Bruford, *The German Tradition of Self-Cultivation: Bildung from Humboldt to Thomas Mann* (London: Cambridge University Press, 1975), 206–263.

56. Felix Salten, "Ammerkung zur Rotary-Idee," *Der Rotarier* 1 (October 1929): 22–23.

57. *Wochen-Bericht* (Dresden) 3/26 (June 22, 1931), RCDB; Viktor von Klemperer, "Memoirs," 53, MM115, ME 559, Leo Baeck Institute Archives, New York.

58. *Wochen-Bericht* (Dresden) 3/26 (June 22, 1931), RCDB.

59. "Minutes of Frankfurt Meeting," November 18, 1929, reported November 20, 1929, 8–9, EAC, RIZ.

60. Hewitt, *Towards My Neighbour,* 130; Nicholl, *The Golden Wheel,* 398.

61. Quoted by Chesley R. Perry to Lester B. Struthers, November 15, 1937, General file, EAC, RIZ.

62. Alex O. Potter to Chesley R. Perry, "Arguments for and against Classification Rules," November 23, 1933, ibid.

63. Nicholl, *The Golden Wheel,* 412–413; Calum Thomson, "Beveridge Report," The History of Rotary Project, http://rotaryclubhistory.org/cities/clubs/50London/Beveridge.htm.

64. Giuseppe Belluzzo, president of Rotary Italiano, to Benito Mussolini, July 31, 1931, fasc. 301, busta 27, G 1, Affari generali e riservati, Ministero della Pubblica Sicurezza, Archivio Centrale dello Stato, Rome; Alfredo Rocco to Benito Mussolini, October 20, 1931, ibid.; Pro-memoria per il capo del governo, February 18, 1930, subfasc. 1, ibid.; Ernesto Cianci, *Il Rotary nella società italiana* (Milan: Mursia, 1983), 97–118; Amelia Belloni Sonzogni, *Rotary in Milano, 1923–1993* (Milan: Rotary, 1993); Armando Frumento, ed., *Nascita e rinascita del Rotary a Milano e in Italia* (Milan: Rotary International, 1976).

65. Kurt Belfrage, "Aims & Objectives Committee" Meetings, Antwerp, March 22, 1935, 9, 13, box 2, EAC, RIZ; Louis E. Steinmann, 3, ibid.

66. Rotarian Newson, "Minutes of Frankfurt Meeting," November 18, 1929, reported November 20, 1929, 13, box 2, ibid.

67. Governor Willems, "Réunion de Paris, 17 Décembre 1927," 14, France 49th district 1926–1927 file, box 3, RIZ.

68. Daniel Baggioni, *Langue et nationalité en Europe* (Paris: Payot, 1997), 320.

69. Antoine Meillet, *Les langues dans l'Europe nouvelle* (Paris: Payot, 1928), 467–483; see also Herbert Newhard Shenton, *Cosmopolitan Conversation: The Language Problems of International Conferences* (New York: Columbia University Press, 1933).

70. "Rotary Club Dresden," *Mitglieder-Verzeichnis der Rotary Klubs,* 1934, 88–91; "Rotary Club Dresden," ibid., 1936, 100–105, both General Affairs, RIZ.

71. "Minutes of the March 1935 Meeting of the EAC of RI," 10, box 3, EAC, RIZ.

72. Wilpert, *Rotary in Deutschland,* 21.

73. J. A. Crabtree to A. O. Potter, January 16, 1934, EAC Subcommittee on Classification, RIZ; cf. Rotary Italiano, *Annuario* (Milan), 1937–38.

74. Russell V. Williams to Karl Von Frenckell, November 17, 1928, 3–4, Dresden file, EO, RIE; Williams to Alex O. Potter, December 7, 1928, ibid.

75. E.g., Lester Struthers to Philip Lovejoy, Zurich, 21 August, 1946, 1, France: Paris, vol. 3, RIZ.

76. Frumento, *Nascita e rinascita del Rotary,* 31, 20.

77. *Il Rotary,* February 1936, 33.

78. "Duluth Rotary Club Sets 60th Birthday Party," *Duluth Sunday News-Tribune,* February 14, 1971.

79. *Wochen-Bericht* (Dresden) 2/28 (April 25, 1929), RCDB.

80. Jesus Rubio Villaverde, *Rotary en España (1920–1992)* (Murcia: Impresopor Imprenta Belmar, 1993), 97.

81. Tocqueville, *Democracy in America,* 432. On the expansionist tendencies of American Protestantism, see R. Lawrence Moore, "American Religion as Cultural Imperialism," in *The American Century in Europe,* ed. R. Lawrence Moore and Maurizio Vaudagna (Ithaca: Cornell University Press, 2003).

82. Felipe Alonso Barcena, "Los rotarios y su codigo moral," *Razon y Fe* 80 (1927): 356; "Rotarismo y masoneria," ibid., 81 (1927): 5–18.

83. An excellent overview of Church-Rotary relations is found in Ernesto Cianci, "Rotary and Catholicism," in *Rotary and Currents of Contemporary Opinion* (Arezzo: n.p., 1985).

84. "Rotary Club e Massoneria," *Civiltà Cattolica,* July 12, 1928, 107–108.

85. Russell V. Williams–Chesley R. Perry, Jan. 12, 1928, subfile C28, 1927–28, C28 Catholic Church and Rotary file, RIE; C. R. Perry–Etienne Fougère, Dec. 5, 1930, and E. Fougère–C. R. Perry, Jan. 7, 1930; subfile C28 France, ibid.; Maurice Duperrey–C. R. Perry, Dec. 2, 1933, subfile C28 France, ibid.; A. O. Potter–M. Duperrey, May 14, 1935, ibid.; A. O. Potter–Robert Burgers, n.d. (spring 1935), C28 France, 1935–36 file, ibid.

86. John Cavanaught, C. S. C., to Fred Warren Teele, C28, 1926–1927 file, C28 Catholic Church and Rotary file, RIE.

87. Edouard Willems to Emmet Richard, February 17, 1936, C28 Catholic Church and Rotary, 1935–1936 file, RIE.

88. *Le Rotary* 71 (November 1934).

89. Governor Luigi Piccione to Alex O. Potter, November 5 and 8, 1934, 46th District (Italy) file, box 3, 1934–1935 letters, RIZ.

90. Mary Vincent, "Spain," in *Political Catholicism in Europe, 1918–1965,* ed. Tom Buchanan and Martin Conway (Oxford: Clarendon Press, 1996), 97–98.

91. "Confidential Memorandum of the visits made by the Reverend D. Gonzalo Arteche to some of the clubs in Spain and South America (1929)," C28 Catholic Church and Rotary 1929–1930 file, RIE.

92. *Wochen-Bericht* (Dresden) 5/37 (March 29, 1933) and 5/38 (April 6, 1933), RCDB; Wilpert, *Rotary in Deutschland,* 62.

93. "Memoirs, Dr. Fritz Salzburg, Dresden, 1935–1937," 82–83, typescript, 1940, courtesy of his daughter Rosemary Heidekraut and Ernest H. Maron.

94. Ibid. See also Dr. Fritz Salzburg, "Manuscript and Documents Submitted to the German Life-History Prize Competition Committee" (1940), 195, Ger 91, BMS, Houghton Library, Harvard University.

95. *Wochen-Bericht* (Dresden) 7/37 (March 19, 1936), regarding the meeting of March 18, 1935, RCDB.

96. Salzburg, "Memoirs"; also Friedrich Salzburg to Rotary Club–Dresden, at-

tention of Club President, Dr. Grünert, November 13, 1935, in Salzburg, "Manuscript and Documents." On the fate of another Jewish Dresdener, a distant relative of Victor von Klemperer, see Victor Klemperer, *I Will Bear Witness: A Diary of the Nazi Years, 1933–1941*, trans. Martin Chalmers (New York: Random House, 1998).

97. Wilpert, *Rotary in Deutschland*, 128, 141, 143.

98. Ibid., 128–147; and "Report of Representative of RI on Conference of 73rd District Held at Hannover, Germany, on 7, 8 and 9 May, 1937," 73rd District (Germany and Austria), 1936–37 file, RIZ.

99. G. Medici del Vascello to Benito Mussolini, August 27, 1937, fasc. 3.29.1524, Presidenza del Consiglio dei Ministri, 1937–1939, Archivio Centrale dello Stato.

100. *Il Rotary*, September 1938, 369.

101. Ibid.; also Frumento, *Nascita e rinascita del Rotary*, 170 ff.

102. Wilpert, *Rotary in Deutschland*, 129–131. A fuller discussion of Rotary International's position on the purges of Jewish club members is found in Walter Struthers to Philip Lovejoy, October 16, 1946, folder Verscheidenes mit Germany zu tun, EAC, RIZ.

103. Frumento, *Nascita e rinascita del Rotary*, 177, 181.

104. *Wochen-Bericht* (Dresden) 9/3, July 23, 1936, RCDB.

105. Ibid., May 24, 1937.

106. Ibid., August 30, 1937.

107. Marc Levin, *Histoire et histoires du Rotary* (Lyons: IBF, 1995), 115–116.

108. David Irving, *The Destruction of Dresden* (New York: Holt, Rinehart and Winston, 1963), 71; "Historical Analysis of the 14–15 February 1945 Bombings of Dresden," USAF Historical Division, Research Studies Institute, Air University, <www.airforcehistory.hq.af.mil/soi/dresden.htm>; Reiner Pommerin, "Zur Einsicht bomben? Die Zerstörung Dresdens in der Luftkrieg-Strategie des Zweiten Welkriegs," in Pommerin, *Dresden*, 227–246.

2. A DECENT STANDARD OF LIVING

Epigraphs: Stanley Hiller, *Exporting Our Standard of Living* (San Francisco: John Howell, 1945), 29; Adolf Hitler, *Hitler's Secret Book*, trans. Salvator Attanasio, ed. Telford Taylor (New York: Grove, 1961), 19.

1. Hiller, *Exporting Our Standard of Living*, preface.

2. For the circumstances in which *Hitler's Secret Book* was written, see Ian Kershaw, *Hitler, 1889–1936: Hubris* (New York: W. W. Norton, 1999), 291–292, 688 n. 202.

3. Hitler, *Hitler's Secret Book*, xiv–xviii, 96. On Fordism in Germany, see Philip Gassert, "Without Concessions to Marxist or Communist Thought: Fordism in Germany, 1923–1929," in *Transatlantic Images and Perceptions: Germany and America since 1776*, ed. David E. Barclay and Elisabeth Glaser-Schmidt (New York: Cambridge University Press and the German Historical Institute, 1997), 217–241.

4. The literature on the standard of living is vast, and, as the entry in the *Encyclopedia of the Social Sciences* (New York: Macmillan, 1938) acknowl-

edges at the beginning, "the concept . . . has yet to be worked into definitive form." See Carl Brinkman, "Standards of Living," ibid., 322–355. For a view of the biases at play in the use of the term, see Serge Latouche, "Standards of Living," in *The Development Dictionary: A Guide to Knowledge as Power*, ed. Wolfgang Sachs (London: Zed Books, 1992), 250–263; and Ivan Illich, "Needs," ibid., 88–101.

5. *Hitler's Secret Book*, 96.

6. Lyndall Urwick to Albert Thomas, July 16, 1929, T 101/0/1, Cost of Living file, Archives of the International Labor Organization, Geneva (hereafter ILO).

7. Memorandum of interview between Lyndall Urwick and Sir Percival Perry, London, September 26, 1929, 1, T 101/0/1, Ford-Filene Enquiry file, ILO. On the expansion of Ford in Europe and the role of its European management, see Mira Wilkins and Frank Ernest Hill, *American Business Abroad: Ford on Six Continents* (Detroit: Wayne State University Press, 1964); and the definitive recent study, Hubert Bonin, Yannick Lung, and Steven Tolliday, eds., *Ford: The European History, 1903–2003*, 2 vols. (Paris: Editions P.L.A.G.F., 2003), esp. 1: 95–168, 319–358; 2: 151–160, 197–198.

8. C. J. Ratzlaff, "The International Labor Organization," *American Economic Review* 22 (September 1932): 447–461, quotation from 449; *Treaty of Versailles* (1919), part XIII, "Labour," preamble. On the ILO, in addition to Ratzlaff, see E. J. Phelan, *Yes and Albert Thomas* (London: Cressent, 1936); and Franco De Felice, *Sapere e politica: L'organizzazione internazionale del lavoro tra le due guerre, 1919–1939* (Milan: Franco Angeli, 1988).

9. Carle Clark Zimmerman, *Consumption and Standards of Living* (1936; reprint, Arno, 1976), 378–417.

10. Draft article by Clarence Streit, May 28, 1929.

11. Copy of telegram, E. A. Filene to Sir Eric Drummond at the League of Nations, July 11, 1929, ibid.; Filene quoted in summary of conversation between Lyndall Urwick and Sir Percival Perry, London, September 26, 1929, ibid.

12. E. A. Filene to A. Thomas, June 7 and 8, 1929, ibid. More generally on the expansion of American foundations abroad, see the recent excellent article by Volker R. Berghahn, "Philanthropy and Diplomacy in the American Century," *Diplomatic History* 23 (summer 1999): 393–419. Progressives of an earlier era also studied the phenomenon. See Merle Curti, *American Philanthropy Abroad: A History* (New York: Rutgers University Press, 1963).

13. Clippings of C.-J. Gignoux, "Triptyque américain," *La journée industrielle*, June 5, 1929; Jean Pupier, "Comment l'Amérique peut espérer conquérir la domination économique du monde," *La journée industrielle*, June 23–24, 1929, both in T 101/0/1, Cost of Living file, ILO.

14. Max Gottschalk to M. Breaud, October 9, 1929, ibid.

15. See *International Wage Comparisons: Documents Arising out of Conferences Held at the International Labour Office in Jan. 1929 and May 1930* (Manchester: Manchester University Press, 1932); W. J. Ellison, "Proposed International Wages and Cost of Living Enquiry," 7 pp., T 101/0/1, Cost of Living file, ILO.

16. Zimmerman, *Consumption and Standards of Living*, 475; Olivier Zunz,

Why the American Century? (Chicago: University of Chicago Press, 1998), 36–37. The paths by which Americans acquired the knowledge offered by European social sciences is studied in Daniel T. Rodgers, *Atlantic Crossings: Social Politics in a Progressive Age* (Cambridge, Mass.: Belknap Press of Harvard University Press, 1998).

17. Telegram, A. Thomas to E. A. Filene, May 31, 1929, T 101/0/1, Cost of Living file, ILO; W. J. Ellison to Herbert Feis, July 13, 1929, ibid. Debate continued thereafter, as evidenced in "Comité nommé per le C. A. en vue d'examiner l'adoption du don de 25.000 offert par M. Filene au nom du 20th Century Fund, Réunion du 9 septembre 1929," Undertaking Entered into Concerning Carrying Out the Enquiry and the Printing and Publication of Results folder, Confidential, 1932, T 101/0/1/0, ibid. See also Bertus Willem Schaper, *Albert Thomas: Trente ans de réformisme social* (Assen: Van Gorcum, 1959), 234.

18. L. Urwick to J. W. Nixon, October 1, 1929, T 101/0/1, Cost of Living file, ILO; Stephen Meyer III, *The Five Dollar Day: Labor Management and Social Control in the Ford Motor Company, 1908–1921* (Albany: SUNY Press, 1981); Clarence Hooker, *Life in the Shadows of the Crystal Palace, 1910–1927: Ford Workers in the Model T Era* (Bowling Green, Ohio: Bowling Green State University Popular Press, 1997), 134–137.

19. Meyer, *Five Dollar Day*, 218–219.

20. Enquiry into Standard of Living of Detroit Workers, T 101/0/1/61, Cost of Living file, ILO; Twentieth Century Fund news release, "International Wage Investigation Begun at Detroit," January 13, 1930, ibid.; J. W. Nixon to L. Urwick, October 8, 1929, with "Enquiry for the Ford Motor Co. Preliminary Plan," ibid.

21. "Ford Enquiry: Present Position," May 1931, Undertaking Entered into . . . folder, T 101/0/1/0, 1932, ibid.

22. Clipping, "La politique des hauts salaires," *Le Temps,* June 12, 1929, T 101/0/1, ibid.

23. Ibid.; Enquiry into Standard of Living of Detroit Workers: Memorandum on Possible Collaboration by National Bureau of Economic Research, n.d. [probably December 1929], T 101/01/1/61, 1931, ibid.

24. Ministre du travail et de la prévoyance sociale [Pierre Laval] to Arthur Fontaine, Delegate of the French Government, ILO, July 25, 1930, T 101/0/1/2/22, ibid.

25. Wilkins and Hill, *American Business Abroad,* 230.

26. Ibid.

27. "Standard of Living of Employees of Ford Motor Co. in Detroit," in ILO, *A Contribution to the Study of International Comparisons of Costs of Living,* 2d rev. ed. (Geneva, 1932), annex I, 159–200; J. W. Nixon, "How Ford's Lowest-Paid Workers Live," annex III, ibid., 208–215.

28. Comparative statistics are suprisingly rare and approximate. *Statistsches Jahrbuch,* 1941–41, p. 109, cited in *Das deutsche Reich und der Zweite Weltkrieg,* 5/1 (Stuttgart: Deutsche Verlags-Anstalt, 1979), 651, in turn cited by MacGregor Knox, *Hitler's Italian Allies* (Cambridge: Cambridge University Press, 2000), p. 30, offers perhaps the most brutally accurate indices of the differences between the United States and European countries, as well as the differences among the latter.

29. See Rosa-Maria Gelpi and François Julien-Labruyère, *The History of Consumer Credit: Doctrines and Practices* (New York: St. Martin's Press, 2000), mainly on France. For conditions in the early twentieth-century United States, see Martha L. Olney, *Buy Now, Pay Later: Advertising, Credit, and Durables in the 1920s* (Chapel Hill: Universirty of North Carolina Press, 1991).

30. J. W. Nixon's memorandum of meeting with E. A. Filene and Director [Albert Thomas], January 14, 1932, Undertaking Entered into . . . folder, T 101/0/1/0, 1932, Cost of Living file, ILO.

31. "Ford Enquiry: Present Position," May 1931, 9, ibid.

32. L. Magnusson to H. B. Butler, December 22, 1931, T 10/0/1/61, Cost of Living file, ILO.

33. Keith Sward, *The Legend of Henry Ford* (1948; reprint, New York: Atheneum, 1968), 218–220.

34. Governing Body of the ILO, "Minutes, Fifth Sitting," January 15, 1932, 29–49, Undertaking Entered into . . . folder, T 101/0/1/0, 1932, Cost of Living file, ILO.

35. ILO, *A Contribution*, 1.

36. Pierre Abelin, *Essai sur la comparaison internationale des niveaux de vie ouvriers* (Paris: Librarie Générale de Droit et de Jurisprudence, 1936), 102–110.

37. "Ford Enquiry: Present Position," May 1931, Undertaking Entered into . . . folder, T 101/0/1/0, 1932, Cost of Living file, ILO; Wilkins and Hill, *American Business Abroad*, 101.

38. Cited in Werner Sombart, *Why Is There No Socialism in the United States?* (1906) (White Plains, N.Y.: M. E. Sharpe, 1976), 11–12.

39. Armand Julin, Governing Body of the ILO, "Minutes, Fifth Sitting," January 15, 1932, 34, Undertaking entered into . . . folder, T 101/0/1/0, 1932, Cost of Living file, ILO.

40. François Simiand, *Le salaire, l'évolution sociale et la monnaie: Essai de théorie expérimentale du salaire*, vol. 2 (Paris: F. Alcan, 1932), 404, 410.

41. François Simiand, *Cours d'économie politique professé en 1929–1930* (Paris: Editions Domat-Montchrestien, 1930), 288, quoted in Maurice Halbwachs, *L'évolution des besoins dans les classes ouvrières* (Paris: F. Alcan, 1933), 8.

42. ILO, *A Contribution*, 106.

43. Abelin, *Comparaison internationale*, 88–96.

44. Meyer, *Five Dollar Day*, 49.

45. Sward, *Legend of Henry Ford*, 56 and, more generally, 50–63; Daniel M. G. Raff, "Wage Determination Theory and the Five-Dollar Day at Ford," *Journal of Economic History* 48 (June 1988): 387–398; David A. Hounshell, *From the American System to Mass Production, 1800–1932: The Development of Manufacturing Technology in the United States* (Baltimore: Johns Hopkins University Press, 1984), 217–325.

46. Paul Mazur, *American Prosperity: Its Causes and Consequences* (New York: Viking, 1928), 7. The early origins of the contrast between New World idealism and European depravity in the treatment of labor are explored in Charles L. Sanford, "The Intellectual Origins and New-Worldliness of American Industry," *Journal of Economic History* 18, no. 1 (1958): 1–16.

47. William Appleman Williams, *Empire as a Way of Life* (New York: Oxford University Press, 1980), 220.

48. Simon N. Patten, *The New Basis of Civilization* (New York: Macmillan, 1907), 23; William Leach, *Land of Desire: Merchants, Power, and the Rise of a New American Culture* (New York: Pantheon, 1993), 213 ff.

49. Figures excluding Russia and Turkey, drawn up by Lyndall Urwick and F. P. Valentine for the International Chamber of Commerce, *Trends in the Organization and Methods of Distribution in the Two Areas,* vol. 5 of *Europe–United States of America* (Paris: International Chamber of Commerce, 1931), 10–12.

50. Alfred D. Chandler Jr. with Takashi Hikino, *Scale and Scope: The Dynamics of Industrial Capitalism* (Cambridge, Mass.: Belknap Press of Harvard University Press, 1990), 52.

51. Philip Scranton, *Endless Novelty: Specialty Production and American Industrialization, 1865–1925* (Princeton: Princeton University Press, 1997); Charles F. Sabel and Jonathan Zeitlin, eds., *World of Possibilities: Flexibility and Mass Production in Western Industrialization* (Paris: Maison de Science de l'Homme; Cambridge: Cambridge University Press, 1997).

52. Lawrence B. Glickman, *A Living Wage: American Workers and the Making of Consumer Society* (Ithaca: Cornell University Press, 1997); idem, "Inventing the 'American Standard of Living': Gender, Race, and Working Class Identity, 1880–1925," *Labor History* 34 (spring–summer 1993): 221–235.

53. Quoted in Glickman, "Inventing the 'American Standard of Living,'" 231.

54. Leach, *Land of Desire,* 189.

55. Theresa S. McMahon, *Social and Economic Standards of Living* (Boston: D. C. Heath, 1925), 106, 110 ff.

56. Zunz, *Why the American Century?* 80–92.

57. Sombart, *Why Is There No Socialism in the United States?* 109.

58. Hazel Kyrk, *A Theory of Consumption* (London: Isaac Pitman and Sons, 1923), 174–177.

59. Simon Nelson Patten, *The New Basis of Civilization* (New York: Macmillan, 1907), 9; Leach, *Land of Desire,* 237; on Patten, see Daniel M. Fox, *The Discovery of Abundance: Simon N. Patten and the Transformation of Social Theory* (Ithaca: Cornell University Press for the American Historical Association, 1967).

60. Robert Lynd, "The People as Consumers," in *Recent Social Trends in the United States: Report of the President's Research Committee on Social Trends,* ed. Wesley Clair Mitchell (New York: McGraw-Hill, 1933); Wladimir S. Woytinsky and Emma Shadkhan Woytinsky, *World Commerce and Governments: Trends and Outlook* (New York: Twentieth Century Fund, 1955), 268; Hugo E. Pipping, *Standard of Living: The Concept and Its Place in Economics* (Helsinki, 1953), 131–132. A broad view of changing objective standards can be found in Clair Brown, *American Standards of Living, 1918–1988* (Oxford: Blackwell, 1994).

61. Margaret Reid, *Consumers and the Market* (New York: F. S. Crofts, 1939), 22–24.

62. Paul H. Nystrom, *Economic Principles of Consumption* (New York: Ronald Press, 1929), 177–230; idem, *Economics of Retailing* (New York: Ronald Press, 1930), 24.

63. Kyrk, *A Theory of Consumption*, 41, 177.
64. Jacob Viner, "W. H. Hutt: Economics and the Public: A Study of Competition and Opinion," *Journal of Political Economy* 46 (1938): 571–575. See also Joseph Persky, "Retrospectives: Consumer Sovereignty," *Journal of Economic Perspectives* 7 (winter 1993): 183–191.
65. André Siegfried, *America Comes of Age: A French Analysis* (New York: Harcourt, Brace, 1927), 436.
66. Antonio Gramsci, "Americanism and Fordism," in *An Antonio Gramsci Reader: Selected Writings, 1916–1935,* ed. David Forgacs (New York: Schocken, 1988), 275–299.
67. Friedrich von Gottl-Ottilienfeld, *Fordismus? Paraphrasen über das Verhältnis von Wirtschaft und Technischer Vernunft bei Henry Ford und Frederick W. Taylor* (Jena: G. Fischer, 1924).
68. François Delaisi, *Les deux Europes* (Paris: Payot, 1929). On Delaisi, see Laurent Badel, *Un milieu libéral et européen: Le grand commerce français, 1925–1948* (Paris: Comité pour l'Histoire Economique et Financière de la France, 1999), 144, 168, 172, 327; Urwick and Valentine, *Trends in the Organization*, 41.
69. See Paul Hirst and Jonathan Zeitlin, "Flexible Specialization versus Post-Fordism: Theory, Evidence and Policy Implications," *Economy and Society* 20 (February 1991): 1–56; and Charles Sabel and Jonathan Zeitlin, "Historical Alternatives to Mass Production: Politics, Markets and Technology in Nineteenth-Century Industrialization," *Past and Present* 108 (August 1985): 133–176.
70. Woytinsky and Woytinsky, *World Commerce,* 383–386; see also Urwick and Valentine, *Trends in the Organization,* 15–16.
71. Edmond Goblot, *La barrière et le niveau: Etude sociologique sur la bourgeoisie française moderne* (1925) (Paris: Presses Universitaires de France, 1967); on Goblot, see Jean Kergomard, Pierre Salzi, and François Goblot, *Edmond Goblot, 1858–1935: La vie, l'oeuvre* (Paris: F. Alcan, 1937).
72. Goblot, *La barrière et le niveau,* 2.
73. Max Weber, *Economy and Society: An Outline of Interpretive Sociology* (New York: Bedminster, 1968); see also Pierre Bourdieu, *Distinction: A Social Critique of the Judgment of Taste* (1979), trans. Richard Nice (Cambridge, Mass.: Harvard University Press, 1984).
74. Thorstein Veblen, *The Theory of the Leisure Class: An Economic Study of Institutions* (1899; reprint, New York: New American Library, 1953).
75. Fred Hirsch, *Social Limits to Growth* (1976; reprint, New York: toExcel, 1999), 60, 173.
76. Lucien De Chilly, *La classe moyenne en France après la guerre: 1918–1924; Sa crise: Causes, conséquences et remèdes* (Bourges: A. Tardy, 1924), 11; Hans Georg, "Our Stand at the Abyss—1921," in *The Weimar Republic Sourcebook,* ed. Anton Kaes, Martin Joy, and Edward Dimendberg (Berkeley: University of California Press, 1994), 182.
77. Lucien Romier, *Who Will Be Master, Europe or America?* trans. Matthew Josephson (New York: Macauley, 1928), 8 ff.
78. Geoffrey Crossick and Heinz-Gerhard Haupt, "Shopkeepers, Master Artisans, and the Historian: The Petite Bourgeoisie in Comparative Focus," in *Shopkeepers and Master Artisans in Nineteenth-Century Europe,* ed. Geoffrey Crossick and Heinz-Gerhard Haupt (London: Methuen, 1984);

see also Philip Nord, "The Small Shopkeepers' Movement and Politics in France, 1888–1914," in ibid.

79. Paul Lafargue, *Le droit à la paresse* (1883; reprint, Paris: Maspero, 1970), 133, 145–146.

80. Quoted in Louise-Marie Ferré, *Les classes sociales dans la France contemporaine* (Paris: Messageries Hachette, 1936), 83.

81. Quoted in Robert Skidelsky, *John Maynard Keynes: The Economist as Savior, 1920–1937* (London: Papermac, 1992), 519.

82. Sward, *Legend of Henry Ford,* 61.

83. On the resistance to changing this attitude, see Gary Cross, *Time and Money: The Making of Consumer Culture* (London: Routledge, 1993), 129–136.

84. Paul-Henry Chombart de Lauwe, *La vie quotidienne des familles ouvrières,* 3d ed. (Paris: Editions du Centre National de la Recherche Scientifique, 1977), 122.

85. George Orwell, *The Road to Wigan Pier* (London: Victor Gollancz, 1937).

86. Maurice Halbwachs, *La classe ouvrière et les niveaux de vie: Recherches sur la hiérarchie des besoins dans les sociétés industrielles contemporaines* (Paris: Librairie Félix Alcan, 1912); Christian Baudelot and Roger Establet, *Maurice Halbwachs: Consommation et société* (Paris: Presses Universitaires de France, 1994); Judith Coffin, "A 'Standard' of Living? European Perspectives on Class and Consumption in the Early Twentieth Century," *International Labor and Working-Class History* 55 (spring 1999), special issue, *Class and Consumption,* ed. Lizabeth Cohen and Victoria de Grazia, 6–26.

87. Jacques Lacour-Gayet, *Histoire du commerce,* vol. 1 of *La terre et les hommes* (Paris: SPID, 1950), 332–346; Ellen Furlough, *Consumer Cooperation in France: The Politics of Consumption, 1834–1930* (Ithaca: Cornell University Press, 1991); also Ellen Furlough and Carl Strikwerda, eds., *Consumers Against Capitalism? Consumer Cooperation in Europe, North America, and Japan, 1840–1990* (Lanham, Md.: Rowman and Littlefield, 1999).

88. Gaston Défossé, *La place du consommateur dans l'économie dirigée* (Paris: Presses Universitaires de France, 1941), 21–23; Pierre Arlet, *La consommation: L'éducation du consommateur* (Sarlat: Michelet, 1939), 120 ff.

89. Gide quoted in Lacour-Gayet, *Histoire du commerce,* 334.

90. Peter Scholliers, "The Social-Democratic World of Consumption: The Path-Breaking Case of the Ghent Cooperative Vooruit prior to 1914," *International Labor and Working Class History* 55 (spring 1999): 71–91.

91. Victoria de Grazia, "The Exception Proves the Rule: The American Example in the Recasting of Socialist Strategies in Europe between the Wars," in *Why Is There No Socialism in the United States/Pourquoi n'y a t-il pas de socialisme aux Etats-Unis?* ed. Jean Heffer and Jeanine Rovet (Paris: Editions de l'Ecole des Hautes Etudes en Sciences Sociales, 1988), 170–181; more generally on the fascinating De Man, see Dan S. White, *Lost Comrades: Socialists of the Front Generation, 1918–1945* (Cambridge, Mass.: Harvard University Press, 1992); and Stanley Pierson, *Leaving Marxism: Studies in the Dissolution of an Ideology* (Stanford: Stanford University Press, 2001).

92. Pierson, *Leaving Marxism,* chap. 2; also Zeev Sternhell, *Neither Right nor Left: Fascist Ideology in France* (1983), trans. David Maisel (Berkeley: University of California Press, 1986), 119–141.

93. Werner Sombart, *Deutscher Sozialismus* (1934), ed. and trans. by Karl F. Geiser as *A New Social Philosophy* (1937; reprint, New York: Greenwood, 1969), 246–248. On Sombart's reactionary turn, see Rolf Peter Sieferle, *Die Konservative Revolution. Fünf Biographische Skizzen* (Frankfurt am Main: Fischer, 1995), 74–105.

94. The rare author speaking to the subject came out of conservative liberal traditions and was trained in jurisprudence rather than political economy. For example: Georges Z. Strat, *Le rôle du consommateur dans l'économie moderne* (Paris: Editions de la Vie Universitaire, 1922).

95. John Maynard Keynes, *The Economic Consequences of the Peace* (New York: Harcourt, Brace and Howe, 1920), 19–20, 23.

96. Halbwachs reproved Keynes on the grounds that he was interested only in demand, not in consumption, and that this lack of empathy for the motives that made people save or spend, so visible in the abstraction of the General Theory's argumentation, weakened its predictive value. Though unfamiliar with Halbwachs, the young American economist James Duesenberry would make a similar point a decade later: to be effective, Keynesian policymakers needed to recognize that the choices behind demand were socially complex, reflecting evolving needs, class relations, and ideals of collective well-being. Maurice Halbwachs, "La 'Théorie Générale' de John Maynard," *Les annales sociologiques,* Série D: *Sociologie économique* 4 (1940): 25–41; James S. Duesenberry, *Income, Saving, and the Theory of Consumer Behavior* (Cambridge, Mass.: Harvard University Press, 1949). More generally, on the spread of Keynes's ideas, see Peter A. Hall, ed., *The Political Power of Economic Ideas: Keynesianism across Nations* (Princeton: Princeton University Press, 1989).

97. Lizabeth Cohen, "The New Deal State and the Making of Citizen Consumers," in *Getting and Spending: European and American Consumer Societies in the Twentieth Century,* ed. Susan Strasser, Charles McGovern, and Matthias Judt (Washington, D.C.: German Historical Institute; New York: Cambridge University Press, 1998), 111–125; Alan Brinkley, *The End of Reform: New Deal Liberalism in Recession and War* (New York: Alfred A. Knopf, 1995), 65–85.

98. Arlet, *La consommation,* 147.

99. Werner Abelshauser, "Germany: Guns, Butter, and Economic Miracles," in *The Economics of World War II: Six Great Powers in International Comparison,* ed. Mark Harrison (Cambridge: Cambridge University Press, 1998), 131; Hartmut Berghoff, "Enticement and Deprivation: The Regulation of Consumption in Pre-War Nazi Germany," in *The Politics of Consumption: Material Culture and Citizenship in Europe and America,* ed. M. J. Daunton and Matthew Hilton (Oxford: Berg, 2001), 165–184.

100. André Piettre, *La politique du pouvoir d'achat devant les faits: Expérience américaine et expérience française* (Paris: Librairie de Médicis, 1938).

101. Julian Jackson, *The Popular Front in France: Defending Democracy, 1934–38* (Cambridge: Cambridge University Press, 1988), 131–138, 159–182.

102. Halbwachs to his mother, November 20, 1930, 152, "Mission à Chicago," Lettres à Yvonne, HBW2.A1–03.3, Institut Mémoires de l'Edition Contemporaine, Paris; Marc Bloch, "La répartition des dépenses comme caractère de classe," *Annales d'histoire économique et sociale* 7, no. 31 (1935): 84; Halbwachs, *L'évolution des besoins*, 105.

103. Halbwachs, *L'évolution des besoins*, 57, 107; Judith G. Coffin, "A 'Standard' of Living? European Perspectives on Class and Consumption in the Early Twentieth Century," *International Labor and Working-Class History* 55 (spring 1999): 6–26, esp. 18–19; Christian Baudelot and Roger Establet, *Maurice Halbwachs: Consommation et société* (Paris: Presses Universitaires de France, 1994); Zimmerman, *Consumption*, 399–400.

104. Maurice Halbwachs, "Budgets de famille aux Etats-Unis et en Allemagne," *Bulletin de l'Institut Français de Sociologie* 3 (17 March 1933): 15, 65–67, 80.

105. Henry Delpech, *Recherches sur le niveau de vie et les habitudes de consommation (Toulouse, 1936–1938)* (Paris: Librarie du Recueil Sirey, 1938), 292, 319; also preface, 11.

106. André Siegfried, *Europe's Crisis*, trans. H. H. Hemming and Doris Hemming (New York: John Wiley and Sons, [1935]), 125 ff.

107. Arlet, *La consommation*, p. 136.

108. There are now two outstanding works on standards of living and consumption politics under Soviet rule. See Elena Osikina, *Our Daily Bread: Socialist Distribution and the Art of Survival in Stalin's Russia, 1927–1941* (Armonk, N.Y.: M. E. Sharpe, 2001); and Julie Hessler, *A Social History of Soviet Trade: Trade Policy, Retail Practice, and Consumption, 1917–1953* (Princeton: Princeton University Press, 2004).

109. Nancy Reagin, "Comparing Apples and Oranges: Housewives and the Politics of Consumption in Interwar Germany," in Strasser, McGovern, and Judt, *Getting and Spending*, 241–261; idem, "*Marktordnung* and Autarkic Housekeeping: Housewives and Private Consumption under the Nazi Four Year Plan, 1936–1939," *German History* 19 (May 2001): 162–184.

110. W. Robert Nitske, *The Amazing Porsche and Volkswagen Story* (New York: Comet, 1958), 121; Hans Mommsen and Manfred Grieger, *Das Volkswagenwerk und seine Arbeiter im Dritten Reich* (Dusseldorf: ECON, 1996), 92–226.

111. Sam E. Woods, Commercial Attaché, Special Report no. 70, Berlin, November 16, 1939, "Rationing of Clothing in Germany," November 16–30 file, box 272, record group 151, Bureau of Foreign and Domestic Commerce, National Archives, College Park, Md.

112. George R. Canty, Trade Commissioner, Special Report, Berlin, "Nazis Organize Spare-Time Movement among Working Classes," December 1, 1933, December 1933 file, ibid.

113. Shelley Baranowski, *Strength through Joy: Consumerism and Mass Tourism in the Third Reich* (Cambridge: Cambridge University Press, 2004).

114. Reinhard Opitz, ed., *Europastrategien des deutschen Kapitals: 1900–1945* (Cologne: Pahl-Rugenstein, 1977), 581; quoted in Volker Berghahn, ed., *Quest for Economic Empire: European Strategies of German Big Business in the Twentieth Century* (Providence: Berghahn Books, 1996), 17.

115. Paul Einzig, *Hitler's "New Order" in Europe* (London: Macmillan, 1941), 43–46.

116. François Delaisi, *La révolution européenne* (Brussels: Editions de la Toison d'Or, 1942).

117. J. Rosen, *Das Existenzminimum in Deutschland* (Zurich: Oprecht, 1939), 139.

118. H. G. Adler, *Theresienstadt 1941–1945: Das Antlitz einer Zwangsgemeinschaft* (Tübingen: J. C. B. Mohr, 1955), 364; more generally, on Nazi food politics, see Boris Shub, *Starvation over Europe (Made in Germany): A Documented Record, 1943* (New York: Institute of Jewish Affairs, 1943); on the rations at Buchenwald, see David A. Hackett, editor and translator, *The Buchenwald Report* (Boulder: Westview, 1995), 146–149.

119. Pierre Bourdieu, "L'assassinat de Maurice Halbwachs," *Visages de la Résistance* 16 (fall 1987): 161–168; Jorge Semprun, *L'écriture ou la vie* (Paris: Gallimard, 1994), 27–33.

3. THE CHAIN STORE

Epigraphs: Edward A. Filene with Werner K. Gabler and Percy S. Brown, *Next Steps Forward in Retailing* (New York: Harper and Brothers, 1937), v; Hermann Levy, *The Shops of Britain: A Study of Retail Distribution* (London: Kegan Paul, Trench, Trubner, 1947), 3.

1. Report of Edward A. Filene's European Trip, 1935, box 6, Filene Papers, Archive, Credit Union National Association, Madison, Wisc. (hereafter CUNA); Distribution Speeches, "How Can Our System of Distribution Be Improved?" June 26, 1935, box 7, ibid.

2. Filene lacks the significant biography he deserves. In general, see Gerald W. Johnson, *Liberal's Progress* (New York: Coward-McCann, 1948); Louis Filler, "Edward Albert Filene," in *Dictionary of American Biography,* Supplement 2, ed. Robert Livingston Schuyler and Edward T. James (New York: Charles Scribner's Sons, 1958), 183–185; John N. Ingham, "Filene, Edward Albert," in *Biographical Dictionary of American Business Leaders,* vol. 1 (Westport, Conn.: Greenwood, 1983), 376–379; "Filene, Edward Albert," in *National Cyclopaedia of American Biography,* vol. 45 (New York: James T. White, 1962), 17–19. On Filene's department store, Robert Hendrickson, *The Grand Emporiums: The Illustrated History of America's Great Department Stores* (New York: Stein and Day, 1980), 129–134; Mary La Dame, *The Filene Store: A Study of Employees' Relation to Management in a Retail Store* (New York: Russell Sage Foundation, 1930).

3. Memo: "Method of Working," March 16, 1934, Method of Working file, box 47, Filene Papers, CUNA.

4. "Summary Report, Project no. 9, Mr. Ford for the Nobel Peace Prize," Nobel Peace Prize, 1930 file, box 23, ibid.

5. Ralph Borsodi, *The Distribution Age: A Study of the Economy of Modern Distribution* (New York: D. Appleton, 1927) 3.

6. Johnson, *Liberal's Progress,* 148. For the voice of Ford, see Henry Ford with Samuel Crowther, *Today and Tomorrow* (Garden City, N.Y.: Doubleday, Page, 1926), 11, 248–249; on GM-Ford competition, see Rich-

ard S. Tedlow, *Henry Ford: The Profits and the Price of Primitivism* ([Boston]: Harvard Business School, Division of Research, 1996), chap. 3; more generally: Allan Nevins, *Ford: The Times, the Man, the Company* (New York: Scribner, 1954); Mira Wilkins and Frank Ernest Hill, *American Business Abroad: Ford on Six Continents* (Detroit: Wayne State University Press, 1964).

7. "Mass Buying Power and Economic Revival," address, VII Congress of the ICC, Vienna, May 29, 1933, 183, 185, 1933 European Trip, part 1, box 4, Filene Papers, CUNA.

8. E. A. Filene to Dr. Alexander Lyons, January 18, 1930, Ford for Nobel Peace Prize file, box 52, ibid.; E. A. Filene, handwritten comments, January 2, 1929, referring to *Henry Ford and the Jews,* by Samuel Crowther; draft of article for *Christian Science Monitor,* March 29, 1922; Edward A. Filene, "Ford: Pioneer, Not Superman," *The Nation* 116 (January 3, 1923): 17.

9. On Ford's anti-Semitism, see Neil Baldwin, *Henry Ford and the Jews: The Mass Production of Hate* (New York: Public Affairs, 2001).

10. Laurence Badel, *Un milieu libéral et européen: le grand commerce français, 1925–1948* (Paris: Comité pour l'Histoire Economique et Financière de la France, 1999), 38–39, 87–88, 213–214 301–302, 465–467; Jean-Paul Caracalla, *Le roman du Printemps: Histoire d'un grand magasin* (Paris: Editions Denoël, 1989).

11. S. J. (Serge Jaumain), "Famille Bernheim," in *Dictionnaire des patrons en Belgique: les hommes, les entreprises, les reseaux,* ed. Ginette Kurgan-van Hentenryk, Serge Jaumain, and Valerie Wontens (Brussels: De Boeck Université, 1996), 46–49; Jacques Lacrosse and Pierre de Bie, *Emile Bernheim: histoire d'un grand magasin* (Brussels: Labor, 1972).

12. On Selfridge, see Erika Diane Rappaport, *Shopping for Pleasure* (Princeton: Princeton University Press, 2000), 145–170; William Lancaster, *The Department Store: A Social History* (London: Leicester University Press, 1995), 94–107.

13. Lillian Schoedler, "Family Background, Education, Work," Sept. 19, 1942, 3, file 120, MC273, Lillian Schoedler Papers, 1891–1963, Schlesinger Library, Radcliffe College.

14. Johnson, *Liberal's Progress,* 231.

15. "Unalloyed vanity" quoted in Jean Milhaud, *Chemins faisant (tranches de vie)* (Paris: Editions Hommes et Techniques, 1956), 48, 59; Badel, *Un milieu libéral,* 215; Albert Thomas, "Note pour M. Butler," July 15, 1929, T 101/0/1, Cost of Living file, International Labor Organization, Geneva (hereafter ILO).

16. Herbert Hoover, "A Problem of Distribution: An Address, January 14–15, 1925," in Chamber of Commerce of the United States, *National Distribution Conference* (Washington, D.C., 1925), 4; Borsodi, *The Distribution Age,* 4–6.

17. Adam Smith, *The Wealth of Nations* (1776), book 1, chap. 3, Edwin Cannan, ed. (Chicago: University of Chicago Press, 1976), 21–25.

18. Theodore N. Beckman, "Criteria of Marketing Efficiency," *Annals of the American Academy of Political and Social Science,* May 1940, special issue, *Marketing in Our American Economy,* ed. Howard T. Hovde, 125, 127.

19. David R. Craig and Werner K. Gabler, "The Competitive Struggle for Market Control," ibid., 84–107.

20. Beckman, "Criteria of Marketing Efficiency, " 139.

21. F. W. Lawe, "Review: *The Distribution of Consumer Goods,*" *Economic Journal,* March 1951, 145, quoted from James B. Jefferys with M. MacColl and G. L. Levett, *The Distribution of Consumer Goods* (Cambridge: Cambridge University Press, 1950), chart 3, "The Cost of Distribution of Commodities and Commodity Groups in 1938."

22. Craig and Gabler, "Competitive Struggle for Market Control," 99–100, 107.

23. Filene, *Next Steps Forward in Retailing,* 148.

24. For the nineteenth century, see George Burton Hotchkiss, *Milestones of Marketing: A Brief History of the Evolution of Market Distribution* (New York: Macmillan, 1938); Harold Barger, *Distribution's Place in the American Economy since 1869* (Princeton: Princeton University Press, 1955).

25. Werner K. Gabler, *Probleme der amerikanischen Warenhäuser* (Zurich: Orell Füssli, 1934). On the role of big merchants in U.S. consumer culture, see William Leach, *Land of Desire: Merchants, Power, and the Rise of a New American Culture* (New York: Pantheon, 1993).

26. Terry Radtke, "Shopping in the Machine Age: Chain Stores, Consumerism, and the Politics of Business Reform, 1920–1939," in *The Quest for Social Justice II: The Morris Fromkin Memorial Lectures, 1981–1990,* ed. Alan D. Corré (Milwaukee: Golda Meir Library–University of Wisconsin, 1992); Ewald T. Grether, "Marketing Legislation," *Annals of the American Academy of Political and Social Science,* May 1940, 167–168; Kurt Mayer, "Small Business as a Social Institution," *Social Research* 20 (1947): 345–350.

27. 1925 European Trip, [p. 5], box 2, Filene Papers, CUNA.

28. Hrant Pasdermadjian, *Management Research in Retailing: The International Association of Department Stores* (London: Newman Books, 1950), 150.

29. Lyndall Urwick and F. P. Valentine for the International Chamber of Commerce, *Trends in the Organization and Methods of Distribution in the Two Areas,* vol. 5 of *Europe–United States of America* (Paris: International Chamber of Commerce, 1931), 133. In general on the obstacles facing large-scale retailers, see, in addition to Gabler, Georges De Leener with Emile James, *Le problème de la consommation* (Paris: Recueil Sirey; Brussels: Institut de Sociologie Solvay, 1938); Roger Picard, *Formes et méthodes nouvelles des entreprises commerciales* (Paris: Recueil Sirey, 1936); Jacques Dansette, *Les formes evoluées de la distribution: Problème économique, problème pychologique* (Brussels: Pauli, 1944).

30. On the European organizations, see Pasdermadjian, *Management Research in Retailing,* 7–10; Badel, *Un milieu libéral,* 38–39; Dr. J. Wernicke and G. Bach, "Geschichte des Verbandes," in *Probleme des Warenhauses: Beiträge zur Geschichte und Erkenntnis der Entwicklung des Warenhauses in Deutschland* (Berlin: Verband Deutscher Waren- und Kaufhäuser, 1928), 13–58.

31. London newspaper, July 7, 1926, Clippings, Trips, 1926–1937, box 3, Filene Papers, CUNA.

32. Charles D. Wrege and Sakae Hata, "Hands across the Sea: Edward Filene

and the International Management Institute: 1926–1934," typescript prepared for the Centennial Anniversary of the Academy of Management, 1986, Filene Papers, Century Foundation Archive, New York City.

33. Leon Urwick, "Albert Thomas and Scientific Management," *Bulletin of the International Management Institute* 6 (June 1932): 1; on the September 29 meeting with Thomas, notes by L. S., 1925 European trip, box 2, Filene Papers, CUNA.

34. Pasdermadjian, *Management Research in Retailing,* 11; see also Hermann Levy, *Retail Trade Associations, a New Form of Monopolist Organisation in Britain: A Report to the Fabian Society* (New York: Oxford University Press, 1948).

35. George L. Ridgeway, *Merchants of Peace: Twenty Years of Business Diplomacy through the International Chamber of Commerce, 1919–1938* (New York: Columbia University Press, 1938), 263 ff.

36. Ibid., 264 ff.

37. Quoted in Badel, *Un milieu libéral,* 217.

38. Ibid., 217–221; see 217 n. 88 on the word *distribution.*

39. P. Scholer, *Le prix de la distribution* (Paris: Dunod, 1949), 3; Communauté Economique Européenne (hereafter CEE), Bureau de Terminologie, *Terminologie de la distribution* (n.p.: Commission des Communautés Européennes, 1964), part 2, notions 27–51: Resultats de l'enquête effectuée en 1962 (December 1962), 11.

40. Jacques Lacour-Gayet, *Histoire du commerce,* vol. 1 of *La terre et les hommes* (Paris: S.P.I.D., 1950), xxi.

41. Scholer, *Le prix de la distribution,* 3, 11.

42. CEE, Bureau de Terminologie, *Terminologie de la distribution* (n.p.: Commission des Communautés Européennes, 1967), part 4, notions 79–103 (December 1966), no. 82, "Marketing," 513.

43. Scholer, *Le prix de la distribution,* p. 85.

44. CEE, Bureau de Terminologie, *Terminologie de la distribution* (1964), part 2, notions 27–51: Resultats de l'enquête effectuée en 1962 (December 1962), no. 29, "Commercio," 253.

45. Alain Desrosières, *La politique des grands nombres: histoire de la raison statistique* (Paris: Editions de Découverte, 2000).

46. Chamber of Commerce of the United States, *Distribution in the United States: Trends in Its Organization and Methods* (Washington, D.C.: Domestic Distribution Department, Chamber of Commerce of the United States, 1931).

47. Leach, *Land of Desire,* 365.

48. Henry Laufenburger, *Le commerce et l'organisation des marchés* (Paris: Recueil Sirey, 1938), 3; Roger du Page and Maurice Lengellé, *L'étude de marché: facteur d'expansion* (Paris: C. A. E., 1955), 23 n. 1.

49. Malcolm P. McNair, Stanley Ferdinand Teale, and Frances G. Mulhearn with Dr. Julius Hirsch, *Distribution Costs: An International Digest* (Boston: Graduate School of Business Administration, 1941), i–iii.

50. Quoted in Milhaud, *Chemins faisant,* 47.

51. *Revue des deux mondes,* August–September 1962, special issue, *Grands magasins, supermarchés: La question du jour,* 4.

52. Fernand Braudel, *The Wheels of Commerce,* vol. 2 of *Civilization and*

Capitalism, 15th–18th Century (1979), trans. Siân Reynolds (Berkeley: University of California Press, 1992).

53. See Vera Zamagni, *La distribuzione commerciale in Italia fra le due guerre* (Milan: Franco Angeli, 1981), 23; idem, "Le conseguenze della crisi del '29 sul commercio al dettaglio in Europa" *Commercio* 9 (1981): 10.

54. William Lancaster, *The Department Store: A Social History* (London: Leicester University Press, 1995); and the venerable study by Hrant Pasdermadjian, *The Department Store: Its Origins, Evolution, and Economics* (1949; reprint, New York: Arno, 1976); Gabler, *Probleme der amerikanischen Warenhäuser;* Michael B. Miller, *The Bon Marché: Bourgeois Culture and the Department Store, 1869–1920* (Princeton: Princeton University Press, 1981); Geoffrey Crossick and Serge Jaumain, eds., *Cathedrals of Consumption: The European Department Store, 1850–1939* (Brookfield, VT.: Ashgate, 1998); Franco Amatori, *Proprietà e direzione: La Rinascente, 1917–1969* (Milan: Franco Angeli, 1989).

55. Bernard Marrey, *Les grands magasins: des origines à 1939* (Paris: Picard, 1979), 100–101, 257 ff.; Catherine Coley, "Les Magasins Réunis: From the Provinces to Paris, from Art Nouveau to Art Deco," in Crossick and Jaumain, *Cathedrals of Consumption*, 225–251; Kathleen James, *Erich Mendelsohn and the Architecture of German Modernism* (Cambridge: Cambridge University Press, 1997); Meredith Klausen, *Frantz Jourdain and the Samaritaine: Art Nouveau Theory and Criticism* (Leiden: E. J. Brill, 1987).

56. Rappaport, *Shopping for Pleasure;* Emile Zola, *The Ladies' Paradise* (1883), trans. Brian Nelson (Berkeley: University of California Press, 1992); Leila Whittemore, "Getting the Goods Together: Consumer Space and Gender in Nineteenth-Century Paris," *Architecture–Research–Criticism* 5 (1994): 14–25; Patricia O'Brien, "The Kleptomania Diagnosis: Bourgeois Women and Theft in Late Nineteenth-Century France," *Journal of Social History* 17 (1983): 65–77.

57. Rémy G. Saisselin, *The Bourgeois and the Bibelot* (New Brunswick, N. J.: Rutgers University Press, 1984), 69–71.

58. Leora Auslander, "The Gendering of Consumer Practices in Nineteenth-Century France," in *The Sex of Things: Gender and Consumption in Historical Perspective,* ed. Victoria de Grazia with Ellen Furlough (Berkeley: University of California Press, 1996), 79–112; Lisa Tiersten, *Marianne in the Market: Envisioning Consumer Society in Fin-de-Siècle France* (Berkeley: University of California Press, 2001).

59. Leach, *Land of Desire*, 99–104; Gabler, *Probleme der amerikanischen Warenhäuser*, 23–24.

60. Edmond Goblot, *La barrière et le niveau: Etude sociologique sur la bourgeoisie française moderne* (1925; reprint, Paris: Presses Universitaires de France, 1967), 30.

61. Gareth Shaw, "Large-Scale Retailing in Germany and the Development of New Retail Organisations," in *The Evolution of Retail Systems, c. 1800–1914,* ed. John Benson and Gareth Shaw (Leicester: Leicester University Press, 1992), 80.

62. Werner E. Mosse, *Jews in the German Economy: The German-Jewish Economic Elite, 1820–1935* (Oxford: Clarendon Press, 1987), 209; Werner E.

Mosse, "Terms of Successful Integration: The Tietz Family, 1858–1923," *Leo Baeck Institute Year Book* 34 (1989): 142 and passim.

63. E. Silberling, *Dictionnaire de sociologie phalanstérienne: Guide des oeuvres complètes de Charles Fourier* (Paris: Marcel Rivière et Cie, 1911), 88–89.

64. "Les Grands Magasins/The Great Department Stores," *Foreign Trade,* September 1933, 15.

65. Werner Sombart, *Händler und Helden: Patriotische Besinnungen* (Munich: Duncker & Humblot, 1915); Herman Lebovics, *Social Conservatism and the Middle Classes in Germany, 1914–1933* (Princeton: Princeton University Press, 1969), 62–63.

66. Hans Buchner, *Warenhauspolitik und Nationalsozialismus* (Munich: Verlag F. Eher, 1929), 3, 22–24.

67. Urwick and Valentine, *Trends in the Organization,* 73–74.

68. Walter Froelich, "European Experiments in Protecting Small Competitors," *Harvard Business Review* 17 (summer 1939): 442–452.

69. Urwick and Valentine, *Trends in the Organization,* 75; Marcel Nancey with the Centre d'Etude du Commerce et de la Distribution, *Où, quand, comment achète-t-on? Tendances* (Paris: CES, 1950); Fernand Simonet, *Le petit commerce du détail: Sa lutte avec le grand commerce de détail* (Paris: Librairie d'Economie Commerciale, 1937); Dansette, *Les formes evoluées,* 70 ff.; Dietrich Denecke and Gareth Shaw, "Traditional Retail Systems in Germany," in Benson and Shaw, *The Evolution of Retail Systems,* 85.

70. See comments on actual and ideal practices by Otto D. Schaefer, director of the Reichskuratorium für Wirtschaftlichkeit, in International Chamber of Commerce, *Helping Retailers to Better Profits: The Comparison of Retail Operating Costs,* brochure no. 86 (Paris, 1934); also Jefferys, *Distribution of Consumer Goods,* 48 ff.

71. Geoffrey Crossick and Heinz-Gerhard Haupt, eds., *Shopkeepers and Master Artisans in Nineteenth-Century Europe* (New York: Methuen, 1984); Philip Nord, *Paris Shopkeepers and the Politics of Resentment* (Princeton: Princeton University Press, 1986). On Germany, see Robert Gellately, *The Politics of Economic Despair: Shopkeepers and German Politics, 1890–1914* (London: Sage, 1974); Uwe Spiekermann, *Basis der Konsumgesellschaft: Entstehung und Entwicklung des modernen Kleinhandels in Deutschland, 1850–1914* (Munich: Beck, 1999).

72. *Revue des deux mondes,* August–September 1962, 23; Jacques du Closel, *Les grands magasins français: Cent ans après* (Paris: Chotard, 1989), 30–33; Gabler, *Probleme der amerikanischen Warenhäuser,* 105–110, 197–201; Dansette, *Les formes evoluées,* 37 ff.

73. J. J. Boddewyn, *Belgian Public Policy toward Retailing since 1789* (East Lansing: Michigan State University International Business and Economic Studies, 1971), 35, 37.

74. Isaac F. Marcosson, *Wherever Men Trade: The Romance of the Cash Register* (New York: Dodd Mead, 1948).

75. R. M. Stephenson, "The German Market for Office Equipment," September 2, 1936, September–October 1936 file, box 265, record group 151, Bureau of Foreign and Domestic Commerce, National Archives, College Park, Md. (hereafter BFDC).

76. Ernst Maheim, "Le consommateur, les classes moyennes et les formes modernes du commerce de détail, première partie," *Revue économique internationale*, November 1936, 229-231.

77. Richard Mutz, *La vente à prix uniques considérée comme nouvelle methode d'organisation du commerce de détail*, trans. René Stolle (Paris: Dunod, 1934). On the one-price store in Europe, see Marguerite Ensêlme, *Les magasins à prix uniques: Leur fonction dans le commerce du détail*, Bordeaux: Faculté de Droit, 1936); Simonet's nuanced study, *Le petit commerce du détail*; Roger Picard, *Formes et méthodes nouvelles des entreprises commerciales* (Paris: Recueil Sirey, 1936).

78. Godfrey M. Lebhar, *Chain Stores in America, 1859-1962* (1952; reprint, New York: Chain Store Publishing, 1963), 404.

79. John K. Winkler, *5 and 10: The Fabulous Life of F. W. Woolworth* (New York: Robert McBride, 1940); Karen Plunkett-Powell, *Remembering Woolworth's: A Nostalgic History of the World's Most Famous Five-and-Dime* (New York: St. Martin's, 1999), 201; *Illustrations from 50 Years of Woolworth, 1879-1929* (New York: Woolworth, 1929).

80. See Mutz, who was a consultant to the firm, *La vente à prix uniques*; see also *Transatlantic Trade*, June 1937; "German Woolworth Company Raises Capital," June 13, 1939, June-July 1939 file, box 270, BFDC; *German-American Commercial Bulletin* 3 (December 1928): 10; *Transatlantic Trade*, January 1930, 19; ibid., September 1933, 8, 14; Frank A. Southard, *American Industry in Europe* (Boston: Houghton Mifflin, 1931), 109; Plunkett-Powell, *Remembering Woolworth's*, 118-121.

81. Notes, L. S., July 6, 1925, 1925 European Trip file, box 2, Filene Papers, CUNA.

82. Uwe Spiekermann, "Rationalisierung, Leistungssteigerung und Gesundung: Der Handel in Deutschland zwischen den Weltkriegen," in *Unterm Strich: Von der Winkelkrämerei zum E-Commerce*, ed. Michael Haverkamp and Hans-Juergen Teuteberg (Bramsche: Rasch Verlag, 2000), 200-201; Noël Cassé, *Etude sur les magasins à prix uniques* (Toulouse: Boisseau, 1935), 20.

83. J. Audibert, "Comment fut créé en France la première chaine de magasins," *Vendre*, September 1930, 151-155; *Frankfurter Zeitung Abendblatt*, August 21, 1928.

84. On Milhaud, see Milhaud, *Chemins faisant*, 48, 59, 138; Badel, *Un milieu libéral*, 215; Antoine Weexsteen, *Le Conseil aux entreprises et l'Etat en France: le role de Jean Milhaud (1898-1991) dans la C.E.G.O.S. et L'I.T.A.P.*, vol. 1 (Paris: Ecole des Hautes Etudes en Sciences Sociales, 1999); Max Heilbronn with Jacques Varin, *Galeries Lafayette, Buchenwald, Galeries Lafayette . . .* (Paris: Economica, 1989), 8-10.

85. Lacrosse and de Bie, *Emile Bernheim*.

86. Figures derived from Giuseppe Mortara, "Lo sviluppo ed il numero dei magazzini a prezzo unico," *Giornale degli economisti*, December 1937, 5. Miller, *The Bon Marché*, 236; Crossick and Jaumain, "The World of the Department Store," in *Cathedrals of Consumption*, 16-17.

87. Cassé, *Etude sur les magasins*, 30 ff.; Mutz, *La vente à prix uniques*, 211.

88. Mutz, *La vente à prix uniques*, 2-3.

89. We must emphasize the relative value of money, as Viviana Zelizer suggests

in "The Social Meaning of Money: 'Special Monies,'" *American Journal of Sociology* 95 (September 1989): 342–377. This relative value is especially pronounced where currency fluctuates; see Hugo E. Pipping, *The Standard of Living: Its Conceptualization and Place in Economics* (Helsinki: Societas Scientarum Fennica, 1953), 178, 230.

90. *Revue des deux mondes*, August–September 1962, 47.

91. Janice Winship, "New Disciplines for Women and the Rise of the Chain Store in the 1930s," in *All the World and Her Husband: Women in Twentieth-Century Consumer Culture,* ed. Maggie Andrews and Mary Talbot (London: Cassell, 2000), 23–45, quotation from 29.

92. Froelich, "European Experiments in Protecting Small Competitors," 449; *Contribution à l'étude du problème des grands magasins: rapport de la Commission fédérale d'étude des prix au Département fédéral de l'Economie publique* (Bern: Secrétariat de la Commission Fédérale d'Etude des Prix, 1933), 29 ff.; Raymond de Roover, "The Concept of the Just Price: Theory and Economic Policy," *Journal of Economic History* 18 (December 1958): 418–434.

93. Charles H. Cooley, "The Sphere of Pecuniary Valuation," *American Journal of Sociology* 19 (1913): 203; idem, "The Institutional Character of Pecuniary Valuation," *American Journal of Sociology* 18 (1913): 543–555; Zelizer, *The Social Meaning of Money,* 33.

94. Geoffrey Gorer, *The American People: A Study in National Character* (New York: W. W. Norton, 1948), 175; Urwick and Valentine, *Trends in the Organization,* 161.

95. Henry Laufenburger, *L'intervention de l'état en matière économique* (Paris: Librairie Générale de Droit et de Jurisprudence, 1939), 24; idem, "Contribution à la théorie économique du commerce," in *Droit social: Revue des rapports professionels et de l'organisation de la production,* April 1944, 2, quoted in Badel, *Un milieu libéral,* 299–300.

96. Memo: International Chamber of Commerce Meeting, Percy Brown to E. A. Filene, April 15, 1937, ICC, 1937 European Trip file, box 17, Filene Papers, CUNA.

97. "A Report on Conditions in Germany," June 15, 1933, 1–9, 1933 European Trip, part 1, box 4, ibid.; B. Connors (secretary to Edward A. Filene) to Chauncey Snow, May 10, 1937, ICC, 1937 European Trip file, box 17, ibid.

98. "How Can Our System of Distribution Be Improved?" June 26, 1935, 5, 6, box 27, ibid.

99. "Additional Notes from EAF visit in Berlin on Nazi situation," 2, 1933 European Trip folder, part 1, box 4, ibid.

100. Simonet, *Le petit commerce du détail,* 70 ff.; see also Levy, *The Shops of Britain.*

101. Froelich, "European Experiments in Protecting Small Competitors." See also idem, "Changes in the Central European Retail Trade," *Journal of Marketing* 4 (January 1940): 259–263; David R. Craig, "Recent Retailing Trends in Europe," *Dun's Review* 47 (December 1939): 5–9.

102. Grether, "Marketing Legislation," 165–175.

103. On Duttweiler, see Sigmund Widmer, *Gottlieb Duttweiler (1888–1962): Gründer der Migros* (Zurich: Verein fur Wirtschaftshistorische Studien,

1985); Sibylle Brändli, *Der Supermarkt im Kopf: Konsumkultur und Wohlstand in der Schweiz nach 1945* (Vienna: Bőhlau Verlag, 2000).

104. Report by LS [Lillian Schoedler] on Mr. Filene's illness and death, Paris, October 1937, folder 13, box 53, Filene Papers, CUNA.

105. Badel, *Un milieu libéral,* 66–67.

106. Douglas Miller, Weekly Economic Report, December 5, 1938, December 1938 file, box 268, RG 151, BFDC.

107. Lacour-Gayet, *Histoire du commerce,* 325.

108. Sam L. Woods, Commercial Attaché, American Embassy, Berlin, Weekly Economic Report, May 4, 1940, June 1940 file, box 273, RG 151, BFDC.

109. Hendrickson, *The Grand Emporiums,* 129.

4. BIG-BRAND GOODS

Epigraphs: David Leslic Brown, "Conduct Your Foreign Advertising on the American Plan," *Printers' Ink,* April 18, 1929; Rainer Maria Rilke, *Selected Letters, 1902–1926,* trans. R. F. C. Hull (London: Quartet Encounters, 1988), 394.

1. Paul Voss, *The Growth of the Leipzig Fair* (Leipzig: Leipziger Messamt, 1933); Leipziger Messamt, *The Leipzig Fair and How It Became the World's Greatest Market* (Leipzig, 1936); Hartmut Zwahr, Thomas Topfstedt, and Gunter Bentele, eds., *Leipzigs Messen, 1497–1997: Gestaltwandel, Umbrüche, Neubeginn* (Cologne: Böhlau Verlag, 1999); A. Allix, "The Geography of Fairs: Illustrated by Old World Examples," *Geographical Review* 12 (1922): 532–569.

2. Fernand Braudel, *The Wheels of Commerce,* vol. 2 of *Civilization and Capitalism, 15th–18th Century* (1979), trans. Siân Reynolds (Berkeley: University of California Press, 1992), 81–94, 114–133.

3. Allix, "The Geography of Fairs," 557–561.

4. Ibid., 561–565; Charles Alengry, *Notre revanche économique par la foire nationale d'échantillons* (Paris: Jouve, 1917).

5. Etienne Fougère, "Sample Fairs and Foreign Trade," International Chamber of Commerce (hereafter ICC) *Digest 55: Fairs and Exhibitions,* January–June 1927, 7–9. ICC *Digest 50: Fairs and Exhibitions,* June–December 1924; Brian Bellasis, "Fairs and Exhibitions: Six Angles from Which to Regard Them," ICC *Digest 52: Fairs and Exhibitions,* June–December 1925, 7–8; Count A. van der Burch, "The Exhibition Problem," ICC *Digest 57: Fairs and Exhibitions,* January–June 1928.

6. Braudel, *Wheels of Commerce,* 94.

7. "A Fair That Is a Fair: Leipzig Shows the Way," *Financial News,* March 7, 1934.

8. Bellasis, "Fairs and Exhibitions," 7–8.

9. Chris Rasmussen, "State Fair: Culture and Agriculture in Iowa, 1854–1941" (Ph.D. diss., Rutgers University, 1992).

10. Paul Voss, "The Leipzig Fair and Its Relations to German-American Trade," *German-American Commerce Bulletin* 3 (June 1928): 5; "Leipzig Trade Fair," ibid. (February 1928): 11.

11. "Doing Business in Europe," *Foreign Trade,* January 1928, 41.

12. Alfred Pearce Dennis, "European Agriculture and the American Export Trade in Food Products," *Annals, American Academy of Political and Social Science* 94 (July 1924): 110–114.

13. Francis P. Miller and H. D. Hill, "Europe as a Market," *Atlantic Monthly,* August 1930, 226–231, and September 1930, 400–410; Miller and Hill, *The Giant of the Western World: America and Europe in a North-Atlantic Civilisation* (New York: W. Morrow, 1930), 23–24.

14. R. M. Stephenson, "The German Market for Office Equipment," September 2, 1936, September–October 1936 file, box 265, RG 151, Bureau of Foreign and Domestic Commerce, National Archives, College Park, Md. (hereafter BFDC); Stephenson, "The German Market for Office Equipment," June 27, 1938, June–July 1938 file, box 269, ibid.; "Competition in Typewriters," *Foreign Trade* 8 (May 1933): 36.

15. L. Michael Fultz, "History of A. A. Waterman," at <www.penbid.com/ Auction/showarticle.asp?art_id=62>; Charles L. Margery, "Le lancement du Parker duofold en France," *Vendre,* November 1929, 349–355.

16. Jens Rösler, *The Montblanc Diary and Collector's Guide* (Hamburg: Christians Verlag, 1993); L. Michael Fultz, "The History of Pelikan Pens," at www.penbid.com/Auction/showarticle.asp?art_id=12, 2003.

17. Robert Read, "The Growth and Structure of Multinationals in the Banana Export Trade," in *The Growth of International Business,* ed. Mark Casson (London: George Allen and Unwin, 1983), 194–195; International Chamber of Commerce, *Document* no. 5 (1937 Congress) (Paris, 1937), 11; Frank A. Southard, *American Industry in Europe* (Ithaca: Cornell University Press, 1931), 127.

18. Karl Marx, *Capital,* vol. 1, trans. Samuel Moore and Edward Aveling, ed. Frederick Engels (New York: International Publishers, 1967), 71, 84–85.

19. Clement H. Watson, "Markets Are People—Not Places," *JWT News Bulletin,* July 1928, 5–6, J. Walter Thompson Company Archives, John W. Hartman Center for Sales, Advertising, and Marketing History, Duke University (hereafter JWT).

20. Walter Benjamin, "The Work of Art in the Age of Mechanical Reproduction" (1936), in *Illuminations,* trans. Harry Zohn, ed. Hannah Arendt (New York: Schocken, 1968).

21. Max Weber, *The Sociology of Religion,* trans. Ephraim Fischoff, ed. Talcott Parsons (Boston: Beacon, 1963), xxxiv, also 2–3, 46–47.

22. Quoted as epigraph in Leipziger Messamt, *The Leipzig Fair,* 4.

23. U.S. Department of Commerce, *European Sales Areas* (Washington, D.C.: U.S. Government Printing Office, 1933), facing 1.

24. "They spent 288,072 in Europe in one month and were not even there!"; *Printers' Ink,* July 25, 1929, 114–115.

25. Michael Schudson, *Advertising: The Uneasy Persuasion* (New York: Basic Books, 1984), 181.

26. Herbert Hoover, cited in Wesley Clair Mitchell, ed., *Recent Social Trends in the United States: Report of the President's Research Committee on Social Trends* (New York: McGraw-Hill, 1933), xxvi; in the same volume see esp. chap. 3, W. F. Ogburn with S. C. Gilfillan, "The Influence of Invention and Discovery"; see also John H. Dunning, "Changes in the Level and

Structure of International Production: The Last One Hundred Years," in Casson, *Growth of International Business,* esp. 104–134.

27. Susan Strasser, *Satisfaction Guaranteed* (New York: Pantheon, 1989), 43. See also Thomas P. Hughes, *American Genesis: A Century of Invention and Technological Enthusiasm, 1870–1970* (New York: Viking-Penguin, 1989); Richard S. Tedlow, *New and Improved: The Story of Mass Marketing in America* (Cambridge, Mass.: Harvard Business School Press, 1996).

28. Richard R. Nelson and Gavin Wright, "The Rise and Fall of American Technological Leadership: The Postwar Era in Historical Perspective," *Journal of Economic Literature* 30 (December 1992): 1931–1964.

29. Dunning, "Changes in Level and Structure of International Production," 106; Strasser, *Satisfaction Guaranteed;* Kathy Lee Peiss, *Hope in a Jar: The Making of America's Beauty Culture* (New York: Metropolitan, 1998).

30. Francis Elvinger, *La lutte entre l'industrie et le commerce: La marque, son lancement, sa vente, sa publicité* (Pairs: Librairie d'Economie Commerciale, 1922), 25–27, 70–77.

31. William Leiss, *The Limits to Satisfaction: An Essay on the Problem of Needs and Commodities* (Toronto: University of Toronto Press, 1976), 80.

32. U.S. Supreme Court Justice Joseph Story, 1841, quoted in Strasser, *Satisfaction Guaranteed,* 43.

33. Robert Lynd, "The People as Consumers," in Mitchell, *Recent Social Trends,* 874–875.

34. Strasser, *Satisfaction Guaranteed,* 28.

35. Charles P. Kindleberger, "Origins of United States Direct Investment in France," *Business History Review* 48 (autumn 1974): 382–413; *American Branch Factories Abroad: A Report on American Branch Factories Abroad, Together with the Economic Factors Involved in the Branch Factory Movement* (Washington, D.C.: U.S. Government Printing Office, 1931).

36. Isaac F. Marcosson, *Wherever Men Trade: The Romance of the Cash Register* (New York: Dodd Mead, 1948), 192.

37. Russell B. Adams, *King C. Gillette: The Man and His Wonderful Shaving Device* (Boston: Little, Brown, 1978), 96–98.

38. Joseph Bourke, "History of the Waterman Pen," http://www.jimgaston.com/waterman.htm.

39. Douglas Miller, "American Business in Germany," *Transatlantic Trade,* May 1930, 5.

40. Watson, "Markets Are People," 5–6.

41. Sinclair Lewis, *Dodsworth* (New York: Harcourt, Brace, 1929).

42. Adams, *King C. Gillette,* 97.

43. The most detailed and elegant analysis is Southard, *American Industry in Europe,* esp. 113–132; see also Graham W. Parker, "American Branch Plants Meet European Competition," *Factory and Industrial Management,* September 1932, 355–357, and October 1932, 375–377. For the later period, see Christopher Layton, *Trans-Atlantic Investments,* 2d ed. (Boulogne-sur-Seine: Atlantic Institute, 1968), 18–26; for the earlier period, Matthew Simon and David E. Novack, "Some Dimensions of the

American Invasion of Europe, 1871–1914: An Introductory Essay," *Journal of Economic History* 24 (December, 1964): 591–605.

44. Southard, *American Industry in Europe*, 113 ff., 201–202.

45. Burton L. Kaufman, *Efficiency and Expansion: Foreign Trade Organization in the Wilson Administration, 1913–1921* (Westport, Conn.: Greenwood, 1974); Harry T. Collings, "United States Government Aid to Foreign Trade," *Annals of the American Academy of Political and Social Science*, September 1926, 134–142; Emily S. Rosenberg, *Spreading the American Dream: American Economic and Cultural Expansion, 1890–1945* (New York: Hill and Wang, 1982), 48–86.

46. William Leach, *Land of Desire: Merchants, Power, and the Rise of a New American Culture* (New York: Pantheon, 1993), 357–363.

47. Lyndall Urwick and F. P. Valentine for the International Chamber of Commerce, *Trends in the Organization and Methods of Distribution in the Two Areas*, vol. 5 of *Europe–United States of America* (Paris: International Chamber of Commerce, 1931), 156.

48. See, for example, Douglas Miller, "Services to American Business in 1932: Office of the American Commercial Attaché in Berlin," February 15, 1933, March 1933 file, box 259, RG 151, BFDC.

49. "Marks of Origin on American Products," April 16, 1934, 1172, April–June 1934 file, Paris 1934 file, box 5, RG 151, ibid.

50. Robert B. Davies, "Peacefully Working to Conquer the World: The Singer Manufacturing Company in Foreign Markets, 1854–1899," *Business History Review* 43 (autumn, 1969): 312–315; Robert Herbert, "When May Goods Be Called German Products?" *Transatlantic Trade*, August 1934, 3.

51. Parker, "American Branch Plants," 357.

52. Gabriel Kolko, "American Business and Germany, 1930–1941," *Western Political Quarterly* 15 (December 1962): 725.

53. *Resolutions Adopted by the Ninth Congress of the International Chamber of Commerce, Berlin, June 28–July 3, 1937*, Brochure 98 (Paris: ICC, 1937).

54. Elvinger, *La lutte*, 170 n. 2.

55. Southard, *American Industry in Europe*, 131.

56. Miller and Hill, *Giant of the Western World*, 193. For the first thorough study of a big brand going local, see Jeff Richard Schutts, "Coca-Colonization, 'Refreshing' Americanization or Nazi Volksgetränk? The History of Coca-Cola in Germany, 1929–1961" (Ph.D. diss., Georgetown University, 2003).

57. "Eastman's article on why Kodak chose J. W. T," June 2, 1930, folder Why Kodak Chose JWT, 1930, International Department, Sam Meek Papers, JWT; "Kodak Survey in Western Europe, September–December, 1953," July–August 1954, 18, Report on international trip, 1954–1955, 6/11 folder, Howard Henderson Papers, JWT.

58. Douglas Miller, "American Business in Germany," 5; Robert L. Sammons and Milton Abelson, *American Direct Investments in Foreign Countries—1940* (Washington, D.C.: U.S. Government Printing Office, 1942), 21, 25; Dunning, "Changes in Level and Structure of International Production," 128. Some of this value showed up in the increase reported by the Bureau

of Foreign and Domestic Commerce on the worth of U.S. investments in distribution, a new category of American investment abroad. This began to be calculated only during the 1930s and included retailing, advertising agencies, and company sales offices.

59. Elvinger, *La lutte*, 169–170.
60. Adams, *King C. Gillette*, 119.
61. Marc Meuleau, "L'introduction du marketing en France (1880–1973)," *Revue française de gestion*, September–October 1988, 2–65; idem, "De la distribution au marketing (1880–1939): Une réponse à l'évolution du marché," *Entreprises et histoire* 3 (1993): 61–74. Marie-Emmanuelle Chessel, "Une méthode publicitaire américaine: Cadum dans la France de l'Entre-Deux-Guerres," ibid., 11 (1996): 61–76.
62. Adams, *King C. Gillette*, 111–112.
63. Case M. 310, Lames de Rasoir, Perrot, January 9, 1932, Centre de Preparation aux Affaires, Chambre de Commerce de Paris; Case M. 316, Lames de Rasoir, Perrot, February 23 and March 2, 1934, ibid.
64. *Libre-Service-Actualité*, January 8, 1962, 25; October 15, 1962, 11; July 23, 1964, 5; October 15, 1964, 10.
65. Hanns W. Brose, *Die Entdeckung des Verbrauchers: Ein Leben für die Werbung* (Dusseldorf: Econ-Verlag, 1958), 3, 39; Dirk Schindelbeck, "'Asbach Uralt' und 'Soziale Marktwirtschaft,'" *Zur Kulturgeschichte der Werbeagentur in Deutschland am Beispiel von Hanns W. Brose (1899–1971)*, special issue of *Zeitschrift für Unternehmensgeschichte* 40, no. 4 (1995): 235–252.
66. Georg Bergler, *Die Entwicklung der Verbrauchsforschung in Deutschland, und die Gesellschaft für Konsumforschung bis zum Jahr 1945* (Kallmünz: Lassleben, 1959).
67. Hanns W. Brose, "Werbewirtschaft und Werbegestaltgung: Der 7. Brief an Herrn M. Mit einem Anschreben an Ludwig Erhard," *Die Deutsche Fertigware* 5 (1938): 87–96.
68. Berit Bass, "Die Braune Grossmesse 1933 in Leipzig," in Zwahr, Topfstedt, and Bentele, *Leipzigs Messen*, 554–555.
69. "A Fair That Is a Fair"; Georg Bergler, "Qualitätssicherung, Markenartikel und Leipziger Messe," *Die Deutsche Fertigware* 6 (February 1934): 21–27; Leipziger Messamt, *The Leipzig Fair*, 24.
70. William L. Smyser, "Fairs and Expositions in Germany during the War," December 27, 1939, 1–15, Special Report: Berlin, December 1939, box 272, RG 151, BFDC; Erich Dittrich, *Südosteuropa und die Reichsmesse* (Leipzig: W. Kohlhammer, 1941); Hartmut Zwahr, "Die erste deutsche Nachkriegsmesse 1946: Widererweckung oder Neubelebung," in Zwahr, Topfstedt, and Bentele, *Leipzigs Messen*, 585–597.

5. CORPORATE ADVERTISING

Epigraphs: Sam Meek to Denys M. Scott, December 5, 1952, Policy Letters, 1925–1957 folder, Howard Henderson Papers, J. Walter Thompson Company Archives, John W. Hartman Center for Sales, Advertising, and

Marketing History, Duke University (hereafter JWT); Blaise Cendrars, "Publicité = poésie" (1927), in *Aujourd'hui 1917–1929* (Paris: Denoël, 1987), 117.

1. P. Brunazzi, "Del cartello pubblicitario," *L'ufficio moderno,* July 1932, 433–434.

2. On advertising as a medium and language, see William Leiss, "The Icons of the Marketplace," *Theory, Culture and Society* 1, 3 (1983): 10–22; idem, *The Limits to Satisfaction: An Essay on the Problem of Needs and Commodities* (Toronto: University of Toronto Press, 1976); and William Leiss, Stephen Kline, and Sut Jhally, eds., *Social Communication in Advertising: Persons, Products and Images of Well-Being* (Toronto: Methuen, 1986). See also Michael Schudson, *Advertising, the Uneasy Persuasion: Its Dubious Impact on American Society* (New York: Basic Books, 1984). On the changing visual repertoire, see T. J. Jackson Lears, *Fables of Abundance: A Cultural History of Advertising in America* (New York: Basic Books, 1994), chap. 1, the thesis of which is tidily summarized in idem, "Reconsidering Abundance: A Plea for Ambiguity," in *Getting and Spending: European and American Consumer Societies in the Twentieth Century,* ed. Susan Strasser, Charles McGovern, and Matthias Judt (Washington, D.C.: German Historical Institute; New York: Cambridge University Press, 1998), 449–466. See also Roland Marchand, *Advertising the American Dream* (Berkeley: University of California Press, 1984). French cultural theorists have been notably attentive to advertising as language; see Roland Barthes, *The Fashion System* (New York: Hill and Wang, 1983); idem, *Mythologies* (New York, Hill and Wang, 1972); and Jean Baudrillard, *For a Critique of the Political Economy of the Sign,* trans. Charles Levin (St. Louis, Mo.: Telos, 1981).

3. On the development of the American industry, see Pamela Walker Laird, *Advertising Progress: American Business and the Rise of Consumer Marketing* (Baltimore: Johns Hopkins University Press, 1998); Daniel Pope, *The Making of Modern Advertising* (New York: Basic Books, 1983); Stephen Fox, *The Mirror Makers: A History of American Advertising and Its Creators* (New York: Vintage, 1985); Marchand, *Advertising the American Dream;* Stuart Ewen, *Captains of Consciousness: Advertising and the Social Roots of the Consumer Culture* (New York: Harper and Row, 1975).

4. Mira Wilkins and Frank Ernest Hill, *American Business Abroad: Ford on Six Continents* (Detroit: Wayne State University Press, 1964); Patrick Fridenson, "French Automobile Marketing, 1890–1970," in *Development of Mass Marketing: The Automobile and Retailing Industries,* ed. Akio Okochi and Loichi Shimokawa (Tokyo: University of Tokyo Press, 1981), 127–154. Files at the Bureau of Foreign and Domestic Commerce, National Archives, College Park, Md. (hereafter BFDC), are rich in reports from American commercial consular officers. See, for example, *Automotive Equipment and Construction Preferences in Foreign Countries,* U.S. Department of Commerce Trade Information Bulletin no. 695 (Washington, D.C.: U.S. Government Printing Office, 1930); and H. C. Schuette, ed., *The Motorization of Germany,* U.S. Department of Commerce Trade Information Bulletin no. 485 (Washington, D.C.: U.S. Government Printing Office, 1927); Douglas Miller, "German Automotive Conditions Re-

flect Native Orderliness," October 23, 1931, October 1931 folder, box 245, RG 151, BFDC.

5. On car marketing in general, see Okochi and Shimokawa, *Development of Mass Marketing*. For advertising more particularly, see "The Job before Us," *General Motors Export Monthly* 1 (June 1922); Georg F. Bauer, "Mass Salesmanship in Automobile Exporting," *Export Advertiser*, June 1929, 32; Louis Cheronnet, "How French Automobile Firms Advertise," *Foreign Trade*, November 1930, 39; J. G. Fevrier, "American Motor Cars Abroad," *Living Age*, December 1, 1929, 421–426; Giuseppe Volpato, "L'evoluzione delle strategie di marketing nell'industria automobilistica internazionale," in *Annali di storia dell'impresa*, vol. 2 (Milan: Franco Angeli, 1986), 119–208; James Flink, *The Car Culture* (Cambridge, Mass.: MIT Press, 1975).

6. Arthur Hartzell, "From the Frontiers of Our Far-Flung Empire," *JWT Newsletter*, June 9, 1927, 291, Newsletter Series, 1916–1987, JWT; idem, *JWT Newsletter*, November 1, 1927, 457–458, ibid.; reprint of "JWT Aim Abroad: Push Gospel of Advertising," *Advertising Age*, March 2, 9, and 16, 1959, Publications file, JWT; "General Motors Advertising," International Branch Management, 1920s file, Howard Henderson Papers, JWT. See also the recent study by Clark Eric Hultquist, "Americans in Paris: The J. Walter Thompson Company in France, 1927–1968," *Enterprise and Society* 4 (2003): 471–501.

7. N. W. Ayer, *Ayer Abroad* (New York: N. W. Ayer, 1931); Ralph M. Hower, *The History of an Advertising Agency: N. W. Ayer and Sons at Work, 1869–1949* (Cambridge, Mass.: Harvard University Press, 1949), 140–146; J. A. G. Pennington, ed., *Advertising Automotive Products in Europe*, U.S. Department of Commerce Trade Information Bulletin no. 462 (Washington, D.C.: U.S. Government Printing Office, 1927).

8. On Hopkins, see Claude C. Hopkins, *My Life in Advertising* (New York: Harper and Brothers, 1927), translated by Louis Angé as *Mes succès en publicité* (Paris: La Publicité, 1930); *La Publicité*, April 1938, 305. On this edition, see Marie-Emmanuelle Chessel, "L'enseignant, le journaliste et le traducteur: Louis Angé (1885–1931)," in *Market Management: revue internationale des sciences commerciales*, no. 3–4 (2003): 18–41.

9. For an introduction to advertising in continental Europe, see, for France, Marc Martin, *Trois siècles de publicité en France* (Paris: Odile Jacob, 1992); Marie-Emmanuelle Chessel, *La publicité: naissance d'une profession, 1900–1940* (Paris: CNRS, 1998). On Germany, see Dirk Reinhardt, *Von der Reklame zum Marketing: Geschichte der Wirtschaftswerbung in Deutschland* (Berlin: Akademie Verlag, 1993); and Uwe Westphal, *Werbung im Dritten Reich* (Berlin: Transit, 1989). On Italy, see Adam Arvidsson, *Marketing Modernity: Italian Advertising from Fascism to Postmodernity* (New York: Routledge, 2003). On Belgium: Véronique Pouillard, "L'Ecole belge de publicité," in *Market Management*, no. 3–4 (2003): 18–41, based on idem, "La publicité en Belgique (1850–1975): Institutions, acteurs, influences," 3 vols. (Thesis, Université Libre de Bruxelles, Faculté de Philosophie et Lettres, 2002–2003).

10. Pope, *Making of Modern Advertising*, chap. 2, esp. 26–29.

11. "The Kodak-Thompson Partnership, Notes on Talk for the Kodak Interna-

tional Group, Rochester, February 26, 1958," 2, Eastman Kodak International Meeting, 1958: Agenda—Kodak International, February 26, 1958, box 6/11, Special Project file, Howard Henderson Papers, JWT.

12. Marchand, *Advertising the American Dream,* xv; Pope, *Making of Modern Advertising,* 18 ff.; Richard W. Fox and T. J. Jackson Lears, *The Culture of Consumption: Critical Essays in American History, 1880–1980* (New York: Pantheon, 1983); Lears, *Fables of Abundance.*

13. On J. Walter Thompson, see Stephen Fox, *The Mirror Makers,* 78–101; Marchand, *Advertising the American Dream;* Pope, *Making of Modern Advertising;* Ewen, *Captains of Consciousness;* "J. Walter Thompson Company," *Fortune,* November 1947, 95–101, 202–206, 214, 216, 218, 220, 223–224, 226, 228–230, 233.

14. Fox, *The Mirror Makers,* 97.

15. Peggy J. Kreshel, "John B. Watson at J. Walter Thompson: The Legitimation of 'Science' in Advertising," *Journal of Advertising* 19 (spring 1990): 49–59.

16. Quoted in ibid., 51.

17. Geoffrey N. Leech, *English in Advertising: A Linguistic Study of Advertising in Great Britain* (London: Longmans Green, 1966); Marchand, *Advertising the American Dream,* 6–7; also Richard Pollay, "The Subsiding Sizzle: A History of Print Advertising, 1900–1980," *Journal of Marketing* 49 (summer 1985): 24–37.

18. "J. Walter Thompson Company," *Fortune,* 244.

19. "The Kodak-Thompson Partnership, Notes on talk for the Kodak International Group, Rochester, February 26, 1958," 2–3.

20. Georges Duhamel, *Scènes de la vie future* (Paris: Mercure de France, 1930), 135–144.

21. Marchand, *Advertising the American Dream,* xxii; see also Otis Pease, *The Responsibilities of American Advertising: Private Control and Public Influence, 1920–1940* (New Haven: Yale University Press, 1958); Roland Marchand, "The Fitful Career of Advocacy Advertising: Political Protection, Client Cultivation, and Corporate Morale," *California Management Review* 29 (winter 1987): 128–156.

22. James Webb Young, *A Footnote to History: Draft of a Plan for Enemy Country Propaganda in the First World War* (Coapa, N.M.: Piñon Press, 1950), unpaginated (p. 1).

23. Quoted in Marchand, *Advertising the American Dream,* 6.

24. James Webb Young, *A Story Still Untold: The Development of America's Socially Conscious Capitalism* (Coapa, N.M.: Piñon Press, 1951), unpaginated.

25. Robert Griffith, "The Selling of America: The Advertising Council and American Politics, 1942–1960," *Business History Review* 57 (autumn 1983): 388–412; Harry Cross to Sam Meek, May 8, 1956, NATO, 1958 file, International Offices and Special Assignments for Samuel W. Meek Subseries, 1926–1961, Howard Henderson Papers, JWT; William P. Wright Jr. to Wolfgang Lehman, December 5, 1958, with attached memos: "Notes for the 10th Anniversary," "Themes for NATO Tenth Anniversary," "NATO," "NATO Campaign: Meeting Report, #3, January 22, 1959," ibid.

26. "Advertising in Germany," January 1928, 1, microfilm, Germany file, JWT.

27. Adrian Head to James Webb Young, *JWT Newsletter,* July 15, 1927, Newsletter Series, 1916–1987, JWT.

28. George Richardson, "JWT in Poland and Sweden," *JWT Newsletter,* July 28 1931, Newsletter Series, 1916–1987, JWT.

29. Douglas C. West, "From T-Square to T-Plan: The London Office of the J. Walter Thompson Advertising Agency, 1919–1970," *Business History* 24 (April 1987): 199–217; reprint of "JWT Aim Abroad: Push Gospel of Advertising," *Advertising Age,* March 2, 9, and 16, 1959, 1.

30. Arthur Hartzell, "JWT in Spain," *JWT Newsletter,* January 15, 1929, Newsletter Series, 1916–1987, JWT. See also "Representatives' Meeting," *JWT Newsletter,* July 29, 1930. Related successes are reported in August 8, 1928; April 30, 1930; December 16, 1930; and July 28, 1931, ibid.; see also Agence Thompson, S. A., *Comment vendre,* 2d ed. (Brussels: Editions Bieleveld, 1937), esp. 34 ff.; and Max Neama, *Publicité à l'Américaine* (Brussels: Editions Bieleveld, n.d.), in the Publications file, JWT.

31. Marcel Bleustein-Blanchet, *The Rage to Persuade: Memoirs of a French Advertising Man,* trans. Jean Bodewyn (New York, 1982), 7 ff.

32. Ibid. See also Bleustein-Blanchet's other memoirs: *Mémoires d'un lion* (Paris: Librairie Académique Perrin, 1988); *Les mots de ma vie* (Paris: R. Laffont, 1990); and, with Jean Mauduit, *La traversée du siècle* (Paris: R. Laffont, 1994).

33. "Le Drugstore 'à la française' s'affirme," *Libre–Service–Actualité,* November 1, 1968, 34–36.

34. For a history of Publicis, see Clark Eric Hultquist, "The Price of Dreams: A History of Advertising in France, 1927–1968" (Ph.D. diss., Ohio State University, 1996).

35. Bleustein-Blanchet, *Rage to Persuade,* 7–8.

36. Marjorie Anne Beale, *Advertising and the Politics of Public Persuasion in France* (microfilm; Ph.D. diss., University of California, Berkeley, 1992).

37. Edward L. Bernays, "Problems of the Advertiser in Europe and America," *Foreign Trade,* September 1928, 53.

38. Jeremy Aynsley, *Graphic Design in Germany, 1890–1945* (Berkeley: University of California Press, 2000), 55–56.

39. A. Le Flobic, "Comment un directeur commerçant a vu l'Amérique," *Vendre,* March 1931, 218.

40. Piero Paolo Pasolini, "17 Maggio, 1973, Analisi linguistica di uno slogan," in *Scritti corsari* (Milan: Garzanti, 1979), 14–17; Serra Ticnic, "United Colors and United Meetings: Benetton and the Commodification of Social Issues," *Journal of Communication* 47 (1995): 3–25.

41. The best account is John Willett, *Art and Politics in the Weimar Period: The New Sobriety, 1917–1933* (New York: Thames and Hudson, 1978).

42. Jac. (Jacob) Jongert, "Posters Designed by Dutch Artists," *Wendingen* 5, no. 2 (1923): 3.

43. Adam Hubertus, "Die Leipziger 'Reklameburg' von Peter Behrens: Ein neuer Weg der Messepropaganda," in *Leipzigs Messen, 1497–1997: Gestaltwandel, Umbrüche, Neubeginn,* ed. Hartmut Zwahr, Thomas Topfstedt, and Günter Bentele (Cologne: Böhlau Verlag, 1999), 505–525, esp. 521.

44. Elias Canetti, *The Torch in My Ear* (1980), trans. Joachim Neugroschel (New York: Farrar Straus Giroux, 1982), 275–276.

45. On Citroën, in addition to Fabien Sabatès and Sylvie Schweitzer, *André Citroën: Les chevrons de la gloire* (Paris: E. P. A., 1980), see Sylvie Schweitzer, *André Citroën* (Paris: Fayard, 1992); and John Reynolds, *André Citroën: The Henry Ford of France* (New York: St. Martin's, 1997); Citroën's own words, translated, are found in André Citroën, "The Future of the Automobile," *Living Age,* August 1929, 451–453. For the views of U.S. commercial attachés, see Harry N. Kelly, "French Automobile Men to Learn English," May 25, 1925, 156, Reports 1925 file, vol. 2, May–August, 1924, Series 16, RG 151, BFDC. For contemporary analyses, see L. Deschizeaux, "La publicité de l'automobile," *Vendre,* June 1930, 473–479; Cheronnet, "How French Automobile Firms Advertise," 39. There are rich historical accounts in Fridenson, "French Automobile Marketing," esp. 139 ff.

46. Cheronnet, "How French Automobile Firms Advertise," 41.

47. Bleustein-Blanchet, *Rage to Persuade,* 8–9.

48. See, for example, J. Neuilly, "L'affiche vend-elle?" *Vendre,* February 1928, 153–157; "L'affiche décade," *La publicité* 1 (April 1925); L. P. B. [L. Balzaretti], "La decadenza del manifesto," *Campana d'Italia,* December 1932; L. Cusmano, "Il cartello in crisi?" *L'ufficio moderno,* December 1928, 679–680; also D. Gualtieri, "Street Advertising in General," in *International Advertising Conference, 1933* (Milan: A. Lucin, 1933), 163–167.

49. Richard Hülsenbeck, "Das Leide der Plakate," *Gebrauchsgraphik* 4 (January 1927): 4.

50. In general, see Harold Hutchison, *The Poster: An Illustrated History from 1860* (New York: Viking, 1968); and Abraham A. Moles, *L'affiche dans la société urbaine* (Paris: Dunod, 1970). On France, see Alain Weill, *L'affiche française* (Paris: Presses Universitaires de France, 1982); on Germany, see Leslie Cabarga, *Progressive German Graphics, 1900–1937* (San Francisco: Chronicle Books, 1994); and Aynsley, *Graphic Design in Germany.* On Italy, see G. Mughini and G. Scudiero, *Il manifesto pubblicitario italiano: da Dudovich a Depero, 1890–1940* (Milan: Nuove Arti Grafiche Ricordi, 1997); and Alberto Casella, Paola Morelli, and Marco Cicolini, eds., *Catalogo Bolaffi del manifesto italiano: dizionario degli illustratori* (Turin: Giulio Bolaffi Editore, 1995). On the Netherlands, see Stephen S. Prokopoff and Marcel Franciscono, eds., *The Modern Dutch Poster: The First Fifty Years, 1890–1940* (Cambridge, Mass.: MIT Press; Urbana, Ill.: Krannert Art Museum, University of Illinois at Champaign-Urbana, 1987); on Britain, see Dennis Farr, *English Art, 1870–1940* (Oxford: Clarendon Press, 1978).

51. Quoted in John Willett, *Art and Politics in the Weimar Period: The New Sobriety, 1917–1933* (New York: Thames and Hudson, 1978), 114.

52. Chessel, *La publicité,* 158–159.

53. J. C. S. Lore, "Die Reklame auf den Hoch und Untergrund Bahnen Berlins," *Gebrauchsgraphik* 3 (September 1926): 31–32.

54. Roger Mauduit, *La réclame: Etude de sociologie économique* (Paris: Librairie Felix Alcan, 1933), 75.

55. Julius Steiner, ed., "Einfülle: Gebrauchs-graphorismen," *Gebrauchs-graphik* 5 (May 1927): 15.

56. H. K. Frenzel, "25 Jahre Deutsches Plakat," ibid. 4 (April 1927): 13. On Frenzel, see Jeremy Aynsley, "*Gebrauchsgraphik* as an Early Graphic Design Journal, 1924–1938," *Journal of Design History* 5 (1992): 53–72.

57. On Magagnoli and Maga, see Gino Pesavento and Antonio Palieri, *Chi è in pubblicità* (Milan: L'Ufficio Moderno, 1953), 202; C. W. Frerk, "The Publicity Poster in Italy," *Advertising World*, June 1928, 224–225, 230; Antonio Valeri, *Pubblicità italiana: storia, protagonisti e tendenze di cento anni di comunicazione* (Milan: Edizioni del Sole 24 Ore, 1986), 51, 55; Herman Behrmann, "Maga," *Gebrauchsgraphik* 3 (July 1926): 41–47.

58. "L'arte di vendere del fumo," *Pugno nell'occhio* 1 (January 1922); "La pubblicità parlata," ibid. (March 1923).

59. Frerk, "Publicity Poster in Italy," 230; H. K. Frenzel, "L. A. Mauzan, 'Ein Erfolgreicher italienischer Plakat-Künstler'—A Successful Italian Poster-Artist," *Gebrauchsgraphik* 6 (March 1929): 53–61.

60. Aynsley, *Graphic Design in Germany*, 119–137.

61. "Lucian Bernhard in New York, ein Interview von Oskar M. Hahn," *Gebrauchsgraphik* 3 (February 1926): 9–10, 12; Fritz Hellwag, "Die Berliner Gebrauchsgraphik," ibid. (May 1926): 3–9; H. K. Frenzel and Frederick Suhr, "Was Weiter? And What Now?" ibid., 5 (October 1928): 33–38; also W. S. Crawford, "Das Plakat—The Poster," ibid., 2 (May 1925): 3–9. The modernist ethos underlying the European representation of commodities is discussed in Reyner Banham, *Theory and Design in the First Machine Age* (New York: Praeger, 1960); Robert Tessari, *Il mito della macchina* (Milan: Mursia, 1973); and Siegfried Giedion, *Mechanization Takes Command* (New York: Oxford University Press, 1948).

62. "Einführung zum Sonderheft münchenen Gebrauchsgraphik," *Gebrauchsgraphik* 3 (January 1926): 3–8; Frenzel and Suhr, "Was Weiter?" 36.

63. Frenzel and Suhr, "Was Weiter?" 33–38; Marchand, *Advertising the American Dream*, 140–150.

64. "Lucian Bernhard in New York."

65. Aynsley, *Graphic Design in Germany*, 85–86.

66. Chessel, *La publicité*, 201.

67. R.-L. Dupuy, "Panorama de la publicité française," *Vendre*, March 1930, 194. On Dupuy, see Pierre Bruneau, *Magiciens de la publicité*, 5th ed. (Paris: Gallimard, 1956), 71–81.

68. J. Murray Allison, "Continental Advertising," *Advertising World*, April 1927 (728–732), May 1927 (16–18), and June 1927 (130–132); Ned Crane, "Bill Day for the Berlin Office," *JWT Newsletter*, November 15, 1927; all Newsletter Series, 1916–1987, JWT.

69. Allison, "Continental Advertising," *Advertising World*, May 1927, 18.

70. Marchand, *Advertising the American Dream*, 10 and passim; see also Fox, *The Mirror Makers*, chaps. 2 and 3.

71. Leiss, "Icons of the Marketplace," esp. 12–13.

72. Leech, *English in Advertising*, 166.

73. "Capitalist realism" is found in Schudson, *Advertising*, 214 ff. T. J. Jackson Lears speaks of "stupid realism" in "The Artist and the Adman," *Boston Review* 11 (April 1986): 5–6. For another formulation, "capital-

ist idealism," see Erving Goffman, *Gender Advertisements* (1979; reprint, Harper and Row, 1987).

74. Schudson, *Advertising,* 218 ff.

75. See in particular Leon Jones, "Pourquoi l'annonce française est différente de l'annonce américaine," *Vendre,* September 1929, 201–204; also Dupuy, "Panorama de la publicité française"; and various articles in *Die Reklame:* Hanns W. Brose, "Goût américain," August 1927, 519–523; G. Haug, "Wirksame verkaufstexte und wie man sie gestaltet," June 1928, 393–395; H. Sakowski, "Amerikanisches-Allzuamerikanisches," October 1930, 640–648; and Vito Magliocco, *La pubblicità in America* (Rome: Edizioni dell' Associazione Nazionale Fascista dei Dirigenti di Aziende Industriali, 1932).

76. Francis Pickens Miller and Helen Hill, *The Giant of the Western World: America and Europe in a North-Atlantic Civilisation* (New York: W. Morrow, 1930), 213–214.

77. Pierre Bourdieu, *Distinction: A Social Critique of the Judgement of Taste* (1979), trans. Richard Nice (Cambridge, Mass.: Harvard University Press, 1984), 4–5, 32, 54 ff.

78. Quoted in Schudson, *Advertising,* 173.

79. Hartzell, "JWT in Spain," 6.

80. Hellmut Lehmann-Haupt, "Amerikanische Reklame Photographie," in *Klimsch's Jahrbuch: Eine Übersicht über die Fortschritte auf graphischen Gebiete* 24 (1931): 19–29; Paule de Gironde, "Si nous faisions une annonce américaine," *Vendre,* March 1929, 80.

81. Bleustein-Blanchet, *Rage to Persuade,* 7.

82. Maurice Halbwachs, "La réclame," *Annales d'histoire économique et sociale* 15 (July 1934): 402. On the rise of advertising agencies, see "De la naissance et de la vie des grandes agences françaises de publicité," *Presse-Publicité,* May 7, 1937, 3–4, 25–26; also Chessel, *La publicité;* Martin, *Trois siècles de publicité.* On the Italian profession, see Pesavento and Palieri, *Chi è in pubblicità.* On Germany, see Hartmut Berghoff, "'Times Change and We Change with Them'": The German Advertising Industry in the 'Third Reich,'" in Roy Church and Andrew Godley, eds., *The Emergence of Modern Marketing* (London: Frank Cass, 2003), 128–147.

83. Paul Knoll, "Die Anzeiger-organization des Ullstein Verlages," in *Der Verlag Ullstein zum Welt Reklame Kongress Berlin 1929* (Berlin: Ullstein, 1929), 124–125; Hermann Ullstein, *The Rise and Fall of the House of Ullstein* (New York: Simon and Schuster, 1943), 109–111, 122.

84. *Presse-Publicité,* May 7, 1938, 6; Mauduit, *La réclame,* 72; Henri Albert Bernard Loustalan, *La publicité dans la presse française* (Pau: G. Lescher-Moutoue, 1933), 7–55, 69–74, 145–183, 273–305, 322–325; Hultquist, "The Price of Dreams" (245), whose estimates show that, at the outside, 15 percent of French illustrated magazines were devoted to advertising, whereas *Life* magazine, which could be considered average, devoted 40 percent of its space to it.

85. Hanns Kropff, "Frauen als Käuferinnen," *Die Reklame,* July 1926, 649–650, 661; see also Hanns Kropff and Bruno W. Randolph, *Marktanalyse: Untersuchung des Marktes und Vorbereitung der Reklame* (Munich: R. Oldenbourg, 1928); on their collaboration with Bernays, see Edward Bernays, *Biography of an Idea: Memoirs of Public Relations Counsel* (New York: Simon and Schuster, 1965), 355–357.

86. Siegfried Kracauer, "Asyl für Obdachlose," in *Die Angestellten* (Frankfurt: Societäts-Verlag, 1930), 91–101, quoted in Anton Kaes, Martin Jay, and Edward Dimendberg, eds., *The Weimar Republic Sourcebook* (Berkeley: University of California Press, 1994), 189.

87. Adolf Guggenbühl, *Reklame in Amerika und bei uns* (Zurich: Verlag Organisator, 1928), 15.

88. Dr. Julius Watkins, quoted in "Representatives' Meeting," *JWT Newsletter,* December 9, 1930, Newsletter Series, 1916–1987, JWT.

89. Guggenbühl, *Reklame in Amerika,* 19–20.

90. Case no. 1022, May 8, May 29, June 5, 1936, 1, Centre de Préparation aux Affaires, Chambre de Commerce de Paris (hereafter CPA).

91. Michelle Wlassikoff and Michel Bodeux, *La fabuleuse et exemplaire histoire de Bébé Cadum* (Paris: Syros-Alternative, 1990); Marie-Emmanuelle Chessel, "Une méthode publicitaire américaine? Cadum dans la France de l'entre-deux guerres," *Entreprises et Histoire* 11 (1996): 61–76; Chessel, *La publicité,* 23, 84, 109, 139, 158.

92. Case no. 1022, 1936, 5, CPA; Chessel, "Une méthode publicitaire américaine?" 72.

93. Case no. 1022, 1936, 6, CPA; Chessel, "Une méthode publicitaire américaine?" 75.

94. L. D. H. Weld, "Germany's Iron Rule over Advertising Does What in U.S. Is Done Voluntarily," *Printers' Ink,* November 18, 1937, 76–88; idem, "Where the Nazis Did One Good Job: They Eliminated Advertising Abuses," ibid., December 9, 1937, 40–48. Edward H. Douglass, head of H. K. McCann Co. in Berlin, gave an even more favorable appraisal, calling it "probably . . . the most advanced legislation to be found in this field," in "Special Laws Must Be Observed by All Advertising in German Market," *Transatlantic Trade,* June 1937, 24–26, quotation from 24.

95. Sam E. Woods, Commercial Attaché, Berlin, "Higher Advertising Turnover in First Half of 1939," August 16, 1939, August 1939 folder, box 271, BFDC.

96. John Barmas, "European Advertising Is Changing," *Advertising Monthly,* June 1938, 28, 30, 46. See also U.S. Department of Commerce, *Foreign Graphic Arts Industries: World Markets for Printing Machinery, Equipment, and Supplies,* Trade Promotion Series, no. 172 (Washington, D.C.: U.S. Government Printing Office, 1937).

97. "Fasching," *Advertising World,* May 1927, 16; "Ist Ihre Ehe glücklich?" *Die Reklame,* September 1932, 520; "Wölkchen am Ehehimmel," *Die Woche,* November 1937, 43.

98. Bleustein-Blanchet, *Rage to Persuade;* "Publicis: Fiche analytique," *Le miroir de l'information* 18 (1958), Policy Letters, 1958–1960, Howard Henderson Papers, JWT.

99. L. R. Coleman to Samuel Meek, September 23, 1944, Antwerp Office Subseries, 1938–1947, box 4, International Office Series, 1928–1952, JWT.

100. On J. Walter Thompson at Antwerp, see Pouillard, "La publicité en Belgique," 1: 159–190.

101. "Advertising Announcement by Myron J. H. Cerny," ca. December 21, 1945, accompanied by memo from H. Henderson, Correspondence Coleman, Lloyd Ring, 1937–1971, box 1/11, Howard Henderson Papers,

JWT; Lloyd Ring Coleman to Howard Henderson, December 2, 1946, ibid.; J. H. Cerny to Donald C. Foote, October 15, 1946, Agence Thompson, Antwerp Office Subseries, 1938–1947, box 4, JWT International Corporation Subseries, International Office Series, Treasurer's Office Records, JWT; Hultquist, "The Price of Dreams," 250–255; John Heidenry, *Theirs Was the Kingdom: Lila and DeWitt Wallace and the Story of the Reader's Digest* (New York: W. W. Norton, 1993), 172.

102. Bleustein-Blanchet, *Rage to Persuade,* 7.

6. THE STAR SYSTEM

Epigraphs: La cinématographie française, October 1, 1926, 2; Hearings before the Subcommittee on International Operations, Committee on Foreign Relations, U.S. Senate, 95th Cong., 1st sess. (Washington, D.C.: U.S. Government Printing Office, 1977), 211–212.

1. Quoted in Patrick McGilligan, *Fritz Lang: The Nature of the Beast* (New York: St Martin's, 1997), 104.

2. Ibid., 108; Tom Gunning, *The Films of Fritz Lang: Allegories of Vision and Modernity* (London: BFI, 2000), 1–11.

3. McGilligan, *Fritz Lang,* 104.

4. Fritz Lang, "Wege des grossen Spielfilms in Deutschland," *Die Literarische Welt* (Berlin), October 1926, 5–6; reprinted in Fred Gehler and Ulrich Kasten, *Fritz Lang, Die Stimme von Metropolis* (Berlin: Henschel, 1987), 242–245; Gunning, *Films of Fritz Lang,* 52–86.

5. Klaus Kreimeier, *The Ufa Story: A History of Germany's Greatest Film Company, 1918–1945,* trans. Robert and Rita Kimber (New York: Hill and Wang, 1996), 125 ff.; Thomas Saunders, *Hollywood in Berlin: American Cinema and Weimar Germany* (Berkeley: University of California Press, 1994), 69–83.

6. McGilligan, *Fritz Lang,* 105; Saunders, *Hollywood in Berlin,* 69–83; Kreimeier, *Ufa Story,* 110–130, 158–172.

7. Fred Hildenbrandt, "Metropolis," *Berliner Tageblatt,* January 11, 1927 (late edition), 2–3. On the film's ambiguous cultural stance, see Andreas Huyssen, "The Vamp and the Machine: Technology and Sexuality in Fritz Lang's *Metropolis,*" *New German Critique* 24–25 (fall–winter 1981–82): 221–237.

8. Mordaunt Hall, "The Screen: A Technical Marvel," *New York Times,* March 7, 1927, 16.

9. On the Hollywood system, the key works are David Bordwell, Janet Staiger, and Kristin Thompson, *The Classical Hollywood Cinema: Film Style and Mode of Production to 1960* (New York: Columbia University Press, 1985); Douglas Gomery, *The Hollywood Studio System* (New York: St. Martin's, 1986); Thomas Schatz, *The Genius of the System: Hollywood Film-making in the Studio Era* (1989; reprint, New York: Metropolitan Books, 1996). On responses to Hollywood films in Europe, see Kristin Thompson, *Exporting Entertainment* (London: British Film Institute, 1985); idem, "Early Alternatives to the Hollywood Mode of Production,"

Film History 5 (1993): 386–404; Ian Jarvie, *Hollywood's Overseas Campaign: The North Atlantic Movie Trade, 1920–1950* (Cambridge, Mass.: Harvard University Press, 1992); Victoria de Grazia, "Mass Culture and Sovereignty: The American Challenge to European Cinemas," *Journal of Modern History* 61 (March 1989): 53–87. For 2001 statistics, see Jens Ulff-Møller, *Hollywood's Film Wars with France: Film-Trade Diplomacy and the Emergence of the French Film Quota Policy* (Rochester: University of Rochester Press, 2001), xiii.

10. In general on the early cinema, see Georges Sadoul, *Histoire générale du cinéma: L'art muet, 1919–1929*, 2 vols. (Paris: Denoël, 1975); Gerben Bakker, "Entertainment Industrialized: The Emergence of the International Film Industry, 1890–1940" (Ph.D. diss., European University Institute, 2001).

11. On Pommer, see Ursula Hardt, *From Caligari to California: Erich Pommer's Life in the International Film Wars* (Providence: Berghahn, 1996); idem, "Erich Pommer: Film Producer for Germany" (Ph.D. diss., University of Iowa, 1989); Wolfgang Jacobsen, *Erich Pommer: Ein Produzent macht Filmgeschichte* (Berlin: Argon, 1989); and Herbert G. Luft, "Erich Pommer," part 1, *Films in Review* 10 (October 1959): 457–469; part 2, ibid. (November 1959): 518–533.

12. Maurice Zolotow, *Billy Wilder in Hollywood* (New York: G. P. Putnam, 1977), 43, quoted in Hardt, "Erich Pommer," 81–82.

13. George R. Canty, April 29, 1933, 4, April 1933, German Motion Picture Industry, March–April 1935 file, box 259, RG 151, Bureau of Foreign and Domestic Commerce, National Archives, College Park, Md. (hereafter BFDC).

14. Georg Jäger, "Der Kampf gegen Schmutz und Schund. Die Reaktion der Gebildeten auf die Unterhaltungsindustrie," *Archiv für die Geschichte des Buchwesens* 31 (1988): 163–191.

15. On the early development of the German cinema, see Hans Wollenberg, *Fifty Years of German Film* (London: Falcon, 1948), 10–16; also Paolo Cherchi Usai and Lorenzo Codelli, eds., *Before Caligari: German Cinema, 1895–1920* (Pordenone: Edizioni Biblioteca dell'Immagine, 1990); Sabine Hake, *German National Cinema* (London: Routledge, 2002), 7–25.

16. On the general question of national film cultures, see, in addition to Hake, *German National Cinema*, Philip Rosen, "History, Textuality, Nation: Kracauer, Burch and Some Problems in the Study of National Cinemas," *Iris* 2 (1984): 69–84; Stephen Crofts, "Concepts of National Cinema," in *World Cinema: Critical Approaches*, ed. John Hill and P. Church Gibson (Oxford: Oxford University Press, 2000), 385–394.

17. Philippe Soupault, *The American Influence in France*, trans. Babette Hughes and Glenn Hughes (Seattle: University of Washington Book Store, 1930), 13.

18. Thompson, *Exporting Entertainment*, 87.

19. Bakker, "Entertainment Industrialized," 130–141.

20. Ibid., 158–159, 161; Richard Abel, *French Cinema: The First Wave, 1915–1929* (Princeton: Princeton University Press, 1984), esp. chaps. 1, 2; also the classic, Sadoul, *Histoire générale du cinéma*, 1: 7–50; 2: 309–373.

21. On the mix of national and local genre in the early film industry, see Charles Musser, *The Emergence of Cinema: The American Screen to 1907*

(New York: Scribner, 1990); Robert Sklar and Charles Musser, eds., *Resisting Images: Essays on Cinema and History* (Philadelphia: Temple University Press, 1990). On early Italian cinema, see Aldo Bernardini, *Cinema muto italiano: arte, divisimo, e mercato, 1910–1914* (Bari: Laterza, 1982).

22. Richard Abel, *The Red Rooster Scare: Making Cinema American, 1900–1910* (Berkeley: University of California Press, 1999).

23. Ibid., 25 ff., 37.

24. Ibid., 99.

25. Ibid., 151–158, 173–174.

26. "Helping the Moving Pictures to Win the War," *Bio,* July 18, 1918, 8, quoted in Thompson, *Exporting Entertainment,* 94.

27. Quoted in Ulff-Møller, *Hollywood's Film Wars with France,* 49–50.

28. Julius Klein, "Trade Follows the Motion Pictures," *Commerce Reports,* January 22, 1923, 191; idem, "What Are Motion Pictures Doing for Industry?" *Annals of the American Academy of Political and Social Science,* November 1926, 79–83.

29. Quoted from *Kinematograph,* July 8, 1931, the trade paper published by Alfred Hugenberg's Scherl Press, in George R. Canty, "Ufa's Reaction to French Contingent," July 29, 1931, October 1931 file, box 254, RG 151, BFDC. See also Ulff-Møller, *Hollywood's Film Wars with France,* 63 n. 15.

30. Thompson, *Exporting Entertainment,* 117; Ulff-Møller, *Hollywood's Film Wars with France,* 48–55.

31. Ruth Vasey, *The World According to Hollywood, 1918–1939* (Madison: University of Wisconsin Press, 1997), 5.

32. See Matthew Bernstein, ed., *Controlling Hollywood: Censorship and Regulation in the Studio Era* (New Brunswick, N.J.: Rutgers University Press, 1999), esp. Ruth Vasey, "Beyond Sex and Violence: 'Industry Policy' and the Regulation of Hollywood Movies, 1922–1939," 102–129.

33. Ivor Montagu, "The Censorship of Sex in Films," in World League for Sexual Reform, *Sexual Reform Congress, London, 8–14: ix: 1929: Proceedings of the Third Congress* (London: Paul, Trench, Trubner), 323–332, quotation from 328.

34. Gregory D. Black, *Hollywood Censored: Morality Codes, Catholics and the Movies* (Cambridge: Cambridge University Press, 1994), 238.

35. Vasey, *World According to Hollywood,* 33, 127.

36. Siegfried Kracauer, "Artistisches und Amerikanisches," *Frankfurter Zeitung* 29 (January 1926), quoted in Miriam Bratu Hansen, "The Mass Production of the Senses," in *Reinventing Film Studies,* ed. Linda Williams and Christine Gledhill (London: Edward Arnold, 2000), 342–343; Saunders, *Hollywood in Berlin,* 183–185.

37. Winifred Holtby, *South Riding* (1936; reprint, Glasgow: Fontana Collins, 1981), 35.

38. J. P. Mayer, *British Cinemas and Their Audiences: Sociological Studies* (London: Dennis Dobson, 1948), 20, 22, 41, 43, 64, 74; see also his *Sociology of Film: Studies and Documents* (London: Faber and Faber, 1946). For intriguing reflections on audience responses to American cinema, see Jeffrey Richards and Dorothy Sheridan, eds., *Mass-Observation at the Movies* (London: Routledge and Kegan Paul, 1987); Jackie Stacey, "Feminine Fascinations: Forms of Identification in Star-Audience Relations," in

Stardom: Industry of Desire, ed. Christine Gledhill (London: Routledge, 1991), 141–163; Stephen Gundle, "Film Stars and Society in Fascist Italy," in *Re-viewing Fascism: Italian Cinema, 1922–1943*, ed. Jacqueline Reich and Piero Garofalo (Bloomington: Indiana University Press, 2002), 315–339.

39. Fabrice Montebello, "Hollywood Films in a French Working Class Milieu," in *Hollywood in Europe: Experiences of a Cultural Hegemony*, ed. David W. Ellwood and Rob Kroes (Amsterdam: VU University Press, 1994), 235, 237–246.

40. Abel, *French Cinema*, 12; André Chevanne, *L'industrie du cinéma: Le cinéma sonore* (Bordeaux: Delmas, 1933), 88.

41. Sadoul, *Histoire générale du cinéma*, 2: 29.

42. On the latter of the two, see Gerben Bakker, "Selling French Films on Foreign Markets: The International Strategy of a Medium-Sized French Film Company, 1919–1928," EUI Working Paper, Department of History and Civilization, European University Institute, San Domenico di Fiesole, 2001.

43. Gilles Willems, "Les origines du groupe Pathé-Natan et le modèle americain," *Vingtième siècle* 46 (April–June 1995): 98–106; Abel, *French Cinema*, 51–64.

44. Ulff-Møller, *Hollywood's Film Wars with France*, 33.

45. Marcel Lapierre, *Les cent visages du cinéma* (Paris: B. Grasset, 1948), 144–145; also Paul Monaco, *Cinema and Society: France and Germany during the Twenties* (New York: Elsevier, 1976), 42; David Strauss, "The Rise of Anti-Americanism in France: French Intellectuals and the American Film Industry, 1927–1932," *Journal of Popular Culture* 10 (spring 1977): 752–759.

46. *New York Herald*, Paris edition, October 3, 1926, quoted in George R. Canty, "Report on the First International Motion Picture Congress," October 12, 1926, BFDC; also J. F. Butler, "Film Industry in France," file Paris, 1925, RG 151, BFDC

47. Ulff-Møller, *Hollywood's Film Wars with France*, 81–83; Canty, "Report on Motion Picture Congress"; Thompson, *Exporting Entertainment*, 112–118.

48. Quoted in Ulff-Møller, *Hollywood's Film Wars with France*, 83–84.

49. Quoted in ibid., 101.

50. Ibid., 103; Paul Léglise, *Histoire de la politique du cinéma français*, vol. 1: *Le cinéma et la Troisième République* (Paris: Librairie Générale de Droit et de Jurisprudence, 1970), esp. 61–102, 261–266.

51. Hardt, "Erich Pommer," 111.

52. Ibid., 85.

53. Saunders, *Hollywood in Berlin*, 88–89, 125.

54. Will H. Hays, *Memoirs* (Garden City, N.Y.: Doubleday, 1955), 509, quoted in Andrew Higson and Richard Maltby, eds., *"Film Europe" and "Film America": Cinema, Commerce and Cultural Exchange, 1920–1939* (Exeter: University of Exeter Press, 1999), 5.

55. Saunders, *Hollywood in Berlin*, 51–83.

56. Hardt, "Erich Pommer," 94–106; Saunders, *Hollywood in Berlin*, 210–212.

57. Hardt, "Erich Pommer," 107.

58. Erich Pommer, "Der internationale Film," *Film-Kurier,* August 28, 1928.

59. Hardt, "Erich Pommer," 172–173; idem, *From Caligari to California,* 127–129.

60. Richard Maltby and Ruth Vasey, "The International Language Problem: European Reactions to Hollywood's Conversion to Sound," in Ellwood and Kroes, *Hollywood in Europe,* 68–93.

61. More generally, see Douglas Gomery, "Economic Struggles and Hollywood Imperialism: Europe Converts to Sound," *Yale French Studies* 60 (winter 1980): 80–93. See esp. René Jeanne, "L'invasion cinématographique américaine," *Revue des deux mondes,* February 15, 1930, 857–884; idem, "La France et le film parlant," ibid., June 1, 1930, 533–554; Alexandre Arnoux, *Du muet au parlant: Mémoires d'un témoin* (Paris: Nouvelle Edition, 1946); and Lapierre, *Les cent visages,* 206–232. The director René Clair recalls his doubts before finally converting to sound in *Réflexion faite: Notes pour servir à l'histoire de l'art cinématographique de 1920 à 1950* (Paris: Gallimard, 1951); so do other contemporaries in the special issue of *Cinématographe* 47 (May 1979): 1–27, devoted to *Du muet au parlant;* Abel, *French Cinema,* 30.

62. Ginette Vincendeau, "Hollywood Babel: The Coming of Sound and the Multiple-Language Version: Cinema, Commerce and Cultural Exchange, 1920–1939," in Higson and Maltby, *"Film Europe" and "Film America,"* 207–224. On Paramount Joinville, see the descriptions by Ilya Ehrenburg, "C'est un film Paramount," *Revue du cinéma,* June 1, 1931, 7–24; and Dudley Andrew, "Sound in France: The Origins of a Native School," *Yale French Studies* 60 (1980): 94–114, esp. 100–101.

63. Léglise, *Le cinéma et la Troisième Republique,* 75 ff., 106–107; Conseil National Economique, *L'industrie cinématographique* (Paris, 1936); Jean-Michel Renaitour, ed., *Où va le cinéma français?* (Paris: Baudinière, 1937), 115; Elizabeth Grottle Strebel, *French Social Cinema of the 1930s* (New York: Arno, 1980), 76–77.

64. Luigi Freddi, "Rapporto sulla cinematografia," June 22, 1934, subfile Freddi, Luigi, file 3/2.2 1397, Series 1934–1936, Presidenza del Consiglio dei Ministri, Archivio Centrale dello Stato, Rome.

65. Quoted in Luigi Freddi, *Il cinema,* vol. 1 (Rome: L'Arnia, 1949), 297. On the response to Americanism more generally, see Gian Piero Brunetta, *Storia del cinema italiano, 1895–l945* (Rome: Riuniti, 1979), 213–219, 227, 409–416; Adriano Aprà, "La 'rinascita' sulla pagina cinematografica del 'Tevere,' 1929-1930," in *Nuovi materiali sul cinema italiano, 1929–1943: Quaderno* 71 (Pesaro: Mostra Internazionale del Nuovo Cinema, 1976), 60–85; and Lucilla Albano, "Volontà-possibilità del cinema fascista: riviste e periodici degli anni trenta in Italia," in *Nuovi materiali,* 10l–136.

66. John L. McBride, "Italian Motion Pictures Industry," January 19, February 6, and February 7, 1935, January–March 1935 file, box 314, RG 151, BFDC.

67. "Attività svolta dell' Istituto nell'esercizio 1933: relazione a S. E. dal Presidente dell'Istituto M. Paolucci de' Calboli," March 31, 1934 file, 20, 36, Series 170.20, Ministero della Cultura Popolare folder, Archivio Centrale dello Stato.

68. McBride, "Italian Motion Pictures Industry," February 7, 1935, 6; Libero Bizzarri and Libero Solaroli, *L'industria cinematografica italiana* (Firenze: Parenti, 1958), 32–41. On Cinecittà: Lucilla Albano, "Hollywood: Cinelandia," in *Cinema italiano sotto il fascismo*, ed. Riccardo Redi (Venice: Marsilio, 1979), 219–232.

69. Libero Bizzarri, "L'economia cinematografica," in *La città del cinema: produzione e lavoro nel cinema italiano, 1930–1970,* ed. Massimiliano Fasoli (Rome: Napoleone, 1979), 40.

70. More generally on this period, see Jean A. Gili, "Pouvoir politique et intérêts économiques: L'industrie du cinéma en Italie pendant le période fasciste," *Film échange* 9 (winter 1980): 67–88. Brunetta, *Storia del cinema italiano,* 293–297, 515–519; see also Libero Solaroli, "Profilo di storia economica del cinema italiano," in *Il cinema come industria,* ed. Peter Bächlin (Milan: Feltrinelli, 1958), 198–199. The most vivid and subtle Italian analysis of the mix of old and new genres is Francesco Savio, *Ma l'amore no: realismo, formalismo, propaganda e telefoni bianchi nel cinema italiano del regime, 1930–1943* (Milan: Sonzogno, 1975).

71. On the Nazis' reorganization of the cinema, see Julian Petley, *Capital and Culture: German Cinema, 1933–1945* (London: British Film Institute, 1979), esp. 29 ff.; David Welch, *Propaganda and the German Cinema, 1933–1945* (Oxford: Clarendon Press, 1983); Kreimeier, *Ufa Story,* 221–224, 255–265; Hake, *German National Cinema,* 61–67.

72. George R. Canty, Weekly Reports, February 6 and 18, March 18, April 1, 8, 15, 22, and 29, 1933, February 1933 file, box 259, RG 151, BFDC.

73. George R. Canty, Weekly Report, April 1, 1933, 2–3, box 259, RG 151, BFDC.

74. Economic and Trade Notes, September 10, 1931, Economic and Trade Notes/Special Reports 1931 (Motion Pictures) file, box 254, RG 151, BFDC.

75. Hardt, *From Caligari to California,* 138–139.

76. George R. Canty, Weekly Report, April 8, 1933, February 1933 file, box 259, RG 151, BFDC.

77. George R. Canty, "Startling Developments in the German Film Situation," November 12, 1932, November 1932 file, box 258, RG 151, BFDC; idem, "The German Film Industry during 1933: Special report," January 15, 1934, January 1934 file, box 261, ibid.; idem, Weekly Report, March 18, 1933, February 1933 file, box 259, ibid.

78. George R. Canty, Weekly Report, April 22, 1933, February 1933 file, box 259, ibid.

79. Petley, *Capital and Culture,* 60; Kreimeier, *Ufa Story,* 226.

80. Hans Helmut Prinzler, *Chronik des deutschen Films 1895–1994* (Stuttgart: Metzler, 1995), quoted in Eric Rentschler, *The Ministry of Illusion: Nazi Cinema and Its Afterlife* (Cambridge, Mass.: Harvard University Press, 1996), 13.

81. As observed by *L'Ambrosiano*'s critic Emilio Ceretti, *Bianco e nero* 3 (June 1939): 110. On the Nazis' emulation of the "star system," see Francis Courtade and Pierre Cadars, *Le cinéma nazi* (Paris: Eric Losfeld, 1972); also Cinzia Romani, *Le dive del Terzo Reich* (Rome: Gremese, 1981).

82. Canty, "German Film Industry during 1933"; Paul Pearson, "Revision of

World Motion Picture Data," August 1, 1939, 16–17, December 1939 file, box 272, RG 151, BFDC.

83. R. M. Stephenson, "Further Defense of American Films in German Press," 11–12, October 22, 1936, German Film Notes, September–October 1936 file, box 265, RG 151, BFDC; idem, "American Films Used as Models," September 17, 1936, ibid.; idem, "German Films Not to Be Laughed At," June 5, 1937, German Film Notes, June 1937 file, box 266; idem, Special Report, "Goering's Mouthpiece Again Sharply Criticizes German Films," October 9, 1937, October 1937 file, box 266, RG 151, BFDC; idem, "German Press Criticism of American Films," June 9, 1939, June–July 1939 file, box 272, RG 151, BFDC; Paul Pearson, "Revision of World Motion Picture Data," August 1, 1939, 16–17, December 1939 file, ibid.

84. R. M. Stephenson, German Film Notes, July 7, 1939, 12–14, June–July 1939 file, box 272, RG 151, BFDC.

85. According to Goebbels's "orders of the day" on February 28, 1941; Willi A. Boelke, ed., *Secret Conferences of Dr. Goebbels, October 1939–March 1943*, trans. Ewald Osers (London: Weidenfeld and Nicolson, 1967), 123–124.

86. Abel, *French Cinema*, 28–30, 35; Andrew, "Sound in France"; Léglise, *Le cinéma et la Troisième Republique*, 93, 152; Lapierre, *Les cent visages*, 499.

87. Nathan D. Golden, "Review of Foreign Film Markets," *Review of Foreign Film Markets during 1938* (Washington, D.C.: U.S. Bureau of Foreign and Domestic Commerce, 1939), iv ff.

88. Marcus S. Phillips, "The German Film Industry and the New Order," in *The Shaping of the Nazi State*, ed. Peter D. Stachura (London: Croom Helm, 1978), 257–281; Mino Argentieri, *L'asse cinematografico Roma-Berlino* (Naples: Sapere, 1986).

89. On the Venice Film Festival, see Francesco Bono, "La mostra del cinema di Venezia: nascita e sviluppo nell'anteguerra, 1932–1939," *Storia contemporanea* 22 (June 1991): 513–549; Marla Stone, "Challenging Cultural Categories: The Transformation of the Venice Biennale International Film Festival under Fascism," *Journal of Modern Italian Studies* 4, 2 (1999): 184–208; also Léglise, *Le cinéma et la Troisième Republique*, 93, 152; Lapierre, *Les cent visages*, 499; Argentieri, *L'asse cinematografico Roma-Berlino*, 37–48.

90. Marla Stone, "The Last Film Festival: The Venice Biennale Goes to War," in Reich and Garofalo, *Re-viewing Fascism*, 293–297.

91. Argentieri, *L'asse cinematografico Roma-Berlino*, 20–21.

92. Ibid., 80; Kreimeier, *Ufa Story*, 331–380.

93. Argentieri, *L'asse cinematografico Roma-Berlino*, 16.

94. Maurice Bardèche and Robert Brasillach, *Histoire du cinéma* (Paris: Denoël et Steele, 1935), 326, 329; Simone Dubreuilh, "Le cinema, art du futur," *Ciné-Comoedia*, August 22, 1936, quoted in Ulff-Møller, *Hollywood's Film Wars with France*, 118, 123 n. 8.

95. Quoted in C. G. Crisp, *The Classic French Cinema, 1930–1960* (Bloomington: Indiana University Press, 1997), 57; see also 55–59. For Europe as a whole see Georges Sadoul, *Histoire générale du cinéma*, vol. 6, part 1: *Le cinéma pendant la guerre, 1939–1945* (Paris: Denoël, 1954), 8–70; Paul Léglise, *Histoire de la politique du cinéma français*, vol. 2: *Le*

cinéma entre deux républiques, 1940–1946 (Paris: Filméditions, 1976); Stéphane Levy-Klein, "Sur le cinéma français des années, 1940–1944," part 1, "L'organisation," *Positif* 168 (April 1975): 23–30, and part 2, "Les réalisations," ibid., 170 (June 1975): 35–44, Evelyn Ehrlich, *Cinema of Paradox: French Filmmaking under the German Occupation* (New York: Columbia University Press, 1985); Jean-Pierre Bertin-Maghit, *Le cinéma français sous l'Occupation* (Paris: Presses Universitaires de France, 1994).

96. Gilles Willems, "The Origins of Pathé-Natan," in *Une histoire économique du cinéma français (1895–1995): Regards franco-américains,* ed. Pierre-Jean Benghozi and Christian Delage (Paris: Harmattan, 1997), translated by Annabelle de Croÿ for the electronic journal *Screening the Past,* no. 8 (November 12, 1999), <http://www.latrobe.edu.au/screeningthepast/classics/rr1199/gwrr8b.htm>.

97. Ehrlich, *Cinema of Paradox,* 85.

98. Quoted in Louis P. Lochner, ed. and trans., *The Goebbels Diaries* (London: H. Hamilton, 1948), 151, 165; see also Boelke, *Secret Conferences of Dr. Goebbels,* 123–124.

99. Rentschler, *Ministry of Illusion,* 20, 201; Karsten Witte, "The Indivisible Legacy of Nazi Cinema," *New German Critique* 74 (spring–summer 1998): 23–29; Patrice Petro, "Nazi Cinema at the Intersection of the Classical and the Popular," ibid., 41–53.

100. Courtade and Cadars, *Cinéma Nazi,* 298–299.

101. Kreimeier, *Ufa Story,* 318–319, 328–329; Rentschler, *Ministry of Illusion,* 193–213; David Stewart Hull, *Film in the Third Reich: A Study of the German Cinema, 1933–1945* (Berkeley: University of California Press, 1969), 253.

102. Golden, "Review of Foreign Film Markets," ix.

103. Walter Wanger, "Donald Duck and Diplomacy," *Public Opinion Quarterly* 14 (1950): 444, 452.

104. Wolfgang Schivelbusch, *In a Cold Crater: Cultural and Intellectual Life in Berlin, 1945–1948,* trans. Kelly Barry (Berkeley: University of California Press, 1998), 137. More generally: Robert R. Shandley, *Rubble Films: German Cinema in the Shadow of the Third Reich* (Philadelphia: Temple University Press, 2001).

105. Quoted in Schivelbusch, *In a Cold Crater,* 137.

106. Ibid., 144; Shandley, *Rubble Films,* 14–15.

107. Quoted in Schivelbusch, *In a Cold Crater,* 140.

108. Hardt, *From Caligari to California,* 163–188; Schivelbusch, *In a Cold Crater,* 144–153.

109. Quoted in Schivelbusch, *In a Cold Crater,* 144; Hardt, "Erich Pommer," 198, 208.

7. THE CONSUMER-CITIZEN

Epigraphs: "Le billet de Robert Guérin," *Vente et publicité,* September 1955, 5; George H. Hildebrand, "Consumer Sovereignty in Modern Times," *American Economic Review* 41 (May 1951): 33.

1. Benjamin Welles, *Spain: The Gentle Anarchy* (New York: Praeger, 1965), 285.
2. "No Loan for Franco," *New York Times,* July 16, 1949, 4.
3. *¡Bienvenido Mister Marshall!,* dir. Luis Garcia Berlanga (UNINXI, 1952); Tatjana Pavlovic, "*¡Bienvenido Mr. Marshall!* and the Renewal of Spanish Cinema," in *Cine-Lit II: Essays on Hispanic Film and Fiction,* ed. George Cabello-Castellet, Jaume Martí-Olivella, and Guy H. Wood (Portland, Ore.: Portland State University Press, 1995), 169–174. See also Aurora Bosch and M. Ferdanda del Ricón, "Dreams in a Dictatorship: Hollywood and Franco's Spain, 1939–1956," in *Here, There and Everywhere: The Foreign Politics of American Popular Culture,* ed. Reinhold Wagnleiter and Elaine Tyler May (Hanover, N.H.: University Press of New England, 2000), 100–115. For background on U.S. involvement in Spain, see R. Richard Rubottom and J. Carter Murphy, *Spain and the United States: Since World War II* (New York: Praeger, 1984).
4. Welles, *Spain,* 289.
5. The authoritative account is José Harris, *William Beveridge: A Biography,* 2d ed. (Oxford: Clarendon Press, 1997). Quotations are from <www.spartacus.schoolnet.co.uk/2WWbeveridgereport.htm>.
6. Blum quoted in Jean Lacouture, *Léon Blum (*Paris: Seuil, 1977), 545.
7. Erhard to Christian Democratic Union Party Congress, August 28, 1948, quoted in Hendrick Kafsack, "Uncle Scrooge and the Miracle," *Frankfurter Allgemeine Zeitung,* English-language edition, August 2, 2001, 8.
8. Willard M. Hogan and Amry Vandenbosch, *The United Nations: Background, Organization, Functions, Activities* (New York: McGraw-Hill, 1952), esp. 258–261. For the historical background, Steven Schlesinger, *Act of Creation: The Founding of the United Nations* (New York: Perseus Group, 2003).
9. Anne Rice Pierce, *Woodrow Wilson and Harry Truman: Mission and Power in American Foreign Policy* (Westport, Conn: Praeger, 2003), 120, 142–143, 147, 181–199.
10. Joseph S. Davis, "Standards and Contents of Living," *American Economic Review,* 35 (March 1945): 1–15; on the AER's quasi-official status: Michael A. Bernstein, "American Economic Expertise from the Great War to the Cold War: Some Initial Observations," *Journal of Economic History* 50 (June 1990): 407–416.
11. T. H. Marshall, *Citizenship and Social Class* (London: Pluto, 1992). An excellent introduction to the politics of postwar Keynesianism is provided by Peter A. Hall, ed., *The Political Power of Economic Ideas: Keynesianism across Nations* (Princeton: Princeton University Press, 1989); the different paths by which governments intervened are carefully studied in idem, *Governing the Economy: The Politics of State Intervention in Britain and France* (New York: Oxford University Press, 1986).
12. François Perroux, quoted in Jules Milhaud, preface to Robert Badouin, *L'élasticité de la demande des biens de consommation* (Paris: A. Colin, 1953), 6.
13. Jean Romeuf, in *Les indices du coût de la vie et des prix* (Paris, 1951), quoted in Maurice Lengellé, *La Consommation* (1956; 6th edition, Paris: Presses Universitaries de France, 1980), 96.

14. Jean-Luc Godard, dir., *Masculin-féminin* (Anoushka/Argos Films, 1966).

15. Hildebrand, "Consumer Sovereignty in Modern Times," 19–33. More generally on the postwar discussion, see Joseph Persky, "Retrospectives: Consumer Sovereignty," *Journal of Economic Perspectives* 7 (winter 1993): 183–191.

16. Joseph Stalin, speech, February 9, 1946, in *Oeuvres*, vol. 14 (Paris: Nouveau Bureau d'Editions, 1975), 189–191.

17. On the rise in Soviet standards of living in the immediate postwar decade, see Julie Hessler, *A Social History of Soviet Trade: Trade Policy, Retail Practices, and Consumption, 1917–1953* (Princeton: Princeton University Press, 2004), 296–328; also Donald Filtzer, "Standard of Living of Soviet Industrial Workers in the Immediate Postwar Period, 1945–1948," *Europe-Asia Studies*, summer 1999, 1013–38. Philip Hanson suggests that in the mid-1960s Soviet levels of consumption were half those of the British; *The Consumer in the Soviet Economy* (London: Macmillan, 1968), 48–82. The big surge came at the turn of the 1970s: Sergei Nikolaenko, "Soviet Consumers: Problems of the Transition to Market Economy," Working Papers, Rutgers Center for Historical Analysis, Rutgers University, 1991.

18. An excellent introduction to the Marshall Plan, its transatlantic and European context, is Barry J. Eichengreen, ed., *Europe's Postwar Recovery* (Cambridge: Cambridge University Press, 1995). The main line of studies, starting with Alan Milward, *The Reconstruction of Western Europe, 1945–51* (Berkeley: University of California Press, 1984), emphasizes the endogenous roots of European recovery and the big bang the American-led recovery achieved with a relatively small investment. This view is incorporated in Gérard Bossuat, *L'Europe occidentale à l'heure américaine: Le Plan Marshall et l'unité européenne, 1945–1952* (Brussels: Edition Complexe, 1992). As the importance of the impact of capital investment has been downplayed, the significance of technology transfers has been more and more highlighted, with much controversy as to the modalities by which U.S. managerial methods operated. Main works include Marie-Laure Djelic, *Exporting the American Model: The Postwar Transformation of European Business* (Oxford: Oxford University Press, 1998); Mattias Kipping and Ove Bjarnar, eds., *The Americanization of European Business: The Marshall Plan and the Transfer of U.S. Management Models* (London: Routledge, 1998); Jonathan Zeitlin and Gary Herrigel, eds., *Americanization and Its Limits* (Oxford: Oxford University Press, 2000); and Dominique Barjot, ed., *Catching Up with America: Productivity Missions and the Diffusion of American Economic and Technological Influence after the Second World War* (Paris: Presse de l'Universitaie de Paris–Sorbonne, 2002).

19. Robert M. Hathaway, *Ambiguous Partnership: Britain and America, 1944–1947* (New York: Columbia University Press, 1981).

20. Charles S. Maier, "The Politics of Productivity: Foundations of American International Economic Policy after World War II," in *The Cold War in Europe: Era of a Divided Continent*, ed. Maier (Princeton: Markus Wiener, 1996), 169–202.

21. *Joe Smith, Travailleur américain* (Paris: Bureau du Travail, European Cooperation Agency, [1950]); Anthony Carew, *Labor under the Marshall Plan: The Politics of Productivity and the Marketing of Management Sci-*

ence (Detroit: Wayne State University Press, 1987); also Federico Romero, *The United States and the European Trade Union Movement, 1944–1951* (Chapel Hill: University of North Carolina Press, 1992).

22. Bertrand de Jouvenal, "La conjuncture," *Vente et publicité,* May 1952, 5. Irwin Wall, *The United States and the Making of Postwar France, 1945–1954* (New York: Cambridge University Press, 1991), highlights the similarly harsh effect of the postwar "plans" on consumers in western and eastern Europe. For Great Britain, see Ina Zweiniger-Bargielowska, *Austerity in Britain: Rationing, Controls and Consumption, 1939–1955* (New York: Oxford University Press, 2000).

23. Bossuat, *L'Europe occidentale,* 186, 351; idem, *La France, l'aide américaine et la construction européenne, 1944–1954* (Paris: Comité pour l'Histoire Economique et Financière de la France, 1992), 2 vols.; idem, *Les aides américaines économiques et militaires à la France, 1938–1960: Une nouvelle image des rapports de puissance* (Paris: Ministère de l'Economie, des Finances et de l'Industrie, Comité pour l'Histoire Economique et Financière de la France, 2001).

24. Harry Bayard Price, *The Marshall Plan and Its Meaning* (Ithaca: Cornell University Press, 1955), 242.

25. Paul Hoffman, *Peace Can Be Won* (Garden City, N.Y.: Doubleday, 1951), 87.

26. Albert Hemsing, "The Marshall Plan's European Film Unit, 1948–1949: A Memoir and Filmography," *Historical Journal of Film, Radio, and Television* 14, no. 3 (1994): 269–297. See also David Ellwood, "From 'Re-education' to the Selling of the Marshall Plan in Italy," in *The Political Re-education of Germany and Her Allies after World War II,* ed. Nicholas Pronay and Keith Wilson (London: Croom Helm, 1985), 219–239.

27. Vittorio Gallo, dir., *The Story of Koula,* film for the European Cooperation Agency, Rome, 1951.

28. Hannah Arendt, "Dream and Nightmare: Anti-American Feeling Is Well on the Way to Becoming a New European 'Ism,'" *Commonwealth,* September 10, 1954, 551–554.

29. David Riesman, *Abundance for What? And Other Essays* (Garden City, N.Y.: Doubleday, 1964), 64.

30. Ibid., preface, 5 n. 4.

31. David Riesman, *The Lonely Crowd: A Study of the Changing American Character* (New Haven: Yale University Press, 1950).

32. "Deux jours à Leipzig, vitrine de deux mondes," *Vente et publicité,* October 27, 1954, 2. For further study, see Katherine Pence, "'A World in Miniature': The Leipzig Trade Fairs in the 1950s and East German Consumer Citizenship," in *Consuming Germany in the Cold War,* ed. David F. Crew (New York: Berg, 2003).

33. Robert Hamilton Haddow, "Material Culture and the Cold War: International Trade Fairs and the American Pavilion at the 1958 Brussels World's Fair" (Ph.D. diss., University of Minnesota, 1984), 12, 16–17.

34. Irving Kravitz, "Work Time Required to Buy Food," *Monthly Labor Review* 70 (November 1949): 487–493.

35. "Condition, attitudes et aspirations des ouvriers," *Sondages: Revue française de l'opinion publique* 18, no. 2 (1956): 39–57.

36. Patricia Maclachlan, *Consumer Politics in Postwar Japan* (New York: Co-

lumbia University Press, 2002); and, more generally on the postwar American hegemony in Japan, see John W. Dower, *Embracing Defeat: Japan in the Wake of World War II* (New York: W. W. Norton, 1999).

37. Howard P. Whidden, "Birth of a Mass Market—Western Europe," *Harvard Business Review*, 33 (May–June 1955): 105.

38. The United States' ardent pursuit of this aim by means of the Ford and other leading foundations, with outlooks akin to that of Edward Filene's Twentieth Century Foundation earlier in the century, is the subject of Volker Berghahn's *America and the Intellectual Cold Wars in Europe* (Princeton: Princeton University Press, 2001).

39. Whidden, "Birth of a Mass Market," 101–107.

40. On this new occupation, see Maria Hohn, *GIs and Frauleins: The German-American Encounter in 1950s West Germany* (Chapel Hill: University of North Carolina Press, 2002). Many themes of the immediate postwar years continue into the 1950s; see Petra Goedde, *GI's and Germans: Culture, Gender, and Foreign Relations, 1945–1949* (New Haven: Yale University Press, 2003).

41. Reinhard Neebe, "German Big Business and the Return to the World Market," in Volker Berghahn, ed., *Quest for Economic Empire: European Strategies of German Big Business in the Twentieth Century* (Providence: Berghahn Books, 1996), 95–121; Gunnar Adler-Karlsson, *Western Economic Warfare, 1947–1967: A Case Study in Foreign Economic Policy* (Stockholm: Almqvist and Wiksell, 1968).

42. Ludwig Erhard, *Prosperity through Competition* (New York: Praeger, 1958), 134; Werner Albelshauser, "The Economic Policy of Ludwig Erhard," EUI Working Paper no. 80, European University Institute, San Domenico di Fiesole, 1984; Henry M. Oliver Jr., "German Neoliberalism," *Quarterly Journal of Economics* 74 (February 1960): 117–149, esp. 136–138; Volker Hentschel, *Ludwig Erhard: Ein Politikerleben* (Munich: Olzog, 1996).

43. Heinz Dietrich Ortlieb, "Unsere Konsumgesellschaft: Glanz und Elend des deutschen Wirtschaftswunders," *Hamburger Jahrbuch für Wirtschafts-und Gesellschaftspolitik* 4 (1959): 224–246, quoted in Ulrich Wyra, "Consumption and Consumer Society: A Contribution to the History of Ideas," in *Getting and Spending: European and American Consumer Societies in the Twentieth Century,* ed. Susan Strasser, Charles McGovern, and Matthias Judt (Washington, D.C.: German Historical Institute; New York: Cambridge University Press, 1998), 441; Konrad H. Jarausch and Michael Geyer, *Shattered Past: Reconstructing German Histories* (Princeton: Princeton University Press, 2003), 269–314. See also Hannah Schissler, ed., *The Miracle Years: A Cultural History of West Germany, 1949–1968* (Princeton: Princeton University Press, 2001); and Crew, *Consuming Germany in the Cold War.*

44. David Potter, *People of Plenty* (Chicago: University of Chicago Press, 1958).

45. Pierre Bourdieu, "Différences et distinctions," in *Le partage des bénéfices: Expansion et inégalités en France* (Paris: Minuit, 1966), 117–129; idem, *Distinction: A Social Critique of the Judgement of Taste* (1979), trans. Richard Nice (Cambridge, Mass.: Harvard University Press, 1984).

46. Louis Pinto, "Le consommateur: Agent économique et acteur politique," *Revue française de sociologie* 31 (1990): 180.

47. Jane Marceau, *Class and Status in France: Economic Change and Social Immobility, 1945–1975* (Oxford: Clarendon Press, 1977), 39 ff.

48. *Enquête sur les tendances de la consommation des salariés urbains: vous gagnez 20% de plus, qu'en faites-vous?* (Paris: Imprimerie Nationale, 1955), 16, 22, 28, 37 ff.

49. On the middle classes, see the exemplary Luc Boltanski, *The Making of a Class: Cadres in French Society* (Cambridge: Cambridge University Press, 1987), 97–144. On youth culture, see among others Uta Poiger, *Jazz, Rock, and Rebels: Cold War Politics and American Culture in a Divided Germany* (Berkeley: University of California Press, 2000).

50. Francesco Alberoni, *Consumi e società,* 2d ed. (Bologna: Il Mulino, 1967), 27, 29.

51. Sandro Rinauro, *Storia del sondaggio d'opinione in Italia, 1936–1994* (Venice: Istituto Veneto di Scienze, Lettere ed Arti, 2002); Löic Blondiaux, *La fabrique de l'opinion: Une histoire sociale des sondages* (Paris: Seuil, 1998); Hartmut Berghoff, "Von der 'Reklame' zur Verbrauchslenkung. Werbung im nationalsozialistischen Deutschland," in *Konsumpolitik: Die Regulierung des privaten Verbrauchs im 20. Jahrhundert,* ed. Berghoff (Göttingen: Vandenhoeck & Ruprecht, 1999), 77–112.

52. Rosa-Maria Gelpi and François Julien-Labruyère, *The History of Consumer Credit: Doctrines and Practices,* trans. Liam Gavin (New York: St. Martin's, 2000).

53. Edward A. McCreary, *The Americanization of Europe: The Impact of Americans and American Business on the Uncommon Market* (Garden City, N.Y.: Doubleday, 1964), 99, 253.

54. Jean Fourastié, *La civilisation de 1960* (Paris: Presses Universitaires de France, 1947), 68–69.

55. Idem, *Pourquoi nous travaillons* (Paris: Presses Universitaires de France, 1959), 94–95.

56. Quoted in Guy Dupuigrenet-Desroussilles, *Niveaux de vie et coopération économique dans l'Europe de l'Ouest* (Paris: Presses Universitaires de France, 1962), 41.

57. Jacqueline Poelmans, *L'Europe et les consommateurs* (Brussels: Labor, 1978), 28, 37.

58. Richard Cooper, *The Economics of Interdependence: Economic Policy in the Atlantic Community* (New York: McGraw-Hill for the Council on Foreign Relations, 1968).

59. Uwe W. Kitzinger, *The New Europeans: A Commentary on Products and People, a Marketing Survey of the European Common Market and Britain* (London: Reader's Digest, 1963), 4.

60. Dupuigrenet-Desroussilles, *Niveaux de vie,* 137.

61. Christopher Layton, *Trans-Atlantic Investments* (Boulogne-sur-Seine: Atlantic Institute, 1968), 29.

62. Ibid.; Robert B. Dickie, *Foreign Investment: France: A Case Study* (Leiden: A. W. Sijthoff, 1970). More generally, see J. J. Boddewyn and D. M. Hansen, "American Marketing in the European Common Market, 1963–1973," *European Journal of Marketing* 11, no. 7 (1977): 548–563. Robert Gilpin highlights the aggressive dynamism of American corporations moving into the 1960s; *U.S. Power and the Multinational Corporation: The*

Political Economy of Foreign Direct Investment (New York: Basic Books, 1975).

63. Layton, *Trans-Atlantic Investments*, 29.

64. J. J. Servan-Schreiber, *The American Challenge*, trans. Ronald Steel (New York: Atheneum, 1969). See also Richard F. Kuisel, *Seducing the French: The Dilemma of Americanization* (Berkeley, 1993).

65. Layton, *Trans-Atlantic Investments*, 76; Marie-Christine Grasse, "The History of the Grasse Perfume Industry," Touch Briefings: Business Briefings, London, 2004.

66. Marc Meuleau, "L'introduction du marketing en France (1880–1973)," *Revue française de gestion*, September–October 1988, 2–65; idem, "De la distribution au marketing (1880–1939): Une réponse a l'évolution du marché," *Entreprises et histoire* 3 (1993): 61–74.

67. Sam Meeks to Tom Sutton, August 12, 1957, Policy Letters, 1954–1957 folder, box 4, Sam Meeks Correspondence, J. Walter Thompson Company Archives, John W. Hartman Center for Sales, Advertising, and Marketing History, Duke University (hereafter JWT).

68. Peter E. Gilow, Personnel, box 27, Individuals and Officers, International Series, E. G. Wilson Series, JWT; Peter Gilow to Tom Sutton, October 13, 1961, Frankfurt Office, Sam Meek folder, International Branch Management file, Henderson Papers, JWT.

69. J. Walter Thompson Company Limited, *Market Research on a European Basis* (London, 1971), 2, 22, Publications Series, JWT.

70. "Welche Theme sollte die Aktion Gemeinsinn bei der derzeitigen wirtschaftlichen und politischen Unsicherheit behandeln," Aktion Gemeinsinn (German Advertising Council) 1961–December 1963, Correspondence file, Frankfurt Information folder, Peter E. Gilow Papers, JWT; also clipping, Hannelore Kroter, "Zwischen Hotshop und garantiertem Werbebefolg," *Industriekurier*, March 11, 1969, 12, ibid.

71. An den Präsidenten von Rotary International, Betr.: Rotary-Club München, August 23, 1945, Vershiedenes mit Germany zu tun file, European Advisory Committee, Rotary International European Office, Zurich; Luther Struthers to E. A. Atkins, June 26, 1947, ibid.; Luther Struthers to Parker, October 14, 1948, ibid.; Lovejoy to Panzar, June 2, 1949, ibid.; "From Belgians, undaunted and unidentified," August 9, 1949, ibid.; Percy Hodgeson to Walther Panzar, September 16 and October 24, 1949, ibid.

72. Bericht über den offiziellen Besuch, March 10, 1956, subfile 2: Germany General IV, 1967, box 3, Country Files: Germany, Rotary International, European Office, Zurich; "Pläne und Kommentäre des Präsidenten," March 3, 1970, Cologne, ibid.

73. *Treaty Establishing the European Economic Community* (*Treaty of Rome, 1958*) (Brussels: Publishing Services of the European Communities, 1967).

74. Union Féminine Civique et Sociale, *Les consommateurs et le Marché Commun* (Paris, 1967), 26.

75. Raymond Aron, quoted in Robert O. Paxton, *Europe in the Twentieth Century*, 2d ed. (San Diego: Harcourt, Brace, 1985), 599.

76. Pierre Massé, "Autocritique des années soixante, vues par un commissaire au Plan," *Bulletin de l'Institut d'histoire du temps présent* (Paris), suppl. no. 1 (1981): 41–44.

77. Jean-Pierre Page, "L'utilisation des produits de la croissance," in *Le partage des bénéfices: Expansion et inégalités en France* (Paris: Minuit, 1966), 115–116.

78. Arthur Marwick, *The Sixties: Culture Revolution in Britain, France, Italy, and the United States, c. 1958–1974* (Oxford: Oxford University Press, 1998).

79. John Martin and George W. Smith, *The Consumer Interest* (London: Pall Mall Press, 1968), 261; Roberta Sassatelli, "Power Balance in the Consumption Sphere: Reconsidering Consumer Protection Organizations," EUI Working Paper, European University Institute, San Domenico di Fiesole, 1995.

80. Jacques-René Rabier, ed., *European Consumers: Their Interests, Aspirations and Knowledge of Consumer Affairs: Results and Analyses of a Sample Survey Carried Out in the Countries of the European Economic Community* (Brussels: Commission of the European Communities, 1976).

81. *221,750,000 consommateurs: Marché commun et Grande-Bretagne* (Paris: Sélection du Reader's Digest, 1963).

8. SUPERMARKETING

Epigraphs: Richard W. Boogaart quoted in "Business around the World," *U.S. News and World Report,* December 19, 1958, 102; speech by Giulio Montelatici, in *Atti del Consiglio Comunale di Firenze,* sess. 5/20, March 1961, 147, Archivio Storico, Comune di Firenze.

1. R. W. Boogaart to W. B. Dixon Stroud, Milan, February 18, 1957, reel 7, International Basic Economy Corporation, Rockefeller Archives Center, Sleepy Hollow, N.Y. (hereafter IBEC); John C. Moffett, "American Supermarkets in Milan, or Sunflowers Grow in Italy," 9, January 16, 1960, thesis prepared for Overseas Training Program, Maxwell Graduate School, Syracuse University, reel 9, IBEC.

2. Nelson Rockefeller, quoted in *Christian Science Monitor,* August 3, 1961.

3. Moffett, "American Supermarkets in Milan," 2; press release, May 2, 1957, 1, reel 7, IBEC. More generally on IBEC and the background to its European undertaking, see Wayne G. Broehl Jr., *United States Business Performance Abroad: The International Basic Economy Corporation* (Washington, D.C.: National Planning Association, 1969); Emanuela Scarpellini, *Comprare all'americana: le origini della rivoluzione commerciale in Italia, 1945–1971* (Bologna: Il Mulino, 2001).

4. R. W. Boogaart, quoted in Moffett, "American Supermarkets in Milan," 3.

5. Boogaart to W. D. Bradford, December 12, 1957, reel 7, IBEC; Moffett, "American Supermarkets in Milan," 4.

6. Jean Dutourd, *Au bon beurre: Ou, dix ans de la vie d'un crémier* (Paris: Gallimard, 1952).

7. Jacques Dansette, *Les formes evoluées de la distribution: Problème économique, problème psychologique* (Brussels: Pauli, 1944), 10.

8. Thomas Horst, *At Home Abroad: A Study of the Domestic and Foreign Operations of the American Food Processing Industry* (Cambridge, Mass.: Ballinger, 1974); Milton C. Hallberg, *Economic Trends in the U.S. Agricul-*

ture and Food Systems since World War II (Ames: Iowa State University Press, 2001). For the later period see "Supermarket Growth Abroad Helps U.S. Food Marketers," *Printers' Ink,* June 17, 1958, 60–62.

9. "Zimmerman, Max Mandell," in *Who's Who in America,* vol. 5 (Chicago: A. N. Maquis, 1974), 807; M. M. Zimmerman, *The Super Market: A Revolution in Distribution* (New York: McGraw-Hill, 1955).

10. M. M. Zimmerman, "Self Service Spreads in Europe," *Supermarket Merchandising* 15 (March 1950): 35.

11. *Premier Congrès International de la Distribution des Produits Alimentaires, Proceedings,* Paris, June 20–23, 1950 (Paris, 1950); Zimmerman, *The Super Market,* 290–291; *Commerce américain et productivité: Rapport de la mission d'étude des techniques commerciales américains* (Paris: Presses Universitaires de France, 1951).

12. *Premier Congrès,* 15.

13. Zimmerman, *The Super Market;* Joseph Cornwall Palamountain Jr., *The Politics of Distribution* (Cambridge, Mass.: Harvard University Press, 1955).

14. Zimmerman, *The Super Market,* 31.

15. Rachel Bowlby, *Carried Away: The Invention of Modern Shopping* (New York: Columbia University Press, 2000). See also Jennifer Cross, *The Supermarket Trap: The Consumer and the Food Industry* (Bloomington: Indiana University Press, 1970), 14–26.

16. Richard Tedlow, *New and Improved: The Story of Mass Marketing in America* (Boston: Harvard Business School Press, 1996), 182–258.

17. Zimmerman, *The Super Market,* 93.

18. *Premier Congrès,* 63–64.

19. Pedrazzoli quoted in Scarpellini, *Comprare all'americana,* 83.

20. Zimmerman, *The Super Market,* 289.

21. Randolph McAusland, *Supermarkets, 50 Years of Progress: The History of a Remarkable American Institution* (Washington, D.C.: Food Marketing Institute, 1980). More generally on the vast social implications of supermarketization, see Lizabeth Cohen, *A Consumer's Republic: The Politics of Mass Consumption in Postwar America* (New York: Knopf, 2003).

22. Pierre Guichard, in *Premier Congrès,* 63 and passim; Michelle Zancarini-Fournel, "À l'origine de la grande distribution, le succursalisme: Casino, Saint-Etienne, 1898–1948," *Entreprises et histoire* 4 (1993): 27–39.

23. *Premier Congrès,* 73.

24. Jacques Pictet, in ibid.; Zimmerman, "Self-Service," 57–59, 62; R. W. Boogaart to W. D. Bradford, February 17, 1957, reel 7, IBEC; Scarpellini, *Comprare all'americana,* 82–84.

25. "L'Europe adoptera-t-elle le libre service à l'americaine?" *Vente et publicité,* September 15, 1953, 1. More generally: Jean-Marc Villermet, "Histoire des 'grandes surfaces': Méthodes américaines, entrepreneurs européens," *Entreprises et histoire* 4 (November 1993): 41–53.

26. James B. Jefferys and Derek Knee, *Retailing in Europe: Present Structure and Future Trends* (London: Macmillan, 1962), 106; K. H. Henksmeier, *The Economic Performance of Self-Service in Europe* (Paris: Organization for European Economic Cooperation, European Productivity Agency, 1960).

27. Moffett, "American Supermarkets in Milan," 3.

28. Memorandum, W. D. Bradford to Members of IBEC Board and Staff: "Supermarket Possibilities in Western Europe," July 23, 1956, reel 7, IBEC; Richard W. Boogaart, "General Summary of Supermarket Possibilities in Western Europe," [July 1956], unpaginated [1], box 37, IBEC Supermarkets–Boogaart, R. W., 1956–1968, IBEC.

29. Stanley Hoffmann, *Le mouvement Poujade* (Paris: A. Colin, 1956).

30. Moffett, "American Supermarkets in Milan," 7.

31. Robert Hamilton Haddow, "Material Culture and the Cold War: International Trade Fairs and the American Pavilion at the 1958 Brussels World's Fair" (Ph.D. diss., University of Minnesota, 1984), 67–69; idem, *Pavilions of Plenty: Exhibiting American Culture Abroad in the 1950s* (Washington, D.C.: Smithsonian Institute Press, 1997), 9 ff.; Godfrey M. Lebhar, *Chain Stores in America, 1859–1962* (1952; reprint, New York: Chain Store Publishing, 1963), 389.

32. Claire Booth Luce to NAR (Nelson A. Rockefeller), December 19, 1956, file 342, box 37, RG 4, Series B AIA-IBEC, Nelson A. Rockefeller Personal Papers, Rockefeller Archives Center.

33. Vittorio Zavagli, "Il supermercato: l'automatismo nei mercati alimentari," *Agricoltura d'Italia,* November–December 1956, 5–6.

34. Quoted in Moffett, "American Supermarkets in Milan," 7.

35. R. W. Boogaart to W. B. Dixon Stroud, February 18, 1957, reel 7, IBEC; Boogaart to IBEC Investment Committee, Milan, March 6, 1957, ibid.

36. Boogaart to IBEC Investment Committee, March 6, 1957, 1–3.

37. Ruggero di Palma Castiglione to Boogaart, March 5, 1957, file 342, box 37, RG 4, Series B AIA-IBEC, Nelson A. Rockefeller Personal Papers, Rockefeller Archives Center; Memorandum, Richard W. Boogaart to IBEC Investment Committee: "Supermarkets–Milan, Italy," March 6, 1957, ibid.

38. Boogaart to W. B. Dixon Stroud, February 27, 1957, reel 7, IBEC; Boogaart to W. D. Bradford, March 26, 1957, ibid. See also Scarpellini, *Comprare all'americana,* 131–132.

39. Moffett, "American Supermarkets in Milan," 10.

40. R. W. Boogaart, "Proposed Schedule," May 2, 1957, reel 7, IBEC.

41. Boogaart to W. D. Bradford, December 13, 1958, reel 9, IBEC.

42. Boogaart to Bradford, December 12, 1958, ibid.

43. Boogaart to Bradford, August 3, 1960, ibid.

44. Boogaart to Bradford, July 17, 1957, reel 7, IBEC.

45. George E. Williamson, "Supermarkets Spread Abroad despite New Political Roadblocks," *Wall Street Journal,* July 18, 1960.

46. Ibid. The *Wall Street Journal* captured the political gist of the loan in the subtitle of Williamson's article: ""Rockefeller Firm in Italy Riles Small Stores, Is Helped by U.S. Aid Loans." Press release: Export-Import Bank of Washington, May 8, 1959, reel 9, IBEC; press release: IBEC, June 12, 1959, ibid. On earlier financial problems, see Boogaart to Bradford, December 17, 1957, March 6 and 14, 1958, reel 7, IBEC. On the loan request, see Boogaart to Bradford, April 28, May 31, and July 9, 1958, ibid.; Boogaart to Bradford, April 25, 30, and 27, 1959, reel 8, IBEC; "Imports as of April, 1959," reel 9, IBEC.

47. Moffett, "American Supermarkets in Milan," 15.

48. R. W. Boogaart to W. D. Bradford, July 7, 1958, reel 7, IBEC.

49. Moffett, "American Supermarkets in Milan," 20.

50. Boogaart to Bradford, October 20, 1958, reel 9, IBEC.

51. Boogaart to Bradford, July 7, 1958, reel 7, IBEC.

52. Moffett, "American Supermarkets in Milan," 34; also *Il Giorno*, May 15, 1959.

53. Boogaart to Bradford, April 28, 1958, reel 7, IBEC.

54. Boogaart to Bradford, March 26, 1957, ibid. In general on Milan in the economic miracle, see John Foot, *Milan since the Miracle: City, Culture and Identity* (Oxford: Berg, 2001).

55. "Plein feux sur Bruxelles: On y brule les étapes," *Libre–Service–Actualité*, October 9, 1961, 2.

56. R. W. Boogaart to W. D. Bradford, March 10, 1960, reel 7, IBEC; Memorandum, Bradford to W. B. Dixon Stroud and H. Levy: "Jewel Tea Co.," March 28, 1960, ibid. On Belgian retailing, see Marcel Michel and Henri Vander Eycken, *La distribution en Belgique* (Brussels: Ducolot, 1974).

57. Zimmerman, *The Super Market*, 91; idem, "Self-Service," 40.

58. *Libre–Service–Actualité*, October 15, 1962, 23; *Entreprise*, March 27, 1965, 69–77; see also ibid., March 4, 1961; René Uhrich, *Super-marchés et usines de distribution: Hier aux Etats-Unis, aujourd'hui en France* (Paris: Plon, 1962), 184; Etienne Thil, *Les inventeurs du commerce moderne: Des grands magasins aux bébés-requins* (Grenoble: Arthaud, 1966).

59. "Plein feux sur Bruxelles," 2.

60. Jacques Lacrosse and Pierre de Bie, *Emile Bernheim: histoire d'un grand magasin* (Brussels: Labor, 1972).

61. *Libre–Service–Actualité*, April 2, 1962, 11.

62. Edward A. McCreary, *The Americanization of Europe: The Impact of Americans and American Business on the Uncommon Market* (Garden City, N.Y.: Doubleday, 1964), 122; *Libre–Service–Actualité*, December 4, 1961; Henri de Torrente, "Les différentes formes de financements des Super-Marchés aux Etats-Unis et en Europe," *Revue-économique franco-suisse;* "Qui est Intershop Holding?" *Libre–Service–Actualité*, September 19, 1963.

63. Lacrosse and de Bie, *Emile Bernheim*, 211–212.

64. "Firenze, 1951–1960: rassegna del comune, relazione prefettizia," 59–62, 83–85, Archivio Municipale di Firenze; on Giorgio La Pira's opposition to the supermarkets, see Roland Hood to W. B. Dixon Stroud, March 13, 1961, reel 9, IBEC. In general on Florence at the turn of the 1960s, see James Edward Miller, *Politics in a Museum: Governing Postwar Florence* (Westport, Conn.: Praeger, 2002), 85–105.

65. R. W. Boogaart to W. D. Bradford, September 16, 1960, reel 9, IBEC.

66. Hood to Bradford, February 21, 1961, ibid.

67. Hood to Bradford, February 27, 1961, ibid.

68. François Gardès, "L'évolution de la consommation marchande en Europe et aux U.S.A. depuis 1960," *Consommation: Revue de socio-économie* 30 (April–June 1983): 3–32; also Louis Levy-Garboua, "Les modes de consommation de quelques pays occidentaux: Comparaisons et lois d'évolution (1960–1980)," ibid. (January–March, 1983): 4–52.

69. R. W. Boogaart to W. D. Bradford, July 7 and 12, 1958, reel 7, IBEC.

70. Boogaart to Bradford, July 12, 1958.
71. See, for example, Angelo Pichierri, "Ceti medi e mobilitazione politica: il caso dei commercianti," *Quaderni di sociologia* 3 (1974): 161–249.
72. Suzanne Berger, "The Uses of the Traditional Sector in Italy: Why Declining Classes Survive," in *The Petite Bourgeoisie: Comparative Studies of the Uneasy Stratum,* ed. Frank Bechhofer and Brian Elliott (New York: St. Martin's, 1981), 71–90.
73. Guido Colonna di Paliano, "Retail Trade in Italy: Problems and Prospects," Banco di Roma, *Review of Economic Conditions in Italy* 25, no. 5 (September 1971): 375–379, is a prescient account by the chairman of the Rinascente group.
74. Roland Hood to W. D. Bradford, April 12, 1961, reel 9, IBEC.
75. Councilman Guglielmo Bacci, in *Atti del Consiglio Comunale di Firenze,* sess. 5/20, March 1961, 156; Berger, "Uses of the Traditional Sector in Italy," 79–82.
76. Councilman Montelatici, in *Atti del Consiglio Comunale di Firenze,* sess. 5/20, March 1961, 147; Sandro Bellassai, *La morale comunista: pubblico e privato nella rappresentazione del PCI (1947–1956)* (Roma: Carocci, 2000), 164–200, 209–230, 292–300.
77. Councilman Mario Leone, in *Atti del Consiglio Comunale di Firenze,* sess. 5/20, March 1961, 162.
78. R. W. Boogaart, quoted in "very general translation" from *Il Giorno,* ca. May 15, 1957, reel 9, IBEC.
79. R. W. Boogaart to H. J. Ostermeyer, Comptroller, IBEC, August 13, 1958, 2, reel 7, IBEC.
80. Roland Hood to W. D. Bradford, June 25, 1961, reel 8, IBEC.
81. Councilman Montelatici, in *Atti del Consiglio Comunale di Firenze,* sess. 5/20, March 1961, 150.
82. Etienne Thil, *Combat pour la distribution: D'Edouard Leclerc aux supermarchés* (Paris: Arthaud, 1964); *Libre–Service–Actualité,* April 16, 1962, 36.
83. *Libre–Service–Actualité,* April 16, 1962, 79.
84. On European women shoppers' habits in general, see European Productivity Agency, *The Consumer's Food-Buying Habits* (Paris, 1958); "Le abitudini d'acquisto delle famiglie italiane: supplemento: indagine condotta dalla 'Misura S.p.A.' per conto dell' Unione Nazionale consumatori," *Mondo economico,* June 27, 1964; "Etudes sur les achats per impulsion dans les grands magasins," *Libre–Service–Actualité,* September 4, 1964, 45–46.
85. R. W. Boogaart to Steve David, February 13, 1961, reel 7, IBEC.
86. Assessore Rodolfo Francioni, in *Atti del Consiglio Comunale di Firenze,* sess. 5/20, March 1961, 151.
87. Hermann Levy, *The Shops of Britain: A Study of Retail Distribution* (London: Kegan Paul, Trench, Trubner, 1947).
88. R. W. Boogaart to W. D. Bradford, December 17, 1957, reel 7, IBEC.
89. Moffett, "American Supermarkets in Milan," 29.
90. *Giornale del mattino,* February 24, 1961, 4; February 28, 1961, 4.
91. Roland Hood to W. R. Bradford, June 25, 1961, reel 8, IBEC.
92. *Giornale del mattino,* March 6, 1961, 4.

93. Ibid., February 28, 1961, 4.

94. Fernand Braudel, *Afterthoughts on Material Civilization and Capitalism,* trans. Patricia M. Ranum (Baltimore: Johns Hopkins University Press, 1977), 63.

9. A MODEL MRS. CONSUMER

Epigraphs: Premier Congrès International de la Distribution des Produits Alimentaires, Proceedings, Paris, June 20–23, 1950 (Paris, 1950), 243; Luuk van Middelaar, "De Democratie kan zonder Ideologie," *NRC Handelsblad,* December 21, 2002.

1. Marthe Vincent, "Les poudres de lavage," 1969, 189 ff., Année 1968–1969, Hautes Ecoles Commerciales Jeunes Filles, Chambre de Commerce de Paris (hereafter CCP); J. Martin, "Les produits pour le lavage du linge en machine," 99–122, Année 1971–72, CCP; idem, "Qui est Procter & Gamble?" *Vente et publicité,* July–August 1956, 67. The canvasser was a stock-in-trade figure of turn-of-the-1960s film and fiction; see Georges Perec, *Things: A Story of the Sixties* (Boston: David Godine, 1990).

2. The transformation of the postwar European household is treated in Michael Wildt, *Am Beginn der "Konsumgesellschaft": Mangelerfahrung, Lebenshaltung, Wohlstandshoffnung in Westdeutschland in den fünfziger Jahren* (Hamburg: Ergebnisse, 1994); Jennifer A. Lohelin, *From Rugs to Riches: Housework, Consumption and Modernity in Germany* (Oxford: Berg, 1999); Claire Duchen, *Women's Rights and Women's Lives in France, 1944–1968* (London: Routledge, 1994). On the American household of the same epoch, see Elaine May, *Homeward Bound: American Families in the Cold War Era* (New York: Basic Books, 1988).

3. Quynh Delaunay, *Histoire de la machine à laver: Un objet technique dans la societé française* (Rennes: Presses Universitaires de Rennes, 1994). See also Patrick Carré, "Les ruses de la 'fee' electricité," in *Du luxe au confort,* ed. J.-P. Goubert (Paris: Belin, 1988), 65–83; and Marie-Noëlle Denis, "Systèmes culturels et technologie: histoire de la machine à laver," *Culture technique* 17 (March 1987): 206–212.

4. On housewifery in postwar France: Claire Duchen, "Occupation Housewife: The Domestic Ideal in 1950s France," *French Cultural Studies* 2, no. 4 (1991): 1–13. More generally, see Susan Strasser, *Never Done: A History of American Housework* (New York: Pantheon, 1982); and Ruth Schwartz Cowan, *More Work for Mother: The Ironies of Household Technology from the Open Hearth to the Microwave* (New York: Basic Books, 1983).

5. Michael Geyer, "America in Germany: Power and the Pursuit of Americanization," in Konrad H. Jarausch and Michael Geyer, *Shattered Past: Reconstructing German Histories* (Princeton: Princeton University Press, 2003), 121–144.

6. "La guerre des poudres à laver," *Libre–Service–Actualité,* March 17, 1966, 40; R. de Rochebrune, "La bataille des détergents: Après l'empoignade des enzymes," *Entreprise,* January 1970, 6; "Etude du marché des détergents de synthèse Panel Stafeco," discussion, March 19, 1960, CR 3878, Centre

de Perfectionnnement dans l'Administration des Affaires, CCP; Vincent, "Les poudres de lavage," 20 ff.; J. Martin, "Les produits pour le lavage," 99 ff.

7. Societé Fournier-Ferrier, discussions 14–21, November 1956, CPA-3.453, CCP; "Procter and Gamble France," *Libre–Service–Actualité,* October 1, 1967, 48–49.

8. Vincent, "Les poudres de lavage," 27.

9. For the history of synthetic detergents, see John Corlett, *The Economic Development of Detergents* (London: Gerald Duckworth, 1958), esp. 105–118; J. Martin, "Les produits pour le lavage," 1–27. On the American firms' major competitor in the world, see D. K. Fieldhouse, *Unilever Overseas: The Anatomy of a Multinational, 1895–1965* (London: Croom Helm, 1978). Excellent on the economic-cultural forces pushing detergents where the need is not yet apparent: Jeffrey James, *Consumption and Development* (New York: St. Martin's, 1993).

10. Vincent, "Les poudres de lavage," 28.

11. Roland Barthes, *Mythologies* (1957), ed. and trans. Annette Lavers (New York: Hill and Wang, 1972) 11, 36–38; Kristen Ross, *Fast Cars, Clean Bodies: Decolonization and the Reordering of French Culture* (Cambridge, Mass: MIT, 1995), 71–106.

12. Jean Baudrillard, *Le système des objets* (Paris: Gallimard, 1968), 249–252; idem, *Consumer Society: Myths and Structures* (1970) (Thousand Oaks, Calif.: Sage, 1998); Ross, *Fast Cars, Clean Bodies,* 73 and 208 n. 5.

13. Henri Lefebvre, *Le temps des méprises* (Paris: Stock, 1975), 34, 115.

14. Jean Dayre, "La première industrie française manque de productivité: 23 million de travailleurs, 35 milliards d'heures de travail par an," *Productivité française* 1 (January 1952): 4; Jacques Rouaud, *60 ans d'arts ménagers,* 2 vols. (Paris: Syros-Alternatives, 1993), 2: 67–69.

15. Merritt Ierley, *The Comforts of Home: The American House and the Evolution of Modern Convenience* (New York: Clarkson Potter, 1999), 180–181; H. H. Kelly, Assistant Trade Consul, "To Give Away American model home at French Salon" January 7, 1926, January–March file, Paris, 1926, vol. 1, RG 151, Bureau of Foreign and Domestic Commerce, National Archives, College Park, Md. (hereafter BFDC); idem, "The Third Salon of Household Labor Saving Devices," January 26, 1926, ibid.; Rouaud, *60 ans d'arts ménagers,* 1: 268–269.

16. Rouaud, *60 ans d'arts ménagers,* 2: 123.

17. Sophie Body-Gendrot, "Une vie privée française sur le modèle americain?" in *Histoire de la vie privée,* ed. Philippe Ariès and Georges Duby, vol. 5 (Paris: Seuil, 1987), 528–579.

18. Mary P. Ryan, *Womanhood in America* (New York: Franklin Watts, 1975), esp. 251–304; also Rayna Rapp and Ellen Ross, "The Twenties Backlash: Compulsory Heterosexuality, the Consumer Family, and the Waning of Feminism," in *Class, Race, and Sex: The Dynamics of Control,* ed. Amy Swerdlow and Hanna Lessinger (Boston: G. K. Hall, 1983), 93–107.

19. Siegfried Kracauer, *The Mass Ornament: Weimar Essay* (1963), trans. Thomas Y. Levin (Cambridge, Mass.: Harvard University Press, 1995).

20. Bruno Frank, *The Persians Are Coming* (1928), trans. H. T. Lowe-Porter (New York: Knopf, 1929).

21. Jean-Philippe Mathy, *Extrême-Occident: French Intellectuals and America* (Chicago: University of Chicago Press, 1993), 74; Manuel Thurner, "The American Girl Inherits Old Europe through Dance: Girlkultur and Kulturfeminismus" (Ph.D. diss., Yale University, 1999).

22. Denis de Rougement, *L'amour et l'Occident* (1939), rev. ed. (Paris: Plon, 1956), 32, 34, 272-273, translated and revised as *Love in the Western World* (Garden City, N.Y.: Doubleday, 1957).

23. Alexis de Tocqueville, *Democracy in America* (1835-1840), trans. George Lawrence, ed. J. P. Mayer (Garden City, N.Y.: Anchor, 1969), 590, 601, 603.

24. *Premier Congrès,* 243, 312-313.

25. Janice Williams Rutherford, *Selling Mrs. Consumer: Christine Frederick and the Rise of Household Efficiency* (Athens: University of Georgia Press, 2003), 57-58, 96 ff., 133-135.

26. Quoted in Simone Weil Davis, *Living Up to the Ads: Gender Fictions of the 1920s* (Durham: Duke University Press, 2000), 85-86.

27. Creative staff meeting, February 1, 1933, 15, box 5, Staff Meeting Minutes Collection, 1927-1938, John W. Hartman Center for Sales, Advertising & Marketing History, Duke University, J. Walter Thompson Company Archives (hereafter JWT).

28. Wesley Clair Mitchell, "The Backward Art of Spending Money," *American Economic Review* 2 (June 1912): 269.

29. Robert S. Lynd, "Family Members as Consumers," *Annals of the American Academy of Political and Social Science,* March 1932, 86 ff.

30. Hazel Kryk, *A Theory of Consumption* (London: Isaac Pitman & Sons, 1923), 20.

31. Robert L. Frost, "Machine Liberation: Inventing Housewives and Home Appliances in Interwar France," *French Historical Studies* 18 (spring 1993): 109-130; Mary Nolan, "'Housework Made Easy': The Taylorized Housewife in Weimar Germany's Rationalized Economy," *Feminist Studies* 16 (fall 1990): 549-578.

32. Madeleine Cazamian, *L'autre Amérique* (Paris: Champion, 1931), 216 ff.

33. Rutherford, *Selling Mrs. Consumer,* 96-135.

34. Duchen, "Occupation Housewife," 4-5; Françoise Werner, "Du ménage a l'art ménager: L'évolution du travail ménager et son écho dans la presse féminine française de 1919 a 1939," *Le mouvement social* 116 (October-December 1984): 64, 71; Martine Martin, "Ménagère: Une profession? Les dilemmes de l'entre-deux-guerres," ibid., 140 (July-September 1987): 95-99; idem, "La rationalisation du travail ménager en France dans l'entre-deux-guerres," *Culture technique* 3 (September 1980): 157-163. Pauline Bernège, quoted in *Premier Congrès,* 243. Rouaud, *60 ans d'arts ménagers,* 1: 55, 123, 132-143, 183, 192; 2: 12, 62, 139.

35. Rutherford, *Selling Mrs. Consumer,* 133-34, 168, 172-178.

36. Pauline Bernège, quoted in *Premier Congrès,* 243.

37. Rutherford, *Selling Mrs. Consumer,* 172-179.

38. Jean Fourastié and Françoise Fourastié, *Les arts ménagers* (Paris: Presses Universitaires de France, 1950), 111.

39. Bertrand de Jouvenal, *Arcadie: Essaie sur le mieux-vivre* (Paris: S.E.D.E.I.S., 1968), 37-38. More generally see Duchen, *Women's Rights and Women's Lives in France.*

40. "Cherchez la femme," *Productivité française*, March 1952, 2; Jean Dayre, "La première industrie française manque de productivité," ibid., 2–9; Jacqueline Bernard, "La période de l'organisation commence," ibid., 10, 13 ff.

41. Rouaud, *60 ans d'arts ménagers*, 2: 17 ff.

42. J. Frederick Dewhurst, *Europe's Needs and Resources: Trends and Prospects in Eighteen Countries* (New York: Twentieth Century Foundation, 1961), 214–216.

43. Jean Festeau, "La distribution des machines à laver," February 9, 1962, CD 4-068, CCP; Delaunay, *Histoire de la machine à laver*, 224; calculations based on ibid., 244–248, 252.

44. Marianne Monestier, "Le credit vous permet: de réaliser des économies de temps et d'argent; de profiter immediatement des progrès techniques," *Marie-Claire*, October 1954, 116, 143. On Cetelem see Philippe Clément and Maurice Roy, *De la 4 CV à la Vidéo: 1953–1983, c'est trente années qui ont changé notre vie* (Paris: Communica International, 1983), 85–98. On consumer credit in the early twentieth-century United States, see Martha L. Olney, *Buy Now, Pay Later: Advertising, Credit, and Consumer Durables in the 1920s* (Chapel Hill: University of North Carolina Press, 1991).

45. Sue Bowden and Avner Offer, "Household Appliances and the Use of Time: The United States and Britain since the 1920s," *Economic History Review* 47, no. 4 (1994): 742–743; Union Féminine Civique et Sociale, *Fiches documentaires d'Action sociale et civique* (Paris, 1963), 14.

46. *Marie-Claire*, October 1957, 128.

47. Ross, *Fast Cars, Clean Bodies*, 78–83.

48. Marguerite Perrot, *Salaires, prestations sociales et pouvoir d'achat depuis 1968* (Paris: Collections de l'INSEE: Ménages, 1971), 48.

49. Christine Rochefort, *Les petits enfants du siècle* (Paris: Grasset, 1961), 108, 25.

50. Dominique Badault, *Equipement du logement et demande de biens durables en Bretagne, 1962–1968: Résultats d'enquêtes effectuées en 1962 et 1968 avec le concours de la DGRST* (Rennes: Centre Regional d'Etudes et de Formations Economiques, 1971), 293, 796, 802.

51. François Gardès, "L'évolution de la consommation marchande en Europe et aux U.S.A. depuis 1960," *Consommation: Revue de socio-économie* 30 (April–June, 1983): 3–32. Also Louis Levy-Garboua, "Les modes de consommation de quelques pays occidentaux: Comparaisons et lois d'évolution (1960–1980)," ibid. (January–March 1983): 4–52; Dewhurst, *Europe's Needs and Resources*, 255–256.

52. André Maurois, "Homme, 1954: Un monsieur exemplaire," *Elle*, October 25, 1954, 31.

53. Françoise Giroud, "Portrait de l'acheteuse," *Vente et publicité*, June 15, 1953, 23; "Les 'arts ménagers' et la publicité," ibid., March 1955, 62. On Giroud see Christine Ockrent, *Françoise Giroud: Une ambition française* (Paris: Fayard, 2003).

54. Timothy Joyce, *The New Housewife* (London: British Market Research Bureau, 1967), 6–7, 9, 12, 19, 21–22, London, Publications, 1967–1972, JWT.

55. Rochefort, *Les petits enfants du siècle; Libre–Service–Actualité,* June 11, 1962, 12; October 2, 1962, 3; Centre d'Etude du Commerce et de la Distribution, *Les habitudes d'achat de la population des grands ensembles d'habitation* (Paris: CECOD, 1965).

56. Jean-Claude Kaufmann, *La vie h.l.m.: usages et conflits* (Paris: Editions Ouvrières, 1981), 79.

57. J. Martin, "Les produits pour le lavage," 114–119.

58. "Poudres à laver le linge: Quelle est la meilleure? *Que Choisir: Union Fédérale de la Consommation,* November 1968, 5; "Les poudres à laver le linge: Un marché naturellement ingrat, ou artificiellement compliqué," *Libre–Service–Actualité,* June 10, 1969, 33–35; J. Martin, "Les produits pour le lavage," 80–84.

59. Giroud, "Portrait de l'acheteuse."

60. "Les poudres à laver le linge," 33.

61. *Femme pratique,* March 10, 1972.

62. Etienne Thil and Claude Baroux, *Un pavé dans la marque* (Paris: Flammarion, 1983), 43–44, 112; Christian Lhermie, *Carrefour ou l'invention de l'hypermarché,* 2d ed. (Paris: Libraire Vuibert, 2003), 79–83.

63. Rouaud, *60 ans d'arts ménagers,* 2: 162–163.

64. Orvar Löfgren, "Materializing the Nation in Sweden and America," *Ethnos* 58, no. 3–4 (1993): 161–196.

65. Daniel J. Boorstin, *The Image: Or What Happened to the American Dream* (New York: Atheneum, 1961), 243.

66. On the Kitchen Debate: Rika S. Sato, "The 'Kitchen' and the Cold War" (B. A. thesis, Princeton University, 1990); Walter L. Hixson, *Parting the Curtain: Propaganda, Culture, and the Cold War, 1945–1961* (New York: St. Martin's, 1997), 151–214.

67. Hixson, *Parting the Curtain,* 210–213.

68. "Visitors' Reactions to the American Exhibit in Moscow: A Preliminary Report," September 28, 1959, box 7: Report on American Exhibition in Moscow, USIA Records Relating to the American Exhibition in Moscow, 1952–1959, National Archives, Washington, D.C.; Shoup Voting Machine Poll, September 4, 1959, box 1: Shoup Voting Machine, ibid.

69. Sato, "The 'Kitchen' and the Cold War," 41.

70. Slavenka Drakulic, *How We Survived Communism and Even Laughed* (New York: Norton, 1992), xiv–xv.

CONCLUSION

Epigraphs: Carlo Petrini, "The Official Slow Food Manifesto," in *Slow Food: The Case for Taste* (2001), trans. William McCuaig (New York: Columbia University Press, 2003), xxii; Aline Sullivan, "Top Brands Ride Out Tide of Anti-Americanism," *International Herald Tribune,* June 14–15, 2003, 15.

1. Petrini, *Slow Food;* Antonio Cianciullo, "Mangio sano, mangio piano: nasce il gastronomo verde," *La Repubblica,* December 10, 1989, 22.

2. The flexible dimension of the new economy and its particular compatibil-

ity with the European environment was heralded in Charles S. Sabel and Michael Piore, *The Second Industrial Divide: Possibilities for Prosperity* (New York: Basic Books, 1984).

3. Joanne Legomsky, "The Europeanization of American Retailing," *Standard and Poor's Industry Surveys*, April 3, 1986, R61–65.

4. Daniel Drache, "From Keynes to K-Mart: Competitiveness in a Corporate Age," in *States against Markets*, ed. Robert Boyer and Daniel Drache (London: Routledge 1996), 31–61.

5. Thomas C. Daniel, *The Helsinki Effect: International Norms, Human Rights, and the Demise of Communism* (Princeton: Princeton University Press, 2001).

6. Generally on the patterns of consumption also called "post-Fordist," "postmodern," or "postmaterialist," see Mike Featherstone, *Consumer Culture and Postmodernism* (London: Sage, 1991). For pioneering work, simultaneously by marketing experts in the United States and Europe, see Susan P. Douglas and Christine D. Urban, "Life Style Analysis to Profile Women in International Markets," *Journal of Marketing*, July 1977, 46–54; Suzanne McCall, "Meet the 'Workwife,'" ibid., 55–65. For a general review of the literature on the phenomenon, see Erik Neveu, "'Sociostyles'. . . Une fin de siècle sans classes," *Sociologie du travail* 2 (1990): 137–154. On the effects of advertising on this trend, see Armand Mattelart, *L'internationale publicitaire* (Paris: La Découverte, 1989); Gerrit Antonides and W. Fred Van Raaij, *Consumer Behavior: A European Perspective* (New York: John Wiley and Sons, 1998); "Special Dossier: À la recherche du nouveau consommateur," *Révue française de gestion* 110 (September–October 1996).

7. Annemoon van Hemel, Hans Mommaas, and Cas Smithuigsen, *Trading Culture: GATT, European Policies, and the Transatlantic Market* (Amsterdam: Bokman Foundation, 1996).

8. Victor Scardigli, *La consommation, culture du quotidien* (Paris: Presses Universitaires de France, 1983), 127.

9. Michèle Ruffat, "L'introduction des intérêts diffus dans le plan: Le cas des consommateurs," in *La planification en crise, 1965–1985,* ed. Henri Rousso (Paris: Editions du Centre Nationale de la Recherche Scientifique, 1987), 115–133; and see now Gunnar Trumball, "Strategies of Consumer-Group Mobilization: France and Germany in the 1970s," in *The Politics of Consumption: Material Culture and Consumers in Europe and America,* ed. Martin Daunton and Matthew Hilton (Oxford: Berg, 2001), 261–282.

10. Scardigli, *La consommation,* 127.

11. A sound introduction to the burgeoning cottage industry of consumer studies is Daniel Miller, ed., *Acknowledging Consumption* (London: Routledge, 1995).

12. Quoted in Omar Calabrese, "Ah, l'edonismo di sinistra," *Panorama*, August 31, 1986, 38.

13. The main source for ARCI's recent past is its self-reflective history, available also in English translation: http://www.arci.it/storia/index.html. See also http://www.arcigay.it.

14. For background, see Alan Warde and Lydia Martens, *Eating Out: Social Differentiation, Consumption and Pleasure* (Cambridge: Cambridge Uni-

versity Press, 1999); Mara Miele and Jonathan Murdoch, "Slow Food," in *McDonaldization: The Reader*, ed. George Ritzer, rev. ed. (Thousand Oaks, Calif.: Pine Forge, 2002).

15. The McDonald's phenomenon has generated a vast disputatious literature. On fast food in general, see Eric Schlosser's elegantly polemical *Fast Food Nation* (New York: Penguin, 2002). For a business history of the enterprise, see John Love, *McDonald's: Behind the Arches* (New York: Bantam, 1995). For an exemplary treatment of the fast-food phenomenon in Europe, see Rick Fantasia, "Fast Food in France," *Theory and Society* 24 (1995): 215–229. The debate over McDonaldization as "rationalization" inevitably touches on overseas trends. See George Ritzer, *The McDonaldization of Society*, rev. ed. (Thousand Oaks, Calif., Pine Forge, 1996); in addition to Barry Smart, ed., *Resisting McDonaldization* (Thousand Oaks, Calif.: Sage, 1999).

16. "La SME cede a un privato il suo 'fast food,'" *La Repubblica*, July 12, 1985, 36; Mariella Tanzarella, "Arriva in Italia il ristorante drive-in," ibid., August 10, 1985, 36; "Il made in Italy alimentare prende la strada del fast-food," ibid., December 7, 1985, 51.

17. Mauro Alberto Mori, "Fast Food in Russia: le Coop sbarcheranno sulla piazza rossa," *La Repubblica*, December 17, 1985, 17; Piero Valentino, "Fast Food italiano in URSS, Pizza sì, Hamburger no," ibid., September 24, 1986, 19.

18. Laura Laurenzi, "È a Piazza di Spagna il tempio fast food più grande del mondo," *La Repubblica*, March 13, 1986, 15; Giorgio Lonardi, "A Cremonini il monopolio del 'fast food' italiano," ibid., January 30, 1988, 54; Enrico Franceschini, "Sua maestà l'hamburger," ibid., November 3, 1988, 24; Alessandra Rota, "E la licenza è un gioco da ragazzi," ibid., March 13, 1986, 15; Mariella Tanzarella, "Uomini di buona voluttà," ibid., May 1, 1992, 30.

19. Schlosser, *Fast Food Nation*, 225 ff.

20. Magdi Allam, "Nasce Meccadonald il re dei fast food nella città dell'Islam," *La Repubblica*, December 29, 1992, 11.

21. Petrini, *Slow Food*, 12, 19; Alexander Stille, "Slow Food," *The Nation*, August 9, 2001; Mara Miele and Jonathan Murdoch, "The Practical Aesthetics of Traditional Cuisines: Slow Food in Tuscany," *Sociologia Ruralis* 42 (October 2002): 312–328.

22. Susan E. Rice and Gayle E. Smith, "Stop the Trans-Atlantic Food Fight," *International Herald Tribune*, May 30, 2003, 6; Ibrahim Coulibaly, "Malien," *Libération*, May 30, 2003, 3.

23. Tyler Cabot, "Naming Rights," *Washington Post*, May 21, 2003, FO1.

24. Joseph S. Nye Jr., *Bound to Lead: The Changing Nature of American Power* (New York: Basic Books, 1990). The definition was subsequently developed in idem, *The Paradox of American Power* (New York: Oxford University Press, 2002), esp. 8–12; and idem, *Soft Power: The Means to Success in World Politics* (New York: Public Affairs, 2004).

25. Benjamin Barber, *Jihad vs. McWorld* (New York: Ballantine, 1996); Zbigniew Brzezinski, *Out of Control: Global Turmoil on the Eve of the Twenty-first Century* (New York: Scribner, 1993).

26. In his widely influential book, *The Clash of Civilizations and the Remaking*

of World Order (New York: Simon and Schuster, 1996), Samuel Huntington spells out the alternative to the "soft" power scenario.

27. Charlotte Beers, "American Public Diplomacy and Islam," Testimony before the Senate Foreign Relations Committee, February 27, 2003, http://www.state.gov/r/us/18098; Simon Roughneen, "Office of Global Communications; A New Departure or More of the Same," September 2, 2002, in http://www.zmag.org/showarticle.cfm?sectionID=11&ItemID=2303.

28. www.whitehouse.gov/ogc/ 05/08/2003.

29. Johanna Neuman, "Ex-Ad Executive Quits Federal Post Pitching America to the World," *Los Angeles Times*, March 4, 2003, A-7.

30. Tim Morris, *Retail Supermarket Globalization: Who's Winning?* (Auckland: Coriolis Research, 2001), 26, 49, 53; Mission Economique, Ambassade de France en Chine, *Fiche de synthèse: La distribution en Chine* (Beijing: Minefi-Dree/Tresor, 2004).

31. Richard Morgan, *J. Walter Takeover: From Divine Right to Common Stock* (Homewood, Ill.: Dow Jones–Irwin, 1991).

32. Sullivan, "Top Brands Ride Out Tide of Anti-Americanism."

33. *Financial Times*, February 26, 2004, 9.

34. Quote from Eric Pfanner, "McDonald's Credits Ads for Lifting Sales," *International Herald Tribune*, June 24, 2004, 17. See also David Barboza, "When Golden Arches Are Too Red, White and Blue," *New York Times*, October 14, 2001; Shirley Leung, "McDonald's in France Focuses on Decor," *Wall Street Journal Europe*, August 30–September 1, 2002, A1, A4; Eric Pfanner, "McDonald's Gets Healthy for Europe," *International Herald Tribune*, March 8, 2004, 13.

35. Prof. Dr. Reiner Pommerin, "70 Jahre Charterfeier des Rotary Club Dresden, 12 Dezember 1928–12 Dezember 1998," talk to the Dresden Rotary Club, 1998, typescript courtesy of the author; private conversation with Ernest H. Maron, July 19, 1999.

Bibliographic Essay

THIS ESSAY HAS TWO PURPOSES: to point readers to studies related to this book's themes and to identify the intellectual building blocks of its arguments. The entangled nature of the American hegemony in Europe mandates the use of both exemplary cases and a wide range of studies of more general interest. Here readers will find references to these works, whereas in the chapter notes they will find the citations to archival sources, specialized literatures, and ephemeral evidence.

AMERICAN EMPIRE

Until very recently the relationship of the United States to Europe was not described in terms of "imperialism" or "empire" in any conventional way. Rather, the relationship was characterized as "empire by invitation," or "empire by consensus," as the effect of "Americanization," or, at the cusp of the twenty-first century, in very general terms as an effect of the "American Century." In the perspective of the post–Cold War world, signaled most prominently by the Al Qaeda attack of September 11, 2001, there has been a torrent of debate about America's imperialism, to which this book adds arguments, but which was not present at its conception. For the best current introduction to the idea of imperialism in American history, see Frank Ninkovich, *The United States and Imperialism* (Malden, Mass.: Blackwell, 2001). The special issue of *Diplomatic History* 23 (spring 1999) on the American Century offers a multifaceted introduction to America's global expansion by seasoned historians. Whether the U.S. relationship with Europe was imperialist has been discussed with varying inflections by both American and European Europeanists, notably by the Norwegian Geir Lundestad in *"Empire" by Integration: The United States and European Integration, 1945–1997* (Oxford: Oxford University Press, 1998) and *The United States and Western Europe since 1945: From "Empire" by Invitation to Transatlan-*

tic Drift (Oxford: Oxford University Press, 2003). See also Charles S.
Maier's clarification of the terms of analysis, "The Politics of Productivity," in his book *In Search of Stability: Explorations in Historical Political Economy* (Cambridge: Cambridge University Press, 1987); and the
Austrian Reinhold Wagnleitner, "The Empire of the Fun, or Talkin' Soviet Union Blues," in the issue of *Diplomatic History* cited above, 499–
524. Although *Empire* by Antonio Negri and Michael Hardt (Cambridge: Belknap Press of Harvard University Press, 2000) is not intended
as a historical work or to argue that the United States is globally hegemonic, the world order the authors characterize as emerging from globalization has several dimensions, such as the striving for a global constitutional framework and porousness of frontiers, which grow directly out of
the decades-old experience of the Market Empire.

Important recent post–Cold War assessments by U.S.-based scholars
treat American hegemony as a given of twentieth-century internationalism, highlighting the pioneering role of U.S. social scientific models and
what are now familiarly known as NGOs, nongovernmental organizations. See in particular Olivier Zunz, *Why the American Century?* (Chicago: University of Chicago Press, 1998); and Akira Iriye, *Cultural Internationalism and World Order* (Baltimore: Johns Hopkins University
Press, 1997). Although U.S. hegemony has continuous features over time,
the relationship between force and persuasion changes profoundly according to place and time; much is to be learned from reading John
Dower's exquisitely crafted *Embracing Defeat: Japan in the Wake of
World War II* (New York: W. W. Norton, 1999) on Japanese responses to
the impositions of their alien occupiers; and from Louis A. Perez Jr.'s
Cuba and the United States: Ties of Singular Intimacy, 3d ed. (Athens:
University of Georgia Press, 2003), the history of a snarled, often bitter
relationship all too close to home.

SHIFTING HEGEMONIES: THE LONG VIEW

American capitalism's global hegemony is best grasped in the framework
of classic studies of systems of capitalist exchange, especially those addressing ruptures and the recasting of their institutions and ideologies, to
the detriment and gain of various regions of the world. Adam Smith's
The Wealth of Nations (1776) is always worthwhile reading: in his astute
invocation of the new "sweet commerce" of the eighteenth century to de-

nounce the closed world of the "Gothic" past, twentieth-century American liberals found a model to counterpose the free-market world service capitalism against the closed world of European imperialism. Karl Marx is relevant here for his writing about the creative destruction of "all that is solid," vividly evoked in *The Communist Manifesto* (1848), as well as for his arguments about commodity fetishism in volume 1 of *Capital*. In *The Great Transformation* (1944), Hungarian economic anthropologist Karl Polanyi brilliantly analyzes industrial capitalism's destruction of social institutions to create markets and the simultaneous struggles of national and local commmunities to use state institutions to "re-embed" civil society.

On the spirit of early capitalism as it gives way to the spirit of late capitalism, see Max Weber, *Essays in Economic Sociology*, (1910–1920) edited by Richard Swedborg (Princeton: Princeton University Press, 1999); and Werner Sombart, *Economic Life in the Modern Age*, edited by Nico Stehr and Reiner Grundmann (New Brunswick, N.J.: Transaction, 2001), both of which are framed by comparing Europe and the United States. A similar contrast lies behind Albert O. Hirschman's "Rival Views of Market Society" (1982), in *Rival Views of Market Society and Other Recent Essays* (Cambridge, Mass.: Harvard University Press, 1986), 105–141. Antonio Gramsci, "Americanism and Fordism" (1931), in *An Antonio Gramsci Reader, 1916–1935*, edited by David Forgacs (New York: Schocken, 1988), is central to pinpointing key features of the "revolution from above" wrought by U.S. hegemony from the late 1920s on. The tendency of interwar economies to turn inward, bringing back the regulations Adam Smith deplored, is studied in Eli F. Heckscher, *Mercantilism* (1931), rev. 2d ed. (London: George Allen and Unwin, 1955). John Maynard Keynes offers perhaps the pithiest summary of Europe's pre–World War I political economy in *The Economic Consequences of the Peace* (New York: Harcourt, Brace and Howe, 1920). The application of the ideas he develops in his *General Theory* (1936), emphasizing the centrality of demand to correcting the capitalist business cycle, is clearly discussed in Peter A. Hall, ed., *The Political Power of Economic Ideas: Keynesianism across Nations* (Princeton: Princeton University Press, 1989). The role played by American corporations in ensuring U.S. economic might is especially strongly highlighted in Alfred D. Chandler Jr. with Takashi Hikino, *Scale and Scope: The Dynamics of Industrial Capitalism* (Cambridge, Mass.: The Belknap Press of Harvard University Press, 1990). On their power in international markets, see Robert Gilpin,

U.S. Power and the Multinational Corporation: The Political Economy of Foreign Direct Investment (New York: Basic Books, 1975).

On late twentieth-century changes in American hegemony, changes that highlight its past strengths and new strategies, see John Agnew, *The United States in the World-Economy: A Regional Geography* (Cambridge: Cambridge University Press, 1987). Since the 1990s a considerable literature has developed on post-Fordist, postmodern, or postindustrial economies. Charles F. Sabel and Jonathan Zeitlin, eds., *World of Possibilities: Flexibility and Mass Production in Western Industrialization* (Paris: Maison de Sciences de l'Homme; Cambridge: Cambridge University Press, 1997), calls attention to the advantages European enterprises could wield from challenging visions of productivity, manufacturing, and progress more appropriate to their region's resources and outlook. Hungarian economist Janos Kornai's *The Socialist System* (Princeton: Princeton University Press, 1993) offers the most systematic effort to demonstrate the incompatibility of consumer choice with state planning. French political economist Robert Boyer and Canadian Daniel Drache, eds., in *States against Markets* (London: Routledge 1996), highlight the responses of different regions to the new pressures of American-led globalization. Historian Paul Kennedy, *The Rise and Fall of the Great Powers* (New York: Random House, 1987), usefully characterizes long-term shifts in global leadership, as does Giovanni Arrighi, *The Long Twentieth Century: Money, Power, and the Origins of Our Times* (New York: Verso, 1994). Kenneth Pomeranz, *The Great Divergence: China, Europe, and the Making of the Modern World Economy* (Princeton: Princeton University Press, 2000), likewise suggests the relative ephemerality of global hegemons by comparing the rapid rise of the European region relative to China in the late eighteenth century.

CHANGING REGIMES OF CONSUMPTION

The argument that the power of U.S. empire rests on America's twentieth-century consumer revolution, as it defined itself against and challenged European commercial civilization, is indebted to a rapidly expanding literature on consumer cultures. Americans have been in the forefront of studies about their own origins as a "people of plenty," a "community of consumption," a "Republic of consumers." The classic work characterizing the consumer dimension of American society is David Potter, *People of Plenty: Economic Abundance and the American Character* (Chicago: University of Chicago Press, 1954). Timothy H. Breen dates this character from the colonies' revolt against England in *The Marketplace of Revolution: How Consumer Politics Shaped American Independence* (New York: Oxford University Press, 2004). Stuart Ewen's *Captains of Consciousness: Advertising and the Social Roots of the Consumer Culture* (New York: McGraw-Hill, 1976); William R. Leach's *Land of Desire: Merchants, Power, and the Rise of a New American Culture* (New York: Pantheon, 1993); T. J. Jackson Lears's *Fables of Abundance: A Cultural History of Advertising in America* (New York: Basic Books, 1994); Gary Cross's *All-Consuming Century: Why Commercialism Won in Modern America* (New York, Columbia University Press, 2000); and Lizabeth Cohen's *Making a New Deal: Industrial Workers in Chicago, 1919–1939* (New York: Cambridge University Press, 1990) and *A Consumer's Republic: The Politics of Mass Consumption in Postwar America* (New York: Knopf, 2003) make consumer culture central to interpreting twentieth-century U.S. history.

For insights into the economic trends, social institutions, and habits of mind underpinning the old regime of consumption, see Fernand Braudel, *Civilization and Capitalism, 15th–18th Centuries*, vol. 1: *The Structures of Everyday Life* and vol. 2: *The Wheels of Commerce*, translated by Sîan Reynolds (New York: Harper and Row, 1986), as well as his *Afterthoughts on Material Civilization and Capitalism*, translated by Patricia M. Ranum (Baltimore: Johns Hopkins University Press, 1977). See also masterly studies by Simon Schama, *The Embarrassment of Riches: An Interpretation of Dutch Culture in the Golden Age* (New York: Knopf, 1987); John Brewer and Roy Porter, eds, *Consumption and the World of Goods* (London: Routledge, 1993); Leora Auslander, *Taste and Power: Furnishing Modern France* (Berkeley: University of California Press, 1996); Norbert Elias, *The Civilizing Process*, translated by Edmund Jephcott (Oxford: Blackwell, 1994); and Daniel Roche, *A History of Everyday Things: The Birth of Consumption in France, 1600–1800*, translated by Brian Pearce (New York: Cambridge University Press, 2000).

"Consumer culture" is a convenient if pat term for speaking about a large array of phenomena, most basically about how people use goods to think about themselves, their communities, and the goals of society generally. One distinguished Western intellectual trend, captured by Karl Marx, "The Fetishism of Commodities," *Capital,* vol. 1, part 4 (1863), emphasizes the social disruption. In this line, read Marcel Mauss, *The*

Gift: The Form and Reason for Exchange in Archaic Societies (1924), translated by W. D. Halls (New York: Norton, 1990); Walter Benjamin, "The Work of Art in the Age of Mechanical Reproduction," in *Illuminations*, translated by Harry Zohn (New York: Schocken, 1988); Siegfried Kracauer, *The Mass Ornament: Weimar Essays*, translated by Thomas Y. Levin (Cambridge, Mass.: Harvard University Press, 1995); Theodor Adorno and Max Horkheimer, *The Dialectic of Enlightenment* (New York: Continuum, 1988); Herbert Marcuse, *One Dimensional Man* (Boston: Beacon, 1991); and Jean Baudrillard, *Selected Writings*, ed. Mark Poster (Stanford: Stanford University Press, 2001). In turn, German, American, and French historical sociology have paid particular attention to the role of consumer patterns in marking status and distinction. See Max Weber, "Classes, Status Groups, and Parties," in *From Max Weber: Essays in Sociology*, translated and edited by H. H. Gerth and C. Wright Mills (New York: Oxford University Press, 1958); Thorstein Veblen, *Theory of the Leisure Class: An Economic Study of Institutions* (1899; reprint, New York: New American Library, 1953); and Pierre Bourdieu, *Distinction: A Social Critique of the Judgement of Taste* (1979), translated by Richard Nice (Cambridge, Mass.: Harvard University Press, 1984). On the role of commodities in expressing individual self and community, see Viviana Zelizer, *The Social Meaning of Money* (New York: Basic Books, 1994); and Dick Hebdige, *Subculture: The Meaning of Style* (London: Metheun, 1979).

The last decade has witnessed a proliferation of European studies on consumer culture. Samples of key arguments are provided in several English-language collections, notably Martin Daunton and Matthew Hilton, eds. *The Politics of Consumption: Material Culture and Citizenship in Europe and America* (Oxford: Berg, 2001); the special issue of *International Labor and Working-Class History 55* (April 1999), titled *Class and Consumption,* edited by Lizabeth Cohen and Victoria de Grazia; Susan Strasser, Charles McGovern, and Matthias Judt, eds., *Getting and Spending: European and American Consumer Societies in the Twentieth Century* (Cambridge: Cambridge University Press, 1998).

AMERICANIZATION

Authors using the term "Americanization" speak to many different issues and subjects. The well-known British publicist W. T. Stead, a quick study, is credited with being the first to apply the term to the United States' rising hegemony in the wake of the Spanish-American War (*The Americanization of the World*, 1898). However, down to the 1920s the term was more commonly used in the United States itself, to speak of the carrots and sticks used to assimilate foreign immigrants. Much is to be said for seeing analogies and continuities between processes of Americanization in the United States and American hegemony abroad: Richard Abel, *Red Rooster Scare: Making American Cinema* (Berkeley: University of California Press, 1999), makes this point well. When speaking of Americanization, it is basic to consider the vexed debate about what structures or outlooks have contributed to making American history "exceptional" with respect to the course of European history: a good start is Ian Tyrell, "American Exceptionalism in an Age of International History," *American Historical Review* 96 (October 1991): 1031–1055.

The term "Americanization" has been so widely used that it is helpful to analyze works according to different approaches. One is to think of *Americanization as cultural dialogue*, whereby local intellectuals work through their own apprehensions and discontents using America as a cultural trope. See especially Dan Diner, *America in the Eyes of the Germans*, translated by Allison Brown (Princeton: Markus Weiner, 1996); and Jean-Philippe Mathy, *Extrême-Occident: French Intellectuals and America* (Chicago: University of Chicago Press, 1993).

No history of European views of America can substitute for the intellectual power and freshness of insight of major works dedicated to making sense of contemporary trends in their own societies by looking at America: notably Alexis de Tocqueville, *Democracy in America*, translated by George Lawrence, ed. J. P. Mayer (Garden City, N.Y.: Anchor, 1969); James Bryce, *The American Commonwealth* (New York, 1895); and Johan Huizinga, *America: A Dutch Historian's Vision—From Afar and Near,* edited and translated by Herbert H. Rowen (New York: Harper and Row, 1972).

Studies of *Americanization as cultural imperialism* in Europe are rare. The concept originated in Europe in the 1920s as European cultural elites worried that economic monopolies would be translated into cultural domination. In the 1960s it was widely applied to the conduct of Western, but especially U.S.-based, media and communications, which in vulnerable Third World countries were accused of allying themselves with agencies of the American state apparatus, including the CIA and the military, and with reactionary local bourgeois elites to snuff out indigenous cultures, thereby imposing the "false consciousness" of mass consumption on a world scale; in notorious cases, notably Chile, these forces combined to overthrow governments that obstructed this endeavor. The major U.S. theorist of this idea is sociologist Herbert Schiller, *Mass Communications and American Empire* (New York: A. M. Kelley, 1969) and *Communication and Cultural Domination* (White Plains, N.Y.: International Arts and Sciences Press, 1976). Anthony Smith pursues similar themes in *The Geopolitics of Information* (New York: Oxford University Press, 1980). John Tomlinson, *Cultural Imperialism: A Critical Introduction* (Baltimore: John Hopkins University Press, 1991), argues that the concept fails to take into account that cultural transfers work differently from economic monopolies and that cartels can shape audience tastes but can neither force people to consume their products nor determine their reception.

The concept of Americanization has worked perhaps best where the process can be measured, as in the case of transfers of business practices. A cluster of studies examines the spread of Fordist production models. Mary Nolan, *Visions of Modernity: American Business and the Modernization of Germany* (New York: Oxford University Press, 1994), illuminates the battle lines over interpreting Fordism. Most works focus on the post–World War II period, notably Marie-Laure Djelic, *Exporting the American Model: The Post-War Transformation of European Business* (New York: Oxford University Press, 1998); Matthias Kipping and Ove Bjarnar, eds., *The Marshall Plan and the Transfer of U.S. Management Models* (London: Routledge, 1998); Jonathan Zeitlin and Gary Herrigel, eds., *Americanization and Its Limits: Reworking U.S. Technology and Management in Post-War Europe and Japan* (Oxford: Oxford University Press, 2000). Dominique Barjot, the French economic historian, has launched a huge multinational project studying Americanization as a processs of diffusion and adaptation of best practices; see Dominique Bargot, Isabelle Lescent-Giles, and Marc de Ferrière Le Vayer, eds., *L'americanisation en Europe au XXe siècle: Economie, culture, politique/Americanization in the 20th Century Europe: Economies, Culture, Politics* (Lille: Centre de Recherche sur l'Histoire de l'Europe du Nord-Ouest, Université Charles de Gaulle–Lille III, 2002); Dominique Bargot, ed., *Catching Up with America: Productivity Missions and the Diffusion of American Economic and Technological Influence after the Second World War* (Paris: Presses de Paris–Sorbonne, 2002).

A large group of works analyze *Americanization as a contest over the reception of U.S. models.* Richard Kuisel, *Seducing the French: The Dilemma of Americanization* (Berkeley: University of California Press, 1993), though impatient with French intellectual anti-Americanism, is sensitive to key paradoxes: namely that even conservatives, notably Charles de Gaulle, might take on board American models in the interest of nation-building; Reinhold Wagnleitner, *Coca-Colonization and the Cold War: The Cultural Mission of the United States in Austria after the Second World War* (Chapel Hill: University of North Carolina Press, 1994), emphasizes the supply side, highlighting the close collaboration of private enterprise and government; Richard Pells, *Not Like Us: How Europeans Have Loved, Hated, and Transformed American Culture since World War II* (New York: Basic Books, 1997), written from an American studies perspective, gives an optimistic view of Europeans' capacity to appropriate American models as they like. Histories specifically dedicated to youth culture give a more complicated picture, as young people, especially from the postwar generation, strategically used Americanization from below as a cultural resource in their battle against old-guard and class-bound cultural codes. See, for example, Uta Poiger, *Jazz, Rock, and Rebels: Cold War Politics and American Politics in Divided Germany* (Berkeley: University of California Press, 2000). Drawing on anthropological and cultural studies, European-based American studies treat American consumer spectacles and goods as cultural signifiers, by and large divorced from larger patterns of hegemonic power. See in particular Rob Kroes, R. W. Rydell, and D. F. J. Bosscher, *Cultural Transmissions and Receptions: American Mass Culture in Europe* (Amsterdam, V[rije] U[niversiteit] University Press, 1993); as well as his *If You've Seen One, You've Seen the Mall: Europeans and American Mass Culture* (Urbana: University of Illinois Press, 1996). Much of the explanatory power of this approach derives from anthropological studies that focus on the strategic reappropriation of cultural goods. See, for example, Richard Wilk, "Consumer Goods as Dialogue about Development," *Culture and History* 7 (1990): 79–100; and Ulf Hannerz, "Cosmopolitans and Locals in World Culture," in *Global Culture*, edited by Mike Featherstone (London: Sage, 1990).

Soft power is another way of thinking about Americanization, largely from the point of view of U.S. foreign policy and, to a surprising degree, with little reference to empirical studies of the impact of "soft resources" historically. The term is attributed to Joseph S. Nye, in the context of debates within the foreign policy establishment starting in the early 1990s about the resources available to the United States to reestablish world leadership; see his *Bound to Lead: The Changing Nature of American Foreign Policy* (New York: Free Press, 1990). Accordingly, soft power was a third resource, together with military and economic power, one that used "attraction" rather than "coercion." In time, soft power was more and more equated with the common habits promoted by the so-called infotainment industries rather than as the shared values promoted by cultural diplomacy. That the globalization of American corporate culture could nonetheless promote world integration around higher and higher levels of access to consumer goods and services is captured by Thomas L. Friedman's quip to the effect that "no two countries with McDonald's have ever gone to war"; see his book *The Lexus and the Olive Tree: Understanding Globalization* (New York: Farrar, Straus, and Giroux, 1999). Benjamin Barber's *Jihad vs. McWorld* (New York: Ballantine, 1996), though not using the expression "soft power," would see it in a new concentration of institutions of democratic civil society to mediate between the inherent destructiveness of corporate-led globalization and the fundamentalist backlash. Soft power appears in a different guise, as fundamental Western values, in Samuel P. Huntington, *The Clash of Civilizations and the Remaking of World Order* (New York: Simon and Schuster, 1996). For the Harvard professor of government, civilization is akin to culture in the old European sense, and the problem central to world order is for the West, with the United States in the lead, to reassert its superiority over the six to seven other world civilizations in which Western cultural penetration and political domination have provoked resentment and heightened attachment to nonwestern values. That the unity between the United States and Europe may prove illusory is U.S. journalist Robert Kagan's thesis in *Of Paradise and Power: America vs. Europe in the New World Order* (New York: Knopf, 2003); in the last decades, the two civilizations have parted ways as the United States has come to embody hard military and economic power, whereas Europe has come to be identified with the arts of exercising soft power. For Joseph S. Nye, *Soft Power: The Means to Success in American Foreign Policy* (New York: Foreign Affairs, 2004), the decline in the U.S. capacity to wield soft power is evidenced in the inability of its foreign policy to convince foreign public opinion of the legitimacy of its goals and values, which in turn has increased its reliance on coercion and economic pressure.

Acknowledgments

I T I S N O T U S U A L L Y the fate of history books to be so completely over-taken by events. When I set out to write this book, two decades ago, I never imagined that by the time it was finished our nation would be regarded both at home and abroad as an imperialist superpower. Nor could I have imagined that the work would be published following a hair-raising thirty-month period in which an American administration unleashed an unprovoked war, withdrew from the international arrangements almost universally regarded as the basis for building a peaceful post–Cold War order, and disparaged as corrupt and illusory the global institutions that had often served to soften American hegemony. In fact the origins of this study lie elsewhere. One is always writing the same book, somebody once said, some primordial issue nagging at the mind. My book is about power and its two faces—consent and force, persuasion and violence, carrot and stick, soft and hard—the movement from one to the other, the thin line between them, the use of one to legitimate the other: first Bourbon Naples's bread and circus, then Mussolini's Fascism, thereafter the seductions and impositions of consumer desire. This version—about the hegemony of American consumer culture over European commercial civilization—has turned out to be by far the most complicated, not so much for its scope and length, but for the difficulty of finding a perspective that would provide that sense of relativity which we all need to break out of our imperial provincialism and understand what we really are.

That couldn't happen, as I used to think, by leaving the United States in order to embrace the critique of America on behalf of its self-conceived opposite, Europe. Speaking of two giants struggling for global hegemony, one needs yet another position, which, given my cultural limits as a Westerner, I could achieve only by straddling these two intimately intertwined yet very different worlds. Born in Chicago after the U.S. victory in World War II, growing up when American power was at its Cold War apogee, I am an American. Becoming an adult, I also became a European, first by disposition and affection, then by marriage, parenthood, and work.

Coming and going, viewing Europe from the United States, and vice versa, my aim has been to capture the structure of conflicts behind clashes of culture, but also, as a historian, to develop a critique of the categories we use to try to make sense of them.

Given the nature of this study, I have often traveled on unfamiliar terrain, with all the risk of blunder and error that comes with trespassing on others' specialized fields. "Who doesn't try, doesn't fail" consoles an old Tuscan proverb. My determination not to take short cuts was strengthened by a wealth of support from many people and institutions. I am especially grateful for grants from the Shelby Cullom Davis Center of Princeton University (1987), the German Marshall Fund of the United States (1990), the Guggenheim Foundation (1998), and leaves and grants from Columbia and Rutgers Universities. More recently I was the beneficiary of a Jean Monnet Fellowship from the Schuman Center of the European University Institute under the warm directorship of Helen Wallace, as well as kind hospitality from Maurice Aymard at the Maison de Science de l'Homme, Heinz-Gerhard Haupt at the Universities of Bielefeld and Halle, Patrick Fridenson of the Ecole Supérieure des Hautes Etudes en Science Sociale, and Danielle Haase-Dubosc at the Columbia University Institute for Scholars at Reid Hall, Paris. I have been helped by the personnel of a score of libraries, archives, and organizations, whose staffs took time from their many regular duties to assist me. I am especially thankful to the cordial staff at Rotary International, Zurich, and its former director Jonathan Fiske; Gabriel Kirkpatrick at the Credit Union National Association, Madison, Wisconsin; Ivan Elsmark of the International Labor Organization in Geneva; Ellen Gartrell, director of the John W. Hartman Center for Sales, Advertising, and Marketing History at Duke University; Udo Germer at the Deutsche Bucherei in Leipzig; and Cinzia Scafiddi at Slow Food, Bra, Italy; as well as the staff at the Century Foundation, New York City; the National Archives at College Park, Maryland; the Chamber of Commerce of Paris; and the Chamber of Commerce and City Archives of Florence.

For years this undertaking has been my *carte d'entrée* to generous networks of intellectual exchange, first and foremost at Columbia University, especially among my colleagues at the Institute for Research on Women and Gender, and before 1994 at the Rutgers Center for Historical Research. My students were my best critics, and none more probing and dearer to me than the members of my undergraduate seminar "America in Europe" at Columbia University and my graduate students at Columbia and the European University Institute. I have spoken on various aspects of the project at about three score other institutions and conferences in Europe, the United States, Canada, and Cuba, each one a special occasion for me and important to shaping this work. I have been the grateful recipient of research assistance from current and former students in the United States and Europe, intellectual interlocutors as well as helpmates, now become or en route to becoming scholars in their own right, in particular Heide Fehrenbach, Jan Lambertz, Paul Lerner, Laura Kopp, Victoria Basualdo, Davide Lombardo, and Nadia Zonis. My debt to the friendship and critical rigor of Arno J. Mayer is inestimable. I am also thankful for incisive comments from Jean-Christophe Agnew, Marcello Anselmo, Leora Auslander, Volker Berghahn, Elizabeth Blackmar, Richard Bushman, Marie Chessel, Michael Geyer, William Leach, Sergio Luzzatto, Frank Mort, Leonardo Paggi, Tom Sedlock, Richard Seidlitz, and Lisa Tiersten. Sydelle Kramer was my pole star, and Joyce Seltzer brought the book into port. Finishing this work, I was accompanied by the affection of Cino Sitia, Nancy Goldring, Miriam Hansen, Martha Howell, and Temma Kaplan, and by the support of my family—especially my beloved daughter, Livia, and my father and mother, Alfred de Grazia and Jill Oppenheim de Grazia (d. 1996), to whom this book is dedicated.

Index

INDEX